EUROPEAN ECONOMIC INTEGRATION

The question of European economic integration has long been a source of intense debate and controversy. Recent changes, such as the 1992 Programme, move towards an economic and monetary union, the reunification of Germany and the disintegration of the eastern bloc have made economic integration seem all the more complex and difficult. Some even wonder whether perhaps the entire process has exhausted itself.

In this text Miroslav N. Jovanović argues that economic integration in Europe is not a lost cause and provides a thorough analysis of the complex issues involved. All the main policy areas are examined in detail, with the political and legal dimensions of European Union involvement and issues such as competition highlighted. Other, less well known policy areas, such as social policy, environmental policy and transport policy, are also examined. Concluding with a look at future possibilities for economic integration, the author argues that only a solution ensuring 'unity with diversity' can guarantee success.

Containing an excellent blend of theory and practice and presenting a highly complex issue in an accessible and non-technical way, this text will be an invaluable resource for students of international economics, international business, and European studies.

Miroslav N. Jovanović is an Associate Economic Affairs Officer at the United Nations Economic Commission for Europe in Geneva.

EUROPEAN ECONOMIC INTEGRATION

Limits and prospects

Miroslav N. Jovanović

Foreward by Alexis Jacquemin

London and New York

First published 1997
by Routledge
11 New Fetter Lane, London EC4P 4EE

Simultaneously published in the USA and Canada
by Routledge
29 West 35th Street, New York, NY 10001

Typeset in Garamond by
Pure Tech India Ltd, Pondicherry

Printed and bound in Great Britain by
TJ International Ltd, Padstow, Cornwall

British Library Cataloguing in Publication Data
A catalogue record for this book is available from the British Library

Library of Contress Cataloging in Publication Data
A catalogue record for this book has been requested

ISBN 0–415–09548–4 (hbk)
ISBN 0–415–09549–2 (pbk)

Својим синовима, Јовану и Николи-Александру,
посвећујем све на свету изузев ове књиге
која је безвредна у односу на
љубав, срећу и наду коју они пружају.

Στους υιούς μου, Γιάννη και Νικόλαο–Αλέξανδρο,
αφιερώνω τα πάντα στον κόσμο, εκτός από αυτό το βιβλίο
που δεν είναι τίποτα μπροστά
στην αγάπη, την ευτυχία και την ελπίδα που προσφέρουν.

To my sons, Jovan and Nikola-Aleksandar,
I dedicate everything in the world *except* this book
which is worthless compared with
the love, happiness and hope that they provide.

CONTENTS

FIGURES

TABLES

FOREWORD

Alexis Jacquemin
Université Catholique de Louvain

Fifty years after the beginning of economic and political reconstruction following the Second World War, Europe sometimes looks like a peculiar cocktail mix – the ingredients of which are Europe's huge resource potential and relative decline in its ability to exploit this same potential. But it is important to recall that right from its origin up to and including the most recent summits, many have viewed European integration with great scepticism.

In the years prior to the signing of the Single European Act, in February 1986, few observers anticipated anything other than stagnation or even decay. For example, the cover of *The Economist* on 20 March 1982, showed a tombstone with the words '*EEC born March 25th, 1957, moribund March 25, 1982, capax imperii nisi imperasset* (it seemed capable of power until it tried to wield it)'.

Today the European Union is immersed in another critical transition period in its history. New uncertainties have emerged, including Europe's high level of structural unemployment, its very complex and difficult process of enlargement, new institutional temptations in the name of subsidiarity or proportionality which could conceivably lead to 'renationalization' of parts of the Community '*acquis*' plus the difficulties of 15 member states agreeing in the Intergovernmental Conference to more efficient institutions, rules and procedures. Dovetailed with this are the great challenges of Economic and Monetary Union and settling the future financing of the European Union for the twenty-first century – adding further layers of complexity.

Should we be surprised by this situation? Not really. The genius of those who invented Europe in the 1950s, Monnet, Schuman, Spaak, Adenauer, was precisely to search for a new European model of society based on a broader and deeper community among peoples, and for institutions that should give direction to a destiny henceforward shared. But they also sought practical policy achievements to create real solidarity among European peoples and so establish common bases for future economic development. This approach was already explicit in the Preamble to the Treaty of Paris creating the European Coal and Steel Community in 1951.

Taking these considerations into account means that to understand the European process of integration, it is necessary to adopt a broad approach, including a historical perspective as well as an evaluation of the main European institutions and policies. It also requires an approach covering both the economics and the politics of the European Union, the internal problems and, of course, Europe's external relations as well.

From this point of view, Miroslav Jovanović's book is a valuable addition to the literature about the construction of Europe. It brings together in a single volume an impressive amount of well researched information and important insights into the phenomenon of integration.

After a sharp analysis of the origin of the European Union and its history, divided into several periods leading to the post-Maastricht challenges, the author develops a systematic examination of the main policies in a European perspective. His work extends from monetary to transport policy, but covers fiscal, agricultural, competition, industrial, trade, regional, capital mobility, labour, social, and environment policies as well. In each of his chapters, Jovanović provides elements for a cost–benefit analysis of these policies, offering balanced views of their relative efficiency. In so doing, he presents, in a concise way, a difficult subject matter, basing his work on a combination of recent economic analysis and the main institutional issues. Instead of trying to close debates, he enriches them through his interdisciplinary approach, while not hiding his own views about the prospects for European Union integration.

Furthermore, he builds up some linkages between the various policies, a research approach that should be reinforced in the future. Indeed all public authorities, including the European Commission, must be, and increasingly are, concerned by the problem of cross-policy coherence, be it at the micro or macroeconomic level. Contradictions between policy can spill over and cause inefficiencies to each instrument, undermining their respective credibility and creating a climate of insecurity for private as well as public actors. One important domain in this area covers the interrelationships between competition, trade and industry policies at EU level,[1] a triptych that plays a central role in the efficiency of any market economy. The rich European experience provides useful lessons here.

Among the messages of Miroslav Jovanović, is his concern for the type of integration that Europe needs. According to him, 'there need to be various measures to preserve unity with diversity in the EU as long as people want that and are able and ready to pay for it'. In this context, globalism appears as a double-edged sword for the future. On the positive side, globalism can allow Europe to make the most of what is its main highly prized asset: its wealth of cultural diversity, which ultimately gives it its capacity for listening, discussing and moving forward. This is reflected in the reference to a specific European model of society.

But, on the other hand, globalization is also a powerful factor in encouraging greater convergence and homogeneity. To survive, diversity, combined with subsidiarity, requires a dynamic economy and an ability to compete at world level. And the competitiveness of an economic system cannot be divorced from the range and scale of the employment prospects it offers its people.

'So are there limits to European economic integration?' The author's answer is negative. But to make this response fully credible, the European Union must continually review its legitimacy by providing meaningful responses to the new common challenges it faces, including those of competitivity and unemployment. As the President of the Commission, Jacques Santer, said in his memorandum on a 'European Pact of Confidence for Employment' (1996), we have to generate 'a dynamic, sustained process based on a coherent, agreed strategy culminating in visible, practical commitments'.

Given the remarkably comprehensive coverage and the pragmatic approach adopted, Miroslav Jovanović's book helps us identify in a very useful way the building blocks necessary for such a process. This book is likely to become a reference work for all those concerned with the future of the European Union.

NOTE

1 See P. Buigues, A. Jacquemin and A. Sapir, *European Policies on Competition, Trade and Industry*, E. Elgar, 1995.

PREFACE

A period of Eurosclerosis and Euro-pessimism in the 1970s and early 1980s received an antidote in the form of the 1992 Programme, devised in 1985. The objective of this 'technical' Programme was to remove non-tariff barriers on internal trade in the European Union, open up the internal market, stimulate competition and, hence, increase welfare in the region. The next logical step to consolidate the earlier achievements in European integration by the elimination of exchange-rate fluctuations was the move towards the economic and monetary union that came with the Maastricht Treaty (1991). European economic and political integration gained momentum. Or, did it? In spite of long and positive declarations of many European Councils on European integration, limitations to the integration process, such as those in the monetary sphere, began to appear. In other areas, such as education, transport policy or environment there are many unexplored prospects for integration.

When big changes occur, such as the 1992 Programme, moves towards economic and monetary union, not to mention the reunification of Germany or disintegration of the eastern bloc, then interest is aroused as opportunities to redesign Europe are rare. The democratic system and market economy of the 15 countries of the European Union, with different degrees of success, provided a fairly flexible foundation for a relatively smooth absorption of the changes brought by these challenges. That is why the system adapted and survived. However, has the European integration exhausted itself? Are there limits to European economic integration? The answer to these questions is negative. For example, if certain ambitious approaches to integration such as economic and monetary union as based on the Maastricht Treaty (and with criteria that are not known in the theory of international monetary integration) are dead, that does not mean that the idea of European integration is dead too. On the contrary. There are many other areas for European integration, including monetary integration. Perhaps, a bit less in the monetary-integration sphere over a longer timescale than established by the Maastricht Treaty may produce a better and more stable European Union in the future, as well as preserve unity with diversity.

The objective of this book is to look into the origin, evolution, operation and prospects for economic integration in the European Union. Economic integration of some of the oldest nations in the world with different organizational traditions and history, full of secular conflicts, is a tremendously difficult, but highly rewarding, political and economic task. Economic integration between relatively small and medium-sized countries can be defended with the same arguments which are used

xiv

for the integration of various regions within a single country. Just as one can always enhance integration of various regions within a single country and exploit unexplored opportunities for national economic integration, one can do the same in the group that comprises various countries. Just as there are mainly political limits to doing this on the national level, there are mainly political limits to further integration in a group that integrates different countries. The main one is the protection of national sovereignty and, hence, distinctiveness.

The term 'European Union' (EU) is used throughout the book as the organizational habitat for the European integration. The one exception is the first chapter on the origin of the EU. Due care was devoted to the evolution of European integration from the European Coal and Steel Community, European Economic Community over European Communities to the EU.

The book is organized as follows. Chapter 1 traces the evolution of the EU. It starts with the ideas about European integration as a means for west European reconciliation following the Second World War. A relatively modest beginning with a sectoral integration (coal and steel) was extended to a wider economic integration in the European Economic Community. Once economic integration started, the process continued to expand in spite of hiccups. European integration grew from the economic sphere to new areas such as foreign policy, security and defence.

Monetary policy, the subject of Chapter 2, together with trade and competition, is the first area where the impact of real integration is felt and tested. An overview of the theory of optimum currency areas precedes the discussion of monetary integration in the EU. Consideration of the theory of monetary integration points to the fact that the Maastricht criteria for monetary integration are arbitrary and even a hindrance to integration in this field.

Chapter 3 deals with fiscal policy and the budget. Once tariffs and quotas are removed on intra-EU trade, the illusion is that such trade is free. Not quite. Differences in taxes may contribute to the distortion of internal trade and factor flows. Although there were certain humble achievements in the approximation of taxes in the EU, there is immense room for improvement. Consideration of the EU budget reveals that, apart from agriculture, the budget does not play a significant role in the economic policy of the EU.

The Common Agricultural Policy (CAP), covered in Chapter 4, is, together with trade and competition, the major economic area in which the EU exerts significant influence. The CAP is based on political compromise between France and Germany, it consumes the bulk of the EU budget, distorts trade and needs to be abandoned. Such economic demand is politically naïve as there is a strong lobby that would prevent such development. None the less, external factors, such as the World Trade Organization, continue to push for the reform in the EU farm policy.

Chapters 5, 6 and 7, respectively, on competition, industrial and trade policy, form an integral part of the book. The division of certain topics among those chapters is arbitrary. For example, consideration of non-tariff barriers is placed in the trade chapter, although it could easily fit into the other two. The EU has largely expanded its involvement into competition matters (state aids or restrictive business practices) which have an impact on industrial policy. Within industrial policy, technology policy shapes the comparative advantage of the EU which in turn, has an impact on competition and trade. The EU is one of the largest international traders. As such, it exerts influence on international trade flows and negotiations within the World Trade Organization and its predecessor. The EU has a system of trade discrimination which 'rewards' preferred partners in trade. The possible eastern enlargement of the EU is discussed within the trade policy chapter and the belief is that it may take place for a select group of transition countries, but that it may take decades.

Regional policy (Chapter 8) is relevant, since with monetary union, balance-of-payments disequilibria are replaced by regional discrepancies. A country or an economic group cannot be considered as well integrated if regional disparities do not have at least a tendency of narrowing. There are still regional gaps in the EU, but the EU budget is still too small to narrow them. In addition, the solution to the 'regional problem' is important for the cohesion of the group. An interesting finding is that while certain member countries give up the national regional policies as inefficient, the EU expands its role in this area.

Chapters 9 and 10, respectively, discuss factor mobility. Capital mobility is still highly concentrated on the 'core' EU countries, although certain EU-rim countries such as Spain show that if the infrastructure and a certain type of labour is provided, that may provide incentives to investors to locate in the country that is in the periphery of the EU. Labour mobility in the EU is quite low because of various social barriers. If labour is mobile in the EU, it derives from third countries.

The rest of the book covers relatively marginal,[1] although expanding, policies of the EU. Chapter 11 treats social policy. This policy at the EU level is nothing like the national policy with the same name. The EU social policy is executed in part through the European Social Fund which gives support to the vocational training of the unemployed. Although the objectives of the European Social Charter are noble, its provisions may introduce additional rigidities in the labour market, very unnecessary in a situation of relatively high unemployment and business demands for a higher flexibility in labour markets.

The environment policy of the EU (Chapter 12) is a relatively novel feature. Although all EU policies must take into account the consequences of their actions on the environment, this expanding policy is still more aspirational than operational. Chapter 13 is devoted to transport policy. Although the Treaty of Rome requested that the EU creates a common transport policy, that has not happened for a very long time. That is one of big disappointments in the process of European integration. There are certain signs that the policy is getting off the ground, but problems arise from a lack of financial resources for large infrastructural projects. Following the experience with the Channel Tunnel, the private sector is very wary of similar projects in the future.

The conclusion of the book is that there is a lot of room for the improvement in the economic integration in the EU. If certain attempts fail such as the Maastricht Treaty-based criteria for monetary integration, that does not mean that the whole process of integration is doomed. On the contrary. The idea of economic integration is always there. The constraints come from the political sphere where national elites, rightly or wrongly, preserve national sovereignty. They tend to forget that in economic integration sovereignty is most often pooled, rather than given up.

I hope that the book will be of interest to economists concerned with international economics, integration and European studies. If it is also of interest to others specializing in economic development, international business and management, as well as policy makers, then this is also to be welcomed.

NOTE

1 EU policy in the field of energy is insignificant, hence there is no special treatment of this issue.

ACKNOWLEDGEMENTS

My involvement in European economic integration began when I was studying the topic at the University of Amsterdam (1980–1981). That period was followed by work in other subjects, such as industrial policy, foreign direct investment and macroeconomic stabilization. However, an interest in integration has always been present, although in the first half of the 1980s I did wonder if my choice of specialization was correct.

Over the years I profited from the human capital of many friends and colleagues. There are several to whom I owe a special gratitude for various kinds of assistance and encouragement in the preparation of this book. They include Asad Beg, Carol Cosgrove Sacks, Victoria Curzon Price, Persephone Economou, Cristina Giordano, William Hill, Birgit Hegge, Piet van den Noort, Dušan Sidjanski, Constantine Stephanou and Joanna Wheeler. The bibliography was prepared by Ljiljana Jovanović, while all the PC-related problems were solved by Slobodan Gatarić. Alan Jarvis and Alison Kirk favoured this project from the outset and were understanding about the delay in the submission of the manuscript.

I am very grateful to all of them. The usual disclaimer applies here: it is I who am responsible for all shortcomings and mistakes. In addition, the expressed views are my own and have nothing to do with the organization in which I work.

Miroslav N. Jovanović
Geneva, December 1996

ABBREVIATIONS

AASM	Associated African States and Madagascar
ACP	African, Caribbean and Pacific
CAP	Common Agricultural Policy
CEEC	Committee of European Economic Cooperation
CET	Common external tariff
CMEA	Council for Mutual Economic Assistance
COCOM	Coordinating Committee on Export Controls
Coreper	Comité des Représentants Permanents
EAGGF	European Agricultural Guidance and Guarantee Fund
EC	European Community
ECB	European Central Bank
ECOFIN	Economic and Financial Committee
ECSC	European Coal and Steel Community
ECU	European Currency Unit
EDC	European Defence Community
EDF	European Development Fund
EEA	European Economic Area
EEC	European Economic Community
EFTA	European Free Trade Association
EIB	European Investment Bank
EMI	European Monetary Institute
EMS	European Monetary System
EMU	economic and monetary union
EPC	European Political Community
ERDF	European Regional Development Fund
ERM	Exchange Rate Mechanism
ESF	European Social Fund
EU	European Union
FAST	Forecasting and Assessment in Science and Technology
FDI	foreign direct investment
GATS	General Agreement on Trade in Services
GATT	General Agreement on Tariffs and Trade
GSP	Generalized System of Preferences
IGC	Intergovernmental Conference
IIT	intra-industry trade

MCA	Monetary Compensatory Amount
MFA	Multi-fibre Agreement
MFN	Most Favoured Nation
MITI	Ministry for International Trade and Industry
NAFTA	North American Free Trade Agreement
NAIRU	non-accelerating-inflation rate of unemployment
NATO	North Atlantic Treaty Organization
NTB	non-tariff barrier
OECD	Organization for Economic Cooperation and Development
OEEC	Organization for European Economic Cooperation
PHARE	Poland, Hungary: Assistance for Economic Restructuring
PPS	purchasing power standard
PSE	producer subsidy equivalent
PSI	production specialization index
R&D	research and development
SCP	structure–conduct–performance
SME	small and medium-sized enterprise
TACIS	Technical Assistance for the Commonwealth of Independent States
TNC	transnational corporation
TRIM	trade-related investment measure
TSI	trade specialization index
UK	United Kingdom
US	United States
USSR	Union of Soviet Socialist Republics
VAT	value added tax
VCR	video casette recorder
WEU	Western European Union
WTO	World Trade Organization

1

THE ORIGIN OF THE EUROPEAN UNION

I INTRODUCTION[1]

The concept of European integration has been a topic for discussion this century among European intellectuals since the early 1920s. Richard Coudenhove-Kalergi argued in 1923 for the creation of a pan-European union. An emerging 'European movement' assembled around 2,000 participants from 24 countries in a Congress in Vienna in 1926. They approved the pan-European Manifesto that was, among other things, in favour of a customs union, common currency, military alliance and the respect of national values. Aristide Briand, the French Foreign Minister, was in charge of the Government Memorandum on organization of the federal union in Europe in 1930, at the time when Adolf Hitler scored his first electoral victories. The Memorandum considered issues such as a common market; customs union; free movement of goods, capital and people; and a community of European people. Altiero Spinelli and Ernesto Rossi, although deported to the island of Ventotene in 1941, secretly circulated the Ventotene Manifesto in which they argued in favour of the creation of the European Federalist Movement. To avoid international anarchy and save the liberty in Europe, they claimed, one needs to establish a federal Europe to which nation states should transfer certain sovereign rights in the common interest of all Europeans (Sidjanski, 1992, pp. 19–26).

The Second World War left many deep scars in Europe. These included not only the destruction of a large part of the population and production potential, but also the position of foreign troops in many countries. There was also a danger that after the joint elimination of Nazism, the confronting forces of the Red Army and the armies of the west would develop into an open conflict between east and the west. That was clearly seen by Winston Churchill who called for a closing of the ranks in the west. In a speech in Zurich on 19 September 1946 he said: 'I am going to say something that will astonish you. The first step in the recreation of the European family must be a partnership between France and Germany' (Jansen, 1975, p. 7). It was a vision that cooperation between former adversaries could defuse potential conflicts in the future.

European intellectuals continued the development of the integration idea after the Second World War. The European Federalist Union was created in Paris in 1946. This multi-party movement was matched by the creation of similar partisan movements among the christian democrats and socialists. Political issues were supplemented by the establishment of the European League for Economic Cooperation on the

1

initiative of Paul van Zeeland in 1947. The League prepared studies on issues such as capital mobility, monopolies, enterprises and currencies. In the same year, the Hague Congress considered two prominent reports dealing with possible ways for European integration. The first one was on federalist issues, by Denis de Rougemont, and the second on economic issues, by Maurice Allais. Those activities by European intellectuals and government officials point to the fact that ideas about European integration were genuine and the post-Second World War regional integration was not artificial.[2]

This chapter starts with a consideration of the Marshall Plan and the first moves towards European integration. That was followed by an expansion in the unity of western Europe and the creation of the European Coal and Steel Community. The next step in integration was the establishment of the European Economic Community and the European Free Trade Association. European integration led next to the enlargement of the European Economic Community. A period of Eurosclerosis (1974–1985) was changed by the Single European Act. The Maastricht Treaty was supposed to pave the way towards the (controversial) economic and monetary union. The intergovernmental Conference is supposed to revise the preceding Treaties of the European Union, make the Union more practical, prepare it for eastern enlargement and for the coming decades. The appendix outlines the structure and operation of the institutions of the European Union.

II THE MARSHALL PLAN

The mistrust and apprehension between the east and the west reduced contact between the two blocs. It was basically taking place only within the United Nations, in particular its regional organization, the Economic Commission for Europe, created in 1947, with the aim fostering contacts among all European countries that would help the economic reconstruction of the region. The cold war increased the gap between the two blocs, and their respective countries tried to find their own way in their political, military and economic recovery and development.

Poverty of a large part of the population is the instigator of social upheavals. Hence came the build-up of the left-wing parties in the post-war period in France, Italy and Greece. Harsh winter conditions (1946–7) and the following dry summer led to a shortage of food. The aggregate production in western Europe was small. Domestic consumption absorbed almost everything that was produced. There were little export surpluses that might have covered the growing demand for imports. The leader of the western world, the United States (US), realized that there ought to be a consolidation of the social system in western Europe by the means of a recovery programme. The programme would inject on a one-off basis a large amount of aid into the west European economies. The expectation was that it would help western Europe recover and grow as a significant market for American goods, services and interests.

In May 1947, three young economists that were working for the US Department of State, Harold van Cleveland, Ben Moore and Charles Kindleberger, sent a paper to George Kennan, Director of Policy Planning Staff. In that letter they called for a 'Coordinated European Recovery Programme' directed 'toward a strong and economically integrated Europe'. Among the 'top secret' documents from that time, there was also a 'Report of the Special "Ad Hoc" Committee of the State-War-Navy Coordinating Committee', in April 1947, which sought a 'reintegration of these countries into healthy regional and world trading and production systems' (Machlup, 1979, p. 10). It was America's strategic interest to have reliable partners in Europe, rather than unpredictable adversaries. All that was an introduction to the famous speech of George Marshall.

The US Secretary of State, George Marshall, gave a speech at Harvard University in June 1947 announcing the European Recovery Programme (known as the Marshall Plan). The plan basically revealed American readiness to help the reconstruction of *all* European countries under two conditions. First, the European countries had to prepare jointly a reconstruction programme. Second, they needed to agree about the volume of the financial-aid package, as well as the share of each country in it. The message of the plan to the Europeans was that they had to integrate in some way if they wanted to get aid from America. Such a stance by the US was based on the top secret documents that argued in favour of European integration (Machlup, 1979, pp. 10, 186), as the US did not have confidence in some 20 atomized states in western Europe. US aid was not offered on a bilateral, but rather on a continental basis.

In July 1947, the foreign ministers of France and Britain invited their counterparts from all European countries, with the exception of Spain, to a conference in Paris to discuss the drafting of a joint reconstruction programme. Poland and Czechoslovakia were the only countries from the East that initially accepted the invitation. Those two countries, however, subsequently declined because of Soviet fear that the Marshall aid programme was an American Trojan horse which would destabilize the Soviet zone of influence. The Paris conference consequently took place with the participation of 16 west European countries.[3] These countries established a Committee of European Economic Cooperation (CEEC) which was supposed to prepare the principles of the Reconstruction Programme and suggest the necessary means for its implementation. The Programme was prepared and submitted to the US Government in September 1947.

In April 1948, the US Government approved the European Recovery Programme (the Marshall Plan). During the life of the Programme (1948–1952), the US spent around $15 billion. The biggest single users of the Programme funds were Britain (around 23 per cent), France (around 20 per cent) and the western zones of occupied Germany (around 10 per cent). The Marshall funds had an enormous stimulating effect on the recovery of west European countries from their post-war economic disarray. Marshall aid was not conditioned in any way, but in fact almost all the funds were spent by the recipients in the US because that was the only country able to provide the goods required.[4]

The member countries of the CEEC discussed the possibility of establishing a permanent organization with the aim of fostering economic cooperation among the member countries. Subsequently, they established the Organization for European Economic Cooperation (OEEC) in April 1948. During the negotiations there were, basically, two schools of thought. The British thought that the OEEC ought to be an organization with minimum authority, just enough to satisfy the American request. In contrast, the French argued that the OEEC needed to have a wider authority. The British approach prevailed in the final agreement as the balance of the European leadership tipped over to the British side. It should be remembered that Britain was still an important partner in the victory over the Nazis and one of the three parties that were dividing the world in Yalta, as well as a large colonial power. One may find here the first bone of contention between Britain (and, perhaps, the Scandinavian states), on the one hand, and France and the other continental European states (that would subsequently create the European Community) on the other.

III UNITY OF THE WEST

The creation of various economic, political and defence organizations in eastern and western Europe reinforced the division of Europe into two blocs. Britain, France and the Benelux countries treated questions of mutual assistance in the event of an attack on any of those countries. In March 1948 they[5] established in Brussels the Western European Union (WEU) which obliges the high contracting parties to collectively defend themselves in the case of an armed attack.[6] Fearing that western Europe might in the long term become too independent (or become communist) in the political and military field, the US decided to remain present in Europe with its military force. The US invited the Benelux countries, Britain, Canada, Denmark, France, Iceland, Italy, Norway and Portugal to unite in their defence efforts. Those countries established the North Atlantic Treaty Organization (NATO) in April 1949. An armed attack on any NATO member country would be taken as an attack on all NATO countries.[7] West European countries accepted the American proposition since that meant a partial reduction in the tax burden on the domestic taxpayers.[8] Italy was included in NATO from its inception, although it is not an Atlantic state. The US had a paramount vision about the question of defence. The Americans, as well as the French, wanted to include Italy in the family of west European states, although it was a member of the Axis, in order to avoid the isolation of Italy which would create fertile soil for the communist onslaught. In addition, Italy could provide strategic contribution to the south flank of the Alliance. The defence club of the west inherited an intercontinental dimension. The WEU fell into hibernation.

Economic cooperation of the west European countries in the post-war period took place within the OEEC. Defence was organized first by the Dunkirk Treaty (1947) of Britain and France (against Germany), then the WEU (against Germany and the Soviet Union), and next NATO (against the Soviet bloc). Political cooperation, as the third pillar of western unity was left aside. But not for long.

Political cooperation also started to develop in Europe. The Hague was the site of the European Congress in May 1948 for the consideration of issues linked with the creation of a united Europe. The Congress was, in essence, to take up two approaches to that issue. The first one was the unionists' model. The British and the Scandinavians (the Protestants) argued that European unity could be achieved through inter-governmental consultations. The second, the federalist model, was favoured by the French (the Catholics). The federalists wanted a more formal organization of European political cooperation. They wanted a political institution with real and supranational powers. The subsequent debate led to the creation of the Council of Europe. The Statute of the Council, according to the British–Scandinavian model, was signed in London in 1949, but its site was and is in Strasbourg.

The Council of Europe is mainly occupied with issues relating to human rights, health, law and human mobility. The real basis for a political union within the Council of Europe was modest, since it excluded the defence issues, while the participation of neutral states precluded the possibility of a common foreign policy. The principle of unanimity in the Council made it difficult to agree on important problems.

The Yalta division of the world found a special partnership in the eastern part of Europe, too. The Soviet Union wanted to consolidate its grip in the east and created political (Cominform, 1947), economic (Comecon, 1949) and defence (Warsaw Pact, 1955)[9] alliances in the east.

IV EUROPEAN COAL AND STEEL COMMUNITY

The rivalry between Germany and France brought about three open wars between the two countries in modern history.[10] France wanted to take advantage of the favourable circumstances following the Second World War. After all, France was a part of the Allied forces that defeated the Nazis. Germany was occupied, and its discredited political and moral position gave France an opening to shape events in western Europe without Britain, albeit with some support from the US.

The occupation of West Germany could not last forever. Therefore, the western Allies established the International Ruhr Authority in 1949. Its aim was to control the production and distribution of coal, coke and steel in the Ruhr region, in order to take hold of West German heavy industry. The economy of West Germany started to recover, and there were certain signs that the country was looking for greater independence. The question that the Allies were facing was, on the one hand, how to permit the development of the mighty West German manufacturing base in order to create a strong shield to withstand the first blow in case of armed conflict with the eastern bloc and, on the other hand, how to prevent the situation of a powerful West Germany again destabilizing peace and security in western Europe. The solution was found in the Schuman Plan.[11]

Robert Schuman, the French Foreign Minister, presented a plan for the establishment of the European Coal and Steel Community (ECSC) on 9 May 1950. Instead of opting for the first federalist action that would embrace all economic aspects, Schuman and Monnet were realistic since they selected a narrow scope: the production of coal and steel.[12] In Schuman's words: 'The solidarity in the production thus established will make it plain that any war between France and Germany becomes not merely unthinkable, but materially impossible' (Jansen, 1975, p. 36). France was ready to sacrifice some of its sovereignty to a supranational body, the ECSC, which would manage a part of France's economy in order to get partial control of West German heavy industry. Konrad Adenauer, the West German Chancellor, saw a chance for his country to improve its subordinate position in the post-war period and to regain equality with other states, so he accepted the plan.

The Schuman Plan was one of the biggest turning points in French history. In the past, France was always looking for allies against Germany. It was either in the east (Poland and Russia) or in the south (Serbia). After the Second World War any partnership with those countries was out of the question. Since coal and steel were the most important levers of economic growth and conventional warfare at the time, France decided to abandon a part of its sovereignty in those industries in order to penetrate the most important manufacturing industries in its former and secular mortal enemy, Germany.

Italy and the Benelux countries accepted the negotiations with France and West Germany about sectoral integration. Those nations signed the Treaty of Paris that created the ECSC on 18 April 1951. The only original text of the Treaty was written in French and deposited in the archives of the French Government (Bayliss, 1985, p. 212).

The objectives of the ECSC are stated in the Preamble of the Paris Treaty. They include the maintenance of peace (mentioned three times in the Preamble), a substitution of old rivalries, an avoidance of bloody conflicts and an anxiety to raise the standard of living. The ECSC ought to contribute to economic expansion, growth of employment and a rising standard of living in the member states (Article 2). The principles of the ECSC are given in Article 3. They include an orderly supply in the common market, equal access to the sources of production for consumers in the Community, the prohibition of price discrimination and the need for an orderly expansion and modernization of production.

The High Authority is in charge of the implementation of the Paris Treaty (Article 8). It may: facilitate investment programmes (Article 54), establish a system of production quotas in the case of manifest crisis (Article 58), influence prices (Article 60), outlaw agreements that prevent, restrict or distort competition within the common market and authorize in advance any transaction that might directly or indirectly bring about a consolidation of industry (Articles 65 and 66) inspired by the French desire to block a reconcentration of West German coal and steel industries. The Treaty was to last for a period of 50 years from its entry into force (Article 97). After ratification, the Paris Treaty became effective on 23 June 1952.

During the negotiations about the Paris Treaty, there was an objection that the ECSC and its executive body, the High Authority, might escape democratic control. A compromise was found in the creation of another body, the Council of Ministers, that was supposed to serve as a link between all national governments and the High Authority (Articles 26–28).

V POLITICAL COOPERATION

At about the same time the ECSC was created, the international political stage was burdened with worrying events. The Korean War (1950–1953) increased the possibility of a conflict between the east and the west, particularly in Europe. The US demanded from its European allies that they increase their defence efforts. The US also wanted to rearm West Germany. The second idea did not look attractive to the Europeans at all, since it was only five years since the end of the Second World War.

René Pleven, the French Prime Minister, offered a plan for the creation of the European Defence Community (EDC) in October 1950. The EDC would integrate the armed forces of all NATO members, including those of West Germany, and it would empower the west European Minister for the Defence to be in charge of that force. The EDC Treaty was signed in May 1952, but the French Parliament failed to ratify it, so that the whole project broke down. The reasons for the failure of the EDC could be found in the awkward situation in which the countries were supposed to have a common defence policy, but without a common foreign policy! The other reason, no less important, was French involvement in Indochina (1946–1954) where it had a significant deployment of troops. If a European army was to be created in those circumstances, then it would mainly consist of soldiers from West Germany! France could not accept that.[13]

The foreign ministers of the six ECSC countries wanted to consider the notion of European political cooperation. They met in Paris in June 1953 with an idea about the creation of the European Political Community (EPC), the aim of which would be to fill the gap in political cooperation among the six countries. The final agreement was reached in Baden-Baden in August 1953. This attempt at political cooperation among some of the west European countries was, again, torpedoed by the French Parliament, which failed to ratify it. That happened because of the existence of a supranational element, the rearming of West Germany and the absence of Britain from the scheme.

A relative success in the creation of the ECSC was not followed by progress in other social fields in western Europe. Cooperation in the defence field failed (EDC) and remained within NATO. As for the area of politics, collaboration remained within the Council of Europe because of the collapse of the EPC. In a situation when most of western Europe was in an impasse, the rescue came, again, from Britain.

Anthony Eden, the British Foreign Secretary, proposed in 1954 to rearm West Germany, but within the framework of the WEU (Britain, France and the Benelux). Paris was the place where, in October, a multitude of agreements prompted several serious political changes. It was decided to cease the occupation of West Germany; to welcome Italy and West Germany in the WEU; to limit production of military goods in West Germany; and to retain troops of the western Allies (US, Britain and France) in West Germany. One of the differences between NATO and the WEU is that the former organization requested the maintenance of a predetermined, but minimal, number of troops. To control West Germany's rearmament, stricter control was needed, as provided by the WEU (Jansen, 1975, p. 53).

VI EUROPEAN ECONOMIC COMMUNITY

The west European experience in the post-Second World War period for the establishment of regional institutions points to the fact that the political union of western Europe might be realized in the long term.[14] What was left for the integration in the short and medium term was the economy. Having their own experience of economic integration,[15] the Benelux countries proposed to the ECSC partners in 1955 an integration of the economic activities that were most closely linked with coal and steel: transport and energy.

The Foreign Ministers of the ECSC countries met in Messina in June 1955 in order to consider the Benelux proposal. Paul-Henri Spaak (of Belgium) was appointed to lead an intergovernmental committee with the task of preparing a report about the possible avenues for integration. Spaak's committee invited the British to join the talks, although that country still argued in favour of a free trade area and within the framework of the OEEC. The ECSC countries argued that profound economic integration is inconceivable within the framework of the OEEC. Britain left the discussions in November, so it was only the six ECSC countries that continued talks. The Spaak Report claimed that there was a need for the creation of a common market among the six countries, with one exception. Atomic energy needed to be covered by a special, sectoral agreement.

During the drafting of the common market agreement, there appeared numerous problems:

- France feared that its manufacturing industry would not be able to withstand open competition from other partner countries. This would come as a consequence of the elimination of tariffs and quotas on internal trade. A compromise was found in the inclusion of agriculture into the agreement, as well as in the avoidance of sensitive issues related to monetary integration. The customs union for the West German manufacturing industry would mean as much as the inclusion of agriculture was supposed to mean for France.
- France, as a traditionally protectionist country, demanded a high rate of common external tariff (CET), while the Netherlands as a traditionally free-trading country, wanted a low CET. The agreement was that the CET would be the arithmetic average of the six countries.
- The association of colonies was one of the most contested issues. With the exception of Luxembourg, all of the negotiating countries were once colonial powers. They would be reluctant to give up those 'special' relations with their colonies or former colonies. The tone of the discussion was set by France which did not want the application of the CET to the African Francophone countries. France wanted the treatment of these countries regarding tariffs and quotas as if they were a part of France. These territories received various aid from France which wanted to share that burden with the new Community and, in particular, with West Germany. Only after West Germany, although reluctantly, agreed to this French request, as well as the inclusion of agriculture into the final arrangement, did the French accept the West German demand for a customs union (tariff and quota-free trade) in the future community.
- Atomic energy was the only area for sectoral integration. There was a fear that the conventional European sources of energy might be depleted. The development, operation and closure of units that produce atomic energy needed large investment. France wanted to reduce the influence of the US on western Europe in this (and other) spheres. A European atomic energy integration organization would give France a chance to have additional control of nuclear research and production of energy in West Germany.

The Foreign Ministers of the six countries accepted the Spaak Report in Venice in May 1956 and decided that the Spaak Committee prepare the agreements for the creation of a common market and an atomic energy community. Britain decided not to take part in the final negotiations and proclaimed in October, as before, that it was interested above all in a free trade area. After a number of consultations, the Treaty that established the European Economic Community (EEC) was signed on 25 March 1957 in Rome, hence its name, the Treaty of Rome. The originals were written in four official languages (Dutch, French, German and Italian).

The Preamble to the Treaty of Rome says that its founders are resolved to preserve and strengthen peace (mentioned only once) and liberty, and urged the other people of Europe who share their ideal to join in their efforts. The Preamble also calls for the improvement of the living and working conditions in the EEC, harmonious development of the regions, common commercial policy and a progressive abolition of restrictions on international trade. The *objectives* of the Treaty are: the promotion of a continuous, harmonious and balanced development; increased stability and standard of living; and closer relations among the member states (Article 2).

The *means* for the achievement of those objectives are: the creation of a common market and a progressive approximation of economic policies of member states (Article 2); the elimination of customs duties and quantitative restrictions on intra-group trade; the freedom of movement for goods, persons, services and capital (four freedoms of movement); the establishment of a CET and a common commercial policy towards third countries; the adoption of common policies in agriculture and transport; the insurance of an undistorted competition in the common market; coordination of economic policies and rectification of disequilibria in the balances of payments; approximation of laws that would enable the proper operation of the common market; the creation of the European Social Fund and the European Investment Bank to improve employment opportunities, support economic expansion and raise the standard of living; and the closer association of overseas countries and territories in order to increase trade and jointly promote economic and social development (Article 3). Any discrimination on grounds of nationality is outlawed (Article 7): that refers, of course, to EEC nationals. The Treaty of Rome was concluded for an unlimited period of time (Article 240).

The economic arguments in favour of the creation of the EEC included a positive impact through increased competition on efficiency in production and employment of resources; an extension of markets demanded by specialization and economies of scale; an expansion of research and development (R&D) and the creation of new or improved goods, services and technologies; a reduction in risk and uncertainty; a tendency towards factor-price equalization; and an improvement in management.

There is a supranational institution in the EEC. It is the Council of Ministers, empowered to reach decisions by a simple or qualified majority vote, while acting on the proposal by the Commission. The Commission is an independent body that initiates and implements decisions of the Council of Ministers. There is also a consultation process with the European Parliament and the Economic and Social Committee. The Court of Justice is in charge of the implementation of the Treaty of Rome throughout the EEC.[16] The Treaty was ratified during 1957 and it came into force on 1 January 1958.

The Treaty establishing the European Atomic Energy Community (Euratom) was concluded at the same time and place as the Treaty that created the EEC. The task of Euratom is: to create conditions for the speedy establishment and growth of nuclear industries (Article 1); promote R&D in the field; set uniform safety standards; facilitate investment; ensure regular and equitable supply of ores and nuclear fuels; exercise the right of ownership regarding special fissile materials; create a common market in specialized materials and equipment; and foster progress in the peaceful uses of nuclear energy (Article 2). The Euratom Treaty was concluded for an unlimited period of time (Article 208).

West Germany was licensed to carry out R&D in nuclear energy, but exclusively for peaceful purposes. It may obtain the nuclear material solely through the Euratom. That gave the Euratom an unrestricted right to inspect all West German R&D in nuclear energy. But what is peaceful R&D in nuclear energy? During such R&D, even if it is done with the best intentions, the result may be totally different from the desired one!

VII EUROPEAN FREE TRADE ASSOCIATION

Having seen that the ECSC countries were determined to continue with an overall economic integration, Britain proposed in 1956 the creation of a free trade area for manufactured goods in the OEEC. The ECSC countries rejected that proposal since it was one-sided. Britain would obtain free access for its manufactured goods in the market of the 'group of six' without giving reciprocal access for farm goods from the continent in its market.

As a response to the creation of the EEC, Britain gathered together the 'other six' countries[17] that signed the Stockholm Convention with a view to creating the European Free Trade Association (EFTA). The small Secretariat (only around 70 people) did not have any supranational authorities, and it was the only body of EFTA. Agriculture was excluded from the arrangement, so the whole business referred to manufactured goods only. Apart from the elimination of tariffs on internal trade, there was almost no other intervention by EFTA. The market forces were left to do the job of integration. There were no common policies whatsoever. Therefore, the history of EFTA appears to be without significance or event. The important things, i.e., market-induced specialization, happened at such a micro level as to escape the commentator's eye (Curzon Price, 1988, p. 100). However, the group was successful in economic terms. Their average GDP per capita was always (significantly) higher than the same indicator in the EEC.

As a purely commercial arrangement (tariff and quota-free internal trade in manufactured goods),[18] EFTA did not have any grand expectations regarding integration compared to the EEC. The reasons are simple. The EFTA countries are in geographical terms very dispersed, they were at different levels of development and, most importantly, the EFTA countries traded much more with the EEC countries than with their partners in EFTA. From the outset, the aim of EFTA was *not* to create strong integration links among its members, *but rather* to find a mutually satisfactory cohabitation with the EEC. In other words, the free trade area among the seven EFTA countries was only a means to an end, rather than an objective in itself (Curzon Price, 1987, p. 4). Since the EFTA countries intended to neutralize the impact of the creation of the EEC on EFTA trade, it appears that EFTA succeeded in its aim.

Just one year after the establishment of EFTA, Britain (the most important EFTA member country) submitted its application for full membership of the EEC. Britain realized that it had to be a part of a stronger and larger economic group. EFTA looked stillborn. It had a kind of negative identity. Members of EFTA started to seem from afar as being not-yet-in-the-EEC.

The creation of the two economic blocs in western Europe revealed that the OEEC failed in its efforts to promote economic cooperation in the region. So the US intended to keep some kind of economic unity in western Europe between the EEC and EFTA. The US, Britain, France and West Germany signed an agreement in 1960 (taking effect in 1961) about a transformation of the OEEC into the Organization for Economic Cooperation and Development (OECD) and an increase in its membership to 20 countries (including the US and Canada). The objective of the OECD was the achievement of the highest sustainable economic growth and employment, promotion of free trade and support of development in the poor non-member countries. The means for the achievement of those objectives were consultations (the OECD is the main international forum for the discussion about the economic matters of the mainly highly developed countries), exchange of macro-economic information and coordination of economic policies and forecasts.

VIII EEC AND BRITAIN

It seemed up until the end of the 1950s that Britain would be neither ready nor willing to accept the 'rules of the game' of the EEC. The reasons could be found in the unacceptability of supranationality, ties with the Commonwealth, membership of EFTA and a system of farm prices (which allowed much higher prices in the EEC than in Britain). The British economy, however, did not develop at a satisfactory pace compared with the other EFTA or EEC countries. A boost to the economy could come from access to a larger market. That was why the Tory Prime Minister, Harold Macmillan, decided to apply in July 1961 to begin negotiations with the EEC about full British membership. Britain did not (initially) like or grasp the idea about the EEC, but thoroughly understood the hard facts. The application was warmly welcomed by the Benelux countries already in the EEC, as well as by the US. The Benelux countries wanted to see Britain in the EEC as a counterbalance to French political supremacy and the West German industrial dominance. The favourable stance of the US could be found in its desire to close the ranks among west European allies.

The EEC Council of Ministers accepted the British application. Negotiations about access started. Charles de Gaulle, the President of France, said in a press conference in Paris in January 1963 that Britain was not yet ready to join the EEC. That was de Gaulle's first veto for the British entry into the EEC. Although de Gaulle's veto was somehow unexpected, many observers were questioning the British sincerity with respect to entry of the EEC. Weeks and months were lost during negotiations on the questions of relatively marginal importance such as the import of cricket equipment from India or kangaroo meat from Australia (Jansen, 1975, pp. 91–92).

The negative French attitude towards British entry of the EEC, in spite of the favourable stance of West Germany and the US, indicated the complexity of relations in the EEC. France did not want the British presence in the EEC, since in the absence of Britain, it was only France that had the monopoly regarding political action in western Europe.[19] As for West Germany, some more time needed to pass before it became a positive force in international relations.

IX LUXEMBOURG AGREEMENT

The six west European countries were joined in three organizations: ECSC, EEC and Euratom. Each one had its own Commission (High Authority in the ECSC), Council of Ministers, Parliament and Court of Justice. In order to avoid the unnecessary duplication of organs a Merger Treaty was signed in Brussels in April 1965. That Treaty (taking effect in July 1967) brought together the bodies of the three distinct Communities into the common organs of the European Communities (EC). One ought to remember that the three Communities had common Parliaments and Courts of Justice since 1958.

11

The work of the Council of Ministers is based on the proposals of the Commission. The Commission was most active at that time in the field of agriculture. Hence, the Council received three proposals in April 1965. The first one dealt with the financing of the Common Agricultural Policy (CAP), the second referred to the creation of EC financial resources, while the third argued in favour of a larger democratic control of the EC's expenditure by the Community's Parliament. France wanted the strengthening of the CAP, but was against the increase in the powers of the Community's institutions. Since there was no compromise by July 1965, the EC entered its deepest crisis since its creation. France left its chair empty in the Council of Ministers. In a press conference (his favourite way of communication), de Gaulle stated in September 1965 that French sovereignty belonged to the French people. The message was that France did not want to accept any longer the majority vote (supranationality) as the mechanism for decision-making in the Council of Ministers.

After seven months of conflict between the Council of Ministers and France, a compromise settlement was reached on 29 January 1966 in Luxembourg (Luxembourg Agreement) about the decision-making process in the Council of Ministers. This agreement about disagreement had two important points:

- When very important interests of one or more countries are at stake, and decisions based on the proposal from the Commission could be reached by a majority vote, the members of the Council of Ministers would endeavour to reach a solution acceptable to all member countries, bearing in mind their common interest, as well as the interests of the EC, and all that in the light of Article 2 of the Treaty of Rome.
- In view of the former point, the French delegation considered that when very important interests were at stake, negotiations had to continue until an uanimous agreement could be reached.

The Luxembourg Agreement meant the virtual end of the undemocratic (but very functional) principle of outvoting in international relations. On the one hand, any minister could declare that the issue at stake is of vital importance for their country, while on the other hand, the Commission (as an independent body of the EC) became more prudent in preparing proposals for the Council of Ministers.

X THE FIRST ENLARGEMENT

The implementation of the Treaty of Rome regarding the elimination of tariffs and quotas on internal trade went much faster and smoother than was envisaged in the Treaty. All tariffs for the EC internal trade were eliminated on 1 July 1968, a year and a half before the Treaty of Rome deadline. At the same time, the Community introduced the CET in its external trade. That was the first big achievement in the EC's integration efforts. Another provision of the Treaty of Rome that was also implemented was the association of non-European countries and territories which had 'special' relations with the EC member countries (Article 131). The association of those countries with the EC started in 1963, when 18 African countries and the EEC signed an agreement on trade and aid in Yaoundé Cameroon (Yaoundé Convention). The Second Yaoundé Convention was signed in 1969.

A relatively unsatisfactory performance of the British economy in the second half of the 1960s made the government in office (Labour) revive the idea of accession to the EC since it might bring important economic benefits (free and secure access to a large and growing market). Britain submitted its second application for membership to the EC in May 1967. With the exception of France, all the EC member countries warmly welcomed the British desire to enter the Community. British entry would reduce French political dominance in the EC. Owing to the British balance-of-payments problems and wishing to keep Britain out of the EC, de Gaulle had a press conference in November 1967 where he stated that the British economy was still too weak to join the EC, and he shut the door on British entry into the Community for the second time.

At about the same time, French industry started to lag behind that of West Germany. Modernization of the manufacturing industry went slowly and protests in May and June 1968 contributed to de Gaulle's departure from the political scene in April 1969. De Gaulle's withdrawal from public life enabled the Hague Summit (December 1969) of the Presidents or Prime Ministers of the EC countries to revisit the opening of negotiations with Britain about entry into the EC, on the basis of the 1967 application which had never been withdrawn. Denmark, Ireland and Norway also submitted applications for entry. Encouraged by the success of integration, as well as growing persistence of other countries to join the EC, Pierre Werner was commissioned to prepare a report about the creation of economic and monetary union in the EC.

The biggest problems for the EC during negotiations with Britain were agriculture, financing of the EC budget and relations with the Commonwealth. Most of British trade before EC entry was with non-European countries where, among other things, Britain purchased food at much lower prices than those prevailing in the Community. As for financial matters, the Community budget was financed by tariffs on imports and direct contributions by the member countries dating from the creation of the EC up until 1970. The Council of Ministers decided in April 1970 that the EC needed to change the previous system and get its own resources. The EC started to be financed from levies charged on imports of agricultural goods, proceeds from the CET and direct contributions by the member states that equal up to 1 per cent of value added tax.

The agreement about the entry of Britain, Denmark, Ireland and Norway into the EC (ECSC, EEC and Euratom) was signed in January 1972 after lengthy and difficult negotiations. The Agreement stipulated a 5-year transition period, quotas for imports of food (butter and cheese from New Zealand) to Britain, the British contribution to the EC budget (because of the disproportionately large share of trade with the non-EC countries) and the association of the countries and territories with 'special' relations with the new members into the EC system.

Britain, Denmark and Ireland supported the Accession Agreement, but this failed to get the support of the Norwegians in a referendum. The EC acquired three new members on 1 January 1973. On the same date came into effect the Brussels series of bilateral agreements of July 1972 between the EC and the rest of the EFTA countries on a free trade area for manufactured products, as Britain and Denmark left EFTA on the day of their entry into the EC. The small EFTA countries stepped part way into the EC. It had been a long-held desire of Austria, since Article 4 of its State Treaty does not permit economic partnership with West Germany, although in the post-cold war era, there is a more liberal interpretation of its provision.[20]

During the British entry into the EC, Tories were in office. The Labour party which submitted the application for entry to the EC was not satisfied with the terms of entry. Labour promised voters that it would renegotiate the terms of British entry. The Labour party had a national programme for the production of coal and steel which wanted to keep the ECSC out of that business in Britain. After they came into office, the Accession Agreement was renegotiated, but the results of the year-long negotiations had not revised the original Agreement in any important way. In the national referendum in June 1975, the British voted in favour of remaining in the EC.[21] The EC offered benefits to every member country. In the case of the three big states, they were most obvious. Britain received EC finances from the regional fund, France benefited from the CAP, while West Germany gained from the EC-internal free trade.

The Rome Treaty envisaged a transition period of 12 years which would establish the EC by the end of 1969. It specified the ways and deadlines for the elimination of tariffs on internal trade and the introduction of the CET. After 1970, the Treaty of Rome was not a precise guide for the future of the EC. That was one of the contributing factors that led the EC into Eurosclerosis.

XI EUROSCLEROSIS

The decision to start negotiations with Britain about entry into the EC was reached during the Hague Summit in 1969. Two years later, in 1971, the same group met in Paris and prepared the grounds for British entry. It became obvious that the summits were quite an effective institution for the resolution of problems, as well as for the guidance of the EC. During the 1974 summit in Paris, the participants agreed to formalize their meetings (at least twice a year) under the name of the European Council.[22]

The European Councils became the highest institution of the EC although they were not mentioned either in the Treaty of Rome or the Treaty of Paris that empowered only the Council of Ministers to pass all the important decisions in the EC. The introduction of the European Councils pushed the development in the EC towards the strengthening of intergovernmental decision-making and away from supranationality. The problem with such a structure was and is that the Council of Ministers tended to pass on very important decisions to the European Council which sometimes has to deal with certain technical issues (such as decisions about production or import quotas). Those negotiations are often linked with the national and political horse-trading, conducted in the small hours of the morning, that reflect transient issues and sometimes do not have very much in common with the real long-term interests of the EC.

The EC intended to expand the coverage of its (common) economic policies outside trade and agriculture. During the turmoil at the international currency markets (1972–1979), the majority of the EC national currencies had a common floating rate of exchange against the US dollar. At the same time, there was an energy crisis coupled with two large external shocks that came from sharp increases in oil prices. The EC countries were occupied with their short-term national problems which pushed EC integration down the list of priorities.

In 1979, the European Monetary System (EMS) established a stricter system for the common float (for the participating countries) by reducing the margins of fluctuations and by providing the system with relatively generous short-term financial assistance. The objective was to influence the EC countries by a sophisticated method of implementing coordinated and comparable economic policies. If it were not for those changes and the largely unnoticed entry of Greece into the EC on 1 January 1981, the 1970s and the first half of 1980s were quite uneventful. On the economic front, productivity was sluggish and labour costs were increasing, so the EC producers were at a competitive disadvantage relative to their rivals in the US and Japan. The EC was in a period without a clear vision about its future, so that those years were often termed Eurosclerosis. None the less, a waking up from hibernation came when it became obvious that the Treaty of Rome was not a good blueprint for the future of the EC after 1968, when the economic performance of the US and Japan seriously threatened the effectiveness of the EC economy.

XII THE SINGLE EUROPEAN ACT

In spite of a tariff- and quota-free trade within the EC, the still excessive non-tariff barriers (NTBs) were segmenting national markets within the EC. That was seriously jeopardizing the ability of the EC manufacturing and services industries to profit from economies of scale and increase their international competitiveness in relation to both the US and Japan, as well as newly industrialized countries. In addition, Article 115 of the Treaty of Rome permitted the Commission to authorize the member countries in economic difficulties to adopt protective measures. They usually took the form of quotas against Japanese cars, or textiles from the developing countries. Article 115 enabled the EC nations in difficulties to block imports from the non-EC countries through another EC country which is not in trouble. That resulted in (sometimes) large differences in prices of identical goods sold in different EC member states. The consequence was a negative impact on the allocation of resources and the integration of the region. Something had to be done.

The White Paper (Cockfield Report) of June 1985 offered the Programme for the Completing of the Internal Market.[23] This supply-side oriented 'technical' programme included 282 legislative proposals and a timetable for their completion by the end of 1992. Since the classical way of economic integration among countries through the elimination of tariffs and quotas on internal trade was exhausted in 1968, the objective of the White Paper was to oust NTBs and create a genuine and homogeneous frontier-free internal market. That was an ambitious task. It has not yet been achieved even in the federal and developed countries such as Switzerland where a free circulation of goods, services, people and capital has not been fully realized because of the diversity of regulations in the constituent cantons. Canada is another example. This country has a free trade deal with the US which liberalizes trade between the two countries; however public procurement policies among Canadian provinces remain important trade barriers within the country. The internal situation in Australia is similar to that of Canada.

At about the same time as the White Paper was delivered, and after a few years of delay from the planned target, the EC finalized negotiations with Spain and Portugal about accession. On 1 January 1986, the EC was enlarged by the two new (southern) members and became the Community of 12 countries.

The intention of the White Paper was to increase the competitiveness of EC goods, services and factors, first, in relation to the American and Japanese rivals through a change in internal rules, rather than subsidies. The White Paper brought the 1992 Programme. It was a kind of EC antidote to Eurosclerosis. The White Paper, a reader-unfriendly document, mentioned the removal of physical, technical and fiscal barriers.[24] Since the 1992 Programme was widely accepted throughout all segments of the EC, it represented the end of lethargy and Eurosclerosis in the EC. It was the biggest boost to the integration process (mark 2) since the signing of the Treaty of Rome (mark 1). One point needs to be remembered. The White Paper and the single internal market programme were not aims in themselves. They were merely a step towards another goal, economic and political union.

The main aspects of the 1992 Programme include the following six features:

- removal of NTBs for internal trade;
- increased competition;
- promotion of cooperation among firms in R&D;
- unification of factor markets through full liberalization of factor (labour and capital) mobility;
- monetary integration;
- social protection (Social Charter).

A smooth implementation of the 1992 Programme required a change in the decision-making process of the EC. That led to the first, although relatively modest, reform of the Treaty of Rome. That was brought about by the Single European Act (signed in February 1986) which came into force on 1 July 1987. What the Act basically did was to speed up the implementation of the 1992 Programme. Except for fiscal matters, rights of employees and free movement of persons (where unanimity remained the rule), the Act increased the importance of majority vote in the Council of Ministers for measures linked with the implementation of the 1992 Programme. That put aside the Luxembourg Agreement. The original spirit of the voting arrangements from the Treaty of Rome was revived.

The Commission gained in importance because it had to prepare proposals to the Council of Ministers for the realization of the 1992 Programme. As for the decisions linked with the creation of the single internal market, the Council of Ministers got new powers. It may act on a qualified majority basis, after consultations with the European Parliament and the Economic and Social Committee, save for the measures that deal with taxation, rights of employees and issues dealing with the mobility of people (Articles 99 and 100a, respectively). For those three issues, unanimity, or to put it in plain English: the *veto* power of each member state, was introduced at British request. Other matters that were officially raised in EC legislation by the Act include: the formal inclusion of the European Council in the EC structure, which is supposed to meet at least twice a year (Article 2 of the Single European Act), although there were no provisions about what the Council is supposed to do; an endeavour to jointly formulate and implement an EC foreign policy (Article 30 of the Single European Act); and the addressing of environmental issues (Articles 130r–t).

The Single European Act shifted the balance of power from the national governments towards the EC. This exacerbated concern by some of the member countries about the transfer of national sovereignty to a relatively distant bureaucracy which lacks political accountability. The relative concentration of decision-making authority about economic issues had certain benefits. Fragmented economic policies and distinct national currencies would not make better off, for example, most of the federal states in the US. The EC had to go ahead. The step following the 1992 Programme 'had' to be towards a monetary union.

XIII THE MAASTRICHT TREATY

Political cooperation (and federalism), one of the necessary conditions for monetary union[25] in the EC, had two basic proponents. While Germany and Italy were in favour of a fast federalization of the EC through such means as a common defence policy,[26] other member countries were thinking about a more gradual process. The preference for gradualism was not only to deter the entry of the EFTA and certain east European countries into the EC; more importantly, EC countries are among the oldest in the world with long and well-established systems of administration and political life. This is hard to change with a bold move over a relatively short period of time.

Ideas about political cooperation and union in the EC abounded, but in reality, there was little progress. The most controversial matters dealt with a common foreign policy and defence, as well as the powers of the European Parliament (since it would not be realistic to expect the European Parliament and the Commission to play the same role as they did in the area of agriculture). In spite of the name, potential European Political Union would not create a single government, but it would increase the power of the European Parliament to reduce the 'democratic deficit' of the EC's institutions.

After the overhaul of the former East Germany and once the memories of the Second World War fade away with a new generation of politicians, a reunited Germany (October 1990) may, in the longer term, present a mighty power that may do something on its own. Throughout the post-war period France was the leading west European state aiming to tie Germany into an arrangement that would prevent Germany going its own way, particularly in the field of security and foreign policy. That started with the ECSC. Although the Franco-German axis was and still is the backbone of west European integration, relations between the two countries were not free of strain. This was obvious in the case of the potential enlargement of the EC. France wanted to reduce the number of new entrants, while Germany was in favour of 'eastern' expansion. Germany wanted future enlargement of the EC to embrace the Scandinavian and east European countries,[27] not only for stability on its eastern border and as a buffer against turmoil in the former Soviet Union, but more importantly because these countries would view EC affairs from a German perspective. In addition, some Germans ask why should they pay through the various EC funds more to Ireland or Portugal than to Poland. Another conflicting point was French apprehension regarding the secession rights of Croatia and Slovenia (Germany succeeded, however, from the start in pushing through that issue at the end of 1991[28] and 'forced' the other 11 EC states to accept the *fait accompli*). The recognition of those two countries for the political establishment of the EC was, in fact, of secondary importance. The newly independent countries could be the Czech Republic and Slovakia, or the Baltic states. What mattered primarily in Maastricht was the fact that it was the 'vote' of 11 EC countries on the question: do they recognize Germany as a great European power, a potential leader of the EU, or not? The answer was yes.

In shaping the future of the EC, Britain continues to play second fiddle. This country has not yet realized that the US has had another number one strategic partner in Europe since the start of the 1970s. It is Germany. The EC countries perceive Britain as the one that has not been fully committed to the continental EC, while Britain perceives itself to be part of a wider 'Atlantic Community'. That has seriously crippled the role that Britain could and should play in the EC. Britain's intention continued to be one in which it would both remain in the EC's club and attempt to maintain its special stakes elsewhere. In addition, a truly EC foreign policy without full British participation may have a limited meaning.

After a period of active diplomacy, frantic negotiations and horse-trading, the European Council, at its meeting in Maastricht on 9 and 10 December 1991, reached a settlement about European Union (EU). France's major goal to bring Germany into a single currency (in 1999) was fulfilled, as were its defence and foreign policy arrangements. Germany got agreement that the monetary policy of the EU would be German inspired and that the European Parliament would increase its powers. The southern countries, led by Spain, got the cohesion fund. The Dutch were able to push through the Social Chapter. Britain obtained from Maastricht two opt-outs. One from the single-currency, and the other from the social chapter.[29] Because of these important exceptions, the Treaty was not a tidy arrangement from the outset and the negotiations brought the EU to the realization that consolidation must occur before expansion. The two exceptions from the Maastricht Treaty are good examples which show that Britain still thinks it is different from other EU countries. Britain, as usual, wanted the Maastricht Summit to do as little as possible.[30] The Treaty on European Union was signed in Maastricht (hence the Maastricht Treaty) on 7 February 1992. After its ratification, mark 3 in the EU's integration, was supposed to start.

The Maastricht Treaty that established the EU is just like the Single European Act, a reader-unfriendly crowd of amendments and additions to the EEC, ECSC and Euratom Treaties. It expands the scope of the activities of the EU beyond its original economic affairs. From a substantive point, the Maastricht Treaty consists of three basic parts (pillars). The first one is the revised Treaty of Rome that includes terms for the economic and monetary union (EMU), the second refers to defence and foreign policy, and the last one deals with justice and home affairs.

No matter how it is interpreted, the Maastricht Treaty is basically about *economic and monetary union*. That is spelt out both in the Preamble and Articles B and G, respectively. Unlike the supply-side oriented and 'technical' 1992 Programme, EMU touches political issues. Although it may be masked behind technicalities, it deals with a single currency and, hence, the political sovereignty of the EU nations. EMU was an expected development following the completion of the internal market. A free flow of goods, services and factors in the EU market, together with an efficient allocation of resources, needs to be supported by stability in exchange rates. Monetary integration seeks to serve as a replacement for a deep(er) political union which did not take solid shape in the Treaty. EMU is to be achieved in three stages. During the first stage, there must be a reinforcement in coordination of economic and monetary policies of the member countries. The second stage started in January 1994 with the establishment of the European Monetary Institute (EMI) in Frankfurt. The EMI is to coordinate the EU members' monetary policies and prepare the conditions for the final stage. The central banks of the member states need to become independent before the end of the second stage when the EMI would be transformed into an independent European Central Bank (ECB).[31]

The Council of Ministers would decide by a qualified majority, not later than 31 December 1996, whether a majority (at least seven) of the EU countries fulfil the five conditions necessary for the third stage of the EMU.[32] If a country fails one (or, perhaps, two conditions), but makes good progress, it may be let into the EMU. Should the Council be unable to decide about the beginning of the third stage, the Maastricht Treaty stipulates that it would begin on 1 January 1999 for the countries that fulfil the necessary conditions for EMU. Those countries would irrevocably fix their exchange rates and the European Currency Unit (ECU), under the name of the 'euro', would later on replace the national currencies. The ECB would follow its primary commitment of price stability and, consequently, set interest rates and conduct foreign exchange operations. In addition, the ECB would support economic growth and employment. The ECB would report regularly to the EU's finance ministers – Economic and Financial Committee meetings of the (ECOFIN) which would issue broad economic policy guidelines – and to the European Parliament.

The second basic part of the Maastricht Treaty are the provisions on the *common foreign and security policy* (Preamble and Articles B and J, respectively). The undefined role of the European Council that came out of the Single European Act (Article 2) was clarified in the Maastricht Treaty (Article D). The job of the European Council is to provide the EU with the necessary impetus for its development, as well as to define the necessary political guidelines. Applied to the foreign and security policy, the EU members 'shall define and implement a common foreign and security policy' (Article J.1) which would lead to 'the eventual framing of a common defence policy, which might in time lead to a common defence' (Article B). A common defence policy is the objective of the EU, not a commitment. So a non-federal (British) view prevailed. The European Council is in charge of the definition of 'the general principles and general guidelines for the common foreign and security policy...The Council shall act unanimously' (Article J.8). The governments of the member states would have to follow the common line. All that is supposed 'to deepen the solidarity between their peoples while respecting their history, their culture and their traditions' (Preamble).

As for the security and common defence policy that might in time lead to common security, the EU is allowed to request the WEU, 'which is an integral part of the development of the Union, to elaborate and implement decisions and actions of the Union which have defence implications' (Article J.4). On French insistence, the WEU is subordinated to the EU (the WEU became the Union's defence wing), while what Britain got out of the deal was the wording that the defence policy would not run counter to the interests of NATO. It was not only Britain that still wants the involvement of NATO in the EU's defence. Some other countries, such as Germany, wanted the American involvement (and taxpayers' money) in defence matters, since that brings savings for the EU's taxpayers.[33] When the eastern bloc disappeared, German money would be better spent on the reunification of the eastern parts of the country, although certain defence efforts need to be made because of the uncertainties that may come from the east. In addition, the US intends to cut expenditure including the one for defence. The Americans want to see the EU more reliant on its own defence. In addition, an event that made many in NATO question American commitment to the Alliance was when the US unilaterally withdrew from the naval blockade in the Adriatic Sea in 1994.

The third major part of the Treaty refers to close cooperation in *justice and home affairs* (Preamble and Articles B and K, respectively). Interior ministers will work together on issues such as crime, terrorism, drugs, immigration, visas, asylum and frontier rules. The decisions ought to be taken unanimously.

Apart from the three basic 'pillars' of the EU, the Maastricht Treaty brought in a number of interesting features to the Union. One of them is *subsidiarity*, a principle that is increasingly advocated by the EU's institutions. It is mentioned in the Preamble and Articles B and G, respectively. On subsidiarity, the Treaty says that the EU would take action 'only if and in so far as the objectives of the proposed action cannot be sufficiently achieved by the Member States and can therefore, by reason of scale or effects of the proposed action, be better achieved by the Community' (Article G). As the EU becomes wider and more diverse in size and deeper in scope, the implementation of decisions may be costlier. Hence, there may be certain economies of scale in the taking of some decisions at EU level. So, the EU needs to be involved only in those affairs which the member states cannot operate in a satisfactory way from a common standpoint. In some cases it is the local level that is better placed and informed to handle certain matters. It is also more accountable and has superior insight about what the electors want and taxpayers are willing to pay. In other cases, e.g., pollution, because of cross-country spillovers, local or regional authorities may overlook those effects, but the EU should not.

The EU's action is not automatic. It would be undertaken only when the benefits of the action exceed its cost. If applied to the limit, the principle of subsidiarity which defines the border between the national and supranational issues would change the EU out of recognition (just think of the British and, perhaps, French reactions because of a further transfer of national sovereignty). Therefore, at least in the beginning, there would be more talk about it than real action. Since subsidiarity is an ambiguous term, it can be interpreted in a number of ways: from a liberal to a dirigiste one. The diplomats may argue that the implementation of subsidiarity may be only the exception in the EU's affairs, while the powers of the member states would be the rule. None the less, the subsidiarity principle masks its real substance. That is, the potential for the continuous expansion of powers of the EU's institutions!

The *European Parliament* increased its authority too. In the new decision-making procedure (Article G) for the measures that relate to the single market, environment, research, trans-European networks, health, consumer protection, education and culture, the Parliament may reject the draft law put forward by the Council of Ministers. The Council may reject the amendments to the law by the Parliament. In either case, the two sides form a Conciliation Committee. If the Committee finds a compromise, it is both the Parliament and the Council of Ministers that have to endorse it. If there is no compromise, the law cannot pass. This procedure, explained in detail below, increased the power of Parliament at the expense of the Council of Ministers. It gave an effective veto power to the European Parliament which emerged as the biggest winner from the Maastricht deal.

Other matters that were mentioned in the Maastricht Treaty are: the *rights of citizens* of the EU to live and work anywhere in the Union; the entitlement of EU citizens while travelling outside of the EU to get diplomatic and consular services from the representatives of any of the EU member countries; and the right to vote and stand for elections in the local and EU elections in any of the member countries. The EU is to contribute to the establishment and development of *trans-European networks* in the areas of transport, telecommunications and energy infrastructure. A *Cohesion Fund* is to support environment and trans-European network projects in the member countries with a below-average GDP per capita. A *Committee of the Regions* was added to the EU structure for consultative purposes. A *Social Protocol*, from which Britain got an opt-out, licensed the EU to regulate on working conditions, employment rights for men and women and workers' participation. The EU is to contribute and encourage (but not legislate) in the areas of cross-border cooperation in *education*, *culture* and *health*.

The *final provisions* of the Maastricht Treaty provide a safety valve if things go wrong. An intergovernmental conference (IGC) is to be convened in 1996 to examine and, if necessary, revise (that will be the case) the objectives of the Treaty (Article N). Any European state may apply to become a member of the EU. If admitted, it must join the whole Union (Article O). It means that the new entrants have to accept some four decades of the EU's legislation and align their policies with the EU during the adjustment period. The Treaty was concluded for an unlimited period of time (Article Q) and was to enter into force on 1 January 1993, or failing that, on the first day following the day of the last ratification of a signatory state (Article S). The Treaty deadline was not honoured. So it entered into force on 1 November 1993 when the last Parliament ratified it. It was – your guess is correct – the Parliament of Britain. On that date, the EC officially became the EU.

XIV A GLIMPSE INTO THE FUTURE

Since the future developments of the EU depend on a plethora of volatile multinational political factors, its future is hard to predict. Various 'dimensions' of the EU are still vague. That includes the external, defence and social 'dimensions'. Even the term 'Union' is unclear. It may be easier to point to problems in the development of an EU which is still being shaped, than to suggest solutions acceptable to everybody. The EU is, indeed, rich in diversity. That should not be very surprising since, for example, even the EC member states themselves have changed. Belgium has transformed itself since the 1970s from a unitary into a federal state. Only the future will tell how that development will end up in Belgium or Italy ('Padania').

One of the first issues to catch the attention of an analyst is that of enlargement of the EU. 'Any European state may apply to become a Member of the Union' (Article O). That is the only Maastricht Treaty based (necessary) condition for a country to be considered for full membership to the EU. In addition to that express requirement, there are several other, tacit, prerequisites for entry. First, the applicant country must have a market economy. Second, the national political system must be stable and democratic.[34] Third, it has to accept and implement, during the negotiated transition period, all of the prevailing EU's legislation, i.e., it has to accept the *acquis communautaire*. Last, it should not jeopardize the EU's financial resources. All those necessary conditions for entry into the EU reveal that the Union has a very high discretionary power and flexibility to select aspiring members. With this in mind, even the chances of the most advanced east European transition economies seem bleak for quite some time in the future, *unless* and until the rules change and the economic situation of such countries improves (the EU has no intentions or funds to support the economies of the member countries that would retrogress towards farming). That may be hypocritical, since, for almost half of a century, the west encouraged those countries to join the free market and democratic world! The message is: calm down Czechs, Poles and Hungarians. This applies to the others too – for quite some time. Thus, according to the most optimistic scenario (meaning relatively smooth negotiations and an adjustment period), the most advanced transition economies may become full members of the EU in some twenty years time!

The one field where coordination and, even, unification of action between the EU and these three prospective member countries is likely in the future is politics. It does not cost the EU money, while the three countries may get the impression that something is going on between them and the EU. But the most that the east Europeans can hope for in the longer term is a kind of arrangement similar to that implemented between the EU and most of the EFTA countries in 1994.

There are, basically, two equally divided groups of countries regarding this issue in the Union. The *deepeners* prefer the consolidation of integration before any new members are admitted into the club. They are strongest in France, Italy and Spain (the Catholic tier). The Protestant *wideners*, led by Britain and supported by Germany, argue in favour of expansion of the EU, in particular, by the rich Scandinavian (Protestant) countries and Austria. These countries would perceive the EU in a liberal way, would dilute Latin activism, and would be good contributors to the EC budget. The *wideners* have had the edge as Austria, Finland and Sweden joined the EU in 1995. In addition, Germany would like to see some of the east European transition countries enter the EU, because these countries would tend to see the Union's affairs in a German way. The southern EU countries are concerned with the possible entry of some of the east European countries, even in the distant future, since they may be democratic (but poor) and would compete with the EU's Club Med, 'olive belt' or 'southern axis' for regional aid.[35] France and Spain would like to see a 'balanced' approach between the potential eastern enlargement of the EU and the policy of openness towards the southern Mediterranean countries. A potentially rejuvenated old division of 'spheres of influence' has a corrosive effect on the unity of the EU as proclaimed by the Maastricht Treaty.

Contrary to Latin activism, the expanded EU would slow down integration and increase the liberals' apprehension regarding the bold interventionist steps in the economy. The ratification procedure of the Maastricht Treaty did not go smoothly at all. Although the Treaty was ratified by all member countries, in most of them it provoked heated debates. The winning majority for the ratification in most countries was very slim, indeed.[36] In Denmark, the first national referendum about the Treaty failed. That could mean in practice the exclusion of Denmark from the EU.[37] After obtaining opt-outs from the foreign and security policies, Denmark repeated its referendum and a (slim) majority in favour was obtained. That may be the sign to the integration enthusiasts to slow down and reflect at least once more about undertaking further grand steps.

The voters may prefer EU *à la carte*. Such flexibility may further complicate the legal structure and operation of the EU, but *that* may be what voters seek and are ready to pay for. If the governments and the Maastricht Treaty are not capable of granting that, they need to be changed.[38]

France has realized that in a wider EU its economic and political weight would diminish, while Germany would become even more influential. The myth about the *grandeur* of France in the EU is most seriously being shaken by the rising political power of Germany after reunification. France seems more to manipulate than to create events now. Germany has already achieved economic dominance in Europe. A strong Franco-German relationship still exists, but it is being modified. It is still necessary for the stability of Europe, but not sufficient. France may soon feel uncomfortable in its political and defence position. Germany is now locked in the EU for quite some time to come, but the question still remains as to how it will use its clout in EU affairs in the future? Would this be 'European Germany', or 'German Europe'?

It must not be forgotten that most of the EFTA countries aspired to join, and actually did join the EU. The new democracies of eastern Europe also wish to become members, as did Greece, Spain and Portugal during the 1970s. In a larger and, perhaps more diluted EU, would decision-making lead to a paralysis in the operation of the EU, as France fears? Would it lead to a further reform of the EU? Would that steel the EU towards federalism, unionism or a two- or multi-speed EU in which a group of countries that are able, ready and willing to go ahead with certain measures create cosy relationships among themselves, while the others are excluded from the arrangement, but openly invited to join when they feel ready to comply with those conditions?

The European Economic Area (EEA) quietly entered into force on 1 January 1994. It was conceived in 1990 as a vehicle for keeping potential new entrants (the EFTA countries) from applying, but it ended up being a waiting room for the new enlargement. The EEA, the world's biggest free trade area with over 370 million consumers, is in essence the virtual entry of the EFTA countries minus Switzerland (the Swiss declined in a referendum to approve it) into the EU, but excluding agriculture, energy, external trade, coal and steel, foreign and security policy. Within the EEA, which is served by an independent EEA Court of Justice, the participating countries enjoy a free mobility of goods, services, capital and people (four freedoms), but only for the internally produced goods and services.

The small EFTA countries achieved from the EEA free entry for their manufactured goods to the largest market in the world which would increase competition for their businesses and, hence, bring efficiency gains. The EU obtained secure access to wealthy consumers and assistance in resisting domestic protectionist appeals. The EFTA countries have always had a liberal trade policy for their manufactured goods. The EEA was to an extent, stillborn, since Austria, Finland, Norway and Sweden applied for a full membership of the EU in order to get a say in the EU's law-making. These applications were welcomed by the EU as the Union needs net contributors to its budget.[39] Austria, Finland and Sweden entered the EU on 1 January 1995. Norway's voters, however, declined to approve the deal.

Slow growth, unemployment and protectionist pressures often provide a fertile soil for introverted and nationalist policies. Those policies may be supported by currency speculation, as occurred in September 1992 when Britain and Italy suspended their membership of the exchange rate mechanism of the EMS, while Spain devalued the peseta. A bigger shock took place at the end of July 1993 with the actual demise of the exchange rate mechanism of the EMS[40] and the EU's federal dreams (at least for some time in the future). The EU was pushed back to the reality of the present, rather than to imagine its future. France thought of the EU as a club of like-minded peers. It was immensely disappointed when Germany refused to cut its interest rate. When major national issues are at stake, EU solidarity is still fragile. The wide increase in fluctuation margins seemed to devide the Maastricht Treaty's intentions to introduce a single currency in the relatively near future. The reunification of Germany was the major instigator of the Maastricht Treaty, as well as the reason for the Treaty's half-hearted implementation.

Lack of enthusiasm for the Maastricht Treaty was reserved not only for monetary affairs. In foreign policy, for example, which is supposed to be agreed unanimously (Article J.8) and which ought 'to deepen the solidarity between their peoples while respecting their history, their culture and their traditions' (Preamble), the EU has, in some cases, done quite the opposite. One of the most obvious cases is the dispute between Greece and the Former Yugoslav Republic of Macedonia. The whole affair revealed the difficulty in creating and implementing a common EU foreign policy. Dealing with problems such as this one will need to be high on the agenda even before the EU is enlarged to 20 or 30 member states.

After the breakup of ex-Yugoslavia in 1992, the 'Republic of Macedonia'[41] had claims not only on Macedonia (the northern Greek province) in its name and constitution, but it also usurped Macedonian (Greek) symbols because it lacked its own. The Maastricht Treaty stands for solidarity among the EU states 'while respecting their history, their culture and their traditions'. Instead of showing solidarity with an EU member country on whose province a newly independent state had certain claims in the constitution, the other EU member countries allied against Greece and pressurized it to accept something that runs contrary to one of the most glorious parts of Greek history, spirit, culture, tradition and territory! What a splendid hypocrisy and implementation of the Maastricht Treaty!

Since negotiations between Athens and Skopje did not lead anywhere, Greece introduced unilateral economic sanctions against the FYR Macedonia in February 1994. The Commission of the EU and other member countries were pressing Greece to revoke that measure on the grounds that it violated the free flow of goods. There were no similar pressures on Skopje which is, after all, outside the EU. When, however, only Germany introduced identical unilateral sanctions against Serbia and Montenegro in 1991, although there were no territorial and other claims on Germany, the Commission was *not* concerned about such a unilateral measure that was preventing a free flow of goods. When Greece does it, that is cause for concern! Small countries are 'really' being asked about certain problems in the EU and their stance is 'respected'![42]

A serious problem for the operation of the EU arose in 1996, when the EU banned the export of British beef and its derivatives in the spring because it feared the spread of the human equivalent of 'mad cow disease' (BSE)[43]. In retaliation, the British government decided to block EU business by a policy of non-cooperation. These kind of tactics had not been seen in the EU since 1965, when General de Gaulle pursued an 'empty chair' policy. After a lot of hot air, a compromise deal was reached. The ban was lifted on certain conditions and Britain resumed its cooperation in the work of the EU.

XV CONCLUSION

The history of the EU could fit into five periods. First was creation and growth (1957–1968); in the second came consolidation and enlargement (1969–1973); third was the period of Eurosclerosis (1974–1984); then arrived a great leap forward and Euro-activism (1985–1992); the latest period is a venture into uncertainty (1993–?). How long the fifth period will last will be seen after the IGC.[44] It may slow down the grand plans presented in the Maastricht Treaty, but the EU may be better organized.

The EU is in a certain (temporary) crisis. On the political front, it has been unable to solve the neighbouring Yugoslav black hole which showed that the Union still plays a relatively minor role in the resolution of grave international crises (although the others did not fare much better).[45] In the economic field it is not capable of creating new jobs and reducing unemployment. As for EMU, the EU is as far away from that as ever.

The objective of the IGC that started in Turin in March 1996 is to revise the Maastricht Treaty and prepare the EU for the coming decades. It is a planned step, as the Maastricht Treaty was only an intermediate stage on the long road of deeper integration. The conference may last till the end of 1997. The major issues that the IGC will have to address and clarify include the following:

- *Eastern enlargement.* Widening cannot wait because of security considerations. In addition, European integration is too important to be left only to the 'exclusive' club of the present members. The EU needs to accept this fact, adapt and expand in order to survive as an open institution. However, nobody can say now when and/or how the enlargement should take place.[46] If EU policies are not altered, eastern enlargement would be too costly to be politically acceptable. Various estimates state that if there is no change in EU policies (for example, the CAP and regional aid), the entry of the Czech Republic, Hungary, Poland and Slovakia would cost the EU budget between ECU 20 to 30 billion a year![47] None the less, the actual costs of entry cannot be estimated prior to knowing the terms of enlargement.
- *Institutional reform.* Could structures that are 'suitable' for 15 countries be adequate for an EU of 20 or more countries? Membership *may* double before the end of the first decade of the twenty-first century. IGC faces a challenging task to reshape the institutions and policy-making in such a way that they are workable in the future EU of 20 or 30 diverse states. However, is deeper union compatible with a wider union? The IGC will have to tackle this issue.

The quota of Commissioners needs to be altered, i.e., reduced to the number of real portfolios. This means that reform proposals will need to consider the issue of allocating each country one post in the Commission; or discuss controversial issues such as rotating Commissioners and deputy Commissioners (for small countries). Reform proposals will also need to consider joint presidencies of several countries that last at least a year or two where each country is in charge of a certain policy area.

- *The EMU* is in great trouble. Relatively slow growth would not permit many countries to restrict government deficits to 3 per cent of the GDP or less. If France cannot follow Germany in the EMU, then there is no point in creating it. Britain has an opt-out; Italy and Spain will not meet the criteria till 1999. By insisting on a stronger federal structure and tough EMU, Germany may risk seriously damaging its relations with France. A tough EMU would create a 'German Europe'. In addition, that would make eastern enlargement much harder. However, it is this enlargement that would make Europe more secure than a deep federalism or strong EMU. Although Germany (together with Britain) would like to see an expanded EU, pushing for the enlargement, as well as a tighter monetary union may end up in neither! Even a majority of the German public is not convinced that the EMU as planned is acceptable. So the question is not whether to postpone (i.e., to kill) the current EMU project that is due to enter its final stage in 1999, but rather how and when to implement it. Stable edifices cannot be made up in a hurry.
- Is the EU going to be structured as a set of *concentric circles* (the idea of Germany and France) and become multi-speed Europe? Politically, this may not be integration-friendly. Britain would like to see the EU of nation states as a *matrix* where countries could pick and chose from the 'menu' policies that they prefer. Some countries may wish to go faster towards a particular goal than others, but they all need to find themselves there in the end. Therefore, the EU equally needs to avoid the *à la carte* option. It may perhaps be better to have a less satisfactory union, but at one speed.
- Germany maintains its *federalist* demands of more power to the EU Parliament and the Commission (a strong Commission is the best ally of the small countries against the dominance of large member states) and a limited right to use the veto. In contrast, the British *nation state ideas* oppose such powers and limitations. In fact, there are many more sovereignty-conscious states in the EU than are admitted in public. However, the British open and hard line stance is making potential allies (such as neutral states)[48] apprehensive. Although it may seem to be the case on the surface, that Britain is 'opposed' in its views about the EU to the other 14 member countries, it is not the case in reality. The problem is that the other countries are either too timid, too small or too weak to align themselves with the British.
- The IGC needs to consider aspirational policies such as *security and defence* (neutral countries may present a problem here), just as the Maastricht Treaty dealt with the EMU. In addition, it may address the issue of reform of already operational policies such as the CAP.

The current IGC presents the most thorough political reform of the EU since its creation. It will face a number of political minefields on the way of preserving unity with diversity in the EU. The Conference may, perhaps, aim at relatively less to make the EU better.

European integration has always been based on the political decision to secure peace in Europe. That is the purpose of the EU although many have forgotten about that! European integration is to mitigate the impact of old rivalries and replace them by mutual economic benefits and social prosperity. Although the post-Maastricht EU received a severe blow with the split of the exchange rate mechanism, the spirit of integration is still there. Dr Samuel Johnson (1709–1784) would probably say that the EU is 'like a dog walking on his hind legs. It is not well done, but you are surprised to find it done at all'! Many Maastricht ideas may be dead, but European integration is not!

APPENDIX: INSTITUTIONS

In order to accomplish its mandate, the EU has institutions that perform legislative, executive, supervisory and consultative tasks. The basic institutions of the EU are the Commission, the Council of Ministers, the European Parliament, the European Council, the Court of Justice, the Court of Auditors, the Economic and Social Committee, the Committee of the Regions, the European Investment Bank and the European Monetary Institute.

When the Merger Treaty (1965) was put into effect in 1967, it unified the so far separate institutions of the ECSC, EEC and Euratom into the single bodies of the EC. It needs to be kept in mind that the Parliament and the Court of Justice were common for all three Communities from 1958. The objective of the merger was to be one step closer to the creation of a single Community that would have a sole treaty which would replace the Treaties of Paris and Rome. That view was not followed up in the subsequent negotiations that led to the Single European Act or the Maastricht Treaty.

I Commission

The Commission plays a central role in the EU. Its assigned tasks are to initiate and execute the Union's policy, to defend the EU's interests in the Council of Ministers and to guard the Treaties of the Union.

The *initiation* of the EU's policies is perhaps the most important function in the whole system of the Union. The Commission formulates recommendations or delivers opinions. The former refer to specific cases, while the latter deal with general policy guidelines. During the formulation of its proposal, the Commission has to make sure that it is impartial. In reality, the Commission does not look after national interests, however, in the decision-making process it makes a note of national sensibilities. Its proposal must conform with the interests of the Union and no favour is to be granted to the benefit of a member state or a group of states unless it complies with the objectives of the EU. As such it *defends* the Union's interests. The Commission also makes sure that the legal acts and policies are consistent. Before drafting its proposal, the Commission has thorough consultations and exchanges of views with the political leaders of the member countries, employers and labour organizations. Once the guidelines of the policy are in place, the discussions continue with high-ranking experts and national civil servants in order to work out technical details of the piece of law to be submitted to the Council of Ministers.

As the *executive* arm of the EU, the Commission carries out the tasks that come from the Treaties and that are mandated by the Council of Ministers. The Commission directly legislates issues that relate to trade, agriculture, competition (restrictive business practices, monopolies and subsidies) and safeguard clauses.[49] In addition, the Commission administers the Union's funds.

As the *guardian* of the Treaties, the Commission makes sure that the provisions of the Treaties are observed and implemented. It is authorized to investigate any suspected infringement of the Treaties. The most numerous violations of the Union's law were in the fields of internal market, agriculture and environment. Although they were infringements of the law, the largest number came from delays in the national implementation of the EU's legislation or a difference in the interpretation of the EU's law between the Commission and the member states that had to be settled by the Court of Justice.

The Commission has 20 Commissioners with a five-year and renewable term in office. The 'big' EU countries (Britain, France, Germany, Italy and Spain) delegate two Commissioners each, while the others assign one each. The conditions for the selection of a Commissioner are competence and capability to act exclusively in conformity with the interests of the EU. The Commissioner must be free and independent from any other interests, including those of his/her country of origin. The Commissioners are appointed on the basis of an agreement of the governments of the member countries. They are not elected, they do not campaign and make public their views about the job they are given to do. Once appointed by their governments, the Commissioners become independent and they can not be dismissed from their office. In theory, the head of the Commission is appointed (not elected) on the basis of the agreement of the European Council and after consultations with the European Parliament.[50] He/she must accept the government's nominees for the Commission and may not influence their choice, but may reward able appointees with important portfolios. The Commission is responsible to the European Parliament which needs to approve the full Commission and, once appointed, the Parliament may dismiss the Commission only as a body (which has not happened so far). None the less, once dismissed, the 'old' Commission remains in office until a new one is appointed. Each member country may block the decision of the Parliament by failing to nominate a Commissioner, but in fact, all involved in the process try to cooperate.

The Commission is a unified body and it acts accordingly. Although each Commissioner is in charge of one or a few portfolios, he/she does not have the same degree of liberty of action as a counterpart in a national ministry. In the decision-making process there are, basically, three procedures. For straightforward matters, the Commission uses the written procedure. The file with the issue and the proposed decision about it is sent to each Commissioner. If there are no disputes within a week (the usual time period) or another specified period, the proposal is taken to be accepted. For routine matters which do not imply political issues, such as agriculture, the Commission may authorize one of its members to take the decision on behalf of the Commission. None the less, the discretionary right in this case is very small, since only the delicate and important subjects are considered on the Commission's weekly meeting. All decisions of the Commission are reached collectively. The influence of the Commission on the shaping of the events was amplified with the expiry of the transition period (end of 1969) set in the Treaty of Rome. Since events after that date were not regulated by the Treaty, the Commission was given greater opportunity to direct the life of the EU after that date. The Commission has a Secretariat-General, a Legal Office, a Statistical Office and around 30 Directorates-General. Its staff numbers some 15,000 officials.[51] The Commission is located in Brussels, but some of its departments operate in Luxembourg.

II Council of Ministers

While the Commission is a common institution of the EU, the Council of Ministers is an intergovernmental body. The dialogue between the Council and the Commission is the moving spirit of the EU. Since the appointment of both bodies, they have been criticized on the grounds that there was a lack of accountability or a democratic deficit. Because the European Parliament is the only directly elected institution of the EU, it won in the Maastricht Treaty the co-decision powers with the Council of Ministers and, hence, introduced democratic control into the EU's affairs. All the Union's institutions fall under the legal control of the Court of Justice.

The Council of Ministers, together with the European Council, are the only bodies of the EU containing directly delegated representatives of the governments of all member countries. The composition of the Council of Ministers varies. It does not have a fixed membership such as the Commission. It can include various ministers, but only one from each country with the right to vote. When the Council of Ministers considers the farm issues, it is composed of the national ministers of agriculture; when the transport issues are at stake, the national ministers of transport are present. Since various Councils tend to reach decisions that can be quite costly, the representatives from the national ministries of finance are often present. None the less, the Council of Foreign Ministers is somehow supposed to be the most senior Council of the EU. The presidency of the Council of Ministers rotates in alphabetical order every six months. The headquarters of the Council of Ministers is in Brussels (although it meets in Luxembourg three months each year).

The Council of Ministers is the Union's legislative body. It acts only on the basis of a proposal from the Commission. If there is no proposal from the Commission, the Council and, hence, the EU is paralysed in its progress. The Commission drafts a proposal which may be amended after the Parliament's opinion. Such a proposal is passed on to the Council of Ministers. The dialogue between the Council and the Commission begins. The Council upholds the national interests, while the Commission stands for the ones of the Union. During the dialogue they try to find joint solutions to problems. If the Council wants to alter a proposal, it has to act unanimously. In other cases, it is only the Commission that has the right to amend its proposal. The Council of Ministers may adopt the proposal as it stands; modify the proposal and accept in unanimously; or fail to reach a decision on it. This kind of decision-making has often been criticized. The Council of Ministers was legislating lavishly, but it was not accountable to anybody, hence the 'democratic deficit'.

Decisions in the Council of Ministers are taken by unanimous, simple or qualified majority vote. If majority vote is permitted, then the decision binds all the countries, even those that voted against the proposal in question. While the Council usually tries to take into account the interests of all member countries, find a compromise and act unanimously, majority rule for an increasing number of questions is still present. Majority rule in some cases may act as a buffer against obstruction and can make unanimity, in certain cases, easier and faster to be achieved. Although the (qualified) majority vote has potential risks, it introduced a certain degree of flexibility in the decision-making procedure, as well as the willingness to compromise. The Luxembourg Agreement authorized the unanimous vote each time a member country declares that an issue is in its vital interest, but without the definition of that interest. The Single European Act and the Maastricht Treaty reintroduced the majority vote procedure for a number of issues, mainly dealing with the creation of a unified internal market. The resolution of the Maastricht Treaty to create 'an ever closer union' (Preamble) may not be achieved in a satisfactory way if the vital interests of one or more nations in the EU are damaged.

When the qualified majority rule is permitted in the Council of Ministers, then the four large countries, Britain, France, Germany and Italy have 10 votes each. Spain has 8, while the small countries, Belgium, Greece, the Netherlands and Portugal have 5 votes each. Austria and Sweden have 4 votes each. Others, Denmark, Finland and Ireland, have 3 votes each, while Luxembourg has 2 votes. The total is 87 votes. The qualified majority is 62 votes. It means that the four largest countries, plus Spain, need to consider the interests of at least 2 or more small countries. The principle is that the qualified majority takes into account the interests of around 70 per cent of the EU's population. The blocking minority is 25 votes (two big and one or two small countries except Luxembourg; for instance the olive oil belt countries: Spain, Italy, Greece and Portugal). The meetings of the Council of Ministers are relatively numerous and often long. They are not pure formalities as are often similar meetings in various international organizations. The meetings of the Council often mean hard negotiations and horse-trading.

The Committee of Permanent Representatives (Coreper)[52] assists the Council of Ministers in its work. The Coreper is composed of the Ambassadors of the member countries of the EU. It is included in all phases of decision preparation and making. If possible, the decisions are taken by the Coreper, so that the Council of Ministers simply endorses them. For crucial decisions, that is not the case. National Ministers are supposed to settle such issues.

The primary sources of EU law are the Treaties of Paris, Rome and Maastricht, the Merger Treaty, the Single European Act, as well as all the Treaties that led to the enlargement of the EU. The secondary sources of law are created by the Council of Ministers, European Parliament and Commission. After consultations with the European Parliament, the Economic and Social Committee and the Committee of the Regions (on regional matters), the Commission submits a proposal to the Council of Ministers which co-decides with the European Parliament. This co-decision is a novelty introduced by the Single European Act and extended by the Maastricht Treaty. The objective is the elimination of the 'democratic deficit' in the Council of Ministers. In the new co-decision process the Council and the Parliament deliver the following four types of legal acts:

- *Regulations* are compulsory and general in their application. They are to be directly implemented in all of the member countries. They overrule the national law if it existed.

- *Directives* are compulsory with respect to the final outcome, but the member countries have the freedom to select how they are implemented.
- *Decisions* are binding for the subjects (governments, associations, enterprises, individuals etc.) that they refer to.
- The implementation of *Recommendations* and *Opinions* is not compulsory.

III European Parliament

The European Parliament is the only institution of the EU that is directly elected. In spite of that, it was puzzling that for more than a quarter of a century, it had only a consultative role, as well as the right to dismiss the Commission and accept or reject (which it did a few times) the Union's budget. Although the opinions of the Parliament could be legally disregarded, in most cases both the Commission and the Council of Ministers respected the views of the Parliament. As is the case elsewhere, it takes a long time for a parliament to gain importance in the governing process. However, it is usually fruitful in the long term. This also happened with the European Parliament.

The expansion-of-authority process of the European Parliament started with the Single European Act and was reinforced in the Maastricht Treaty (Article G). The Parliament got the right to co-decide with the Council of Ministers on matters relating to the conduct of the internal market, mobility of labour and capital, trans-European infrastructure networks, consumer protection, research, environment, health, cultural matters, and the like.[53] The decision-making scheme of the EU is given in Figure 1.1.

If an act is to be adopted it has to be initiated by the Commission which has to send its proposal to the Parliament for the first reading. After the European Parliament communicates its opinion to the Council of Ministers, the Council is to adopt a common position that is to be passed on to the Parliament for the second reading. Regarding the common position, the Parliament may:

- approve it,
- not take a decision,
- propose amendments, or
- reject it.

If the Parliament *approves* the common position, then the act is adopted. The 'double signature' symbolizes the co-decision process between the Parliament and the Council. If it *fails* to take a decision, the Council is allowed to accept the act. In the case when the Parliament proposes *amendments* to the common position, the Council may accept them within three months. If the Council fails to do that, it may, together with the Parliament, convene the meeting of the Conciliation Committee (composed of an equal number of the representatives of the Council and the Parliament) with the task of reaching an agreement on a common text. The same procedure is also possible in the case when the common position is *rejected* by the Parliament. The conciliation process is supported by the Commission which helps both the Council and the Parliament to modify their positions. Both the Parliament and the Council have six weeks to approve the common text of the act in question. If one of the two bodies fails to do that or if there is no agreement on the common text, the proposed act is

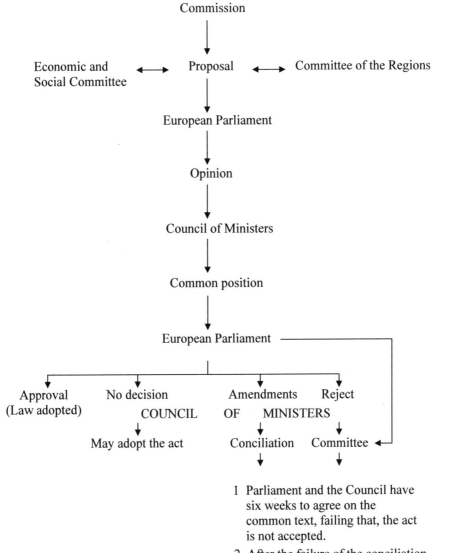

Figure 1.1 The decision-making process in the European Union

not adopted. However, there is one more provision that is heavily contested by the Parliament. After the failure of the Conciliation procedure, the Council of Ministers may within six weeks confirm its previous common position (which may include some of the Parliament's amendments) and adopt the act. The Parliament has still a chance to overrule the Council's decision by an absolute majority of its members if it acts within six weeks after the Council's decision. That opportunity, in practice, may not be fulfilled. The problem is absenteeism. The amendments of the Parliament require a majority vote of the entire Parliament (not just the ones that are present and voting). Often hardly more than a half of the Members of the Parliament bother to attend the meetings, so many amendments fail.

The new powers of the Parliament may alter the agenda of its sessions. The Parliament has over the years dissipated its time and energy on issues that it does not control: the killing of kangaroos in Australia, animal welfare, human rights in Chile, Salvador, Sudan, etc.[54] None the less, the new co-decision, cooperation and the dialogue between the Parliament and the Council may steadily develop into a new and important part in the Union's set up.

The European Parliament has 626 members which represent 370 million people. Each member country has a quota in it.[55] The Parliament was directly elected for the first time in June 1979. Before that, it was composed of the members of the national Parliaments. The members of the European Parliament do not sit there divided into national groups, but rather according to their political orientation. The Socialists (221 members) and the European People's Party (173 members) are the largest political groups.[56] No matter how one looks at the distribution of the seats, neither the Socialists, nor the centre-right can dominate. However, unlike in national parliaments, there is neither majority, nor opposition. Since there is no EU government, there is no ruling majority or an opposition. The Parliament has 20 committees that prepare the work of the plenary sessions. The Parliament sits in Strasbourg. Its secretariat is in Luxembourg, while its committees meet in Brussels. The Parliament may sit in Brussels, but only if the sessions are relatively short.

IV European Council

Although the European Council has been in operation since the early 1970s and was *de facto* the supreme body of the EU, it was introduced *de jure* into the Union's structure in the Single European Act (1987). The Council is made up of Heads of Governments (Head of State in the case of France) and the President of the Commission. Its work is assisted by the Foreign Ministers. The role of the Council was reinforced by the Maastricht Treaty (Article D). Its function is to provide the EU with the necessary impetus for development, and to lay down general political guidelines for the future. The meetings of this Council are free of any formalities and take place at least twice a year. Matters discussed include not only the EU's business, but also intergovernmental issues. The country holding the Union's rotating (in alphabetical order) presidency may not have much power. It is only the first amongst equals for six months. However, what this country can do is set the agenda. It can chose what the European Council discusses. The European Councils reach the major political decisions that concern the EU. If they need to become the Union's law, those decisions are passed on to other EU's institutions in order to proceed with the usual agenda.

V Court of Justice

The structure of the European Union is complex. The implementation of the Union's law may sometimes be difficult. Therefore, the Court of Justice has to intervene each time when the implementation of the primary or secondary law of the EU comes into question. The Court is supposed to provide interpretations of the Union's law and, when asked, may give its opinion about an issue. When delivered, that opinion becomes binding.

The Court has 15 Judges and 9 Advocates-General appointed according to the agreement of the member countries for 6 years. They sit in Luxembourg. Since everyone affected by the EU's legislation has the right to file charges to the Court, the task of the Advocates-General is to conduct a preliminary investigation of the case and give their non-binding, but highly respected (although not always accepted)[57] opinion to the Judges. Court hearings are public, but the discussions about the judgments and the majority vote system for reaching judgments is always closed to the public. Outside the chamber for deliberation, there is no dissenting minority among the Judges. They all are unanimous in their views. Judgments are signed by all the Judges that took part in the case in order to avoid trouble for the Judges after the expiry of their term.

For the execution of its decisions, the Court relies on the administration of the member countries on which the ruling applies. In order to make sure that its decisions are implemented, the Court has the capacity to impose serious fines on member states that do not carry out their obligations. The matters that appear most often in the Court relate to agriculture, competition, internal market and social issues. The Court of Justice represents the highest legal authority in the EU. There are no appeals against its judgments. A Judge can be dismissed from the Court only by a unanimous vote of his colleagues.

The Court of Justice is assisted in its work by the *Court of First Instance* (15 Judges) that deals mainly with cases brought by the individuals. This new Court was introduced in the Union's structure under the Single European Act and started its operation in 1989. The job of this Court is to speed up the judicial process by relieving the workload of the Court of Justice. The Maastricht Treaty reinforced its role. Its jurisdiction covers competition issues, charges by individuals and firms (but not states) against the EU's institutions and disputes between the EU and its staff. Appeals against judgments of the Court of First Instance may be filed in the Court of Justice.

VI Court of Auditors

The ever expanding resources that the EU disposes of (its budget for 1995 was around ECU 80 billion) ask for the accurate auditing of those resources. The EEC and Euratom, on the one hand, and the ECSC, on the other, had separate auditing boards. Both of them were merged by a Treaty in the Court of Auditors in 1975. The new Court started its operation two years later in Luxembourg. It has 15 members that are appointed for a renewable period of three years. This Court scrutinizes the inflow and outflow of resources in all bodies of the EU, as well as the Union's budget. At the end of each fiscal year, the Court of Auditors publishes its annual report. The statements of that report provide influential guidelines for the collection and expenditure of the Union's funds.

VII Economic and Social Committee

The Economic and Social Committee is only a consultative body in the EU's structure. It has 222 members in Brussels that represent employers, employees and various interest groups (agriculture, consumers, environment, transport and others). They are appointed for a four-year term in their private capacity by the Council of Ministers. Opinions of the Committee provide a blend of views of various groups that may be affected by the decisions of the EU. As such, they provide a helpful input to the Commission and the Council of Ministers during the preparation of the Union's laws. Apart from its consultative role, the Committee has not yet found or won any other place in the structure of the EU.

VIII Committee of the Regions

Local authorities in a number of EU countries are exerting or gaining increasing influence in the countries' legislative process. The Maastricht Treaty reacted to these developments by the creation of the Committee of the Regions. This Committee gives an opportunity to the regional authorities of the member countries to be involved in the Union's legal matters. It needs to be consulted on proposals that have a bearing on the regions. The Committee has 222 members in Brussels and it needs to earn a certain respect and status in the Union's structure. Since the regional authorities gain influence in the governing structure of the member countries, they have a chance to wield influence in the future in the EU's matters too.

IX European Investment Bank

The European Investment Bank raises funds on the capital markets to finance investment projects which contribute to the development of the EU. The Bank is allowed to grant loans to third countries if the projects are of relevance to the EU, such as roads, ports or railways, or as a part of development aid. The Bank was established in 1958 and operates from Luxembourg. It is a non-profit-making lender that granted loans totalling ECU 20 billion in 1994.

X European Monetary Institute

The European Monetary Institute was established in 1994 in Frankfurt. It started to prepare grounds for the single currency, the euro, that was supposed to be introduced in 1999. At the same time the Institute was expected to be transformed into an independent European Central Bank. The Institute is in charge of coordination of monetary policies of member countries and the preparation of the final stage of EMU.

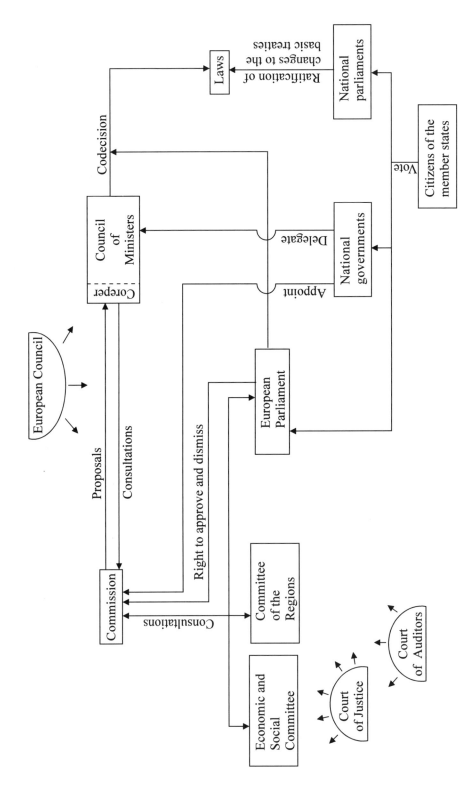

Figure 1.2 Operation of the institutions of the European Union

XI Conclusion

If one regards the inception of the EU as being 1952, with the creation of the ECSC, then its institutions live in their fifth decade. From the long-term standpoint, the Union's system demonstrated its viability and endurance. Figure 1.2 presents the organizational scheme of the Union's institutions. The EU is a fully recognized international organization since most of the countries in the world have diplomatic relations with it. An increasing number of countries aim at joining the EU. The Union takes part in the annual summits of the most important developed market economies (G-7). As the Union's business and membership expands, additional powers are given to already existing bodies, as well as the new ones that are being created. The Single European Act and the Maastricht Treaty amplified the role of most of the Union's institutions. That was most evident in the case of the European Parliament. The powers of the Council of Ministers suffered from all those changes. It remains for the Parliament to demonstrate, in practice, that it can meet the challenges assigned to it by the new structure of the EU. As already noted, the IGC needs to address the organizational and policy-making problems of the EU in order to make it manageable in the coming decades when the Union may even double its number of members.

NOTES

1 The Roman Empire (first century BC to the fifth century AD) fulfilled many goals regarding integration of the European continent, although it covered parts of northern Africa and the Middle East. There existed a common currency, free trade, common defence, foreign policy and legal system, as well as a certain autonomy of the regions. After the decline of the Roman Empire, it was only Charlemagne (742–814) who was able to create and maintain a partial integration of Europe at the beginning of the ninth century. In the post-classical history, Napoleon succeeded, through the military conquest, in integrating a large part of Europe during the 1809–1812 period. This century, Hitler tried to do the same during 1939–1945.

2 For a profound political analysis of the origin and future of European integration consult Sidjanski (1992).

3 Austria, Belgium, Britain, Denmark, France, Greece, the Netherlands, Ireland, Iceland, Italy, Luxembourg, Norway, Portugal, Sweden, Switzerland and Turkey.

4 Sweden was another country, but its supply capacities were limited.

5 The original five member countries were joined by West Germany and Italy in 1954, as well as Spain and Portugal in 1988.

6 An armed attack is a wider notion than a war, since a (classical) war has its established rules.

7 NATO does not have, however, a clear cut answer to the problem of armed conflict between its members. For example, Turkey often claims sovereignty over certain Greek islands. These expansionist claims have been on the verge of provoking armed conflicts several times. Tensions have been defused (temporarily) only after excessive pressure from the US on the two countries.

8 Greece (location) and Turkey (location and the contribution in manpower) entered NATO in 1951; West Germany joined in 1954, while Spain did so in 1982.

9 The Warsaw Pact was created after the entry of West Germany into NATO.

10 The French–Prussian war (1870–1871) and the two world wars.

11 The Schuman plan was drafted by Jean Monnet, a high officer of the French government in the field of planning. The political responsibility for its implementation was taken by the French Foreign Minister, Robert Schuman.

12 The low-profile, sectoral approach to integration in the areas of coal and steel was relatively easy to negotiate. There was a limited number of production facilities, they were relatively large, and there was a high degree of cartelization of business. Control over this production can be exercised in an easier and more effective way than in other production fields with many competitors and an easy entry and exit from business. In any case, the sectoral approach was a good training ground for the pan-economic integration that came in the following years.

13 The territorial controversies between France and West Germany were finally settled in 1957 when France returned Saarland. Since 1945 that part of Germany was in the French zone which was attached economically to France, from 1948 until its handover.

14 The experience of Germany in the creation of a political union may be instructive here. The German customs union (*Zollverein*), led by Prussia, was set up in 1834. It was only after the war with France, in 1871, that political union came about.

15 The Belgian, Dutch and Luxembourg governments signed a Convention about the creation of a customs union in 1944. The Convention was implemented in 1948.

16 The institutions of the Community are elaborated later in the text.

17 Apart from Britain there were Denmark and Norway, as well as the neutral countries: Austria, Sweden and Switzerland. Portugal joined the group a little later, but took part in the establishment of the organization. Iceland joined in 1970. Finland became an associate member in 1961, while it entered the group in 1986 as a full member.

18 EFTA refers only to the manufactured goods. Agricultural goods are left out of the agreement. That was not very popular in those countries with a relatively developed agricultural and fisheries sector, such as Denmark, Norway and Portugal.

19 Certain observers would argue that it was merely the continuation of friction between the Catholics and the Protestants.

20 The small countries, members of the EFTA, had an interest in staying out of the EC since they did not have to accept the CET of the Community which was at a higher level than their own tariffs on external trade, and they did not take part in the CAP which in some cases (for example, Switzerland or Finland) offered smaller subsidies to the farm sector than was the case in the EFTA countries. In addition, the costs of staying outside the EC would have meant sacrificing the chance to influence the economic policies of the new generation in the EC. However, this view is based on an assumption that small countries are, in reality, being asked for their opinion and, more importantly and optimistically, that the opinion is (highly) respected. We shall see later whether that is, in fact, the case.

21 The group of the developing countries with which the EC has 'special' relations expanded to African, Caribbean and Pacific countries after the British entry. That was reflected in 1975 when the Yaoundé Agreements were replaced by an extended Agreement signed in Lomé (Togo).

22 The European Council should not be confused with the Council of Europe (the European talking-shop in Strasbourg).

23 Lord Arthur Cockfield was the Commissioner who was the author of many legal acts that brought the 1992 Programme. Being dissatisfied with such initiatives, the government of Margaret Thatcher did not reappoint him for a further term in 1989.

24 The European Parliament estimated *annual* losses for the EC coming from the NTBs (internal costs). From an incomplete EC internal market, the losses were 12 billion ECUs from frontier formalities, 40 billion ECUs from diverse national standards and technical regulations, 40 billion ECUs from discriminatory practices (domestic-firms preference) during public procurement and, in addition to all that, 10 billion ECUs because of high production-costs (meagre economies of scale) coming from the limited size of national markets (*European File*, No.17, 1987).

25 In a monetary union where the money supply is jointly and centrally controlled, a country in economic difficulties is not able to devalue its currency or to 'inflate' its way out of economic trouble. Therefore, smooth political cooperation in the Union is a necessary condition for its existence and survival.

26 The relatively slow progress in the federalization of western Europe is different from the history of the US. In the initial days of the US, it was the member states that transferred

foreign, defence and tax policies to Washington, DC. These are federal rights that the EC states have been very slow to cede to a central authority.

27 The desire to have the political and economic stability on Germany's eastern border, as well as a discouragement of migration plays a role in the German policy towards the new 'democracies' in the east.

28 During the final negotiations in Maastricht, and the horse trading phase, Germany offered to support the British opt-out from the single currency arrangement, but in return requested and got British backing for the instant recognition of the independence of Germany's Nazi-period ally, Croatia. (Germany does not forget its allies!) Neither bargaining chips (the monetary arrangement and the Croatia's independence) qualify for the list of splendid successes in international diplomacy.

29 The argument of Britain against the inclusion of the social issues in the deal was that it would make the EC producers uncompetitive.

30 After a certain period of time had passed, quite a few commentators would subscribe to the British view.

31 There would be, in fact, the European System of Central Banks. It would be composed of the ECB and the central banks of the member states.

32 The five necessary criteria that a country needs to fulfil are. (1) a high degree of price stability (inflation within the margin of 1.5 per cent of the three best-performing EU countries); (2) a sound public financial position (budget deficit of less than 3 per cent of the GDP); (3) a national debt of less than 60 per cent of the GDP); (4) the observance of the 'normal' fluctuation margins (no devaluation within the EU's exchange rate mechanism for at least two past years); and (5) the durability of convergence of economic policies, which needs to be reflected in long-term interest rate levels (interest rate needs to be within the 2 per cent margin of the three best performing EU countries).

33 WEU is upset by several crucial problems. Unlike NATO, the WEU does not have an integrated military command; it does not have as efficient command and communication system as NATO has; and the WEU has no airlift for moving troops and hardware to match that of the Americans. To create an entirely European system would cost money which the taxpayers in the EU would not want to pay.

34 This includes free elections, a multi-party parliament, respect of rights of minorities, good neighbourly relations and no territorial disputes.

35 The entry of the east European transition countries need not worry EU Mediterranean countries, at least for another fifteen years or so. The most developed of the 'new democracies' lag a lot behind Portugal in economic terms. But that is not the biggest stumbling block to their entry. A more important one is that the EU, in particular its defence wing, does not even dream about importing new political problems such as disputes over minorities and borders.

A factor that contributed to the apprehension of Denmark regarding the EU was the growing political clout of Germany. In addition, Denmark, as a small country, feared that its national interests would be neglected. The same reason contributed to a negative vote in Switzerland in 1992 to a deal that would fully include this country in most of the activities of the EU.

36 In France, for example, it was 'only' 51 per cent with some 3 per cent of invalid votes!

37 There are no provisions to deal with the expulsion of a member country from the EU (it is neither allowed, nor prohibited). However, in theory, it could happen. The countries that want to go ahead with a deal could draft and accept a new treaty that could leave the dissenting country outside the club. By implication, that may continue until those, presumably weak, poor and small countries are put aside. Ultimately the 'ideal' union would consist only of a single country. Alternatively, ostracism was practised in ancient Greece. Those that were powerful and dangerous to the state (rather than the weak) were expelled from the city for 5 to 10 years.

38 The comment by the Italian statesman Massimo Taparelli Marchese d'Azeglio (1798–1866): 'We have made Italy, now we must make Italians', does not easily apply to international arrangements that integrate countries.

39 The neutrality of most of the EFTA countries was seen to be an obstacle to those countries joining the EU. None the less, the concept became quite flexible (except in Switzerland) after the dissolution of the east European bloc.

40 The need for Germany to obtain funds to finance the reintegration of its eastern part increased interest rates. The country placed its national interest ahead of the EU's by refusing to cut German interest rates, and produced a currency crisis. To ease the strain, a way out was found in an increase in the earlier margins for the fluctuations of the currencies participating in the exchange rate mechanism of the EMS. They were widened from ±2.25 per cent to ±15 per cent on either side of the central parity. The 'dirty float' began. A condition for the establishment the EMU is that 'normal' (without a definition) fluctuation margins for currencies need to be observed for at least two years. However, what is 'normal' in a situation when the exchange rate mechanism of the EMS remains only in name! As long as currencies are allowed to move against one another, the genuine single market will not be secure.

41 The Slav Macedonia, a communist invention mainly of the 1940s, has *never* existed before, either as a state or a religious entity, even the existence of the nation is highly controversial. Those who are interested in this issue may wish to consult message No. 868.014 of 26 December 1944 by the US Secretary of State.

42 The Commission took Greece to the EU Court of Justice in order to exert additional pressure on that country to lift its embargo on the FYR Macedonia. The Court, however, refused the Commission's request for an interim emergency ruling that would make Greece lift its embargo in June 1994. This was a serious blow to the Commission as it was not able to convince the Court that the sanctions caused damage to the EU. Tensions between Athens and Skopje were defused, at least for the time being, by a deal in September 1995. Greece lifted its embargo in return for a change of flag and the alteration of the Constitution of the FYR Macedonia.

43 A series of articles in the *Lancet* point to the fact that there will be serious concern about BSE for quite some time in the future.

44 IGCs provide relatively rare opportunities to redesign the EU. So far, there have been only seven IGCs in the EU. The first one started in 1950 and culminated in the signing of the Treaty of Paris that created the ECSC; the second one began in 1955 in Messina and ended up with the Treaty of Rome; the third one was initiated in 1970 in order to revise Article 203 of the Treaty of Rome on the financing of the budget; the fourth one started in 1985 and led to the Single European Act; the fifth and the sixth IGCs started simultaneously in 1990. One dealt with the extension of the Single European Market to the economic and monetary union, while the other focused on political union. They both produced the Maastrich Treaty. The seventh IGC started in Turin with the goal of making the EU more manageable once it increases, or even doubles, the number of member countries.

45 The fragile Dayton Peace Accord (1995) reflected the fact that the warring parties were temporarily tired of war.

46 Nobody can predict at present whether the new members will first enter NATO or the EU. Joining NATO is politically easy, but technically difficult. The reverse is true for entry to the EU.

47 Cyprus and Malta were promised that they could commence negotiations six months after the end of the IGC. The same holds for the Central European countries. Turkey applied for membership of the EU in 1987. In spite of the likely Greek veto, many in Europe consider this country to be too underdeveloped, too unmanageable and to have too many cultural differences to qualify.

48 Austria, Finland, Ireland and Sweden.

49 A safeguard clause is embodied in Article 115 of the Treaty of Rome.

50 France and Germany decided on their own in June 1994 that the new head of the Commission was to be the then Prime Minister of Belgium Jean Luc Dehaene. They thought that the other EU countries would go along with their choice. This arrogant attitude irritated many other member countries, although Britain was the most vocal and blocked that choice, not necessarily because it was not happy about the candidate, but

more importantly because of the distorted procedure. A compromise candidate was later found in the then Prime Minister of Luxembourg, Jacques Santer.

51 Although that size of the staff may seem large, it is often much smaller than some of the important ministries in the EU's member countries. A big part of the Commission's staff is in the translation service since all the documents need to be published in all of the 11 official languages of the EU. Hence the size of the translation and interpretation service. The proponents of rationalization voice their suggestion that if the operation of the United Nations can be handled in six languages or if the EFTA uses only one language for its business (English – a language that is not the official language of any of its member countries), the EU may start to think along these lines too. It needs to be kept in mind that many of the EU's affairs are carried out through the administrations of the member countries which need to be informed in a timely and punctual way. Hence, there is a need for an efficient translation function.

52 The French acronym Coreper (Comité des Représentants Permanents) for this body is often used even in English.

53 The Parliament has the right of consent regarding the application of new member countries and important international agreements. It was withholding or stalling its assent to agreements with countries that had a poor record of human rights.

54 The discussion about the existence of aliens in outer space was on the Parliament's proposed agenda in January 1994, until a last minute withdrawal!

55 The quotas are distributed as follows: Germany 99; Britain, France and Italy have 87 each; Spain 64; the Netherlands 31; Belgium, Greece and Portugal have 25 each; Sweden 22; Austria 21; Denmark and Finland have 16 each; Ireland 15; and Luxembourg 6.

56 Turnout in the elections in 1994 was 56 per cent, the lowest ever. Explanations might be the perception that the Parliament is too far away from the man in the street and that it has complex procedures.

57 The *Continental Can* case (1973) is an example.

2

MONETARY POLICY

I INTRODUCTION

Monetary policy is a key element in the economic strategy of the economic and monetary union (EMU). As it is one of the most sensitive policies, the Treaties establishing the EU made special references to these issues. In fact, the Maastricht Treaty is almost entirely about EMU. Integration of monetary policies in the EU is necessary not only for the stability of rates of exchange, prices, balances of payments and investment decisions, but also for the protection of the already achieved level of integration, as well as for the motivation for further integration in the future.

Relatively small countries may have an incentive to integrate into the monetary field in order to avoid domination by large countries. The joint money may overcome the disadvantage (vulnerability on external monetary shocks) of atomized currencies and it may become a rival to the monies of larger countries in international currency markets. A common currency among the integrated countries may become an outward symbol, but it is not a necessary condition for a successful monetary union.

A monetary system between countries should be distinguished from a monetary union. Countries in a *monetary system* link their currencies together and act as a single unit in relation to third currencies. A *monetary union* among countries is an ambitious enterprise. It exists if there is either a single money (*de jure* EMU) or an irrevocable fixity among the rates of exchange of the participating countries together with a free mobility of goods and factors (*de facto* EMU). This prevents any alterations in the rates of exchange as indirect methods of non-tariff protection or a subsidy to exports. It also means that the member countries should seek recourse to the capital markets in order to find funds to cover their budget deficit. Within an EMU, it should be as easy, for example, for a Frenchman to pay a German within Europe, as it is for a Welshman to pay an Englishman within the United Kingdom (Meade, 1973, p. 162).

A monetary union requires: convertibility (at least internal) of the participating countries' currencies; centralization of monetary policy; a single central bank or a system of central banks that control stabilization policies; unified performance on the international financial markets; capital market integration; identical rates of inflation; harmonization of fiscal systems; replacement of balance-of-payments disequilibria with regional imbalances; similar levels of economic development or a well-endowed fund for transfers of real resources to the less developed regions; continuous consultation about and coordination of economic policies among the participating countries, as well as the adjustment of wages on the union level.

There may, also, exist a pseudo exchange rate union (Corden, 1972). In this kind of set-up, member countries fix exchange rates of their currencies and freely accept each others' monies. However, since there is no pooling of foreign reserves and no central monetary authority, such a union is not stable. Since there is no mechanism to coordinate national policies, an individual member country may choose to absorb real resources from the union partners by running with them a balance-of-payments deficit. In addition, such a country may change the effective exchange rates of other members by creating a deficit in the union's balance of payments with the rest of the world. A full EMU is not vulnerable to such instability. Foreign exchange rates are pooled and monetary policy is operated by a single monetary authority. In a pseudo exchange rate union, there is imperfect coordination of national monetary policies, but in a full EMU, the problem is solved by policy centralization (Cobham, 1989, p. 204).

This chapter starts with the traditional single criterion theory of monetary integration. A superior, that is, cost–benefit model, further develops consideration of monetary integration. Parallel currencies are presented before the analysis of the past and present monetary arrangements in the EU.

II TRADITIONAL MODEL

1 Exchange rate regimes

Both flexible and fixed exchange rates have their virtues and vices. The benefits of a flexible exchange rate include their free floating according to demand and supply. This improves the allocation of resources and in liberal societies removes the need for government interference. There is no need whatsoever for foreign currency reserves, because balance-of-payments disequilibria are adjusted automatically. A country is free to pursue independently its national priorities with respect to inflation, employment and interest rate targets. Any possible mistake in economic policy may be straightened out by continuous and smooth changes in rates of exchange.

There are, of course, several arguments against free floating. The most serious one is that the rate of exchange divides the economies of different countries. As such, it reduces the benefits of economies of scale. The floating rates of exchange stimulate speculation, uncertainty and instability. All the alleged claims about a smooth adjustment without the need for changes in reserves were disproved during the 1970s. Any change in the rate of exchange would have an impact on home prices. Its repercussions would be swifter in the countries which have a relatively greater degree of openness. There is, however, another problem with the floating rate of exchange. It is overshooting. Although some changes in economic policy are only announced and not yet implemented, the floating rates of exchange move and overshoot their long-run equilibrium.

The objections to fixed exchange rates are the mirror-image of the virtues of the flexible rates. They include the following. Fixed exchange rates do not permit every country to pursue independently its own policy goals regarding employment and inflation. Countries have to subordinate their monetary policy to the requirements of the external balance. When the time comes for adjustment in the rate of exchange, it may be relatively large and disruptive in relation to the smooth, potentially frequent and small changes in the exchange rate in the case of the free float. The system of fixed rates of exchange requires reserves of foreign currencies for intervention in the currency market in order to defend the fixed parity. These funds would arguably be better spent on alternative productive uses, such as education or research.

The arguments in favour of fixed rates of exchange are those which justify the introduction of a single currency in a country. This system stimulates cooperation among countries as opposed to floating rates which encourage 'economic national-ism'. The most important feature of fixed rates of exchange is that they bring stability; prices are less inflationary; the allocation of resources is improved because decisions about investment are not delivered exclusively on the basis of short-term market signals; uncertainty is reduced and trade flows are stabilized. All this stimu-lates economic integration among countries. That is why the establishment of a free internal market in the EU in 1993 'needs' to be followed by a monetary union.

There is no general rule about which system of exchange rates is better. If a country has a balance-of-payments deficit, then it has to restore competitiveness. This can be done by a reduction in private and public consumption, so it requires cutting wages directly or devaluation which in turn cuts wages indirectly. But note, the choice of the exchange system here does *not* play a role at all. Reductions in real income are necessary under either exchange rate system.

It is a formidable task to reach a definitive conclusion about the 'correct' system of exchange rates. The above choices contrast the costs against the benefits of a particu-lar system. In practice, the choice may often be between costs of one system and the costs of the other. In such situation it comes as no surprise that economists are not unanimous. In an EMU, small countries may overcome, the disadvantage which stems from their relatively small economic size and thus create an area of economic stability. They may also reap the fruits of economic cooperation in an area where expectations may be held with a significant degree of accuracy.

Discussion about the exchange rate regimes (fixed, floating or managed), sheds light only on one side of a country's monetary policy in an international context. The other side deals with the domestic monetary policy. Linkages between the national money supply and rates of interest, as well as price levels must be also considered. Otherwise, the debate may be in vain.

Monetary integration means in its highest form that each member of an EMU is free to use its own currency for any kind of payments to partners. The minimum definition of the monetary integration is absence of restrictions, while the maximum definition requires the use of a single currency (Machlup, 1979, p. 23). Monetary integration may exist even without the integration of markets for goods and the integration of such markets may exist without monetary integration. The former case is exemplified by countries in the West African Monetary Union which have a single currency, the CFA franc, and a similar monetary policy to France (their former colonial master), but there is little real integration of markets for goods, services and factors among them. The latter case may be found in the EFTA, where member countries have integrated their markets for manufactured goods, but there is no formal integration of the monetary policy among them.

2 Factor mobility

The traditional single-criterion model of monetary integration started with the theory of optimum currency areas. This theory was a purely scholastic exercise during the 1960s. After a long while the theory was revived. That was prompted by the intentions to bolster the EMS, as well as by the breakup of formerly federal states in central and eastern Europe, in particular, the USSR, which presented problems of how to handle the new and separate currencies in most of the newly independent states.

The theory of optimum currency areas was started by Mundell (1961). Economic adjustment can take place on international and national levels. On the international level, the basic issue of adjustment is whether the countries with trade deficits would accept inflation or deflation in their respective economies. On the national level, the pace of inflation in countries that have a single currency, but several regions, is regulated by the desire of the central authorities to permit unemployment in the regions with deficit. If the objective is the achievement of a greater degree of employment and stable prices in a world where there is more than one currency area, then this case asks for floating exchange rates based on regional instead of national currencies. As with Mundell, a region is the optimum currency area. Factor mobility is the criterion that determines a region. Within the currency areas factors are mobile, while among them, factors are immobile. Fluctuating rates of exchange are the adjustment mechanism between various currency areas, while factor mobility is the equilibrating mechanism within them.

Factor mobility as the criterion for an optimum currency area ought to be considered carefully. The difficulty with this model is that a region may be an economic unit, while the domain of a currency is an expression of national sovereignty which seldom coincides with a region.[1] In addition, factor mobility may change over time. Strong integration of goods and factor markets can tighten the budget constraint. Borrowing today implies higher taxes tomorrow. If factors (labour and capital) are free to move, that may give incentives to mobile factors to move to lower-tax jurisdictions which would erode the tax base in a high-tax country. Investors know that the ability of a government to borrow today is limited by its capability to tax tomorrow, as well as its ability to tax tomorrow being restricted by factor mobility. Hence, investors would refuse or reduce their lending to governments threatening to exceed their borrowing capacity. The higher the integration of factor markets, the sooner this would take place (Eichengreen, 1993, p. 1335).

Mobility of capital is sensitive to the degree of economic activity and the outlook for economic prosperity. In the nineteenth century, labour and capital were flowing towards the Americas and Australia as the areas of promising development which needed those factors most. During the 'golden' 1960s, however, labour and capital were flowing towards the growing developed and relatively rich regions and countries.

Labour is not a homogeneous factor. Its full mobility may exist only in relatively small geographic areas or within a very specialized professional category. The experience of the EU is the best proof. The flow of labour in the EU in the 1960s and up to mid-1970s came mostly from workers from the Mediterranean countries that were not members of the EU (with the exception of Italy). Those labour flows may not be taken as intra-EU labour mobility.

Regions within a single country grow at different rates. The same holds for countries in an EMU. These developments cause strain which is exacebrated if there are fewer possibilities for adjustment such as factor mobility and fiscal compensations. However, it still does not (yet) make a sensible case for southern Italy to have a separate currency, which creates a separate economy, from the northern part of the country. The cost of such a monetary disintegration would be high.

3 Openness

The second major approach focused attention on the degree of openness of a country (McKinnon, 1963). Commodities in a country may be distributed between tradables and non-tradables. The ratio between these goods determines the degree of its openness to trade. As a rule, the smaller the country, the greater the relative degree of its trade interaction with other countries. A high degree of openness embodies relatively high specialization of a country and it may be taken as the criterion for the optimum currency area.

When the tradable goods represent a significant part of home consumption (unless most of the consumer's goods are imported), then by a change in the rate of exchange, a country may hardly change real wages. Such a country (presumably small) is advised to enter into an EMU for it may not be an optimum currency area as a single unit (Corden, 1972). The greater a country's openness, the smaller the chances for the effective independent use of exchange rate as an instrument for economic stabilization.

Relatively small economies are advised to link their currencies with that of their major trading partner. This is the case when the former colonies link their currency to that of their former master (the CFA franc zone) or when some of the transition economies of central and eastern Europe link their currencies to the German mark. The second piece of advice to small economies which conduct a significant part of their trade among themselves is to link their currencies together. In the case of a single currency all financial dealings may be simpler. This is part of the reason why the 50 federal states in the US[2] or 16 German *Länder* may not be able to separately issue and operate their own currencies in an efficient way. Another piece of evidence may be found in the serious difficulties in handling monetary affairs in most of the independent states that emerged from the former USSR.

If small open economies operate near full employment, then internal fiscal measures are advised for the adjustment of the balance of payments. Fixed exchange rates would be more productive in this case than flexible ones as they would have a less damaging effect on prices. A variation in the exchange rate would have a small response in the change in the level of imports because of high dependency on imports. Therefore, a variation in the rate of exchange should be much higher than in the countries which are relatively less open.

An alteration in the exchange rate would have a direct and significant impact on real income. Consumers and trade unions would request indexation of wages with the change in prices and exchange rate. If money illusion exists – the impression that changes in nominal (money) wages are identical to changes in real income – then a change in the exchange rate may be an effective means for the adjustment of balance of payments. However, money illusion is not a long-term phenomenon. It is no longer even a short-term event. An alteration in the exchange rate may not be effectively employed for the adjustment of balance of payments independently of other instruments. Flexible rates of exchange may be an efficient means for the adjustment of balance of payments of relatively large economies which are linked by small trade relations.

The assumptions in this model are that the equilibrium in the balance of payments is caused by microeconomic changes in demand and supply and, also, that prices in the outside world are stable. The argument about the relative stability of prices in the outside world may not be substantiated for the period lasting around two decades since the early 1970s. When the prices in the outside world are fluctuating, that is directly conveyed to the home prices through a fixed exchange rate. Openness of an economy may be the criterion for an optimum currency area if the outside world is more stable than the economic situation in a small open economy. Fixed exchange rates may force small open economies to pursue more rigorous economic policy than under the fluctuating exchange rates regime which may permit a policy of monetary 'indiscipline'. That is so, because if money illusion does not exist, then the possibility for the alteration of the exchange rate as an adjustment instrument becomes almost useless.

The Benelux countries and Denmark have participated in the EMS since its creation. Other small European countries (for example, Austria, Finland, Norway, Sweden and Switzerland) initially decided to stay out of the EMS and manage their exchange rates unilaterally, although these countries pay close attention to the developments in the EMS. The membership of most of those countries in the EU would make them strong insiders in the system. The argument for openness fails to explain why these countries are still keeping national control over the exchange rate in spite of strong trade relations with the member countries of the EMS. In addition, it fails to explain why relatively large countries such as Germany and France opted for the EMS. However, the basic flaw of the optimum currency area theory is that it failed to distinguish between the case for fixed exchange rates and the situation when separate states join together in a common currency (McKinnon, 1994, p. 61).

4 Diversification

The third major contribution stated that countries whose production is diversified do not have to change their terms of trade with foreign countries as often as the less diversified countries (Kenen, 1969). An external shock in the form of a reduction in foreign demand for a country's major export item may have a relatively smaller impact on the diversified country's employment than on a specialized country's economy and employment. Moreover, links between home and foreign demand, as well as export and investment, are weaker in the diversified country than in a specialized one. Big and frequent changes of exchange rate are not necessary for a diversified country because of the overlap in the reduction and increase in demand for various export goods. This overlap may keep the proceeds from exports on a relatively stable level. In conclusion, Kenen suggested that fixed rates of exchange were suitable for diversified countries. Diversification was his criterion for the

47

optimum currency area. It helps the stabilization of home investment and adjustment of the economy to external shocks. The US may be the closest example of such an economy. Countries with specialized economies and relatively low levels of diversification have a need to take part in currency areas with flexible rates of exchange. Such countries are more vulnerable to external shocks than are diversified economies. Examples may be found in Denmark, Iceland, New Zealand and most of the African countries.

While McKinnon dealt with internal shocks to an economy, Kenen considered external ones. Kenen's argument may be weakened in the situation where the reduction in foreign demand occurred during a general fall in demand in a recession. That reduces total demand, so a country's diversification does not help much in the mitigation of the fall in the demand for exports.

5 Other strands

Coordination of economic policies could be a criterion for an EMU (Werner, 1970). Economic policies which are not coordinated among countries may be the major reason for the disturbance in the equilibrium of the balance of payments. Coordination of economic, in particular monetary, policies from a supranational centre requires political will on the part of the participating countries. A declaration towards such an objective was epitomized in the Maastricht Treaty.

One criterion for monetary integration may be a similar level of inflation among the potential member countries (Fleming, 1971). Diverging ratios of employment to inflation among these countries would cause hardship. Countries with a balance-of-payments surplus would be driven to accept a higher level of inflation than in the situation when they are free to choose this ratio. Conversely, countries with deficits may be asked to tolerate a higher level of unemployment than they would be willing to accept in the situation when they are free to choose this level.

An optimum currency area may be defined as a region in which no part insists on creating money and having a monetary policy of its own (Machlup, 1979, p. 71). A monetary union which imposes minimum costs on the participating countries may be called an optimum currency area (Robson, 1983, p. 143). An optimum currency area may be alternatively defined as an area in which net benefits of integration (increase in welfare in the form of greater stability in prices and smaller disturbances coming from abroad), outweigh the costs (restraint to individual uses of monetary and fiscal policies) (Grubel, 1970, p. 323). An optimum currency area aims at identifying a group of countries within which it is optimal to have fixed exchange rates while, at the same time, keeping certain flexibility in the exchange rate with the third countries (Thygesen, 1987, p. 163). Very small currency conversion costs and openness is likely to make the EU an optimal currency area, while high levels of government spending would make the EU less likely so (Canzoneri and Rogers, 1990, p. 422). An optimum currency area may also be defined as one that attains the macroeconomic objectives of internal balance (low unemployment and inflation) and external balance (a sustainable position in the balance of payments) (Tavlas, 1993a, p. 32).

The notion of an optimum currency area is theoretical, rather than practical. A region may be an economic unit which does not necessarily coincide with the domain of a currency. An optimum currency area may be able to sustain itself on its own. Its definition may ask for liberalization of all activities within it and its protection against the outside world. Despite their relevant arguments, these definitions can hardly be applied to countries in the real world, because the states are constituted in a sub-optimal way, so that full economic efficiency (regardless of the external world) can seldom, if ever, be achieved. A single criterion model has a narrow scope. Therefore, it is unable to present costs and benefits of an EMU. The next task is to amend this shortcoming.

III COSTS AND BENEFITS

1 Issues

A more practical and fruitful way to analyse an EMU is to study the optimum economic policy area, rather than the optimum currency area. A single state becomes increasingly ineffective as an independent policy-making unit in the modern era of continuous changes in technology, relatively easy and cheap dissemination of information and frequent market changes. This is true for all countries in the world, but it is not true for all of them equally. Therefore, not all of them seek international solutions to their national problems. In a situation where economic problems assume global proportions there is only one optimum policy area: the world (Panić, 1988, p. 317–330). The most pressing international economic problems cannot be solved by countries acting in isolation. Solutions to these problems can be found in coordinated national economic management. A system of safeguards which would include assistance in the form of transfer of (real) resources to the countries which experience difficulties, is an essential feature for the survival of an efficient multilateral system of trade and payments.

The shortcomings of the traditional single criterion and optimum currency model of international monetary integration may be overcome by the 'new theory' of monetary integration that relies on the cost–benefit model. This model offers superior policy implications. The costs which may be brought by a country's participation in monetary integration may be traced to the losses of a country's right to alter independently its rate of exchange, its ratio between inflation and unemployment, its ability to handle regional development policy, as well as its seigniorage. Monetary integration brings in a number of benefits. These include a dismissal of the exchange problems within the group of countries in the arrangement, an increase in influence in monetary affairs and an increase in monetary stability. The larger the integrated area, the larger are the gains. Both the costs and benefits of monetary integration are analysed next.

2 Costs

First, the creation of a supranational body to conduct monetary policy (money supply, rate of interest and rate of exchange) in an EMU may be perceived as a significant loss of the participating countries' sovereignty. This is the first cost, which may provoke adverse political, as well as psychological consequences in the countries that take part in the arrangement. The most vulnerable issue may be the loss of the right to alter independently the rate of exchange. The loss is complete against the currencies of the partner countries and partial against other countries. A right, often used selfishly, is gone. However, the gains here come from the pooling of monetary policies of the member countries that can exercise a much greater leverage over their monetary policy in comparison to the situation which preceded integration.

When policy makers want to adjust the balance of payments by means of alterations in a country's rate of exchange, then the most critical issue is the fall in real wages. Labour may accept a fall in real wages under the condition that the other alternative is (longer-term) unemployment. A reduction in the rate of exchange introduces an increase in the price for imported goods, as well as for some home produced goods and services. The impact of the devaluation depends on the openness of a country. A reduction in real wages introduces an advantage in the cost of labour and a relative decrease in the price of export goods in the short run. This classical scenario may be seriously questioned. Money illusion does not have a significant impact on labour any more. Every increase in inflation and corresponding fall in real wages under the assumption that there is no change in productivity, stimulates labour and concerned trade unions to ask for increases in wages. Short-term cost advantage of devaluation are eroded by such increases.

Devaluation as an instrument of economic policy may not alone eliminate deficits in the balance of payments. The government may state that its policy objective is not to use devaluation in the fight against inflation. Such a policy goal may act as an important incentive to firms to resist higher costs because their goods would become uncompetitive at foreign and, potentially, home markets if trade were free. A recession may be another, although less desirable, cure for inflation. Shrinking markets give firms incentives to keep prices low, while rising unemployment forces trade unions to resist increases in wages.

The exchange rates started to float in the early 1970s and did so for a decade. The experience has provided sufficient evidence that a country's autonomy in a situation of floating exchange rates is overstated. The majority of countries are small and open. This leads to the conclusion that the sole use of the exchange rate as the adjustment mechanism of the balance of payments is of limited significance. Fiscal policy[3] and labour mobility are the necessary supplements. Devaluation of a national currency is a sigh of failure to manage the economy soundly and carefully according to international standards. The standards of international economic prudence demonstrate that it is the national bureaucracy who is the only loser from the deprivation of the right to devalue the national currency. Therefore, the loss in autonomy in the management of a country's rate of exchange as a policy instrument is of little real significance.

If, however, the rate of exchange of a group of countries such as the EU is fixed to an anchor currency such as the German mark, as was the case in the EMS till August 1993, the situation may change. If international capital markets are free, the loss of the autonomy in fixing the exchange market does not matter as long as the economic cycles match each other. If the cycles differ, as has been the case in the EU, partner countries may be reluctant to follow the monetary policy of the anchor currency, since it may not match the necessary policy actions of the other participating countries.

Second, it was argued that floating rates of exchange permit unconstrained choices between unemployment and inflation in a country. On those grounds, countries may seem to be free to pursue their own stabilization policies. An EMU constrains the independent national choice of the rates of growth of inflation, unemployment and rate of interest. This national choice, as a second cost of monetary integration, is constrained by the choice of other partner countries. A loss of the right to deal independently may significantly jeopardize national preferences with respect to possible choices. The country with relatively low inflation and balance-of-payments surplus may, in accordance with its economic and political strength, impose its own goals on other partner countries, because this country may have much less pressure for adjustment than the other countries. A common currency levels the competitiveness of the group in the monetary field. If a region's factor productivity is lower than the average one in the group, then the regional/country authorities will have to 'tolerate' unemployment. Labour mobility (outflow) may be a solution to the problem. The higher the labour mobility, the more diversified the output pattern, and the more flexible prices and wages, the smoother the adjustment. Applied to the EU, only the relative diversification of the economic structure may pass the test for a smooth adjustment. Other macroeconomic criteria (labour mobility and flexible wages) do not fare well.

This consideration was examined with geometric rigour by de Grauwe (1975). It was proven that the countries differ regarding the position of their Phillips curves, rates of productivity growth and the preferences of governments between unemployment and inflation. These are the differences that explain why, in the absence of an EMU, rates of inflation among countries would be equal only by accident. For a smooth operation of an EMU, the requirement is not only balanced growth, but also equal unemployment rates, otherwise the EMU may not survive without intercountry compensatory transfer of resources. The mere integration of economic policy goals may not be effective without agreement on the means for achieving the agreed targets. If countries cope with a common problem and employ different tools, the outcome of harmonizing only economic policy objectives may be more harmful than helpful.

The Phillips curve suggests that there is a measurable, inverse relation between unemployment and inflation. The government could reduce unemployment by means of demand stimulus such as an increase in budget deficit while the price for this policy is increased inflation. In Friedman's model, the rate of unemployment is independent of the rate of inflation. The followers of this school criticize Phillips for not seeing that continuous inflationary policy provokes changes in the expectations about inflation in the future. They argue that there is only one rate of unemployment which is consistent with a constant rate of inflation. That is the natural rate of unemployment or the non-accelerating-inflation rate of unemployment (NAIRU). No matter what a government does, the rate of unemployment may not fall below the national NAIRU. This rate is not fixed. It is determined by the real factors which include minimum wage legislation, tax policy, dole money, labour mobility, the impetus for vocational training, payroll taxes,[4] as well as the choice between work and leisure. Most of these factors are made by economic policy. Every attempt to lower the rate of unemployment below the NAIRU by means of monetary expansion would only accelerate inflation. Hence, the loss of this economic policy choice is also of limited significance.

The main way to decrease unemployment is to reduce the NAIRU. It can be done by reducing the social security benefits below the minimum wage for unskilled labour, shortening the time during which those benefits apply and by controlling the wage demands of trade unions. Economic policy should be active in combating unemployment. The long-term unemployed have obsolete experience and training which makes them less attractive to potential employers. Those unemployed compete less vigorously on the labour market and place less downward pressure on wages. The NAIRU increases with the expansion of the long-term unemployed. Economic policy should withdraw social benefits from those who refuse vocational training and/or jobs with the exception of those who are beyond the agreed age. The problem of the EU and its member countries is that they have not dealt with the long-term unemployed. These countries handed relatively generous benefits for long periods to the unemployed. Around a half of the unemployed in the EU are out of work for over a year, while the same ratio in the US is less than 10 per cent.

The Canadian experience during 1950–1962 with a fluctuating rate of exchange was illustrative. Canada intended to have monetary independence in relation to the US. Theoretical arguments (illusions) about greater national independence and freedom regarding employment policy in a flexible exchange rate situation seemed attractive. Canadian hopes were high. At the end of this period a mismanaged government intervention succeeded in destabilizing prices in Canada and growth stagnated. The decision to abandon flexible exchange rates showed that the benefits in the stability of employment and economic independence are smaller than the cost paid in economic instability and efficiency. Given the contemporary capital market integration among open economies, significant differences among the rates of interest among different countries may not exist. Hence an open economy may not rely independently on this instrument of economic policy. In a situation where two or more currencies are close substitutes and where there exists free capital mobility, the central banks of these countries cannot conduct independent monetary policies even under fluctuating rates of exchange. Small open economies may be advised to link their monetary policies to those of their major partners in trade and investment.

Third, a serious problem in a monetary union may be traced in the inflow of capital into the prosperous regions. The regions losing this capital expect compensatory transfers from the prosperous ones. Those countries which feel that their destiny is to be losers from an EMU would not enter such an arrangement. The system of transfers may be a bribe to these regions/countries to participate. When there are budget deficits and expenditure cuts, the funds for transfers may not be found easily. None the less, the gainers may be quite happy to compensate the losers and protect the net gains from integration.

Fourth is the loss (if it is a loss) of seigniorage (also called the inflation tax) in an EMU. Instead of selling debt, a government may print money and, hence, raise revenue in order to cover its budget deficit. The government is taxing (inflation tax) the holders of cash held by the public and the commercial banks' low-interest bearing deposits/reserves held at the central bank.[5] In an EMU, inflating a national way out of economic crisis is not possible. Therefore, a country in need is supposed either to reduce its debt or to sell more reserves or both.

To sum up, an EMU introduces significant losses in constitutional autonomy of participating states, but real autonomy to conduct independent monetary policy for a small country in the situation of convertibility, synchronized economic cycles and openness for trade and investment would remain almost intact.

3 Benefits

The benefits of monetary integration are numerous and intuitive in their nature. They are hardly quantifiable and difficult to comprehend by the non-economist. The most important benefit of monetary integration is that it improves the integration of markets for goods, services and factors. Exchange rate risk for trade flows among the integrated countries is eliminated (false pricing that reflects distortions in the money exchange market is abolished), transaction[6] and hedging costs are reduced, so investors can make decisions with a high degree of long-term confidence. Without a single currency, a German investor would look at an investment project in Britain as a riskier one than the same project in Germany. Intra-union direct investment is not controlled. That improves competition and allocation of resources. This brings an increase in influence in monetary affairs, as well as connections among major trading partners. Further, by coordination of monetary and fiscal policies, the participating countries are led to fewer distortions while combating macroeconomic disequilibria. This introduces a greater monetary stability. In the situation with stable prices, interest and exchange rates, trade flows are not volatile, as there is no exchange rate risk and uncertainty. This increases competition, economies of scale and mobility of factors that further improves the allocation of resources and increases economic growth. The central financial institution may be entitled to finance regional inequalities.

The pooling of national reserves of foreign currencies is also advantageous for the member countries of an EMU. By internalizing their foreign trade, these countries reduce their demand for foreign-currency reserves. These reserves may not be necessary for trade within the group, but they may still be needed for trade with third countries. Anyway, there are economies in the use of reserves. Their level is reduced and overhead costs are spread on the participating countries. A single currency in the EU would save on the exchange reserves of the member states around $200 billion (*European Economy*, 1990a, p. 178). That money could be easily spent on alternative and more productive uses.

The net effect of monetary integration may not be easily and directly quantified. Just assume a reversed case. There were tremendous costs from the monetary disintegration of countries such as the former USSR or the former Yugoslavia. Imagine the losses of the monetary disintegration of the US or Germany where each federal state independently handles its own currency! If there does not exist a control group of similar unintegrated countries, then there is no yardstick against which one may compare the relative performance of the countries which created an EMU. The cost which may be brought by monetary integration in the form of an increase in prices or unemployment are relatively easy identifiable, borne by the few and perhaps of a short-term nature. If that nature is not short-term, then an indefinite intra-union system of transfer of resources is a necessary condition for the survival of the scheme. The benefits which accrue from monetary integration are long-term, they come in small amounts to everybody and are hard to quantify with great precision. In any case, those benefits create potential for the new capital formation (a permanent growth bonus) which would accelerate growth of output.

The 'new theory' of monetary integration suggests that there are somewhat fewer costs (loss of autonomy to handle domestic macroeconomic policies) and somewhat more benefits (gains in credibility in the combat against inflation) associated with monetary integration (Tavlas, 1993a, p. 682). The benefits of an EMU are larger, the greater the intra-union factor mobility, the more diversified the economies, the higher the flexibility of wages, the greater the internal trade and the higher the synchronization of business cycles among the member countries. The EU may pass most of those tests except for labour mobility and flexibility of wages.

IV PARALLEL CURRENCIES

There may be a question whether an irrevocable fixity of exchange rates is a sufficient condition for monetary integration or whether the introduction of a single currency is necessary in an EMU. Suppose that there are various currencies in an EMU which are tied by a fixed exchange rate. If there is an increase in the supply of any of these currencies, then convertibility may be maintained only by intervention, either in the form of the absorption of this currency by the monetary authorities or by reduction in demand (restriction in transactions) for this currency. The first method represents monetary expansion, while the other is an act of disintegration.

A common currency may be an outward symbol, but it is not the necessary condition for a successful EMU. Capital mobility and irrevocably fixed exchange rates of currencies in an EMU may create a single currency *de facto* in everything except, possibly, name, while a single currency would make a monetary union *de jure*. A single currency would be ultimately necessary, because it would make the irrevocable fixity of exchange rates of the participating currencies completely credible. Countries would not have even a remote possibility of finding their way out of economic difficulties in devaluation and/or inflation.[7] In addition, a single money would eliminate possible conversion charges, prices in the area would be fully transparent and there would be external benefits (such as introduction of a better symmetry in the international monetary system).

An evolutionary approach to the introduction of an EMU may be that a common currency may exist side by side with the currencies of the member countries. Once agents are used to dealing with the common currency, it may gradually replace the monies of the participating countries. This is the case of parallel currencies. An important issue here is that the new, parallel currency, ought to be linked to the pace of economic activity, otherwise price stability may be in danger. In addition, it may bring an extra complication in the monetary affairs among the integrated countries. A gradual convergence among the currencies would make the participating currencies yield an identical return. They would become perfect substitutes. Monetary unification may take place.

Gradual monetary integration suffers from a serious flaw. It is a lack of credibility. During the transition phase, the participating countries may find a way to step out temporarily from the arrangement. A system that permits some, even though remote, autonomy in the national monetary policy in the situation of a free capital mobility is subject to speculative attacks (the most obvious example in the EU took place in July 1993). On the one hand, the longer the transition to a single currency, the greater the fragility of the system. On the other hand, a fast acceptance of a single money may provoke harsh regional disequilibria for which the countries may not be prepared (for example, a lack of regional funds). Policy-makers need to balance the two sides before they decide. They also have to take into account the increase in unemployment in East Germany after reunification with the western part of the country in 1990. It directly resulted from an instant merger of the two economies on a very different level of development before they were ready for a full EMU. Should the same be repeated in the EU?

The above theoretical model about parallel currencies has two caveats. It ignores network effects and switching costs (Dowd and Greenaway, 1993a, p. 1180). For example, after the breakup of the former USSR, the rouble was a currency which did not fit well into the new realities. Certain newly independent states continued to use roubles because of the network effects. They did so because most of their trading partners were using them too. In addition, the switching costs from one currency to another are quite high. At the limit, it would be preferable to use only one money because of the network effects, conversion charges and switching costs. If the benefits of a single currency outweigh those costs, welfare is maximized and it is justified, from the economic point of view, to switch to a single currency. In the case of the EU, the German mark would be the best candidate to serve as the EU common currency. The mark has the biggest existing network, while the Bundesbank is more credible than any of the existing central banks in the EU (Dowd and Greenaway, 1993a, p. 243).

Currencies of the member countries in an EMU are perfect substitutes. On the one hand, it would be meaningless to speak here about a parallel currency, since any parallel currency would be indistinguishable from national currencies in everything but name. The concept of a parallel currency becomes meaningful only in an intermediate stage of an EMU, when different currencies are not perfect substitutes because of transaction costs and/or exchange rate expectations. Reductions in exchange rate variability would diminish the usefulness of a parallel (basket) currency as an instrument of risk diversification, unless transaction costs in the parallel (common) currency decline by more than the transaction costs in the component currencies. On the other hand, a parallel currency is unlikely to develop in the case when national currencies are only very imperfect substitutes, because of high conversion costs. Widespread use of a parallel currency alongside national currencies can therefore be expected only under a high degree of monetary integration (Gros, 1989, p. 224).

A common currency may replace national currencies after some period of adjustment. Stability in the monetary sphere may be a result. However, the new and single money in the area would not solve the problem of budget deficits of the member countries that would be revealed, in part, as regional disequilibria.[8] Gresham's law says that in a situation where there are two currencies (in his example, gold and silver coins) circulating side by side in the economy, then 'the bad money will drive out the good', except in the case where there is a fixed exchange rate between the two monies. This result has not materialized in some countries.[9]

V MONETARY INTEGRATION IN THE EUROPEAN UNION

1 Background

Integration in the EU has advanced at a pace faster than that envisaged in the Treaty of Rome. The customs union was fully established among the founding member countries in 1968, which was a year and a half ahead of schedule. This was one of the most significant initial achievements of the group.

The original version of the Treaty of Rome provided the legal basis for the EU involvement in monetary policy. Article 103 requested that countries regard their national economic policies and their coordination as a matter of common concern. Article 104 allowed the member countries to pursue their own economic policies, but they must ensure the equilibrium of the national balance of payments and confidence in their currencies, and also aim for a high level of employment and stability of prices. Article 105 required that the member states coordinate economic policies. Article 106 declared the readiness of the member states to remove capital controls. Article 107 asked that each member country must treat its exchange rate policy as a matter of common interest. The domestic rules that manage capital market and the credit system ought to be applied in a non-discriminatory way (Article 68). A safeguard clause could be found in Article 73 since it entitles the Commission to permit a member state to take protective measures in the field of capital movements if such movements bring disturbances in the operation of the national capital market. Article 108 referred to the balance-of-payments difficulties of the member states. In that case, the Commission shall investigate the situation and make recommendations including mutual financial assistance of the member countries. According to Article 109, a member country might, as a precaution, take the necessary protective measures in the situation of a sudden crisis in the balance of payments, but the Commission may suspend such measures. The Single European Act requested, in the amended Article 102a of the Treaty of Rome, that the member countries strengthen cooperation in the fields covered by Article 104 and respect the rules of the EMS. The above provisions were thoroughly altered by the Maastricht Treaty (Articles B and G, respectively, will be discussed below) in order to provide a base for the EMU.

2 Ideas

After the initial success in the establishment of a customs union, the EU contemplated the establishment of an EMU. There were two schools of thought about how to implement this idea. They were the 'monetarists' and the 'economists'. The first school (Belgium, France and Luxembourg) argued that a promising EMU requires an irrevocable fixity of exchange rates of the participating countries from the outset. The member countries would, then, be driven to coordinate their economic policies in order to mitigate and, eventually, eliminate the discrepancies in their economies that are necessary for a full EMU. They also argued in favour of a well endowed fund for the support of the adjustments of the balance of payments. Complete freedom of capital movements should be permitted only after the establishment of a full EMU. The last request of this school was that supranationality should be on a relatively low level.

The school of 'economists' (Germany and the Netherlands) argued that fixed exchange rates for a group of countries that are on relatively different levels of development is a formidable task. They argued that the coordination of economic policies should be the primary task, because it would bring economic harmonization among the participating countries. They argued in favour of a free movement of capital from the outset and felt that fixed exchange rates may be introduced only after the fulfilment of the above conditions.

The Werner Report (1970) was offered as the blueprint for the EMU in the EU. The Report asked both for fixed rates of exchange and free mobility of capital. Thus, it represented a compromise between the two schools. Over optimism (EMU by 1980) was not rewarded, because the report overestimated the will of the member states to abandon their monetary authority in favour of a supranational body, in particular in the light of the turmoils on the currency markets during the 1970s. This approach may have also failed because it wanted to fix rates of exchange without prior monetary reform among the member countries.

3 European Monetary System

The early 1970s were characterized by significant turbulence on the monetary scene. Currencies were fluctuating, so this state of affairs endangered the functioning of trade flows in the EU. The Council of Ministers requested the member governments not only to follow the ± 2.25 per cent margins of fluctuation in relation to the dollar, but also to reduce the level of fluctuation among their respective currencies. This introduced the 'European snake' (common margins of fluctuation). If one plots the daily fluctuations of the currencies of the EU member states, then one would get a snake-like ribbon. The width of the snake depended on the fluctuation of the strongest and the weakest currencies remaining always within the ± 2.25 per cent fluctuation margins of the dollar tunnel. The creation of the 'snake' was mainly a European reaction to the hectic situation of the dollar on the international money market.

The main feature of the 'snake' was intervention. When the sum of the fluctuations in the 'snake' exceeded the margins, intervention was supposed to take place (the strongest currency should purchase the weakest one). The dollar tunnel disappeared in 1973, so the 'snake' found itself in the lake. The currencies in the 'snake' entered and left the system quite often. This introduced uncertainty in trade relations in the EU. Apart from external pressures to which the 'snake' was unable to resist, an internal shortcoming (different national monetary policies) also played a role. Something should have been done about that.

The member countries of the EU wanted not just to preserve the already achieved level of economic integration, but also to add to it. A further step was the creation of the European Monetary System (EMS). The approach was completely different from the one which established the 'snake'. Instead of preparing various economic plans for political consideration, the EU member countries first delivered their political decision about the establishment of the system and then, agreed about the technical/operational details of the system. The EMS was introduced in 1979.

The objectives of the EMS are: stabilization of exchange rates through closer monetary cooperation among the member countries, promotion of further integration of the group and contribution to the stabilization of international monetary relations.

A key role in the EMS is played by the European Currency Unit (ECU). The ECU is basically a 'cocktail' of fixed proportions of currencies of the EU member countries. The share of every currency in the ECU depends on the economic potential of the country (aggregate GDP), its share in intra-EU trade and the need for short-term monetary support. The composition of the ECU is presented in Table 2.1. Alterations in its composition may occur every five years or when the share of each currency changes by at least 25 per cent in relation to the originally-calculated value. In addition, the make-up of the ECU can change when the currency of a new member country enters the 'basket'. The currency composition of the ECU was 'frozen' by Article 109g of the Treaty of Rome (as revised by the Maastricht Treaty). That is why the currencies of Austria, Finland and Sweden are not included in the basket.

Table 2.1 Composition of the ECU (%)

Currency	Weight in the basket			
	1979–84	*1984–89*	*1989–94*	*1995*
1 German mark	33.0	32.0	30.1	32.7
2 French franc	19.8	19.0	19.0	20.8
3 Pound sterling	13.3	15.0	13.0	11.2
4 Dutch guilder	10.5	10.1	9.4	10.2
5 Belgian franc	9.3	8.2	7.6	8.4
6 Italian lira	9.5	10.2	10.15	7.2
7 Spanish peseta	—	—	5.3	4.2
8 Danish krone	3.1	2.7	2.45	2.7
9 Irish pound	1.1	1.2	1.1	1.1
10 Portuguese escudo	—	—	0.8	0.7
11 Greek drachma	—	1.3	0.8	0.5
12 Luxembourg franc	0.4	0.3	0.3	0.3
Total	100.0	100.0	100.0	100.0

Source: European Monetary Institute (1996)

The exchange rate mechanism (ERM) of the EMS has been in the centre of controversy since its inception. Every currency in the EMS has its own central rate versus other partner currencies and the ECU. In relation to the partner currencies in the system individual currencies could fluctuate within a ±2.25 per cent band with the exception of the Spanish peseta and British pound which were permitted to float within a ±6 per cent limit. In 1990, 11 years after the creation of the EMS the special (±6 per cent floating band) treatment for the Italian lira ended. When a currency reaches its limit (upper or lower) of fluctuation in relation to another EMS partner currency, then intervention in the national currency by one of the two central banks is compulsory. Intervention within the margins of fluctuation may be either in the national currencies of the members of the EMS or in dollars.[10]

Fluctuation of each EMS currency versus the ECU is slightly stricter. The Commission has individualized each currency's margin of fluctuation. It was strictest for the German mark (±1.51 per cent) and widest for the Irish pound (±2.22 per cent). (Currencies granted 'special treatment' had wider margins of fluctuation than the standard ones in relation to the ECU.)

There was an implicit objective behind the relatively strict margins of fluctuation for currencies in the EMS. It was to encourage member countries to accept similar economic policies and to converge. This convergence does not necessarily aim at averaging out the economic performance criteria. Although the EMS has not produced a full convergence of the macroeconomic indicators of the member countries, it seemed for quite some time that it was heading towards the desired outcome. The best signal was that most member countries remained in the EMS despite certain strains.

In order to prevent frequent interventions, the EMS has introduced an early-warning system in the form of a divergence indicator. The divergence threshold is ±75 per cent of a currency's fluctuation in relation to the ECU. The role of this indicator is ambiguous. As soon as the divergence threshold is reached, the countries in question are not formally required to do anything, even to consult. Therefore, this innovation has not so far played an important role in the EMS. None the less, consultation and cooperation of the monetary authorities of the EU member countries have compensated, at least in part, for this shortcoming of the EMS.

The strongest arguments for the non-participating countries to join the ERM of the EMS seemed to be predominantly political. It was not going to help integration for these countries to stay aloof from one of the most significant achievements of the EU. In addition, and more importantly, the creation of a genuine internal market for goods, services and factors would be incomplete without a single market for money.

The EMS funds for exchange market interventions are relatively well endowed. The very short-term financing facility for compulsory intervention provides the participating central banks with an unlimited amount of partner currency loans. None the less, the Bundesbank does not, in practice, accept intervention without limits. The short-term monetary support disposes of 14 billion ECUs for the financing of temporary balance-of-payments deficits, while the medium-term support facility disposes of 11 billion ECUs (but the use of this mechanism is subject to conditions).

A country with the best performance in inflation, balance of payments, employment, growth and the like has least pressure to adjust and, in relation to its size, it may influence the shaping of other countries' economic variables. Hence, Germany was able to dominate within the EMS which operated asymmetrically in formulating monetary policies of other member countries that had to bear the adjustment burden. Since inflation has been reduced and other monetary variables reasonably aligned among most member countries, the EMS operated in a more symmetric way before the reunification of Germany in October 1990.

The EMS may sometimes slow down the rate of economic adjustment of a member country. When countries borrow on the international financial markets, these markets do not exclusively consider the credit-worthiness (reserves, deficits, experience in adjustments and outlooks) of the borrowing country. These markets consider the membership of the EMS and its possibilities for financial support. In this indirect way, the financial markets take into account the reserves of the other EMS countries. These markets believe that the partner countries will help the borrowing country in financial difficulties. This is a recognition of the relative success of the EMS. However, it may prevent a country accepting greater monetary discipline. A heartless government may erode the real burden of debt by using inflation. In any case, a country which follows a policy of a relative monetary indiscipline would reduce domestic reserves and lose credit-worthiness in the long run. Foreign creditors may reasonably demand higher interest rates which usually deter private investment greater than consumption and, hence, reduce the future economic potential of the country. An agreed limitation for national borrowing needs to be a part of an EMU.

Apart from funds for exchange market interventions, other EMS adjustment mechanisms include home price and income alterations, rates of interest, control of capital flows, as well as increased cooperation and exchange of information. Controls of internal trade flows are, of course, prohibited.

The rates of exchange in the EMS were semi-fixed. The EMS did not have as its goal the petrifaction of rates of exchange among the member countries. The adjustments of the central rates may take place either every five years or according to need. When all other mechanisms for intervention are used up, the country in question may ask for permission to change the central rate of its currency. The Council of Ministers decides about these changes (usually during the weekend when the financial markets are closed). The effects of realignments (or put in plain English, devaluations) may be eaten away by inflation. So, the best and, surely, the hardest way for the stability of the system is that the deficit countries increase productivity above the EU average.

In spite of its relative rigidity, the EMS made the rates of exchange quasi-flexible. If a currency is in the type of trouble which may not be solved by intervention, then the system permitted adjustments (revaluations and devaluations) of the central rate of exchange. This kind of adjustment happened relatively often during the first years of the existence of the EMS.

A change of the central rate of a currency (devaluation) is still a permitted means for the restoration of competitiveness among the EMS member countries. In some distant situation with no national currencies, even *de facto*, the restoration of national competitiveness could be achieved by an increase in productivity, reduction in wages or by labour migration to advanced regions or by all three. The US is an example where wages are flexible and labour is highly mobile. At the same time a single currency has a smooth internal performance. The US inter-regional adjustments are eased by a system of implicit federal government transfers of real resources. The federal government spends much and taxes little in the backward or ill-performing states/regions, while it does the reverse in the advanced states/regions. A similar mechanism does not yet exist in the EU. The EU, with its vast internal market, does not yet have economic stabilizers on the American scale that are supposed to ease the adjustment troubles of both countries and regions within them. There are, however, growing structural funds in the EU. The adjustment does not only ask for the transfer of real resources, but also for measures to enhance mobility of factors from low- to high-productivity regions. On this account, the EU has so far failed.

All member countries of the EU have exchanged for ECUs 20 per cent of their gold reserves (the role of gold is partly reaffirmed) and 20 per cent of their dollar reserves with the EMI (until 1994, the European Fund for Monetary Cooperation). These assets are swapped on a revolving quarterly basis for ECUs. Hence the ECU is not a newly created reserve asset which is an addition to the existing stocks of reserves such as the special drawing rights are. The creation of the ECU transforms a part of the existing reserve assets into another asset. The amount of ECUs issued changes every quarter in relation to the changes in member countries' volume of reserves, the price of gold and the dollar exchange rate. There were around 54 billion ECUs issued in 1996.

The ECU is used as: an accounting unit for intervention; a means of settlement among central banks; a part of international financial reserves; a basis for the calculation of the divergence indicator; a unit for the store of value (because of its relative stability) and a unit for financial transactions and statistics of the EU administration. There are, also, ECU-denominated bonds. Although the ECU is still remote from day-to-day use by individuals, many banks open personal accounts in ECUs and offer an interest rate which is a weighted average of interest rates of the participant countries in the ECU. They also offer travellers' cheques denominated in ECUs. Interest rate differentials reflect mainly differences in the national rates of inflation. Once the exchange rates start to move with inflation differentials, the profitability of holding ECUs may cease.

The ECU is used by the monetary authorities as the official ECU, while businesses and the public use the private or commercial ECU. Nevertheless, the ECU market is not fragmented. All dealings are in a single ECU, as the definition of both is the same. A central bank may hold ECUs. If the national currency comes under pressure, the bank can sell ECUs and purchase the national currency. This may be a cheaper and less visible way of intervention than by a direct borrowing of other currencies to buy domestic when the exchange rate is falling. The major reason for the relative spread in the use of private ECUs is the demand of business for the simplification of transactions and, possibly, avoiding capital controls where they existed. The ECU is attractive because of its greater stability in relation to its components. Except for the intra-firm trade, firms do not have big incentives to use the ECU when the rates of exchange are not stable (since they may wish to exploit the difference in prices). Non-European investors prefer to deal in a single currency rather than several different currencies. The market value of the ECU is not directly influenced by the value of the dollar as it is not incorporated in the ECU basket as is the case with the special drawing rights. Therefore, the dollar holders can buy the ECUs and hedge against the dollar exchange risk.

Britain did not have capital controls, hence the volume of funds for intervention in order to protect a certain exchange rate needs to be quite large. Such interventions may endanger the British monetary targets. Britain is a significant oil exporter, so the pound is a petro-currency. As such, it is much more sensitive to the actual and expected changes in the price of oil than any other EU currency. The reaction of the pound usually went in the opposite direction from other EU currencies. As long as the exchange rate of the dollar (in which the price of oil is denominated) remains uncertain and as long as Britain remains a significant oil exporter, this potential over-reaction of the pound may remain. None the less, after a long period of absence, Britain decided to join the ERM of the EMS in 1990. Since the British goal was monetary stability and to fight inflation, it was a wise decision. In addition, the EMS fully included one of the world's major currencies. During the first year of participation in the ERM, Britain reduced its rate of inflation to the German level (4 per cent). It took France a decade to achieve the same goal.

A shock came in September 1992. The demand for funds to cover the excessive costs of the reunification of Germany put pressure on its budget. In order to contain the inflationary pressure, Germany raised interest rates. At about the same time, the US wanted to revive demand by cutting interest rates. The dollar became cheaper, while the German mark became dearer. The divergency prompted speculations that hit the weaker currencies hard in the EMS. Currency market speculation forced Britain, followed by Italy, to suspend their membership of the ERM. The EMS was on the brink of a breakdown. A single EU currency would avoid such a crisis. None the less, Britain had certain benefits from the 25 per cent depreciation in the value of the pound in the following months. For example, Philips moved the manufacturing of cathode tubes from the Netherlands to Britain. Hoover also relocated the production of vacuum cleaners from France to Britain.

Adjustments in the rates of exchange together with capital controls were used by some countries in the EMS, for example Italy and France, to control the domestic monetary system by an easier way than through other, relatively unpopular methods, such as recession. To an extent, they were able to follow for some time, a different course in national macroeconomic variables from their foreign partners. Capital, one of the major lubricants of the economy was 'forced' to remain at home. In addition, an outflow of capital would push interest rates up. That would slow down the economy, perhaps at the very moment when it needs to grow. However, the problem is that capital controls retard structural adjustments that need to take place in any case. Although the short-term effect of controls may bring certain policy successes, the long-term costs of the structural transformation would increase. That is why interest rate policy may be now a preferable instrument.

Capital controls are effective ways to manage monetary affairs in a situation where money markets expect adjustments in the exchange rate.[11] Then, controls drive holders to keep (in the country) the currency that is about to be devalued. Controls may be permanent or temporary (as emergency measures to prevent speculative capital flows). In the absence of capital controls, devaluation of weak currencies cannot be postponed; however, controls make the delay of devaluation possible. None the less, delays increase uncertainty about the rate of exchange in the future and, hence, jeopardize investment decisions. With capital controls, a relatively modest increase in the national rate of interest would achieve the desired monetary policy result. Without capital controls, the only instrument that can be used to the same effect is a sudden and, usually, large, increase in the rates of interest. The main defence of capital controls is not found in the fact that they are costless, but rather that they are less costly than the movements of exchange rates and interest rates that would happen without those controls (Folkerts-Landau and Mathieson, 1989, p. 8).

The removal of the remaining capital controls in the EU in 1995 was one of the notable achievements of the 1992 Programme. It made the residents throughout the EU sensitive to differences in interest rates. TNCs, including banks, as major beneficiaries of the dismantling of capital controls, are able to easily and swiftly change and diversify the currency composition and maturity of their financial portfolios. By doing that, TNCs and other money holders may jeopardize the objectives of monetary policy of individual member countries in a situation with easy and cheap currency substitution. An increase in the national rate of interest in order to reduce the supply of money and cool the economy would have the opposite effect. Increased interest rates would suddenly attract an inflow of foreign capital and increase the national supply of money. (Such swift changes are not very likely in the flow of goods and services.) Conversely, if the intention of the national government is to stimulate home economic activity by a reduction in interest rates, the effect would be the opposite from the intended one. Capital would fly out of the country to locations where rates of interest are higher. Without capital controls investors speculate about which currency is to be devalued next. Enormous capital flows can destabilize exchange rates. With a daily trade of around 1 trillion dollars on foreign exchange markets and with more than one money in the currency market, it is possible to gamble. No national intervention can triumph over the speculators. That was proved in the EU in the summers of 1992 and 1993. The grand dreams of an EMU in the relatively medium term were, in fact, pushed into the (distant) future.

Without capital controls, large differences in interest rates among the EMS countries cannot be sustained. In the new situation, the EU member countries have no other rational choice but to pool their national monetary policies and cooperate. Any increase in monetary instability among EU currencies would provoke the mobility of funds in search for a greater security, thus making it impossible to maintain EMS parities without even greater harmonization of national monetary policies (Panić, 1991). Since it was the Bundesbank that calls the tune in the EMS, pooling of monetary policies among the countries of the EU may increase the sovereignty of smaller countries because they would, in the new situation, have some say in the EU monetary policy-making process. Although the national central banks may become increasingly independent from the national governments, they need to enhance their reliance on other national central banks in the EU.

A reduction in the variance of economic indicators among the countries may illustrate their economic convergence. A narrowing of the differences in performance criteria among countries does not necessarily mean that their standards of living are becoming more equal. Membership of the EMS may be used by the national government as a convincing argument in pursuing a prudent national economic policy in the fight against the opposition. The EMS has introduced convergence in domestic monetary policies and inflation rates, but it has not been fully backed up by corresponding progress in the fiscal sector and external balance.

A mere convergence in the rate of inflation and other monetary variables may not be enough for the smooth operation of the single EU market. The EMS was not able to increase significantly the use of the ECU, the role of the European Fund for Monetary Cooperation was marginalized and the present form of the system was unable to bring spontaneous monetary integration. Those objectives might be achieved if there was a European central bank, a system of central banks or a common monetary authority. This did not happen before the implementation of the Maastricht Treaty because of a fear that monetary issues would be passed on to a remote bureaucracy. The governments were afraid of losing monetary sovereignty (the right to cheat on their citizens, firms and other holders of their money without a promise to convert paper money into gold). Another fear was that they may not be able to pursue their own stabilization policy. Those anxieties were not well founded. In order to carry on with the national stabilization, balance of payments, regional, industrial and other policies, the governments would still have at their disposal taxes, certain subsidies, some procurement and budget deficits. The only (severe) restrictions to their sovereignty to choose stabilization policies are that they could not employ exchange rate changes and have different rates of inflation from their partner countries.

It must be always kept in mind that in an EMU, national governments could still have a chance to tax and spend in the way they think is most appropriate. Budget deficits would still be possible, but subject to only one condition. It is that this excess budget expenditure must be financed by borrowing (on commercial terms) instead of printing domestic money. For example, the borrowing and expenditure of the cantons in Switzerland and provinces in Canada are not subject to constraints. The *Länder* in Germany restrict borrowing only to the extent that it is necessary to finance investment, while the federal states in the US limit their outlays, applying a kind of balanced budget. It is only in Australia that the federal government continuously supervise state debts.

The freedom to tax and spend in an EMU, however, is not absolute. As soon as a country's national finances jeopardize the stability of the union, such as excess imports that depress the value of a common currency, the union's authority may step in. It may impose limits on the borrowing from the central bank and other sources, ceilings on the budget deficit, a request for non-interest bearing deposits and impose fines. In a single currency area, foreign debt has to be serviced by export earnings. The national debt, however, does not present an immediate real burden on the economy because it represents a transfer between present and future generations.

There may be a temptation for a country in a monetary system to run a budget deficit for quite some time according to current needs. Although governments are often safer borrowers in relation to private ones,[12] capital markets would increase interest rates to heavy borrowers when their credit-worthiness is jeopardized. Big budget deficits keep long-term interest rates on a higher level than would otherwise be the case. This reduces the size and effectiveness of the cuts in short-term interest rates. The governments of the EU countries generally failed to do that during the 1980s, hence the lack of power to employ fiscal policy to prop up recovery in the 1990s. If a state in federations such as the US and Canada increases its borrowing, then the value of government bonds falls throughout the country. In such cases, the federal government may step in and correct the distortion. However, this kind of well developed corrective mechanism does not yet exist in the EU.

IV EUROPEAN MONETARY UNION

During the discussions that led to the Maastricht Treaty, there were two extreme possibilities for the final shape of the EU Central Bank and a number of mixed ones. One extreme is on the model of Germany's Bundesbank. It is independent from the government in the conduct of monetary policy and possibly, thereby, quite successful. The Bundesbank ensures stable prices, high employment, balanced foreign trade, as well as a constant and reasonable economic growth. The other extreme is the Bank of France. In this bank the government has a full stake, so France would like to see a kind of accountability of the EU Central Bank to the public bodies. As Germany was the engine of EU monetary stability until 1992–1993, the Maastricht Treaty opted for this kind of a central bank for the EU. The Bank is supposed to be very tough on inflation.

The main argument in favour of a common central bank is that it reduces uncertainties and conflict about and among national monetary policies. It does so by providing a forum in which national views can be represented and resolved, as well as by reducing the discretion that national monetary authorities have in the implementation of (divergent) policies. In the absence of a central bank, national conflicts would be resolved by market forces with adverse externalities for efforts to promote greater stability of exchange rates (Folkerts-Landau and Mathieson, 1989, p. 15). However, a question still remains: do the appointed central bankers possess superior knowledge about the country's long-term needs than the governments that represent the elected opinion of the public?

Many EU member countries preferred to see a 'German-influenced' Union's bank, rather than the continuation of the prevailing system that is 'German controlled'. In the system with binding rules and procedures, the smaller EU countries may be represented on the Bank's board where they could, at least to an extent, shape policy. Therefore, their sovereignty may be *increased* in comparison to the previous situation. Independent central banks, such as the judiciary, are constitutional institutions since they are not accountable to the elected government or parliament. Their autonomy comes from a general consensus about the long-term economic objectives and from the fact that their instruments may be badly abused by the political majority of the day (Vaubel, 1990, p. 941).

The Delors Report (1989) gave a new impetus to the creation of the EMU. It envisaged the EMU in three stages. Astutely, it did not state any specific date apart from mid-1990 for the beginning of the first stage. During the first phase, member countries would strengthen the coordination of their economic and monetary policies. The removal of the remaining capital controls would require this in any case. All countries would enter the ERM of the EMS. Stage two would be marked by the creation of the European Central Bank (a system of central banks or a monetary authority). The major macroeconomic indicators would be set for all member countries including the size and financing of the budget deficit. In addition, the margins of fluctuation in the ERM would be narrowed. The first two stages would not be fully stable, as there would be the potential for speculative attacks. In the last stage of the creation of the EMU, a common central bank would be the only authority responsible for the conduct of the monetary policy throughout the EU. The exchange rates among the national currencies would be permanently fixed without any fluctuations. A single currency would emerge. It may be a necessary condition for a genuine single market where a national competitiveness would not be influenced by alterations in exchange rates. This was the blueprint for the finalization of the Maastricht Treaty.

In 1990 the British proposed an alternative plan that would introduce a 'hard ECU' as the thirteenth currency at that time, in stage two, as a parallel currency. It would be an additional anti-inflationary control on governments that intend to ease national monetary policy. It would be issued by the Central Bank in exchange for deposits of national currencies. The 'hard ECU' would be managed in such a way that each national central bank would compensate the Union's Central Bank for any loses caused by devaluation of its currency and that any inflating national central bank would buy back its national currency with, for example, dollars or yens. Wide acceptability of the 'hard ECU' would prevent national central banks from inflating. The problem with this plan was that the British saw it as an end in itself, not as a vehicle towards a single EU currency. This plan received little support during negotiations about the EMU.

After the currency disturbances of September 1992, when Britain and Italy left the ERM, a new and bigger shock took place at the end of July 1993 when the actual demise of the ERM of the EMS occurred. Germany's need to obtain funds to finance the reintegration of its eastern part increased interest rates. The country placed its national interest ahead of the concerns of the EU by refusing to cut interest rates.[13] That produced a currency crisis. To ease the strain, a possible solution was found in increaseing the margins for the fluctuations of the currencies participating in the ERM. They were widened from ±2.25 per cent to ±15 per cent from the central parity. The 'dirty float' began. The EMS revealed its fragility. However, a step back from the EMU path was a better option than the total suspension of the EMS. The widening of the possibilities to fluctuate within the ERM increased the room for differences in the national economic policies. Even though this was a possibility, it was not exercised. The countries endeavoured to keep the exchange rate of their currencies within the 'old' margins of fluctuation. None the less, the mere existence of the allowed wider margins for fluctuations introduced an element of uncertainty.

A condition for the establishment of the EMU is that the 'normal' (without a definition) fluctuation margins for currencies need to be observed for at least two years. However, what is 'normal' in the situation when the ERM remains only in name! The wide increase in the fluctuation margins made a mockery of the Maastricht Treaty's intentions to introduce a single currency in the relatively near future. One needs to remember that exchange rate movements of 15 per cent are quite common outside the EU.

The Maastricht Treaty that established the EU is in essence mostly about the EMU. That is voiced both in the Preamble and Articles B and G, respectively. It is an expected step after the establishment of a free internal market in 1993. For a free flow of goods and services, as well as for an efficient allocation of resources, a necessary condition is a degree of stability in exchange rates and a removal of conversion costs.

According to the Maastricht Treaty, the EMU is to be achieved in three stages. During the first, there was to be a reinforcement of coordination of economic and monetary policies of the member countries. The second stage started in January 1994 with the establishment of the EMI in Frankfurt. This took place in an unsettled exchange rate environment. The EMI is to coordinate the EU members' monetary policies and prepare the conditions for the final stage. The central banks of the member states need to become independent before the end of the second stage when the EMI would be transformed into an independent European Central Bank (ECB). There would be, in fact, the European System of Central Banks. It would be composed of the ECB and the central banks of the member states.

According to the letter of the Treaty, the Council of Ministers would decide by a qualified majority, not later than 31 December 1996, whether a majority (at least eight) of the EU countries fulfil the following five necessary criteria for the third stage of EMU (Article 109j and Protocol on the Convergence Criteria):

- a high degree of price stability (inflation within the margin of 1.5 per cent of the three best-performing EU countries);
- sound public financial position (budget deficit of less than 3 per cent of the GDP);[14]

- a national debt of less than 60 per cent of GDP;[15]
- the observance of the 'normal' fluctuation margins (no devaluation within the EU exchange rate mechanism for at least two preceding years); and
- the durability of convergence of economic policies that needs to be reflected in the long-term interest rate levels (interest rate has to be within the 2 per cent margin of the three best performing EU countries).

If a country fails one (or, perhaps, two conditions), but if it makes good progress on those issues, it may be let into the EMU. If the Council is not able to decide about the beginning of the third stage, the Maastricht Treaty stipulates that it would begin on 1 January 1999 for the countries which fulfil the necessary conditions for EMU. Those countries would irrevocably fix their exchange rates and the ECU would subsequently replace the national currencies under the name of the 'euro'. The ECB would follow its primary commitment of price stability and, consequently, set interest rates and conduct foreign exchange operations. In addition, the ECB would support economic growth and employment. The ECB would report regularly to the EU finance ministers (meetings of the ECOFIN which would issue broad economic policy guidelines) and to the European Parliament. In any case, the implementation of the five criteria for the third stage of the EMU, if implemented strictly, would have a deflationary effect on the economy of the EU.

The Maastricht convergence criteria are arbitrary. Economic theory suggested other conditions for monetary integration such as flexibility in labour markets, labour mobility and fiscal transfers. The Maastricht criteria could be met once the countries are *in* the EMU; however, *before* such a union takes place it may be extremely hard to meet the criteria. 'The Maastricht treaty has it back to front.... On balance the Maastricht convergence criteria are *obstacles* to a monetary union in Europe' (de Grauwe, 1994b, pp. 159–161). The question is: is the difficult road towards the EMS as structured by the Maastricht Treaty becoming impossible?

It is certain that very few countries would meet the Maastricht convergence criteria for the EMU. If the EMU takes place only among the select group of countries, the excluded countries would face divergence, rather than convergence in certain macroeconomic variables, because of the fact that they are left out of the arrangement. Exchange rates between the full EMU countries and the ones that are outside would remain volatile. That would have an adverse impact on the EU single market. Therefore, one may wish to put less emphasis on convergence criteria and more on strengthening of the future monetary institutions of the EU. First, if the Board of Directors of the ECB fails to maintain price stability, there should be a procedure for their removal. Second, if a country (such as Belgium or Italy) fails to satisfy budgetary standards, it would be denied voting power on the Board of Directors of the ECB (de Grauwe, 1995, pp. 19–20). These ideas have economic merit, but they are politically naïve.

The way out may be found either in changing criteria or in altering the timetable. If the criteria are changed, the arrangement may not be acceptable to Germany. Hence, the answer is self-evident. The problem with changing the timetable is that once this occurs and deadlines are altered, for instance postponed for a few years, this may terminate the whole project. After all, the 'process of creating an ever closer union' (Preamble for the Maastricht Treaty) is not necessarily only linked to the EMS (at least as structured so far)! The abandonment of 1999 deadline does not mean the departure from the idea about the EMU.

The reunification of Germany was the major instigator of the Maastricht Treaty, as well as the reason for the Treaty's disappointing implementation. The EMS became too rigid to adjust to disequilibrating blows such as the reunification of Germany and the consequent budget deficits. The high German interest rates (because of the decision to pay for the reunification[16] by borrowing, rather than by raising taxes) and the need of the economies in recession to get cheap loans, produced the upheaval the speculators desired. If EMU is founded on foreign policy considerations, it comes as no surprise that the German voters are highly sceptical about it. The exchange rate crisis was a good reminder to the policy-makers that markets cannot be avoided. The capital markets would always probe the decisiveness of the governments to defend the narrow bands of exchange rate. As long as the economies are in recession, governments would not enter such contest. The wreckage of the ERM of the EMS is one of the symbols of the evident 'weakness' of governments and the power of markets.

V CONCLUSION

Monetary integration is an area where genuine economic integration among countries was tested. The EU countries wanted to supplement the customs union and the frontier-free internal market with an EMU that would secure trade flows. The politicians succeeded in achieving a more modest goal. The EMS was a voluntary and complicated system of semi-fixed exchange rates supported by a certain cooperation of the central banks. Success in the attainment of the original objectives of the EMS were obvious. The EMS introduced a certain degree of monetary stability up to 1992 by a reduction in inflation differentials and by a lowering in the volatility of the exchange rates. Since August 1993, the EMS, in fact its ERM, has all but disappeared. The ambitious Maastricht Treaty objective of achieving a full EMU[17] in the medium term, by 1999 at the latest, will be almost certainly scaled down.

The experience of a full EMU among the 50 states of the US needs to be considered, but only with caution. There is a high labour mobility in the US, certain transfers of funds and the shocks that hit the federal states are much more alike than those in the EU. The federal fiscal system in the US provides transfers to and lessens taxes in the depressed states. However, that comes, in part, from a high labour mobility and, hence, the need for a strong federal tax authority because of potential tax evasion. Nothing similar to the US federal tax system exists (or is in sight) yet in the EU. It may not be necessary in the EU, because local/regional/state tax authorities may be quite efficient simply because of the low European labour mobility. Yet, a single currency in the EU may be necessary as it would stimulate internal stability, trade and production and specialization.

Less developed regions/countries in the EMU and the ones with deficits in the balance of payment would be deprived from employing devaluation as a means of adjustment. These countries/regions would have to do better than the others in the EU in reducing costs and increasing productivity. Hence the need for regional, industrial and social policies and aid at the EU level. Otherwise, the less developed and deficit countries/regions may threaten to use protectionism and jeopardize the whole EMU programme. Once the countries are seriously committed to integration and place the long-term interests of the EU above the short-term national ones, it is harder to stop than to go ahead with it. One of the major problems with this view is that Germany, the hegemonic country in the EMS, did not do that in 1993!

The rationale for a common EU economic policy exists in the case where the Union is better placed to do certain things than the member countries (subsidiarity). One can hardly think of a better example for this than monetary and trade policies. An EMU would further promote and strengthen integration in the EU, but, as structured so far, it is not the only approach to an 'ever closer union'. Economic efficiency would be increased because of the improved allocation of savings and investment due to the elimination of exchange rate risk and reduction in the cost of capital. However, a mere EMU would not be the end of the story. Fiscal harmonization and budgetary coordination would be the next step, as they would contribute to the full effectiveness of the stabilization policy.

NOTES

1 Separate countries may, *de facto*, share a common currency. For example, Estonia's Law on Security for Estonian Kroon (1992), Clause 2, directly links the exchange rate of the kroon to the German mark. The Estonian Central Bank is forbidden to devalue the kroon. However, devaluation may take place, but only if the law is changed. The usual parliamentary procedure is necessary for that action. There have been no cases in history so far, when the authorization for the devaluation of a national currency has been enthusiastically authorized by a parliament.

2 Some Californians may argue, perhaps rightly, that this may not be so in the case of their own state.

3 The impact of fiscal policy for the fast fine-tuning of the economy should not be exaggerated. A country's fiscal policy is almost, as a rule, an annual event. It passes through a long parliamentary procedure. Therefore, it is the monetary policy that is continuously at hand to equilibrate the economy. Fiscal policy is not its replacement, but rather a less flexible supplement.

4 If payroll taxes are high, firms are less willing to hire new, or keep, existing staff.

5 If a government cannot or does not want to tax businesses and individuals, it may print money and tax everybody through inflation. Keynes wrote about such an inflation tax that 'a government can live for a long time... by printing money. The method is condemned, but its efficacy, up to a point, must be admitted... so long as the public use the money at all, the government can continue to raise resources by inflation' (Keynes, 1923, p. 23).

6 Businesses in the EU yearly convert several trillion ECUs at an annual cost in conversion charges of over ECU 15 billion or about 0.4 per cent of the EU's GDP (*European Economy*, 1990a, p. 63). This is the *only* cost of monetary non-union that may be relatively easy to estimate.

7 There were many international pledges to fixed exchange rates that have broken down! As soon as markets question the promise by the participants in the deal, that creates incentives for speculation.

8 See Chapter 8 on regional policy.

9 In the early 1980s firms in the former Yugoslavia were permitted to sell their home-made durable goods to domestic private buyers for hard currency. These buyers received price rebates and priority in delivery. Due to shortages and accelerating inflation, domestic private hard currency holders increased their purchases in order to hedge against inflation. The growth of this type of home trade relative to 'normal' trade in the (sinking) domestic currency has been increasing. The discrimination of home firms against domestic currency has spread. Firms were happy because they received hard currency without the effort

required to export, while consumers were happy because they were able to get what they wanted. Subsequently, domestic sales for hard currency were banned because they reduced the effectiveness of domestic monetary policy. This is an example where a weak domestic currency (prior to state intervention) has been crowded out of domestic trade by a relatively strong foreign currency (German mark). Hard currency has not, however, been driven out of private savings in Yugoslav. Around four-fifths of these savings were in foreign hard currency in Yugoslav banks. This was the way to protect savings from rising home inflation and negative interest rates on savings in the home currency. A new restatement of Gresham's law had the reverse meaning: good money drives out the bad one.

10 Greece and Portugal did not participate in the ERM as those countries were at a lower level of development relative to the core EU countries, so they wanted time for a gradual adjustment. This made the EMS incomplete even in its initial phase. A few other countries were out of the ERM, but they joined this part of the EMS later.

11 An alternative policy instrument could be (interest free one-for-one) deposit requirements.

12 An appraisal of the relative safety of a borrower introduces many problems. The value of assets in the private sector is determined by the net present value of the stream of profit that those assets earn. As for the public assets, there are many that do not yield a financial return (military bases, for example). Their value can be assessed in an indirect way through replacement costs.

13 Solidarity in the EU is still quite fragile when major national interests are in question. The Bretton Woods currency system collapsed because of similar reasons. Countries refused to forgo control over domestic money supply for the sake of external equilibrium.

14 The budget-deficit condition provoked most criticism. A country with a heavy public debt has a good reason to have episodes of inflation: it is to reduce the real burden of its debt.

15 While annual budget deficits may occur, depending on the business cycle, the overall national debt may need to be controlled in a different way than that proposed in the Maastricht Treaty. Instead of putting a cap on the public debts (and on the budget deficit) which are, indeed, at various levels among the EU countries, a more effective way may be to install instruments that discourage trends of growing debts and deficits, and that encourage their continuous reduction.

16 The annual fiscal transfers from the western part of Germany to the eastern part were around DM 150 billion. They would be necessary for around a decade.

17 The emu is a large flightless bird!

3

FISCAL POLICY AND THE BUDGET

I INTRODUCTION

It is a common assumption in the standard theory of customs unions that, by the elimination of tariffs and quotas, trade within an integrated area becomes free (but for the existence of the common external tariff). It is also assumed that foreign trade is fostered by relative differences in national production functions and resource endowments. This is merely an illusion. It is not only the tariff and quota systems that distort the free flow of trade, but fiscal impediments such as subsidies and taxes also create distortions.[1] The focus of the 1985 White Paper (European Communities, 1985) and the 1992 Programme was mostly on the elimination of frontier controls. After the creation of a genuine internal market in 1993 and steps towards EMU, light needs to be shed on tax harmonization in the EU. Should taxes be unified throughout the EU, or should they be set independently by each country and markets left to equilibrate trade flows and, supposedly, introduce approximation in taxes? Or should national preferences derived from a variety of geographical or social reasons be reflected in tax diversity among the EU countries?

This part of the book deals with the structure and harmonization of taxes, as well as the budget of the EU. It starts with fiscal-policy issues. Sections 3 and 4, respectively, present a discussion of direct and indirect taxes. An analysis of the EU budget is contained in section 5. At the end, the conclusion is that there is a great deal of room for improvement in the fiscal and budgetary integration in the EU.

II FISCAL POLICY

The fiscal policy of a country deals with considerations regarding the demand, size, revenues and expenditure of the public sector. It influences both the provision and consumption of a range of goods and services. In addition, it affects the allocation of resources (efficiency), economic stabilization (reduction in the fluctuation of macro-economic variables around desired, planned or possible levels) and equity in the distribution of the national wealth. Fiscal policy can also reflect strategic behaviour of national governments. By offering a preferential tax treatment to transnational corporations (TNCs), governments may change/improve their competitiveness in relation to other countries. Applied to an EMU, fiscal federalism (a supra-national fiscal authority) needs to take care of a certain transfer of resources from the prosperous countries/sectors to the needy ones, as well as to promote mobility of resources.

Harmonization of the fiscal system among countries has two meanings. First, the lower form of fiscal harmonization may be equated with cooperation among countries. These countries exchange information and/or enter into loose agreements about methods and types of taxation. Second, at its higher level, fiscal harmonization means the standardization of mutual tax systems regarding methods, types and rates of taxes and tax exemptions (Prest, 1983, p. 61).

A prudent fiscal policy should ensure that the government at all its levels (local, regional and central) should spend only on those activities where it can use resources in a superior way to the private sector. Taxes should be high enough to cover that cost, but levied in a way that distorts the economy as little as possible (although there are some valid social cases for distortion which include conservation of energy and control of pollution). The budget should be roughly in balance during the economic cycle. The problem that must be avoided is to resist the burdening of a too narrow tax base, otherwise tax rates would be high and distorting. As for the collection of taxes, they ought to be other than taxes on trade and company profits. Those two types of taxes cause most distortion. Unfortunately, they are the most common taxes in the developing world. Taxes on trade (both export and import) prevent specialization, while loophole-ridden taxes on company profits distort investment decisions. Sales taxes (value added tax) may be the most favoured alternative.

The integration of fiscal policies in an EMU refers to the role of public finance and the part played by the budget. The theory of fiscal integration deals with the issue of optimal fiscal domains in an EMU (Robson, 1987, p. 89). It studies the rationale, structure and impact of fiscal (tax and budgetary) systems of the integrated countries. Integration of fiscal policies implies not only a harmonization of national systems of taxes and subsidies, but also issues such as public expenditure, transfers (redistribution) within and between countries, regions, economic sectors and individuals; the combat of cyclical disturbances; stabilization policy; and tax evasion. The highest type of fiscal integration among countries represents a unified system of taxes and subsidies, as well as the existence of a single budget that is empowered to cope with all economic issues of common concern. This has, however, only been achieved in centralized federal states.

Fiscal neutrality among the integrated countries refers to a situation in which a supplier or a consumer of a good or service is indifferent towards being taxed in any of the integrated countries. This is an important prerequisite for the efficient allocation of resources and for the operation of an EMU.[2] The fiscal authorities should be quite cautious while assessing taxes and spending tax receipts. If they tax a significant part of a profit or income, then they may destroy incentives for business, savings and investment. They may stimulate factors to flow to the locations where they may maximize net returns. This can, however, be a powerful tool for the direction of certain business activities towards specific locations (tax havens). Such a policy may find a certain social justification (equity), although it may be questionable from the efficiency standpoint.

The member countries of an EMU may basically finance a common budget according to the principles of benefit and ability to pay. First, the principle of benefit is based on the rule of clear balances or *juste retour* (a fair return). Those that get favours from budget expenditure ought to contribute to these public funds in proportion to the benefits they receive. Second, the economic advantages of integration do not accrue to the participating countries only through the transfers of (common) public funds. The most important benefits come from a secure intra-group free trade, mobility of factors, specialization, acceleration in economic activity and the like. Such a neo-classical expectation may not ask for 'corrective measures' since all countries and regions gain from integration. However, in a situation of imperfect markets and economies of scale, this expectation may not materialize. The principle of ability to pay features highly. Individual contributions and receipts from the common budget do not have to be equal. Net contributions reflect a country's ability to pay. The nominal net contributory position of a country can well be more than compensated for by various spillovers that stem from the membership of an EMU. Therefore, the *juste retour* principle may get a new dimension: it is a discreet, but continuous, flow of resources from the rich and thriving to the less well off member countries and the ones in (temporary) need.

Fiscal policy has a direct (blunt) effect on income of factors, as well as consumption of goods and services. This is in contrast to monetary policy that does the same, but in an indirect (fine tuning) way through financial markets. By a simple change in transfers and rates of taxes and subsidies, the fiscal authority may directly affect expenditure and consumption. However, the problem with fiscal policy is that it is usually passing through a long parliamentary procedure and its changes may take place once (or only a few times) a year. Monetary policy may do the same job as fiscal policy, but in a discreet manner and, potentially, much faster. By changing interest or exchange rates, a government may react swiftly to the emerging crises and opportunities. Such a quick reaction is not possible with fiscal policy. Hence comes the need for the coordination of fiscal and monetary policies in an EMU. If they work one against the other, neither will be effective and the result may be damaging. Stabilization and investment policies for a small country may be more effective in an EMU, than in a situation where these policies are pursued in an independent, uncoordinated and often conflicting way with countries that are major economic partners. If intra-union trade is high in proportion to the total external trade of the unionized countries, then the stability in the group exchange rates is a necessary condition for the protection of these flows.

The issue that needs to be addressed next is the classification of taxes. According to their base, taxes may be levied on income (direct taxes) and consumption (indirect taxes). Direct taxes are charged on the incomes of firms and individuals (factor returns), as well as on property ownership. These taxes are effective at the end of the production process. They have an impact on the mobility of factors. A change in these taxes has a direct impact on taxpayers' purchasing power. Indirect taxes are applied to consumption. They affect movements of goods and services. An alteration of these taxes changes the prices of goods and services.

III DIRECT TAXES

1 Corporate taxes

The international aspect of corporate taxation refers to the taxation of TNCs. Differences in corporate taxes among countries in which a free capital mobility is permitted may endanger the efficient allocation of resources if capital owners tend to maximize their net profits in the short run. Other things being equal, capital would flow to countries with a relatively low level of corporate taxes (although this is only one of the variables that influence investment decisions). TNCs decide about their transborder business activities not only according to production-efficiency criteria, but also according to other conditions that include differences in tax rates, subsidies, market growth, trade regime, competition, stability and so on.

Corporate taxes may be collected according to several *methods*. There are the classical, integrated and dual or imputation systems. A classical, or a separate, system represents one extreme. According to it, a firm is taken as a separate entity, distinct from its shareholders. Corporations are taxed irrespective of whether profits are distributed or not. At the same time, shareholders' income is taxed notwithstanding the fact that the corporation has already paid taxes on its profit.

An integrated system represents another extreme which is relevant for theoretical considerations. Here, a corporation is viewed simply as a collection of shareholders. Corporate tax is eliminated while shareholders pay tax on their portion of corporate profits. Hence, personal income tax and corporate tax are integrated in full. It is, however, very hard to implement this system because of the practical problems of allocating corporate income to possibly thousands of shareholders.

The dual (two-rate, split-rate) system falls between the two extreme methods. A corporation pays tax at a lower rate if profits are distributed than when they are not.

Imputation is another intermediate system for taxing corporations. In contrast to the dual system, however, relief is provided here at shareholder level. Corporations pay taxes just as in the classical system, while shareholders receive credit, usually in the year they receive dividends, for the tax already paid by the corporation.

Computation of corporate profits has provoked immense controversy. The authorities of several states in the US[3] apply the unitary or formulary apportionment method for the taxation of TNCs. This arbitrary and controversial method was inspired, in part, by the problem of transfer pricing. A TNC derives its income not only in its place of residence, but also from the operations of its subsidiaries. The rationale for the unitary method is that profits of the TNC accrue from its global operations, so that a TNC needs to be taken as a single unit. The tax authorities, in particular in California, reach beyond the borders of their own jurisdiction. Because of the increasing diversity and volume of international transactions and the globalization of business activities, it is hard to assess exactly the individual affiliate's contribution to the overall profit of a TNC (UNCTAD, 1993, p. 209). If instead of the employment of the still prevailing (and perhaps superior) cost-plus or resale-minus method, the unitary system is applied, then the tax authorities relate sales, assets and/or payroll expenditure of the affiliate under their jurisdiction to the TNC's worldwide sales, assets and/or payroll outlays. The business community adamantly and rightly disputes such a mechanical view that averages the global operations of a TNC across the board. Profit uniformity at all stages of production and at all international locations does not prevail.

In a globalized international economy there may be continuous multi-jurisdictional conflicts regarding the taxation of TNCs. The national tax authorities take a semi-arbitrary unitary method and assess the share of global profits of the TNC that should be taxed within the confines of their jurisdiction. This approach contrasts sharply with the traditional separate accounting rules (arm's-length method) for tax assessment among distinct fiscal authorities because it is not (necessarily) arbitrary. Although the unitary method has elicited support from certain intellectuals, the business community is adamantly opposed to this kind of taxation. Opposition comes not only from increased administrative costs for the TNCs, but also from the fact that it runs contrary to the US constitutional provision that the federal government (not the ones in the constituting states) is in charge of foreign commerce.

If the unitary principle is applied in only one or a few (but not all) locations where a TNC operates, the following two cases are possible. First, if the operation of the affiliate is more profitable than the average overall profitability of the TNC, then the local authority that applies the unitary method of corporate taxation would collect less tax revenue than it could by the application of the cost-plus method. Second, if business operations of the affiliate are less profitable than the average-universal profitability of the TNC, than the local tax office would collect more tax than under the alternative collection method. The second case directly harms the profitability of the affiliate, reduces the corporate funds for the potential investment and, hence, the long-term interests of the host country. In 1994, after 17 years of legal battle, the US Supreme Court decided in favour of California regarding the unitary method of taxation (Barclays Bank lost the case). The Court held that unitary taxation did not violate the foreign commerce clause. The implications of the decision are not fully clear. If profitability of a TNC is higher in California than elsewhere in the world, such a company may benefit from unitary tax assessment. California, however, allows taxpayers to choose between unitary tax assessment and the 'water's edge' method (taxation of income within the confines of the US), a system close to the universally accepted arm's-length method.

The main distortion that is brought by unitary taxation is that it is different from the standard arm's-length taxation principle. In addition, states using the unitary method adopt a formula favourable to themselves. Many states employ different formulae (more distortions) and the outcome is the creation of a potentially higher aggregate taxable income than the aggregate economic income.

The main objective of corporate taxation is not to increase the price of goods and services, but rather to capture a part of the firm's profit. Frequent changes in the corporation-tax systems should be avoided. They increase uncertainty and administrative burden on firms. Unless they are favourable for business, these variations distort the decision-making process about investment and may have a long-term negative effect on capital that would prevent or reduce investment in such locations.

A firm may pass on the tax burden to consumers in the form of higher prices for its goods and services or to its employees by reduced wages, or a combination of the two. By passing on the tax burden, it may decrease, in part or in full, the impact of tax on its profit. The possibility of passing on the tax burden depends on the idiosyncrasies of the goods/services and the labour market. If a firm is free to set its prices, then it relies on competition if this passing on is possible. If prices are regulated, then the method of passing on the tax burden is different. Suppose that the prices do not rise. A firm may reduce the quality of its output in order to save profits. In the reverse case when prices do not fall, it may improve the quality of its output and after-sales service in order to increase its competitiveness and save or increase its market share.

The importance of the distribution of the tax burden between individuals and firms may be analysed in the following example. Suppose that P_d stands for the price paid by consumers. If one imposes a tax of t dollars per unit of output on the suppliers, then the price P_s which they receive is:

$$P_s = P_d - t \tag{3.1}$$

The condition for equilibrium is:

$$P_s(q) = P_d(q) - t \tag{3.2}$$

Assume that one imposes the same tax of t dollars per unit of purchased good on the buyers. The price paid by consumers is:

$$P_d = P_s + t \tag{3.3}$$

The condition for equilibrium in this case is:

$$P_d(q) = P_s(q) + t \tag{3.4}$$

Note that the two conditions for equilibrium 3.2 and 3.4 are the same. Thus the quantity, P_s and P_d in equilibrium are independent of whether the tax is levied on demanders (individuals) or suppliers (firms). The volume of government revenue does not change. What changes, is the composition of revenue, which may provoke intense political debate. This is obviously not understood by many tax authorities.

There is a school of integrationists who argue that income has to be taxed as a whole in spite of differences in its source. It says that all taxes are ultimately borne by the people. This view conflicts with the school of absolutists who argue that firms are separate legal entities that need to be taxed in their own capacity (under the assumption that they may not pass on the tax burden either to their employees or consumers). Another reason for the separate treatment of corporations is that they use government services without fully paying for them. This impacts on the reduction of costs of operation. Tax authorities may use their policy to regulate the investment of firms and to control their monopoly position. On these grounds, tax instruments may influence the behaviour of the business sector.

If private capital flows are a significant feature in economic relations among countries, some of those countries may have an incentive to negotiate tax treaties in order to avoid double taxation and, possibly, achieve tax neutrality. Tax neutrality between investment in home country A and foreign country B is achieved when firms are indifferent (other things being equal) about investing, producing and selling in either country. In this case, the foreign country's tax equals the corporate tax plus the withholding tax (tax on the transfer of profits). If under a condition of free capital mobility country A's firm finds country B's taxes equal to country A's, then there is tax neutrality between these two countries.[4] If not, investment would flow to the country that has relatively lower taxes.

Cooperation among the tax authorities in partner countries is necessary for the smooth operation of the economies of the integrated countries. This demand is amplified if the desired goals are a free mobility of capital, free competition, efficient allocation of resources, 'fairness' in the distribution of revenues among the member countries and the elimination of administrative difficulties. This is of special importance in a situation with fixed exchange rates and free capital mobility. The measures to reduce the risks of tax evasion can take the form of a generalized withholding tax to all EMU residents and/or the commitment of banks to disclose information about interest received by the Union residents. Therefore, the need to create conduit companies, as intermediary subsidiaries that take advantage of tax treaties in order to reduce withholding taxes, would be eliminated. As tax harmonization deals with difficult and deeply rooted national customs, the EU has put the harmonization issue aside. The Single Market Programme from 1993 and the moves towards EMU are supposed to perform the sophisticated, behind-the-scenes market-led pressure on the countries to approximate taxes, since the high-tax countries, other things being equal, would lose the competitiveness of their goods and services, as well as becoming less attractive locations for foreign direct investment (FDI).

2 Corporate taxes in the European Union

The basic treaties of the EU are short on tax provisions. There are just a few provisions in the Treaty of Rome that refer to the general issue of taxation. Article 95 stipulates that imported products from partner countries may not be taxed more highly than comparable domestic goods. This introduced the principle of destination for value added tax (VAT), as well as non-discrimination in EU internal commerce. Article 96 introduced tax neutrality. It states that any repayment of tax on the goods exported to EU partner countries may not exceed the taxes actually paid on the good in question. Article 99 seeks harmonization of indirect taxes, while Article 100 indirectly demands approximation of laws that affect the establishment or operation of the common market. Article 100a excludes fiscal matters from the majority voting procedure. The unanimity principle has prevented fast progress in the approximation of fiscal matters in the EU.

Table 3.1 illustrates, in a simplified way, differences in corporate tax systems in the EU countries. It does not take into account any of the surtaxes, surcharges, local

Table 3.1 Systems and rates of corporate taxes in EU countries in 1996

Country	System	Rate(%)
1 Austria	Classical	34
2 Belgium	Classical	40
3 Denmark	Classical	34
4 Finland	Imputation	28
5 France	Imputation	37
6 Germany	Dual and imputation	30 (distributed) 45 (retained)
7 Greece	Corporate tax, no tax on shareholder	35 (40 for foreign companies)
8 Ireland	Imputation	38
9 Italy	Imputation	36
10 Luxembourg	Classical	34
11 Netherlands	Classical	35–37
12 Portugal	Imputation	36
13 Spain	Imputation	35
14 Sweden	Classical	28
15 United Kingdom	Imputation	33

Source: International Bureau of Fiscal Documentation (1996).

taxes, credits, exemptions, special treatment of small and medium-sized enterprises and the like, that apply in nearly all EU countries. The differences in systems and rates of corporate taxes point at the distortions of tax neutrality for investment in the EU. Therefore, the Commission thought about proposing a single corporate tax rate for the EU, but stepped back from the idea. A special Committee proposed a minimum tax rate (30 per cent) and a maximum rate (40 per cent) that may be introduced in the EU countries. The proposed rates will be meaningful only if the tax base is also harmonized.[5] The problem is identified, but the solution is not always easy to find. A TNC is ready to pay relatively higher corporate taxes in country A if it supplies the business sector with educated labour, infrastructure, lower social contributions, even trade protection, relative to country B where the corporate tax rate is lower.

Harmonizing or equalizing corporate tax rates in the EU aims at introducing an identical distortion across the EU. However, the corporate tax distorts another important variable for firms. That is the form of financing. A corporate tax punishes enterprises that raise their capital through equity, rather than debt. That is because interest payments can be deducted from taxable profits, while the return on equity cannot. Probably the best solution may be to completely eliminate corporate taxes. Taxes on corporate profit could be collected from shareholders' income and/or on corporate cash flow before the interest is paid (not as now, after deductions for the interest payments). That would be in line with a tendency to stay away from taxes that hurt capital formation.

Differences in corporate taxation distort the operation of the EU internal market. The Ruding Committee (1992) reaffirmed this observation, but recommended that the existing system of corporate taxation be retained. The state in which the profits of a TNC originate should continue to tax them in full (i.e., both distributed and retained profits should be taxed). If the profits are transferred to the parent country, this state should exempt them from taxation or allow a tax credit for taxes already paid in the country where they were made. This reflects difficulties in harmonization of taxes on the international level. It seems that tax reform *within* the countries needs to precede tax reform *between* them.[6]

Juridical double taxation arises when a single economic income is taxed twice. If a firm (TNC) operates in two countries, its profit may be taxed by the two national tax authorities. It is often forgotten that what matters for TNCs is not the fact that profits are taxed twice, but rather the level of total taxation. If the profit of country A's TNC earned in country B has been taxed by country B, then country A may exempt this TNC from taxes on that part of its income earned in country B. Another method for solving this problem is that country A provides credit to its TNCs on taxes paid in country B. In this case the tax burden on country A's corporation operating in country B is the same as the one made from purely home operations in country A, provided that country B's taxes are lower or equal to those in country A.

A solution to the double taxation problem may also be found elsewhere. One of the possible answers is the unitary method (with all its controversies) of collecting corporate taxes. A second is the profit-split method. Income of the distinct affiliates of a TNC is split in relation to the functions they perform and the associated risk. The difference between the profit-split and the unitary method is that the former applies a functional analysis that is unique to each transaction, while the latter averages out all transactions. A third potential solution is the mutual agreement procedure where the national tax authorities discuss and try to correct tax discrepancies. In fact, they try to find a smooth way for the application of an existing method. The EU *Convention on the Elimination of Double Taxation in Connection with the Adjustment of Profits of Associated Enterprises* (1990) provides for binding arbitration related to the adjustment of profits of associated enterprises. A fourth solution may be found in advance pricing agreements. This is, again, the application of an existing method. A TNC may acquire an advance agreement from the tax authority on the system for the allocation of its profit. This method represents a departure from the usual tax procedure (tax audits may take place even a few years after a transaction occurred) since it refers to the unknown future evolution (UNCTAD, 1993, pp. 207–210).

3 Personal income tax

Differences in personal income taxes between countries and different regions within them may affect the mobility of labour. Actual labour mobility depends on a number of factors that include the chances of finding employment, improved standard of living, social obstacles, social security benefits and immigration rules. Differences in personal income taxes may be neither the most decisive nor the only incentive for labour to move. This difference is significant only for the movement of the upper-middle class and the wealthy.

It is a generally accepted principle that taxes are applied in those countries in which income originated. In addition, most countries tax the global income of their residents, but with foreign tax relief. A person originating from country A who works part of the year in country B and the rest of the year in country A would pay income tax on pay earned in country B and ask for tax credit while paying income tax in country A for the rest of the taxable income. This person's tax payment would be the same as if the whole income had been earned in country A, unless country B's income tax is higher than the one in country A.

A tax ratio relates tax revenues to the GNP of a country. This ratio has been increasing over time. There are at least three reasons for such evolution. First, the welfare state has increased social care transfers. They are financed mostly by social security levies. Second, economic development and increasing opportunities had their impact on the growth of taxable incomes. Taxpayers were climbing into higher brackets, so these proceeds increased. Third, inflation has increased nominal tax revenues and devalued their real value.

Personal income tax is taken to be one of the most genuine rights of a state. There is little chance that this tax can be harmonized in an EMU. The EU is fully aware of this issue, so it has little ambition in the sphere of personal income taxation. On the one hand, a free mobility of labour in the EU may provide a behind-the-scenes pressure for harmonization of national personal income taxes. On the other hand, that pressure may not be too intense because of the still great social obstacles[7] to moving from one country to another.

A notable exception has often been the taxation of income of frontier and migrant workers. Tax agreements generally avoid double taxation, both in the country of destination (where the income was made) and the country of origin (where the income maker resides). Troublesome issues remain regarding deductions, allowances and applicable rates. Granting an allowance to a non-resident worker may involve a concession. This would be the case when the same allowance is offered by the country of residence. Generally, full taxation in the country of residence with a credit for tax paid in the source country would be the solution (Cnossen, 1986, p. 558).

IV INDIRECT TAXES

Indirect taxes are levied on the consumption of goods and services. They influence the retail price, hence they affect patterns of trade and consumption. Sales and turnover taxes, excise duties and tariffs are the basic indirect taxes. In contrast with direct taxes, indirect taxes are seldom progressive. The principles for the levying of these taxes will be considered before the analysis of indirect taxes.

1 Principles of destination and origin

Tax authorities are aware of the possible impact that indirect taxes have on trade in goods and services. Therefore, they introduced a guarding device in the form of the destination and origin principle for taxation. This is of great importance to countries that integrate. According to the principle of destination, taxes on goods are applied in the country of their consumption. That is the norm accepted in the General Agreement on Tariffs and Trade (GATT). According to the principle of origin, taxes apply in the country of their production.[8]

The destination principle states that consumption of all goods in one destination should be subject to the same tax irrespective of its origin. This principle removes tax distortions on competition between goods on the consuming-country's market. The goods compete on equal tax conditions. This principle does not interfere with the location of production. It is widely accepted in international trade relations. The problem is that this principle may create the illusion that it stimulates exports and acts as a quasi-tariff on imports. This issue will be discussed shortly.

The origin or production principle asserts that all goods produced in one country should be taxed in that country, despite the possibility that those goods may be exported or consumed at home. If the production tax on good X in country A is lower than the same tax on the same good in country B, then if exported at zero transport and other costs, good X produced in country A would have a tax advantage in country B's market over country B's home made good X. This introduces a distortion that interferes with the location of production between the countries. For allocational neutrality, a harmonized rate of tax, between the countries, is a necessary condition.

Even within a customs union or a common market, there may exist fiscal frontiers if the member countries accept the principle of destination. The fiscal authorities of each country should know the limits of where and when they are entitled to tax consumption of goods or services. The origin principle may have an advantage, for it does not require fiscal frontiers. That saves scarce resources.

Taxes levied according to the destination and origin principles differ in their revenue impact. These two principles determine to which government the proceeds accrue. A full economic optimization cannot be achieved if there are different tax rates levied on various goods. Suppose that country A levies a VAT at the rate of 25 per cent on cars only, while the partner country B applies a uniform tax at the rate of 10 per cent on all goods. Suppose that both countries apply the destination principle for tax collection. In this case, production in either country would be maximized because it would not be affected by the tax. Consumption would, however, be distorted. The relative consumer prices would be distorted because cars are dearer relative to clothes in country A, than they are in country B. Consequently, country A's consumers buy less cars and more clothes than they would do otherwise. The opposite tendency prevails in country B. In this case, trade between the two countries would not be optimal. Conversely, suppose that the two countries collect taxes according to the origin principle. In this case trade would be optimized for the relative consumer prices would be the same in each country. So, although trade would be optimized, taxation would still distort the maximization of production. That is because producer prices, net of tax, would be reduced in a disproportionate way. Country A producers would be stimulated to produce clothes, rather than cars, while the opposite tendency would prevail in country B. Once the indirect tax is not levied at a uniform rate on all goods, the choice is between the destination principle that maximizes production, but does not optimize trade and the origin principle that optimizes trade, but does not maximize production (Robson, 1987, p. 122–123).

The principle of destination introduces a possibility of tax evasion that is not possible (if the records are not faked) with the origin principle. If taxes differ, then a consumer may be tempted to purchase a good in the state in which the relative tax burden is lower and consume it in the country where the tax burden is relatively higher. Consumers may easily purchase goods in one country and send or bring them to another one, or order these goods from abroad. This tax evasion depends on the differences in taxation, cost of transport and cooperation of buyers and sellers which do not inform the tax authorities if they know that the object of certain purchases is tax evasion. The revenue effect of a tax at a rate of 40 per cent in a country where tax evasion is widespread (the 'olive oil belt' countries of the EU) may be much smaller than the revenue impact of the same tax at a rate of 10 per cent in the country where tax evasion is not a common practice.

The tax system in the US relies on corporate and personal income taxes applied according to the origin principle. The west European tax authorities rely upon consumption taxes with the application of the destination principle. If the Europeans export goods to the US, they may have an advantage embodied in the difference in the tax systems. The US may contemplate the introduction of a border tax adjustment. This step may involve an addition to or reduction in the taxes already paid in Europe. The objective would be to keep competition in the US market on the same tax footing.

While the origin principle does not involve a visible border tax adjustment, the destination principle includes it to the full extent of the tax. The long-run effect of either principle is, however, the same. In general equilibrium, any short-run advantage by one country would be eliminated in the long run by changes in the rate of exchange and domestic prices (Johnson and Krauss, 1973, p. 241). The US is a net importer of manufactured goods from Europe and Japan. It is advantageous, however, for the US to have these two exporting countries administer taxes on a destination, rather than origin basis (Hamilton and Whalley, 1986, p. 377). This is correct in the short run. In the long-run general equilibrium, the operation of exchange rates and factor prices (Johnson-Krauss law) would, presumably, eliminate any short-run (dis)advantage to these countries.[9]

2 Sales and turnover taxes

Sales and turnover taxes are payments to the government that are applied to all taxable goods and services except the ones that are subject to excise duties. Turnover tax is imposed during the process of production, while if the tax is applied during sales to the final consumer it is called a sales tax. There are two *methods* for the collection of the sales tax. One is the cumulative multi-stage cascade method, while the other method is called the VAT (value added tax). Apart from these two multi-phase methods for the collection of the sales tax, there is a one-stage method. This method is applied only once, either at the stage of production or at the wholesale or retail sales phase. The following analysis will deal with the multi-phase methods.

3 Cumulative multi-stage cascade method

According to the cumulative multi-stage cascade method for the collection of sales tax, the tax is applied every time goods and services are transferred against payment. The tax base includes the aggregate value of goods that covers previously paid taxes on raw materials and inputs. The levying and collection of this tax is relatively simple: the tax burden may appear to be distributed over a larger number of taxpayers and the rate of sales tax applied by this method is relatively lower than the rate applied by the VAT method.

Firms may be stimulated by this method of collection of sales tax to integrate vertically in order to pay tax only at the last stage of the production process. This may have a favourable impact on the expansion of the business activities of firms (diversification). It may, however, cause a misallocation of resources. This artificial vertical integration may erode the advantages of specialization and the efficiency of numerous relatively small firms if the vertically integrated firm ceases to use their output or if it absorbs them.

4 Value added tax

This method of collecting sales tax operates every time a good or service is sold, but it applies only on the value that is added in the respective phase of production. That is the difference between the price paid for inputs and the price received for output. The application of VAT starts at the beginning of the production process and ends up in the retail sale to the final consumer. VAT avoids double or multiple taxation of the previous stages of production. Every taxpayer has to prove to the tax authorities, by an invoice, that the tax has been paid in the previous stages of production. Hence, there is a kind of a self-controlling mechanism.

At the early stages of economic development, countries have relatively simple tax systems which apply to only a few goods and services. As they develop, they tend to introduce a tax system that is more sophisticated, that has a wider and more neutral tax base and coverage, and one that is more efficient. Taxes on international trade (exports and imports) ought to be replaced by sales taxes that are collected by the VAT method. A relatively low rate of tax applied according to this method can raise a lot of revenue. It does not distort the economy, because it is neutral to the production mix of home and imported factors. In addition, it does not discriminate between production for home and foreign markets. VAT is neutral regarding the vertical integration of firms, so specialized small enterprises may remain in business. If sales tax is collected according to the VAT method, then it would be harder to evade it in comparison to tax collected only at the retail stage.

VAT, on the principle of destination, is accepted in the EU as the method for collecting sales tax. The system is harmonized, but there is a wide range of variation in the rates of this tax among the EU countries. If the objective is to have a single rate of this tax, then there exists considerable room for improvement in the future. The elimination of fiscal frontiers in the EU in 1993 put certain market pressure on tax authorities to 'align' national VAT rates and prices, otherwise they would lose business, particularly in the frontier regions.

The 1985 White Paper proposed the setting up of the EU Clearing House System. Its role would be to ensure that VAT collected in the exporting member country and deducted in the importing member country was reimbursed to the latter. This system would play a crucial role in developing across-the-EU-bookkeeping and computerization. In principle, it would create a situation for taxing people in the EU identical to the one that prevails in member countries. In spite of the potential benefits of such a system, it was criticized on the grounds that it would be bureaucratic and costly.

In practice, however, the existence of widely diverging rates of tax and tax exemptions may expose the system to the risk of fraud and evasion. The EU was aware that some fraud and evasion do exist at present, but the scale of such distortions after the removal of fiscal frontiers without harmonization would, potentially, increase. Therefore, a minimum standard VAT rate of 15 per cent on most goods became a legal obligation in the EU from October 1992. It is relatively understandable for Britain (as well as Ireland and Greece) to argue against alignment since cross-border shopping is not a common feature in these countries as they have no common land frontier with the rest of the EU. However, Austria, the Benelux countries, France and Germany, have no such such arguments, as cross-border shopping is important for these member states.

A move towards the origin principle (collection of tax during production) would require a system for the redistribution of revenues (refunds) from the country where the goods were produced and taxed to the one where they are consumed. The effect of such a system would be as if the tax had been levied on consumption. Although there were concerns in some member countries because of the need to find alternative employment for thousands of customs officers, the fiscal frontiers among the EU countries were removed in 1993. That was the most visible benefit of the implementation of the 1992 Programme.[10] Consumers are free to purchase goods in any EU country and bring them home with very few restrictions, provided that the imported goods are only for their personal consumption. There are, of course, exceptions. But, only two. The purchase of new cars is taxed in the country of registration, while mail-order purchases are taxed in the country of destination.

In any case the tax system of the EU is only transitional, until 1997 when the entire tax system will be reassessed and made permanent. The final tax system will be moved towards the origin principle, but it is likely that the 1997 deadline will not be met. According to the interim system (introduced in 1993) companies pay VAT in the country of consumption. This system replaced time-consuming tax controls and payments at the EU internal borders with a demanding centralized reporting system carried out by companies themselves. The final system would allow firms to pay VAT in the country of origin, as if all EU member countries were a single country. The burden of redistribution of VAT revenue would then fall on the member states. This would be advantageous to businesses as they would not have to differentiate between domestic and intra-EU sales. None the less, there would be two problems. First, a clearing-house system would have to redistribute revenue around the EU as countries that export a lot would benefit from the system, while the ones that import a lot would lose. Second, the origin-based tax system will enhance the need for a greater harmonization of VAT rates. In the meantime, the current transitory system seems to be operating quite well. This will, of course, be taken into account during the reassessment of the tax system.

Table 3.2 illustrates differences in VAT rates in the EU countries. The underlined rates are the standard ones, as well as the lower rates for food, clothing and other essential items. Portugal has lower rates in its autonomous regions. Ireland and Britain use the zero rate for food, books and children's clothing. The other countries generally apply an exception with credit (which comes down to the same thing as a zero rate) to exports and supplies assimilated to exports, such as supplies to embassies, to ships leaving the country and the like. In Ireland and Britain these supplies are also covered by the zero rate.

A broad-based VAT can be criticized on the grounds that it is regressive. The reason for the regressive impact of VAT in the EU could be found in the

Table 3.2 VAT rates in EU countries in 1996

Country	VAT rate (%)
1 Austria	10, 20
2 Belgium	1, 6, 12, 21
3 Denmark	25
4 Finland	6, 12, 17, 22
5 France	2.1, 5.5, 20.6
6 Germany	7, 15
7 Greece	4, 8, 18
8 Ireland	0, 2.8, 12.5, 21
9 Italy	4, 10, 16, 19
10 Luxembourg	3, 6, 12, 15
11 Netherlands	6, 17.5
12 Portugal	5, 17
13 Spain	4, 7, 16
14 Sweden	6, 12, 25
15 United Kingdom	0, 17.5

Source: International Bureau of Fiscal Documentation (1996)

structure of the national demand. Consumption to which VAT applies, usually embraces a relatively higher proportion of the GNP in the less advanced member countries than in the richer ones. Other components of demand, such as investment, that is presumably higher in the advanced countries, is not burdened by VAT. The low-income segment of the population can be helped by transfer payments. This can make VAT directly progressive. Zero rating, exemptions and multiple rates do not always directly assist the low-income groups of the population as intended.

The EU conducted an extensive survey in the second half of the 1980s. About 20,000 businesspeople from 12 member countries were asked to rank the worst barriers to free trade. The most damaging of all were overt obstacles. Different national technical standards, administrative and customs formalities were top of the list. Variations in rates in VAT and excise duties came at the bottom of the list of eight barriers (Emerson *et al.*, 1988, p. 44–46).

5 Excise duties

Excise duties are a type of indirect taxes that are levied for the purpose of rising public revenue. They are applied in almost every country to tobacco, spirits and liquid fuels. Excise duties are also applied in some countries to coffee, tea, cocoa, salt, bananas, light bulbs and playing cards. These duties are levied only once. It is usually at the stage of production or import. Another property of excise duties is that they are generally high in relation to other taxes. While VAT is proportional to the value of output, excise duty may be based either on the *ad valorem* principle (retail or wholesale price) or it may be a specific tax. Within the EU, tobacco products are subject to both. There is a specific tax per cigarette and an *ad valorem* tax based on the retail price of the cigarettes concerned (Kay, 1990, p. 34).

Table 3.3 presents the rates of excise duties in the EU member countries and the minimum EU rates. There is a wide variety in the rates of excise duties among the member countries. This difference is due to the various choices of fiscal and health authorities. If the difference in excise duties among countries exceeds the cost of reallocation of resources or transport, it will have a distorting effect on the allocation of resources or the pattern of trade. The difference in excise duty on 1,000 litres of petrol of ECU 191 between France and Spain is significant when one keeps in mind that it costs just a few ECUs to transport this amount of fuel by pipeline.

VAT is calculated on the price of a good that includes the excise duty. Any change in excise duties would produce differences in VAT revenue. Hence the need for harmonization of excise duties too. A solution to maintaining the national fiscal frontiers within the EU could be achieved in a way similar to the one by which the US preserves different liquor duties among its states. Liquor and cigarettes should bear the national tax authority stamp. Only the nationally stamped goods could be purchased legally within a state. Import for personal consumption would be unlimited, while bulk intra-EU commercial transport and trade in these goods without the proper tax clearance would be forbidden. The rates proposed by the Commission should be viewed just as a yardstick for approximation as it would be most difficult

Table 3.3 Excise duty rates in EU countries in 1992

Country	Pure alcohol (ECU per hl)	Wine (ECU per hl)	Beer (ECU per hl)	Cigarettes		Petrol (ECU per 1,000 l)
				ECU per 1,000	ad valorem (%)	
1 Austria	739	0	1	17	41	406
2 Belgium	1,607	37	1	9	50	479
3 Denmark	3,698	87	3	80	21	467
4 Finland	5,016	284	11	12	50	532
5 France	1,381	3	1	5	55	585
6 Germany	1,327	0	1	43	25	562
7 Greece	550	0	1	3	54	406
8 Ireland	2,757	272	9	72	17	378
9 Italy	593	0	1	3	53	527
10 Luxembourg	1,037	0	1	3	54	408
11 Netherlands	1,540	50	2	38	21	566
12 Portugal	715	0	1	7	56	479
13 Spain	552	0	1	3	50	394
14 Sweden	5,132	284	10	81	0	498
15 United Kingdom	2,634	180	5	74	20	462
EU min.	550	0	1	—	—	337

Source: Commission of the the the EU (1995)

and highly uncertain to try to unify excise duties throughout the EU member countries.

The goods that are subject to excise duties are normally stored in bonded warehouses that are controlled by the public authorities. Once the goods are taken out for consumption, the excise duty is levied. If the goods are exported, the excise duty is not charged upon the presentation of a proof of export. The importing country of these goods controls the import at the frontier where it establishes liability for the excise duties of these goods. This ensures that excise duty is charged in the country where the goods are consumed. After the removal of tax and other frontiers, the wide divergence in excise duties would distort trade, because of a real danger of fraud and evasion. The White Paper proposed as a solution: a linkage system for bonded warehouses for products subject to excise duties and approximation of these charges in the EU.

The benefits that accrue from the elimination of fiscal frontiers in an EMU include the following gains. Investment decisions of the firms are improved as the tax system increases the degree of certainty in relation to the situation when every country manages its own taxes. A removal of tax posts at the frontiers saves resources and, more importantly, increases the opportunities for competition. Of course, certain facilities for random anti-terrorist, health, veterinary and illegal immigration checks may be necessary. Finally, harmonization of the tax system would enhance the equalization of prices and lower the distortions due to different systems and rates of taxation.

V BUDGET OF THE EUROPEAN UNION

1 Introduction

Together with the law and its enforcement, the budget, its revenue and expenditure, is one of the most important instruments that an economic and/or political organization may employ to fulfil its role. The budget should cover not only administrative costs, but it should also dispose of funds by intervention in the economy. Otherwise, the role of such an organization would be limited to mere consultation and, perhaps, the research of certain issues. Most international organizations cover only their administrative expenses. A rare exception is the EU that returns and redistributes around 96 per cent of its receipts. The budgets of the member countries reduce their expenditure on their own interventions in areas where the EU has competence and where it intervenes.

The theory of fiscal federalism looks at a central fiscal authority and considers its relations with the lower administrative levels. In a general case, this consideration is complicated by the existence of different currencies that take part in the venture and that are not irrevocably linked through the fixed rate of exchange. If an EMU is to conduct an effective stabilization policy it should be endowed with the power to tax and borrow. This implies that its budget may be not only in balance, but more importantly, in temporary deficit or surplus over an economic cycle. An EMU may not necessarily directly tax firms and individuals, as it may tax the member governments. In order to maximize welfare, the EMU needs to decide about the preferred distribution of functions among distinct governments (principles of: subsidiarity, cooperation or competition). It should also act upon that decision and allocate public goods and services that ought to be provided commonly, and others, that are to be supplied at the national or local level.

A common approach to the macroeconomic management of an EMU is subject to a number of pitfalls. The first is the issue of a common stance on major macroeconomic variables. Even if the member countries agree on the main objectives (rate of exchange, inflation, rate of interest, balance-of-payments position, unemployment and the like) they also have to agree on the economic policy instruments and their timing. Even though the countries concur about the important macroeconomic goals, they may use different, and often conflicting, methods of achieving the stated objectives. Instead of improving the economic situation such an economic policy may well worsen it. Therefore, it is not only the main economic goals that the member countries should agree upon, they should also concur on the means of attaining the agreed objectives. Common fiscal and monetary policies need to be in harmony with each other in an EMU.

An integrated fiscal policy in the absence of an integrated monetary policy and vice versa, in an EMU may be a waste of time. Of course, the agreed economic policy would not need to have equal effects on all member countries. Similarly, in a single country, public economic policy does not have identical effects on all regions or industries. A solution to this problem may be found in the creation of built-in stabilizers, such as a transfer of resources among the member states or among regions within a country. In spite of the above disputes among economists, there is a certain agreement that economic stabilization can be influenced in the short run by a joint action of fiscal and monetary policies. It may control expenditure, employment and output around their 'natural' levels and avoid the excess demand that creates inflation. If economic ties among countries are highly interlaced, then the optimal solutions to economic issues may be found in the joint action of the countries concerned, rather than in an atomized and uncoordinated way.

2 European Union

The EU is on its way towards an EMU. None the less, the absolute and relative size of its budget is rather small in relation to its share of the joint GNP of the member states, as well as the potential impact on the economic life of the EU. As such, it differs from the national budgets since it neither plays a significant role in economic stabilization, nor in the allocation of resources (apart from agriculture). In addition, its stabilization role is further jeopardized by the request that it must achieve annual balances without the provision to take loans to finance possible deficits (Article 199 of the Treaty of Rome).

The budget of the EU is subject to the principle of annuality. That is to say, the financial operations need to be executed within the given budget year. This eases the control of the work of the EU executive branch. The financial year is equal to the calendar year. The Union, however, has sometimes to engage in multiannual financial operations, which are continuously expanding. Therefore, those dual requirements are reflected in the entry of two distinct appropriations. First, the commitment appropriations refer to the total cost in the current financial year of the obligations that are to be carried out over a period of more than one financial year. Second, the payment appropriations cover expenditure (to the limit entered in the current annual budget) that result from the commitments undertaken in the current financial year and/or preceding financial years.

The Treaty of Rome (Article 203) sets two types of the EU budgetary outlays. They are the compulsory and non-compulsory expenditures. The distinction between the two kinds of expenditure is basically political, so it is often a source of conflict between the Parliament and the Council of Ministers. The vague definition of the two kinds of expenditures was clarified in 1982 by a joint Declaration of the Commission, Council of Ministers and Parliament. It stated that compulsory expenditure from the budget is obligatory for the EU in order to make it meet its obligations. It refers both to the internal and external tasks that stem from the Treaties and other Acts. All other expenditure is non-compulsory. The Council has the last word on compulsory expenditure, while the Parliament decides on the non-compulsory outlays. The Parliament may increase the amount of non-compulsory expenditure by amending the draft budget. The maximum rate of increase in relation to the preceding fiscal year depends on the trend of the increase in the GNP in the EU, average variation in the budgets of member states, trend in the cost of living, as well as on the approval by the Council. Before drafting a new budget, the Presidents of the three institutions have a trialogue meeting to determine the grouping of the new budget chapters and the ones for which the legal basis might have changed.

3 Budgetary procedure

Article 203 of the Treaty of Rome lays down the budgetary procedure (sequence of steps and deadlines) that need to be respected by the Commission, Council and Parliament. The prescribed budgetary procedure begins on 1 September and ends on 31 December of the year preceding the budget year in question. In practice, from 1977, the procedure starts much earlier. The sequencing of the annual budgetary procedure is as follows (European Communities, 1993, p. 9):

- The Commission is to prepare and send to the Council and Parliament the preliminary draft budget by 15 June. It does so by compiling and putting together the requests of all spending departments. The Commission also arbitrates between conflicting claims on the basis of the priorities set for the year in question. The preliminary draft budget can be amended in order to allow for the inclusion of new information that was not available prior to June.
- The Council is to adopt the preliminary draft budget before 31 July, but prior to doing so, it must have a conciliation meeting with a delegation from the Parliament. The adopted draft budget is sent to the Parliament for the first reading in the early half of September.
- The Parliament conducts its first reading of the draft budget during October. It may amend the non-compulsory expenditure by an absolute majority of its members. As for the modifications to the compulsory expenditure, they require an absolute majority of votes cast. The Parliament is supposed to pass the amended draft back on to the Council by 19 November for the second reading.
- After the conciliation meeting with the Parliament, the Council conducts its second reading of the draft budget during the third week of November. The draft budget is altered following the amendments (for the non-compulsory expenditure) by the Parliament or proposed modifications regarding compulsory expenditure. Unless the entire budget is rejected by the Parliament, this is the stage when the Council determines the final amount of the compulsory expenditure. The amended draft budget is returned to the Parliament by 4 December for the second and final reading.
- As the Council decides on compulsory expenditure, the Parliament spends most of its time reviewing the non-compulsory outlays. For that part of the budget, the Parliament may accept or refuse the proposals by the Council. The budget is accepted (before the New Year) and could be implemented when the Parliament approves it, acting by a majority of its members. Three-fifths of the votes cast must be in favour. As certain unforeseen and exceptional events may take place during the year when the budget is implemented, the Commission is entitled to propose amendments to the ongoing budget. Those changes are subject to the same procedural rules as the general budget.

4 Expenditure

The budgetary crises in the 1980s, prompted the EU institutions to reconsider the budgetary procedure and discipline. The budget was sometimes balanced by accounting tricks dubbed 'creative accounting'. Certain payments were deferred till the following year, when it was expected that the financial conditions would improve. As part of the reform, the Commission, the Council and the European Parliament concluded the binding Interinstitutional Agreement in 1988. A reference point for the budgetary expenditure was the financial perspective for 1988 to 1992. The new Interinstitutional Agreement covers the period 1993 to 1999.

The financial perspective marks the maximum amount of payment appropriations for the various chapters of the EU expenditure. It is not, however, a multiannual budget, as the usual annual budgetary procedure is still a key element for the decision about the exact volume of the budgetary expenditure (but up to the ceiling provided by the financial perspective). The three institutions agree to respect the annual expenditure ceiling for each expenditure item. The ceilings, however, need to be sufficiently large in order to allow for the flexibility necessary for budgetary management. The ceiling may be revised in either direction, but that depends only on unforeseen events (such as German reunification, violent disintegration of the former Yugoslavia or aid to Rwanda) that took place after the Interinstitutional Agreement was signed.

The reform of the budget of 1988 had three additional aspects. First, the total 'own' resources of the EU budget were not linked to the VAT contribution. Instead, resources required to cover the budgetary expenditure had a ceiling in appropriations for payments. That overall ceiling was fixed for each year from 1988 to 1992 as a percentage of the Union's GNP (e.g., 1.15 per cent in 1989 and 1.2 per cent in 1992). The new ceilings would gradually increase from 1.20 per cent to 1.27 per cent in the period which ends in 1999. Second, the budgetary discipline, as a shared responsibility of the Commission, the Council and the Parliament, was increased. Its major objective was to check farm expenditure. The means to achieving this is a guideline that may not increase by more than 74 per cent of the annual rate of growth of the GNP of the EU. Third was the coordination and increase in effectiveness of the three Structural Funds (European Agricultural Guarantee and Guidance Fund, European Regional Development Fund and European Social Fund). The objectives included the adjustment of regions whose development was below the EU average, the structural conversion in the regions hit by industrial decline, the fight against long-term unemployment, the occupational integration of young people and the adjustment of the farm structure and development of rural areas.

The European Council (Edinburgh, 1992) reaffirmed the basic goals of the EU budgetary policy. Following the doubling of the Structural Fund appropriations from 1988 to 1992, the EU was able to continue its regional and social development efforts. The expenditure in the future would mainly affect the EU *regions* in which the average GNP per capita is less than 75 per cent of the EU average. The expenditure from the Cohesion Fund in *countries* where the per capita GNP is less than 90 per cent of the EU average (Greece, Ireland, Portugal and Spain) is to help those countries comply with the EU legislation. That needs to be done by financing transport infrastructure or environmental projects. In addition, expenditure on internal policies is supposed to increase in the future. The main priority would be the financing of the trans-European transport, telecommunications and energy networks. Emphasis will be given to the cross-frontier links between the national networks. As for external action, the EU will pay attention to emergency aid (primarily to the countries in the vicinity: transition countries and the Mediterranean region, basically to prevent undesired migratory inflows of people), as well as loan guarantees.

The expenditure of the EU has expanded and diversified remarkably since its inception. Table 3.4 presents budgetary expenditure for 1994. The guarantee expenditure of the CAP disposes of a little more than a half of the entire budget. Hence in relative terms, not much remains for many other economic policies of the EU. Structural funds of the EU include the European Regional Development Fund (ERDF), European Social Fund (ESF), the Guidance Section of the Agricultural Fund and, from 1993, the Cohesion Fund. Expenditure on transport and fisheries are also included in this chapter. The share of structural funds is 32 per cent of the budget. A notable feature of the components of this chapter is that their shares are continuously rising in the general budget over time. The (ab)use of structural funds may become a serious stumbling block in the future, just as the agricultural expenditure has continued to be for decades.

Table 3.4 The 1994 budget expenditure (ECUs millions)

Chapter	Commitments		Payments	
	Amount	%	Amount	%
1 Common Agricultural Policy (guarantee expenditure)	37,465.0	51.0	37,465.0	53.5
2 Structural, regional, fisheries and transport operations	23,454.5	31.9	21,528.8	30.7
3 Social operations (training, youth, culture and others)	560.6	0.8	539.5	0.8
4 Energy and environment	185.9	0.3	174.5	0.2
5 Consumer protection, internal market, innovation, trans-European networks	567.6	0.8	464.5	0.7
6 Research and technological development	2,767.4	3.8	2,555.4	3.6
7 Cooperation with developing and other foreign countries	4,507.7	6.1	3,348.3	4.8
Operating appropriations	69,826.7	95.1	66,395.9	94.8
8 Administrative operations	2,428.0	3.3	2,428.0	3.5
Commission total	72,254.7	98.4	68,823.9	98.3
9 Other institutions	1,189.6	1.6	1,189.6	1.7
Total	73,444.3	100.0	70,013.5	100.0

Source: The Community Budget: The Facts and Figures (Brussels: EC, 1994)

Other chapters of the budget are very much less important in relative terms. In terms of payments, training of the unemployed, youth and culture disposed of 0.8 per cent of the budget; energy and environment 0.3 per cent; while consumer protection, internal market (harmonization of standards and laws, and exchange of information) and trans-European networks are allocated 0.8 per cent. Research and technological innovation in the areas considered strategic for the future (such as information technology, telecommunications, biotechnology and controlled thermonuclear fusion) have 3.8 per cent, while various types of aid to the third (developing and transition) countries absorbs 6.1 per cent of the budget. Administrative operations cost the EU only 3.3 per cent of the budget, while the rest of the budget is redistributed mostly to member countries. This distinguishes the EU from other international organizations whose budgets are used mainly for administrative expenditure.

5 Revenue

The budget of the EU was financed by national contributions of the member states by 1970. Thereafter the EU got its 'own' resources that include customs duties, agricultural levies and a budget-balancing resource of up to 1 per cent of the VAT base (the base was increased to 1.4 per cent in 1985). Own resources of the EU budget represent a one-time tax revenue allocated to the EU. They accrue automatically to the EU without any need for additional decisions of the national governments. A reform in 1988 of finances altered and expanded the EU's own financial resources. These resources are customs duties; agricultural, sugar and isoglucose levies; VAT resources; the fourth resource; and miscellaneous revenue.

Table 3.5 presents the EU budget revenue in 1994. Customs duties and agricultural levies are the 'natural' proceeds of a customs union. First, customs duties (CET) that are applied on imports of goods from non-member countries represent 18 per cent of revenue. Their relative impact is diminishing over time as tariffs are being continuously reduced through the GATT rounds of tariff negotiations. This trend may be partly compensated for by an increase in the volume of trade with external countries, but recession can reduce the level of economic activity and, consequently, reduce imports.

Table 3.5 The financing of the 1994 budget (ECUs millions)

Country	Agricultural levies	%	Customs duties	%	VAT	%	Fourth resource	%	Total	%
Belgium	109.4	4.0	858.4	31.1	1,178.5	42.6	617.3	22.3	2,764.0	100.0
Denmark	44.0	3.2	270.0	19.6	666.1	48.4	396.6	28.8	1,376.8	100.0
Germany	449.0	2.1	3,780.0	17.9	11,357.8	53.8	5,513.5	26.1	21,100.3	100.0
Greece	32.4	3.2	184.5	18.1	562.0	55.2	240.1	23.6	1,019.1	100.0
Spain	183.3	3.2	566.5	10.0	3,361.6	59.5	1,542.7	27.3	5,654.1	100.0
France	383.9	2.9	1,620.0	12.1	7,710.7	57.4	3,728.1	27.7	13,442.6	100.0
Ireland	14.7	2.7	144.5	26.6	268.6	49.5	114.8	21.2	542.5	100.0
Italy	322.7	3.3	1,050.3	10.7	5,428.6	55.2	3,041.7	30.9	9,843.3	100.0
Luxembourg	0.2	0.1	14.9	10.0	93.6	62.9	40.0	26.9	148.7	100.0
Netherlands	162.4	3.7	1,462.5	33.4	1,858.0	42.5	895.3	20.4	4,379.1	100.0
Portugal	117.8	10.3	154.1	13.5	607.9	53.3	259.8	22.8	1,139.6	100.0
United Kingdom	219.1	2.7	2,513.7	31.1	2,755.9	34.1	2,598.8	32.1	8,087.5	100.0
Other									515.9	
Total	2,039.0	2.9	12,619.4	18.0	35,850.5	51.2	18,988.8	27.1	70,013.5	100.0[a]

Source: *The Community Budget: The Facts and Figures* (Brussels, EC, 1994)
Note: [a]This row includes the relative contribution of other sources of 0.7%

Second, agricultural levies (3 per cent of the budget revenue) are variable charges applied on imports of farm goods included in the CAP, and imported from third countries. They are a variable source of revenue for they depend on the volume of imports that relies in part on weather conditions and partly on trade concessions the EU offers to foreign partners. Another element in this fluctuation is that the world market prices for agricultural goods often change. The EU is becoming increasingly self-sufficient in a number of agricultural products of the temperate zone, hence there is a reduction in demand for imports. Sugar and isoglucose levies are charges on producers that are supposed to make them share the financial burden of market support for production and storage.

Third, the VAT contribution includes 51 per cent of the revenue. It is calculated for each member country by the application of a uniform rate of 1.4 per cent to the national VAT base. This base may not exceed 55 per cent of the national GNP.

Fourth is a new category known as the fourth resource. It is closely related to a country's ability to pay. This revenue item provides 27 per cent of the EU budget. Together with the VAT resources, it is the only dynamic component of the budgetary revenue as it is derived from the application of a rate to the GNP of each member country. It is an additional source as it is calculated during the budgetary procedure in order to top-up the difference between the budgetary expenditure and (insufficient) revenue that accrues from other sources.

The fifth revenue item is of negligible size relative to the total budget. It covers miscellaneous revenue such as deductions from the salaries of the EU civil servants, fines and possible surpluses from preceding years.

6 Winners and losers

A formal obligation to contribute to the EU budget exists for every member country. It differs from the actual net contribution to or net receipt from the budgetary operations. The disequilibrium between the payments to and receipts from the EU budget brought tensions between Britain and the rest of the EU for quite some time.[11] Tables 3.6 and 3.7 are supposed to provide an answer to the often asked questions of who pays and who gains, respectively, from the EU budget. Those two issues may have certain nominal relevance for the day-to-day (unpleasant) political debates. None the less, it must be remembered that economic integration is not an enterprise with short-term or, even, long-term clear financial balances. Rather, integration is an undertaking that offers a longer-term enhancement for the utilization of resources and potential of the participants. Therefore, a country that is a net contributor to the budget should not be seen as a loser from the integration venture (e.g., Germany), but rather as a participant that is gaining elsewhere: a secure, unrestricted and long-term free access to partner-country markets for its goods and services.

Table 3.6 shows that Germany (30 per cent), France (19 per cent), Italy (14 per cent) and Britain (12 per cent) were the biggest contributors to the EU budget in 1994. 'Where it all goes to' in the same year is presented in Table 3.7. France was the biggest recipient of the budgetary resources (16 per cent), followed by Spain (13 per cent) and Germany (12.8 per cent).[12]

7 Problems

The preceding analysis revealed that both the EU budget expenditure and revenue were not related either to the EU need to influence economic life (save for agriculture) as the national governments can do or, until, recently to the relative economic wealth of the member countries. Instead of singling out economic areas that need to be influenced on the EU level and, then, creating the necessary funds, the EU still continues to adopt policies that fit into its limited funds. It should not be forgotten

Table 3.6 The financing of the 1994 budget: relative contribution of each country (%)

Country	Agricultural levies	Customs duties	VAT	Fourth resource	Total
Belgium	5.4	6.8	3.3	3.3	3.9
Denmark	2.2	2.1	1.9	2.1	2.0
Germany	22.0	30.0	31.7	29.0	30.1
Greece	1.6	1.5	1.6	1.3	1.5
Spain	9.0	4.5	9.4	8.1	8.1
France	18.8	12.8	21.5	19.6	19.2
Ireland	0.7	1.1	0.7	0.6	0.8
Italy	15.8	8.3	15.1	16.1	14.1
Luxembourg	0.0	0.1	0.3	0.2	0.2
Netherlands	8.0	11.6	5.2	4.7	6.3
Portugal	5.8	1.2	1.7	1.4	1.6
United Kingdom	10.7	19.9	7.7	13.7	11.6
Other					0.7
Total	100.0	100.0	100.0	100.0	100.0

Source: The Community Budget: The Facts and Figures (Brussels: EC, 1994)

Table 3.7 Payments made in 1994: by sector and by member state (ECUs millions)

Country	EAGGF Guarantee	EAGGF Guidance	EAGGF Guidance Fisheries	Regional Fund	Social Fund	Administration	Others	Total	%
Belgium	1,174.4	36.4	6.4	77.9	87.3	600.6	529.8	2,512.8	4.2
Denmark	1,278.9	23.1	41.5	14.8	38.7	3.7	85.4	1,495.1	2.5
Germany	5,271.6	458.9	17.1	726.8	611.9	24.0	619.0	7,729.2	12.8
Greece	2,723.5	294.1	38.3	912.0	444.6	3.1	428.7	4,844.2	8.0
Spain	4,426.9	392.4	135.0	1,361.2	660.2	5.3	853.7	7,834.7	13.0
France	8,048.8	355.7	28.4	460.8	453.3	23.0	554.6	9,924.3	16.5
Ireland	1,527.1	124.0	4.9	213.3	339.8	2.6	179.1	2,390.9	4.0
Italy	3,481.4	283.2	45.1	665.1	385.8	17.7	341.0	5,219.2	8.7
Luxembourg	12.7	6.5	0.1	3.0	4.0	303.6	89.2	419.1	0.7
Netherlands	1,935.9	26.6	4.7	60.0	173.1	17.1	198.6	2,416.0	4.0
Portugal	713.5	397.6	52.4	1,120.7	260.8	2.4	495.4	3,042.6	5.0
United Kingdom	3,001.9	100.4	21.0	788.6	685.4	46.7	614.7	5,258.6	8.7
Allocation unavailable	0.0	—	—	6.6	—	2,515.9	4,695.1	7,217.7	12.0
Total	33,605.4	2,498.9	395.0	6,410.8	4,144.8	3,565.5	9,684.3	60,304.8	100.0

Source: Official Journal of the European Communities (C 303, 14 November 1995)

however, that it is neither the absolute nor the relative size of the budget that matters. What matters is the size of funds needed relative to the necessary encouragement to change certain behaviour in a desired direction. In some cases this amount can be rather minuscule, such as the development of small and medium-sized enterprises where a simple freedom of establishment, tax incentives and loan guarantees can do the job. In others, such as agriculture or adjustment out of obsolete industries, the amounts required to change behaviour in the desired way can be quite large.

When the member countries of the EU agree to pursue a common policy, one can also expect that the means for carrying out that policy may also be transferred upwards towards the EU institutions. The problem is that the member countries take the EU as the appropriate plane for the conduct of common policies in certain cases, but they are quite unyielding (mainly Britain) when the new funds have to be collected. Reforms of the EU budget are resisted by the regions and countries that benefit from the present structure (mainly the agricultural regions in the north and the less developed ones in the south). An increased expenditure on economic activities (other than agriculture), without extra funds, can jeopardize the current distribution of costs and benefits. Without the ability to increase or substantially reorganize spending, the EU should endeavour to coordinate its own expenditure with that of member countries. The application of common rules on the size and trend in the public expenditure are expected to lead to the final stage of the EMU. They need to be followed, since fiscal 'indiscipline' by one or several member countries may affect the fiscal policy of the EU as a whole.

The EU budget absorbs only around 1 per cent of the combined GNP of its member countries. Compared with the national budgets, (agriculture apart) it plays only a limited role in the redistribution of income and the allocation of resources. Its role in economic stabilization has not been fulfilled. The influential MacDougall Report (1977) noted that in federal states such as the US and Germany, federal spending was in the neighbourhood of 20–25 per cent of GNP. Such an increase in the EU spending cannot be reasonably expected in the near future. In the pre-federal stage of the EU, a budget that absorbs 5–7 per cent of the combined GNP (without transfers for defence) could have an impact on economic stabilization and even upon regional disparities. Such a budget may be able to influence social (unemployment, education, health, retirement), regional and external aid policies. Resources may be found either in the transfer of funds from national budgets and/or in an increase in the 'fourth' budgetary resource. The problem is that the member countries are still reluctant to increase the budgetary powers of the EU. If the EU gets more resources for its budget, the total public expenditure in the EU, compared with the similar uncoordinated outlays of the member states, may be reduced because of economies of scale. A budget with increased resources may represent a built-in stabilizer for macroeconomic management. In addition, transfers among regions may enhance economic convergence and strengthen the cohesion of the EU.

In contrast to a variety of revenue sources employed to supply national budgets, the EU budget is financed from a narrow range of taxes. On the expenditure side of the EU budget, there is a high concentration of resources in one area: farming. That contrasts with the much diversified public expenditure in the member countries. However, the possibility of changing such a pattern of revenue and expenditure in the EU still remains in the hands of the member countries and depends on their willingness to enhance the powers of the EU. The EU should avoid a situation in the future in which the member countries have a single monetary policy and, at the same time, largely decentralized and uncoordinated fiscal policies.

Apart from all the stated problems, the EU has a strong indirect means for controlling a significant part of public expenditure in all member countries. That is, EU competition policy. State aids absorb a significant part of national budgets. To control these outlays does not require extra expenditure from the EU budget. One may expect that in the near future a major reform of the EU budget will, unfortunately, not happen. An event like this would have to be coupled with considerable political sensitivity. What may take place instead is a reform, or rather restructuring (in relative terms), within the framework of the existing budget. Increased contributions to the EU budget according to the level of national wealth or the principle of the ability to pay should be further encouraged.

VI CONCLUSION

A country or a group of countries that frequently change fiscal systems and move away from liberalization, may be regarded as potentially risky destinations for investment. This may provoke a reduction in the inflow and an increase in the outflow of capital to relatively more stable and growing locations. Complete unification of fiscal systems, however, may not be a prerequisite for the smooth functioning of an EMU. The US is the best example in support of this argument. The federal states in the US have differences in their respective tax systems. This system has functioned relatively satisfactorily without the tax posts between the states for a number of decades. However, one must note that the differences in the tax systems among the federal states in the US are not that great. There exists a significant degree of harmonization among tax systems in federal units.

A genuine internal market in the EU requires a degree of harmonization of indirect taxes among its member countries. Otherwise, the member governments would have to accept substantial diversions in revenues. It is widely believed that a difference in sales tax of up to 5 per cent can introduce distortions that may be acceptable among the integrated countries and that would not bring unbearable budgetary problems. However, difficulties arise when national budgets have different trends regarding their public deficits. Alterations in the national tax systems in such situations can bring serious political problems.

As for the possibility of a significant degree of harmonization (or, in an extreme case, unification) of fiscal systems in the EMU, there are certain reasons for pessimism. A tax policy is one of the most fundamental national sovereign rights. Recall the vehement British opposition to the inclusion of fiscal matters in the majority-voting issues in the Single European Act. The achievement of national goals within a fiscal policy do not necessarily coincide at all times with those of other partners. Although an EMU may agree on the basic objectives, their achievement may be left to the member countries which sometimes wish to use different and often clashing instruments. None the less, the sophisticated market led approach (bottom-up) to integration in tax matters that derived from the Single European Act (a removal of fiscal frontiers) may compel national tax authorities to align their tax rates and systems. Otherwise, other things being equal, businesses may move to and settle in those countries where tax treatment is most favourable. This bottom-up approach of the EU is a significant shift from the earlier policy proposals that were arguing in favour of full tax harmonization (top-down).

The public is sensitive to changes in tax systems. Full fiscal harmonization in the EMU may require an increase in taxes in some countries (Germany) while it may require their decrease in others (Denmark and Ireland). In the low-tax countries there is an opposition to tax increases, while in the high-tax countries, there is a fear of revenue losses. Therefore, a partial fiscal harmonization (only on agreed taxes) may be a good initial step. Harmonization of the fiscal systems of the countries that are in the EMU requires caution, gradualism and, more than anything else, the political will which economic theory may not be able to predict.

The Maastricht Treaty has enhanced the role of the EU institutions. New EU-wide policies and responsibilities require the EU to play a much more prominent role than it performed before the Maastricht Treaty. This will involve an increase in common resources, as well as the coordination of fiscal, monetary, social and regional policies. The EU ought to have the authority to tax and spend in its own right, at least up to an agreed limit. How to persuade national governments to abandon a part of their fiscal sovereignty in favour of the EU in order to reap the benefits of fiscal integration is a question to be dealt with in politics and diplomacy.

NOTES

1 See Chapter 5 on competition policy.
2 The allocation of resources is production efficient if all producers face the same tax for the same good or service. It is consumption efficient if all consumers face the same tax for the consumption of the same good or service.
3 Alaska, Arizona, California, Colorado, Connecticut, District of Columbia, Illinois, Indiana, Iowa, Kansas, Massachusetts, New Hampshire, New Jersey, New York, Ohio, Rhode Island and West Virginia. Because of controversies regarding the unitary system of computation of corporate profits, certain states have considered abandoning this system.
4 This assumes that country A grants either an exception or a full foreign tax credit.
5 There is also a problem of inflation. Depreciation may be calculated according to historic costs, but how should capital gains that reflect inflation be taxed? Luckily, the governments of most EU countries continue to be tough on inflation.
6 Cnossen (1995) provides a survey of options for the reform of corporate taxes in the EU.
7 For example, language, seniority, xenophobia, social and family ties.
8 The application of the principle of origin is a consideration, but so far only in those countries that integrate.
9 The new theory of trade and strategic industrial policy disputes the Johnson-Krauss argument. In the real situation with imperfect markets (increasing returns to scale, externalities and economies of learning), once the production of, for example, aircraft or fast trains, starts at a very restricted number of locations in the world, it perpetuates itself. There is no room in the world even for five producers of wide-body passenger aircraft. In this case, the exchange rate argument (Johnson-Krauss) is of little help for the small and medium-sized countries.
10 Apart from making life and travel easier for EU residents, the business community saves too. They are spared the preparation of some 60 million customs and tax documents a year. The abolition of border checks saves around ECU 8 billion a year to EU member states (*Business International*, 15 July 1991, p. 237). In 1988, the EU introduced the Single Administrative Document to replace some 30 documents that were required in order to allow goods to move within the EU. This document has not been required for internal trade since 1993, but is still used for goods that cross an EU external frontier.
11 Britain won an arrangement in 1984 which let it get a refund from the EU budget.
12 The difference of ECU 10 billion between the totals in Table 3.4 and Table 3.7 is attributable to the following factors. Table 3.4 gives commitments and payments in 1994. Table 3.7 presents effective payments in 1994, as well as payments obligated in 1993, but made a year later.

4

COMMON AGRICULTURAL POLICY

I INTRODUCTION

During the past decades agriculture has been a statistically shrinking economic sector in the developed market economies. The share of agriculture in the GNP of the EU was 3 per cent, while its share in the region's employment was less than 6 per cent[1] in 1994. Agriculture was employing around 20 million people at the time of the creation of the EU. More than three decades later, the number of people directly employed in agriculture was a little over 8.5 million. If one adds the dependent family members to those that work in the farm sector, the number relying on this sector for their livelihood is around 40 million people. Apart from the customs union, the Common Agricultural Policy (CAP) is often described as *the* genuine economic policy of the EU, as well as one of its greatest achievements in economic integration – and, perplexingly, as its weakest link!

This part of the book is structured as follows. As agriculture is a special economic activity, section II explains why it is so. The following two sections cover the objectives and the implementation of the CAP, respectively. Section V examines the operation and consequences of the CAP. Because of the controversy, reforms of the CAP are considered in section VI. Before our conclusion, there is a separate section on the Common Fisheries Policy.

II DISTINCTIVENESS OF AGRICULTURE

Since the time of its creation, not only has the relative share of those employed in agriculture decreased in total, but the share of agriculture in the GNP has also declined in the EU. If that is so, why does agriculture command such a prominent position in the economic and political life of many countries, as well as in the EU?[2] The answer to this question can be found in at least seven elements:

- One of the basic and oldest reasons for the special attention given to the agricultural sector of the economy is strategic. Governments supported domestic food production in order to ease the situation in the country in the event of war, crisis or foreign economic blockade. Linked to this consideration is the fact that farmers are scattered all around the country and that the peasants (at least used to) have larger families in order to get cheaper labour. In the event of war, this segment of the population could give a valuable contribution both to manpower and to the coverage of the national territory. In modern times, farmers are the part of the population that bothers to vote. Therefore, each political party must take into account the concerns of the powerful farm lobby.[3]

- If one assumes that the national population is able to satisfy the basic needs for food, as is the case in the developed market economies, then price elasticity of demand (E_{dp}) for food is less than 1 (equation 4.1). Such price inelasticity makes the price (p) of food fall if there is an increase in the quantity (q) supplied.

$$E_{dp} = \frac{\frac{\Delta q}{q}}{\frac{\Delta p}{p}} = \frac{\Delta q}{\Delta p} \frac{p}{q} < 1 \qquad (4.1)$$

One may find here a difference between farm and manufactured goods and compare potatoes and cars as representative products of the two sectors. If the price of French potatoes falls on the German market, then the German farmers would be able to sell their potatoes on the domestic market only if they reduce the price of their potatoes to match the price (other things being equal) of their French competitors. If, however, Renault slightly lowers the price of its cars in the German market, one may not expect a corresponding increase in the German demand for Renaults and a matching fall in the demand for Volkswagens. The reason for such a state of affairs and in the behaviour of consumers is that most of the farm goods are standardized, while the manufactured goods carry with them a number of psychological attributes such as status, taste or past experience. Hence, one may conclude that (1) international economic integration in farm goods brings gains to the farmers of the exporting country to the detriment of farmers of the importing country, and that (2) integration in manufactured goods brings gains to everyone (Petith, 1976, p. 132).

- The relative price of food in the developed market economies is not only on the decline because of the low price elasticity of demand, but also because of the low income (y) elasticity of demand (E_{dy}) that is less than 1 (equation 4.2).[4]

$$E_{dy} = \frac{\frac{\Delta q}{q}}{\frac{\Delta y}{y}} = \frac{\Delta q}{\Delta y} \frac{y}{q} < 1 \qquad (4.2)$$

- Agricultural production depends on natural conditions. They include not only biological cycles, but also climate, droughts/floods, earthquakes, diseases and pests. On the one hand, the impact of some of these factors diminishes over time because of irrigation, drainage, mechanization, fertilizers, pesticides, herbicides, vaccines, glasshouses, genetic engineering and artificial selection. On the other hand, a disturbance of the natural cycle can be detrimental, such as giving hormones to calves in order to accelerate their growth which could make the meat unfit for human consumption.[5] Similarly, the use of chemicals may be unfriendly to the environment.

The biological cycle is often a limiting factor in farm production. For example, if one year a farmer sows wheat and, then, unexpectedly there is an increase in the demand and price for maize, the farmer's switch to the maize production can take place only during the next sowing season. The situation is, however, different in most of the manufacturing industry. In oil refineries a simple turn of the handle can alter the production of gas into the production of diesel. This simple 'turn of the handle' is not possible in agricultural production. If capital is invested in a particular product, it may not be easily or swiftly withdrawn.

- Agriculture is not only a producing economic sector, it is also a significant consumer of goods and services. The farm sector purchases machinery, transport equipment, chemicals, construction material, fuel, energy, insurance, legal services and the like. In addition, a part of R&D in the manufacturing sector has a specific farm dimension. At the same time, the price of farm goods influences the price of labour that all sectors have to pay, and through that, the price of low value added final goods and services.
- Agriculture plays a role in the conservation of the environment and of the human habitat. There is a distinct demand for the preservation of the idyllic peasant's life, particularly in countries where only a small segment of the population makes a living in the farm sector. In addition, an excessive use of chemicals may degrade the quality of the environment. Therefore, many public bodies and a number of private firms are devoting increasing attention to the conservation of the environment.
- The prices of most of the temperate-zone farm goods on the world market reflect only a part of the planet's production. In most cases those prices are not only highly volatile, but also distorted. For some goods such as temperate-zone fruits, vegetables, beef or wine, there is hardly any 'world market' at all.

Taken together, the above elements can provide the answer to why the agricultural sector attracts special and disproportionately large attention in the economies of the developed market economies relative to its direct contribution to GNP and employment.

III OBJECTIVES

During negotiations (1956) about the creation of the EU, France insisted on the inclusion of agricultural goods in the customs union. What the internal free trade offered to German manufacturers, the CAP was to offer to French farmers. This 'deal' was agreed between the two major negotiators. In addition, the CAP united the country with a large farm output (France) and the one with high prices for farm goods (Germany). Article 3 of the Treaty of Rome requires the introduction of a common policy in agriculture and it has a special Title on agriculture (Articles 38 to 47).

Article 39 lists five *goals* of the CAP:

- The CAP is 'to increase agricultural productivity by promoting technical progress and by ensuring the rational development of agricultural production and the optimum utilisation of factors of production, in particular labour'.
- It has 'to ensure a fair standard of living for the agricultural community, in particular by increasing the individual earnings of persons engaged in agriculture'. 'A fair standard of living' is, however, not defined. One may think that this means an equalization of average individual incomes in agriculture and manufacturing.
- The CAP has 'to stabilise markets'.

- It has 'to assure the availability of supplies'.
- The supplies have to 'reach consumers at reasonable prices'. However, 'reasonable prices' are not defined by the Treaty of Rome.

Article 40 refers to the permitted measures and forms of the CAP. In order to attain the objectives of the CAP, there needs to be a common organization of farm markets. The *measures* to attain the goals of the CAP may include the regulation of:

- prices,
- aids and funding,
- storage, and
- external trade.

Depending on the good, such organization would take one of the following three *forms*:

- 'common rules on competition;
- compulsory coordination of the various national market organisations;
- a European market organisation'.

The Commission is charged by the Treaty of Rome to 'submit proposals for working out and implementing the common agricultural policy, including the replacement of the national organisations by one of the forms of common organisation' (Article 43). In addition, one of the objectives of the EU is to contribute to the harmonious development of world trade and progressive abolition of restrictions on international trade (Article 110). The Single European Act brought Article 130r which refers to the issue of environment. It accepts the 'polluter pays' principle and states that 'environmental protection requirements must be integrated into the definition and implementation of other Community policies'. The Maastricht Treaty (Article 3a) obliges the EU to keep 'an open market economy with free competition'. According to the Treaty of Rome, agricultural products mean 'the products of the soil, of stockfarming and of fisheries and products of first-stage processing directly related to these products' (Article 38). Although the farm products also include fish, the fisheries policy in the EU has developed on its own. It is outlined at the end of this chapter.

The CAP is in essence a price policy for a large number of agricultural goods of the temperate zone. It encourages production and, at the same time, 'taxes' consumption.[6] The CAP is not, however, a single compact policy, but rather a combination of different product rules. The CAP has two dimensions, internal and external. The first is to ensure a determined price level on the EU domestic market. If the price of a farm good falls below the intervention price (the level under which EU intervention is compulsory), the excess supplies must be purchased by the intervention agencies in unlimited quantities in order to keep the internal EU price of the good at the guaranteed minimum level. The external dimension of the CAP maintains the lowest level of prices for imports of farm goods. This threshold price protects the internal EU farm market both from foreign competitors and from fluctuation of prices in the external market. At the same time, the EU subsidizes exports of internal surpluses of farm goods abroad. This policy became a stumbling block in international trade negotiations and created a number of frictions in international trade. In fact, the CAP is the most obvious example of an inward-oriented sectoral integration arrangement that has resulted in trade diversion. The outcome of the CAP was a high degree of self-sufficiency or surpluses in most of the temperate-zone agricultural products. In addition, overall costs of the CAP were quite high, not only in terms of misallocation of resources and frictions in international trade, but also in terms of complex administration and degradation of the environment.

Farming, particularly in continental Europe, is a part of the social structure, a way of life in the region that has survived for several thousand years. There is a relatively high degree of national self-sufficiency in the production of food, as well as highly protectionist and interventionist national institutions. On the other hand, the pattern of certain types of farming in countries such as the US, Canada or Australia is different: large-scale farming started by the European immigrants just a few centuries ago. It is basically linked with commercial land use, while in Europe, this commercial activity is most intimately and deeply connected to national social structure. Hence, the strong support of European countries for national farming interests in spite of certain financial costs.

IV IMPLEMENTATION

The establishment of a customs union for manufactured goods is simpler than for the farm commodities. A customs union that deals solely with manufactured goods needs only an elimination of tariffs and quotas (the assumption is that there are no other NTBs) on internal trade, an establishment of rules on competition, as well as an introduction of the CET. Introducing a similar arrangement for farm goods is a much more formidable task. That is not only because of the natural dimension of the production process, but also because of the general need and political desire to keep a part of the population in the farm business.

The six founding member countries of the EU had a strong political will to implement the integration provisions of the Treaty of Rome. This made negotiations about the shape of the CAP relatively easy in Stresa (Italy) in 1958. The implementation of the CAP started in 1962. It was a gradual process which was expected to collect the receipts from the import levies in sufficient quantity to finance the CAP outlays. Later on, however, an increase in domestic output reduced imports and, consequently, receipts from variable levies. Hence, the tax proceeds from import levies were insufficient to cover EU expenditure on the CAP.

Following the provisions of the Treaty, although with some delay, Walter Hallstein, the President of the Commission, submitted to the Council of Ministers the final version of the Proposal on the CAP in 1964. At the same time he asked the Council to accept the proposal unanimously or to accept the resignation of the Commission. The national interests of the member countries were overridden by common ones, hence the Proposal was accepted. That was the first and only time when the Commission so convincingly achieved this. The CAP became fully operational in 1967.

Prior to the introduction of the CAP, the member countries of the EU practised different and often complicated intervention systems in agriculture. These support systems could be classified in five basic groups:

- *Market control*: was common in the founding six member countries of the EU. In this system, the government guarantees to purchase a certain quantity of farm goods at a determined (high) price. If the supply of the good is over and above the guaranteed limit, the administration may purchase the excess supply at (lower) market prices. In addition, if production is over the agreed quota, the authorities may charge these producers a penalty.
- *Direct income payments*: in order to keep a certain level of standard of living, farmers receive payments from the chancellor of the exchequer without any relation to the quantity of their production. Sweden practised a similar system.
- *Deficiency payment*: there is a free market determination of prices of farm goods in this system. However, the government guarantees prices that are higher than the ones on the domestic market. The difference between the (lower) market price and the (higher) guaranteed price is covered by transfers from the budget to the farmers. Britain used this system of support before entering the EU in 1973. At that time, prices of food in Britain were lower by around 30 per cent compared with those in the EU. After entry, Britain abandoned this system as a part of the *acquis communautaire*. This change was not as hard as it may appear, since an abandoning of the original system was on the way in Britain for some time because of the need to reduce public expenditure. While the price-support system demands control at the external border, the deficiency-payment system requires control both at the external border and at the level of individual farms.
- *Variable levies on imports*: the administration sets a threshold price for imports of farm goods and charges a variable levy on imports that is equal to the difference between the lower and fluctuating 'world market price' and the higher domestic threshold price. The system may be combined with quotas.
- *Other policies*: these include subsidies such as the ones for exports, capital investments or R&D.

Compared with the system of free trade where the consumers have freedom of choice and where they opt (other things being equal) for the cheapest source of supply, none of the above systems gets a pass mark. None the less, the direct-income payments system seems to introduce least distortions, but the real problem is where to find resources for its operation.

The EU selected the system of variable levies and quotas for imports for the CAP. France would get a free access to the EU farm-market and the system would be supported by price policies, rather than income payments. The established system has three basic principles:

- there is a common market for agricultural goods that may circulate freely in the EU, prices are the same throughout the EU and administrative and health standards are harmonized;
- there is an EU preference for domestically produced farm goods over imported ones; and
- there is financial solidarity regarding the cost of the CAP among the member countries of the EU.

The CAP is operated through national customs and intervention agencies, and it is financed through the EU budget.

V OPERATION AND CONSEQUENCES

1 Protection of the internal market

The CAP covers almost the entire farm production in the EU. The only significant agricultural commodity that is beyond its scope is the potato. Although there are certain differences in the systems of protection/intervention for various goods, the basic idea is generally the same. It is exemplified in the case of wheat.

Figure 4.1 illustrates the support-price system for wheat. The policy rests on three different types of prices. These are the target price, the threshold price and the intervention price.

- The *target price* is the price of wheat in Duisburg (Germany). That is the region where cereals are in shortest supply in the EU. This is the highest possible price in the EU and it includes the costs of transport and storage.
- Imports into the EU are forbidden below the *threshold price*. The threshold price is calculated on the basis of target price. Costs of transport and distribution from the frontier (Rotterdam) to the region with the highest shortage of wheat (Duisburg) are subtracted from the target price in order to determine the threshold price. This price is applied in all ports through which imports enter the EU.
- If there is an increase in the internal EU production and supply of wheat, the internal price falls. The *intervention price* is the minimum price that the EU guarantees to the domestic producers. This price is around 8 per cent lower than the target price. Until the proposed reforms of the CAP in the 1970s and 1980s, the intervention agencies were obliged to purchase an unlimited quantity of the domestically produced good if it conformed with specified standards.

These prices are set once a year (usually in April) by the Council of Ministers and they are valid for the period of the following 12 months. The difference between the CIF price and the intervention price represents the protection and aid that the CAP gives to the domestic producers relative to the foreign suppliers. There is no *a priori* knowledge about the cost of the CAP at the time the prices are set. Falling world cereal prices or a generous harvest may upset EU farm expenditure.

When wheat is imported in the EU from abroad, the difference between the price of imports CIF Rotterdam and the threshold price is bridged by a *variable levy*. This levy is calculated on a daily basis as the CIF price may constantly change. Such a system ensures that imported wheat always enters the EU at a fixed threshold price. Receipts from variable levies form a part of the receipts of the general budget of the EU. On rare occasions, as happened in 1973–1974, when the price of cereals on foreign markets was higher than the threshold price, the EU applies the variable levy for exports of the goods abroad.

The CAP made the EU self-sufficient in most of the agricultural goods it covers. There were, in fact, substantial surpluses of farm goods in the EU. Therefore, the EU exported them abroad. As the prices for these goods are higher in the EU than abroad, the EU hands out *variable refunds* for exports. The role of these refunds is to bridge (reduce) the difference between the target price and the price on the 'world market'. As prices on foreign markets fluctuate, the refunds are calculated daily and

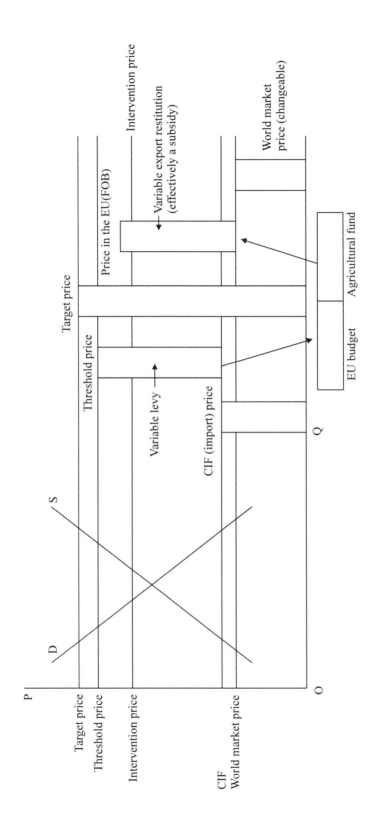

Figure 4.1 The Common Agricultural Policy price support system for wheat

are paid from the EU farm fund. These refunds are similar to the inverse version of the variable levies charged on imports of agricultural goods to the EU.

The above analysis reveals that the implementation of the CAP rests on two pillars. The first one is the intervention price, while the second one includes variable levies for imports into and variable refunds for exports of farm goods from the EU. Around 70 per cent of the entire farm output of the EU (cereals, milk, sugar and meats) benefited from this intervention. The following quarter of the EU farm production (eggs, poultry and select fruits and vegetables) profited only by protection from cheap imports. The rest of the agricultural business (olive oil, tobacco, cotton, hops and a few others) receive a certain fixed subsidy from the EU.[7]

2 Monetary compensatory amounts

The prices of farm goods are set in the common accounting units and then converted into the national currencies of the member countries. During the time when the rates of exchange were fixed, there were no problems regarding such conversion. However, the French franc devalued and the DM revalued in 1969. That changed price parities for agricultural goods in the EU market. The introduction of fluctuating rates of exchange brought the 'green rates of exchange' for the prices of farm goods covered by the CAP. The 'green' rates were set by the Council of Ministers, at least once a year, in order to stabilize domestic output prices.

In order to avoid the disequilibria in the internal farm trade, the EU introduced the monetary compensatory amounts (MCAs). Agriculture is an economic sector just like the others. There is nothing special about its exposure to exchange market fluctuations. The MCAs depend on the difference between the central and the 'green' rates of exchange. Once an EU country *revalues* its currency, it hands out a compensatory amount on its exports of farm goods in order to give it a subsidy.[8] The objective is to give the same amount of national currency per unit of output to the home producers as was the case prior to revaluation. The same country charges a tax on imports of farm commodities from partner countries in order to preserve the balance of relative prices of farm goods in the EU. Without MCAs, the country with the highest intervention prices would be flooded with farm goods from the EU partner countries. That would distort trade flows. If an EU country *devalues* its currency, the procedure is reversed. Exports are taxed with a compensatory amount, while imports are subsidized.

The MCAs represent taxes and subsidies on imports and exports in intra-EU farm trade. They have, in effect, split the EU agricultural market into a group of national markets that were 'divided' by a special system of taxes and subsidies on imports and exports. In fact, that introduced a variant of the system of multiple exchange rates in the internal market for agricultural goods. Because of such splintering of the market, the Cockfield Report (*Completing the Internal Market*) of 1985 requested the abolition of MCAs (Point 38, p. 12).

This complex system of trade barriers hinders competition among farmers in the EU. MCAs gave artificial support to the output of farmers that live in countries with strong currencies and they hinder output in other countries. Wherever there are taxes and subsidies such as the MCAs, there is a temptation for fraud. For example, when the Belgian franc was weak in the early 1980s, the Belgian farmers were smuggling their pigs and cows into the Netherlands where they hid the origin of their merchandise. The Belgians later imported pork and beef from the Netherlands and pocketed an import subsidy of ECU 300 per tonne. Similar contraband exists between Northern Ireland and the Irish Republic, as well as elsewhere.

The system of support for farm prices was modified in 1984. The added switchover system practically linked the CAP prices to the DM. Hence, revaluations of the DM have not led to a larger gap between Germany's 'green' and market rates. Instead, a revaluation of the DM led to a rise in the ECU value of CAP prices. That has, in turn, increased prices in other member states. The switchover system was potentially inflationary and protectionist. A positive development was that exchange rates were relatively stable during the 1980s. New MCAs could come from parity changes. As this was rare, the attention of policy-makers was directed towards the dismantling of MCAs. By the beginning of the 1990s, almost all MCAs had been dismantled. However, the currency instability following that period worked against the elimination of this system of 'support'.

The system for the support of prices of farm goods was revised in 1993. The key element was a system that automatically adjusted green rates with the market rates of exchange. The MCAs became unnecessary, as small variations in the exchange rates are thought to be irrelevant in disrupting internal trade flows. As the reform was founded on the assumption of stability in the exchange markets, the events in 1992 brought frequent changes in the CAP prices and green rates. From August 1993 EMS margins of fluctuation were widened from ±2.25 to ±15 per cent (effectively a free float). Large fluctuations of DM and corresponding CAP prices can take place. As the switchover system may be prompted only by the official realignments in the EMS, a revaluation of the DM may not cause the realignment in prices, i.e. CAP prices in Germany may be reduced without compensation under the switchover system. Hence, Germany (and the Netherlands) demanded a modification in the system that would activate it even by fluctuations in the exchange rates. Britain was against such a proposal. None the less, the automatic mechanism was altered at the end of 1993. The alteration permits gaps of up to 5 per cent between CAP prices among the member states (von Cramon-Taubadel and Thiele, 1994, pp. 264–265).

The removal of border controls was the consequence of the implementation of the 1992 Programme. Hence, the impossibility for the continuation of MCAs. An agreement was reached in December 1992, at the last minute, on how to proceed after the internal-market programme was in place. The 'green rates' would continue to apply, but the Commission was authorized to change them as required to avoid the necessity of MCAs. The Agricultural Ministers agreed in 1995 to introduce a 'dual green currency system', one for direct currency payments, and the other for price support payments. It is intended to protect the income of farmers in countries where currency revaluations endanger the value of CAP prices in national currencies. The principal components of the agreement include three items. First, in countries in which revaluations took place before the end of 1995, there would be a freeze in the rates for payments of aid for reforms such as set-aside land, till the end of 1998. Second, compensation payments for farmers in countries whose currency revalued was limited to a period of three years and it is due to decline during that period.

Third, member states are permitted to pay farmers a flat aid from the national budgets to compensate for the losses suffered because of the movements in the exchange rates in 1994 and 1995. Half of these payments would come from the EU budget. That entire aid is to be given over a period of three years and is supposed to decline during that period. In addition, farm prices were unpegged from the DM in June 1995.

3 European Agricultural Guidance and Guarantee Fund

The European Agricultural Guidance and Guarantee Fund (EAGGF) was created in 1964 in order to help the implementation of the CAP. It disposed of almost ECU 40 billion in 1995 (Table 4.1). This fund has two sections, one for guidance and the other for guarantees. The Guarantee section, 92 per cent of the EU expenditure on the CAP in 1995, covered outlays that include intervention on the EU market for farm goods, gave refunds for exports of agricultural goods to third countries and financed food aid to foreign countries. The Guidance section of the EAGGF disposes of modest funds relative to the other section. Outlays from the Guidance section cover expenditure that refers to the structural policy. Outlays from this section usually co-finance 25 per cent (exceptionally up to 65 per cent) of the costs linked with the alteration in the structure of production within a designated area. The change in the structure of production refers to the costs that include the provision of infrastructure, vocational training and modernization. Although the total direct cost of the CAP is relatively high in budgetary terms, the cost per EU consumer per day was ECU 0.3 per day in 1995! As it was a relatively small amount,[9] the consumers were not able or, rather, not interested in organizing a consumer lobby that would strongly present their case in the EU. In addition to expenditure on the CAP, there are also charges under this policy. The most significant are levies on imports of farm goods (major source of receipts) and those on sugar. None the less, these charges cover only a relatively small part of expenditure on the CAP. The coverage ratio was only 5 per cent in 1995.

Table 4.1 Budgetary expenditure on and charges under the Common Agricultural Policy, 1991–1995

Indicator	1991	1992	1993	1994	1995
EAGGF Guarantee (million ECUs)	32,386	32,107	34,748	34,787	36,972
EAGGF Guidance (million ECUs)	2,011	2,715	3,386	2,619	2,827
Total agricultural expenditure[a] (million ECUs)	34,542	35,000	38,338	37,532	39,947
Net cost of the CAP					
– as % of EU GDP	0.6	0.6	0.7	0.6	0.6
– per capita ECU	92.1	94.7	104.6	101.3	108.2
Charges under the CAP (million ECUs)	2,763	2,209	2,144	2,304	2,182
Of that:					
– Ordinary levies (million ECUs)	1,621	1,207	1,029	922	946
– Sugar levies (million ECUs)	1,142	1,002	1,115	1,382	1,236

Source: EC (1995), *The Agricultural Situation in the Community, 1994 Report*. EC: Brussels
Note: [a]Includes expenditure additional to the EAGGF

Table 4.2 EAGGF Guarantee expenditure by select product,
1994 and 1995

Product[a]	1994 (million ECUs)	%	1995 (million ECUs)	%
Arable crops[b]	12,840	36.9	14,779	38.9
– Refunds	1,633		1,263	
– Intervention	11,207		13,516	
Milk products	4,344	12.5	4,059	10.6
– Refunds	1,926		1,942	
– Intervention	2,418		2,117	
Beef/veal	3,569	10.3	5,255	13.9
– Refunds	1,730		1,351	
– Intervention	1,839		3,904	
Sugar	2,170	6.2	1,947	5.1
– Refunds	1,463		1,399	
– Intervention	707		548	
Fruit/vegetables	1,665	4.8	1,833	4.8
– Refunds	216		166	
– Intervention	1,449		1,667	
Wine	1,179	3.4	1,515	4.0
– Refunds	81		70	
– Intervention	1,098		1,445	
Sheep/goat meat	1,740	5.0	1,264	3.3
– Refunds	—		—	
– Intervention	1,740		1,264	
Olive oil	2,060	5.9	893	2.4
– Refunds	55		73	
– Intervention	2,005		820	
Others	5,220	15.0	5,428	17.0
Total EAGGF	34,787	100.0	36,973	100.0

Source: EC (1995), *The Agricultural Situation in the Community, 1994 Report*. EC:
Luxembourg
Notes: [a]Refunds include food aid.   [b]From 1994, following the new budget nomenclature,
appropriations relating to cereals, oilseeds, peas and field beans and set-aside will be brought
together under Chapter BI.10, 'Arable crops'

As regards the EAGGF Guarantee section outlays per commodity (Table 4.2),
more than a third of expenditure was allocated to arable crops in 1994 and 1995. That
was followed by beef/veal and milk products (both over 10 per cent). EU intervention in the purchase of other farm products consumed relatively less funds. One of
the major problems of the CAP since its inception was refunds (read subsidies) for
exports of EU agricultural goods to third countries. In 1994 refunds for exports for
four major farm-commodity groups were ECU 6.6 billion or 18 per cent of all of the
EAGGF outlays. That has constantly created frictions with other international
exporters of agricultural goods.

Storage of agricultural goods also consumes a significant share of EU farm expenditure. In 1973, EU expenditure for storage was 10 per cent of the total EAGGF
Guarantee outlays. It rapidly increased over time to reach 25 per cent in 1986 before
falling erratically to 18 per cent in 1992.

4 The consequences of the Common Agricultural Policy on the European Union

4.1 Intervention, structure of output and self-sufficiency

Whenever a government guarantees purchases of a certain good at a specified price that covers the local costs of production and profit, and when there is a protection against imports, then one can produce everything everywhere, no matter how expensive it may be! The CAP guaranteed the purchase of the home production of the selected agricultural goods that conformed with the specified quality standards. That boosted the production of farm goods in the EU.

The involvement of the CAP was predominantly to support the income of farmers. Structural issues such as technical modernization, size of holdings and employment in agriculture were left to the national authorities. National expenditure in the farm sector supplements that of the EU. This expenditure included subsidized loans, tax exemptions, social security and other subsidies. The EU gave incentives for the increase in the agricultural production, while at the same time, it assumed responsibility for the purchase of farm output and to dispose of excess supplies. The financial solidarity that came with the CAP made possible the externalization of the cost of national investments in agriculture.

Subsidization of the farm sector is not an exclusive feature of the EU. Other OECD countries subsidize their agriculture too. In some cases, and depending on the indicator, that support is much higher than in the EU (Table 4.3). Producer subsidy equivalents (PSEs) measure 'annual monetary transfers to agricultural production from domestic consumers and taxpayers as a result of agricultural policies' (OECD, 1995, p. 109). The higher the PSE, the lower the efficiency of farm production. The farm sector of the OECD countries received ECU 147 billion in PSEs in 1994.[10] Although there were certain annual fluctuations regarding annual subsidies during the period 1986–1994, the annual volume of support remained roughly stable.

Table 4.3 Producer subsidy equivalents and transfers to the farm sector in select OECD countries in 1994

Country	PSE (billion ECUs)	PSE (%)	Total transfers[a] (billion ECUs)	Share of total transfers in GDP (%)	Total transfers per capita (ECUs)	Total transfers per full-time farmer (ECUs)
Australia	0.909	10	1.035	0.4	58	2,798
Austria	2.757	62	3.802	2.2	473	20,551
Canada	3.368	27	5.017	1.1	173	11,889
Finland	2.513	67	3.287	3.6	641	22,888
Japan	38.974	74	75.097	1.8	592	25,099
New Zealand	0.100	3	0.124	0.3	36	1,007
Norway	2.144	75	2.901	3.2	666	32,452
Sweden	1.500	51	1.794	1.1	203	21,460
Switzerland	4.462	82	4.904	2.1	700	31,438
United States	22.036	21	79.238	1.4	305	31,051
EU	80.480	50	113.180	1.7	322	16,147
OECD	147.000	43	292.900	1.8	331	13,731

Note: [a]Transfers from taxpayers and consumers minus budget revenues generated by the farm sector
Source: Agricultural Policies, Markets and Trade in OECD Countries (1995). Paris: OECD

In 1994, the PSE was highest in Switzerland (82 per cent), Norway (75 per cent), Japan (74 per cent), Finland (67 per cent) and Austria (62 per cent). The same indicator was 50 per cent in the EU which was much higher than the 21 per cent in the US,[11] 10 per cent in Australia or 3 per cent in New Zealand.

As a result of the CAP and its 'market organization', there was a commitment by the EU to purchase and dispose of farm goods through its executive agencies. Figure 4.2 presents the consequences of fixing prices and guaranteeing purchase. Suppose that in the market for wheat SS and DD represent supply and demand curves, respectively. Equilibrium in the market is at E and the market clearing price is OP_e, while the corresponding quantity of output is QQ_e. If the price is fixed above the market-clearing level, for instance, at OP_h then, the demand curve gets a kink and becomes DD_h. As the supply curve is unchanged, equilibrium is at point E_h. The free-market purchase of wheat is QQ_2, quantity Q_2Q_e presents a reduction in consumption, while Q_eQ_3 is hyperproduction. Triangle a illustrates welfare loss for the consumers, while triangle b stands for a misallocation of resources. Suppose that a lower level than OP_e is used to fix the price, for instance OP_1. Equilibrium is at point E_1, the quantity consumed is OQ_1, while quantity Q_1Q_4 stands for a shortage. The example with the fixing of prices above the equilibrium level conforms with the price distortions that are induced by the CAP, while the fixing of prices at the level below the equilibrium represents the case with rents.

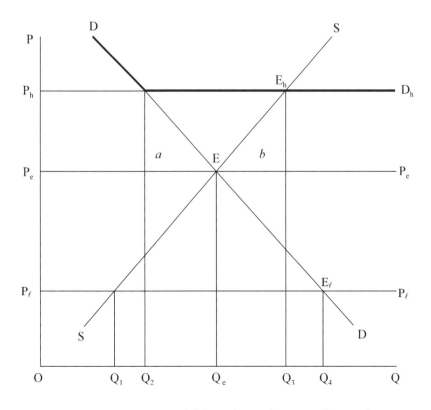

Figure 4.2 Consequences of fixing prices and guaranteeing purchases

111

Table 4.4 Shares of individual products in final agricultural production in 1993 (%)

Products subject to EEC market organizations	EUR 12[c]	Belgium	Denmark	Germany[c]	Greece[c]	Spain	France	Ireland	Italy	Luxembourg	Netherlands	Portugal[c]	United Kingdom
Wheat	6.2	2.7	8.4	5.0	4.3	3.8	7.6	1.4	4.8	2.0	0.8	1.6	10.8
Rye	0.1	0.0	0.7	0.9	0.0	0.1	0.0	0.0	0.0	0.1	0.0	0.3	0.0
Oats	0.1	0.0	0.2	0.0	0.0	0.1	0.1	0.2	0.1	0.3	0.0	0.1	0.3
Barley	1.8	0.7	3.2	2.4	0.3	3.3	2.0	2.1	0.4	2.2	0.2	0.1	3.6
Maize	2.0	0.0	0.0	0.5	3.0	0.6	4.7	0.0	3.4	0.0	0.1	2.1	0.0
Rice	0.4	0.0	0.0	0.0	0.6	0.5	0.1	0.0	1.4	0.0	0.0	1.0	0.0
Sugarbeet	2.4	4.8	2.4	3.7	1.5	2.1	2.9	1.7	1.6	0.0	1.9	0.5	2.1
Tobacco	0.7	0.1	0.0	0.1	5.3	0.5	0.2	0.0	1.0	0.0	0.0	0.5	0.0
Olive oil	1.8	0.0	0.0	0.0	7.9	6.1	0.0	0.0	4.3	0.0	0.0	4.5	0.0
Oilseeds	0.9	0.1	1.4	0.8	0.1	1.2	1.9	0.0	0.5	0.4	0.0	0.2	1.4
Fresh fruit[a]	4.7	3.9	0.5	7.4	7.5	6.7	3.3	0.2	4.8	1.2	1.5	5.0	2.1
Fresh vegetables	9.5	13.6	1.8	3.4	12.8	15.8	7.1	2.7	14.3	1.0	10.8	9.9	7.6
Other fruit and vegetables[b]	1.9	0.1	0.9	0.1	2.5	4.4	1.2	0.0	3.1	0.0	0.1	2.5	0.7
Wine and must	5.7	0.0	0.0	3.8	2.2	2.7	11.4	0.0	7.8	9.4	0.0	5.8	0.0
of which: quality wine	0.0	0.0	0.0	0.0	0.0	0.0	8.3	0.0	0.0	0.0	0.0	0.0	0.0
Seeds	0.6	0.1	0.8	0.5	0.1	0.1	1.7	0.0	0.0	0.0	2.1	0.0	0.3
Textile fibres	0.5	0.1	0.0	0.0	12.2	0.3	0.1	0.0	0.0	0.0	0.0	0.0	0.0
Hops	0.1	0.1	0.0	0.4	0.0	0.0	0.0	0.0	0.0	0.0	0.0	0.0	0.1
Milk	16.6	14.4	25.0	24.0	11.2	7.6	17.9	33.2	11.2	45.5	23.0	13.7	23.9
Beef/veal	12.0	20.0	8.2	14.2	3.3	7.4	15.0	39.1	9.8	27.1	10.7	9.7	14.6
Pigmeat	11.7	19.3	30.9	17.8	3.0	11.3	6.4	5.9	6.8	7.4	13.8	13.9	7.4
Sheepmeat and goatmeat	2.1	0.2	0.1	0.4	6.5	4.8	1.3	5.0	0.7	0.0	0.5	3.4	5.4
Eggs	2.4	3.0	1.2	2.9	2.3	3.1	1.7	0.7	2.5	1.0	3.3	3.2	3.5
Poultry	4.8	3.6	2.5	2.3	2.9	4.5	6.7	3.0	5.8	0.1	3.8	8.6	7.3
Silk worms	0.0	0.0	0.0	0.0	0.0	0.0	0.0	0.0	0.0	0.0	0.0	0.0	0.0
Subtotal	89.0	86.8	88.2	90.6	89.7	87.0	93.3	95.2	84.3	97.7	72.6	86.1	91.1
Products not subject to EEC market organizations													
Potatoes	1.8	3.4	1.4	1.7	2.6	1.9	1.3	1.6	1.2	1.2	1.9	4.7	2.9
Other	9.2	9.8	10.0	7.7	7.7	11.1	5.4	3.2	14.5	1.1	25.5	9.2	6.0
Subtotal	11.0	13.2	11.4	9.4	10.3	13.0	6.7	4.8	15.7	2.3	27.4	13.9	8.9
Grand total	100.0	100.0	100.0	100.0	100.0	100.0	100.0	100.0	100.0	100.0	100.0	100.0	100.0
Value in million ECUs	197,563	6,357	6,058	26,215	8,486	17,003	43,997	4,419	31,272	196	15,222	3,934	18,002

Source: EC (1995), *The Agricultural Situation in the European Union, 1994 Report*. EC: Brussels
Notes: [a]These are products listed in Annex II of Regulation (EEC) No 1035/72. [b]Dried pulses, citrus fruit. [c]1992

Shares of member states in the final agricultural output of products that are subject to the CAP and the ones that are outside the EU 'market organization' in 1993 are given in Table 4.4. The largest producers of farm goods in the EU are France, Italy, Germany, Britain and Spain in declining order. Those five countries jointly produced more than two-thirds of the value of the entire farm output. Being large countries in the region, their hefty shares do not come as a surprise. The Netherlands is a relatively small country in the EU, but it contributed over 8 per cent to the value of total EU farm output, just a little less than the contribution of Britain or Spain. Hence, even a small and highly efficient country received relatively large benefits from the CAP.

The commodity structure of the farm output in the EU for 1992 is given in Table 4.5. The striking feature of the output structure was relative high concentration on a few products. Out of 25 commodities that are subject to the CAP 'market organization' only three products (milk, beef/veal and pork), contribute 40 per cent to the total farm output, while 22 others include most of the rest. Because of the climate, the production of the 'three commodities' is concentrated in the central and northern countries of the EU.[12] The share of southern countries in the output of these goods was much smaller. None the less, the contribution of southern countries was more pronounced in the output of fresh vegetables.

Apart from vegetables and potatoes, the original six member states of the EU were not self-sufficient[13] in farm products at the time of the establishment of the EU. As a direct consequence of the CAP, as well as progress in technology, the EU reached a high degree of self-sufficiency in almost all temperate zone agricultural products (Table 4.6). Greatest self-sufficiency existed in cereals, sugar and milk-based products. Having reached such a high level of self-sufficiency, attention needs to be paid to the other dimensions of the agricultural sector. One of them is the protection of the environment. A broad use of fertilizers, herbicides and pesticides could increase farm output in the short run, but may downgrade soil and have adverse effects in the medium and long term for the environment. There needs to be greater concern for the impact of farming on the environment (soil, air and water), as well as on the health and growth of plants and animals (not to mention humans) in the future.[14]

The only 'deficit' in the internal production is in fresh and citrus fruits, as well as in maize.[15] This means that the concessions (quotas) that the EU offered to foreign exporters for all other farm goods deal with political issues, rather than with the 'deficit' in internal EU production relative to consumption.

As there are substantial surpluses of farm goods, the EU had to dispose of them in several controversial ways. Milk is sometimes distributed free of charge to schools in order to supply the children with the nutrients necessary for growth, as well as to foster the habit of consuming milk from an early age. Butter is sold at privileged prices to hospitals, army and humanitarian organizations, while the general public was able to enjoy those prices only at Christmas. Cake manufacturers and bakeries might sometimes procure butter at privileged prices in order to reduce the competitive pressure from other fats such as margarine. A portion of the surpluses is donated to poor or crisis-ridden countries as humanitarian aid. Finally and most importantly, surpluses are exported to third countries with refunds (read subsidies). Surpluses of farm goods cannot be freely distributed or constantly sold at reduced prices to domestic consumers. If that were the case, internal EU prices would fall and the

Table 4.5 Shares of individual products in final agricultural production in 1992 (%)

Products subject to EEC market organizations	EUR 12	Belgium	Denmark	Germany	Greece	Spain	France	Ireland	Italy	Luxembourg	Netherlands	Portugal	United Kingdom
Wheat	6.2	3.4	7.5	5.0	5.1	—	10.3	2.2	4.8	2.7	1.0	1.6	11.8
Rye	0.1	0.0	0.7	0.7	0.0	—	0.0	0.0	0.0	0.1	0.0	0.3	0.0
Oats	0.1	0.0	2.5	0.0	0.4	—	2.7	3.1	0.4	0.3	0.2	0.1	0.3
Barley	1.8	0.8	0.1	2.4	0.1	—	0.1	0.3	0.1	2.3	0.0	0.1	4.4
Maize	2.0	0.0	0.0	0.5	3.2	—	4.5	0.0	3.0	0.0	0.0	2.1	0.0
Rice	0.4	0.0	0.0	0.0	0.4	—	0.1	0.0	1.2	0.0	0.0	1.0	0.0
Sugarbeet	2.4	4.6	2.0	3.8	1.6	—	2.6	1.7	1.9	0.0	2.0	0.0	2.3
Tobacco	0.7	0.0	0.0	0.1	7.3	—	0.2	0.0	1.2	0.0	0.0	0.5	0.0
Olive oil	1.8	0.0	0.0	0.0	9.1	—	0.0	0.0	3.4	0.0	0.0	4.5	0.0
Oilseeds	0.9	0.1	1.1	0.9	0.1	—	1.5	0.0	0.7	0.2	0.0	0.8	2.1
Fresh fruit	4.7	5.1	0.4	5.7	7.9	—	2.9	0.3	7.6	0.9	1.2	5.0	2.1
Fresh vegetables	9.5	12.0	1.8	3.1	12.7	—	6.3	2.9	15.2	1.0	11.0	9.8	7.5
Other fruit and vegetables	1.9	0.0	1.1	0.1	2.8	—	1.9	0.0	4.9	0.0	0.1	2.5	1.0
Wine and must	5.7	0.0	0.0	3.9	1.7	—	12.4	0.0	8.9	13.2	0.0	5.8	0.0
Quality wine	0.0	0.0	0.0	0.0	0.0	—	9.0	0.0	0.0	0.0	0.0	0.0	0.0
Seeds	0.6	0.1	0.7	0.4	0.1	—	1.2	0.0	0.0	0.0	2.0	0.0	0.3
Textile fibres	0.5	0.1	0.0	—	9.3	—	0.0	0.0	0.0	0.0	0.0	0.0	0.0
Hops	0.1	0.0	0.0	0.4	0.0	—	0.0	0.0	0.0	0.0	0.0	0.0	0.1
Milk	16.6	14.3	23.6	24.8	8.7	—	16.2	32.1	11.4	42.4	22.0	13.6	21.8
Beef/veal	12.0	18.4	8.4	14.7	3.1	—	14.5	37.6	8.6	25.2	10.6	9.6	13.7
Pigmeat	11.7	25.1	35.0	18.4	3.6	—	7.4	6.5	7.0	7.9	17.8	13.8	8.0
Sheepmeat and goatmeat	2.1	0.1	0.1	0.4	8.0	—	1.2	4.5	0.7	0.0	0.5	3.4	4.9
Eggs	2.4	2.4	1.0	3.0	2.7	—	1.6	0.7	2.3	0.9	3.1	3.2	3.2
Poultry	4.8	3.1	2.3	2.4	2.9	—	6.3	3.2	5.2	0.1	3.6	8.5	6.7
Silk worms	—	—	—	—	0.0	—	0.0	0.0	0.0	0.0	0.0	0.0	0.0
Subtotal	88.9	89.7	88.4	90.6	90.8	—	94.2	95.1	88.4	96.8	75.2	86.3	90.2
Products not subject to EEC market organizations													
Potatoes	1.8	1.9	1.9	1.8	1.9	—	0.9	1.7	1.5	1.3	2.3	4.7	3.6
Other	9.3	8.4	9.7	7.6	7.3	—	4.9	3.2	11.7	1.5	22.4	9.0	6.2
Subtotal	11.1	10.3	11.6	9.4	9.2	—	5.8	4.9	13.2	2.8	24.8	13.7	9.8
Grand total	100.0	100.0	100.0	100.0	100.0	—	100.0	100.0	100.0	100.0	100.0	100.0	100.0
Value in Million ECUs	197,563	6,559	6,459.0	26,722	8,616.0	—	44,905	4,420	37,793	189	16,012	3,577	18,471

Source: EC (1994), *The Agricultural Situation in the Community, 1993 Report.* EC: Luxembourg

Table 4.6 Self-sufficiency in select agricultural products (%)

Product	Year	EU	Belgium/Luxembourg	Denmark	Germany	Greece	Spain	France	Ireland	Italy	Netherlands	Portugal	United Kingdom
Cereals	1985–6	110	54	117	94	104	83	201	90	80	28	33	120
	1991–2	120	51	151	114	93	99	226	104	84	28	51	124
	1992–3	120	54	113	114	114	99	249	98	92	29	34	125
Fresh vegetables	1985–6	107	116	70	37	157	131	91	81	125	204	144	63
	1991–2	106	124	55	38	143	117	89	80	119	253	121	88
	1992–3	106	140	55	38	157	117	89	83	123	254	123	88
Fresh fruit (excluding citrus fruit)	1985–6	87	61	38	53	125	116	89	15	128	57	95	22
	1991–2	85	40	20	22	171	94	86	15	114	63	84	19
	1992–3	85	81	20	22	122	94	86	14	117	63	78	19
Citrus fruit	1985–6	75	0	0	0	163	299	3	0	113	0	100	0
	1991–2	71	0	0	0	177	231	3	0	106	0	88	0
	1992–3	70	0	0	0	145	231	2	0	106	0	88	0
Wine	1985–6	104	68	0	57	119	118	108	0	121	0	113	0
	1991–2	115	38	0	88	139	118	93	0	114	0	123	0
	1992–3	115	119	8	88	120	117	113	0	127	0	117	0
Potatoes	1985–6	101	108	98	99	108	100	101	87	96	146	94	92
	1991–2	100	146	95	92	92	94	100	77	84	164	72	92
	1992–3	100	142	88	92	99	100	105	83	91	135	90	92
Sugar	1985–6	123	227	220	130	97	109	203	145	81	153	2	56
	1991–2	128	224	223	141	92	89	213	173	94	197	1	53
	1992–3	128	222	189	141	88	79	235	150	116	167	1	65
Fresh milk products (excluding cream)	1985	102	124	105	104	98	99	111	100	97	93	100	100
	1991	102	134	104	113	97	97	103	101	96	88	90	98
	1992	102	140	103	113	95	97	102	101	95	86	99	98
Whole-milk powder	1985	316	239	2,517	140	33	106	721	2767	13	573	92	234
	1991	272	238	10,800	136	61	92	569	2,400	9	653	100	155
	1992	272	211	10,300	136	0	99	500	3,100	9	2,667	120	150
Butter	1985	110	120	183	121	56	155	118	484	57	444	104	74
	1991	121	99	165	96	27	170	98	1,255	75	248	108	60
	1992	121	101	194	96	29	180	92	1,233	76	510	131	54
Meat (total)	1985	102	122	324	91	70	97	100	270	74	240	97	81
	1991	102	150	319	90	71	96	105	299	73	230	90	87
	1992	102	152	329	90	66	97	107	299	75	231	88	85
Beef	1985	107	130	324	118	35	95	119	655	62	200	87	87
	1991	108	178	213	120	32	95	119	977	62	173	76	92
	1992	107	196	205	123	25	102	127	992	65	138	70	83
Pork	1985	102	145	370	87	71	97	81	116	71	270	97	71
	1991	104	180	381	86	73	97	88	126	67	280	91	72
	1992	104	178	414	86	65	98	91	126	65	278	88	75
Oils and fats	1985	63	31	93	49	129	98	63	62	52	32	36	28
	1991	70	37	99	65	117	80	82	59	42	33	30	34
	1992	70	30	99	65	117	80	82	59	42	33	3	2

Source: EC (1995), The Agricultural Situation in the Community, 1994 Report. EC: Brussels

whole CAP intervention system would collapse. As part of the reform package, the cost of handling surpluses in the future may fall on the national, rather than the EU budget.

4.2 Consequences for farmers

The best answer to whether the CAP helps a farmer to begin agricultural production, remain in it or leave farming altogether would be to consider the situation when there was no CAP. Such a comparison would, however, be uncertain, difficult and dubious. None the less, there are certain ways, though full of methodological pitfalls, to compare wages in different sectors.

A comparison between incomes in the farm and manufacturing sectors is difficult and unreliable. Most of the farmers live in the countryside where rents are lower than in urban areas. Residents in the cities have higher outlays for clothes and footwear, as well as for transportation relative to farmers who may live close to their farms. Farmers are sometimes said to live poor, but die rich. For the years for which the comparable set of data was available, the income of the average *farm* household exceeded that of the average of *all* households in all member states apart from Portugal. In the Netherlands, for example, the income of a farm household was twice as high as that of the average household. Comparison of *averages* is contro-

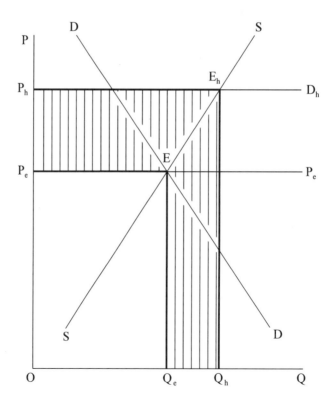

Figure 4.3 Income of farmers in the European Union

versial and it is coupled with problems such as concealed deviations that exist in the data regarding both the level and source of income. For instance, in Germany in 1981, 4 per cent of all farm households had incomes of less than a half of the average income of all households, while 5 per cent of the agricultural households had income that was more than double the national average (Frohberg, 1994, p. 183)!

A graphical illustration of the income of farmers is given in Figure 4.3. DD and SS present demand and supply, respectively, for a farm good subject to the CAP 'market organization'. Free market equilibrium is at E, but if the CAP fixes price at P_h, then the new equilibrium is at E_h. If quantity is multiplied by price, the income of farmers equals rectangle $OP_hE_hQ_h$. In a free market situation the income of farmers would equal a smaller rectangle OP_eEQ_e. The difference between the two rectangles is the shaded area that equals income subsidies that EU farmers receive from the CAP.

Half or all farm holdings in the EU were relatively small (up to 5 ha) in 1989 (Table 4.7). Those small holdings were most widespread in the southern countries (Club Med). The share of small holdings was highest in Portugal (74 per cent), Greece (70 per cent), Italy (67 per cent) and Spain (55 per cent). Large farms, those over 50 ha, predominated in Britain (34 per cent) and Luxembourg (30 per cent), while in most of the other countries the farm area was mostly concentrated around the average size of units that had 20–50 ha.

The general farm support provided by the CAP is in a sense one-sided. It favours output in the northern regions of the EU where the production is large-scale, it takes place on large farms and it is based on goods of animal origin and on certain cereals. In the southern regions, however, crops predominate that do not have such a large share in the CAP expenditure as 'northern' products. In addition, they are produced on small farms. Therefore, the owners of large farms in the north of the EU derive the greatest benefits from the CAP. This structure of farm support is far from the goal of ensuring 'a fair standard of living for the agricultural community'.

4.3 Consequences for consumers

One of the achievements of the CAP was the security of food supplies from domestic production. If the origin of farm commodities is put aside, then the security of food supplies could be achieved in a cheaper way. For example, agricultural goods could be purchased abroad where they are cheaper compared with prices in the EU. The outlays for storage in the EU would be the same for an identical quantity of goods, but there would be a saving equal to the difference in the value of the stored goods, as the ones purchased in the foreign markets are cheaper than the ones available from EU domestic production.

The CAP system of variable levies and guaranteed purchases at specified prices for agricultural goods aims at supporting the income of farmers. The deficiency-payment system, like that used in Britain prior to the entry into the EU in 1973, supports the income of consumers. The CAP system, not only increases the cost of food and taxes (national contributions to the EU budget), but also increases production expenditure, as a part of wages is influenced by the cost of food. None the less, producer prices of farm goods in the EU have not risen faster than consumer prices for food! During the period 1985–1991, the annual rate of change of producer prices for *agricultural*

Table 4.7 Number and area of holdings in the EU in 1980, 1987 and 1989

	Farm size class (ha UAA)[a]	Holdings × 1,000			% of total	
		1980	1987	1989	1987	1989
EUR 12	1–5	—	3,411.0	3,173.1	49.2	49.3
	5–10	—	1,163.0	1,038.7	16.8	16.1
	10–20	—	936.0	848.3	13.5	13.2
	20–50	—	946.0	894.8	13.7	13.9
	⩾50	—	473.0	483.4	6.8	7.5
	Total	—	6,929.0	6,438.3	100.0	100.0
Belgium	1–5	25.9	21.8	20.1	27.7	27.5
	5–10	18.1	14.3	12.7	18.1	17.4
	10–20	24.3	19.3	16.8	24.5	22.9
	20–50	19.1	18.8	18.7	23.9	25.5
	⩾50	3.8	4.6	4.9	5.8	6.7
	Total	91.2	78.8	73.3	100.0	100.0
Denmark	1–5	12.9	1.5	1.3	1.7	1.6
	5–10	20.5	14.0	12.1	16.3	15.1
	10–20	30.8	21.8	20.1	25.3	25.0
	20–50	40.4	33.9	31.3	39.4	38.9
	⩾50	11.8	14.8	15.6	17.2	19.4
	Total	116.3	86.0	80.4	100.0	100.0
Germany	1–5	275.8	196.9	183.1	29.4	29.0
	5–10	149.1	118.4	108.4	17.6	17.2
	10–20	181.3	148.5	134.6	22.1	21.3
	20–50	177.9	166.2	159.8	24.8	25.3
	⩾50	31.3	40.7	45.6	6.1	7.2
	Total	797.4	670.7	631.5	100.0	100.0
Greece	1–5	541.3	488.0	478.1	69.4	70.0
	5–10	149.9	140.7	130.1	20.0	19.0
	10–20	46.6	53.5	53.8	7.6	7.9
	20–50	12.4	17.5	18.0	2.5	2.6
	⩾50	1.6	3.8	3.2	0.5	0.5
	Total	751.8	703.5	683.2	100.0	100.0
Spain	1–5	849.5	821.1	750.4	53.3	54.7
	5–10	274.2	292.0	244.7	19.0	17.8
	10–20	183.1	189.5	165.7	12.3	12.1
	20–50	132.8	144.6	124.9	9.4	9.1
	⩾50	84.4	92.7	87.0	6.0	6.3
	Total	1,524.0	1,539.9	1,372.7	100.0	100.0
France	1–5	234.0	166.0	187.9	18.2	20.3
	5–10	165.5	107.2	113.9	11.7	12.3
	10–20	240.0	174.7	163.3	19.1	17.6

Farm size class (ha UAA)[a]	Holdings × 1,000			% of total	
	1980	1987	1989	1987	1989
20–50	345.0	299.2	288.3	32.8	31.2
⩾50	151.0	164.7	172.1	18.1	18.6
Total	1,135.0	911.8	925.5	100.0	100.0
Ireland 1–5	33.9	34.9	17.6	16.1	10.5
5–10	35.4	32.9	24.1	15.2	14.3
10–20	67.7	63.3	48.3	29.2	28.8
20–50	66.6	66.3	58.4	30.5	34.8
⩾50	19.7	19.5	19.6	9.0	11.6
Total	223.3	216.9	168.0	100.0	100.0
Italy 1–5	1,312.3	1,340.1	1,170.2	67.9	67.4
5–10	322.3	333.0	284.3	16.9	16.4
10–20	166.8	171.3	155.2	8.7	9.0
20–50	86.9	91.6	87.6	4.6	5.0
⩾50	38.0	38.0	38.4	1.9	2.2
Total	1,926.3	1,974.0	1,735.7	100.0	100.0
Luxembourg 1–5	0.9	0.7	0.7	18.9	19.1
5–10	0.5	0.4	0.4	9.9	9.7
10–20	0.7	0.5	0.4	12.4	11.6
20–50	1.8	1.2	1.1	32.5	29.4
⩾50	0.8	1.0	1.1	26.2	30.2
Total	4.7	3.8	3.6	100.0	100.0
Netherlands 1–5	31.0	29.2	27.8	24.9	24.8
5–10	26.1	21.6	21.5	18.4	19.1
10–20	37.3	29.3	25.4	25.0	22.6
20–50	30.8	32.0	31.6	27.3	28.1
⩾50	3.8	5.2	6.0	4.4	5.4
Total	129.0	117.3	112.3	100.0	100.0
Portugal 1–5	272.4	278.4	309.2	72.5	74.4
5–10	43.9	57.8	56.1	15.0	13.5
10–20	18.3	27.5	27.4	7.2	6.6
20–50	8.7	12.9	13.6	3.4	3.3
⩾50	6.2	7.4	9.3	1.9	2.2
Total	349.5	384.0	415.6	100.0	100.0
United Kingdom 1–5	29.4	32.8	26.7	13.5	11.3
5–10	31.2	30.2	30.5	12.4	12.9
10–20	39.8	37.1	37.4	15.3	15.8
20–50	67.6	61.8	60.7	25.4	25.7
⩾50	81.3	81.0	81.0	33.3	34.3
Total	249.2	242.9	236.3	100.0	100.0

Source: EC (1994), *The Agricultural Situation in the Community, 1993 Report*. EC: Luxembourg
Note: [a] Utilized agricultural area

119

products was 2.8 per cent, while the same rate of consumer prices for *foodstuffs*[16] and beverages was 4.5 per cent.[17]

One of the objectives of the CAP, as specified by the Treaty of Rome, is that supplies have to 'reach consumers at reasonable prices'. However, 'reasonable prices' are not defined by the Treaty. 'Reasonable prices' change their meaning, not only across the different income groups of consumers, but also over time. There is statistical evidence that the prices of farm goods in the EU were increasing at a slower rate than the incomes of consumers. None the less, one may not infer from these relative changes that consumers were supplied at 'reasonable' prices. The prices of agricultural products subject to the CAP 'market organization' are on the same level as the highest ones for farm goods – those that prevail on the German market, the country that is one of the wealthiest in the EU. In addition, there is a weak correlation between the price of agricultural goods at the farm gate and the retail prices of food for final consumers (the base good passes through a chain of transformation, value is added, in addition to the costs of marketing and distribution). Hence, a comparison between the two prices is subject to a great deal of methodological difficulties.

The CAP has created social problems too. The groups of the population with the lowest incomes (the poor, the students and the retired) have relatively the highest expenditure on food. One can find here one of the greatest controversies of the CAP. It is the income transfer from the poor consumers to the rich farmers! In fact, the major beneficiaries of the CAP include large farmers;[18] those who transport, store and trade in surplus products; and all bureaucrats (mostly in the national offices) that deal with the CAP.

4.4 Consequences for foreign countries[19]

Protecting the income of farmers in the EU is achieved, among other ways, by restricting foreign competition in the EU market. That is done by the employment of an efficient and flexible system of variable levies on imports of agricultural products. None the less, the EU is at the same time the largest importer of agricultural commodities in the world. On the export side, the EU is (together with the US) the largest exporter of farm items. As such, it influences the quantity and structure of international production, prices and trade in farm goods.

The EU has an undisputed impact on the price of farm goods because of its large share in the world trade in these commodities. While exporting farm commodities abroad, the EU applies a refund (subsidy) that bridges the difference between the higher prices for farm goods prevailing on the EU market and the lower prices at which those goods are sold to foreign partners. If one defines dumping as sales of domestic goods to foreign partners at prices below those on the domestic market (minus the sales tax) and/or at prices below the costs of production, then the CAP system of refunds represents a textbook example of dumping. Such sales distort international specialization, because more efficient producers than those in the EU are denied export markets, as well as sales. Until the conclusion of the Uruguay Round, however, trade in agricultural goods was outside of the scope of the GATT. Thus, little could be done about EU farm-trade policy.

Tables 4.8 and 4.9, respectively, list major partners in agricultural trade of the EU during the 1991–1993 period. On the exports side, major customers for EU goods

Table 4.8 Principal customer countries for agricultural and food exports of the EU (12), 1991–1993 (ECUs millions)

No.	Main client countries (based on 1993)	Exports			Corresponding imports			Trade balance		
		1991	1992	1993	1991	1992	1993	1991	1992	1993
1	United States	4,483	4,646	4,819	7,177	7,711	7,367	−2,693	−3,064	−2,548
2	Russia	0	1,222	2,961	0	455	808	0	767	2,153
3	Switzerland	2,785	2,721	2,717	993	1,029	1,043	1,792	1,692	1,674
4	Japan	2,501	2,523	2,702	221	182	157	2,280	2,341	2,545
5	Austria	1,676	1,728	1,788	1,272	1,298	1,197	404	430	591
6	Sweden	1,633	1,718	1,663	1,643	1,750	1,738	−10	−32	−75
7	Saudi Arabia	1,235	1,303	1,133	16	10	29	1,218	1,293	1,104
8	Poland	1,027	959	1,125	1,216	1,150	1,016	−190	−191	109
9	Hong Kong	854	984	1,124	49	52	69	805	932	1,055
10	Canary Islands	1,018	1,082	1,096	1,025	1,024	1,260	−6	58	−164
11	Algeria	909	866	922	22	28	27	887	838	895
12	Canada	842	834	876	1,579	1,496	1,352	−737	−661	−476
13	Norway	621	675	722	1,401	1,604	1,525	−780	−929	−803
14	Egypt	432	444	673	148	131	133	284	312	540
15	Taiwan	351	426	560	81	95	91	269	331	470
16	Libya	413	364	500	3	4	9	410	360	491
17	Finland	512	518	497	907	927	1,001	−395	−409	−505
18	Turkey	311	322	470	1,253	1,151	1,194	−942	−830	−724
19	United Arab Emirates	438	420	470	7	4	6	430	416	464
20	Mexico	324	496	458	248	218	204	77	278	254
21	Czech Republic	0	15	454	0	0	322	0	15	133
22	Australia	393	407	408	1,290	1,476	1,140	−897	−1,070	−733
23	Singapore	328	366	380	153	158	163	175	208	217
24	Israel	312	303	371	755	735	593	−443	−431	−222
25	Hungary	187	240	354	994	913	780	−807	−673	−425
	Total of 25 countries (A)	23,585	25,582	29,245	22,454	23,600	23,225	1,130	1,982	6,021
	Total of third countries (B)	35,983	38,759	41,803	56,866	56,871	54,599	−20,883	−18,112	−12,796
	% A/B	65.5	66.0	70.0						

Source: EC (1995), The Agricultural Situation in the European Union, 1994 Report. EC: Brussels

Table 4.9 Principal supplier countries for agricultural and food imports of the EU (12), 1991–1993 (ECUs millions)

No.	Main supplier countries (based on 1993)	Imports			Corresponding exports			Trade balance		
		1991	1992	1993	1991	1992	1993	1991	1992	1993
1	United States	7,177	7,711	7,367	4,483	4,646	4,819	−2,694	−3,064	−2,548
2	Brazil	3,896	4,158	4,146	333	199	285	−3,563	−3,959	−3,861
3	Argentina	3,172	2,729	2,496	82	122	166	−3,091	−2,607	−2,330
4	Sweden	1,643	1,750	1,738	1,633	1,718	1,663	−10	−32	−75
5	Thailand	1,593	2,038	1,609	272	296	348	−1,321	−1,742	−1,260
6	Norway	1,401	1,604	1,525	621	675	722	−780	−929	−804
7	China	1,494	1,440	1,422	298	196	155	−1,196	−1,244	−1,267
8	Canada	1,579	1,496	1,352	842	835	876	−736	−661	−476
9	Malaysia	1,236	1,264	1,276	166	157	187	−1,070	−1,107	−1,088
10	Ivory Coast	1,419	1,341	1,270	177	175	190	−1,241	−1,166	−1,080
11	Indonesia	1,126	1,195	1,269	79	102	115	−1,047	−1,092	−1,154
12	Canary Islands	1,025	1,024	1,260	1,019	1,082	1,096	−6	58	−164
13	New Zealand	1,211	1,193	1,209	52	52	63	−1,160	−1,141	−1,147
14	Austria	1,272	1,298	1,197	1,676	1,728	1,788	404	430	591
15	Turkey	1,253	1,151	1,194	311	322	470	−942	−830	−724
16	Australia	1,290	1,476	1,141	393	407	408	−897	−1,070	−733
17	Switzerland	993	1,029	1,043	2,785	2,721	2,717	1,792	1,692	1,674
18	Poland	1,216	1,150	1,016	1,027	959	1,125	−190	−191	109
19	Finland	907	927	1,001	512	518	497	−395	−409	−505
20	Colombia	1,109	1,040	996	27	37	50	−1,082	−1,002	−946
21	Russia	0	455	808	0	1,222	2,961	0	767	2,153
22	South Africa	1,095	993	789	216	220	212	−878	−773	−577
23	Hungary	994	913	780	187	240	354	−807	−673	−426
24	Morocco	919	809	770	267	330	301	−651	−479	−469
25	India	678	654	750	33	66	59	−644	−588	−690
	Total of 25 countries (A)	39,697	40,835	39,425	17,490	19,023	21,630	−22,207	−21,812	−17,795
	Total of third countries (B)	56,866	56,871	54,599	35,983	38,759	41,803	−20,883	−18,112	−12,796
	% A/B	69.8	71.8	72.2						

Source: EC (1995), The Agricultural Situation in the European Union, 1994 Report. EC: Brussels

were the US, Russia, Switzerland, Japan, Austria and Sweden. Those six countries together absorbed 56 per cent of the entire exports of agricultural goods and food items in 1993. The commodity structure of exports was dominated in declining order by the following items in 1991: beverages and tobacco; cereals; milk and eggs; fruits and vegetables; and meat. On the imports side, the major suppliers of the EU were the US, Brazil, Argentina, Sweden, Thailand and Norway. Those six countries supplied 47 per cent of all EU imports in 1993. The commodity structure of imports was roughly in line with 'shortages' of farm goods at the EU market. It was dominated in declining order in 1991 by: fruits and vegetables; fish; timber and cork; coffee, cocoa, tea and spices; animal feed; oilseeds; and beverages and tobacco. The overall trade balance in agricultural and food products was in deficit. During the 1991–1993 period, the annual deficit was around ECU 15 billion. The highest deficit in farm trade was with Brazil, the US, Argentina, Thailand, China and the Ivory Coast. Those six countries jointly accounted for more than two-thirds of the deficit in 1993. Considerable surpluses in the farm and foods trade were accumulated in the same year with Japan, Russia, Switzerland, Saudi Arabia and Hong Kong.

In spite of relatively substantial imports and exports (ECU 55 billion and ECU 41 billion, respectively, in 1993) of agricultural and food commodities of the EU, imports of those items would be higher and exports lower if the EU were without the CAP. The foreign countries that are hardest hit by the CAP are important food producers and exporters of goods that compete with the products covered by the CAP 'market organization'. They include the US, Australia, New Zealand, Brazil, Argentina and the transition countries of central and eastern Europe. As such, the CAP hinders unimpeded international division of labour and specialization. An increase in the prices of farm goods in the EU provokes an increase in production and supply, as well as a partial reduction in domestic consumption per capita. As a consequence, there is an increase in exports from the EU and a fall in imports into the EU. Hence, the prices of farm goods fall on the international markets. The countries that export farm goods are adversely affected by the CAP,[20] while the ones that are food importers benefit from the CAP. That is the main reason why an international front of developing countries against the CAP has never been established.

VI REFORMS

After the setting up of the CAP and the display of its trade-diverting effects, together with its large budgetary expenditure, it became obvious that the CAP had to be reformed. The first reform was proposed by the Commissioner, Sicco Mansholt, in 1968. The *Mansholt Plan* encompassed a set of proposals that should have changed the shape of the CAP by 1980. The Plan suggested an increase in the size of holdings, their specialization and modernization, withdrawal of 5 million hectares of land from farming for afforestation and recreational purposes, as well as a reduction in the number of those employed in the EU(6) farming from 10 million in 1968 to 5 million in 1980 (this would be achieved by an early retirement system for older farmers and the retraining of others). There were various reasons why the plan was not accepted. These included a 'mechanical' approach to the agricultural sector; there were no annual rates at which the change had to take place; it was too radical and hence politically dangerous to implement; and it was without foresight on what would take place after 1980. The Plan was much more radical than its successors, which were more modest in their aims, as the Commission 'learned the lesson' from the Council's rejection of the proposals for an extensive overhaul. None the less, the *Mansholt Plan* presented early ideas about how to change the CAP.

In spite of the rejection of the *Mansholt Plan*, the Commission continued with its aspirations to reform the CAP. These attempts, although on a less ambitious scale, were embodied in the various papers from 1973 to 1985 that were often much more analytical than original regarding the reform. The ideas about reforms coincided with a period of big change in the international market (two oil crises). A restructuring of the economy featured high on the agenda, while a substantial reform of the CAP was left for another time. In addition, once established, the CAP has demonstrated its strong resilience to profound change.

There was, however, a good opportunity to alter the CAP. It was after the first enlargement of the EU in 1973 that brought in Britain, Denmark and Ireland. As a large importer of food, Britain would be a net contributor to the EU budget. Therefore, the expectation was that this would prompt Britain to support a reduction in the CAP price support. In addition, the enlargement made the EU an important player in the world market for agricultural goods. However, the CAP remained basically unaltered. As a result, self-sufficiency in most of the goods covered increased and EU farm expenditure doubled between 1975 and 1985.

Throughout the 1980s, the CAP was in continuous crises. This was not only because of the growing surpluses in all major farm products, but also because of a rapid increase in expenditure. Being aware of the problem, the EU implemented various measures during that decade. None the less, they had only a very limited impact on the alleviation of the major CAP problems of costs and surpluses. The measures included *co-responsibility levies*. These levies on the production of sugar had existed since the start of the CAP. Their goal was to make producers of sugar bear a part of the CAP expenditure on this commodity, as well as to reduce production. Levies were charged on the production of milk in 1977 and cereals in 1986. In practice, the burden of the levy was passed on to the consumers. *Guaranteed thresholds* on cereals reduced support prices for the year to come if production surpassed the agreed level. However, the pre-set production quotas were placed on relatively high levels so their actual impact was quite limited. The experience with *marketing quotas* for milk was similar. *Product diversification*, such as conversion of production from milk to beef, also had limited results. The same happened with the *subsidies on domestic consumption*, with the addition of fraud in the distribution of funds.

The first real reform of the CAP since its inception took place in 1992 with the Plan by Commissioner Raymond MacSharry. The amendments to the CAP were not as profound as many economists would have liked. In addition, its coverage of farm products was limited. The reform was not directly linked to the EU internal market programme (1992), but rather to internal financial strain and to external events (the inclusion of agriculture in the Uruguay Round). The main features of the *MacSharry Reform* include reduction in prices for cereals and beef in order to bring them closer to the levels that prevail on the world market, as well as the use of compensatory payments, subject to the reduction in the number of livestock and the area sown in the period 1993–1996. The goal is to shift the CAP from the support and control of prices on the internal market to direct payments to farmers as a compensation for lower prices. The specific points of the reform include:

- Intervention prices for most of the products are to be reduced by 33 per cent. Farmers are to receive compensatory payments if they set 15 per cent of the (productive) cereal land aside. Smaller farmers are to get compensations without conditions.[21] This element decouples output levels from compensations. If farmers set aside[22] 15 per cent of their land, that would not be translated directly into an identical drop in output, but rather to a smaller one. That is because the farmers would not put aside their most productive land.[23] Compensation would be paid from the EU budget. However, this type of common financing would be phased out and passed on to the national governments and budgets over a period of 10 years. The national fiscal authorities would be entitled to continue with such handouts, but which must follow the competition rules of the EU.
- Intervention prices for beef and veal are to be reduced by 15 per cent. The major fall in the prices for beef and veal would come from a fall in feed prices.
- Elimination of price support for oilseeds and protein crops.
- Intervention prices for butter are to be reduced by 15 per cent.
- There are few changes in the systems for the production of pigs, poultry, wine and sugar.
- Compensation for an early retirement of farmers over 55 years old.
- A farm environmental package was supposed to aid chemical-free production and the use of land for the protection of nature, afforestation and leisure.

The *MacSharry Reform* is supposed to introduce at least two kinds of gains to the EU. First, a reduction in prices would diminish incentives to overproduce and, second, a fall in prices would eliminate a part of the tax that is paid by consumers. The problem with this reform is that it benefits farmers that have below-average yields, while it offers a disincentive to those that are farming efficiently. In fact, the reform 'penalizes' large and efficient farmers.

The reform was presented by the EU as an exclusively 'internal' matter. It was, however, a big concession to the Uruguay Round partners. Following a long stalemate in negotiations, the *MacSharry Reform* was enough to get the Uruguay Round re-started. Some of the negotiating partners, such as Japan, thought the reform went too far, while others, such as the Cairns Group, considered that it offered little.[24] In short, the farm deal of the Uruguay Round required a conversion of NTBs affecting agricultural products into tariff equivalents (tariffication) and their reduction by 36 per cent over six years; tariffs should be prohibited from increases in the future; new NTBs should not be introduced in the future; domestic subsidies should be lowered by 20 per cent; and direct export subsidies should be reduced by 36 per cent during the period 1995–2000. *If* prices fall and *if* the domestic EU production drops and *if*, at the same time, domestic demand increases, the reform may bring some gains to the foreign exporters.

VII COMMON FISHERIES POLICY

Fishing was not a significant economic activity in the original six member states of the EU. Article 38 of the Treaty of Rome includes fish in the definition of agricultural products. That is the only primary legal source for this policy in the EU. The fisheries industry is distinct, not only because of changes in the volume of catch, but also because the catch is heterogeneous and perishable. It is also linked with regional issues, as those employed in this industry are in areas on the periphery of the EU.

The Second World War interrupted many fishing activities. The consequence was the flourishing of marine fauna. Hence, there was an impression until the 1960s that the seas and oceans were inexhaustible. Fishing fleets were expanding, which led to over-fishing and a failure to replenish certain species of fish. The growth rate of catch started to slow down. The time came for the reappraisal of fisheries. Hence, the EU started to develop its Common Fisheries Policy in the mid-1960s. France was the principal proponent of this policy as its fisheries industry was highly protected. It wanted to preserve certain EU safeguards for domestic fishermen.

The approaching 1973 enlargement of the EU with Britain, Denmark and Ireland[25] would double the Union's catch of fish. This has heated and speeded up the debate about the fisheries policy. The Council adopted the Commission's proposal in 1970 to introduce the Common Fisheries Policy. Although the policy was created, it did not become a reality until more than a decade later. The thrust of the policy was the rule of equal access to EU waters by the Union's fishermen and a free internal market for fish. This was very hard for Norway to accept. The Commission delivered a new set of proposals for the revision of the policy in the mid-1970s. They included the protection of halieutic resources by setting the quotas for the total allowable catches. They would not be defined by commercial, but rather by biologic rules, i.e., there should always be a minimum stock of fish in the sea that could be able to reproduce itself.

In the meantime, the UN Convention on the Law of the Sea (1982) gave international legitimacy to an exclusive economic zone of 200 miles around coastal countries. As a result, fish stocks fell under the authority of the coastal countries. They are in charge of the management of the sea's resources. If this is done in a rational way, that may provide a permanent and significant contribution to the supply of food.[26]

After lengthy negotiations, in particular with Denmark, the Common Fisheries Policy took off the ground in 1983. It covers wider issues than just who fishes, where and how much. The policy is based on the following principles:

- non-discriminatory access to the fishing waters for the EU domestic fishermen (although there is an exclusive zone of 12 miles for the coastal countries, while the balance to 200 miles is open to the EU fishermen);[27]
- conservation of halieutic resources (total allowable catches are calculated for various species);
- market support (the guide price is set by the Commission and when the price falls below the predetermined withdrawal price, supplies may be withdrawn from the market);
- modernization of the fisheries industry; and
- a common approach to foreign countries while negotiating fish deals.

Although the policy is now implemented and Spain and Portugal[28] made a smooth entry into the system, the policy has not yet had a deep impact on the industry compared with the one the CAP had on farming. Overfishing is still a problem. For the policy to operate properly, there needs to be a 'policing' of the arrangements. Surveillance standards vary markedly from one country to another. Hence, the EU established its own Fisheries Inspectorate that is supposed to check the enforcement agencies of the member countries.

VIII CONCLUSION

As agriculture is a special economic and social activity in Europe, it may be unfair to assess its accomplishments by employing free trade criteria. The CAP replaced the various national farm support systems that existed prior to the establishment of the EU. In spite of the controversies created by the CAP, the objectives of the farm policy in the EU, as given in Article 39 of the Treaty of Rome, were largely met by the CAP. The possible exception may be the protection of the income of small farmers mainly located in the south of the EU. The implementation of the CAP brought with it several problems. They include not only highly concentrated and excessively large expenditure from the EU budget, disputes in trade, 'discrimination' between northern and southern products and large and small farmers, but also surpluses in many agricultural goods. Those excess supplies are not cyclical, but rather structural. Because of all those difficulties, the EU has tried to reform the CAP on many occasions. However, the problem was that those 'reforms' were merely attempts to partially adjust a CAP which is full of arbitrary elements based on political compromises. There has never been any intention to dismantle the CAP.[29] That would be politically too explosive. Hence, the past reforms were directed more to the partial alteration of the *form*, rather than the *substance* of the CAP. The only real reform of the CAP since its inception was the one introduced by MacSharry, which observed the historical spirit of the CAP. Although it was not presented officially in such a way, the reform was carried out under external pressure (Uruguay Round). In the future, the CAP will be more and more subject to WTO rules, including those on subsidies.

Future reforms of the CAP, basically aimed at reducing its cost, could lower the burden on taxpayers, reduce consumer prices, ease the possible integration of some of the transition countries with the EU, calm tensions in international trade and reduce environmental damage in Europe.[30] They could follow three possible routes. First, there may be a further and total decoupling of farm output and income support. Second, support may be given only to those that are most in need from the social and economic viewpoint. Third, subsidies given from EU resources may be gradually passed on to the (tight) national budgets. Since nearly 40 per cent of the farmers in the EU have a second job, future welfare of the small farmers would depend more on the health of the local economy and regional development policies than on the CAP.

All future 'support' to the EU farm sector would have to observe more closely the competition rules than was the case in the past. Future rounds of multilateral trade negotiations under the auspices of the WTO will definitely refer to the further liberalization of the farm trade. Regarding the possible 'eastern' enlargement of the EU, it would be simpler to absorb those countries into the EU if the responsibility for the farm sector is passed on to the member countries, rather than kept at the EU level. Without changes in the CAP, the cost of enlargement of the EU with Visegrad countries would cost the EU between ECU 12 and 35 billion a year![31] There are three basic options to ease the possible enlargement of the EU. First, to reform the CAP, second, to delay enlargement and, third, to give the newcomers a long transition period prior to the full integration into the CAP.

Reforms of the CAP that started in 1992 have already achieved certain positive results. For example, EU reserves of unsold cereals, butter and beef have almost disappeared; farm prices and dumping abroad have fallen sharply; and the EU took steps in 1995 to reduce its export subsidies by 21 per cent till 2001, as required by the Uruguay Round deal. Although the EU output was reduced, the EU expenditure on the CAP increased due to the direct income subsidies to both small and large farmers.

NOTES

1 Nearly 40 per cent of those that work in the farm sector have another gainful activity (*European Economy*, 1994a, p. 24).
2 Governments have been intruding in the farm production ever since Joseph advised Pharaoh to hoard grain during seven fat years. In Europe, for example, Corn Laws had protected the British landowners from imports of foreign cereals for two centuries. A liberal movement, supported by the growing number of industrialists prompted parliament to reform the laws in 1846. The countries on the continent followed the British example shortly afterwards. The farm business was prospering as there was a growing demand for meat in the cities. This lasted only some three decades. The war between Germany and France, as well as recession, made most of the countries abandon liberal trade in farm goods. That was the end of the only exposure of the agricultural sector to free trade.
3 The entire territory of Finland is located above the line at which Sweden found that farming was problematic. The frontier of Finland with Russia is 1,200 km long. It is hardly policeable. Therefore, one way of keeping the frontier regions populated is to offer subsidies to the agricultural sector.
4 An elasticity of substitution between certain food items may be pronounced. Examples include margarine and butter or beef and veal. As income increases, the diet pattern may change in favour of higher-quality items.
5 Recall the 'mad cow disease' frenzy in Britain and the subsequent EU ban on imports of British beef in early 1996.
6 At the time of the introduction of the CAP prices for food were relatively high. In addition, consumers had vivid memories about the scarcity of food during the Second World War. Hence, there were no protests when the CAP was introduced.
7 In dealing with the same basic price, but for different commodities, the EU uses different terms. This introduces confusion. For example, the target price for beef and veal is called the guide price, while for tobacco, its name is the norm price. Pork, poultry and eggs are considered to be processed cereals. Producers in foreign countries have access to cereals cheaper than those available in the EU. During the determination of the sluice-gate price (the threshold price) the EU takes into account the low prices for cereals available from foreign exporters. The basic price for pork is tantamount to the target price. The function of the threshold price is played by the preference price for fruits and vegetables.
8 As the DM was revaluing, the MCAs were protecting the income of German farmers.
9 One should not forget that there are national subsidies of various kinds to the farm sector that roughly equal those given by the EU. National subsidies are particularly generous in the field of social security benefits.
10 *Total* transfers to agriculture in the OECD countries were estimated at ECU 293 billion in 1994. The same transfers were ECU 113 billion in the EU, ECU 79 billion in the US and ECU 75 billion in Japan (OECD, 1995, p. 275). They include PSEs, consumer subsidy equivalents and the expenditure of other policies related to agriculture. Such huge subsidies distort international trade, consumption patterns and the allocation of resources.

11 The US uses, among other policy instruments, the Export Enhancement Program and voluntary export restraint arrangements to support domestic production. The research service of the US Department of Agriculture has one of the largest collection of economists in the world. However, the highest paid agricultural economists are not found in those countries with a vibrant farm sector, but rather in Brussels or Tokyo, where there is a dynamic 'farm-subsidy industry' (*The Economist*, A survey of agriculture, 12 December 1992, p. 9).

12 Around a quarter of the largest farm producers in the EU receive up to three-quarters of all CAP-induced support. The high level of support has tended to be capitalized in the value of land and it has stimulated capital-, rather than labour-intensive farm production (Sarris, 1994, p. 115).

13 Self-sufficiency is represented by the ratio of domestic consumption to domestic output.

14 The impact of the CAP on the environment is considered in Chapter 12 on environment policy.

15 Maize was not represented in Table 4.6. The degree of EU self-sufficiency in this commodity was 77 per cent (1985–1986) and 94 per cent (1991–1992).

16 Foodstuffs are processed agricultural goods.

17 EC (1994), *The Agricultural Situation in the Community, 1993 Report*. EC: Luxembourg, pp. T74–T75.

18 Because of the bias of the CAP towards 'northern' farm products, around 80 per cents of CAP outlays go to around 20 per cent of farmers (*European Economy*, 1994a, p. 27).

19 See Chapter 7 on trade policy.

20 Most of the lightly protected countries that export farm products met in Australia in 1986. The circle was named the Cairns Group after the town where the meeting took place. The purpose of the group was to keep the farm trade high on the agenda of the Uruguay Round negotiation. The Cairns Group consists of 14 countries: Argentina, Australia, Brazil, Canada, Chile, Colombia, Fiji, Hungary, Indonesia, Malaysia, the Philippines, New Zealand, Thailand and Uruguay. In spite of the relative smallness of these countries, if taken together, their combined farm output is the largest in the world.

21 Large farmers in Britain opposed such discrimination.

22 'Set aside' is a euphemism for paying farmers not to grow crops. This policy has many drawbacks: it is expensive to administer, as well as requiring constant checking by inspectors and satellites. Whenever there is a disbursement of funds for similar purposes, the system is prone to abuses. For example, a random check of Italian inspectors of farms in Sardinia in 1995 found irregularities. In one case, a farmer collected the cheque and sold his land to five different buyers. In addition, he was shot dead by the police in a shooting incident!

23 Statistically, the average output per unit of cultivated land may increase.

24 For the details of the Uruguay Round deal on farm trade see Chapter 7 on trade policy.

25 Norway was also negotiating with the EU, but later on, the voters declined to approve the deal because of the fisheries policy.

26 The developing countries are the major beneficiaries of the new system.

27 Although this is the ideal, until 1996, there were problems in the access of Spanish and Portuguese boats to the fishing waters of Britain and Ireland. In addition, there was domestic pressure on the British government to withdraw from the Common Fisheries Policy.

28 The entry of the two countries doubled the EU fleet.

29 It took almost 40 years to build the CAP, if one could dismantle it in half that time it may be a success. But remember, it took the EU 25 years to implement reforms proposed by Sicco Mansholt in 1969.

30 The main policy suggestion is that public authorities should stay away from setting prices and should not employ a protectionist policy. If intervention is necessary, it should be only to the extent that is necessary to rectify market failures and profit from positive externalities. The precise balance of policy measures is hard to determine in advance as policymakers are subject to strong and well organized farm lobbies.

31 *The Economist*, 8 July 1995, p. 32.

5

COMPETITION POLICY

I INTRODUCTION

Free market competition provides everyone with the widest opportunities for business and produces the best allocation of resources. By so doing, competition improves efficiency in the use of factors of production. That conclusion has been accepted by the neo-classical economic theory as a truth. It has provided the intellectual backing for competition (anti-trust) policy. Therefore, the EU has its own rules for market behaviour. They refer to the restriction of competition, abuse of the dominant position and state aids. The importance of competition policy was enhanced by the Single Market Programme completed in 1992.

Competition policy is a mixture of two irreconcilable impulses. On the one hand, there is an argument for a concentration of business, which rationalizes production and which benefits from economies of scale. On the other hand, there is a case for anti-trust policy[1] which prevents monopolization and, through increased competition, increases welfare. The challenge for a government is to balance these two tendencies. It needs to keep the best parts of each of the two opposing tendencies, profit from a harmonious equilibrium between allocation and productive efficiency and employ competition policy as a tool for increasing the standard of living.

The discussion starts with the welfare effects of a monopoly, it continues with a consideration of the basic concepts of competition and market structure. A growing awareness of the beneficial influence of competition on innovation is considered in a separate section. As intra-industry trade absorbs a significant proportion of total trade (and influences competition), it is presented in a section of its own. Another section considers competition policy in the EU. The conclusion is that the 1992 Programme instigated a profound reorganization of competitive business structure. It remains to be seen if that would be enough to increase the competitiveness of the EU producers of goods and services on the domestic and international market.

II MONOPOLY

In an ideally competitive market, the marginal revenue (MR) curve of a firm is flat (Figure 5.1). No firm can influence the market price. Each firm is a price taker.[2] Hence, the MR curve of every firm equals market price. In a simple model with linear demand, cost and revenue curves, respectively, the MR curve cuts the horizontal axis OQ (representing the quantity produced) at point E. At that point MR is zero. To the left of E on the horizontal axis, MR is positive and, moving from O to E, *total*

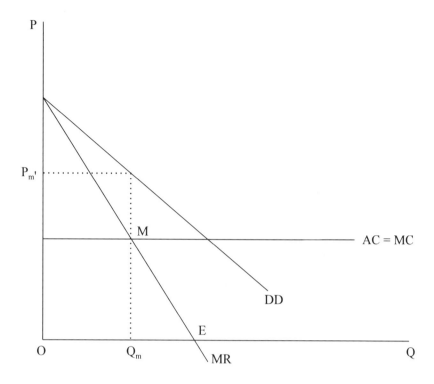

Figure 5.1 Welfare effects of a monopoly

revenue is increasing. To the right of E on the same axis, MR is negative and, moving from E to Q, total revenue is decreasing. At E, total revenue is at maximum.

The market structure of a monopoly is at the opposite end from perfect competition. Entry into such an industry is costly, risky and time consuming although, potentially, highly profitable. While in perfect competition no firm has any power whatever over the market price, a monopoly (an exclusive supplier) has the power to influence the market price of a good or a service if there are no substitutes. To counter this, governments may choose to intervene and prevent/rectify such non-competitive behaviour. That can be done by regulation of the conduct of monopolies and/or by liberalization of imports.[3] If the monopolist wants to maximize total revenue, he would never supply a quantity that is bigger than OE.

With constant returns to scale, average costs are constant, hence the average cost (AC) curve is horizontal. The consequence of this simplification is that marginal costs (MC) equal AC. This permits the finding of the point where profit is at the maximum if demand curve is DD. It is maximized at point M, where MR = MC. At that point, a monopolist produces OQ_m and charges price $OP_{m'}$. The quantity produced is smaller and the price charged by the monopoly is higher than in the case with perfect competition.

This is an obvious, although very simple, example of how a monopoly (or a cartel) undermines the welfare of consumers and allocates resources in a sub-optimal way from the social standpoint. In addition, if left alone, a monopoly is not pressed to do anything about it. Such a safe and quiet life does not force the monopoly to innovate and increase efficiency, as would be the case with free competition. A quiet life could make a monopoly innovation-sluggish in the longer term. None the less, there is a potentially inverted effect in the short run. If a firm thinks that an innovation may bring it a monopoly power, in the short run, that firm would venture into a process that may lead into an innovation. If successful, this *may* bring inertia, less flexibility and reluctance to adjust in the longer term. However, such inflexibilities may not be found only on the side of firms. Labour, in particular labour unions, may pose obstacles and slow down the innovation process. Machines, it may be argued, may destroy jobs.[4] If this were ever true, it may be correct only in the short run. Technological progress and alternative employment, often requiring a superior labour profile, more than compensate for the alleged short-term social loss. Only those that are reluctant to adjust to the new situation suffer. Although technology has advanced rapidly over the past centuries, unemployment has not risen with it. Increases in productivity, output and job openings have risen together over the long term.

If a monopoly exists, one should not rush to the conclusion that its presence *per se* leads to economic inefficiency. It is possible that in industries with high entry barriers, sunk costs and economies of scale (for example, aerospace), a single efficient producer may have a lower monopoly price for the good than would be the price of many inefficient producers in the same industry. In such cases it may not be efficient to break up a concentrated industry. The authorities may more effectively tax excessive profits of firms in such industries and/or make sure that they are reinvested. If the market grows sufficiently, then the authorities need to encourage other, potentially efficient producers, to enter this kind of business.

Policies that were intended to increase competitiveness sometimes produced unexpected results. During the 1950s the US wanted to dismantle large and mighty corporations. So, the government broke up AT&T. Little attention was paid during the debate to the place of Bell Labs and the fact that it had played a major part in innovations in telecommunications over the preceding century. Deregulation of the industry prohibited the US telephone operating companies to manufacture phones or switching equipment. As a result, US exports grew moderately, while imports exploded (Lipsey, 1992, p. 295).

From these examples stem convincing arguments in favour of a competition policy. The intention of this policy is to improve efficiency in the use of factors with the objective of increasing welfare. However, in a real market situation that is full of imperfections (economies of scale, sunk costs, innovation, asymmetric information, etc.) one may easily find arguments in favour of a certain concentration of production (mergers) and protection of intellectual property rights. It may sometimes be argued that it is quite costly to trade intangible technology assets at arm's length. That is because 'it is a combination of skills, equipment and organization embodied in people and institutions as much as in machinery and equipment' (Sharp and Pavitt, 1993, p. 147). If an inventor fears that his patent rights[5] are not sufficiently protected (enforcement, length of the patent right, level of penalties), he would keep the innovation as a secret for himself or create disincentives for R&D in the future. A part of the innovation process may lean towards outcomes that may not be easily imitated. The conflict between the static and dynamic efficiency in production, as well as between the welfare of producers and consumers is obvious. Once technology becomes older and is no longer in the core business activities of the innovator, there is a higher chance that the innovator will spread technology through licensing.

Appropriation of returns from innovation does not create a huge problem if the innovator is a non-profit institution such as a research institute, university or government. Non-profit sources of innovation have the greatest public dimension to their work. The results of their efforts may enter directly the distribution phase of the process. It is estimated that around half of total investment in R&D is financed by the business community and between half and two-thirds of R&D is carried out by private firms (Dosi, 1988, pp. 1123–4). The appropriation problem arises when there is a conflict between public interest in the spread of information and knowledge, and private interest in retaining and employing that knowledge for lucrative purposes. If the private knowledge that may have been acquired through risky investment of resources is not protected, at least for a certain period of time, an unprotected spread of it may remove the valuable incentives for innovation that propel efficiency and, hence, contribute to growth in the future.

An analysis of alternative ways of protecting competitive (monopolistic) advantages of new and improved processes and products, by Levin *et al.* (1987), found that patents are the least effective means for the appropriations of returns. Lead time over competitors, moving fast down the learning curve (unit costs of production fall as output increases over time) and sales/service effort were regarded among the surveyed firms as a superior means for the appropriation of returns than patents. Firms may sometimes refrain from patenting products or processes to avoid the revelation of the actual fact or the details of the innovation, because of the possible disclosure of information to competitors and imitators. At the same time, firms have every incentive to advertise the advantages of new or improved products and disseminate them to consumers. Therefore, secrecy about innovation is both difficult and undesirable. Additional profits can be made by the production of complementary assets. So, not only innovation and manufacturing (technological leadership), but also and equally important, distribution and after-sale service (commercial leadership) are of great advantage in capturing markets and profits. Japanese companies in the business of producing cameras, audio and video goods (and some segments of the passenger car market) have almost ousted most of their international competitors through an uninterrupted tide of technical improvements and distribution/service network.

The benefits of increased competition will materialize only if firms compete and do not collude to avoid competition. Competition stimulates innovation. It may, in turn, bring new technologies with large sunk costs, concentration of production and other entry barriers. If this is the case, then neither markets, nor monopolies (oligopolies) need to be left alone. Otherwise, consumer welfare would be distorted and the allocation of resources may take place in a sub-optimal way from the social standpoint. Hence, the need for a competition policy, not only in the market of a single country, but also in the widest possible area. The rule of law, based in part on economic theory, may modify market distortions.

III CONCEPT

One of the most obvious initial effects of international economic integration is the improvement in efficiency in the use of factors due to increased competition on the enlarged market. The competitiveness of firms has two aspects: national and international. In either case, a competitive firm is the one that is able to make a profit without being protected and/or subsidized. The goods and services of a country are internationally competitive if they can withstand competition on the world market, while, at the same time, the domestic residents keep and increase their average standard of living.

There are three concepts of competitiveness. *Cost competitiveness* relates to the difference (i.e., profit) between the price at which a good is sold and the cost of its production. If a firm is able to reduce production costs by cutting down input prices, by innovating and/or organizing production and distribution in a superior way not available to its competitors, it may improve its relative profit margin. A firm has a *price competitive* product if it matches other firms' products in all characteristics, including price. This type of competitiveness can be improved if the firm unilaterally reduces the price of its good (other things being equal) and/or upgrades its attributes and provides a better service. *Relative profitability* exists when there is the possibility of price discrimination (e.g., domestic and foreign markets). Then the different profit margins in those respective markets indicate relative profitability.

The measurement of competitiveness of an integrated *group* of countries includes the intra-group trade ratio (intra-group export/intra-group import) and extra-group trade ratio (extra-group export/extra-group import). In addition, the competitiveness of an integrated *country's* economic sector (or industries within it) may be measured in the following two ways.

The *trade specialization index* (TSI) provides details about the integrated country j's specialization in exports in relation to other partner countries in the group. If this index for good i is greater than one, country j is specialized in export of good i within the group. TSI (5.1) reveals country j's comparative advantage within the group.

$$\text{TSI} = \frac{\dfrac{X_{i,j}}{X_{\text{ind},j}}}{\dfrac{X_{i,g}}{X_{\text{ind},g}}} \tag{5.1}$$

$X_{i,j}$ = export of *good i* from country j to the partner countries in the integration group
$X_{\text{ind},j}$ = total *industry* exports to the group from country i
$X_{i,g}$ = intra group exports of *good i*
$X_{\text{ind},g}$ = total *industry* exports within the group

The production specialization index (PSI) is identical to the TSI, except for the fact that export (X) variables are replaced by production (P) ones. PSI shows where country j is more specialized in production than its integration partners. This index reveals country j's production advantage, as well as its domestic consumption pattern. Interpretation of both the TSI and the PSI may be distorted if the production and export of the good i in country j is protected/subsidized. The revealed 'advantage' would be misleading as is the case of exports of farm goods from the EU due to the CAP.

Goods that are produced and traded by a country may be categorized by their economic idiosyncrasies. There are five, sometimes overlapping, types of goods (Audretsch, 1993, pp. 94–95):

- The Ricardo goods have a high natural-resource content. Those commodities include minerals, fuels, wood, paper, fibres and food.
- Product-cycle goods include the ones that rely on high technology and where information serves as a crucial input.[6] This group includes chemicals, pharmaceuticals, plastics, dyes, fertilizers, explosives, machinery, aircraft and instruments.
- R&D-intensive goods include industries where R&D expenditure is at least 5 per cent of the sales value. These are pharmaceuticals, office machinery, aircraft and telecom goods.
- High-advertising goods are the ones where advertising expenditures are at least 5 per cent of the sales value. These include drinks, cereals, soaps, perfumes and watches.
- Goods that are produced by high-concentration industries include tobacco, liquid fuels, edible oils, tubes, home appliances, motor vehicles and railway equipment.

These five types of goods were compared among the rich western countries (mainly the OECD), poor western countries (mainly the north Mediterranean countries) and now the transition countries of central and eastern Europe in 1975 and 1983. The findings were as follows. First, in 1975 the western countries had a comparative disadvantage in the Ricardo goods while the other two groups had a comparative advantage. In 1983, the central and east European countries exhibited a comparative disadvantage in Ricardo goods, together with the rich western countries, reflecting their inability to compete with resource-rich developing countries. Second, the rich western countries have a constant comparative advantage in product cycle, R&D-intensive and advertising-intensive goods over the other two groups of countries. Third, the rich western, as well as the central and east European countries have a competitive advantage in highly concentrated industries over the poor western nations (Audretsch, 1993, pp. 95–96).

While competition in goods is more or less global, competition in many services is localized. A big part of competitive activity in manufactured goods has a price component, competition in many services has predominantly a non-price dimension. Reputation and past experience of services often plays a crucial role in deciding about the choice of the supplier of a certain type of service. Local providers of certain types of services, as well as ones with a high (international) reputation have a specific market power. This kind of local market influence of producers of goods is in most cases non-existent, as goods may be (easily) traded. Because of a generally lower degree of competitiveness in the service industries than in the manufacturing ones, as well as because of the protection of consumers, administrative regulation in the services sector is quite high.

The competitiveness of a country's goods and services may be increased through depreciation of a home currency and/or a reduction in wages. The healthiest way to increase competitiveness, however, is to increase productivity. Developing, intermediate and advanced countries trade more or less successfully all over the world. The level of living standard, however, depends on each country's productivity. But the ability to trade depends only on the ability to produce something that is wanted, while the rate of exchange ensures that exports can be sold. This was the message of David Ricardo in the early nineteenth century and is as important (and as little understood) today as it was in Ricardo's time (Lipsey, 1993b, p. 21).

The new theory of trade and strategic industrial policy argues that with imperfect competition, there are no unique solutions to economic problems.[7] The outcome depends on assumptions about the conduct of economic agents. There is a strong possibility that in a situation with imperfect competition, firms are able to make above-average profits (rents). Intervention in trade, competition and industry may, under certain conditions, secure those rents for the domestic firms. This trade policy of beggar-thy-neighbour or 'war' over economic rents may look like a zero-sum game where everybody loses in the long-term through a chain of retaliations and counter-retaliations. However, potentially, there is at least one good argument in favour of intervention. With externalities and spillovers, governments may find reasons to protect some growing, high-technology industries. These are the industries where accumulated knowledge is the prime source of competitiveness. As such, the expenditure of those industries on R&D and the employment of engineers and scientists is (well) above the average for the economy. Sunk costs and R&D may be supported by governments since the positive effects of introducing new technology are felt throughout the economy and beyond the confines of the firm that initiates it. The whole world may benefit in some cases, from new technology whose development is supported by government intervention. For example, spacecrafts had to be equipped with computers. They had to be small and light. A spillover from the development of such equipment was the creation of personal computers. Therefore, the new theory says, with externalities and under certain conditions (no retaliation), intervention may be a positive sum game where everyone potentially gains in the long run. The critics of the new theory did not show that this theory was wrong, but rather that it was not necessarily correct. In fact, what was not understood was that the new theory provided only a programme of research, rather than a prescription for policy (Krugman, 1993, p. 164).

IV MARKET STRUCTURE

In a situation without trade and where a monopoly in country A produces good X while there is free competition in country B in the market for the same good, one can expect that prices for good X would be lower in country B. If free trade is permitted, country B would export good X to country A. This example showed that the difference in market structure between countries may explain trade, even though the countries may have identical production technologies and factor endowments.

Competition policies may be classified according to the structure–conduct–performance (SCP) paradigm. The thrust of the SCP paradigm is that performance in a defined market depends on the interaction between the structure of the market and the conduct of buyers and sellers in it.

- *Structure* refers to the organization of production and distribution, i.e., which enterprises are permitted to enter into which business activities. It structures the number and size of buyers and sellers; product differentiation; and relationship (horizontal and vertical integration) between buyers and sellers.
- *Conduct* sets how firms behave in their business. This refers to the competitive strategy of suppliers such as (predatory) pricing, innovation, advertising and investment.

- *Performance* refers to the goals of economic organization such as efficiency, technological progress, availability of goods and the full employment of resources.

The most common indicator of market structure or the degree of competition is the proportion of industry output, sales, investment or employment attributable to a subset (usually three to ten) of all firms in the industry. It shows the intensity of the competitive pressure on the incumbents. If this ratio is relatively high, then it illustrates that market power is concentrated in relatively few firms. It is, however, important to be cautious in dealing with these ratios. While an employment-concentration ratio may show a monopoly situation, a sales concentration ratio may not. Competitiveness is not only linked to market shares, but as a dynamic phenomenon, to the relative growth of productivity, innovation, R&D, size and quality of the capital stock, mobility of resources, operational control, success in shifting out of ailing lines of business, education of management, training of labour, incentives and the like. Therefore, it is false to fear that a potential exodus of jobs from the EU to the transition countries of central and eastern Europe or to the south Mediterranean countries (because of the relatively low labour costs there) would undermine the global competitiveness of the EU economies. If it were true, the EU would be flooded by goods from those countries. That is, however, not the case. There are many factors other than the relative labour costs that influence competitiveness. In most of the 'other factors' the EU fares much better than the competitors from the respective two regions. Anyway, this ratio is a useful second-best barometer of the oligopolistic restriction of competition.

The Hirschman–Herfindahl index (HHI) is an alternative and more complete measure of market structure than the concentration ratio. It is being increasingly used in the public fight against oligopolies.

$$\text{HHI} = \sum_i s_i^2 \times 100 \tag{5.2}$$

The HHI (5.2) is the sum of squared market shares of each firm in the defined market. It is between 0 and 100. The index is 100 when there is a monopoly, while it is relatively small in competitive industries. The HHI accounts for all the firms (i.e., both their absolute number and relative difference in size) in the defined market, while the concentration ratio accounts only for a select number of firms in the same market.

Integration may provoke several scenarios regarding competition. On the one hand, an increase in industrial concentration may be a consequence of the choice of firms to take advantage of economies of scale. Economies of scope[8] may increase concentration because they favour diversified firms which are often large. On the other hand, smaller firms may benefit, as in Japan or in Italy, because they may be included in the network of large ones. In addition, reduced cross-border transaction costs make it easier for smaller firms to penetrate the markets of partner countries. This may reduce concentration.

Firms compete by product differentiation, quality, R&D and advertising, as well as by price. The exceptions are, of course, raw materials and semi-finished goods. Major changes in the capacity of a firm linked to big sunk costs do not happen frequently. It is, however, more difficult to test the impact of non-price rivalry, like a competitor's

R&D, design activities and non-technical matters such as management and marketing, than their prices. It also takes a longer time to retaliate in these areas than to change prices (Schmalensee, 1988, p. 670).

V INNOVATION[9]

The process of technological change is driven by the existence of unexploited opportunities for the solution of problems such as the transformation of electricity into sound or light into electricity. The process has three distinct, but interrelated phases: invention (discovery of something new), innovation (putting invention into commercial use) and spread. If firms innovate (i.e., realize their technological capabilities to develop, produce and sell goods and services) and introduce new technologies and new goods/services, due to the new circumstances (integration), in order to preserve or improve their market position, then efficiency may increase. From a given set of resources one may expect to get either more and/or better quality output. That directly increases national welfare on average. In fact, integration for a small (or medium-sized) country enables economic development and progress at a lower cost than does autarky. There is, however, an opposing force. When there are imperfections, such as economies of scale and externalities, firms make rents.[10] Free competition leads to concentration that may reduce competition in the future. The new theory of trade and strategic industrial policy advocates that there may be fierce competition even among a few firms, such as in the aircraft industry, or in the US long-distance telephone call market, or in the Japanese market for electronic goods (although largely reserved for a half a dozen home conglomerates).

An innovation changes the mix of factors used in the production and/or consumption of goods and services. Usually, an innovation brings a reduction in the necessary quantity of factors in the production of a good or service as shown in Figure 5.2 with an arrow. That makes output cheaper and, consequently, more competitive. Suppose that the production of a good requires two factors, f_1 and f_2, respectively. If one needs to use per unit of output OA of factor f_1 and OB of factor f_2, then one gets rectangle OACB. An innovation reduces the area of rectangle OACB (note the direction of the arrow). In certain cases, when a factor such as oil or some other raw material becomes scarce, an innovation may reduce the consumption of this factor, but disproportionally increase (at least temporarily) the use of the other factor. Hence, in such a special case, the area of the rectangle OACB may increase as the result of innovation.

Economic integration opens up the markets of the integrated countries for the local firms. One can reasonably expect that competition may have a positive effect on innovation, but what are the effects of such a process in the long run? If innovation decentralizes, and if it increases competition, then competition and innovation reinforce each other. If, however, innovation centralizes over time and larger firms are necessary for costly and risky innovation that may be undertaken by only a few firms, then the extension of markets for firms would have a positive effect on innovation only in the short run. Therefore, one needs to ensure that short-run positive effects do continue in the long run (Geroski, 1988, pp. 377–379). In order to keep the 'necessary' level of competition within the integrated area, the countries

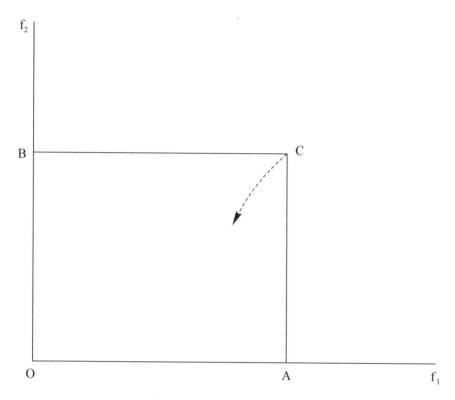

Figure 5.2 Effect of innovation on the use of factors

involved may wish to do that in an elegant way. That is to reduce the level of common external tariff and non-tariff protection.

The impact of competition is not restricted only to prices and costs. Competition also yields other favourable effects. It stimulates technical progress, widens consumer choice, improves the quality of goods and services, and also rationalizes the organization of firms. It is important to remember that firms seldom suffer from competition because their output is priced in a non-optimal way or because their production capacity is insufficient, rather they lose because they fail to develop new products and new production processes as efficiently or as quickly as their competitors (Lipsey, 1993a, p. 13). If a firm does not make its own product obsolete through innovation, some other entrepreneur will do that.

Innovations are constantly changing the method of combining factors in the production process, i.e., technologies.[11] These changes can range from minor to revolutionary. They could have four levels (Lipsey, 1993a, p. 3):

- incremental innovations, each one is small, but their cumulative effect is large;
- radical innovations, these are discontinuous events such as the development of a new (plastic) material or a new source of power;
- changes in the technology system affect an economic sector and industries within it, those were the changes in and around the chemical industry in the nineteenth century; and
- technological revolution changes the whole technoeconomic paradigm.

Innovation is an important economic impulse. There is, however, no simple answer to the question of whether international economic integration stimulates or prevents innovation by firms. There are two opposing views. First, a monopolist faces a secure market for the output. It can anticipate normal or super-normal profits (rents) from an innovation and can also reap all of the profits from its implementation. So, it is easier for such a firm to innovate than for a firm that does not have this market foresight, influence and market security. On the other hand, without the pressure from competition, the monopolist may not feel the need to innovate. The impression of long-term stability favours a conservative way of thinking which may restrict innovative activity. Monopolists may not wish to 'rock the boat', and can prevent or delay the implementation of innovations either in their own production or in the production activity of others.

The group of countries that generate the largest part of innovations is relatively small and stable over time. Britain was the leader in innovative activities during the era of the industrial revolution. It was joined in the second half of the nineteenth century by Germany, the US, France, Switzerland and Sweden. Membership of this select group of countries has been stable for over a century. The only major new-comer to the group was Japan in the post-Second World War period. Towards the end of the twentieth century, a few newly industrialized countries, in particular South Korea, might have joined this still select club of nations.[12] The general evidence on why some countries innovate more than the others is still imperfect. None the less, there are several factors that jointly supply part of the answer to that question. Differences in the scale of the local market (remember that integration increases the size of the market),[13] competition and supply of skills provide important ingredients in the complex links between technological opportunities and entrepreneurial decisions. R&D plays a crucial role in the innovation process as it provides a source of knowledge. However, the most important part of the answer to the question of relative stability in the number of countries that, in general, innovate most is that innovation reflects the *cumulative* and interrelated nature of the acquired knowledge, change in technological capabilities and economic incentives.[14] It does not only relate to the creation and absorption of new knowledge, but also to its adaptation and extension within an innovation-friendly environment. Put together, that establishes strong grounds for the creation of dynamic comparative advantages, certain irreversibilities[15] and the economic growth[16] of firms and nations as success breeds the potential for further success. The higher the level of accumulation of knowledge and capital stock, the higher are the benefits on technological progress[17] and vice versa. The law of diminishing returns does not apply to the accumulation of knowledge (Lipsey, 1994, p. 20). That is also reflected in the export performance of those countries measured by the shares in world exports of industries in which innovations take place, as well as in differences in labour productivity. Innovation is concentrated in a few firms in industries with heavy entry barriers such as aerospace, chemicals, automobiles, electrical and electronic industries, while it is spread among many firms in machinery and the production of instruments (Dosi, *et al.* 1990).

Empirical studies draw attention to the fact that monopolization or concentration is not the main factor explaining innovation. Cumulative knowledge made Germany excel at chemicals and high-quality engineering; Britain at pop music and publishing;

Italy at fashion and design; and the US at computers, software and films. Innovations are more numerous in industries that are less concentrated and where there are no serious barriers to entry. New entrants may have greater motivation to test and develop new products and technologies than the already established firms. In many industrialized countries, the average size of firms is becoming smaller not bigger. That reflects the demand for more custom-made goods that are produced in smaller batches with factors that may be smoothly moved across various alternative uses. But that is only on average. The industries with the most advanced technology are often the most concentrated, most profitable and largest. Modern technology is augmenting capital, in particular human capital.[18]

It is one thing to invent, find new or improved goods or services (product differentiation) and/or uncover a new way to produce already existing goods and services, and quite another to commercialize that success. The basic VCR technology was a result of the invention by Ampex in the US in the 1950s. The first VCR aimed at the consumer market was launched in 1971 by Philips, a Dutch producer, several years before Sony appeared with its own version. Other Japanese manufacturers followed, with a small time lag. Since then, the Japanese began to dominate the international market for (home) video equipment. A different approach was chosen by Philips after this firm invented compact discs. To avoid a repetition of the experience with VCRs, Philips developed the final technology for compact discs jointly with Sony.

Similarly, commercial jet technology was a British invention. Rolls-Royce was the first producer. That contributed to the production of the first jet transport aircraft. Later on, the US took the lead (Boeing and McDonnell-Douglas) and this was, subsequently, seriously challenged by the European Airbus (a consortium of government-supported British, German, French and Spanish firms). Government support of Airbus provoked a sharp reaction from the US (forgetting that US aircraft producers were generously subsidized through defence contracts). That led to the GATT Agreement on Trade in Civil Aircraft (1979). While 'supporting' the civil aircraft programmes, the signatories 'shall seek to avoid adverse effects on trade in civil aircraft' (Article 6.1). This is a statement that may have a number of different interpretations.[19] As such, it was insufficient to ease tensions in the aircraft industry. A Bilateral Agreement (1992) between the US and the EU was supposed to introduce a framework for all government 'involvement' in the development of commercial aircraft with 100 seats or more. However, it did not refer to past damage. The deal did not eliminate, but just constrained subsidies (for innovation and R&D). It set quantitative limits on both direct and indirect (military) subsidies for the development of new aircraft. The allowed limit for the direct subsidy for the development cost of a new aircraft was set at 33 per cent. Identifiable benefits from indirect subsidies were limited to 4 per cent of each firm's annual sales (Tyson, 1992, p. 207).

A positive effect on innovation (creation of technology) in the EU was expected to come from the completion of the 1992 Programme. An enlarged market would stimulate competition giving an incentive to innovation which would promote competition to the benefit of the consumers. If corrective measures (in support of trade, competition or industrial policy) were added, they would not necessarily violate a free trade system in the long term. They would simply add an adjustment mechanism to the already highly imperfect and sub-optimal market situation.

Perfect competition eliminates inefficient firms from a market, and at the same time rewards the efficient ones. In the words of Schumpeter, this process is called creative destruction. If inter-country factor mobility is allowed for, the supply of factors (labour, capital, land, technology, organization and entrepreneurship) increases. Competition probably operates best when a firm believes that it is in the process of becoming a monopolist (at best), or an oligopolist (at least). However, consumers may be made worse off if the equilibrium industry structure is monopolistic or oligopolistic. This would be soothed somewhat if oligopolistic firms introduce the most efficient innovations as rapidly as perfectly competitive firms would and if governments prevented such a market structure from behaving in a noncompetitive way.

Reliance on various foreign technologies is an inevitable fact for small open economies. Such countries often do not have the necessary resources to develop basic technologies for all lines of production. If this situation is regarded as detrimental, then economic integration may increase the pool of resources (human, technological and financial) for innovation and the development of new technologies, products and inputs, which may mitigate the potential disadvantage of smallness.

In a relatively well integrated area such as the EU, one would expect that the prices of similar goods in different countries would be similar, due to competition and trade. The stronger the competition and the larger the volume of trade, other things being equal, the smaller the differences in prices. Pre-tax prices for the same good may differ only for the cost of transportation, handling, insurance and, to an extent, marketing. However, the evidence has not substantiated this expectation. The EU was aware of those barriers to competition other than tariffs and quotas (NTBs), so, at the end of 1992, it implemented an ambitious programme to create a genuine internal market. There are, however, various local factors that prevent full equalization of prices. In some regions there may be small markets for certain goods and services. In order to do business there, firms may price their goods relatively higher. Due to special requirements about the necessary ingredients in some countries, the same basic good (for instance, chocolate) may be priced differently. If there are local substitutes, then foreign suppliers may modify the price of their goods. Some goods (wine) may be regarded as luxuries in one country and be taxed accordingly, while in another country, they may be regarded as basic necessities. This widens the price gap for the same good in different countries, even different regions of the same country. In a perfectly competitive market (together with free entry and exit) for a good, free competition ensures equality of prices and drives profits to zero. In imperfectly competitive markets there is room for price variation and, therefore, for greater profits.

VI INTRA-INDUSTRY TRADE

While increased competition offers potential gains regarding the efficient allocation of resources in production and in increased consumption, there is nothing to ensure that these gains would be realized in practice. If a government has this pessimistic view and if it believes that domestic production would be wiped out by foreign competition, then it may pursue a policy of protection on the grounds that it is better to produce something inefficiently at home, than to produce nothing at all. This disastrous scenario has not been identified in reality. The very existence of the EU, deepening in integration and with continuous enlargement is the best example of a positive scenario. Firms in different EU countries have not been thrown out of business by competition from firms in partner countries. Instead, many of them have continuously increased their business over the long run. They have specialized in certain lines of production that are supposed to satisfy distinct demand segments throughout the EU. Trade takes place in these differentiated products. This phenomenon is known in theory as intra-industry trade.[20] Generally, product differentiation tends to dominate product specialization in the internal trade of the EU.

There are also other examples that support the thesis of a smooth intra-industry adjustment in trade. Successive rounds of negotiations within the GATT, reduced tariffs. The ensuing intra-industry adjustment in trade and specialization among developed countries occurred relatively smoothly. Contrary to the expectation of the factor-endowment theory, intra-industry adjustment prevailed and it carried fewer costs than would be the case with inter-industry adjustment. Even if there are fears that foreigners would eliminate domestic firms through competition, exchange rates may act as an important safety valve to prevent such development and ease the transition to the new situation.

With an increase in income, consumers are no longer satisfied with identical or standardized goods. They demand and pay for varieties of the same basic good, often tailored to their individual needs. Intra-industry trade refers to trade in differentiated commodities. This happens when a country simultaneously exports and imports goods (final or semi-finished) that are close substitutes for consumers. Differentiation of goods begins when various characteristics are added to the basic good or component. All that is amplified by strong advertising campaigns. So, gains from trade in differentiated goods may materialize through an increase in consumer choice.

The variety of goods produced in a country, as the new theory suggests, is limited by the existence of a scale economies in production. Thus, similar countries have an incentive to trade. Their trade may often be in goods that are produced with similar factor proportions. Such trade does not involve the big adjustment problems common for more conventional trade patterns (Krugman, 1990a, pp. 50–51). In fact, one of the most distinctive properties of the liberalization of trade in the EU was an increase in intra-industry trade coupled with modest adjustment costs (Sapir, 1992, pp. 1,496–1,497).

The core of the neo-classical international trade and customs union theory refers to two goods. Therefore, it cannot consider preference diversity and intra-industry trade in a satisfactory way. The neo-classical theory's 'clean' model of perfect competition cannot be applied there. The potential for intra-industry trade increases with the level of economic development, similarity in preferences (tastes), openness to trade and geographical proximity which reduce costs of transport and after sale service. A significant part of trade among developed countries consists of intra-industry trade. Preferences may be such that variety is preferred to quantity, so a part of the volume of trade is not only due to different factor endowment, but also to different national preferences (tastes). The response of successful firms to such business challenges is to find a special market niche and to employ economies of scope, rather than scale.

There is a finding that incentives for intra-industry trade come from the relative level of per capita income and country size, product differentiation, participation in regional integration schemes, common borders, as well as similar language and culture. A negative influence on this type of trade comes from standardization (reduction in consumers' choice), distance between countries (increases the cost of information/service necessary for trade in differentiated goods) and trade barriers that reduce all trade flows (Balassa and Bauwens, 1988, p. 1,436).

Intra-industry trade is relatively high among developed countries. It refers to trade within the same trade classification group. One may, therefore, wonder if intra-industry trade is a statistical, rather than an authentic phenomenon. In addition, it may be argued that two varieties of the same product are not always two distinct goods. The criteria for data aggregation in international trade statistics (SITC) are similarity in inputs and substitutability in consumption. They often contradict each other. Many of the three digit groups in SITC include heterogeneous commodities. SITC 751 (office machines) includes typewriters, word processing machines, cash registers and photocopying machines, while SITC 895 (office and stationery supplies) includes filing cabinets, paper clips, fountain pens, chalk and typewriter ribbons. On these grounds one may believe that intra-industry trade is a pure statistical fabrication. However, this is hardly so in reality. If one studies trade groups that have more than three digits, differences may and would appear. The index of intra-industry trade (IIT) in a country is represented by the ratio of the absolute difference between exports and imports in a trade classification group to the sum of exports and imports in the same classification group.

$$\text{IIT} = 1 - \frac{|X_j - M_j|}{X_j + M_j} \qquad (5.3)$$

The IIT index (5.3) equals one for complete intra-industry specialization (a country imports and exports goods in a group in the same quantity) and is zero for complete inter-industry specialization. The *ex ante* expectation that trade liberalization would shift the IIT index closer to one in the case of developed countries has been substantiated in numerous studies. Among the EU countries, the IIT index was the highest in 1987 for France (0.83), Britain (0.77), Belgium (0.77), Germany (0.76) and the Netherlands (0.76), while the lowest was in Portugal (0.37) and Greece (0.31) implying that these two countries had a high inter-industry specialization (*European Economy*, 1990a, pp. 40–41).

Some goods that belong to the same classification group may be perfect substitutes, they may have identical end uses (e.g. plates). However, goods such as plates may be made of china, glass, paper, plastic, wood, metal or ceramic. Every type of this end product requires different factor inputs and technology. Similar examples may be found in tableware, furniture, clothing, etc. These differences among goods that enter a single SITC group may not be important for statistical records, but they are often of crucial importance to consumers. Demand for a variety of products increases with a rise in income. Increased income gives consumers the possibility of expressing variety in taste through, for example, purchases of different styles of clothing. A customs union may change consumers' preference ordering since the choice of goods in the situation prior to a customs union or reduction in tariffs may be quite different.

Integration in the EU increased intra-industry trade within this group of countries, while integration in the former Council for Mutual Economic Assistance (CMEA) had as its consequence greater inter-industry trade (Drabek and Greenaway, 1984, pp. 463–464). Preferences in the centrally planned economies were revealed through plan targets. They were different in comparison with economies in which market forces reveal consumers' preferences. In market economies competition takes place among firms, while competition in centrally planned economies occurred among different plans that were offered to the central planning body. A free trade area between the US and Canada (1987) was not expected to alter crucially the pattern of trade between these two countries. One reason was that the last step in the reduction in tariffs agreed during the Tokyo Round of the GATT negotiations took place in 1987. After this reduction, trade between the US and Canada became largely free, that is 80 per cent of all trade was duty-free while a further 15 per cent was subject to a tariff that was 5 per cent or less. Another reason was that there is greater similarity in consumers' tastes in North America than in the EU.

Since a large part of trade among developed countries has an intra-industry character, this may lead to the conclusion that the Heckscher–Ohlin (factor proportions) theory of trade is not valid. Intra-industry trade (a relatively large share of total trade among the developed countries) is not based on differences in factor endowments among countries.[21] Countries tend to specialize and export goods that are demanded by the majority of domestic consumers. It is the demand that induces production, rather than domestic factor endowment. Countries have a competitive edge in the production of these goods and thus gain an advantage in foreign markets, while they import goods demanded by a minority of the home population (Linder, 1961). The US, Japan and Germany have the greatest comparative advantage in goods for which their home market is relatively big. These are standardized goods for mass consumption.[22] Because of the larger and more homogenized market that made production runs large, labour productivity in the manufacturing industries was some 50 per cent higher in the US than in Germany in 1986. Such an estimate might have exaggerated the difference in productivity as there was little allowance for the high quality of German manufactured products (Pratten, 1988, pp. 126–127). As an example, being preoccupied with large quantities of output and economies of scale made the taste of American chocolate, for a European, absolutely appalling.

Intra-industry trade may be described in terms of monopolistic competition and product differentiation. Perfect competition is not a realistic market structure, so perfect monopolistic competition is the ideal market structure in a situation with differentiated goods (Lancaster, 1980). Armington's assumption states that products in the same industry, but from different countries, are imperfect substitutes (Armington, 1969, p. 160). In other words, buyers' preferences for different(iated) goods are independent. Armington's assumption overestimated the degree of market power of a particular producer.

Table 5.1 gives data on the shares of intra-industry trade in total trade in the major OECD countries. It shows that the share of intra-industry was growing, on average, from the mid-1960s for the following two decades. During that period intra-industry trade was more important for the EU countries and North America (high intra-industry specialization reveals imperfect competition) than for Japan or Australia which had relatively high inter-industry specialization.

Table 5.1 Intra-industry trade in major OECD countries: share in total trade (%)

Country	1964	1967	1973	1979	1985
Belgium/Luxembourg	62	66	69	73	74
France	64	67	70	70	72
Germany	44	51	60	60	65
Italy	49	45	54	48	55
Netherlands	65	66	63	65	67
United Kingdom	46	55	71	80	76
Australia	18	18	29	22	25
Canada	37	49	57	56	68
Japan	23	22	24	21	24
United States	48	52	48	52	72
Mean of major OECD countries	46	49	55	55	60

Source: *Structural Adjustment and Economic Performance* (OECD, 1987, p. 273)

Instead of taking goods themselves as the basis for analysis, 'address models' of goods differentiation take characteristics that are embodied in commodities as their starting point (Lipsey, 1987a). The computer is a good that may be considered as a collection of different attributes such as memory, speed, print, graphics and the like. Figure 5.3 illustrates two characteristics of a set of goods (computers).

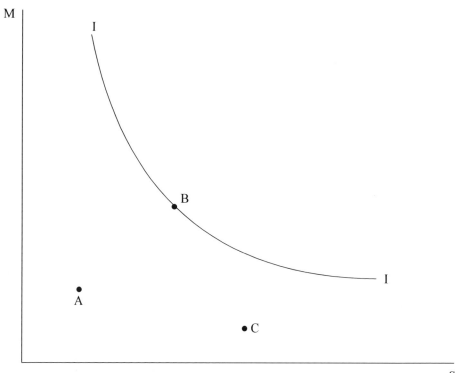

Figure 5.3 Characteristics of computers

146

Each good (computer) A, B and C, respectively, has a certain combination of characteristic S (speed) and characteristic M (memory). Each good is defined by its location in the continuous space of characteristics, hence it has a certain 'address'. Consumers' preferences are related to characteristics, not goods. Some consumers prefer memory over speed, while others have opposite tastes. On the assumption that all three goods have the same price in Figure 5.3 let a consumer have tastes embodied in the indifference curve II. This consumer maximizes utility with the purchase of good B. Each good in this model has close and distant neighbours. There are many goods and many consumers. Everyone attempts to attain his own highest indifference curve. That gives rise to intra-industry trade. Address models of localized (monopolistic) competition may be an important part of the explanation of intra-industry trade.

All general explanations of trade in differentiated goods refer only to final goods in trade among developed countries. In addition, intra-industry trade is linked to imperfect product markets (monopolization) and consumers' demand for a variety of goods. Economies of scale may be the other important part of the explanation of trade in differentiated goods, as countries with a similar endowment of factors would still trade. Imperfect information on the part of consumers about goods may have its impact on intra-industry trade, but its effect would disappear in the long run because of advertising and other ways of spreading information.

The Heckscher–Ohlin theory gave students the impression that the factor proportions theory of trade is orthodox. Linder's theory tended to be less rigorous and thus has not made the same impression on students. None the less, Leamer (1984) found evidence which supports the classical theory. Linder's theory does not reject factor proportion theory, it only explains that factor proportions are not the only cause of trade. One may conclude that the factor proportions theory determines trade and specialization *among* different SITC classification groups, while economies of scale and diversity in tastes determine production and trade *within* SITC classification groups. As most changes in demand take place *within* certain clusters of goods, that is a sign that changes in technology are important driving forces of trade.

VII EUROPEAN UNION

1 Introduction

The Commission of the EU has a special responsibility for the proper operation of competition in the EU because it 'handles' a much larger number of firms than any member country. Basic rules (including exceptions) of the EU on competition policy could be found in the Treaty of Rome and Rulings of the Court of Justice. In essence, there should be no barriers to internal trade. Freedom of movement for goods, services, people and capital (four freedoms) are contained in Article 3 of the Treaty of Rome. The EU does not tolerate any discrimination on the grounds of nationality[23] (Article 6). 'The internal market shall comprise an area without internal frontiers in which the free movement of goods, persons, services and capital is ensured' (Article 7a). This provision is the one that was supposed to oust NTBs for internal trade and ensure very liberal competition rules for the EU residents. Freedom of movement of goods is elaborated in Articles 9–37.[24] Free movement (and establishment) of persons, services and capital is regulated by Articles 48–73. In addition, national tax provisions must not discriminate against goods that originate from other member states of the EU (Articles 95–99). In addition, Article 130 requests both the EU and its member states to ensure the necessary conditions for competitiveness of the EU industry.

Competition rules are founded on the postulate that the concentration of (private) economic power within monopolies, oligopolies, cartels or other market structures that have similar negative effects on consumers, need to be outlawed and/or regulated and monitored. Individual economic freedom needs to be fostered through rules of market competition. The objective of this approach is to allocate factors according to the criteria of efficiency and, hence, contribute to an increase in the average standard of living.

The EU accepted in 1985 a technical blueprint, known as Programme 1992,[25] with 282 measures for the attainment of a genuine single internal market in the EU by the end of 1992. Its major thrust was the removal of NTBs to internal trade in the EU. That was supposed to increase competition and improve competitiveness of the EU goods and services relative to exporters in the US, Japan and newly industrialized countries. The Programme removed border formalities, introduced mutual recognition of standards, established a single licence and home country control for financial services, and also opened national public procurement contracts to suppliers from other EU member countries.[26] The principal gains from the Programme would not come from the reduction in the costs of internal-EU trade that resulted from the removal of NTBs, but rather from the longer-term dynamic benefits of increased competition on the expanded internal market. The anti-competitive market behaviour of various local monopolies would be checked. Competition in the EU would be, however, furthered when the EU-internal liberalization is coupled with external liberalization. There are at least two reasons for the external opening of the EU in order to make competition vigorous. First, intra-EU trade is mostly in differentiated products (intra-industry). Second, a part of intra-EU trade takes place between subsidiaries of a single TNC. Extra-EU competitive pressure is necessary to ease this oligopolistic structure and increase the competitiveness of both traditional and new-growth industries (Jacquemin and Sapir, 1991).

This chapter will concentrate on rules that regulate the actions of firms and governments to reduce competition on the EU market. Two articles of the Treaty of Rome govern the actions of *firms*. Article 85 refers to restrictions of competition, while Article 86 prohibits the abuse of a dominant position. *Governments* may also jeopardize the process of competition. This occurs in the case of state aids (subsidies). Article 92 regulates this issue. Aid above a certain level must be notified to the Commission for the examination of its legality and compatibility with the goals of the EU.

In order to execute its duties as the guardian of the Treaty of Rome, the Council of Ministers issued Regulation 17/62 (1962). The Commission has the right to request relevant information from all enterprises, their associations and member states. If the information is not provided, the Commission may impose a daily fine of up to ECU 1,000 until the information is provided. The Commission is also empowered to investigate the case. This includes 'dawn raids' (surprise visits) to the premises of the parties involved. Inspectors may examine books, accounts, business records, take copies and ask questions. However, all this must be with the approval of the party visited since the investigators are not permitted to use force. As the information obtained may comprise business secrets, the Commission may use it exclusively for the purpose of the handling of the case in question. If an infringement of the rules is found, the Commission may fine the culpable party/parties. The maximum fine equals 10 per cent of the total annual turnover of the enterprise concerned. While setting the fine, the Commission considers both the weight and the duration of the violation of the Treaty of Rome. A review of the fines imposed by the Commission reveals that the fines have been increasing over time. The guilty parties may appeal against decisions of the Commission to the Court of First Instance. A further appeal may be brought before the Court of Justice.

2 Restriction of competition

Article 85 of the Treaty of Rome prohibits 'as incompatible with the common market' all explicit or implicit, as well as horizontal or vertical agreements (collusion) among firms that may have a negative impact on internal EU trade 'and which have as their object or effect the prevention, restriction or distortion of competition within the common market', unless authorized by the Commission of the EU. Private practices that restrict competition according to this Article include:

- direct or indirect fixing of prices and other trading conditions;
- limitation or control of production, markets, technical development, or investment;
- sharing of markets;
- application of dissimilar conditions to equivalent transactions with different clients; and
- tying in contracts unconnected to transactions.

It has been recognized for quite some time, at least in the smaller countries on the European continent, that there is a certain need for some concentration of business. Hence, Article 85 (3) states exemptions from the general rules of competition. Its application is often based on political compromise. Hence the potential danger (uncertainty) that comes from the lack of transparency. An agreement, decision or practice may be declared as compatible with the common market if it contributes to an improvement in production or distribution of goods, or to the promotion of economic or technical progress, 'while allowing consumers a fair share of the resulting benefit'. In addition, to be exempt from the rules of competition, the restrictive agreement must be necessary for the accomplishment of the desired business end (appropriateness principle). If certain kinds of business practices occur frequently and if they are compatible with the rules of competition, the Commission may grant a block exemption. For example, in 1985 Regulation 418/85 granted a block exemption, until the end of 1997, to agreements among firms on joint R&D and joint exploitation of those results (manufacturing or licensing to third parties).[27] The Commission also recognized the importance of cooperation for technical progress.

Manufactures in the EU wield a strong lobbying influence on economic policy. One of the examples (Article 85 (3) of the Treaty of Rome) has been the block exemption of car producers from the full rigour of competition since 1985

(Regulation 123/85), on the grounds that cars are a very special kind of consumer goods: they are specialized goods that require distinct attention and after-sale service. Producers were able to request a tightly controlled exclusive dealership, as well as demand that garages use the original spare parts (consumers may benefit from the better knowledge of the specialist dealers, service and safety). In addition, producers could control the geographical market segmentation, as well as the quantity and prices of the cars sold. Although there is little competition between retailers of the same type of car, there is still solid competition among different producers of cars. Car manufacturers have received these favours from the Commission, but have failed to fulfil their part of the bargain, i.e. to let consumers shop around the EU for the best deals. There are still significant differences in prices for the same car among the member countries of the EU and guarantees are not honoured throughout the region. The price for such uncompetitive behaviour is paid by the consumers in higher prices and reduced choice. For example, prospective buyers of cars from Austria wanted to purchase cars in Italy because the identical models were cheaper by as much as 30 per cent in 1995 (this was due in part to the depreciation of the lira). The Italian car dealers refused to sell cars to non-nationals. In other countries dealers also often refuse to sell cars to the non-nationals or discourage them from purchasing cars through excessively long delivery times, various surcharges or warnings that after-sales service would not be honoured abroad. The block exemption was, however, extended in 1995 for a period of seven years (Regulation 1475/95). The new exemption allows for multi-dealership as a means of avoiding 'exclusive' dealership. This is, however, an insignificant gesture as the second franchise has to be on different premises, under different management and in the form of a distinct legal entity. If the Commission is really keen on increasing competition and efficiency in the EU car industry, then it needs to abandon limits on imports of cars from Japan.

Examples of uncompetitive behaviour may be found elsewhere. Fragrance producers have a similar right to license only upmarket shops to sell their products. After all, could competition laws ever force Burger King to sell McDonald's hamburgers or *vice versa*?

The merger/acquisition-control procedure of the EU has seven, often overlapping, stages. They are: pre-notification discussions, notification, investigation, negotiation, decision, political evaluation and judicial scrutiny. The strength of the EU procedure in comparison with the past and with other jurisdictions is that it is:

- fast (a majority of the cases are resolved within a month),
- flexible (as the pre-notification discussions resolve the question of the necessary background information for the decision), and
- it has a 'one-stop shop' (the Commission is the single body in charge of receiving notifications, investigation and decision).

The Commission may approve a merger, clear it with conditions, or block it. Although the EU procedure is made simpler, it has at least one weakness: the lack of transparency. The Commission has considerable discretionary room for manoeuvre in the decision-making process.[28]

Exemptions from the competition rules of the EU are possible under Article 85 (3) of the Treaty of Rome. To obtain an exemption, the firms involved need to demonstrate that the benefits of the deal outweigh the anti-competitive effects. The firms need to prove to the Commission that the deal improves production and/or distribution of goods and that it promotes technological progress. In addition, the deal needs to pass on a 'fair share' of the resulting benefits to consumers. The procedure for clearance was quite long. It could have taken up to two years to obtain an exception. From 1993, if a deal (principally, but not exclusively, joint ventures) between firms has implications for the structure of an industry, the parties are to receive a favourable or a warning letter within two months of the mandatory notification of the Commission about such an agreement. First examples include an approved dual venture between Olivetti and Canon for the dual development and production of printers and fax machines. The reason for the exception was the avoidance of duplication of development costs and the transfer of technology from Canon (Japan) to Olivetti (Italy). The joint venture by Asea Brown Bovery for the development and production of high-performance batteries was also approved on the grounds that it brings innovation, reduces dependence on imported oil and, indirectly, improves the quality of life of consumers. The merger between Aérospatiale-Alenia/de Havilland was, however, prohibited on the grounds that it would create a dominant position in the worldwide market for medium-sized (40–59 seats) turbo-propelled aeroplanes.

Competition rules apply not only to the written and enforceable deals among undertakings, but also to tacit ones (such as concerted practices). The *Dyestuffs* case (1969) was one of them. The biggest EU producers of aniline dyes increased their supply prices by identical margins with a time lag of only a few days. That happened on three occasions (in 1964, 1965 and 1967). Professional organizations from the textile and leather industries were among those that complained to the Commission. The parties charged denied the existence of any gentlemen's agreement and argued that in a closely knit industry each producer followed the price leader. None the less, the Commission had enough circumstantial evidence of collusion and fined the ten guilty parties for concerted practice. The total fine was ECU 0.5 million. The firms involved in this case were BASF, Bayer, Hoechst and Cassella Farbwerke Mainkur (from Germany); Francolor (France); ACNA (Italy); ICI (Britain); and Ciba, Sandoz and Geigy (Switzerland). The Court of Justice upheld the decision of the Commission on the grounds that the national markets for dyestuffs were fragmented and that synchronized price rises did not correspond to the normal conditions of the market. One of the important issues that came out of this anti-cartel case was that the Commission and Court applied the EU competition rules on an extra-territorial basis. British and Swiss enterprises were a part of the aniline dye gentlemen's agreement. Even though they came from the outside world, they were fined by the EU for the non-competitive market behaviour. The principle that was established in this case was that each firm must independently determine its business policy on the common market.

Concerted practices did not take place only on the producer level, but also at the point of distribution, such as in the *Pioneer* case (1979). Pioneer of Japan, the producer of hi-fi equipment, had exclusive distributors MDF (France), Melchers (Germany) and Shriro (Britain). The price of the same equipment was higher in France than either in Britain or Germany. MDF complained to Pioneer about imports from Britain and Germany into France. The four parties had a meeting in Belgium after which both Shriro and Melchers either refused to take orders from firms that wanted to ship equipment to France or asked them not to do it. The fine imposed by the Commission for the prevention of parallel trade was ECU 6.95 million. It was subsequently reduced by the Court to ECU 3.2 million.

Article 85 has been invoked, for example, in the *Polypropylene* case (1986). A fine of ECU 58 million was imposed by the Commission on 15 major EU producers of petrochemical goods. They violated competition rules by colluding to carve up the market and fix prices. The Court reduced the fine to ECU 54 million. Similar cartel charges were imposed in two cases in 1988 against firms that produced base chemicals, including PVC. The first one involved 14 firms, while in the second one there were 17. The fine for such non-competitive behaviour was ECU 23.5 million and ECU 37 million, respectively.

In another exclusive purchasing controversy, the *Delimitis* case (1991), a national German court asked the EU Court of Justice to interpret Article 85 when applied to the exclusive purchasing commitment in supply contracts for beer. In principle, an exclusive purchasing obligation restricts the buyer from procuring goods or services from the seller that takes part in the contract. However, that is in principle. In practice, the Court ruled that the mere existence of an exclusive purchasing duty does not restrict competition *per se*. Such agreement would restrict competition only if other business rivals were inhibited from entering or expanding in the relevant market.[29] This depends on the total volume of sales in the market, the duration of the deal, the opportunities for the newcomers to obtain enough sales locations, and the market dominance of the existing firms. A decision on whether an agreement restricts competition or not depends on a complex analysis according to the above criteria. If an exclusive purchasing contract does not violate these criteria, then it does not restrict competition according to the Court of Justice and *vice versa*.

Competition policy requires skilful handling in a system that integrates countries. Breaking up a price-fixing cartel is obviously a competition issue. Deciding, however, how many big chemical or car companies the EU should have is a political question. There should be certain control over mergers with an EU dimension. All industries in the EU have used mergers and acquisitions in their business strategy.[30] That was pronounced in the second half of the 1980s when firms were facing the possibility of a genuine internal market that was supposed to come from the completion of the 1992 Programme.[31] A tool of the Programme was the elimination of the unnecessary regulation (NTBs) that was splintering national markets for goods, services and factors in the EU. Mergers, acquisitions, strategic alliances, joint ventures and networking were used by the business community to respond to this challenge. All that was supposed to consolidate the positions of firms in the new, frontier-free and highly competitive market. Such a business policy had an indirect positive effect on standardization. It was tolerated by the Commission because of efficiency considerations.

After an acceleration in the second half of the 1980s and a peak in almost all types of concentration deals in 1989–1990, concentration activity has continued to decelerate ever since (Table 5.2). Firms adjusted their business structure and operation several years prior to the final implementation of the 1992 Programme.

The greatest number of concentration deals was in the manufacturing industry and within that, paper manufacturing. It was followed by food and drink,[32] sugar-based production and chemicals. That is explained by the expected removal of NTBs in

Table 5.2 Mergers and majority acquisitions, 1987–1993

Year	National mergers[a]	EU internal[b]	EU international[c]	International EU[d]	Outside EU[e]
1987–8	2,110	252	499	160	114
1988–9	3,187	761	659	447	310
1989–90	3,853	1,122	655	768	356
1990–1	3,638	947	550	729	376
1991–2	3,720	760	497	605	326
1992–3	3,004	634	537	656	381

Source: XXIIIrd Report on Competition Policy 1993 (Brussels: European Commission, 1994)
Notes: [a]Deals among firms of the same country. [b]Deals involving firms from at least two different member states of the EU. [c]Deals in which EU firms acquire firms of non-EU origin. [d]Deals in which the bidder is from outside of the EU and acquires one or several EU firms. [e]Deals in which there was not any involvement of EU firms

Table 5.3 Mergers and majority acquisitions by major economic activities in the EU, 1987–1993

Economic activity	1987–8	1988–9	1989–90	1990–1	1991–2	1992–3
Agriculture	16	22	45	45	37	22
Energy and water	53	77	75	88	102	81
Minerals and chemicals	215	452	594	589	489	452
Metal, engineering and cars	588	975	1,229	1,137	1,154	941
Manufacturing	560	1,090	1,307	1,306	1,230	1,061
Distribution and hotels	547	863	1,173	899	1,025	797
Transport and telecommunications	95	178	253	257	238	224
Banks, finance and insurance	748	1,046	1,309	1,194	968	918

Source: XXIIIrd Report on Competition Policy 1993 (Brussels: European Commission, 1994)

internal trade. The metal-based production (mechanical and electro-based engineering and vehicles) had also relatively high concentration activity. The suppliers of the public procurement goods concentrated with the intention of withstanding potentially strong competition. Larger business units are able to share R&D costs in those two industries. Wholesale distributors reacted to the elimination of NTBs by concentration of their activities. The same was true for the providers of financial services (Table 5.3).

The major motive for mergers and acquisitions throughout the period was a strengthening of market position. It was followed by a development of commercial activities (market expansion) and rationalization of business (*European Economy*, 1994a, p. 20). The objective was preparation for the intensive competition of an enlarged market. Companies in Britain, Germany[33] and France were the most favoured targets for intra-EU mergers. At the same time, firms from these three countries were the most active buyers of companies in the EU. Parent companies from Britain, Germany and France (the 'trio') were also active in purchasing non-EU firms. While British firms preferred to purchase companies in North America, the German and French parent firms have more evenly distributed their non-EU purchases among North America, western (non-EU) and eastern Europe. As for the non-EU acquirers of EU firms, North American buyers were most active in the EU 'trio'. They were followed by firms from Switzerland, Sweden and Japan.

A new trend in relations among firms was that firms in low and medium technologies use mergers and acquisitions in their business strategy, while the ones in high technology employ cooperation and collaboration (joint ventures). That breaches the historical pattern of relations among firms, which traditionally relied on the protection of their knowledge and experience in manufacturing and marketing. The high costs of developing new and upgrading existing technologies made them share this R&D expenditure.

If the structure of the market remains competitive, mergers and acquisitions are supposed to bring at least two efficiency gains. One is related to management, while the other is linked to a reduction in transaction costs. These benefits need to be weighed against the possible costs that come from the potential inefficiencies that may arise from concentration. If the initial expectations about efficiency gains are not fulfilled and do not predominate, a new merged enterprise may suffer from differences in corporate cultures, inflexibility and poor coordination of business. A number of studies that examined full legal mergers in various countries in the EU found a lack of substantial efficiency gains. Economies of scale were not significant either. Mergers had little or no effect on the post-merger profitability. There was no significant difference in the returns per share three years after the merger.[34] Costs of changes in business organization were often greater than the benefits claimed by the promoters of takeovers. The main reasons for these disappointments include the high prices paid for the target firms, an over-estimation of the business potential of the acquired firm and a mismanagement of the integration process with the acquired firm (Jacquemin, 1990a, pp. 13–14; 1990b, p. 541; Jacquemin and Wright, 1993, p. 528). This is most obvious in the cases of mergers of firms in the production of steel or cars, as well as in airlines. Hence, mergers were used as defensive business-policy instruments. A big wave of mergers in the US (and Britain) during the 1960s and 1970s proved to be a myopic way out of business trouble. Instead of supporting adjustment, mergers obstructed it by protecting firms from competitive pressure. That was reflected in the relatively slow response of US firms to the oil crises and to Japanese competition. Firms in the EU would be wise to avoid a repetition of the US experience. The presence of Japanese TNCs with their top technology and business organization in the EU may be the best motivation to EU-domestic firms to restructure business and become more competitive.

Given the substantial number of mergers and acquisitions, the degree of concentration in the EU has increased. That may *increase* competition on the internal EU market and abroad through rationalization of production and economies of scale. At the same time, an increased concentration of business may *restrict* competition. Therefore, the EU introduced an important legal instrument for the *ex ante* control of mergers in 1990.[35]

The EU needed a sound competition policy in order to prevent the creation of pan-EU oligopolies (corporate fortresses) that replace the national ones and that counter competitive pressure from open markets. According to the Merger Control Regulation 4064/89 of 1989, which came into effect in September 1990, the Commission has a say if a bid has an EU dimension,[36] i.e., if it crosses each of the following three thresholds:

- if annual worldwide turnover of the new (merged) company is above ECU 5 billion (general threshold),
- if sales in the EU of each party are more than ECU 250 million (*de minimis* threshold), and
- if each party makes more than 66 per cent of sales in any EU country.

The decisive determinant according to these thresholds is *turnover*, not domicile/ nationality of the parent enterprise.[37] If the proposed merger has a dominant position that may restrict competition (if the new firm can increase prices by, for example, 10 per cent without losing market share), the Commission has the authority to stop the deal. Anyhow, the Commission has not blocked a deal with a post-merger/acquisition market share below 40 per cent. Therefore, the purpose of the Merger Control Regulation is to prevent *ex ante* the creation of unwanted market behaviour that comes from the abuse of dominant position in the EU market.

If the governments of the EU countries are seriously committed to efficiency in the economy, cooperation and savings, they would have to consider modifications to Article 223 of the Treaty of Rome. This Article allows any member state to take such 'measures as it considers necessary for the protection of the essential interests of its security which are connected with the production of or trade in arms, munitions and war material'. An occasion to review this right to shelter defence contractors might be the IGC that is supposed to revise the Treaty of Rome in 1997. If some kind of protection is necessary, it may be given only to a select group of the most 'sensitive' technologies. As the arms industry is so special, hopes about the revision of Article 223 are, unfortunately, not high.

The end of the cold war resulted in a drop in the defence budgets. While the US defence contractors reacted to that by mergers and alliances, their counterparts in the EU moved in an erratic and slow way.[38] The pooling of the helicopter business of Aérospatiale (France) and Daimler-Benz Aerospace (Germany) into Eurocopter in 1992 or the purchase of Heckler and Koch (Germany) by Royal Ordnance (Britain) are more exceptions rather than the rule. All these alliances remained within the confines of the EU. The defence firms were (and still are) 'national champions' in the EU. Defence procurement has been conducting overt or covert industrial policy at a tremendous cost to domestic taxpayers. Standardization of hardware in the EU, together with a common procurement agency, may bring savings and increase competitiveness.

3 Dominant position

If a firm has or reaches a dominant position in the market, it may significantly affect competition. This market position may be secured in several ways. They include the following five:

- Firms may have innovative skills not only for products (goods/services), but also for management and planning. They may enter into the kind of risky investments in R&D, production and/or marketing that deters their competitors. Such first-mover advantages may result in dominance in the market and super-normal profits (Microsoft's MS-DOS and Windows, as well as Nintendo's Game Boy are obvious examples). The lifecycle of a product is shortening. Hence the importance of innovating. In fact, most firms compete through a perpetual creation of quasi-monopolistic positions that are based on innovation of various kinds.[39] A classical view that firms are only an input-conversion mechanism does not correspond to the contemporary world. In addition to their input-conversion and value-adding functions, firms are also involved in learning-by-doing and innovation activities. Concentration in industries with various entry barriers may occur as a direct consequence of a firm behaving efficiently. A policy that promotes R&D among firms in the EU may provide them with an improved footing for oligopolistic competition at home and abroad with foreign rivals that come mainly from Japan and the US.

- A dominant position in the market can be reached through mergers and acquisitions. That is the typical way of securing a dominant position in the English-speaking countries.
- A firm may obtain or shelter its dominant position through anti-competitive business practices. Examples of this include exclusive dealership and predatory pricing. Exclusive dealership may not always reduce welfare. For example, compared to the situation with free entry and exit among dealers/retailers, permanent and exclusive dealership (including after-sales service) may be a preferable and more welfare-enhancing solution.
- A dominant position may be captured through a competitive and risky pricing policy. If there are important scale and learning economies with a significant fall in prices as output increases over time, a risk-loving firm may choose to set current prices on the basis of the expected (low) costs of production in the future or on the average cost of production over the lifecycle of the select output.
- Yet another way by which firms come to dominate a market may be when the public authorities grant them such a licence. Examples could be found in 'natural' monopolies such as public utilities (supply of water, gas, electricity, postal service, rail transport, local telephone service). In these industries the minimum efficient scale is so large that a single firm is necessary to serve the entire national market.

Article 86 of the Treaty of Rome refers to the issue of the dominant position on the market. It does not prohibit the possession of a dominant position (monopoly or monopsony) *ex ante*, but rather the *abuse* of it. This article has only an *ex post* effect. In order to determine whether an infringement of the EU market has taken place, the Commission looks at three factors:

- the existence of the dominant position;
- its abuse (in pricing or control of production or distribution); and
- the negative effect on trade among the member countries.

Big firms are permitted by the Treaty of Rome to have market dominance, but they are forbidden to exercise it. This is romantic and naïve! Whoever gets the power will behave as a monopolist. The temptation is almost irresistible. Anyway, the legal formulation recognizes that there is a need for a certain level of concentration[40] in some industries for reasons of efficiency. It is inevitable for the attainment of the efficient scale of production, both for home and foreign markets. Otherwise, protected and inefficient national firms, with higher costs of production than foreign competitors, will continue to impose welfare losses on consumers. That is the reason why many/most European countries have relaxed their anti-trust policies. Otherwise, small domestic firms could be protected only at high cost and a loss in the efficiency in production. Concentration of production is a potential barrier against foreign competition on the home market and a springboard for penetration into foreign ones.

A refusal to supply goods or services was taken to be an infringement of Article 86. In the *United Brands* case (1976) the Commission found that United Brands, the major supplier of (Chiquita) bananas to most of the EU countries, abused its dominant position by refusing to supply green bananas to Olesen, a Danish ripener and distributor. Although Olesen had taken part in an advertising operation with one of United Brands' competitors, the Court found that the reaction of United Brands to competitive threat was excessive and, hence, abusive. Ceasing to supply bananas was a significant intrusion into the independence of small and medium-sized firms. United Brands was fined ECU 1 million by the Commission. The Court reduced the fine to ECU 0.85 million.

Another abuse of the dominant position can be found in the *Commercial Solvents* case (1972). Commercial Solvents had a dominant position in the EU market in the supply of raw materials required for the production of certain drugs. Till 1970, ICI, its subsidiary in Italy, acted as a reseller of those materials that were made by the parent in the US. Zoja, an Italian company, started purchasing inputs from ICI in 1966. In 1970, ICI started producing and upgrading the basic raw materials. Commercial Solvents decided that it would not supply any more of the basic raw material in the EU, only the upgraded one. In late 1970 Zoja placed an order for the usual commodity. The reply of Commercial Solvents was that none was available (although the requirements of Zoja were just a small percentage of Commercial Solvents' global output of that product). The Commission fined Commercial Solvents ECU 0.2 million for abusing its dominant position. The Court later halved that fine and requested Commercial Solvents to correct its business behaviour.

Exclusionary practices violate Article 86 too. *Hoffmann-La Roche* (hereafter, Roche) (Switzerland) was the company that entered in a number of arrangements that gave fidelity rebates to customers. In the case on vitamins (1976), the Commission found that there was an abuse of the dominant position by Roche. The company bound customers through an exclusive or preferential purchasing commitment for all or a substantial proportion of their purchases of 13 groups of vitamins in favour of Roche. Those vitamins were used in pharmaceuticals, food and animal feed. In return, Roche offered fidelity rebates that were in the range of 1 and 5 per cent (in one case it was 12.5 to 20 per cent). The Commission found it unacceptable to offer a price differential on the basis of the supply of all (or a substantial part) of a customer's requirements, rather than on the basis of the quantity of each good required. The purchases of vitamins of one group were tied to the purchases of vitamins of another one. The agreements usually contained the 'English clause', i.e., if buyers received an offer from another supplier that was more favourable than the one from Roche, buyers were obliged to inform Roche about such offer. If Roche was not able to match the offer by the third party, then the buyers were free to purchase externally, without losing the rebate in the future. The Commission fined Roche ECU 0.3 million. Subsequently, the Court upheld the findings of the Commission, but reduced the fine by a third.

One of the most well known merger cases was the *Continental Can* case (1973). Continental Can, a US firm and the leading world producer of metal containers, established a holding company, Europemballage in Belgium. Later on, it acquired a majority holding in Schmalbach, a major German can maker. Europemballage made a bid to acquire Thomassen & Drijver-Verblijfa, the Dutch can producer. The Commission was opposed to the acquisition of the Dutch firm. Continental Can appealed against the Commission's decision to the EU Court of Justice on the grounds that the Commission had failed to prove in which segments of the market the company had abused its dominant position. Other arguments used by Continental Can against the Commission were that it had not taken into account the potential competition of plastic and glass containers, as well as the relatively easy entry into the industry. The Court upheld the plea of Continental Can and ruled against the Commission. One of the most important issues that came out of this case was that the Court used Article 86 of the Treaty of Rome and applied it to mergers and acquisitions.

The Commission was tough in the *Tetra Pak* case (1991). This Swedish/Swiss company is the largest world supplier of the packaging inputs for liquid foods (juices and milk) in cartons. Elopak, its Norwegian rival, was frustrated about certain practices of Tetra Pak that were violating Article 86 on the EU market. Tetra Pak controlled over 90 per cent of the market for both machines and cartons in the aseptic business, while market dominance in the non-aseptic business was around 50 per cent. Among the abusive practices employed by Tetra Pak were obligations to use Tetra cartons in Tetra machines, there were also loyalty discounts and inspection clauses, predatory pricing, division of national markets and price discrimination. The Commission fined Tetra Pak ECU 75 million for these abusive business practices.

The highest fine ever, of ECU 248 million, was imposed by the Commission in the *Cement* case (1994). The Commission fined 33 firms in the cement business for operating a cartel for ten years from 1983. The original charge was against 78 companies. The investigation took eight years because firms hid the evidence well. Although the overall fine was high, the fines against the culpable firms amounted to 3–4 per cent of their individual annual turnover in Europe. The Commission sent a clear signal to other firms thinking about operating a cartel that such market conduct would not be tolerated.

4 State aids

Perfect competition in the neo-classical economic model can be undermined by protection and subsidization. The distinction between the two distortions is subtle. On the one hand, tariff and non-tariff *protection* allow the protected suppliers to charge higher prices on the local market than would be the case with free imports. Such protection provides an 'implicit subsidy' paid directly from consumers to producers. On the other hand, *subsidies* go to the domestic producers, not directly from consumers, but rather from taxpayers to the government and, then, to producers. The two types of 'support' have the same objective. Where they differ, is in transparency and in the method of supplying funds to the select industries or firms within them.

Those that consider the market functions efficiently use that argument as an argument against subsidies (state aids). Although there are many cases where such a view is valid, there are others where the neo-classical argument does not always hold. In the case of imperfections such as externalities (R&D or pollution), economies of scale, imperfect mobility of factors and sunk costs, intervention may be justified. Therefore, industrial and regional policies may be used as a justification for the existence of state aids. Article 92 of the Treaty of Rome recognizes this issue and regulates it.[41] It prohibits any aid that distorts or threatens to distort competition among the member countries. This means that Article 92 does not apply to aid given as a support to firms or for the production of goods and services that do not enter intra-EU trade (local consumption), as well as aid for exports outside the EU (regulated by Article 112).

There are, however, a few exceptions to the general rule of incompatibility of state aid. Article 92 affirms that aid, compatible with the Treaty, is given on a non-discriminatory basis to individuals for social purposes, as well as aid to the regions affected by calamities. Aid that *may be* considered compatible with the Treaty is given to projects that are in the EU's interest and aid for regional development in the 'areas where standard of living is abnormally low' (for the purpose of social cohesion in the EU). The Council of Ministers (based on a Proposal from the Commission) has the discretionary right to decide that other aid may be compatible with EU rules. This includes aid to SMEs,[42] conservation of energy, protection of environment, promotion of national culture or the alleviation of serious disturbances in a national economy. If an industry comes under competitive and/or restructuring pressure, the Commission considers the social and other impact of such adjustment according to the guidelines of 1979. The Commission may permit aid under conditions based on principles that include:

- temporariness (a clear time limit);
- transparency (the amount of aid has to be measurable);
- selectivity (aid is supposed to be given to firms and industries that have a reasonable chance of standing on their own after the restructuring period); and
- appropriateness (aid has to match the basic needs of the assisted firm/industry to operate during the restructuring period[43] after which the assisted firm/industry needs to become economically viable on its own).

In order to ease the workload and concentrate on the large and potentially the most damaging cases, the Commission introduced a *de minimis* rule in 1992. According to this rule, governments are not requested to notify aid that does not exceed ECU 100,000 over a period of three years. The Commission reckons that such aid does not distort competition. In addition, aid linked to environmental issues may be allowed if it enables improvements that go beyond the required environmental standards.

Article 92, as well as Court practice provide the Commission with a wide discretionary margin in the decision-making process. None the less, the Commission employs two criteria. First, is compensatory justification. To 'clear' aid as compatible with the rules, aid has to conform with goals set out in Article 92 and it needs to be proven that without state aid, free markets would not be capable of accomplishing the same end. Second, is transparency. Each grant of aid has to be justified and measurable. Member states must notify the Commission about the form, volume, duration and goals of the aid. If two months after the notification the Commission does not take any explicit decision, aid is regarded as being tacitly accepted. The Commission may decide 'not to raise objections', which means that the case has received preliminary approval, but the Commission needs to have further information to reach a final decision. The Commission may open the procedure (Article 93) and request the concerned parties to submit their comments. Following that, the Commission takes a final decision on the compatibility of aid with the EU rules.

Article 92 does not define state aid. None the less, the Commission and the Court of Justice interpret aid in a broad sense. They take it to mean any benefit given by a government in a form that includes subsidies, special public guarantees, supply of goods or services at preferential conditions and favours regarding credit terms, that are offered to one or more firms or their associations. Loans and guarantees given by the state or its agency does not necessarily constitute aid. The aid element exists only when such injections of funds are offered on conditions that would not be acceptable to an investor in 'normal' market circumstances.

Governments can still try to disguise industrial aid as regional aid. It is difficult to trace such support if companies make losses. R&D aid can similarly be abused. The 'support' to the manufacturing and services sectors needs to be at the R&D stage. Otherwise, foreign competitors, mainly from the US, would complain that EU subsidies distort international competition. Any EU member state can finance basic and applied research in the private sector according to the agreed sliding scales.[44] The Commission's Framework on state aid for R&D of 1995 has several criteria for the compatibility of such aid with the common market. They include the following:

- There is a distinction between 'industrial research' and 'pre-competitive development activity'. As one gets closer to the market place for final goods, the potential distortion of competition for aid increases.
- State aid for R&D should create an incentive for the recipient firm to carry out R&D in addition to that which it would undertake in the normal course of its business operation.
- Aid for 'industrial research' may be up to 50 per cent of the cost, while aid for 'pre-competitive development' may be up to 25 per cent of the cost. None the less, there are special additional bonuses of 10 per cent for projects that involve SMEs, of 15 per cent if the project is a priority under the EU R&D programme and up to 10 per cent if R&D is undertaken in regions eligible for regional aid.
- Maximum aid for R&D in the EU (allowable under the GATT Agreement on Subsidies and Countervailing Measures) is 75 per cent for 'industrial research' and 50 per cent for 'pre-competitive development activity'.
- Member states have to notify the Commission about all individual aid packages for projects exceeding ECU 25 million where aid exceeds ECU 5 million.

The State-aid Department of the EU Commission has a staff of 50 officials responsible for monitoring state aid and carrying out other tasks in the field. They cannot be expected to examine every item of state aid, especially if one considers that every region in each member country has the staff (often significantly more numerous than the Commission's) to dispense aid. Therefore, the Commission's priority is the prevention of the biggest and most competition-distorting examples of aid.[45] The Commission has to make sure that aid is given to the most disadvantaged regions and that it is compatible with the Treaty rules. All these formidable issues linked to competition are increasingly becoming a paradise for lawyers.

The overall level of state aid in the EU declined from 2.1 per cent of the GDP in 1988–1990 to 1.9 per cent in 1990–1992 (Table 5.4). Average aid per person employed also declined from ECU 777 to ECU 704 in the same period, however it increased in Germany from ECU 1,031 to ECU 1,090 (mainly because of the support to the eastern *Länder*) and in Luxembourg.[46] Overall aid also declined as a share of total public expenditure throughout the EU. The declining trend in state aid reflects not only a strict implementation of competition policy in the EU, but also reduction in public expenditure in the member countries.

Table 5.4 Overall state aid in member states, 1990–1992 and 1988–1990, as % of GDP per person employed and relative to government expenditure

	% of GDP		ECU per person employed		% of total government expenditure	
	1988–90[a]	1990–2	1988–90[a]	1990–2	1988–90[a]	1990–2
Belgium	2.8	2.3	1,107	966	5.4	4.5
Denmark	1.1	1.0	414	399	1.9	1.7
Germany	2.5	2.4	1,031	1,090	5.0	4.8
Greece	3.1	2.2	551	335	6.2	4.2
Spain	1.8	1.3	544	420	4.3	2.9
France	2.1	1.8	870	801	4.1	3.6
Ireland	1.9	1.5	593	502	4.4	3.6
Italy	2.8	2.8	1,177	1,165	5.5	5.1
Luxembourg	3.9	3.9	1,456	1,513	7.7	7.8
Netherlands	1.1	0.9	391	338	2.0	1.7
Portugal	2.0	1.4	255	178	4.5	3.0
United Kingdom	1.2	0.6	398	189	3.2	1.5
EUR 12	2.1	1.9	777	704	4.4	3.8

Source: Fourth Survey from the Commission on State Aid in the European Union (1995). Brussels: Commission of the European Union
Note: [a]1988–90 averages in 1991 prices

The declining trend in total public aid was also observed in annual state aid to the manufacturing sector from 3.8 per cent of value added (or ECU 40.7 billion) in 1988–1990 to 3.7 per cent (or ECU 37.8 billion) in 1990–1992 (Table 5.5). The highest share of aid in manufacturing output was in Greece (12.3 per cent) and Italy (8.9 per cent), while the lowest was in Britain (1.5 per cent) in 1990–1992. Germany's new *Länder* represented a special case. Aid per person employed was almost 3.5 times higher than the EU average in 1990–1992. The lowest state aid per employee was in Spain and Britain, while the highest was in Italy, Greece, Luxembourg and Belgium.

Table 5.6 reveals that grants and tax reductions were the most common types of aid in the EU (84 per cent of total state aid). All other types of aid had little relevance, although guarantees and soft loans are worth mentioning. State aid to the manufacturing sector had a predominantly regional-development function (Table 5.7). Half of it was disbursed on regional objectives in 1990–1992. Among the horizontal objectives (38 per cent of aid), support to R&D,[47] SMEs and export were the most prominent.

Table 5.5 State aid to the manufacturing sector: annual averages,
1990–1992 and 1988–1990

	% of value added		*ECUs per person employed*		*Million ECUs*[a]	
	1988–90	*1990–2*	*1988–90*	*1990–2*	*1988–90*	*1990–2*
Belgium	5.0	4.3	1,743.6	1,526.5	1,280.1	1,119.3
Denmark	2.3	2.0	684.8	637.6	365.0	335.6
Former Germany[b]	2.6	2.1	1,098.9	978.8	8,487.9	7,133.9
New *Länder*	—	n.a.	—	4,385.3	—	4,848.7
Greece	16.9	12.3	2,419.9	1,578.4	1,764.4	1,032.1
Spain	3.7	1.7	1,079.0	493.2	2,901.7	1,349.2
France	3.7	3.0	1,449.1	1,138.1	6,423.7	5,043.7
Ireland	3.9	2.9	1,821.3	1,410.5	389.4	307.4
Italy	7.8	8.9	2,425.1	2,610.5	12,161.5	12,526.0
Luxembourg	3.4	4.1	1,369.4	1,572.6	51.0	57.7
Netherlands	3.2	2.6	1,266.0	978.3	1,177.3	928.7
Portugal	7.3	5.2	910.5	625.4	735.9	479.2
United Kingdom	1.9	1.5	756.1	525.1	4,067.4	2,660.6
EUR 12	3.8	3.7	1,372.1	1293.1	40,703.5	37,822.1

Source: *Fourth Survey from the Commission on State Aid in the European Union* (1995). Brussels:
Commission of the European Union
Notes: [a]1988–90 averages in 1991 prices. [b]In its borders before October 1990

Table 5.6 State aid to the manufacturing sector, 1990–1992: breakdown according to
type of aid (%)

	Type of aid						
	Group A		*Group B*	*Group C*		*Group D*	*Total*
	Grants	*Tax reductions*	*Equity participations*	*Soft loans*	*Tax deferrals*	*Guarantees*	
Belgium	50	30	1	9	0	9	100
Denmark	83	4	0	4	0	8	100
Germany	46	37	0	8	1	8	100
Greece	55	19	0	13	0	13	100
Spain	79	0	2	16	0	3	100
France	31	28	5	9	3	25	100
Ireland	67	24	5	0	0	3	100
Italy	48	44	5	3	0	0	100
Luxembourg	82	5	0	13	0	0	100
Netherlands	80	15	0	1	0	5	100
Portugal	75	9	0	6	0	10	100
United Kingdom	89	6	0	1	3	1	100
EUR 12	51	33	3	6	1	7	100

Source: *Fourth Survey from the Commission on State Aid in the European Union* (1995) Brussels:
Commission of the European Union

Table 5.7 State aid to the manufacturing sector, 1990–1992: breakdown of aid according to sector and function (%)

Sectors/function	Belgium	Denmark	Germany	Greece	Spain	France	Ireland	Italy	Luxembourg	Netherlands	Portugal	United Kingdom	EUR 12
Horizontal objectives	82	68	21	64	50	71	31	30	34	72	34	45	38
Research and development	13	31	9	1	17	27	4	3	12	26	3	7	10
Environment	0	15	1	0	3	0	0	0	0	5	0	1	1
SME	26	1	4	12	10	11	7	9	16	20	1	15	9
Trade/export	16	8	1	15	1	30	20	9	0	2	0	15	9
Economization of energy	7	11	2	0	2	1	0	3	0	14	1	0	2
General investment	12	0	0	3	6	1	0	2	5	3	18	6	2
Other objectives	7	2	4	32	10	0	0	5	0	2	10	0	4
Particular sectors	2	30	8	6	34	18	0	8	0	10	55	25	12
Shipbuilding	1	24	2	0	12	1	0	1	0	4	37	2	2
Other sectors	1	6	6	6	22	16	0	7	0	6	19	23	9
Regional objectives	16	2	72	30	16	11	69	62	66	18	11	30	50
Regions under 92(3)c	16	2	5	0	3	7	0	4	66	18	0	20	6
Regions under 92(3)a	0	0	36	30	14	5	69	58	0	0	11	10	43
Berlin/Zonenrand			31										
Total	100	100	100	100	100	100	100	100	100	100	100	100	100

Source: *Fourth Survey from the Commission on State Aid in the European Union* (1995). Brussels: Commission of the European Union

VIII CONCLUSION

Relatively small countries that are in the process of developing employ industrial policies that may not always be competition friendly. Relatively large and developed countries value competition quite highly. As the concentration of the business in certain industries increases, there is a trend to tighten anti-trust policy and keep a certain level of competition in the internal market. Increased competition would in most cases, without any doubt, put a downward pressure on prices and costs. This outcome would enable economic growth with a reduced inflationary pressure. It is, however, not clear how this would happen in practice. Competition may reduce prices of goods and services. It may increase output, but keep prices constant. In this case a reduction in prices would be offset by an increase in demand. The most likely outcome in practice would be that competition would produce a blend of benefits which accrue from an increase in output and a decrease in prices.

Programme 1992 enhanced the dynamic process of competition through an easing of the market segmentation and, paradoxically, increasing concentration in business. Concentration permitted the employment of economies of scale and an increase in technical efficiency in production. In addition, it enhanced R&D through a joint sharing of high costs.

Among the driving forces behind the 1992 Programme were: a change in global competition and the relative loss of EU competitiveness in comparison with the US in computers and aerospace industries, Japan in cars and consumer electronics, and developing countries in textiles and apparel, as well as a potential loss in a number of other industries. Businesses reacted to the single-market programme by consolidations through mergers and acquisitions, as well as joint ventures. An increase in internal EU competition that came through the elimination of internal barriers gave the EU the chance to benefit from the so far unexploited economies of scale that would, over time, reduce the costs of production and increase global competitiveness, not only of manufacturing, but also of services. This would all provide an additional bonus to investment and growth of the EU's economy. Hence, not only innovating firms and the ones that use state-of-the-art technologies, but also consumers are able to gain from the opportunities provided by increased competition. Those that are dynamic and flexible, and can respond to challenges by adjusting and exploiting these opportunities (for example, as part of the labour force) will benefit from the integration process. This newly created trade and competition will not determine whether there are jobs, but rather what kind of jobs are available.

NOTES

1 Competition policy does not protect individual competitors, but rather the process of competition.
2 Hayek criticized the neo-classical model that is based on perfect competition in the following way: 'But I must be content with thus briefly indicating the absurdity of the usual procedure of starting the analysis with a situation in which all the facts are supposed to be known. This is a *state* of affairs which economic theory curiously calls "perfect competition". It leaves no room whatever for the *activity* called competition, which is presumed to have already done its task' (Hayek, 1978, p. 182).
3 Liberalization of imports has the strongest impact when rates of exchange are stable. Volatility in the exchange rate market may enhance/loosen the effect of this policy instrument.

4 The response of the Luddites in the early nineteenth century to the introduction of looms and jennies was to destroy them.

5 Patent rights seek to protect somebody's codifiable innovation and knowledge, while trademarks protect the reputation of a firm. Other knowledge that comes from learning, trial and error (externalities) is largely unprotected because it may not be put into 'blueprints'.

6 Timely, correct and cheap information is becoming a crucial input in the decision-making process. A banker that is handling large funds over his PC terminal is a long way from the British general Sir Edward Pakenham who lost the battle of New Orleans and his life on 8 January 1815 15 days after the Treaty of Ghent ended the war, but several days before the frigate arrived at his headquarters with the news about the end of the war (Lipsey, 1992, p. 288).

7 The neo-classical doctrine relies on an elegant, but unrealistic, assumption that markets are perfect. Without such a hypothesis, there is no case for optimality in resource allocation.

8 Economies of scope are the outcome of the need for flexible (innovation driven) methods of production. That is because the total production costs of the manufacturing of two separate goods may be higher than the costs of producing them together.

9 See Chapter 6 on industrial policy in manufacturing and services – the section on technology policy in the EU.

10 Rents are proceeds that are in surplus of what is necessary to cover costs of production and to yield an average return on investment. They are due to barriers to entry such as large sunk costs, economies of scale, externalities, advertising, regulatory policies, distribution and service networks, asymmetric information, as well as consumers' loyalty to a certain brand.

11 Innovations do not only change the way of producing goods and services, but also our values and the way we live in an integral manner. For example, Hollywood films changed the way we lived and worked, how we saw the world, how the young courted (they were taken by the car away from the eyes of parents and chaperons) (Lipsey, 1993a, pp. 3–4).

12 While R&D and innovatory activities in the US are mainly led by the military and double-use industries where demand is limited, these activities are in other countries more consumer related; they are directed towards the development of those goods and services for which demand exists everywhere. In addition, R&D is chiefly mission oriented towards big problems in countries such as the US, France and Britain. In countries such as Germany, Japan, Sweden or Switzerland, R&D is directed more towards the solution of practical problems.

13 Apart from the integration of separate markets, other *supporting* adjustment devices include deregulation and privatization.

14 The era of imaginative individuals as major sources of innovation belong to the nineteenth century and before. To fly to the Moon, it takes the work of a vast team of experts.

15 These irreversibilities include savings in factor (including energy) inputs per unit of output.

16 Economic growth may be propelled by the following three components (or by their combination): investment in capital and/or human resources, trade, and technological change.

17 The time needed to double national income per capita in the early stages of industrialization has fallen dramatically. It took Britain around 60 years after 1780 to do that, some 35 years to Japan after 1885, Brazil 18 years after 1961 and China 10 years after 1977. The main reason is technological progress. Countries are able to purchase foreign technology to make their home factors more productive. There is also another dimension to new technology. While it represented an increase in the physical capacity to influence the environment and production that was brought by the industrial revolution in the nineteenth century, the current industrial revolution is more in the domain of qualitative dimension.

18 'The great majority of innovations did *not* come from formal R&D (even in organisations like Du Pont... which had strong in-house R&D facilities). Most... came from production engineers, systems engineers, technicians, managers, maintenance personnel and of course production workers' (Freeman, 1994, p. 474).

19 International agreements are usually ambiguous. This permits diplomats to interpret them at home in their own favour. Conversely, constitutions and other domestic laws are (supposedly) clear. This is because the domestic politicians want the voters to understand them in order to win their votes.

20 Strong advertising campaigns create awareness about 'differences' among, basically, very similar and substitutable goods (for instance, cars, soaps or TV sets). In addition, a large part of intra-industry trade is in parts and components.

21 Linder (1961, p. 102) noted that ships that brought European beer to Milwaukee took American beer back to Europe.

22 Verdoorn suggested that differences in methods of manufacturing between the US and European firms was not in the size of firm/plant but in the length of the individual production run. The diversity of technical processes performed in the same type of plant was much smaller in the US than in Europe (Hague, 1960, p. 346). Compared with plants in the same industry, production runs in the US were several times larger than in Europe, even though the plants were owned by the same TNC (Pratten, 1971, pp. 195, 308–9; Pratten, 1988, pp. 69–70). On the other hand, even in the most efficient developed countries, manufacturing takes place, to a large extent, in plants of only moderate size. Differences in plant productivity are best explained by factors such as (1) inappropriate labour relations, in particular where many thousands of workers need to be employed together; (2) inadequate level of technical training; and (3) an unsatisfactory structure of incentives (Prais, 1981, pp. 272). In support of one of these arguments, there is a finding that strikes grow exponentially with plant size (Geroski and Jacquemin, 1985, p. 174).

23 This refers to the nationality that belongs to the EU.

24 An exception to the general freedom of movement of goods is possible only in cases when such movement jeopardizes public morality, security and the health of humans, animals or plants (Article 36).

25 This programme is also known as the White Paper or the Cockfield Report.

26 Public procurement contracts that cross certain thresholds must be advertised in the *Official Journal* of the EU. For example, the threshold for public works is ECU 5 million, supply contracts in telecommunication is ECU 0.6 million and in the supply of water energy and transport is ECU 0.4 million. The supply of military goods is excluded from these rules. There are, of course, loopholes in the rules. For example, certain public works may be split into a number of smaller ones that are below the limit. Another way of avoiding EU scrutiny is to underestimate the value of the goods and services procured.

27 Regulation 418/85 includes a list of authorized and forbidden clauses in the agreement.

28 A special and still unresolved issue refers to takeovers by foreign firms. If a foreign buyer comes from a country with relatively cheap capital (low rate of interest) relative to the country of the target firm, such an acquirer has an advantage over other potential buyers that have access to financial markets charging higher interest rates. If the authorities in the country of the target firm want to keep the domestic ownership of such a business, they could restrict takeovers by foreign firms and/or give subsidies to domestic acquirers. A much better policy for dealing with such direct interference in business would be to keep the domestic macroeconomic policy in order and, hence, have a domestic capital market competitive with the international one.

29 A relevant market for a good is defined mainly, but not exclusively, on the basis of relatively fast substitutability in demand.

30 The exceptions are airlines and fibres. The two industries have already been highly concentrated for quite some time.

31 If to start a business requires substantial sunk costs, then mere deregulation (the 1992 Programme) may not be enough. Further measures (such as subsidies) may be necessary to provide an investment impetus to firms.

32 The degree of concentration was much lower in the food and drink than in the chemical industry. It was higher on the national than on the EU level because of the barriers to trade (European Communities, 1991, p. 227).

33 Privatization in the former East Germany accounted for a part of the merger and acquisition activity in Germany.

34 This result was similar to the one reached in many studies on mergers in the US.

35 Another important tool for the control of dominance at the EU market and enhancing competition was the conclusion of the Uruguay Round in 1994. After ratification, the deal would liberalize further international trade, increase competition and, hence, modify/limit the non-competitive behaviour of the concentrated EU industries in the internal market.

36 Smaller mergers are under the control of national authorities.

37 These thresholds also apply to firms that originate outside of the EU.

38 The US is currently developing only one advanced fighter jet. At the same time, there are three advanced fighter jets being developed in the EU: the Eurofighter 2000, Dassault Rafale and Saab Gripen. It may be difficult to sustain such prodigality for the next generation of fighter aircraft.

39 If competitive firms want to keep their lead, they need to follow developments not only in their own industry, but also in unrelated, but potentially competing ones. Examples of 'learning by watching' may be found in the almost overnight disappearance of the market for cine cameras after the appearance of camcorders, redressing of the market for mechanical watches after the invention of digital ones or a shift from dot matrix to laser printers.

40 The growing concentration of the semiconductor equipment and materials industries by a few Japanese enterprises created a strategic threat to both commercial and defence interests. For example, because of the concerns of the socialist members of the Japanese Parliament in 1983, the MITI reportedly ordered Kyocera (a domestic manufacturer of high-technology ceramic products) not to take part in contracts to sell ceramic nose cones to the US Tomahawk missile programme (Graham and Krugman, 1991, p. 116). In another example, Nikon, one of only two Japanese suppliers of certain kinds of semiconductor producing machinery, withheld its latest models from foreign customers for up to two years after making them available to Japanese clients (Tyson, 1992, p. 146). An 'explanation' was that the 'regular' customers needed to be served in a better way and prior to the others. The behaviour of IBM was no different. This firm has also refused to sell its components to other clients (Sharp and Pavitt, 1993, p. 144).

41 This Article, however, neither outlaws nor discourages state ownership of enterprises.

42 EU Guidelines for state aid for SMEs (1992) outline that these firms (fewer than 50 employees) may receive support of up to 15 per cent of investment cost. Enterprises with 50 to 250 employees may receive the same aid up to 7.5 per cent of their investment cost, while larger firms may get the same only in the assisted regions of the EU.

43 In the case of steel, shipbuilding or textiles, restructuring often means reduction in production capacity.

44 A special type of public aid is in the form of public purchases. In Italy, for example, a law required that 30 per cent of contracts need to be awarded to firms based in the southern part of the country. The EU Court of Justice ruled in 1990 that such a law violated the public procurement directives. In other countries such as France or Germany there is no explicit buy-national law. None the less, publicly owned enterprises (railways, PTT) are 'expected' to prefer home made goods and services over foreign ones.

45 The biggest state aid case that came before the Commission was the $9.2 billion rescue package for Crédit Lyonnais, the French state owned bank. It was approved in 1995. One cannot avoid the impression that the approval did not have political motivations.

46 State aid in Luxembourg to railways is extremely large.

47 Intervention in R&D may be made for a variety of reasons. For example, the international market for semiconductors and semiconductor equipment industries is dominated by the Japanese. In this highest-technology industry, government intervenes heavily all around the world. In such cases, a defensive national trade policy cannot be a substitute for supportive domestic policies. If the US fails to introduce an industrial policy and make the domestic industry a winner, then the US may well become a long-run loser in the rigged game of international competition (Tyson, 1992, p. 154). A similar analogy may apply to the same industry in the EU.

6

INDUSTRIAL POLICY IN MANUFACTURING AND SERVICES

I INTRODUCTION

Explicit industrial policy as a part of overall economic policy was not in the centre of research interest in the industrialized countries until the mid-1970s. This is due to underlying economic developments. During the 1960s and early 1970s these countries experienced relatively fast economic growth with low rates of inflation and unemployment. Prices of raw materials were stable and relatively low, while labour was flowing without major disturbances from agriculture to the manufacturing and services sectors. Excess demand for labour was met by a steady inflow of labour from abroad. This period was also characterized by sporadic government intervention to influence the pattern of national manufacturing and services production. Relatively free markets were operating smoothly without significant disruption. During this period, the GATT was active in the lowering of tariffs.

The golden era of the 1960s was followed by a period whose first characteristic was a sharp increase in the price of oil in 1973. This triggered rises in inflation, unemployment and a deceleration in the rate of growth throughout the world. International competition increased sharply because suppliers were fighting in shrinking markets. It seemed that the free market system was not capable of coping satisfactorily with this situation. There appeared an awareness about a need for alternative strategies (i.e. ones based on intervention in manufacturing, services and trade) to cope with the new situation. Industrial policy could be seen as a supply-side response to market imperfections. Discussion was less about the formation of capital and more to do with its allocation. It was also more about the adjustment policy than about an industrial policy (a term not liked by either politicians or neo-classical economists). None the less, the gloves were now off for the debate about industrial policy in the developed market economy.

This chapter is structured as follows. An explanation of the rationale (market failure) for an industrial policy is followed by a consideration of the meaning of this policy. Various issues related to industrial policy are considered in a separate section, and so too is the problem of picking winners or losers in industry. Industrial policy in the manufacturing sector, including the technology policy of the EU, is presented, before the analysis of industrial policy in the services sector. At the end of the chapter, certain doubts are raised about the possibility of implementing a sound industrial policy both in a single democratic country or in economic unions because of various interests and coordination problems.

II BACKGROUND

The classical economic model based on free trade and perfect competition predicted that *laissez-faire* is universally beneficial and costless. The new theory of strategic[1] trade and industrial policy demonstrated cases where intervention (including an industrial policy) can play a useful role in mitigating the shortcomings of market imperfections. In general, economic adjustment (reallocation of resources) is prompted by an increase in GNP, as well as changes in demand, technology, prices, foreign competition, marketing and organization of markets, which all contribute to a potential loss in current competitiveness. This adjustment is neither smooth nor easy, nor costless, hence the need for an industrial policy. Instead of relying on the inherited and nature based advantages, industrial policy may help in the conscious shaping of a country's comparative advantage through the supplies of trained labour and an educated management of a specific profile (e.g., engineers vs. priests) tax, infrastructure, public purchase and R&D policies. One thing, however, has to be clear from the outset. Both intervention (action) and *laissez-faire* (non-intervention) have an impact on the structure of industry. The challenge for a government is to profit from the balance between the best parts of the two approaches. That, however, is not at all easy.

Countries in the EU and the US responded to the circumstances during the 1970s primarily by protectionism. These and other industrialized countries realized that the solution to lagging productivity, recession and deteriorating export performance may be found in policies that affect the development of national industry. None the less, inadequate economic performance is not a sufficient condition for the justification of industrial policy. The question is *not* whether the economy is operating (un)satisfactorily, *but* rather whether an industrial policy might have achieved a better result than a free market system (Adams, 1983, p. 405). Any policy has to be tested according to its gains and losses in a dynamic context.

Once free markets lose credibility as efficient conductors of an economy, intervention (with various economic policies) seems inevitable. The question is, how can a government intervene in the most efficient and least harmful way? The choice might be between the risk of leaving the economy to the imperfect entrepreneurs and, possibly, the even greater risk of having it run by imperfect governments (Curzon Price, 1981, p. 20). However, there is no *a priori* reason why an economy run by imperfect governments is at an even greater risk than when the economy is run by imperfect businesspeople and vice versa. Both of them are second-best conductors.

Risk taking (entrepreneurship) has always been a significant engine of economic growth. But the benefits of risk taking are not without peril. The greatest part of the cost of adjustment to a changed situation is borne by those that are powerless. Therefore, governments have quite often followed a defensive policy whose objective was to ensure employment in the short run and evade social tensions, at least during their own term at the office. The socialization of risk in the form of various economic policies may bring a safer life, but it may also prevent both a free operation of individual entrepreneurial activity and an even greater increase in the size of the economic pie. This process may be seen as placating the public's desire to see a happy marriage between progress and stability (Blais, 1986, p. 41). Interestingly, the British experience has shown that rescuing declining industries (coal) to protect jobs has not been a safe route to re-election. Taxpayers and consumers have become more aware of the costs of such an exercise. However, the influence of trade unions in declining industries can still mobilize a powerful lobby in many countries. Those who have full confidence in the operation of a free market system say that the market would take care after itself. Why bother to change those things which would happen anyway? This school of thought does not consider a number of serious market imperfections.

The most influential reasons for intervention may be found in the loss of a competitive position, the management of expansion of new and decline of old industries, the handling of industries subject to scale effects and externalities, as well as attracting footloose industries (Lipsey, 1987a, p. 117). Fostering strategic industries[2] which have strong forward and backward linkages with the rest of the economy can be a very attractive policy goal. These industries supply external or non-priced gains to the rest of the entire economy. Growing industries such as semiconductors and electronics have a much more profound spillover effect on the economy than the furniture or clothes industry.

Another classification of the reasons for an industrial policy groups them in three broad categories. There are respectable, false and non-economic arguments in favour of intervention (Curzon Price, 1990, pp. 159–167):

- Respectable arguments include *market failures* because, in practice, a perfect competition model does not always lead to a stable equilibrium. But the problem is that a market failure such as wage rigidity or monopolies can be traced to a previous intervention by the government. *Domestic distortions* may be used as another pretext for intervention. A uniform VAT system may be neutral regarding the consumption of goods or services. If one wants to reduce the VAT rate on food, a part of resources may shift to that industry at the time when telecommunication or data processing may employ them in a superior way. *Infant industries* provide an appealing reason for intervention, but the problem is that there are many old 'infants' that may never become self-sustaining. Is Airbus one of them? One can build an intellectually respectable case for an industrial policy on *positive externalities* and spillover effects (Krugman, 1993, pp. 160–161).[3] They include the benefits from setting common technical standards for production and/or operation of goods, e.g. telecommunications. However, there may be costly mistakes in targeting, such as computers in France, Concorde (Britain and France) or petrochemicals and aluminium in Japan prior to the first oil shock. The process may become too politicized and subject to strong lobbying just like in the case of *public goods* that everyone wants and consumes, although these goods can be produced with a commercial loss.
- The first false argument in favour of intervention is the issue of *employment*. If employment subsidies extend the life of jobs in the declining businesses, those funds are taken from the growing industries that may need them to expand their operations and that may improve job opportunities both in quality and quantity in the future. The proponents of the *balance-of-payments* argument for intervention often forget that resources that move into the protected industries may leave those industries in which export opportunities may be superior. Hence a drop in imports may provoke a fall in exports.

170

- Non-economic arguments may be quite strong. It is often hard to dispute the issue of *national security*. This is a political process that escapes the prediction scenarios of an economist. The problem is that it may be pushed to the limit where most of the industries may be labelled to be essential for national defence. In general, possible nuclear warfare and 'smart bombs' reduce the weight of the national security argument for intervention. Long-term supply contracts from allies and stockpiling may be considered prior to intervention. *Social arguments* for intervention that distributes, rather than creates wealth, such as regional development or the protection of the environment may have certain non-economic weight during the discussion about intervention.

The relative shares of the manufacturing industry and agriculture in GDP and employment have been continuously declining in the industrialized countries over the past decades. The GDP and employment in these countries on average consists mostly of services (60 per cent), while the rest is distributed between manufacturing, 35 per cent, and agriculture, 5 per cent. Hence, the process of de-industrialization leads countries to the post-industrial society. These countries would be better called service rather than industrialized economies, because manufacturing industry is a statistically 'shrinking' sector in relation to services.[4] One has to be very cautious with such generalizations. Many services (around half) are directly linked to the manufacturing of goods such as transport, financial, telecom and other business services that cover everything from cleaning hotels to business consultancy and advertising. These services are not directly aimed at individuals for their personal consumption. If they are added directly to the relative share of manufacturing and agriculture, these sectors may significantly increase their relative share in the national economy. In fact, they are most intimately linked to each other. In regions with poor services, the manufacturing industry performs below its potential. Hence, the relation between manufacturing and services is not one way. New manufacturing technologies require new, better and/or more services, while services (such as R&D) may create new manufacturing technologies that may, in turn, create a demand for services etc. Profound changes in the structure of manufacturing and services have blurred the division between the two economic sectors.

A relative increase in the demand for services and growth of this sector was made possible by an increase in the productivity of the manufacturing sector. This provided more resources for the services sector of the economy. An increase in productivity lowered the price of manufactured goods, hence there appeared to be an increase in disposable funds for the consumption of services. This makes industrial policy interesting to consider.[5] The importance of manufacturing was considered by the MIT Commission on Industrial Policy. The Commission found for the US that (Dertouzos *et al.*, 1990, pp. 39–42):

- Imports of goods and services were ten times as large as exports of services in 1987. It is necessary to manufacture and export goods in order to pay for imports. The more the resources are relocated to services the lower the chances of equilibrating the foreign balance.
- Moving resources from manufacturing industry into services would cause a shift from a sector with a relatively high productivity growth to one where it is lower.
- Almost all R&D is done by the manufacturing sector.[6]

- The national defence depends on the purchase of a lot of manufacturing goods. If the country starts to rely on foreign suppliers, national security may be in jeopardy.

III WHAT IS THE MEANING OF AN INDUSTRIAL POLICY?

The literature on modern industrial policy started its development in the early 1980s. There appeared various definitions of industrial policy. Before surveying them, one should bear in mind the difference between competition and industrial policy. The former is directed towards the freeing of market forces, while the latter is seeking to channel them (Geroski, 1987, p. 57). In addition, industrial policy may sometimes have strong anti-competitive effects.

Some definitions of industrial policy are specific and selective. Industrial policy can be defined as coordinated targeting. It is the selection of parts of the economy such as firms, projects or industries for special treatment (targeting), which is coupled with a coordinated government plan to influence industrial structure in defined ways (coordination) (Brander, 1987, p. 4). Industrial policy implies policies that relate to specific industries, such as correcting restrictive business practices (Pinder, 1982, p. 44). Industrial policies can be those government policies that are intended to have a direct effect on a particular industry or firm (McFetridge, 1985, p. 1). Industrial policy is aimed at particular industries (and firms as their components) in order to reach the ends that are perceived by the government to be efficient for the country as a whole (Chang, 1994, p. 60). This definition does not, however, distinguish between the short- and long-term time perspective. Different policies need to be employed to achieve efficiency if that perspective changes.

Other definitions of industrial policy are broad, often overloaded, and include many areas of public policy. For example, industrial policy includes all government actions that affect industry such as domestic and foreign investment, innovation, external trade, regional and labour policies, environmental features and all other aspects (Donges, 1980, p. 189). Industrial policy can be any government measure or set of measures used to promote or prevent structural change (Curzon Price, 1981, p. 17). Industrial policy may mean all measures that improve the economy's supply potential: anything that will improve growth, productivity and competitiveness (Adams and Klein, 1983, p. 3). Another view of industrial policy can take it to mean a government policy action aimed at or motivated by problems within specific sectors. The 'problems' are presumably in both declining and expanding (manufacturing or service) industries. The solutions to these problems need not necessarily be sector-specific although that is a possibility (Tyson and Zysman, 1987a, p. 19). The initiation and coordination of government activities in order to influence and improve the productivity and competitiveness of particular industries or the whole economy is industrial policy (Johnson, 1984, p. 8). Industrial policy can be defined as the set of selective measures adopted by the state to alter industrial organization (Blais, 1986, p. 4). Another definition states that its focus has been on the ideal relation between governments and markets. Industrial policy need not be equated with national planning. It is, rather, a formula for making the economy adaptable and dynamic (Reich, 1982, pp. 75 and 79). The term industrial policy describes that group of policies whose explicit objective is to influence the operation of industry (Sharp and Shepherd, 1987, p. 107). An industrial policy implies intervention by a government which seeks to promote particular industries in some way. This may be either to stimulate an industry's production and growth or to promote export sales (Whalley, 1987, p. 84). This definition does not, however, include government influence on the decline of and exit from an industry. Industrial policy may be equated with intervention employed to cope with market failures or price system and that affects allocation of resources (Komiya, 1988, p. 4). All acts and policies of a government that relate to industry, constitute industrial policy (Bayliss and El-Agraa, 1990, p. 137). Industrial policy is defined by the World Bank 'as government efforts to alter industrial structure to promote productivity-based growth' (World Bank, 1993, p. 304).[7] Industrial policy includes all actions that are taken to advance industrial development beyond what is allowed by the free market system (Lall, 1994, p. 651). To formulate a definition of industrial policy can be difficult. One US Supreme Court Justice tried to find a definition of pornography and said: 'You know it when you see it, but you can't define it' (Audretsch, 1989, p. 10). This may be the case too with industrial policy.

A critical definition of industrial policy states that it is the label used to describe a wide ranging, ill-assorted collection of micro-based supply-side initiatives that are designed to improve market performance in a variety of mutually inconsistent ways. Intervention is typically demanded in cases with market failures and where major changes need to be effected quickly (Geroski, 1989, p. 21).

Industrial policy may mean different things for various countries at different times. Developing countries consider industrial policy as a means of economic development. They may favour certain industries over others. Once these countries become developed, industrial policy may be directed towards fostering free competition. In the ex-centrally planned economies, industrial policy meant planning and imposing production and investment targets in each sector and industry within it.

Industrialized countries have had implicit industrial policies for a long period. They were embodied in trade, competition, tax, R&D, standardization, education, public procurement and other policies that have derived effects on the industrial structure. This is due to the interdependence of economic policies within the economic system. Therefore, some countries have joint ministries of industry and international trade. This is the case, for instance, with the British Department of Trade and Industry (DTI) and the Japanese Ministry of International Trade and Industry (MITI), although there are differences in powers and role in the economy between the two ministries.

In most developed countries the whole period after the Second World War was characterized by reductions in tariffs, as well as measures to prevent the demise of declining industries. The industrial policies of governments may be a simple continuation of old protectionism by more sophisticated means (Pinder *et al.*, 1979, p. 9). Governments' tax and transfer policies have had an impact on demand, which affected manufacturing production. By direct production and supply of public goods, as well as through public procurement governments have influenced, at least in part, the industrial structure of their economies. Other government policies, such as foreign policy have nothing directly to do with an increase in the economic pie of the country. However, they can influence industrial structure and employment. This is the case when some governments ban the exports of high-technology goods abroad.

Various economic policies have their impact on industrial policy. It is not only trade policy, but also social, regional, energy, transport and others. Hence, most definitions of industrial policy include, at least implicitly, the need for a stable economic environment and a coordination of different economic policies. Only then may specific targeting of industrial policy make its full contribution to economic growth and improvement in productivity and competitiveness with the final objective an increase in the standard of living. On those grounds, broad definitions of industrial policy may embrace all of these facets. Hence, industrial policy is an economic policy that shapes a country's comparative advantage. Its objective is to influence the change in national economic structure (reallocation in resources) in order to enhance the creation and growth of national wealth, rather than to distribute it.

Three (non-mutually exclusive) broad types of industrial policy include macroeconomic, sectoral and microeconomic orientation. Macroeconomic orientation is least interventionist because it leaves the operation of industries and firms to market forces. This policy orientation simply improves the general economic climate for business. Sector-specific orientation becomes relevant when market failures affect certain industries. It tries to amend the particular market shortcoming. Microeconomic orientation of industrial policy may direct a government to act directly towards specific firms or industrial groups (Jacquemin, 1984, pp. 4–5).

There are another three broad types of industrial policy. They are market oriented, interventionist or mixed. The first type (market oriented) fosters competition and free markets. The second (interventionist) policy may be conducted as in centrally planned economies. In practice, industrial policy is most often a mixture of the former two. The majority of countries may be classified as 'massaged-market economies'.[8] The only thing which most often differs between countries is not whether they intervene or not, but rather the degree and form of intervention in industry.

Industrial policy may be adjustment-prone or adjustment-averse. Adjustment-prone industrial policy stimulates the adjustment of various industries to enter into the new production, remain competitive or ease the exit from the selected lines of production. Adjustment-averse industrial policy is the policy of protection which impedes changes in an economy by preserving the status quo.

IV INDUSTRIAL POLICY ISSUES[9]

The standard comparative-advantage and factor-proportions theories of international trade may be satisfactory for an explanation of trade in primary goods. They are, however, less so in understanding trade in industrial goods. Manufacturing can be seen as a collection of industries with no factor abundance base. On those grounds it is difficult to explain why France exports perfumes while Japan exports copiers, cameras and VCRs, or why the Swiss export chocolate, chemicals and watches.

A country's comparative advantage is not only given by resource endowment, but is shaped over time by the actions of both business and government. Economic policies of a government may affect comparative advantage over time by influencing the quantity and quality of labour, capital, incentives and technology. The comparative advantage in manufacturing industries is not an unchangeable facet of nature, but often the outcome of economic policies which affect incentives to save, invest, innovate, diffuse technology and acquire human capital.

Until 1970s market imperfections were at the margin of orthodox economic analysis, but these imperfections are in the heart of analysis of the new theory of trade and industrial policy. A country's size; regional disequilibria; skill, mobility and unionization of labour; R&D sunk costs; economies of scale; competition and bankruptcy laws are just a few imperfections. To ignore them is to miss the point that their effects can be mitigated by economic policy (Tyson, 1987, pp. 67–71). In the field of industry, a government disposes of a number of instruments. They include trade policy (tariffs and NTBs) that may reduce competition and antitrust policy that increases it; preferential tax treatment; non-commercial loans and loan guarantees as a support to the risk capital; exports, insurance and other subsidies; public procurement; support to education and vocational re-training; assistance to workers to improve their professional and geographical mobility; and provision of public or publicly financed R&D.

Free competition within an economic union brings costs of adjustment to which the governments, voters and citizens are not indifferent. It is often forgotten that increased competition brings benefits from economic restructuring. Costs of adjustment are often highly concentrated on the (vociferous) few and are usually temporary, while the benefits are dispersed over a long period of time and throughout the society, but in relatively small instalments to everyone. In the real, second-best and imperfect world, there may be enough scope for both market mechanism and select intervention (economic policy).

The role of governments as organizers of national economies is coming under increasing inquiry. In spite of a general agreement about the need to reduce the extent of public intervention in the allocation of resources in a national economy, it is a fact that the countries that had the most impressive economic achievements during the past two decades were the ones whose governments exerted strong and positive influence over all facets of commercial affairs (Dunning, 1994a, p. 1).

A general reduction in tariffs and NTBs, as well as economic integration, may increase a country's market. However, free markets are short-sighted about producing the necessary structural adjustments from the vantage point of long-term needs of the society. The adjustment (the transfer of resources from the lagging to the growing industries) may not necessarily be a swift, cheap and smooth process. In addition, that is a risky operation as the future of the expanding industries is not very certain in the long run. If smart (a big if), adjustment policies (intervention) can facilitate these shifts by providing incentives and support to the private businesses to adjust to the new situation, then intervention may find certain justification.

One can make predictions about the model of economic adjustment based on the characteristics of a country's financial system. First, if this system relies on capital markets that allocate resources by competitively established prices, the adjustment process is company-led. The allocation decisions are the responsibility of firms as is in the US. Second, in a credit-based financial system where the government is administering prices, the adjustment process is state led (such as the past experiences of Japan and France). Lastly, in a credit-based system where price formation is dominated by banks the adjustment process can be described as negotiated, as found in Germany (Zysman, 1983, p. 18).

The question still remains: can imperfect governments make this shift any better than imperfect markets? Generally not, but this does not mean that market solutions are always superior than other ones. Just as the dangers of market failure are often exaggerated, so are the competences of governments. None the less, there are certain cases where a government's intervention (policy) may fare better than a free market solution. There are a number of reasons, along the lines of the new theory, why intervention may be justified.

First, the time horizon that private markets consider is relatively short. They may not foresee the long-term needs of countries in changing circumstances, or their capabilities, as well as opportunities with a high degree of accuracy. Japanese manufacturing is financed to a large extent by bank credits while the US industry uses this source of finance to a much lower degree. This means that the manager of a Japanese firm who asks for a loan can inform the home bank manager that he is looking for patient capital since he expects profits to come in the ship that is due to arrive in the forthcoming few years. The manager of an American firm in the similar situation has to be sure that he can see the smoke of the ship in the distance. Hence, US industrial production is much more affected by the short-term interests of shareholders than Japanese. The major goal of Japanese and German bank and enterprise managers is to ensure a firm's long-term competitive position in the market and favour risky investments such as commercialization of new technologies. In contrast, the US system opts for readily measurable physical (mergers and acquisitions) over intangible assets such as education or R&D. A government policy may change this short-term foresight towards longer-term economic considerations.

Second, in a different case, risk-averse governments may organize stockpiling in order to cushion the effect of a possible crisis. Private markets may not have the desire and/or funds to do the same in the long run. A government may estimate cost of this kind of risk in terms of GDP that would be sacrificed in the case of an unexpected reduction in the availability of certain inputs.

Third, governments may wish to keep some facilities for home production as a bargaining chip with foreign suppliers when negotiating prices in long-term supply contracts. This would deter foreign monopolies from charging monopoly prices.

Fourth, market forces are quite efficient in allocating resources among producers and allocating goods and services among consumers in simple and static settings. Much of the power of markets in these circumstances emerges from the fact that prices convey all the necessary information to participants. That enables them to act independently, without explicit coordination, and still reach a collectively effective solution. It is possible that markets can, at least in principle, solve simple and static problems in a remarkably efficient way, but it is not very surprising to find out that the free market game does less well in more demanding circumstances such as market imperfections. Adjustment problems appear because of the unsatisfactory operation of the market/price game viewed from the long-term vantage point. It is the aim of forward-looking intervention to put the economy on the way towards the desired long-term equilibrium.

Fifth, basic research provides significant positive externalities (spillovers) throughout the economy. These social gains are in most cases difficult for private markets to grasp because the private risks and costs may be very high in the light of uncertain benefits and their appropriation. In addition, without intervention, such as patents and other intellectual property rights, free markets cannot guarantee sufficient pecuniary returns to the private innovator. The fruits of successful basic research fuel technological progress in the country. This research is funded in full or in part by the government in direct (subsidy) or indirect (tax relief) ways in most countries. Governments and private businesses share risk.

Sixth, industrial policy may ease economic adjustment in a more efficient and equitable way than free market forces. This policy may provide support for R&D, education and training, support for geographical and professional mobility of labour, investment subsidies, protection and other support for the improvement of infrastructure during the initial fragile period of a new industry. Free market forces fail to do so. As for the adjustment and exit from ailing industries, government policy may offer unemployment benefits and vocational training. Industrial policy can, to an extent, both anticipate and shape these changes. It can be involved either directly in picking the winners/losers or indirectly by creating a business environment where firms can make choices in the potentially successful and desirable way.

Seventh, agriculture is a sector in which every government intervenes. Due to the impact of weather conditions, free market forces cannot achieve stability of supply and stabilize incomes of the farm population relative to the labour force in the manufacturing sector. In addition, governments tend to secure the domestic supply of farm goods in the event of war, as well as protect the landscape and environment.

The eighth reason for the introduction of an industrial policy is that this policy may be able to respond, with various internal and external (retaliatory) measures, to the economic policies of foreigners. Left alone, the market forces may take advantage of foreign policies in the short run, but if the long-term strategy of foreigners is to undermine the importing country's home production by means of predatory pricing in order to create an international monopoly, then the long-term effect may be detrimental for the importing country's welfare. An industrial policy may be a suitable response because it may alter the possible free market outcome.

Tariffs (trade policy) were historically the most important instrument of industrial policy. Due to a number of rounds of multilateral reduction in tariffs under the GATT, the use of this instrument was restricted and reduced, but there appeared other means of intervention. Some of them personify protectionist pressures against adjustment, while others are adjustment oriented. They include subsidies for exports, production, R&D and investment; NTBs; tax, exchange rate and credit policy; public purchases; price and exchange controls; regulation of the market (such as licensing); technical standards; direct production by the state; provision of infrastructure; competition and concentration policy.

The most benign intervention is one that does not harm other businesses and sectors. The most effective instruments of an industrial policy include macroeconomic stability, education and provision of infrastructure. Low inflation, stable exchange rate and slightly positive real rates of interest may be the best tools of an industrial policy. Savings will increase and entrepreneurs would have the chance to observe and shape their future with a relatively high degree of accuracy. Well-educated management and well-trained labour (investment in human capital) provide the economy with the most valuable assets, capable of solving problems. Moreover, in many cases private businesses are not interested in investment in infrastructure (sewerage systems, certain roads or bridges, etc.), so the government needs to step in.

Many of these instruments may be applied to a single target simultaneously, and may sometimes be in conflict. If the objective is an increase in efficiency, then competition and concentration may be conflicting. It was accepted that many industries may not operate efficiently without a certain degree of concentration that is dictated by minimum efficient economies of scale. So, a certain degree of concentration has to be accepted. Small countries usually do not have very restrictive anti-monopoly laws, because efficient production for their home (unprotected) market and possibly foreign ones often allows the existence of only one efficient production unit. Countries such as France foster the policy of concentration and efficiency, while others such as the US, due to the huge home market, have strong anti-monopoly legislation which favours free competition. Inward-looking industries that are in the ailing phase of their lifecycle traditionally lobby in every country for protection, while the emerging industries which are oriented to the widest international market, support free trade.

It was a strong belief in Europe during the 1960s that big American-style companies were the key factor of economic growth for a country. These enterprises may, among other things, spend substantial funds on R&D and increase their international competitiveness. Hence, mergers and acquisitions were encouraged. That policy left Europe with a number of sleepy industrial giants who were ill equipped to face the challenges of the 1970s and 1980s (Geroski and Jacquemin, 1985, p. 175). However, experience has shown that those countries that spend most on R&D do not necessarily have the highest rates of growth. It was also realized that SMEs,[10] largely forgotten or marginal in the traditional economic analysis, are important factors for economic revival and employment. Subsequently the policy which strongly encouraged mergers and acquisitions was abandoned. Jobs created by SMEs are greater in number than those created by large companies per unit of investment. This may be one of the outcomes of a business policy of (large) firms that want to avoid conflicts with organized labour. Product differentiation demands production on a smaller scale and decentralization of business. This is radically different from the prevailing theoretical expectations of the 1960s.

An expansion of SMEs started after the first oil shock (1973). However, jobs created by SMEs often have the disadvantage of being relatively less secure than those in big firms. Being small, these firms need to be flexible if they want to withstand competition. Flexible SMEs often use hit-and-run methods in their business which is linked with low sunk costs, since they can act faster regarding new business opportunities than rigid large firms. However, SMEs often do not have the ability to behave 'strategically' and exert such a strong lobbying power as big businesses can. None the less, SMEs are necessary for the balanced growth of an economy, as they provide links among various sub-sectors. In general, neither large businesses nor SMEs may be efficient in isolation. They both need each other. Big businesses may use specialized SMEs as subcontractors and buffers against fluctuations in demand.

While industrial policy deals with select industries, policy on SMEs refers to a group of firms of a specific size. It is supposed to rectify market imperfections that work against relatively smaller firms (uncertain future; high risk; absolutely low value of assets, but their quality may not necessarily be low). This policy also supports the beneficial attributes of SMEs, such as organizational flexibility, fast and smooth flow of information, product differentiation and custom-made goods and services.

Subsidies may be a distorting instrument of industrial policy. They may diminish incentives to profitable firms if they are always taxed to provide the government with revenue for subsidies to inefficient enterprises. A subsidy that stimulates the introduction of new capital may distort a firm's choice among technologies. That is relevant for firms that use capital and labour in different proportions. If a firm has to pay the full cost of capital it might choose another technology. A one-time subsidy to investment may help a firm to buy time and adjust to an unexpected change in demand or technology. If the value of subsidies and other favours is smaller than the additional value added in the given industry, than subsidization may be justified (but this calculation can be quite difficult). If subsidies are provided on a permanent basis for the protection of employment in an industry or firm, its management does not need to perform its role as efficiently as it would in enterprises or industries where market criteria predominate. A permanently subsidized industry or firm is a very likely candidate for nationalization.

A common view of the world holds that firms play Cournot–Nash games against all other players (each firm decides on a course of action, e.g. output, on the assumption that the behaviour of the other firms remains constant), while the governments play a Stackleberg game (this agent knows the reaction functions of all others) against firms and Cournot–Nash against other governments (Brander and Spencer, 1985, p. 84). Unfortunately these are all games that may produce relatively unstable solutions and fluctuations in prices. Collusion among the players may lead to a relatively stable (Chamberlin) solution.

The promotion of the adjustment of some industries does not always go smoothly. Some ailing industries are well established, relatively large employers of labour and possess a strong political lobby. This is often the case with the steel industry. Some steel firms are, however, quite successful in their adjustment, such as the US Steel Company which closed 13 steel making units and diversified out of steel. This company invested funds in a shopping centre in Pittsburgh, Pennsylvania, and a chemical business in Texas. Steel making accounted for only 11 per cent of the US Steel's operating income (Trebilcock, 1986, p. 141). Other steel companies prefer a steady life. They neither innovate nor compete, but they are able to mobilize powerful political forces and government policy instruments (tariffs, quotas, subsidies) in order to resist adjustment (contraction in output and labour redundancies). Response to shocks such as an increase in labour costs was met by a number of US firms by sticking to the same technology, but investing abroad where labour costs were lower. The response of Japanese firms to the same shock was to change technology and increase productivity. In addition, certain Japanese TNCs, operating in the US, increased the US content of their goods over and above the domestic content of their US counterparts in the same industry. A number of US firms wanted to compete on the home market with the Japanese TNC not necessarily on the basis of productivity, but rather on the grounds of low labour costs. Therefore, many US firms started to source heavily from abroad (developing countries) or to transfer labour-intensive operations to these locations. Japanese TNCs operating in the US were increasing productivity, so by the mid-1980s, for example, colour TVs sold in the US by the domestically owned firms had less local content than those made by Japanese competitors. Honda and Nissan each had a local content of over 60 per cent in their cars produced in the US in 1987. That was expected to increase to 75 per cent over the following ten years (Graham and Krugman, 1991, pp. 78–79).

The newly industrialized countries have substantially increased their competitiveness in traditional industries such as steel and shipbuilding. Their output position is irreversible in the medium and, perhaps, long term. These industries cannot recover in developed market economies on the grounds of reductions in wages. Such a policy would involve a waste of resources, as trade unions would resist cuts in wages to match the level of wages prevailing in the newly industrialized countries which have productivity at a level comparable to that one in developed market economies.

Sufficient subsidies would always keep output (in ailing industries) at a level which would not survive in free market conditions. Emerging industries, where investment risk is quite high, have to offer the prospects of relatively higher rewards than elsewhere in the economy in order to attract factors. Gains in productivity in these new businesses may be able to cushion increases in pecuniary rewards to investors without increases in prices. However, faced with the possibility for higher wages in one industry, trade unions might press for increases in wages elsewhere in the economy. Without increases in productivity, the result might be an increase in prices throughout the economy. None the less, the emerging industries where productivity is higher than elsewhere in the economy might still remain a lap ahead of other businesses in the same race.

The policy of shoring up a 'dying' industry for an excessively long period is like moving forwards, but looking backwards. Paying compensation to redundant labour might be preferable to the policy of shoring up ailing firms. Compensation to redundant labour needs to be provided by public authorities because the whole of society benefits from industrial change and adjustment. Shareholders of dying firms should not be compensated for the depreciated value of their shares. They should channel their funds to the growing businesses that need fresh capital for expansion, not to the ones that are declining and that do not need it (Curzon Price, 1981, pp. 27–29).

In contrast with the declining industries, the emerging ones need venture capital: they may be quite small, numerous, unstable and with an uncertain future. When they are in trouble their voice may not be heard as loudly as the voice of declining industries. Investment in the emerging firms is risky because many of them collapse before they reach maturity.[11] However, these firms are the most propelling agents of the modern economy. Although many of them disappear from the market, many of them stay and new ones are created. A high birth rate of new firms is the best expression of the vitality of the system which creates incentives, so that many new enterprises may be started and risk accepted. Alfred Marshall drew the analogy between the forest (industry, sector or the whole economy) and the trees (individual firms). The trees may grow and decay for individual reasons (such as the prodigal character of the owner's wife), but what is important for the economy is that the forest grows.

When the economic adjustment is spread over a number of years, it might appear that it is easier and less costly per unit of time. Some 'breathing space' for the structural change (slowing down the attrition or keeping the ailing industries alive) might be obtained, but this argument is not always valid. First, the damage to the rest of the economy is greater the longer a depressed industry is allowed to prolong its agony and, second, it is not obvious that the prolonged adjustment is really any easier to bear than a quick surgery. Even the direct costs may turn out, in practice, to be higher (Curzon Price, 1981, p. 120).

All protectionist measures offered to an industry ought to be conditional, otherwise the problems of an industry may be exacerbated. If the protected industry is in decline, then its adjustment may be postponed or reversed by production or employment subsidies. This increases costs to the society in the long run because the desired change (transfer of resources from low-profit to high-profit industries) does not take place. The adjustment policy needs to be of limited duration. It should involve both public funds and private capital, and should also make the cost of action as transparent as possible. In addition, the recipients of assistance should be expected to develop comparative advantages prior to assistance ending. Market processes should be encouraged and managerial practices improved.[12]

Direct subsidies for R&D or indirect subsidies in the form of public procurement are powerful instruments for the support of industries that introduce new goods and services. The volume of demand and its structure provides the most important incentive for production. This is also crucial for strategic industries, the ones whose activities provide external and unpriced gains through linkages and externalities to the rest of the economy (examples include the machine tool industry, computers, telecommunications and data-processing).[13] If start-up costs create a barrier to entry into strategic industry, the government may step in and help out. If the governments of other countries are subsidizing their strategic industries, the case for intervention by the domestic government may look very tempting. In the early unstable phase of the introduction of a new good or service, a secure government demand provides a powerful impetus for the firm to shape the product and open new markets. If this production does not become self-sustaining within a specified period of time, then it may never become profitable and resources that may be allocated for protection may be used elsewhere in the future with a greater efficiency in improving competitiveness. The costs of subsidies need to be considered before intervention. A subsidy to one firm is a tax on others. If there are possibilities for big returns in the future, such tax might be worth bearing, but the gains are impossible to judge in advance. Once a government starts handing out subsidies, demands for more keep expanding without end. It is then that political power, rather than 'economic sense' determines who gets what. The long isolation of an industry from market forces may remove incentives for the swift reaction to signals that come from competition in international markets.

Protection may be given to an industry on the condition that the schedule of protection/intervention is revised downward over time. If protection is not temporary and selective, it may create serious adjustment problems and increase costs in the future. The strategy of selection and the transitory nature of protection may provide a limited adjustment period to an industry by mitigating the full impact of international competition. This programme does not ensure the existence of inefficient industries and firms, but rather their adjustment and exit from declining businesses. The self-liquidation of protection is perhaps the only means for maintaining the incentives to adjust. If the adjustment programmes offer funds to firms, then there must be an obligation that these funds are spent on specified activities. The adjustment programmes should be overseen by technical advisory boards that represent a wide community (Tyson and Zysman, 1987b, p. 425).

Public intervention was in many countries primarily, but not exclusively, directed towards the problem industries. They were usually coal, steel, textiles, footwear and agriculture. However, there appeared a growing interest in intervening in the emerging industries. Intervention there is in the form of providing or subsidising innovation, R&D in firms, special tax treatment of new technologies (tax holidays and subsidies), training of labour, education of management, government procurement, provision of infrastructure, as well as more general instruments such as planning, policy guidelines and the exchange of information.

The level of industrial policy may be general and specific. The choice is between discrimination and non-discrimination. The degree of intervention should be as high as possible. That means that it needs to be general, i.e. available to every industry and enterprise. Once the policy is installed, the market is the best tool for fine tuning the economy, creating and taking advantage of unforeseen opportunities, as well as selecting the firms or industries that should take advantage of the policy instruments. Market forces prevent players from inefficient employment of resources. The policy should be tailored to suit local needs (industry or firm) in cases where there are no externalities. In addition, it ought to be used only as a last resort because the government does not have perfect knowledge and may well make the wrong choice, as was the case with the French and British Concorde project.

V PICKING THE WINNER/LOSER

The new theory of trade and strategic industrial policy found, in contrast to the neoclassical theory, certain manufacturing and service industries that are relatively more important to an economy than others. Those are the industries with economies of scale, wide forward and backward linkages and unpriced spillover effects (externalities) on the rest of the economy. Favours to those industries *may* create a new irreversible competitive advantage for a country.[14] It needs to be clear from the outset that the findings of the new theory are not prescriptions for economic policy, but rather an agenda for further research (Krugman, 1993, p. 164). If industrial policy is selective, then it is coupled with the policy of picking the winner (creating a national champion) or picking (bailing out) the loser. This has always been difficult, risky, and has demanded considerable and costly information. If this were not so, then you would probably not bother reading this book, but rather look at the stock market report, invest and increase the value of your assets by several zeros daily. If the choice of the winner of tomorrow is wrong and requires permanent subsidies, then such an industry/firm may become a loser the day after tomorrow. If one intervenes, it is important to have reasonable aims and use policy tools preferably in an indirect way, and to be ready to pull back whenever there are undesirable events in order to prevent even greater damage.

Picking the winner can usually be found in countries whose domestic market is small and unable to support the competition of several firms that operate at the optimum level of efficiency. National free market policies can be fostered in large countries such as the US, which leave market forces to select the best suppliers. Smaller countries have usually to rely on selective policies which are potentially riskier. They have to make the best use of the limited available resources. Those resources have to be concentrated on select industries (specialization). Such industrial and trade policy may be termed 'cautious activism' which should not be taken to mean protectionism.

While France relied on a relatively centralized economic model, Germany fostered a decentralized one. However, both countries have achieved a relatively comparable level of economic success (de Ghellinck, 1988, p. 140). While picking the winner, the government chooses between supporting emerging industries and propping up ailing ones (protection of the existing structure which is adjustment-averse). The balance between the two depends upon both the power of the involved industries and the intentions of the government.

The policy of singling out industries or firms for special treatment means disregarding the problems of all others. The 'neglected' businesses may be at a relative disadvantage because they cannot count on direct support from the state if they happen to be in need. In addition, they are taxed in one way or another to provide funds for the public support of the 'privileged' businesses. That drains funds for investment in the promising enterprises. The neglect of emerging and expanding industries can reduce the appetite of entrepreneurs for risk-taking and jeopardize the growth of the economy in the future. If a government cannot formulate the basic structural objectives of national economic policy, then it would have to leave that to the politically strongest segment of industry.[15] The policy would be formulated in a hurry in response to the political pressures of the moment which would probably result in the protection of troubled industries. Independence, resistance to business pressures and clear economic objectives by a government remove *ad hoc* economic policies. Otherwise, the industrial policy of the country would be an instrument for supporting the obsolete industries and a brake on expanding ones (Tyson and Zysman, 1987a, p. 22). The history of trade and industrial policy (just look at the GATT rounds of negotiations) revealed how hard it is to fight the entrenched interests of producers.

Output grows fastest in the emerging industries. These industries may not necessarily create a significant volume of direct employment, but due to linkages and other externalities, they have a strong potential for the creation of indirect jobs. There has been, however, a notable technological improvement in declining industries such as textiles and steel. So, the distinction between the two kinds of industries is, in general, mostly for analytical purposes. A wise move for the risk-averse developing country may be to choose first the establishment of a good 'declining' industry, rather than an uncertain expanding one. Of course, the potential consequences of this choice may be a decline in the standard of living relative to countries that have opted for a different development model and are successful (?!) in its implementation.

Targeting is linked to three basic issues. They are: (1) which industries or firms should receive support; (2) what kind of support should be provided; and (3) for how long? The industries that are singled out for 'special treatment' are usually the ones that are significant employers and those that have important externalities. In addition, if the private markets do not favour risky investments such as the development of alternative sources of energy, then the government may also single out such investments for special treatment.

If domestic regulations regarding safety standards are stricter and more costly than abroad, than, other things being equal, this may put home firms at a relative disadvantage in competition with foreigners. This might be used as an argument for demanding some public 'support'. Political reasons such as national defence and pride might influence decisions about the support of certain industries. Assistance should cease as soon as the beneficiary becomes profitable; or once it becomes obvious that it would never happen; or after the expiration of the specified period of time for assistance.

Japan is an example of a country that has reaped the fruits of conscious targeting of certain industries. This country was always one step ahead of competitors regarding new technologies[16] in the targeted industries. During the 1960s the targets were steel and shipbuilding because of their significant externalities. Another target was the production of toys. During the 1970s the targets were machine tools and cars. The target for the 1980s was electronics (copiers, computers, audio and video equipment). The target for the 1990s are semiconductors. This may be taken as an example of the shaping of comparative advantage in a dynamic context. Japanese 'targeting' was first and foremost an information-collecting, interpretation and transmission process which helped individual firms to make investment decisions. In addition, it guided the government in allocating, basically, indirect support to businesses. Japan was emphasizing intervention in technological *areas* that created a large bilateral trade surplus with the US, rather than in *firms*.[17]

Japanese targeting has not been successful in all cases, however, for a variety of reasons. For example, this country targeted the production of aluminium and petro-chemicals before the first oil shock, after which such choice was not justified. The MITI was against the development of cars during the 1960s since the US and Europe were ahead of Japan in these industries. In spite of the official opposition to the expansion of the car manufacturing industry, Japanese corporations were against the MITI and pushed ahead with the manufacture of cars. Their policy was sound and yielded positive results.

Elsewhere in the developed market economies, the policy of targeting may not be that smooth. After the Second World War, industrial policy relied partly on unorganized labour that was flowing from agriculture and abroad into the manufacturing industry. This situation has since changed. Trade unions organize labour that can influence (i.e. postpone) economic adjustment, even though it may be to the long-term detriment of the economy.

France is a country whose concern was in the creation of large and efficient firms to compete in international markets. This country was not very concerned with home competition. France's Interministerial Committee for Development of Strategic Industries targeted the key industries, defined the strategy and picked a firm as a national champion to implement the programme. The programme was implemented through a contract between the government and the firm. The government did not, however, have perfect foresight. Mistaken judgements have been made in very costly projects such as computers and Concorde. Although the Concorde project was a success in the high-technology industry, it was a commercial failure (the project started in 1962 when fuel was cheap).

The French strategy in computers was to try to build large mainframes in order to compete directly with IBM, rather than begin with small computers or peripheral equipment. This was too ambitious for the relatively undeveloped French firms to cope with, so the attempt failed. The mistake might have been avoided if the government industrial policy-makers had consulted more with private experts. Private firms also make mistakes, but they are less likely to ignore market forces (in particular when they use loans) than government officials. That was the main reason why the Japanese targeting was more successful than French. The early French mistakes, however, were not in vain. During the Airbus[18] project, the government learned to select the segment of the market for which demand would be high. It also tied customers by early purchasing of aircraft parts in exchange for orders (Carliner, 1988, p. 164).

Direct targeting of certain industries or firms has not been a striking feature of US industrial policy. This system was established in such a way as to foster individual freedom, not to discriminate among firms or industries. The only exceptions are agriculture and sporadic bailouts of firms such as Lockheed (1971) or Chrysler (1979). Government consumption on all levels, however, gives a big overall demand pull to the economy due to a huge general expenditure and the budget deficit. Since a part of public expenditure is defence-related, selective public procurement or subsidized insurance indirectly influences the development and expansion of high technologies. Hence, the argument that the US government does not intervene in the economy does not hold water at all. In special situations (e.g, during the Second World War), the US had an explicit industrial policy.[19] In addition, the US has become the major producer of food in the world as a consequence of calculated economic and other policies that involved various (including credit) subsidies.

Human capital and human resource management are the key factors in increasing a country's comparative advantage in a rapidly changing technology and market situation. Basic choices such as the education of priests or engineers, singers or mathematicians, lawyers or designers influence a country's competitiveness. Macroeconomic policy may just support, in an important way, the creation of comparative advantage, but it is human capital (properly organized, valued and continuously educated) that presents the major lever in the enhancement of a country's competitive advantage.

During the nineteenth and early twentieth centuries, bright pupils in Britain were steered towards the classics at Oxford and Cambridge, while technical subjects were reserved for the less gifted. The situation was reversed in France, Germany and Japan. After the Second World War, British industry began to recruit widely from the universities. A career in industry, even if a third choice after the Foreign Office and the BBC, became socially acceptable for the sons (and increasingly the daughters) of the establishment (Sharp and Shepherd, 1987, pp. 83–84).

Some may argue that government planners and other public officials in Japan, France and Germany may be more competent and sophisticated than the managers of private firms in those countries. The best and most ambitious students aspire to government service. In North America, society has a different attitude. Many people look on government jobs as inferior to those in the private sector because, among other things, they are less well paid. It is not surprising to find that Japan, France and Germany have an industrial policy, while the US and Canada do not, at least not overt industrial policies. Nevertheless, shoddy economic policies in these two countries may be easily amended if civil servants were given a freer hand by the system (Brander, 1987, p. 40).

VI EUROPEAN UNION

1 Legal base

General economic conditions supported a liberal (non-interventionist) economic strategy when the EU was established. Therefore, the Treaty of Rome did not explicitly ask for the introduction of an industrial policy, as was the case with trade, agriculture, social issues or transport.[20] The Treaty empowered the EU to regulate only the rules of competition (Articles 85, 86 and 92, respectively) and external trade. At the same time, industrial policy itself remained in the hands of national governments. Those EU rules were the means of conducting industrial policy. The use of all other policy instruments was severely restricted. A step towards the elimination of internal NTBs came with the Single European Act. Article 8a defined the internal market of the EU as 'an area without internal frontiers in which the free movement of goods, persons, services and capital is ensured'. The EU acquired overt competence in industrial policy affairs in the Maastricht Treaty (Article 130). According to that Article, the Commission and the member states have to assure that there exist conditions for the competitiveness of EU industry. In accordance with a system of open and competitive markets their action shall be aimed at speeding up the adjustment of industry to structural changes; encouraging an environment favourable to initiative (particularly small and medium-sized enterprises); encouraging an environment of cooperation among firms; fostering better exploitation of the industrial potential of policies of innovation, research and technological development.

2 Rationale

The grounds for the introduction of an industrial policy in the EU can be found in at least seven related areas:

- If uncoordinated, national policies introduce a wasteful duplication either of scarce resources for R&D or investment in productive assets of sub-optimal capacity, and if minimum efficient economies of scale demand access to a market that is wider than the national one, then there is a case for a common EU approach to the issue. Some competition in the diversity of R&D, ideas and production is necessary because it can be the source of creativity. None the less, the authorities need to find a harmonious balance between competition and coordination, in order to profit from them both. Hence, certain coordination of industrial policies at the EU level contributes to the efficiency of the policy.
- A common or a coordinated industrial policy in a large and expanding EU market may wield a deeper (positive or negative) impact on the economy than any isolated national policy can, no matter how big the national market of a member country.
- With a free mobility of factors in the EU, any disequilibria in a national economy may first provoke an immediate and a large outflow or inflow of capital and, later, other factors if the disequilibria are not corrected. If a government wants to cool off the economy and increase the rate of interest, the consequence may be the opposite from the desired one. High rates of interest would provoke a large inflow

of foreign hot capital and the economy could become 'overheated'. Therefore, the deeper the integration in the EU, the less effective become national macroeconomic policies that are pursued in isolation. A common or coordinated EU policy in such circumstances is a superior choice than the sum of national ones.

- Although EU firms are rivals on the EU internal market, they are allies in competition against firms from third countries both in the world and in the internal EU market. If national economic policies which are used to tackle the same problem are different and have undesirable and unwanted spillover effects on EU-partner countries, then there are grounds for the introduction of subsidiarity, i.e., a common industrial policy of the EU.
- Another argument may be found in 'unfair' trade and industrial practices of foreign rivals. An EU industrial policy may be a counter-measure.
- No matter how disputed in theory, the concern about employment always carries weight in daily politics.
- Last, but not least, there is the situation of externalities which create market failure (difference between private and social benefits). When there are undesired spillover effects beyond the frontiers of a single country from, for example, large investments in certain businesses that pollute, then the response to such outcomes could be found in a common EU policy.

In spite of the arguments in favour of an EU industrial policy, one should not get the impression that it has to be a substitute for national policies. On the contrary, they should be complementary. In fact, EU policy needs to refer only to areas where it has the potential to fare better than national policies can. In general, policies at the EU level need to be as general as possible, while local ones need to be custom made. There has to be coordination between the EU and national/local policies in order to avoid the implementation of clashing instruments, even when there is an agreement about the major goals to be achieved.

One of the principal things that the Treaty of Rome tried to achieve was to increase the competitiveness of domestic firms relative to the US at the time of the creation of the EU. The intention was to take advantage of economies of scale which were provided by an enlarged EU market. It was primarily the expansion of domestic demand that stimulated the development of both the US and, later, Japan. Competitiveness was created in the two countries on the basis of the secure, even protected, large domestic market. A large domestic market in any EU member state was lacking in comparison either with the US or Japan. The creation of the EU was conceived to redress this 'disadvantage'.

In the small European countries industrial policy was often defensive (subsidies to protect employment), rather than aggressive (risky entry into the new industries). Relatively weak anti-merger laws created the potential for the establishment of large European corporations in the 1960s which could, it was thought at that time, successfully compete with their US and Japanese rivals. However, the problem was not merely the size of firms in the EU. Fragmented by NTBs, the internal market of the EU had as a consequence economic rigidity and shielded many national firms both from the EU-internal competition and the necessary adjustment. The consequence was that in certain industries and relative to the US and Japan, the EU became close to a 'manufacturing museum'.

Protectionism has been the instrument of the EU industrial policy in spite of costs and the postponement of adjustment. Resistance to abandoning obsolete technologies and industries permitted others, most notably Japan, to gain the competitive edge and penetrate the EU market with many high-technology goods. The EU manufacturing has strong points in industries where the growth of demand is slow. Competitive advantage is relatively smaller in the expanding industries. Without domestic restructuring and with the exception of German, Dutch firms and companies from a few other countries, foreign TNCs that are located in the EU and that operate in the expanding industries may be among the major beneficiaries of the gains from Programme 1992. If the instruments of protection and cartelization (in the coal and steel industry) are not coupled with other tools of industrial policy (contraction of obsolete industries or assistance for a limited time for the introduction of new technologies), then such a policy would be ineffective. It may be pursued by those who choose and who can afford to be wasteful.

3 Evolution

The first attempt to introduce a 'real' industrial policy by the EU dates back to 1970. The Commission's *Memorandum on Industrial Policy* (the Colonna Report) was a project to shape the structure of EU industry and set priorities for common action. As there were no strong legal basis for the introduction of a common industrial policy in the Treaty of Rome, the Report restricted itself only to ambitious general statements and five recommendations. First, the Report foresaw the creation of a single EU market (such as the one in the US or Japan) based on the abolition of internal barriers to trade. Second, it sought the harmonization of legal and fiscal rules to ease the establishment of enterprises throughout the EU. It envisaged the creation of a European Company Statute. Third, although the EU had existed for more than a decade, firms were very slow to merge businesses across national boundaries. As TNCs were perceived to be important vehicles for improvements in competitiveness and technology relative to foreign rivals, there was a need for the support (intervention) of intra-EU mergers and acquisitions.[21] Fourth, changing demand conditions entail economic adjustment. This transition could be made smoothly by encouraging geographical and occupational mobility of labour and upgraded business management. The last recommendation was an extension of the EU solidarity regarding foreign competition, R&D and finance. Consideration of the Report ran into difficulty as there were two opposing views. On the one hand, Germany did not want any interference into industrial policy either on the national or the EU level. On the other hand, France was in favour of coordinating national economic policies. Other countries sided with one or other of these views.

The next step in the shaping of the EU industrial policy was a *Memorandum on the Technological and Industrial Policy Programme* (the Spinelli Report) of 1973. Basically, it was a scaled-down version of the Colonna Report. The new Report argued in favour of exchange of information, coordination of national R&D policies, joint R&D projects and the elimination of national technical barriers. The broad strategy did not succeed in full because of different economic philosophies among the member countries. After the oil crisis member countries pursued nationalistic industrial policies and were not very interested in a joint approach to the issue. In fact, they passed on to the EU the adjustment of the problem industries (steel, shipbuilding, textiles and in some cases even cars) via trade, social and regional policies, while keeping the management of expanding industries in national hands. During this period there was only a certain coordination of technical standards and joint actions in R&D.

A profound step towards the elimination of NTBs on internal trade, competition and, hence, industrial policy came with the introduction of the programme, *Completing the Internal Market* (the Cockfield Report) of 1985. This supply-side oriented 'technical' Programme had 282 industry-specific legislative proposals for the elimination of NTBs, as well as a timetable for their implementation by the end of 1992. The adoption of the Cockfield White Paper (1985) and the Single European Act (1987) provided the EU with the means to implement the 1992 Programme. The objective was the achievement of a genuine single internal market through the adoption and implementation of 282 measures (Directives). This was the outcome of the political determination of the member states to eliminate NTBs on internal trade and change their 'atomized' industrial policies. The EU tried to employ its resources in a superior way by a reduction of physical, technical and fiscal barriers to internal trade (elimination of X-inefficiencies). The classic-integration method (elimination of tariffs and quotas) in the EU exhausted its static effects at the end of the 1960s. A new approach, the ousting of NTBs, favoured full factor mobility. It was implemented in order to create a genuine frontier-free internal market in the EU. The stress was on the change in rules, rather than on additional funds. The creation of a homogeneous internal market, such as the US one, which benefits from enormous economies of scale, was not expected. The Europeans have, on average, far more refined and deeply rooted tastes, hence they benefit from variety. They demand and are often ready to pay for increased quality and diversity. The 1992 Programme was concerned with an improvement in competition and market access to diverse national, regional and local markets, as well as an introduction of flexible modes of production.

The abolition of customs duties and quotas in the EU benefited only those industries that serve *private* consumers. There is also another market, the one for goods and services that are consumed by *governments*. Industries that were employing new technologies failed to serve the entire EU market for these goods and services and benefit from economies of scale due to the existence of NTBs. These national industries compete for public funds and orders. That is why EU firms tended to cooperate more with partners in the US or Japan, than among themselves. By a joint venture with a Japanese firm, an EU enterprise made up for its technological gap without forgoing the protectionist shield and/or privileges in the form of public procurement, major export contracts, tax reliefs and R&D accorded by the state (Defraigne, 1984, p. 369). The outcome of such a policy was an absence of EU standards for high-technology goods, as well as the existence of relatively big and protected national corporations, which were not very interested in intra-EU industrial cooperation. These firms were unable to respond swiftly to changes in the international market. Obvious examples of this sluggishness was relatively slow adjustment after the oil shocks.

EU company law will help carry out the objectives of the Treaty of Rome regarding the harmonious development of economic activities in the Union. Therefore, the Commission proposed the European Company Statute in 1989. Arguments in favour of the Statute include the elimination of difficulties deriving from the current national tax systems for firms that operate in several EU countries. Business in the entire EU market would be made simpler if the firms were incorporated under a single code of law. On the other hand is the case against the Statute. Increased interference by the EU may jeopardize the national sovereignty.

The Commission was not without further ideas about industrial policy. A communication on *Industrial Policy in an Open and Competitive Environment* (the Bangemann Communication) of 1990 had, basically, the following three proposals. First, industrial policy needs to be adjustment-friendly. That has to take place within the framework of liberal trade policy. Second, EU industrial policy has to be in accord with other common policies. They need to reinforce each other. Third, difficulties within industries or regions need to be settled by the employment of horizontal measures. The means for the achievement of these ideas should include an improvement in the operation of both the internal market and the international market, as well as the creation of investment-friendly environment for risk-taking in the EU.

The impact of the opening up of the internal EU market as a consequence of the 1992 Programme is most obvious in highly regulated (and hence fragmented) industries such as pharmaceuticals. A major regulatory change in the EU took place with the initiation of the European Agency for the Evaluation of Medicinal Products in 1995. The opening up of the EU market would alter the business practices of firms in the industry in the following seven ways (Chaudhry *et al.*, 1994):

- *Market authorization*: National regulatory authorities that control the introduction of new products at different rates wield influence not only on trade, but also on the health and life of patients. To change that, the European Agency for the Evaluation of Medicinal Products became the single decision-making body of the EU in 1995. A pharmaceutical firm can, however, use a two-tier system. It may choose either a centralized procedure leading to a single authorization for the entire EU (this procedure is mandatory for products derived from biotechnology) or a decentralized method based on mutual recognition of national marketing authorizations. The probable choice of the firm would be to select the country with the least amount of regulatory delay and, then, apply the principle of mutual recognition to a product.
- *Dependence on domestic market*: More than 60 per cent of sales of pharmaceutical firms located in France, Germany, Greece, Italy, Portugal or Spain were to the domestic market. That was the consequence of preferential government procurement from local firms, insistence on local R&D and local content requirements. Following the opening up of the EU market, the business of the firms that were selling primarily on the national market will be in jeopardy.
- *Parallel trade*: The EU Court of Justice ruled in favour of parallel importers (*Centrafarm v. Sterling Drug*, 1974), i.e. purchasing of drugs in a low-price market, repacking and diverting them to other markets. The principle is that ethical drugs are permitted to move freely from one country to another if the importing country provides a marketing authorization. If there are price differentials for the same drug between the EU countries, this type of trade would continue to exist.

- *Regulated prices*: Price differences for drugs among EU countries exist because of various factors that include price-control schemes, different costs of production, variations in exchange rates, differences in reimbursement systems, transfer pricing, patent status, package sizes, rebates and taxes. Sometimes the difference in price for the same drug between the country in which it is the cheapest and the one where it is most expensive is 10 times! The opening up of the EU market would tend to bring a slow convergence in prices for drugs. The progress would be relatively slow as many of the distortions mentioned would continue in the future too.
- *Expenditure for R&D*: Competition would stimulate innovation. R&D for new drugs that are directed at the regional and global market would increase. R&D in the pharmaceuticals industry has always been mission oriented regardless of integration.[22]
- *Rationalization of operation*: Producing a drug involves the manufacture of the active substance and, subsequently, the conversion of this ingredient into dosage forms. The first part has been centralized in the EU, while the second one has been decentralized. Many of the plants were not benefiting from economies of scale as they were operating between one-third and one-half of their capacity. Plant closures, as a consequence of market opening in the EU, would bring benefits in the form of economies of scale.
- *Mergers and acquisitions*: The integration of various firms in the pharmaceutical industry is expected to consolidate the industry. Examples include the purchase of Syntex by Hoffmann-La Roche and a mergers between Smith Kline and Beecham or Bristol-Myers and Squibb.

When a large corporation from a declining industry closes down in an old industrial city, the first reaction of the state is often to offer subsidies to large new corporations to settle there. If an industrial rhinoceros is caught or attracted, it is usually loyal in this area only as long as the carrot lasts. If the firms are uncertain that the incentives will last up to the end of the investment/production programme, they will not enter into this business. Risk-averse enterprises may in this situation request larger incentives and/or single out projects with relatively high rates of return. Locally created jobs can be found in the development of SMEs. Of course, SMEs may not create enough jobs in the short run to make up for the loss of posts in an area where a large corporation closes down. However, SMEs have accounted for more than a half of net created jobs in countries such as the US in the past decade or two. SMEs can flourish in the EU even more than was the case until now. Some 17 million SMEs employed around 70 million people in the EU in 1994 (*European Voice*, 4 January 1996, p. 22). Their output can be efficient on the grounds of economies of scale and specialization because they can serve one segment of the entire EU, rather than the local or national market (if demand for their output exists there).

A policy of support for SMEs is different from one that fosters the development of a few national champions that are easy to control. Until the 1980s, even the EU regarded SMEs as unstable and maginal. It is true that the life of many SMEs is much shorter than the life of big firms, many of SMEs disappear from the market before they reach maturity, but many new ones are always being created. That should not be a worrying sign at all. It shows that the economic system is healthy and that enables many new business opportunities to be tried out. Since the mid-1980s, the EU approach towards SMEs has changed. Many industrial policy programmes have started to support this type of enterprises. SMEs are of vital importance when the market is in the process of opening (1992 Programme). Euro-Info Centres act as 'marriage agencies' for SMEs and support the establishment of business networks among those firms. This evolutionary and cumulative process has to be sustained by an educational system that supplies businesses with labour that is and will be in demand. None the less, the EU must be much more explicit in its industrial policy towards SMEs in the future than was the case in the past.

The opening up of the EU market prompted by the 1992 Programme brought several advantages to SMEs. They include the rationalization of distribution networks; cheaper and fewer inspections of conformity standards; diversification of suppliers; more efficient stock control; and savings in time and cost of transport. None the less, there are certain drawbacks. Many SMEs do not fully understand the operation of the EU market. For example, many SMEs are familiar with the concept, but relatively few of them know the conditions under which they can use 'CE' marking which shows that the good was produced in the EU and that it meets EU standards. The EU policy regarding SMEs will have to refer to these and similar issues.

4 Technology policy[23]

Shaping factors of industrial structures of the developed market economies since the 1960s included changes in technologies, foreign competition, environmental factors, changing employment patterns, as well as an ageing population. With this in mind, the Commission of the EU was initially more concerned with those industries in crisis. None the less, from the 1980s it started to be involved with industries of the future. These are the ones that have strategic importance for competitiveness. Therefore, the EU created various technology-push programmes in the mid-1980s. In the creation of those programmes, the Commission has always had to balance the interests of Directorates-General for competition that argue in favour of *laissez-faire* and those of electronics and telecommunications that argue in favour of an industrial policy (intervention). These programmes have (indirectly) created a technology policy for the EU. With the exception of Euratom, R&D has long been in the domain of national governments. A part of the inspiration for such approach came from the Japanese experience and the public support offered to industries by the MITI in the form of an exchange of information, cooperation and partial funding of R&D projects. The legal base for the EU action in R&D was given in the Single European Act (Title VI). Although there had been certain earlier moves in this direction, the member governments decided for the first time to pass on significant funds for R&D from national to the EU programmes. According to the Single European Act, the EU shall strengthen its scientific and technological bases and encourage competitiveness at international level (Article 130*f*). The Commission and the member states are supposed to coordinate policies and programmes carried out at the national level (Article 130*h*). The EU needs to adopt a multiannual framework programme for its R&D projects (Article 130*i*). In the implementation of its long-term R&D programme the EU may cooperate with third countries or international organizations (Article 130*m*). The goal is to have closer links between research institutes and entrepreneurs throughout the EU in order to alter the old perception that science (i.e., R&D) in Europe is culture, while it is business in the US.

In the situation where strong national elements still prevail, the EU should endeavour to coordinate national policies, and promote cooperation in R&D and production, as well as support the flexibility of the industrial structure. Coordination of national policies should be in the decaying industries in a way that avoids integration-unfriendly beggar-thy-neighbour policies. In the light of the irreversible changes started by the 1992 Programme, operations in the expanding industries should introduce common EU standards that provide room for large-scale production and improvement in competitiveness. The objective is to avoid the creation of incompatible standards as happened with the PAL and SECAM television systems. The EU has opted for the MAC standard in the emerging high-definition television system. Although it would be applied throughout the EU for the next generation of television, it may be different from the Japanese and US (perhaps superior) standards. Making the EU market different from foreign ones would reduce benefits from economies of scale, but it would also provide a temporary shield to EU producers from external competition which may be the 'real' objective of devising different standards. If the EU, Japan and the US accept three different standards for high-definition television and if the experience is a good guide, it seems likely that the Japanese may excel in the production of TV sets that satisfy all three standards.

The dependence of the EU on third-country suppliers of high-technology goods has several causes. On the supply side, there is a gap between investment in R&D in the EU countries on the one hand and US and Japan on the other; relatively insufficient allocation of human resources in R&D in Europe; and delays in the passing on of the results of R&D into production and marketing. On the demand side, there are still various national 'attitudes' (buy domestic) that are limiting potential demand for high-technology products in the EU countries; lower receptiveness of European firms to new products compared with their US or Japanese rivals; a lack of stronger links between producers and consumers in Europe; and inadequate training in new technologies (Jacquemin and Sapir, 1991, pp. 44–45).[24] Various EU technology programmes are supposed to redress this situation.

Philips and Thomson were leading the lobby of European companies that were pushing national governments for the completion of the EU internal market as the principal cure for countering the Japanese ability to be always a few steps ahead in the business game. The Round Table of European industrialists was successful in eliciting support of governments for the 1992 Programme. When the US announced the 'Star Wars' project in 1983, EU industrialists started to worry. First the Japanese took over a large part of the market for consumer electronics, then the Americans were on the way to taking over advanced industrial goods. Following that, the Round Table (rent-seekers) was pushing for the creation of a transnational industrial policy in the form of the EU support for high-technology research projects. In spite of the budgetary restrictions, the big EU industrialists were successful once again (Curzon Price, 1993, p. 399–400).

The EU policy in R&D is carried out in the form of 4-year Framework Programmes that started in 1984. The purpose of these medium-term instruments is to integrate and coordinate all assistance/aid that is given to R&D in the EU.[25] These programmes lay down objectives, priorities and the budget for the EU-sponsored R&D. By distributing funds on selected research actions, the EU sets guidelines for specific R&D programmes. Based on the findings of the FAST (Forecasting and Assessment in Science and Technology) programme,[26] the EU initiated a score of publicly supported programmes for industrial cooperation among the EU firms at the R&D stage. Most of the programmes would be beyond the financial capability of participating countries if they were supposed to finance them on their own. These programmes include the following 'winners':

- A dozen renowned enterprises in information technology from Britain, France, Germany, Italy and the Netherlands wanted to pool resources, share risk and extract certain subsidies.[27] Their pressure group (the Round Table) was lobbying both national governments and the Commission to adopt the European Strategic Programme for Research in Information Technology (ESPRIT) and try to 'correct market failures' in R&D. The Commission was receptive to the idea and together with the Round Table won the approval from the national governments. The EU adopted the Programme, i.e. picked a winner, in 1984. Within ESPRIT the EU finances half of the cost of the project that is in line with the EU terms of reference and that is proposed by two or more firms from different EU countries. The other half of the funds has to come from the participating firms and national sources. The project has to refer only to pre-competitive R&D. The Commission has been refusing to subsidize joint production. The reason is that it wants to avoid all accusations from the US about subsidies.[28]
- Research and Development in Advanced Communication for Europe (RACE) is a spillover programme from the ESPRIT. It aims at advancing telecommunication network in Europe in the future by means that include standardization and coordination of national telecom services.
- Basic Research in Industrial Technologies in Europe (BRITE) aspires to revitalize traditional industries in the EU. It is to be done through the introduction of new technologies in these industries. It is unclear what is so 'strategic' in these industries. Perhaps, the concern here is more about employment, than anything else. Public money is spent on projects that financial markets find unattractive.
- Biotechnology Action Programme (BAP) is small relative to its 'strategic' potential in the future.
- European Collaborative Linkage of Agriculture and Industry through Research (ECLAIR) is, like the BAP, relatively small, but with great potential for providing solutions about food in the future. It contributes to the establishment and reinforcement of inter-sectoral links between agriculture and manufacturing.

EUREKA (European Research Cooperation Agency) was a programme started by 17 countries (from the EU and the EFTA) on the French initiative in 1985. It was a response to the Strategic Defence Initiative ('Star Wars') of the US. Its objective is the development and *production* of high-technology goods. It is not confined only to pre-competitive R&D as the other programmes are. Other countries (such as Turkey) may be included in some of its programmes. EUREKA is, however, *not* an institution of the EU. It has a small secretariat in Brussels and it has gained popularity in the business community.

The Fourth Framework Programme (1994–1998) disposes of ECU 13.2 billion. The five beneficiaries are cars, trains, aeronautics, vaccinations and educational software. These EU-wide programmes ought to be supported by a number of national plans that spread and reinforce links among the parties that are involved in R&D and implementing the results of these efforts. A lot of public money has been poured into R&D over the past decade in the EU, but the results have been very slow in coming. Of course, the effects of basic R&D cannot be predicted with a high degree of certainty. As public funds are limited and as the results of R&D are more important than the origin of the work, companies from foreign countries may take part in R&D projects of the EU on a case-by-case basis, but without any financial help from the Commission. Production in the world is becoming more and more globalized. Therefore, 'forcing' cooperation in R&D only within the EU may waste a part of the taxpayers' money. What global production in the world demands is an open (global) industrial and trade policy system.

Inter-firm strategic alliances in the development of technology in the EU increased sharply during the 1980s. In addition, there was a relatively vigorous involvement by the Commission in projects on the cost-sharing basis. Over 70 per cent of private (largely non-subsidized) strategic-technology alliances were related to joint R&D of new core technologies in informatics, new materials and biotechnology. A major field of cooperation was in information technology as over 40 per cent of all strategic-technology alliances were in this field (Hagedoorn and Schakenraad, 1993, p. 373). A comparison between the established 'private' cooperation in R&D and that sponsored by the EU found that they resemble each other in leading enterprises. In fact, the 'subsidized R&D networks are added to already existing or emerging private networks and merely reproduce the basic structure of European large firm co-operation' (Hagedoorn and Schakenraad, 1993, p. 387). If so, one fails to understand why leading and large firms in the EU need subsidies! If the 'official' network largely reproduces the already existing 'private' one, then it may be redundant. Financial resources may be used elsewhere (for instance, programmes that are not in the field of informatics, such as biotechnology or education or infrastructure). Is such replication of R&D networks the outcome of the lobbying strength of powerful firms or is it necessary to accelerate R&D in the private sector because of significant externalities? This has to be addressed in the future.[29] Perhaps such a waste of scarce public money could be checked by the WTO rules on subsidization.

The experience of Japan is also instructive. During the 1960s the MITI targeted the production of steel and shipbuilding as the beneficiaries. Intervention (support) was quite extensive. At that time Japanese corporations had an identical business choice and were investing in those industries. These private investments would have happened even without government intervention. At about the same time, Japanese firms wanted also to start developing the car and electronics industries. These two industries were not on the priority list of the MITI. None the less, private businesses went ahead alone in their investments and were successful without puiblic support (if one disregards the relatively closed domestic market).

An altered and improved new industrial strategy of the EU and its member states needs to take into account first and foremost the crucial role played by the development of human capital for the long-term competitiveness of the economy. In addition, there may be a certain need for selective intervention in the form of subsidies, promotion of cooperation and exchange of information during the pre-commercial phase of R&D projects that may give (oligopolistic) advantages to EU producers relative to foreign rivals. If deemed appropriate, selective intervention in the new technologies needs to be aimed at those expanding industries where the EU businesses already have or could create internal resources. That means that the EU efforts and funds should not be focused solely on the replication of industries where the US and Japan are strongest (cooperation with them may be a wiser option), but primarily where there are grounds for the development of genuine EU technologies and comparative advantages.[30] One of them could be found in biotechnology. Not only now, but also in the coming decades there will be an increased overlap between mechanical, electronic, chemical, medical and biotechnology industries. The EU has a reasonable chance of becoming a leader in this field.

5 The way forward

The competitiveness of a country's goods and services in the modern world is created rather than inherited. The leader in certain lines of production cannot be certain that this position will be secure in the long run. Therefore, one can find scope for industrial cooperation in the EU. It could be established both in the pre-commercial and during the commercialization stages of R&D. In this way, inefficient duplication or multiplication of R&D would be eliminated and resources saved and directed elsewhere. However, creation of knowledge is not enough to keep a country on a competitive edge. That knowledge needs to be applied in practice. Here the US fares much better than the EU. The US system and culture offers wide opportunities to start and re-start promising businesses. If someone with sound profit-making ideas fails (for whatever reasons) in Boston, there are still other chances in Seattle or San Francisco. In Europe, the situation is different. If your business start-up fails, do not think about another one for a while, unless you cross the Atlantic!

As the 1992 Programme eliminated most NTBs on internal EU trade, its largest impact was and will continue to be felt in sensitive businesses.[31] Those are the ones that were shielded by relatively high NTBs and which had as their impact large price distortions. They include the production of goods that are publicly procured either in the high-technology business (office machines, telecommunications and medico-surgical equipment) or in the traditional manufacturing industries, such as electrical and railway equipment, pharmaceuticals, wine and boilermaking. Businesses that were protected with relatively modest NTBs would also continue to be affected by market liberalization. They include motor vehicles, aerospace equipment, basic chemicals, machine tools for metals, as well as textiles and sewing machines.

Outsiders were afraid that the 1992 Programme could lead to the creation of 'Fortress Europe', created by a mixture of intra-EU liberalization and an increase in the existing level of external protection. However, the EU neither had such a plan, nor considered it served its long-term interests. If a 'fortress' was mentioned, it was only in the context of a potential bargaining chip with major trading partners. It was expected that the 1992 Programme would lead, among other things, to increased competition and efficiency which would reduce prices in the EU. Therefore, even without a change in the existing level of nominal protection, the real level might rise. An extra increase in the existing level of protection would be neither necessary nor desirable. On the contrary, increased efficiency may prompt the EU to reduce the current level of protection as happened in the Uruguay Round deal. None the less, the 1992 Programme has influenced the timing of external FDI in the EU. Many foreign TNCs entered the EU in order to become an 'internal' resident of the EU prior to the full implementation of the 1992 Programme. They wanted to pre-empt any temptation to create a fortress from 1993.

Potential changes in the rules of origin and local content may, however, discriminate against 'internal' goods with a relatively high external-import content. This may be reinforced by the discriminatory application of testing procedures and standards. A fortress mentality may be introduced in the EU through the social(ist) over-regulation of labour issues. If this is done in the future, it will cause a flurry of protectionist winds that will make the security of current jobs more important than the long-term efficiency and adjustment of the economy.

The impetus to the economic life once offered by a customs union as mark 1 in the process of integration in the EU was exhausted by the end of the 1960s. Something more and new was needed. The genuine EU internal market with an unimpeded flow of goods, services and factors from 1993, ended mark 2 in the integration process. It provided the EU with the new propelling force. The member countries decided to re-introduce the principle of majority voting (save for fiscal, national border controls, working conditions and environmental issues) in order to ease the procedure for the implementation of the Programme.

The EU member countries realized that the costs of 'non-Europe' were too high to be ignored. The EU without frontiers, for domestic residents of course, as envisaged in the White Paper could increase the GNP in the EU up to 7 per cent and employment by 5 million new jobs, if accompanied by matching national policies (Emerson et al. 1988, p. 165). The 'sacrifices' for those real gains were more freedom for business and less regulation. The opponents of the 1992 Programme have not been able to create a more attractive and feasible economic strategy and ultimately gave these efforts up. Only the inefficient ones and the others that fail to compete and adjust would lose in the new situation. As there was no moratorium on bankruptcies throughout the EU, that is an indication that business has absorbed the 1992 Programme without any serious, negative shocks. However, the Programme was no more than the first step. One has to keep in mind that the 1992 Programme is merely a medium-term strategy. The Maastricht Treaty rearranged the decision-making process in the EU and set the agenda for the EMU. If (a very big if) that is realized according to the plan and timetable, one does not know yet what would come after that. This is a highly political question because it is linked to a transfer of other responsibilities to the EU level.

Tables 6.1, 6.2 and 6.3, respectively, show annual percentage changes in GDP, manufacturing output and capital formation in the EU countries during the period 1987–1995. Memorandum items in the tables are indicators for the US and Japan. Although the performance of individual countries differ, there is a general harmony in economic cycles of the EU countries. The most obvious example was in 1993 when most of the EU countries were in recession. That was the first year when the 'genuine internal market' in the EU started to operate! In addition, industrial production and investments in the EU started to suffer even from 1991. It would, however, be cynical to associate those negative macroeconomic trends with the potential failure of the

197

Table 6.1 Real gross domestic product in the EU countries, US and Japan, 1987–1996
(annual % change)

Country	1987	1988	1989	1990	1991	1992	1993	1994	1995	1996
1 Austria[a]	1.7	4.1	3.8	4.6	2.8	2.0	0.4	3.0	1.8	0.7
2 Belgium	2.2	4.9	3.6	3.8	2.2	1.8	−1.6	2.2	1.9	1.2
3 Denmark	0.3	1.2	0.6	2.0	1.3	0.8	1.5	4.4	2.8	2.0
4 Finland[a]	4.0	5.4	5.4	0.3	−7.1	−3.6	−1.2	4.4	4.2	2.8
5 France	2.3	4.5	4.1	2.2	0.8	1.3	−1.5	2.9	2.2	1.2
6 Germany	1.4	3.7	3.4	5.1	5.0	2.2	−1.2	2.9	1.9	1.3
7 Greece	−0.7	4.1	3.5	−0.2	3.2	0.8	−0.5	1.0	2.0	2.5
8 Ireland	4.6	4.5	6.4	7.1	2.9	5.0	4.0	6.5	10.3	6.5
9 Italy	3.1	4.1	2.9	2.2	1.2	0.7	−1.2	2.2	3.0	0.8
10 Luxembourg	2.9	5.6	6.8	3.2	3.1	1.9	0.0	3.3	3.2	2.6
11 Netherlands	0.9	2.6	4.7	3.9	2.3	2.0	0.8	3.4	2.1	2.5
12 Portugal	5.3	3.9	5.2	4.1	2.1	1.1	−1.2	0.9	2.6	2.3
13 Spain	5.6	5.2	4.8	3.7	2.2	0.7	−1.2	2.1	2.8	2.3
14 Sweden[a]	2.8	2.3	2.4	0.7	−1.1	−1.4	−2.2	2.6	3.0	0.8
15 United Kingdom	4.8	4.4	2.1	0.5	−2.0	−0.5	2.3	3.9	2.6	2.3
United States	3.1	3.9	2.5	0.8	−1.0	2.7	2.2	3.5	2.0	2.3
Japan	4.1	6.2	4.7	4.8	4.3	1.1	−0.2	0.5	0.9	3.5

Source: National statistics and UN ECE
Note: [a]Joined the EU in 1995

Table 6.2 Industrial production in the EU countries, US and Japan, 1987–1995
(annual % change)

Country	1987	1988	1989	1990	1991	1992	1993	1994	1995
1 Austria[a]	1.0	4.4	5.9	7.4	1.8	−1.1	−2.0	4.0	5.4
2 Belgium	2.2	6.5	3.4	3.8	−2.0	−0.5	−5.2	1.8	4.2
3 Denmark	—	—	—	—	—	—	—	—	—
4 Finland[a]	4.2	5.8	2.4	0.4	−9.8	2.5	5.1	11.5	7.5
5 France	1.9	4.7	4.1	1.9	0.2	−1.1	−3.7	3.8	1.5
6 Germany	0.4	3.6	5.0	5.1	2.9	−1.9	−6.3	−1.3	2.1
7 Greece	−1.5	5.1	1.9	−2.4	−1.4	−1.2	−2.1	0.9	2.3
8 Ireland	9.1	10.6	11.6	4.6	3.2	9.3	5.6	11.0	18.8
9 Italy	2.6	6.9	3.9	−0.7	−0.9	−1.3	−2.2	6.8	5.5
10 Luxembourg	—	—	—	—	0.1	−0.8	−2.5	5.9	1.4
11 Netherlands	1.0	0.1	5.1	2.3	3.9	0.2	−1.1	3.0	2.3
12 Portugal	4.4	3.7	6.8	8.9	0.1	−3.4	−2.6	−0.2	4.6
13 Spain	4.7	3.0	4.5	0.1	−0.9	−2.9	−4.7	7.0	4.7
14 Sweden[a]	2.6	1.3	3.6	−2.7	−5.6	−3.5	−0.2	10.5	10.6
15 United Kingdom	3.2	3.6	0.4	−0.5	−3.9	−0.2	2.1	5.0	2.5
United States	5.0	5.5	2.5	1.0	−1.7	3.3	3.5	5.9	3.2
Japan	—	11.0	4.8	4.2	1.8	−5.7	−4.2	1.2	3.3

Source: National statistics and UN ECE
Note: [a]Joined the EU in 1995

1992 Programme. Integration is after all no more than a *supporting* instrument to the general national macroeconomic policies. Once they are in order, integration can contribute to their reinforcement.

Table 6.3 Real gross fixed capital formation in the EU countries, US and Japan, 1987–1996 (annual % change)

Country	1987	1988	1989	1990	1991	1992	1993	1994	1995	1996
1 Austria[a]	3.1	6.0	6.1	5.8	6.3	1.7	−1.6	6.7	2.3	0.7
2 Belgium	5.6	15.2	14.5	8.3	−1.5	0.2	−6.7	3.0	3.0	3.1
3 Denmark	−3.8	−6.6	1.0	−0.9	−5.7	−7.2	−2.3	3.0	10.2	5.2
4 Finland[a]	5.4	10.5	14.1	−4.9	−20.3	−16.9	−19.2	−0.3	7.7	9.2
5 France	4.8	9.6	7.0	2.9	0.0	−3.1	−5.8	1.6	2.8	0.7
6 Germany	2.1	4.6	6.5	8.7	5.8	3.5	−5.6	4.3	1.5	−2.0
7 Greece	−5.1	8.9	10.0	4.8	−4.5	0.5	−2.7	0.6	5.8	9.5
8 Ireland	−2.3	3.3	15.8	9.5	−8.2	−1.9	−0.5	8.7	10.1	9.0
9 Italy	5.0	6.9	4.3	3.3	0.6	−1.7	−13.1	0.2	5.9	1.7
10 Luxembourg	14.5	14.2	9.7	2.5	9.8	−2.1	3.9	2.4	3.5	3.7
11 Netherlands	1.1	4.5	4.9	3.6	0.2	0.6	−3.1	1.6	6.7	3.3
12 Portugal	15.1	15.0	5.6	6.0	2.4	5.4	−4.8	3.9	5.4	5.0
13 Spain	14.0	14.0	13.8	6.9	1.3	−4.1	−10.6	1.8	8.2	4.3
14 Sweden[a]	7.6	5.8	11.8	−0.5	−8.9	−10.8	−17.2	−0.2	10.6	9.4
15 United Kingdom	9.6	14.2	7.2	−3.1	−9.5	−1.5	0.6	2.9	−0.2	4.4
United States	−0.5	4.2	0.1	−2.8	−8.0	5.7	5.1	7.9	5.2	5.3
Japan	9.6	11.9	9.3	8.8	3.7	−1.1	−1.8	−2.3	0.8	4.2

Source: National statistics and UN ECE
Note:[a] Joined the EU in 1995

The year 1992 came and passed, but the economies of the EU have not yet exhibited a big expansion in economic activity in spite of the large-scale expectations about the beneficial effects that would come from the implementation of Programme 1992. Has something gone wrong? Perhaps not. Economic integration, including the single market programme is a process. It is not a programme with clear deadlines after which one may measure the overall effects with a small margin of error. Research on the effects of the 1992 Programme suffers from an identification problem. It is a common shortcoming of all studies that deal with the effects of international economic integration. It is hard to know which changes in the economy and the reaction of enterprises are due to the 1992 Programme and which would have happened anyway (for example, because of imports of improved foreign technology or globalization of business and competition)! It may take another decade or so until all the effects of Programme 1992 are fully absorbed by the economies of the EU. Perhaps – again a 'perhaps' – the biggest effect on the economies of the EU already took place at the end of the 1980s. Partial support for this thesis can be identified in the peak in business concentration deals in 1990. It needs to be kept in mind that the 1992 Programme is *a*, rather than *the* reason for change.

The EU direct intervention in the manufacturing industry was primarily aimed at declining industries such as steel, shipbuilding and textiles during the 1970s and early 1980s. From 1985, the major emphasis of the policy changed. The EU became much more involved in the expanding high-technology industries through its R&D policy. This should not be taken to mean that the EU is no longer concerned with the 'obsolete' industries, or that it was not interested in the support and development of advanced industries in the past. On the contrary. EU involvement with both types of manufacturing industries existed before, and it continues in the present. What changed, was only the order of priorities.

VII SERVICES

1 Issues

While physical existence determines goods, such a direct relationship does not exist for services. A service may be given to various recipients. It can be supplied to a person for a haircut, education, entertainment or transport; to a legal entity such as a firm or government, for banking or construction; to an object such as an aeroplane for guidance, repairs or airport services; or applied to goods for transport or storage. Certain services can be provided to a variety of recipients. For example, banking, insurance, transport, telecommunication, leasing, data processing and legal advice could be offered to both individuals, businesses and governments.

In general, the services sector in the developed market economies contributes by more than a half both to GNP and to employment. The share of services has been continuously increasing. These de-industrialization tendencies have been shifting emphasis towards the services sector as one of the key solutions to the problem of unemployment and growth. Employment in the manufacturing sector in the EU declined from 33 million to 30 million between 1980 and 1990. At the same time, employment in the services sector increased from 44 to 54 million. Newly created jobs in the services sector more than compensated for job losses in manufacturing. Production of almost all services takes place in every country. The same however, is not true for the manufacturing of cars, lorries, aircrafts or steel. Hence, the alleged importance of the creation of new jobs in the services sector.

Notwithstanding its importance and impact on the economy, the services sector has been neglected in economic analysis for a long time. Classical economists such as Adam Smith and Karl Marx neglected services as the residual sector of the economy on the grounds that it does not have durable properties and no facility for physical accumulation. Production and consumption of services is simultaneous and it demands a degree of mobility of factors. Therefore, the classical economists turned their attention towards physical goods.

On the 'technical' side, services differ from other business activities in at least the following five ways (Buigues and Sapir, 1993, p. xi):

- The production and consumption of services happen at the same time and at the same place. Therefore, they are regarded as non-tradeable since they cannot be stored. Because of a relatively low level of internationalization, the right of establishment (FDI) is essential for the provision of services abroad. Although services account for around a half of the GDP of the EU, their share is around 20 per cent in total trade. This epitomizes the non-tradeable nature of many services. On the other hand, services account for around half of all FDI in the EU. Internationalization of services is lowest in distribution, road transport and construction; average in telecommunications, financial and business services; and relatively high in air transport and hotel chains.
- The quality of services can not be easily verified in advance of consumption. Non-price competition such as reputation often plays a key role during the decision-

making process by the consumers. This is important in longer-term relations such as in financial services. Experience plays its role even in one-time relationships in certain cases and places.[32]

- Governments in all countries intervene in services more than in other economic activities because of market failures. They include imperfect competition in a number of services, asymmetric information between providers and consumers (sellers potentially know more about the service such as an insurance policy than the buyers) and externalities.[33] Public intervention influences entry, operation, competition and exit from the sector. Regulation is high and competition low in financial services, air transport and telecommunications. Therefore, only a few big companies exist in those industries. Reputation plays a big role in finance, economies of scope in air transport, while in telecommunications there are relatively large sunk costs and economies of scale (most of the countries have a single public firm providing the service). Competition tends to be higher and regulation easier in road transport, business services, construction and hotels.
- Debates about the (im)possibility of the government to intervene (in)efficiently to correct the above market failures, as well as changes in technology contributed to an ebb in deregulation in the sector first in the US at the end of the 1970s, then in Britain during the early 1980s which subsequently spread to the rest of Europe.
- Services are characterized by a relatively slow growth of labour productivity. Their rate of productivity growth during the period 1970–1990 was half of what it was in the manufacturing sector. There are at least two explanations for such a development. First, competition in services is obstructed by a high degree of regulation and, second, the substitution of capital for labour is more limited in services than in manufacturing. Technological innovations, however, increased labour productivity in telecommunications and air transport during that period.

Differences between services and other economic activities are not confined only to the 'technical' side. There is also a social dimension. First, half of the employees in services were women in 1990. That is in sharp contrast with the manufacturing sector where women have only one in five jobs. Second, there are many more part-time employees in the services sector than in manufacturing. Third, and linked with the former issue, is an expansion of temporary work contracts in services. Fourth, there is a relatively high level of non-employees. Fifth, labour unions are not spread in the services sector. The exceptions are transport and telecommunication services. Sixth, SMEs are dominant types of business organization in most service industries.

There are other reasons that make the analysis of services tricky. One is a lack of any profound theory. A wide definition states that a service is a change in the condition of a person, or a good belonging to some economic unit, which is brought about as a result of the activity of some other economic unit (Hill, 1977, p. 317). Without a proper definition, the measuring unit is lacking. Trade statistics, however, lists thousands of items for goods on the one hand, but records only a handful of services on the other. Although many services are not tradeable, progress in information and telecom technology has made many services eligible for international trade. Nevertheless, trade in many services is not recorded. The service part of a good, such as repair, may be incorporated in the total price of traded goods. Apart from transport and telecom services, an entry into and exit from a service industry is in principle, relatively cheap and easy. None the less, there are regulatory barriers to such (dis)orderly operation in the service businesses. TNCs release little data on their internal trade in services, while other establishments in the sector only reluctantly make public this information, as this may endanger their competitive position. In addition, information can be easily, swiftly and cheaply distributed which jeopardizes property rights. Such a lack of hard statistical information makes trade in services difficult to study.

It is easier to sell goods than services in foreign markets. While barriers to trade in goods can be eliminated at the border, problems for the suppliers of services usually start once they pass the frontier control. The provision of services often requires the right of establishment and national treatment of enterprises. Service providers actually need to be present in person in order to offer many services to their receivers.

Experts may enter and settle in foreign countries, but their qualifications and licences may not be recognized by the host authorities. Public authorities regulate the supply of services to a much higher degree than they do with the production of goods. They often regulate public shareholding, quality and quantity of supply, rates and conditions of operation. Fiscal incentives are often more easily given to firms in the manufacturing industry than to firms in the services sector. Because of a wide coverage of regulation of industries in the services sector, an easing or a removal of control of the establishment in services can have a much greater impact on trade and investment in this sector than would be the case in trade and production of goods.

Small and open countries that are net importers of goods may not choose to rely solely on their domestic manufacturing industry, which need not operate on an efficient scale. These countries may seek to develop service industries which may create proceeds to pay for imports of goods. In general, the Netherlands developed trade, Austria tourism, Norway and Greece shipping, while Switzerland and Luxembourg are highly specialized in financial services.

The issues linked to trade in services have often been neglected in the past. The rules relating to these problems were not negotiated. Once trade in services passed the $1,000 billion point in 1993 (almost a third of world trade in goods) it came as no surprise that services were included in the Uruguay Round Accord and the WTO.

The services sector of an economy changes its structure over time. Traditional services (such as transport, legal, banking and insurance) are enriched by new and fast growing ones (such as telecommunications, information, data processing, engineering and management consultancy). Services and the jobs they create may be broadly classified into two groups: (1) those that require high skills and pay (such as business, financial, engineering, consulting and legal advice); and (2) those that are geared to consumer and welfare needs. The suppliers of services in this second group receive poor training, have a high turnover and low pay (such as jobs in shops, hotels and restaurants). Economic development in its post-industrial phase should be aimed at the creation of jobs in the former group rather than in latter (Tyson, 1987, p. 79).

2 European Union

Articles 52 to 68 of the Treaty of Rome grant the right of establishment to EU residents, freedom to supply services throughout the region and freedom of movement of capital. Article 90 states that public enterprises and the ones with special or exclusive rights to provide services of general economic interest 'shall be subject to . . . the rules on competition, in so far as the application of such rules does not obstruct the performance, in law or in fact, of the particular tasks assigned to them'. Compared with trade in goods, those rights have not yet materialized in practice on a large scale. The main reason took the form of various national restrictions (NTBs). In fact, around a half of the 282 measures that came from the 1992 Programme related to services such as finance, transport and telecommunication. It was in the financial services (banking and insurance) that the 1992 Programme was advancing most swiftly. On the one hand, this was due to impressive changes in technology (data processing and telecom services); on the other, to international efforts to liberalize trade in services under the auspices of the Uruguay Round.

But do the changes prompted by the 1992 Programme have the same effects on the services sector as they have on the manufacturing? The question is, in fact, whether the Programme will impact on the geographical location of services in the EU as happened with manufacturing? For certain services that are tradeable because of data-processing and telecommunication services, such as accounting, there will be some centralization and reallocation of business. For most others, significant changes are not expected in the short and medium term. Skilled accountants are able to move around the EU and offer their services, but the Greek islands (tourism) will always remain where they are!

The financial services deal with promises to pay. In a world of developed telecom services, these promises can move instantaneously all around the globe. Customs posts do not matter in this business. None the less, restrictive rights of establishment may limit the freedom to supply these services. Traditionally, the monetary power was jealously protected and saved for the domestic authorities. This has changed in the past decades. International mobility of capital can hardly be stopped, therefore countries try to make the best use of it. Financial services not only generate employment and earnings themselves, but, more importantly, the efficient allocation of resources and competitiveness of the manufacturing sector depends on the wide choice, efficiency and low cost of financial services.

The still evolving legislative framework for the single EU market in services is based on the following four principal elements:

- *Freedom of establishment.* Enterprises from other EU countries may not be discriminated and receive the national treatment in the country of operation. This is important in the services sector because of the necessity for direct contact between providers and consumers of services. There needs to be a single licence for the provision of services throughout the EU. This means that a firm that is entitled to provide services in one EU country has the same right in another EU country. The country that issues such a licence is primarily responsible for the control of the licensed firm on behalf of the rest of the EU.

- *Liberalization of cross-border trade in services.* This element increases the possibility of cross-border provision of services without the actual physical establishment of business in the host country. A gradual inclusion of cabotage (internal transport service within a country) in air and road transport are the key changes of the Programme.

- *Harmonization of the national rules.* This eases the transborder establishment of business and provision of services. This is relevant for telecom (technical standards) and financial (solvency) services.
- *Common rules of competition.*

According to the First Banking Directive (1977), the EU-resident banks are free to open branches throughout the Union, but this was subject to host-country authorization. Foreign banks could not compete successfully with local banks, as the costs of establishment differ widely among countries. In addition, foreign banks may be excluded from certain services (securities) which are reserved for local residents. The Second Banking Directive (1989) brought a major breakthrough in the EU banking industry as it introduced the single banking licence. From 1993, member countries of the EU accepted the home-country control principle, as well as a mutual recognition of each other's licensing rules for the banks. Full harmonization of the banking laws in the EU countries is, however, neither easy nor necessary. The banking laws among the states in the US differ, but this has never been a big handicap to the economic performance of the country. As financial services became globalized, the challenge to the EU and its member countries was to adjust to this change and remain competitive, become mature (although the absolute level of business may remain the same or expand, the relative share of the business may decline) or lose out to other competitors. If third country banks wish to benefit from the single market in the EU, a draft of the Second Banking Directive asked for reciprocal treatment from them. Subsequently, it became evident that it would be an unrealistic proviso in relation to US banks. These banks are not allowed to enter certain financial operations (such as securities) beyond the boundaries of federal states. It would be unreasonable to provide the EU banks operating in the US with a more favourable treatment than the domestic US banks have, and/or that the US would change the domestic rules because of different regulation in the EU. Ultimately, the reciprocity provision will not apply to subsidiaries of US banks that were established in the EU prior to 1 January 1993.

The insurance business is very special and complex indeed. There are few homogeneous products and there is usually a long-term relationship between the parties. If a consumer purchases a bottle of Scotch whisky, he can still enjoy drinking it, even if the producer goes out of business. The same is not true for an insurance policy. Control in the insurance business is exercised by the regulation of entry into this business. In the EU, insurers are granted the general right to establish, but they were often permitted to solicit business only through local agencies. This is particularly true for compulsory insurance.[34] The rationale for such restrictions may be found in the protection of consumers' interest because of the asymmetric information between the seller and the buyer (the seller may know much more about the policy than the buyer such as a housewife),[35] but it may be employed for the protection of local business too. It is difficult to determine where a sound case for the protection of local consumers ends, and where a barrier to trade in the insurance business and the protection of local industry begins. Buyers of an insurance policy may see the benefit of relatively higher regulation, but may not wish to accept the higher costs that the extra regulation brings.[36]

Progress in the EU was faster in the non-life than in the life insurance business. The 1988 Directive 1988 on the freedom to supply non-life insurance distinguished between two kinds of risks. First, the home-country regulation applies to mass risks (commercial risks) and large risks (transport, marine, aviation). Second, the national regulation that applies to personal insurance is the one where the policy-holder resides. Progress in the integration of the insurance business in the EU has not advanced as much as in the field of banking. The EU insurance companies were allowed to compete only under the host country rules which significantly reduced the possibilities for real competition. In fact, the insurance industry is least affected by the globalization of business. Highly protected national insurance markets would require a lot of harmonization before real competition takes place in this field and before a 'single EU insurance passport' is introduced in this business. The process may take longer than was the case in banking because distortions in the insurance business were much more complex, and because the reasoning from the *Cassis de Dijon* case has not yet been applied to insurance services.

As a part of the implementation of the internal-market programme, personal insurance policies started to be sold and advertised freely in the EU in 1994. But the insurers and the consumers were not rejoicing in full. One reason is that national tax treatment would still favour local companies. These firms have a wide network of tied agents that may not be easily and swiftly replicated by foreign competitors. Another one includes national restraints on the sale of certain types of policies. For example, Italy banned the sale of kidnap insurance because of the concern that it would encourage abductions.

Uncoordinated national laws can no longer provide the basis for future development of financial services in the EU. This is increasingly important in the light of rising globalization and a loss of the EU-specific dimension in business, especially in banking. If the EU wants to preserve or, even, increase the existing amount of business and employment that goes with it, the crucial thing is that it fosters the development of an open and efficient market for financial services. Consumers would get a wider choice, better quality and cheaper financial services – all essential for the competitiveness of the manufacturing industry and the whole economy.

The *Debauve* case (1980) dealt with advertising. It showed how complicated cases in the services sector can be. Belgium prohibited advertising on TV. None the less, cable TV programmes that originated in other countries without such restrictions and were marketed in Belgium did contain advertising. The issue was whether the government of Belgium has the right to ban advertising on channels received in the country, but which originate in other countries. The EU Court concluded that in the absence of EU action, each member state can regulate and even prohibit advertising on the TV on its territory on the grounds of general interest. The question here is what was the 'general interest' in this case? A typical argument for regulation would be the protection of consumers (viewers). An increase in the choice of channels would not be against the interests of the viewers regardless of whether foreign programmes contain advertising. Therefore, the argument that the welfare of those in Belgium who wished to watch foreign channels would be improved by the ban, could not hold water (Hindley, 1991, p. 279). If Belgian viewers watch foreign programmes (with or without advertising), they would watch fewer domestic channels. Hence, support for the public financing for the domestic TV would decrease. An additional reason for the Belgian policy was the protection of the advertising revenue of local newspapers.

Both large-scale and flexible modes of production require an efficient and reliable transport service. The sophistication in demand by the consumers and a reduction in the own-account transportation have redressed the demand for this service. Just-in-time delivery system (frequent, punctual and reliable shipments) was the outcome of sophisticated logistics which reduced costs of storage. All that would be reinforced and advanced by competitive transport services. The majority of firms in the haulage industry are small or medium-sized. Around 95 per cent of the companies have less than six vehicles. This reflects the fact that road haulage markets are mainly local (Carlén, 1994, p. 89). Two-thirds of all goods transported by road in the EU are within a distance of 50 km, a further 20 per cent within distances of 50 to 150 km, leaving only 14 per cent for distances over 150 km (Commission, 1992, p. 11). While in most of the EU countries road transport is geared towards domestic services (most obviously in Greece, Spain and Portugal), the Netherlands and Belgium direct around a half of their respective road transport services to other countries because of their ports of Rotterdam and Antwerp.

The operation of commercial transport vehicles and the supply of transport services was highly restricted throughout the EU. Free competition did not exist. It could be understood because all countries apply qualitative controls (safety standards), but they also used quantitative controls. Cabotage was generally prohibited, while bilateral permits negotiated between member states regulated haulage between them.

The EU was relatively successful in introducing special transport permits valid for a limited duration throughout the EU. However, the number of these permits was relatively small in relation to demand. The shortage of international haulage licences acceptable for business throughout the EU has created a black market for them. The price of an annual permit for a lorry to carry goods around the EU could be as high as a fifth of a lorry's operating costs. International road transport in the EU was fully liberalized from 1993. Liberal rules for the EU road haulage including cabotage, would significantly increase the efficiency of transport and reduce costs of this service to the manufacturing sector, trade and distribution.[37] There is a quota of around 30,000 authorizations (valid for two months) for cabotage in the EU. It will be progressively increased until 1998, after which EU hauliers will be free to pick up or deliver their cargo anywhere in the EU without restriction. The Single Administrative Document for carrying goods among the member countries of the EU is a significant step in the direction of improving the transport service.

One of the fastest growing industries in the services sector is telecommunication. That is because of profound technological changes since the 1960s which include communication via satellite, microwaves and digital technology. New goods and services, such as fax machines and mobile phones, appeared. The natural monopoly argument for the provision of long-distance services have vanished, although it may still be valid for the local phone service because of the economies of scale and sunk costs. Local phone companies, however, have access to several competing long-distance networks. The EU policy in the telecom field has been slow and late to appear. During the mid-1980s, the EU concentrated its efforts on R&D and common standardization. Subsequently, the intention to have an open network was translated into a Directive in 1990. In addition, public contracts that exceed ECU 0.6 million in the industry have to be transparent and officially published. For the future, the goal is to have a universal telecom service by 1998. This means that the EU consumers should have the right to have a phone connected, access to new services, services of a specified quality, and benefit from a new system of problem solving between the consumer and the provider of the service.

Business services have high rates of growth too. They include accountancy, auditing, legal, R&D, information, data processing, computing and various engineering and management consultancy services. Different technical standards, licensing of professionals and government procurement of services represent barriers to the free supply of services throughout the EU. A liberal treatment of these services may reduce their costs and increase the efficiency of business. In a world with continuous changes in technology, markets, laws and the like, as long as consultants manage to stay at least one step ahead of their clients, their services will survive.

3 The way forward

The policy of the EU towards services should be founded on three major freedoms: the freedom to establish business, the freedom to offer services and the freedom to transfer capital. Deregulation in the services sector would increase competition which would reduce costs for consumers, increase opportunities and improve the competitive position of the entire economy. Apart from deregulation, the promotion of the development of an EU-wide service industry need to be encouraged. The initial steps towards this objective include recognition of qualifications, single banking and insurance licences, removal of restrictions on transport and the opening up of government procurement over a certain (small) threshold to all EU suppliers.

Although the general interests of a member country does not always conform with the overall interest of the EU, the EU Court has often been reluctant to question the national stance. That has limited the effectiveness of Articles 59–66, as well as Article 90 of the Treaty of Rome. While the *Cassis de Dijon* case was applied to internal trade in goods, the application of the same principle to services is waiting for a more appropriate moment. The 'soft' stance of the EU regarding restrictive agreements and abuse of dominant position in services may not be easily explained only by the properties of services; but one also needs to consider the influence of entrenched businesses, lobbies and the public protection of specific interests. None the less, the attitude is slowly changing in favour of the view that regulation which limits competition, prevents, rather than stimulates, efficiency in services such as telecommunication, transport and finance.

As the provision of most of the services has a local character (many of them are non-tradeable), there will be no major change in their location, as the local incumbents have established operating retail networks and goodwill (accounting may be an exception). Because of this, national regulation will remain dominant in many industries within the services sector in the future. The structure of ownership, however, may change as local firms enter into a network of large TNCs in the industry. However, one should not exaggerate the potential expansion of TNCs in the services sector as most of mergers and acquisitions have a strong national dimension. An international, i.e. EU dimension, in the services sector is growing in the insurance industry. Allianz, the biggest insurer in the EU made 48 per cent of its premium income outside Germany in 1990, compared with only 18 per cent in 1985 (Sapir, 1993, p. 37).

The impact of the 1992 Programme on services may not be immediately obvious. Its materialization would take a long time in the future. The 1992 Programme may bring certain benefits to consumers of services. However, any large-scale benefits may be absent because of important barriers that include the reputation of the already established service firms, past experience, excess capacity and cultural differences. It may be wrong to expect that the genuine internal market would cause an equalization of prices of services throughout the EU. Prices would only tend to converge because of increased competition. None the less, certain price differences would still persist due to differences in productivity, taxation and the requirements of the local markets.

VIII CONCLUSION

Consideration of the various problems which appear during the creation and implementation of an industrial policy in the manufacturing and services sectors of a country has given an insight into the magnitude of the problems in this field which face schemes to integrate countries. There is at least one forceful argument that favours the introduction of an industrial policy. The neo-conservative school argues that a free market system is the best existing method for solving economic problems. However, this cannot be accepted without reservations. Neither the economic performance of the US prior to the New Deal, nor contemporary economic performance in the most successful industrialized countries such as Germany, Japan or Sweden supports this view. Strategic government intervention and comprehensive social welfare programmes, rather than free markets, have been the engines of economic success throughout the advanced industrial world (Tyson and Zysman, 1987b p. 426). In fact, free markets are no more than 'fine tuning' policy choices by the government.

If a country's policy is flexible towards the manufacturing industry in response to market signals (as in Japan) or if it shapes the market (as in France), it has a greater opportunity of adapting than countries which have largely prevented change (such as Britain). Industrial policy that ignores market signals and supports declining industries creates confusion over future developments and increases the cost of that inevitable change. These costs may be much higher in the future than they were in the past because of social rigidities and rapid changes in technology. The success of an industrial policy may be tested by its effectiveness in shifting resources from ailing industries, not how effective it is in preventing this adjustment.

The policy of picking the winner (a strategic industry with important externalities) *ex ante* may propel the economy of a country in the future. This may have a favourable outcome for the country or the EU if the choice is correct, if this policy is coordinated with the suppliers of inputs, and if it is limited to a defined period of time in which the national champion is expected to become self-reliant. The other interventionist approach of the rescue (*ex post*) may simply postpone the attrition of the assisted industry and increase the overall costs of change to society. The shifts away from obsolete industries into modern ones seem easy in theory, but can be quite difficult, costly and slow in practice. This, of course, is a matter of political choice.

Inability to do something is different from an unwillingness to do it. The EU opted for the creation of an environment that favours change. None the less, its direct industrial policy which is in many respects a set of R&D policies, may remain relatively modest because of the lack of funds. Other dimensions of industrial policy would be implemented within the domain of competition and trade policies. There is some hope that the 'social dimension' in the future of the EU will remain only a set of non-obligatory standards that will not mislead the EU into a complacency that will kills the impetus for continuous change for the better.

The shaping of an industrial policy in every country requires detailed data about the available factors, competition, externalities, policies of the major trading partners, as well as the tax, legal and political environment. Even then, industrial policy prescriptions should be taken with great caution. At the time when Britain was industrializing, the textile industry was the leader in technology. The capital required for the start-up of a firm was much smaller than for a steel mill which was the chief manufacturing industry when Germany started to industrialize. The problems of development had to be solved by government incentives (intervention) and bank loans. Modern industries not only require capital investment (in many cases this entails a reliance on banks) but also, and more importantly, they require investment in highly qualified personnel. Education policy is always shaped to a large extent by the government.

There are certain reasons for pessimism about the possibility for the creation and implementation of an effective industrial policy in a decentralized country or a group that integrates countries. There are many agents and issues which should be taken into account during the decision-making process. Various agents have their special impact on industrial policy. They include ministries of trade, finance, social affairs, education, regional development, defence and foreign affairs. Most of these departments exist at the federal, regional and local levels. There are also labour unions, banks and industrial associations. They all have diverse and often conflicting goals. The complexity of coordination, communication and harmonization of all those players increases exponentially with their number. In spite of all these organizational difficulties, the rewards are challenging.[38] However, numerous agents may of course, be a source of creativity, but in practice they often turn out to be a source of disagreement over the distribution of instruments of industrial policy. The interaction of all those players has an amalgamating effect on the national industrial policy. To reconcile all the diverse aspirations of the players is a great political demand.

Luckily, the evidence in the cases of Japan and Germany may serve as an example to other countries for the shaping of national industrial policies. The crucial property of a promising industrial policy is that if it cannot be organized on the central level (subsidiarity), then it ought to coordinate measures taken at lower levels. Without a consensus about the basic objectives of the industrial policy among the major players and their commitment to these goals, the success of this policy would not be fulfilled. Exchange of views, mutual understanding, trust, support and agreement about the goals and means of industrial policy between the governments at all levels, business community and labour is the essential element of its effectiveness.

While the EU creates conditions for competition, its member countries implement their own national industrial policies. The divergence in the industrial policy philosophies among member countries and a lack of funds have prevented the EU from playing a more influential role. The variety of national uncoordinated policies brought confusion and uncertainty regarding the future actions of the EU. Until the member countries take advantage of a vast internal market, they may in future lose the competitive edge in many industries to Japan, the US and the newly industrialized countries. To be durable and successful an EU industrial policy will require an agreement of the member states about their objectives and policy means. A new philosophy of the Commission regarding industrial policy in the EU is based on the idea that this policy needs to offer primarily a stable macroeconomic environment. It is hoped that enterprises will be left alone in such an atmosphere to do their best to remain competitive. The 'golden' rules for a respectable industrial policy include the following.

- The policy should not harm other parts of the economy.
- The policy needs to be continuous and stable.
- The policy instruments should reinforce each other.
- Inflation needs to be low, rates of interest positive, and exchange rates stable. In such an environment incentives exist for savings and investment.
- Public borrowing needs to be small to give better opportunities to the private sector to obtain investment funds.
- If necessary, intervention needs to be general and offer support to industries, rather than to individual firms.
- There always needs to be an element of choice among various courses of action, as well as the flexibility to respond to crises and opportunities.
- If certain support (such as subsidies, tariffs or quotas) is offered, it should have a timetable, be transparent and be of limited duration after which it has to be withdrawn.
- There needs to be a reference to investment in human capital. Well trained labour and educated management are the most valuable assets an economy can have. The policy needs to support the acquisition of new skills and promote the flexibility required for adapting to constant changes in the economy and technology.[39]
- Measures to ease adjustment frictions are often a necessary element in an industrial policy. Emphasis needs to be on the expanding, rather than declining industries.
- The policy need not neglect the creation of SMEs that establish valuable links throughout the economy, not only among the big firms, but also between producers and consumers.
- There needs to be a consensus among the major players (employers, employees and the government) in the economy about the global economic goals and the means for their achievement. The players should also be committed to the achievement of the agreed goals. This implies that the long-term vision of these goals needs to be realistic.
- Public support for R&D and innovation should increase the exchange of information among the interested parties.
- As private capital is generally uninterested in investment in infrastructure, the government needs to step into this field.

Although industrial policy is wider than trade or competition policy, the frontier between them is obscure. Whether an industrial policy has increased the national

GDP in relation to what would have happened without it can be debated for a long time without a solution that would satisfy everyone. A promising industrial policy should neither shield the expanding industries from competition for an excessively long time, nor prevent the attrition of declining industries forever. It ought to facilitate the movement of factors from obsolete to modern industries. It has to be well coordinated at all levels of government with other economic policies that affect the manufacturing and services sectors. Without successful communication, harmonization and coordination, intervention in industry would be similar to the work of a brain-damaged octopus! This holds both for single countries and for integration schemes. None the less, traditional behaviour is sometimes hard to change in reality, even though the need for change is recognized. The EU has chosen a path which creates the conditions for this transformation according to the market criteria of efficiency. It is up to the economic agents to take advantage of these opportunities.

NOTES

1 Strategic is not taken here to have any military sense, but rather its meaning refers to businesses that have important forward and backward links with other industries, as well as strong and positive externalities (spillovers) on the rest of the economy.
2 Technologies that are 'critical' for a large country's competitiveness and/or defence include those that deal with new materials, energy sources and the environment; biotechnology and pharmacy; manufacturing including production of tools; information gathering, communications, data processing and computers; transportation and aeronautics including navigation. Because of large sunk costs and economies of scale, small and medium-sized countries do not have the means and the need (if they have the possibility to acquire through trade some of those goods, services or technologies) to develop all or most of those technologies and operate them in a commercially viable pattern. What these countries may do instead is to select a 'critical' mass of 'critical' technologies or some parts of them (e.g., components, basic chemicals etc.) and try to excel in those market niches as is the case with Switzerland, Austria, the Benelux or Scandinavian countries.
3 There is a growing awareness that *most* external economies apply at a regional or metropolitan level, rather than at an international one. Therefore, the fears that external economies would be dissipated abroad is mostly wrong (Krugman, 1993, pp. 161, 167).
4 It needs to be noted that a part of the manufacturing jobs from the developed countries have gone to the developing world.
5 Akio Morita, the chairman of Sony Corporation argued that 'an economy can be only as strong as its manufacturing base. An economy that does not manufacture well cannot continue to invest adequately in itself. An economy whose only growth is in the service sector is built on sand. Certainly, the service sector is an important and growing economic force. But it cannot thrive on its own, serving hamburgers to itself and shifting money from one side to another. An advanced service economy can thrive only on the strength of an advanced manufacturing economy underlying it … The notion of a postindustrial economy that is based principally on services is a dubious one' (Morita, 1992, p. 79).
6 Over 90 per cent of R&D expenditure in the US is accounted for by the manufacturing sector (Bhagwati, 1989, p. 449).
7 Does this mean that aid to ailing industries falls out of the scope of industrial policy?
8 The term 'massaged-market economies' was first used by Lipsey (1993a, p. 12).
9 See Chapter 5 on competition policy.
10 A common definition of a SME takes the number of employees as the determining factor. Small enterprises are taken to be those with up to 25 employees, while medium-sized ones have up to 250 workers.
11 Entrepreneurs (sometimes 'maniacs with a vision') often have genuine ideas, but many of them do not have the necessary knowledge of how to run a business.

12 There was an argument that protectionism did not cost the US economy any more than the trade deficit did. The real harm done by protectionism (reduction in the efficiency of production because of fragmentation of markets, as well as prevention of specialization and economies of scale) is more modest than was usually assumed in the case of the US. The major industrial nations suffer more, in economic terms, from the relatively unattractive problems for economic analysis such as 'avoidable traffic congestion and unnecessary waste in defence contracting than they do from protectionism. To take the most extreme example, the cost to taxpayers of the savings and loan bailout alone will be at least five times as large as the annual cost to U.S. consumers of all U.S. import restrictions' (Krugman, 1990a, p. 36). The reasons why *protectionism* features relatively highly on the public agenda could be found in politics and symbolism. Politically, free trade offsets economic nationalism, while symbolically, free trade is a cornerstone of liberal democracies. In addition, voters from the protected businesses, such as agriculture and declining manufacturing industries, are the ones that bother to vote in a very large proportion, unlike the rest of the population.

13 New technologies are less and less sector or industry specific. The same holds for modern firms. Many of them may not be easily put in the group of enterprises that belong only to one industry or sector.

14 A relatively modest beginning for an industry can have irreversible effects for a particular location, region or a country. For example, there are interesting stories of why certain firms/industries are located where they are. There was a recession in Seattle (Washington) after the First World War. The economy of the region was based on fishing, production of timber and ship/boat building. At about the same time demand for aircraft (made of wood) started to emerge. There were unemployed boat-builders and other inputs. Workers had the know-how to make wooden boats, and they could easily make a fully covered boat (the body of an aeroplane), they knew how to fix a propeller and that is how it all began for Boeing. The US film industry started in California because that state has excellent light. Although modern filming and lighting technology does not depend on natural light at all, the clustering of the film industry in California continues. Nestlé was established in Vevey (Switzerland). There was a brook that could be used to turn a mill-wheel (with a hammer). It was used for the cracking of cocoa nuts and the production of cocoa powder and, hence, chocolate. There has been no production in Vevey for a long time, but Nestlé has kept its headquarters there.

15 Groups that lobby in Brussels include 400 trade associations, around 300 large firms, 150 non-profit pressure groups, 120 regional and local governments and 180 specialist law firms (*The Economist*, 15 April 1995, p. 26). Fiat or Mercedes-Benz, for example, have 50 to 100 people in their offices in Brussels. There are around 4,000 lobbyists in Brussels which has become a decision-making centre of the EU in its own right (Fraisse *et al.*, 1993, p. 227). A very high concentration of lobby services in Washington DC made in some cases the collection of certain (private) interests stronger than those of the government.

16 The lack of natural resources made Japan invest in the development of human and technological capital.

17 In spite of the success in certain high-technology industries, average living standards in Japan are below those of the US. Part of the explanation may be found in the relatively high proportion of Japanese national resources that are devoted to the stagnant industries relative to the US.

18 Airbus is a publicly sponsored consortium of British (British Aerospace), French (Aérospatiale), German (Deutsche Airbus) and Spanish (CASA) enterprises. It was established without the involvement of the EU and under the French law as a *Groupement d'Intérêt Economique*. This means that the accounts of the group are available only to the four shareholders. Unlike Boeing's profitability that is open to the public, Airbus's accounts are concealed from the public and the profit disguised in the accounts of its shareholders. It is, therefore, hard to assess the commercial success of the best known consortium in Europe. Why then does Boeing not pressure the US administration to do something about this? As around a half of the value built into the Airbuses has US origin, the producers of these

components have a strong lobbying power in Washington DC and could counter that of Boeing.

Airbus received in subsidies for new models of aircraft in the period 1970–1994 between $10 billion and $20 billion, depending on whether the source of the data is Europe or America (*The Economist*, 8 July 1995, p. 14). If these subsidies have been given for such a long time and in such a large volume, one wonders if the man-made comparative advantage was really successful!

19 The policy goal was to produce war materials. There was little concern about anti-trust laws, international competitiveness or competing national objectives (Badaracco and Yoffie, 1983, p. 99). Governments have always affected industrial development through trade policy, public procurement, taxes and subsidies, as well as the provision of public goods.

20 The two sectoral treaties on the ECSC and Euratom, considered industrial policies in economic fields characterized by a high concentration of business; high sunk and capital investment costs; importance for the defence; and the uncertainty that comes from the cyclical nature of demand. The two sectoral treaties try to overcome these market failures by a common policy.

21 The absence of an EU corporate law presented a serious problem. Large national corporations that tried to merge on the EU level such as Fiat-Citroën, Agfa-Gevaert, Dunlop-Pirelli or Fokker-VFW, gave those projects up. A notable exception is Airbus Industrie (set up in 1970). The pan-EU TNCs that survived to adolescence were those (Philips, Shell, Unilever) that had existed long before the establishment of the EU.

22 See Chapter 5 on competition policy.

23 See Chapter 5 on competition policy – the section on innovation.

24 In the US small high-technology firms sell as much as half of their output to the federal government and benefit from R&D support. In contrast, public procurement in Europe is effected through a small number of large national suppliers. This suggests that the fostering of free entry and mobility within flexible industries may be a better policy choice than supporting a few giants that react to changes only with delay (Geroski and Jacquemin, 1985, p. 177).

25 The First Framework Programme (1984–1987) disposed of a budget of ECU 3.7 billion, the Second Framework Programme (1987–1991) had a budget of ECU 6.5 billion, while the Third Framework Programme (1991–1994) was allocated ECU 8.8 billion.

26 FAST is a shared-cost programme involving a number of research and forecasting centres in the EU. It is an instrument for studying future developments, as well as the impact and social uses of sciences and technology.

27 One wonders why renowned and leading-edge companies need support and cartelization at all?

28 Indeed, the Commission tried to argue that it does not operate a large-scale industrial policy, but rather a series of R&D programmes (Curzon Price, 1990, p. 178).

29 Decisions that are taken at EU level are easy targets for special lobbies as they are too distant for the public to monitor. The co-decision procedure between the Council and the Parliament introduced by the Maastricht Treaty tried to redress this shortcoming. This is a step forward compared with the past, but there is still the danger that EU technology policy may become a sophisticated way of creating a new protectionism.

30 The EU invested in industries in which there is a high risk of failure and where Japan and the US are the strongest. A relative failure of electronics in the EU is due, in part, to the fact that domestic firms were sheltered from foreign competition. On the other hand, where competition was global, for example, in commercial aircraft, Airbus had certain successes.

31 They include businesses in both the manufacturing and services sectors. The impact on services is discussed below.

32 Do you remember your first (or for that matter even second or third) cab drive from the airport in a south European country as a foreigner? If not, you will!

33 Positive externalities take place in services, such as telecommunications, where the value for one user increases with the total number of all users. A negative externality may be found, for example, in financial services where the failure of one bank may cause troubles to a number of others (Sapir, 1993, p. 27).

34 The number of car accidents per motor car or per inhabitant may be higher in one country relative to another. Hence, due to greater risk, certain differences in insurance premiums among countries would remain in spite of increased competition.

35 'As patriotism is the last refuge of scoundrels (according to Dr. Johnson), the welfare of widows, orphans, and the incompetent is the last refuge of supporters of regulation. Individuals free to make their own decisions will indeed make mistakes. Even if potential buyers are clearly informed of the regulatory regime, some will not understand its significance. Even if large amounts of information are available on that significance, some will not bother to obtain it.... Protection of the foolish against error provides a rationale for almost infinite extension' (Hindley, 1991, pp. 272–273).

36 Everyone may appreciate the benefits of a car such as a BMW or a Mercedes. But it is quite another thing for consumers to be willing to pay or have the means to pay for such a motor car. A small Fiat may be the absolute limit for many of them.

37 The US offered a convincing example of deregulation of inter-state transport services in 1980.

38 Without the highest degree of coordination one would not be able to fly to the Moon and return safely to the Earth.

39 Education may be a subsidized input for which the business sector has not paid the full cost. None the less, countervailing duties cannot be introduced by foreign partners as education often takes a long time and cannot be easily and directly valued as with other subsidies, such as those for exports.

7

TRADE POLICY[1]

I INTRODUCTION

The Preamble to the Treaty of Rome states that the EU desires to contribute to the progressive abolition of restrictions on international trade by means of a common commercial policy. Internal trade in the EU would be free of all customs duties and quantitative restrictions (Article 3). The EU is ready to contribute to the development of international commerce and lower barriers to trade by entering into reciprocal agreements devised to reduce tariffs below the general level (Article 18). The objective of the EU in commercial policy is 'to contribute, in the common interest, to the harmonious development of world trade, the progressive abolition of restrictions on international trade and the lowering of customs barriers' (Article 110). Member countries need to coordinate their trade relations with third countries (Article 111). Probably the most important provision of the Treaty regarding trade is that the common commercial policy is based on uniform principles, in particular regarding tariffs and trade arrangements with third countries (Article 113).[2] In the case of economic difficulties, the Commission may authorize the affected member state(s) to take the necessary protective measures (Article 115).[3] There are two other safeguard provisions in the Treaty. If there is a sudden crisis in the balance of payments, the member state concerned may take the necessary protective measures (Article 109). In the chapter on full elimination of quantitative restrictions on internal trade, Article 36 allows member states to prohibit or restrict trade or the transit of goods that jeopardize public morality, policy or security, or endanger the health or life of humans, animals or plants. Member states should operate in international economic organizations only on the basis of common action (Article 116). This provision is supposed to enhance the bargaining power of the EU. Small member countries particularly benefit from it. There is also an agreement to associate the non-European countries that have special (read: ex-colonial) relations with the EU (Article 131).[4] The associated countries would have the same treatment in trade as the members of the EU (Article 132). The EU may conclude association agreements with a third country, group of countries or an international organization (Articles 228 and 238). Any European state may apply for membership in the EU (Article 237). Article 100a refers to the establishment and operation of the internal market. Save for fiscal, free movement of persons and rights of employees, the earlier principle of unanimity is replaced by one of qualified majority in the decision-making process.

This chapter is structured as follows. It starts with the basic theory of customs unions. Then follows an overview of trade relations of the EU which includes

215

international trade negotiations, NTBS, imports, exports and balance of trade. Next comes a look at the trade relations of the EU with its most important trading partners: the EFTA, the US, Japan, the transition economies of central and eastern Europe and the developing countries. At the end, the conclusion is that the EU has taken bold steps to liberalize economic relations with its foreign partners, but it also has the means to step back from such commitments when the internal economic situation is unfavourable.

II THEORY OF CUSTOMS UNIONS[5]

1 Introduction

All types of international economic integration provoke interest because they, to varying degrees, both promote and restrict trade. Trade is liberalized, at least partly, among the participating countries, while it is also distorted with third countries as there are various barriers between the integrated group and the rest of the world. On these grounds the analysis of international economic integration is complex. A customs union is the type of international economic integration which has received the most attention in research and is the most rigorously developed branch of the neo-classical theory. This section is limited to an analysis of the basics of the static and dynamic models of customs unions.

The tariff system may discriminate between commodities and/or countries. Commodity discrimination takes place when different rates of import duty are charged on different commodities. Country discrimination is found when the same commodity is subject to different rates of duty on the basis of country of origin. Lipsey (1960, p. 496) defined the theory of customs unions as a branch of tariff theory which deals with the effect of geographically discriminatory changes in trade barriers. While this is true in the static sense, however, a customs union in a dynamic setting may be, among other things, a means for economic development.

The efficiency criterion used most often in economics is that of Pareto optimality. An allocation of resources is said to be Pareto-optimal if there does not exist another feasible allocation in which some agents would be better off (in a welfare sense) and no agents worse off. By a judicious definition of welfare, the Pareto-optimal allocation is that allocation which best satisfies social objectives. Pareto optimality (the first best solution) is achieved exclusively in the state of free trade and factor mobility, so that other states, in which there are distortions (tariffs, subsidies, taxes, monopolies, externalities, minimum wages, local content requirements, to mention just a few), are sub-optimal. It may happen that the Pareto-optimal allocation cannot be achieved because of one or several distortions. Can a second-best position be attained by satisfying the remaining Pareto conditions? The theory of the second best answered in the negative (Lipsey and Lancaster, 1956–7). In the presence of distortions, if all the conditions for Pareto optimality cannot be satisfied, then the removal of some of the distortions does not necessarily increase welfare, nor does the addition of other distortions necessarily decrease welfare! Welfare may remain unaffected, increased or decreased. This implies that there can be no reliable expectation about the welfare effect of a change in the current situation. The theory of the second best has a disastrous effect on welfare economics. However, Lipsey (1960) was not discouraged enough to be put off writing a seminal article on the theory of customs unions.

The intuition behind the classical theory of customs unions is the proposition that the potential consumption of goods and services in a customs union is higher than the sum of the individual consumptions of the potential member countries in the situation in which trade among these countries is distorted by tariffs and quotas. In this situation one should, at least partly, remove these impediments.

2 Static model

A static model of the theory of customs unions considers the impact of the formation of a customs union on trade flows and consumption in the united countries. The classical (orthodox or static) theory of customs unions relies on a number of explicit and implicit assumptions. This approach makes theoretical consideration easier, but it also simplifies reality to the extent that the policy recommendations are to be considered with great care.

Assume that there are only three countries. Country A, a relatively small country in relation to the other two, forms a customs union with country B. Country C (which may represent all other countries in the world), is discriminated against by the customs union by means of a CET. Tariffs are levied on an *ad valorem* basis in all countries. Rates of tariffs are the same both for final commodities and inputs, so that the rate of nominal protection equals the rate of effective protection. The assumption of equal rates of tariffs prior to integration removes the possible dispute about the level of the CET. Tariffs are the only instrument of trade policy and there are no NTBs to trade. The price of imported goods for home consumers (P_{mt}) is composed of the price of an imported good (P_m) and tariff (t):

$$P_{mt} = (1 + t)P_m \qquad (7.1)$$

where $t \geqslant 0$. State intervention exists only at the border and trade is balanced. Free or perfect competition, exists both in markets for goods and services, as well as in markets for factors. Perfect competition or complete equality of opportunity exists in all economies, except for the existence of tariffs.

Production costs per unit of output are constant over all levels. To state it more formally, production functions are homogeneous of degree one, i.e. to produce one more unit of good X, inputs must be increased by a constant proportion. Costs of production determine the retail price of goods. Producers in an industry operate at the minimum efficient scale at the production possibility frontier. Countries embark upon the production of certain goods on the basis of the prices (relative abundance or scarcity) of home factors.

The theory of customs unions refers to the manufacturing sector: a fixed quantity of factors of production is fully employed. There are no sector-specific factors such as specific human and physical capital, entrepreneurship and the like. In a dynamic model these specific factors can be transformed in the long run, but this would require adjustment costs which are ruled out in the static model. Mobility of factors is perfect within their home country, while commodities are perfectly mobile between the integrated countries. This means that TNCs are ignored. There are no transport, insurance or banking costs.

All countries have access to the same technology and differ only in their endowment of factors. Economies are static, with static expectations. This is to say that rates of growth; technologies; tastes; propensities to consume, save, import and invest are given and unchangeable. There is no depreciation of the capital stock. All goods and services are homogeneous, i.e. consumers do not have a preference for the consumption of goods and services from any particular supplier. They decide upon their purchases exclusively on the basis of price differences. All goods and services have unit income elasticities of demand, i.e. every increase or decrease in income has a proportional change in demand for all goods and services in the same direction. This means that demand is 'well behaved'. Non-tradeable commodities do not exist. There is no intra-industry trade or 'cross-hauling', i.e. a country cannot both export and import identical goods or close substitutes. There are no inventories. All markets clear simultaneously. Such equilibrium must be both sustainable and feasible, i.e. firms can neither profitably undercut the market price nor make loses.

In this model there is no uncertainty. Firms and resource owners are perfectly informed about all markets while consumers are fully familiar with goods and services. Fiscal (taxes and subsidies) and monetary (rates of exchange, interest, inflation and balance of payments) operations are ruled out. Finally, a country which is not included in a customs union is assumed not to retaliate against the integrated countries.

The above assumptions are clearly highly restrictive, but greatly simplify the analysis so that the essential properties of the model can be highlighted. The objective of the following analysis is to make a point, rather than to be realistic.

2.1 Partial equilibrium model

The partial equilibrium model deals with the market for *a single good*. International trade can be a response to differences in the availability of resources (factor proportions), differences in technology and efficiency in production (production functions), economies of scale, differences in tastes, differences in market structures and/or differences in output or factor taxes. Suppose that three countries produce the same commodity, but with varying levels of efficiency: their production functions differ. This model, is described in Table 7.1.

Table 7.1 Unit cost of production of a commodity

Country	A	B	C
Unit cost of production	60	50	35

Country C has the lowest unit cost of production, hence this country will become the world supplier of this commodity in a free trade situation. Suppose now, that country A wants to protect its inefficient domestic producers from foreign competition for whatever reason. This intention of country A can be criticized from the outset. Tariffs are an available means of protection which have distortionary effects. The most important effect is that they move the country away from free trade towards autarky. Gains from specialization are sacrificed because resources are diverted away from the pattern of comparative advantage. In addition to reducing potential consumption, tariffs redistribute income in favour of factors which are used in production in the protected industry and decrease the possibility of their more efficient employment elsewhere in the economy. If country A wants to protect her home production of this good it must levy a tariff. This tariff of, for example, 100 per cent, not only increases the price of the imported commodity to country A's consumers, but more importantly it shifts consumption away from imports towards country A's domestic production. In these circumstances, country A could increase domestic consumption of this good if it enters into a customs union with either of the countries in this model. Table 7.2 presents prices of the imported commodity with the tariff on country A's market.

Table 7.2   Price of an imported commodity in dollars, with the tariff on country A's market

Import duty (%)	Price of a commodity from	
	Country B	Country C
100	100	70
50	75	52.5

If country A forms a customs union with country B, then consumers in country A could import the good from country B at a cost of 50 dollars per unit, rather than to buy it from domestic suppliers at the cost of 60 dollars as before. Hence, they are better off than in the case with a non-discriminatory tariff. If country A creates a customs union with country C, then country A's consumers are in an even better position compared to a customs union with country B. Now, they purchase the good at a unit price of 35 dollars. In both cases, consumers in country A are better off than in the situation in which they were buying the domestically produced good. The final effect in both cases is trade creation.

The formation of a customs union encourages *trade creation* as a result of a change from a dearer to a cheaper source of supply. Other things being equal, this is a potential move towards free trade because a less efficient protected domestic supplier is replaced by a more efficient foreign one. Country A gives up the production of a good in which it has a comparative disadvantage in order to acquire it more cheaply by importing it from a partner country, so trade is created. This welfare enhancing effect depends crucially on the assumption that the freed domestic resources can find alternative employment elsewhere in the economy.

Suppose now that prior to the formation of the customs union, the duty on imports was 50 per cent in country A. Table 7.2 shows that in this case the supplier of country A would be country C. Country A's domestic industry offers this good at a unit price of 60 dollars, country B at a price of 75 dollars, while country C is the cheapest source of supply at 52.5 dollars. If instead, country A enters into a customs union with country B and if the CET for the commodity in question is 50 per cent, then country A would purchase this good from country B. In this case country A pays 50 dollars per unit to country B, while at the same time, a unit of the good from country C costs 52.5 dollars. The outcome in this case is *trade diversion*. Trade creation and trade diversion are often called Vinerian effects after Viner (1950) who first introduced those terms.

Trade diversion works in the opposite way from trade creation. The cheapest foreign supplier is changed in favour of a relatively dearer one from the customs union. Due to the CET, business is taken away from the most efficient world producer and trade in this commodity is reduced. This creates a global welfare loss. Trade within a customs union takes place at a protected (higher) level of prices. A higher union level of prices relative to the international one brings benefits to internal exporters. Importers lose as they pay the partner country suppliers a higher price per unit of import and their country forgoes tariff revenue which is not levied on intra-union imports.

The net impact on world efficiency of a move to a customs union depends on which of the two Vinerian effects prevails. It may be positive, negative or neutral. Hence, according to this theory, the favourable attitude of the GATT towards customs unions and free trade areas as trade liberalizing moves cannot be accepted without reservation.

Major economic policies of the EU such as the Common Commercial Policy (customs union) or the CAP are mostly shaped according to the interests of the producers. The interests of the consumers are largely neglected in the EU. Hence, the possibilities for a trade diverting bias in the EU should come as no surprise. None the less, the slowly expanding role of the European Parliament may increase more forcefully the interest of the consumers into the EU decision-making structure.

Trade diversion may be more beneficial than trade creation for consumption in the country that gives preferential treatment to certain suppliers. That is because this country does not sacrifice home production. The source of benefits is *anticipated* trade creation since, by assumption, bilateral trade flows must balance. The comparison here is between trade creation and the autarkic volume of domestic production. An integrating country will not benefit from trade creation unless it increases its exports to the partners (as compared to the pre-union level) which from partner's point of view can represent trade diversion (Robson, 1987, p. 52).

Trade flows among countries A, B and C may have the following patterns. Suppose that country A and country B form a customs union. If only country A produces this good, but inefficiently, then the choice between domestic production and imports from country C depends on the height of the CET. If both countries in the customs union produce the good, but inefficiently, then the least inefficient country will supply the customs union market subject to the protection of the CET. If neither country in the customs union produces the good, then there is no trade diversion. The customs union is supplied by the cheapest foreign supplier. If only one country in the customs union produces the good in question, but in the most efficient way, then this country will supply the market even without a CET. By offering a common level of protection, the CET may promote a more efficient allocation of resources within the customs union.

Figure 7.1 illustrates the effects of a tariff and a customs union on economic efficiency for a single good in country A's market. SS represents country A's domestic supply curve, similarly, DD shows the domestic demand curve. Country B's supply curve is BB, while country C's supply curve for the same good is CC. Both foreign countries can supply unconditionally any quantity of the demanded good at fixed

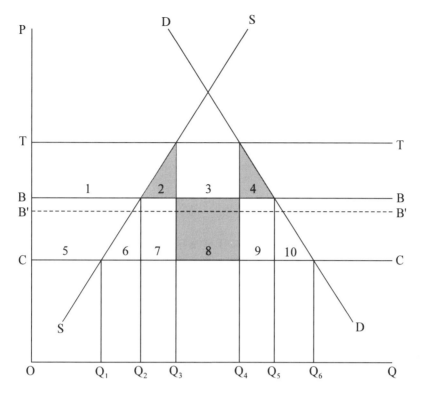

Figure 7.1 Effect of a tariff and a customs union on production and consumption in country A

prices. Both foreign supply curves are flat (perfectly elastic). It is a consequence of the smallness of the country in our example. This country cannot exert influence on its terms of trade, but in a customs union with other countries this is likely to change. Prior to the imposition of a tariff, at price OC home demand for the good is OQ_6. Domestic producers supply OQ_1 while country C supplies Q_1Q_6.

Suppose that country A introduces a tariff on imports such that the price for domestic consumers is OT. Now, country A can expand domestic production from OQ_1 to OQ_3 and curtail home consumption of the good from OQ_6 to OQ_4. The government collects tariff revenue equal to $CT \times Q_3Q_4$. This choice by country A may be questioned. There are at least two good reasons to object to trade restrictions in the medium and long term. First, new barriers to trade can provoke retaliation from foreign countries where domestic exporters intend to penetrate. Second, and more subtle, if intermediate goods exist, all trade barriers raise the price of imported inputs. Therefore, they act as a tax on exports.[6] With the tariff, country A employs more resources in an industry in which it does not have a comparative advantage. Bearing in mind the assumption that the amount of resources is fixed and stepping out shortly from the partial equilibrium model, the fact is that resources are diverted away from business activities in which this country may have a comparative advantage. If a home industry is not competitive, a tariff may save jobs in this business in the short term. This may, however, lead to reduced activity in other home industries. If the uncompetitively produced home good is an input in other industries, their export performance may be compromised and investment reduced with the overall consequence of increased unemployment in the longer term.

Policy-makers can easily identify jobs that are saved by various forms of protection, but they do not easily recognize the adverse consequences of this protection, hence the need for a general equilibrium model. Through protection in the long term, resources are wasted on inefficient production. Everybody loses except the government (because of increased revenues) and the protected industry. In the short run the problem is that the general equilibrium consequences of a given policy are not easily quantifiable. This policy of import substitution as opposed to a policy of export promotion may be substantiated only on the grounds that foreign markets for country A's exports are closed.

Returning to Figure 7.1, assume that country A which imposed a non-discriminatory *ad valorem* tariff on imports, enters into a customs union with country B. The price of imports from country C with a common external tariff of CT is OT. Country B will supply country A's market. Country A's inefficient production contracts from OQ_3 to OQ_2 while consumption increases from OQ_4 to OQ_5. *Trade expansion* due to the creation of the customs union equals the sum of the reduction in home production Q_2Q_3 and the increase in home consumption Q_4Q_5. Country A's government does not earn any tariff proceeds from imports of the good from the customs union partner, country B. Trade expansion inevitably effects rationalization in production. This takes place through an improved employment of existing factors, increased size of production units (reallocation of resources within sectors). The consequences of these rationalizations are decreased unit costs of goods and services, as well as increased standards of living on average.

Trade-expansion effects, however, should not be over-emphasized. The downward adjustment of domestic tariffs to the CET need not result in an increased trade expansion effect in a customs union. This alignment will lead first to a reduction to normal levels of the profit margins of the protected domestic producers. If there is excess capacity in the protected industries, a possible increase in the domestic demand which comes as a consequence of the fall in price, will be met first by the country's own production (if it exists), rather than through imports. Thus the trade expansion effects due to the creation of a customs union will not be as large as would be suggested by the difference in tariffs before the creation of a customs union and after it. Therefore, the scope for trade diversion is, indeed, smaller than it may initially appear. It is just the potential for trade and competition that does this good work for consumers, as well as producers in the long term.

Consumer surplus is defined as the difference between the consumers' total valuation of the goods consumed and the total cost of obtaining them. It is represented by the area under the demand curve and above the price that consumers face. Any decrease in price, other things being equal, increases consumers' surplus. Country A's consumers benefit when their country enters into a customs union with country B in relation to the situation with an initial non-discriminatory tariff. Their gain is given by the area $1 + 2 + 3 + 4$. These consumers are, however, worse off in comparison to the free trade situation in which country C is the supplier. This loss is given by the area $5 + 6 + 7 + 8 + 9 + 10$. Domestic producers lose a part of their surplus in a customs union compared to the situation with a non-discriminatory *ad valorem* tariff (area above SS up to the price OB which they receive). This is represented by area 1. From the national standpoint, area 1 nets out as part of both the consumers' gain and the producers' loss. Country A loses tariff revenue (area 3) which it collects in the initial situation. Hence, the net gain for country A is area 2 + 4.

The formation of a customs union has increased trade and consumption in country A in comparison to the initial situation with a non-discriminatory tariff. In the situation prior to the formation of a customs union, country A imports the good from country C, pays for it an amount equal to $Q_3Q_4 \times OC$ and collects revenue equal to the area 3 + 8. After the formation of a customs union, area 3 is returned to consumers in the form of lower prices for the good, while area 8 represents a higher price charged by the customs union partner country. The return of area 3 to consumers may be regarded as Hicksian compensation. When tariffs change, compensation is seldom paid. Hence, demand curve DD may be regarded merely as an approximation of the compensated Hicksian demand curve. It is important to note that country A pays, for the same amount of imports Q_3Q_4, a higher price to the customs union partner ($Q_3Q_4 \times OB$) than was paid to the country C suppliers prior to the customs union formation. The country has a greater outflow of foreign exchange and does not collect revenue which it did when it imposed a non-discriminatory tariff on imports from country C. The outflow of foreign exchange from country A was equal to $Q_3Q_4 \times OC$ while area 3 + 4 illustrates the transfer from consumers to producers within the home country.

The net welfare result of the creation of a customs union in country A depends on the relative size of the Vinerian effects; trade creation (area 2 + 4) minus trade diversion (area 8). Instead of a revenue generating obstacle to trade (tariff) a government may introduce cost increasing barriers (various standards; customs, health and testing documentation) whose effect may be a reduction in trade. (Let the effect of the NTBs be BT in trade with country B.) If the set of NTBs is removed, the effect on domestic consumers and producers would be the same as in the situation when the tariff is removed. The government which has never earned revenue from the set of non-tariff regulations, would lose nothing. The social gain from reducing these barriers is area 2 + 3 + 4

If one introduces dynamics into this model, in the form of increasing returns to scale, country B, as the customs union supplier of the good, faces an increased demand. Production would become more efficient and the price might fall from OB to, say OB'. This enhances trade creation and decreases the size of the trade diversion effect.

Figure 7.1 belongs to the family of standard microeconomic partial-equilibrium figures. Unfortunately, they all deal just with a part of the business cycle, that is, only with the first third of the cycle when demand rises. Other cases, such as stagnation or reduction in demand, are seldom considered.

Patterns of consumption would change following the creation of a customs union. Inter-country substitution occurs when one country replaces the other as the source of supply for some good. Inter-commodity substitution happens when one commodity is substituted, at least at the margin, for another commodity as a result of a shift in relative prices (Lipsey, 1960, p. 504). The latter occurs for example when country A imports from the customs union partner country B relatively cheaper veal which replaces at least some of the pork produced in country A and at least some of the chicken imported from country C, and when consumers in a customs union replace a part of the demand for theatre and opera by relatively cheaper stereo and video equipment.

One can ask if there are superior alternative policies to the creation of a customs union? Unilateral, non-discriminatory reductions in import tariffs may seem to be a superior policy to the formation of a customs union. It seems better to obtain exclusively trade creation as a result of unilateral tariff reductions than to create a customs union which causes both trade creation and trade diversion (Cooper and Massel, 1965, p. 745–746). This argument cannot be accepted without serious reservations. A customs union offers something which is not offered by a unilateral reduction in tariffs. That is, an elimination of tariffs in customs union partner countries. A unilateral reduction in tariffs exaggerates the price reduction effects on consumption, while it eliminates the possibility of penetration into customs union partner countries' markets.

In spite of the trade diversion costs of a customs union, the terms of trade of member countries may turn in their favour, so that on balance, each member country may be better off than in the unilateral tariff reduction case. The classical approach to the theory of tariffs is mistaken. This approach, on the one hand, finds gains in the replacement of domestic goods for cheaper foreign goods, while on the other, expansion of domestic exports does not bring gains in this model to the exporting country (except a possible improvement of the terms of trade), but rather to the foreigners.

Suppose that transfer payments between countries are allowed for. Then any customs union is potentially favourable for all countries considering participation, since they can be compensated for losses when they join. This means that a customs union among countries can be extended to $n + 1$ countries. By expansion, this implies that there is an incentive to extend the customs union until the whole world is included, until free trade prevails throughout the world (Kemp and Wan, 1976). This may lead to the classical proposition that a customs union is a step towards free trade. This conclusion depends on the existence of inter-country transfers within the customs union. This is a severe restriction and the greatest weakness of this approach. The more countries there are in a customs union, the greater will be the potential need for compensation. If compensation schemes are adopted in reality, they are often the products of political bargaining and not purely of economic impact. These schemes are too complicated and never compensate in full, since they are never perfect, which limits the actual size of customs union. This leads to the conclusion that non-economic reasons may also play a prominent role in economic integration. The experience of the EU illustrates that political considerations are an important factor for integration, in particular regarding expansion in the number of member countries.

2.2 General equilibrium model

A partial equilibrium model considers the market for a single good. It assumes that all prices other than that of that good are fixed. A general equilibrium model considers *all markets*. All prices are variable and competitive equilibrium requires that all markets clear. All markets are connected by a chain of inputs and substitutes,

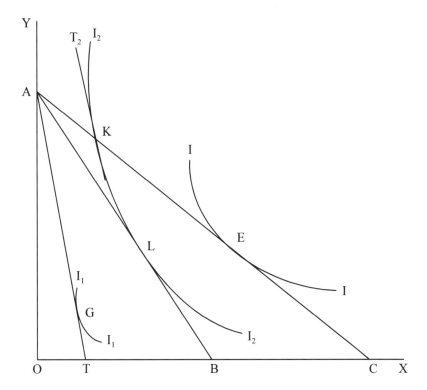

Figure 7.2 Welfare in a trade diverting customs union

information, technology, mobility of factors and goods, income (if one spends more on something, less will remain for other things), etc.

Consideration of the general equilibrium model will start with the 3 × 2 model. In this case there are three countries A, B and C, as well as two goods (markets) X and Y. Lipsey (1957 and 1960) was the first to study these cases in a customs union framework. The model included full specialization and constant costs. A small country A imports good X from country C which is the foreign supplier with the lowest price.

Consider a case illustrated in Figure 7.2, where substitution in consumption is allowed for by smooth and convex indifference curves. There are three countries A, B and C, and two goods X and Y, respectively. In the free trade case, country A trades with country C and achieves indifference curve II. Suppose now that country A introduces a non-discriminatory tariff on imports. The relative price in country A is now AT.

Suppose that this tariff does not give enough incentive to home entrepreneurs to embark upon production of good X. Country A achieves the indifference curve I_1I_1 with equilibrium at point G. If the government either returns all tariff proceeds to consumers or spends the entire amount in the same fashion as the consumers would have otherwise done, then the equilibrium should be on line AC (as country C is the best foreign supplier). The equilibrium point is at point K, which is where the line T_1 (parallel to AT which illustrates compensation of consumers) intersects with terms-of-trade line AC. The extent of the rightward shift in the terms of trade line depends on how much people are willing to import at these prices and, hence, the volume of tariff revenue to be returned to them. T_1 is deliberately drawn in such a way that K and L lie on the same indifference curve. The tariff has changed the structure of production and relative prices. Consumption of the home good increases, while imports and exports decrease.

Suppose that country A forms a trade-diverting customs union with country B. The terms of trade line with country B is illustrated by line AB. Suppose that K and L lie on the same indifference curve I_2I_2. The formation of a customs union has not changed country A's welfare, although the structure of consumption has changed. If the best situation is at point E, then the formation of a customs union for country A is a move from one sub-optimal position K, to another sub-optimal position L. Country A is indifferent. If country A obtains in a customs union terms of trade which are worse than OB/OA, then country A is worse off than in the situation with a non-discriminatory tariff. If country A, however, obtains terms of trade which are better than OB/OA, then a trade-diverting customs union can be welfare improving for this country. Hence, the classical statement that trade diversion is always a bad thing is rejected.

2 Dynamic model

The classical theory of customs unions assumes that the static effects of resource reallocation occurs in a timeless framework. If one wants to move the theory of customs unions towards reality one must consider dynamic effects. Instead of considering only the possibility of trade in commodities, dynamic models analyse the possibility of allocations across time. The static effects of international economic integration have their most obvious and profound influence in the period of time immediately following the creation of, for example, a customs union. Gradually, after several years of adjustment, the dynamic effects will increase in importance and become dominant.

Current flows of trade may not remain constant. In fact, they change over time. Changes in the equilibrium points in, for example, in Figure 7.1 are described as instantaneous changes. Such changes in equilibrium points, however, may not always be possible. Delays in reaction on the part of countries and consumers in a customs union could be caused by their recourse to stocks. Hence, they do not immediately need to purchase those goods whose price has decreased as a consequence of the formation of a customs union. They also may have some contractual commitments that cannot be abandoned overnight. Finally, and nowadays less likely, consumers may not be aware of all the changes. Up to the nineteenth century state intervention was negligible, but markets remained disconnected because of imperfect information and relatively high transport costs. A time interval between the implementation of a policy change (creation of a customs union) and its favourable effects may include an initial period of economic deterioration in certain regions which may be followed by improvements due to the J-curve effect.

Consideration of dynamic, i.e. restructuring effects, would be limited to the analysis of economies of scale, specialization and terms of trade as the impact of opening up of markets on increased competition was dealt with in the chapter on competition policy (5).

Returns to scale refer to the relation between input requirements and output response with its impact on costs. Economies of scale comprise a number of things, from simple technical scale to phenomena such as: processing complex information; direction, control and improvement of independent activities; and experience. If a firm's output increases in the same proportion as its inputs, then that firm's technology exhibits constant returns to scale or, one may say, that a firm has constant marginal costs. If a firm's output increases by a greater proportion than inputs, then this firm's technology has increasing returns to scale or it enjoys decreasing marginal costs (or increasing marginal product). If a firm's output decreases by a smaller proportion than input requirements, then the firm suffers from decreasing returns to scale or increasing marginal costs.

The pure theory of international trade is concerned mostly with perfect competition. In a situation in which the minimum efficient scale is relatively large, only a few firms may exist simultaneously. Competition in such markets is not perfect. When markets are enlarged by international economic integration or opened by projects such as the 1992 Programme which increase competition, firms may expand their production and specialize in order to achieve lower costs (economies of scale).

The existence of internal NTBs to trade is the cause of unexploited economies of scale in the EU market. An empirical study of potential economies of scale in EU industry reported that in more than a half of all branches of industry, 20 firms of efficient size could coexist in the EU, whereas the largest national markets can support only 4 each. The EU internal market can offer the potential for efficiency and competition. Twenty efficient firms are more likely to ensure effective competition than 4 firms (Emerson *et al.*, 1988, p. 18). This finding ignores the logic behind the role of concentration in modern industries and the contribution which a few oligopolies, exploiting economies of scale and carefully monitored by appropriate regulatory authorities, can and do make to economic welfare. Besides, there may be fierce competition even among the 4 firms. Just take a look at competition in the US long distance telephone call business or the fierce competition of a few Japanese electronic conglomerates both in the domestic and international market.

Changes in technology exert a continuous pressure on the efficient size of plant. Hence, the minimum efficient size of plant changes over time. Large-scale production is profitable only if there is secure access to a wide market. It is reasonable, therefore, to argue that firms which operate on a wide market are likely to be closer to the minimum efficient plant size than the ones which act within a more restricted framework. However, recent developments in technology are diminishing classical scale economies associated with mass production in large plants. Modern technology increases the role of smaller, but highly specialized plants.

Economies of scale are largest in transport equipment, electronics, office machines, chemicals and other manufactured products. These are the industries in which demand has the highest growth and where technology changes fast. The common element in these industries is the vast investment required to produce even a small amount of output. Advance technology is not necessary for increasing returns to scale, but increasing returns to scale are frequently in high-technology industries. In addition, those industries are under continuous pressure from international competition. Industries with relatively smaller returns to scale are the ones with stagnant demand and relatively low technology content. They include food, textile, clothing and footwear industries.

Adam Smith pointed out that specialization is limited by the extent of the market. A customs union increases the market area for firms in the participating countries, hence it opens up opportunities for specialization. If they trade, countries may gain not only from an exchange of goods and services, but also from specialization and a wider choice of goods. Trade increases the bundle of available goods and services in relation to what is available in autarky. Specialization and alteration in the output mix in a country may take the full advantage of its factor endowment.

Economies of scale may be internal to individual firms. That may also be external to these firms (this is the case when the whole industry grows and when all the firms in that industry enjoy the fruits of this growth). The attention here will be focused on technical (as one of the types of) economies of scale. The peculiarity of economies of scale is that they are not consistent with perfect competition. With imperfect market structure many welfare outcomes are likely to happen. A perfectly competitive firm takes the price for its output as given. A firm with increasing returns to scale in such a market will find it profitable to produce one more unit of output since it can do so at less than the prevailing price. In so doing, it will tend to increase output until it dominates the market, while efficiency may set the price for its output.

Consider the case in Figure 7.3 which illustrates the impact of economies of scale on price in the exporting country A. The vertical axis shows the price in country A for good X. Increasing returns to scale are implied by the downward-sloping AC_a curve. The producer of this commodity has a monopoly position in the domestic market. There is no producer in country B, but this country has a tariff on imports of good X for fiscal reasons. Domestic demand in country A is represented by the curve D_a and the demand for the product in country B is represented by the curves D_b and $D_{b'}$. The former is the demand curve incorporating a tariff in country B on imports of good X, while the latter reflects demand for this good if no tariffs are levied.

The initial equilibrium in this market is represented by the intersection of the joint demand curve D_{a+b} and the AC_a curve as implied by the monopoly position of the country A producer. If countries A and B enter into a customs union, then the tariff on imports of good X into country B will be eliminated, increasing the demand for this good. Thus, the curve representing demand in country B is D_b, and the joint demand in the customs union is D_{a+b}. Faced with this increased demand the producer in country A will expand output. With increasing returns to scale this output expansion lowers the marginal and average costs of production and leads to a fall in the equilibrium price from P_1 to P_2. The elimination of the tariff has an unambiguously positive effect: all consumers can purchase a greater quantity of good X at a lower price, and profits to the producer have increased.

The above result is called the *cost-reduction effect*. It is distinct from trade creation since the existing supplier reduces the price for good X. There is an additional effect: suppose that there was an initial tariff on imports of good X but it was insufficient to induce domestic production of X in country A. After the creation of a customs union with country B, the market area for country A is increased. Costs of production may fall, hence production of good X may begin in country A replacing imports into both customs union partners from country C. For country A this is *trade suppression*

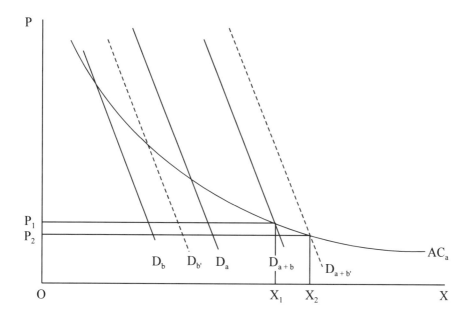

Figure 7.3 Economies of scale and their impact on price in exporting country A

while for country B, this represents trade diversion. While learning by doing, country A may become a more efficient producer of good X than country C, so in the longer run, this policy may pay off. The country in which production with increasing returns to scale occurs enjoys double gains (employment and increased production). Governments in the customs union may cooperate in order to evenly distribute the industries with increasing returns to scale, otherwise they may end up in an investment subsidy war to attract such industries.

In perfectly contestable markets, price equals marginal cost (firms just cover production costs of the last unit and profits are zero). Economies of scale introduce imperfection into the market system since firms set prices at average cost and make profits. Therefore, economies of scale lead to more specialization compared with the situation with constant returns to scale. The existence of these firms is protected by barriers to entry such as sunk costs and capital requirements.

After a certain level of output some costs, in particular depreciation of equipment, may increase disproportionately in relation to output, and partly offset the reduction in costs that accrues from increasing returns to scale. For example, the ends of the blades on very large turbines move at the speed that can be close to that of sound. At such speed metal fatigue increases disproportionately in relation to a turbine's capacity. A strike in a firm with an increasing returns to scale technology may have a profound impact on the profitability of a firm. Such threats by trade unions may be mitigated by warnings of a removal of barriers to trade and imports.

Returns to scale have not been thoroughly studied in the theory of customs unions because it is difficult to model them. Therefore, one should be very careful while using the classical theory either as a description of what is likely to happen in a customs union or as a guide to policies that will ensure that such a union fulfils the expectations. Another important fact is that a substantial part of production is linked to economies of scope rather than scale. While economies of scale imply a certain level of standardization in tastes and production, economies of scope deal with product or process diversity. Economies of scope allow firms such as Benetton to respond swiftly to changes in the supply of inputs and shifts in demand, because they come from a common control of distinct, but interrelated production activities. For example, the same kind of fabric can be used in the production of various goods.

Economies of scale are coupled with market imperfections which make possible various welfare outcomes. Distortions, such as deviations from marginal cost pricing or the existence of barriers to entry mean that the creation of a customs union does not necessarily either improve or worsen welfare. With economies of scale and other distortions, the welfare effects of customs union creation and patterns of trade are much more affected by government policy than they are in the neo-classical theorists' world of comparative advantage and factor proportions.

The terms of trade is the ratio of the quantity of imports that may be obtained in trade for a certain quantity of exports or, alternatively, it is the relative price of imports to exports. If home demand for good X is elastic, then the home country's tariff on imports may reduce both consumption and imports of this good. If this country can act as a monopsonist it may turn prices on the international market in its favour, which improves its terms of trade (at least in the short term). The same powers may be wielded by a customs union. Third countries may not only lose exports by possible trade diversion, but also have to increase their effort in exports to the customs union in order to mitigate the impact of adverse terms of trade changes.

If a customs union is large enough to influence its terms of trade on both the export and import side (externalization of integration), then the customs union sets the international prices for these goods. Other countries, supposedly small ones which are the price takers for the standardized goods, must accept the prices which prevail in the customs union less the CET and less the cost of transport if they want to sell in the customs union market. A big customs union may exercise its monopoly and monopsony powers at the expense of third countries' consumers who pay domestic tariffs and producers which pay the customs union's CET if they want to export there.

Monopoly power is not without its disadvantages. If a customs union is large enough to influence prices on international markets, then in the absence of offsetting changes in the rest of the world, an increase in the customs union's supply of good X would simply decrease the price of that good. On the side of the customs union's demand for good Y from abroad, an increase in demand would increase the price of good Y. The greater the demand in the customs union for good Y and the greater the supply of good X and the greater the trade of the customs union, the greater will be the deterioration of the customs union's terms of trade. With both monopoly and monopsony powers, as well as without changes in the outside world, the customs union is made worse off by its desire to increase trade. This situation may be called immiserizing customs union.

Terms of trade effects of customs union do not only have an external dimension. In addition, there is an internal meaning. Trade flows among the member countries are also affected. The unionized partners are not only allies in their relations with third countries, but also competitors in the customs union internal market. The elimination of tariffs and quotas on trade in a customs union has a direct impact on internal trade and prices. A union member country may gain from an improvement of customs union terms of trade with third countries, but this gain may be reduced by worsened terms of trade with the customs union partner countries.

The countries which are in a customs union may experience a shift in productivity due to increased competition and the rapid introduction of new technologies. If one excludes all demographic changes, then any increase in labour productivity has the direct effect of increasing real income under the assumption of unchanged quantity and velocity of money. This has a direct impact on the terms of trade because prices of home goods fall.

The bargaining power of countries that have entered into a customs union is greater than the power they exert as individuals prior to entering the union. What matters here is not the absolute, but rather the relative size of the union against its trading partners. The EU is often advised by third countries, especially the US, to adopt more liberal trade policies. The capacity and willingness of the EU to accept such advices depends, at least in part, on similar actions by its major trading partners: the US, Japan and, increasingly, by developing countries such as Korea and Taiwan.

III THE IMPACT OF THE EUROPEAN UNION ON INTERNATIONAL TRADE

1 Trade negotiations

The first thing that one needs to have in mind while considering various rounds of trade negotiations under the auspices of the GATT is that they have an important impact on world trading arrangements in the long term. Negotiations during distinct rounds may take almost a decade. In addition, there is usually a transition period of another decade, so the impact of trade concessions that each round brings is felt only in the distant future.

The experience has shown that real negotiations take place only among a select number of negotiators. So far, they have been the US and the EU. Japan appeared as the third major negotiator in the late 1960s, but the basic negotiations still take place between the EU and the US. Many (developing) countries have shown little interest in negotiations, at least in recent decades. They were free-riding since the most-favoured-nation (MFN) clause extended to them all the concessions that were exchanged among the three major players. There is an increasing, but still minor, influence by the newly industrialized Asian countries on negotiations. In fact, the openness of the markets of the developed economies for trade and FDI in the future will increasingly depend on similar concessions being offered by the developing countries – at least, the newly industrialized ones.

There have been seven rounds of tariff negotiations,[7] but our attention will be focused only on four. The *Dillon Round* of trade negotiations brought a relatively modest reduction of tariffs. A more significant step took place during the *Kennedy*

Round when tariffs on manufactured goods were reduced by 35 per cent on average. Unlike the earlier round which reduced excessive protection, this round cut deeper into protection. It provoked a serious structural adjustment of the economies, at least in the developed world. During this round the US wanted to include trade in farm goods into negotiations, as at that time, a fifth of the US exports into the EU were agricultural goods. The EU has proved its bargaining power, as it resisted those pressures and protected the CAP. The *Tokyo Round* reduced tariffs on manufactured goods by a third on average. The inclusion of farm goods and NTBs into negotiations was a big success. None the less, the results of the round in these new areas remained small.

It is widely accepted that the Dillon, Kennedy and Tokyo Rounds of trade negotiations were attempts by the US and other developed market economies to reduce the discriminating effect that came from the creation and enlargement of the EU. The outcome of these rounds was that the average tariff decreased from 11 per cent at the time of the introduction of the CET in the EU to 7.5 per cent after the completion of the Tokyo Round reductions (Yannopoulos, 1988, pp. 26–27). One could have argued that the pace of multilateral trade liberalization during the 1960s and beyond, as well as the extension of GATT coverage of new areas such as services, agriculture and NTBs would have been delayed without European integration. Hence, European integration was friendly with multilateral liberalization of trade.

The *Uruguay Round* of trade negotiations had a very ambitious agenda. Hence the reason for numerous standstills during negotiations. The developed countries wanted to update the GATT system by the inclusion of new areas such as trade in services, intellectual property rights or trade related investment measures (TRIMS).[8] In addition, there were proliferating penumbra measures that needed a certain international structuring. These included market-sharing deals such as orderly marketing and voluntary export-restriction agreements.[9] There was also desire to include trade in textiles and agricultural goods in the deal. The new GATT rules were expected to introduce an 'insurance policy' regarding security and predictability about the market access in the future.

A word needs to be said here about international trade in agricultural commodities. The EU was generally in favour of a liberal international-trade regime for manufactured goods, unlike the temperate agricultural products. The root of the problem regarding trade in farm goods was the American demand to exclude these goods from the GATT. This country succeed in weakening the GATT rules that applied to trade in farm goods during the 1950s. The US wanted to preserve its domestic autonomy in handling farm policy that was highly interventionist and protectionist after the Second World War. When the EU and Japan implemented their own farm policies, that were permissible by the earlier American action, the US and other exporters of temperate agricultural goods found their export potential to the EU curtailed. Thus, the Congress's solution to the American problems of the 1940s and 1950s (i.e., to exclude agriculture from the GATT) served as an impediment to worldwide liberalization of trade in farm goods (Lipsey and Smith, 1987, p. 6). Perhaps the US has learned a lesson from this example for its trade policy in the future.

The GATT principles of non-discrimination, reciprocity[10] and the impartial settlement of disputes were originally conceived to ameliorate international trade at the border. At the time of the creation of the GATT (1947), border measures were, perhaps, the most important protectionist instruments. As tariffs were reduced over time, grey-area measures expanded. These penumbra trade tools shifted protectionist techniques. Protection now takes place not at the border, but within the domestic market. The Uruguay Round was a sign that the multilateral trading system was seeking ways to address these new challenges.

The Uruguay Round settlement established the World Trade Organization (WTO) in January 1995. The WTO is the only multilateral institution that may curb the operation of large trading blocs. The WTO is an 'umbrella' organization for the GATT and the General Agreement on Trade in Services (GATS). The major results of the Uruguay Round can be summarized as follows:

- Tariffs on industrial goods would be reduced by a little more than a third (38 per cent). That would decrease the average tariff on industrial goods in the developed market economies from 6.3 per cent to 3.9 per cent by 1999. Such a reduction is supposed to enhance competition and increase efficiency in the employment of resources.
- The US and the Cairns Group[11] were able to push trade in agricultural goods very high up the agenda. Trade in farm goods was subject to little 'international discipline'. While the EU and Japan argued against changes in the past rules, the US wanted a complete liberalization by the year 2000. The compromise included a partial liberalization in farm trade: (1) All NTBs need to be converted into tariffs (tariffication) – that tariffication may produce very high, even prohibitive, tariff rates of 200–500 per cent *ad valorem*.[12] (2) These tariffs are to be reduced by 36 per cent on average by 2001 in the developed countries, while in the developing countries, the average reduction needs to be 24 per cent by the year 2005. (3) Production and export subsidies in the farm sector need to be reduced – developed countries will have to reduce export subsidies (the value of budgetary outlays) by 36 per cent over six years, while the corresponding figure for the developing countries is 24 per cent over a period of 10 years.

  Although, the establishment of a full international framework for trade in farm goods will take quite some time, the current deal provided the framework for further negotiations, as well as the first step on the road towards a more stable and predictable trade in farm goods.
- Developed market economies need to reduce their 'support' to the farm sector by 20 per cent, while the same request regarding developing countries is 13.3 per cent. Subsidies that are not directly related to production are exempted. These include environmental protection, regional development, structural adjustment and income support. Hence, subsidies are allowed. Many kinds of subsidies may be easily hidden under the permitted chapters. That may offset, in part, the 64 per cent reduction in export subsidies from their average level in 1986–1990.
- In textile trade, average tariffs need to fall from 15.5 per cent to 12.1 per cent. The average tariff protection may still look high, but it will take over the protective measures from quotas, which is an achievement. A renegotiation of the Multi-Fibre Agreements (MFA)[13] was of vital importance for developing countries. The arrangement has three stages. First, at least 16 per cent of goods covered by MFAs need to be covered by the WTO regulation; second, the coverage is to expand by

another 17 per cent in 1998 and, third, to a further 18 per cent in 2002. The rest is to be integrated into the WTO system by 2005. This 'rest' consists of sensitive items, so liberalization would not touch it for a decade. None the less, the classical example of protection for the textile industry runs the risk of being seriously shaken in the future.[14]

- The Kyoto Customs Convention (1973) on the determination of rules of origin is vague. As it is not applied by the US, its practical value is limited. The WTO is to draft rules of origin that would be applicable in all of its members. This noble task of harmonization that is supposed to increase certainty in trade relations may run into problems as it is difficult to predict the progress in the preparation, acceptance and implementation of new rules.

- Regarding technical standards, the EU in its internal trade implements mutual recognition of national standards. In the WTO, there has only been a call to trading partners to follow international standards. So far, so little!

- Article VI authorizes the use of anti-dumping duties if the injured country proves that domestic producers are (potentially) harmed by such imports.[15] Predatory pricing (through dumping) falls on the profit of firms. This practice is subject to anti-dumping duties. Export subsidies, however, cause the outflow of public funds. This practice is subject to countervailing duties.[16] The GATT outlaws export subsidies (Article XVI).[17] But these subsidies are not the only ones that distort trade. A subsidy is defined to be a financial contribution by a government or any public body. Such a financial contribution includes a direct transfer of funds, potential transfers of funds such as loan guarantees, discriminatory public procurement, forgoing of revenue by tax authorities and public provision of goods or services. The WTO even entered into *domestic* economic policy since it can start action if a domestic subsidy injures a trading partner. If a domestic subsidy is an aid package to a disadvantaged region, for research and pre-competitive activities or ecological matters, the WTO does not intervene. However, what if the opaque subsidies are 'sold' as permitted ones?

- Temporary safeguards are allowed under Article XIX of the GATT Charter if there is a sudden and serious injury or potential injury to domestic industry from an unexpected surge in imports. This provision continues to be important. For example, a sudden fall in the exchange rate of the dollar helps US exporters. This may provoke the concern of importers. However, if increased quality and productivity is at stake, such as Japanese cars or electronics, then, instead of trying to increase domestic productivity and penetrate the Japanese market, the US and and the EU restrict the entry of Japanese goods into their domestic markets. According to the Uruguay Round provisions, all penumbra measures such as voluntary export restraint agreements are ruled out. Other NTBs need to be eliminated within a period of four years after the entry of the Uruguay Deal into force.[18] As there is the possibility of introducing safeguards without retaliation for a period of three years, it opens doors for potential abuse of those rules. Safeguard measures, however, would not apply against a good originating in a developing country if its share of imports in the country of destination is 3 per cent or less.

- The new organization, the GATS, is to provide a forum that will take care of the liberalization of trade in services. This is of increasing importance, since trade in services has not been on the international agenda for negotiations as was the case with trade in goods. The deal introduces the MFN principle in trade in services. A regulatory framework would increase certainty in world trade in services over $1,000 billion (almost a third of trade in goods) in 1993. Previously, trade in services was referred to as 'invisible' transactions. In spite of numerous exceptions,[19] such as, that they do not exceed a 10-year period (although that period may be extended) and vague formulations, the inclusion of services is a great achievement of the Uruguay Round. The subsequent round of negotiations on the liberalization of trade in goods and services will start five years after the entry into force of the Uruguay Round Agreement. This continuous liberalization device for trade in services is an important accomplishment of the Uruguay Round.

- Together with the deal regarding services, the major novelty of the Uruguay Round was the arrangement on intellectual property rights. Although intellectual property rights are regulated by several Conventions and by the World Intellectual Property Organization, the WTO is supposed to introduce an additional element for the protection of these rights.

- An efficient and impartial settlement of disputes needs to enhance the role of the WTO, revive multilateralism and prevent the implementation of unauthorized unilateral measures by an individual member country (read: the US). If the informal settlement of a dispute is not successful, then there is a Dispute Settlement Panel that may issue a verdict. There is a possibility that it may be contested before the Standing Appellate Body. After its decision, the injured party may request compensation. If there is no agreement on the settlement with the perpetrator, the injured party may impose sanctions. If applied strictly, this dispute settlement system is supposed to eliminate the unilateral dispute settlement measures, as practised by the US.

The Uruguay Round of tariff negotiations brought the most profound changes in international trade negotiations in history. There is a legal framework for trade in important areas (agriculture, services) that were beyond the scope of the GATT. Estimates about the global increase in income put it around $200 billion a year. That is roughly 1 per cent of the annual world product. Is that not too little to justify such a big fuss?

Estimates about the potential gains from the implementation of the Uruguay Round Agreement are generally based on the classical assumption that a set of traded goods is both complete and fixed. In such a case, the gains from trade liberalization (elimination of tariffs and other barriers to trade) appear to be quite small. Prices in the economy could be changed by government (tariff) intervention, so the quantity of produced and traded goods would change, but the list of the manufactured and traded goods would remain the same. Suppose now, that the list of goods is expandable. The neo-Schumpeterian economic model assumes that there are no limits for the introduction of new goods and services in an economy. Assume, in addition, that the introduction of a new commodity requires a large amount of fixed costs.[20] This is especially true in the case of the developing countries. Perfect competition and free trade exclude (major) fixed costs from consideration. Once the fixed costs are included in the picture, their presence is often used as a justification for government intervention. When important fixed costs enter the model, a substantial amount of the good needs to be sold in order to make profit. In such a case, a tariff on the good in question may reduce demand. If such a reduction in (international) demand is important, then the commodity may never appear on the market. Losses from such a development or gains in the reversed case may not easily be estimated, at least, not for now. In any case, if the new goods are left out of consideration, then this kind of analysis may bring substantial underestimates of the welfare cost of trade restrictions (Romer, 1994).

The major beneficiaries of gains that come from trade liberalization would be the EU and the US. It is because they are the largest international traders and they have, perhaps, the biggest distortions in trade. The final package deal of the Uruguay Round was supposed to satisfy all parties. On the one hand, the developed market economies obtained from the deal some regulation of trade in services and protection of intellectual property rights. On the other, the developing countries and transition economies found gains in the reduction of tariffs, the ousting of NTBs, as well as the liberalization in trade in textiles and farm goods. They, or some of them, will be able to increase their exports of textiles and farm goods.

2 Non-tariff barriers[21]

The GATT was quite successful in the continuous reduction of tariffs on industrial goods during the post-war period. Unfortunately, on the reverse side of these achievements, NTBs have mushroomed and eroded the beneficial liberalizing effects of tariff cuts. NTBs are all measures other than tariffs that reduce international trade. Some of them are overt (quotas), while others fall into a grey area such as the application of technical standards or rules of origin. Although they are costlier in terms of resource efficiency and they do not create customs revenue, they expanded because the GATT does not permit unilateral introduction of new tariffs, while at the same time domestic pressure groups may be quite successful in eliciting protection. NTBs are the strongest in the 'sensitive' commodity groups; in fact, the use of NTBs may determine which commodity groups are sensitive. The implementation of the Treaty of Rome eliminated tariffs and quotas on internal trade in the EU in 1968. As for NTBs, that was the task of the 1992 Programme.

While tariffs add to the costs of goods such as those of transport, NTBs act like import quotas, but do not generate revenue for the government. NTBs nowadays present the most important and dangerous barriers to trade that fragment markets in a more successful way than tariffs have ever done. Tariffs were reduced under the auspices of the GATT/WTO to relatively low levels, and on the average, so that they represent no more than a fig leaf to cover the economic inefficiency of a country. None the less, national administrations try to obtain short-term political gains through protectionism at the expense of long-term economic benefits. Hence, NTBs are high on the agenda for all international actions to liberalize trade.

Consideration of NTBs has always been difficult. One reason is the creativity of their authors, but also, and more importantly, the lack of data. Administrations either do not record the use of NTBs or if they do, this is done only partially. It comes as no surprise that the reported impact of NTBs can lead to considerable underestimations. Our classification of NTBs is presented in Table 7.3.

The greatest concern which stems from a growing use of NTBs is a lack of transparency; hence, they are prone to great abuse, which increases uncertainty

Table 7.3 Non-tariff barriers

Major group	Type
1 Government involvement in international trade	Subsidies (production, exports, credit, R&D, cheap government services)
	Public procurement (local, regional, central)
	State monopoly trading
	Exchange rate restrictions
	Embargoes
	Tied aid
2 Customs and administrative entry procedures	Customs classification
	Customs valuation
	Monitoring measures (antidumping and countervailing duties)
	Rules of origin
	Consular formalities
	Trade licensing
	Deposits
	Calendar of import
	Administrative controls
3 Standards	Technical
	Health
	Environment 'green standards'
	Testing and certification
	Packing, labelling, weight
4 Others	Quotas (tariff free ceilings)
	Local content and equity rules
	Tax remission rules
	Variable levies
	Bilateral agreements
	Buy domestic campaigns
	Voluntary export restriction agreements
	Self-limitation agreements
	Orderly marketing agreements
	Multi-fibre agreement
	Ambiguous laws
	Cartel practices
	Permission to advertise

about access to foreign markets. Tariffs are economic policy instruments that are obvious. Market forces can thus react to this economic policy tool through adjustment measures. The operation of NTBs demands monitoring measures as they do not operate through markets. This procedure requires additional 'policing' which increases both costs to firms and uncertainty because of the administrative discretion. In relation to tariffs, NTBs are less desirable as they circumvent market forces and, hence, introduce greater distortions, uncertainty and prevent efficient specialization.

A government at all its levels (local, regional and central) is an important consumer of goods and services. It can use its procurement policies either to protect home business (small firms in particular) and employment or to support young industries during their first fragile steps in order to help the creation of a country's comparative advantage. *Public procurement* can also be employed as an instrument for the implementation of regional policy and/or aid to disadvantaged groups of population (for instance women and minorities).

An open public procurement market in the EU is seen as one of the major potential benefits that EU firms may exploit. The EU-wide competitive tendering directives require the publication of all tender notices above a certain (rather low) financial threshold in the *Official Journal of the European Community*. This is supposed to avoid an under-estimation of the value of the contract in order to evade an open tendering. Coupled with compliance with the EU technical standards and an allowance for a reasonable time for the submission of the offer, this may increase fairness of the bidding procedure. The Commission may exclude foreign firms from the public procurement market if the EU enterprises do not have a reciprocal access to public contracts in the countries from which these firms originate. In spite of this possibility, there is a chance for inertia (read: buy domestic). A public authority has a chance to split a large public contract into a series of small ones that follow each other and avoid the need to advertise in order to award the business locally.

It is widely accepted that the eligible goods for tariff- and quota-free trade in all integration arrangements are all goods with the exception of those that jeopardize public morality, public security and order, as well as human, animal or plant life or health. An important NTB can be found in *technical standards* (a set of specifications for the production and/or operation of a good). The intention of this hidden barrier to trade is in many cases to protect the national producer despite the long-term costs in the form of higher prices that come from lower economies of scale and reduced competition.

One of the most famous cases of an NTB within an integrated group was that of a fruit-based liqueur *Cassis de Dijon* from 1979. Germany forbade the importation of this French drink on the grounds that liqueurs consumed in Germany should have more than 25 per cent of alcohol, while *Cassis de Dijon* had 5 per cent less than Germany's threshold. The case was considered by the EU Court of Justice which ruled that the ban on imports of this liqueur was not legitimate. The importance of this ruling is paramount. It created a precedent in the EU for all goods that are legally produced and traded in one member country. These goods cannot be banned as imports to other partner countries on the grounds that national standards differ. The gateway to competition in all goods manufactured in the EU was wide open. The exception is the case in which the imports of a good can jeopardize an important national interest. If differences in the national standards do exist, then consumers can be protected by a warning on the good which states this difference. None the less, this case is insufficient to create a uniform EU market and increase the competitiveness which goes with it. Harmonization may remove such shortcomings even though it can be criticized on the grounds of its over-regulation, reduction in choice and the relatively long time it takes to implement. The *Cassis de Dijon* precedent was also used when the EU forced Germany in 1987 to open its market for beers from other EU countries in spite of the fact that those beers do not comply with the German beer purity law (*Reinheitsgebot*) of 1516 which specified that beer must be composed only of water, barley, hops and yeast. This decision has not, in spite of fears, jeopardized Germany's beer production.

Another imaginative NTB is illustrated by the *Poitiers* case. The French government wanted to protect the home market from imports of Japanese VCRs. There was, however, no home production of VCRs; the domestic manufacturer Thomson was importing Japanese VCRs and distributing them under its own name. The government requested, just before Christmas, 1982, that all Japanese VCRs must pass through customs inspection in the town of Poitiers in order to make sure that they all have instruction manuals in French. This town is in the centre of France, far from all main ports of entry for these goods, while its customs post had only eight officers and was not well equipped. This action increased costs (transport, insurance, interest, delays) and reduced the quantity of VCRs imported and sold to 3,000 units a month. This measure, perhaps, would make some sense in the situation when the government wanted to restrain rising consumer expenditure that was causing a short-term drain on the balance of payments. In such cases, however, a more appropriate measure might be an excise duty or high sales tax. The lesson that should be learned from this case is that when importing goods whose efficient manufacturing depends on scale economies and learning curve effects, the ideal time to protect is before external suppliers have captured most of the domestic market. The clamour in the media about this case was so loud that the French government had no other choice but to revoke this measure. After Christmas, of course![22]

The importation of the *Japanese cars* into Italy was subject to a quota. That arrangement was initiated by Japan in 1952. At that time, the Japanese were afraid of the penetration of small Italian cars into their market. The quota allowed for the annual importation of 2,800 passenger cars and 800 all-terrain vehicles directly from Japan. Once this situation changed, and when the Japanese became highly competitive in the production of cars, this NTB hit back at Japan.[23] From 1987 the Commission has not been supporting Italy's claim to use Article 115 and block indirect imports of Japanese cars through other EU countries. Hence, the imports of Japanese cars has soared.[24] Other EU countries have annual 'caps' on the imports of Japanese cars. For example, the 'cap' for Japanese cars in the French car market is around 3 per cent, while in Britain, the same limit is around 10 per cent of domestic sales. A tacit limit for the share of Japanese car producers in the German market is around 15 per cent. All these measures have negative effects. On the one hand, the consumers lose as they pay more for both the domestic and imported cars, while on the other hand, the EU car industry is postponing its inevitable structural adjustment and potentially losing the competitive edge relative to the Japanese. The governments of the EU countries simply bow to the short-term interests of strong domestic lobbies. There was a 'car deal' between the EU and Japan in 1991. The EU offered the Japanese an increase in the market share from 11 per cent in 1991 up to 17 per cent until 2000, when all quotas are, in principle, supposed to go. The problem is that the EU wants to include in the quota those Japanese cars manufactured in the EU. The deal is, however, subject to different interpretations. The EU argues that the maximum number of imported Japanese cars and those produced in Japanese subsidiaries in the EU is based on forecasts of market growth. This assumes that if market grows less than forecast the EU may renegotiate the deal. The Japanese interpretation of the deal is that the EU has committed itself not to restrict the sale of Japanese cars in the EU. Another accord between the EU and Japan of 1995 is supposed to simplify EU exports of cars and commercial vehicles to Japan through the mutual recognition of vehicle standards, as well as the possibility that the Japanese inspectors who issue certification to imported cars do their job in Europe.

There are, also, many cases of NTBs that deal with standards (technical specifications). Belgium allows the sale of margarine only in oval containers, while square ones are reserved solely for butter. The standard width of consumer durables in the EU countries is 60 centimetres, while in Switzerland this standard is a few centimetres smaller. The City of London demands that taxi cabs are spacious enough to allow gentlemen to sit comfortably in an upright position with their hats on. All these technical specifications do not have a crucial impact on the protection of life and health. Their final effect is to reduce competition and increase the price to consumers. Trade policy is a policy of details that easily escape the scrutiny of voters. Small and well organized groups of producers may wield a strong influence on the government attitude to trade policy.

Harmonized standards for some matters such as safety, health or the environment are essential, while mutual recognition (an agreement to acknowledge diversity) may be a solution for the traded goods still waiting to be harmonized. The long-term effect of such a policy is that firms would face one set of rules instead of up to 15 different ones. This may increase the gains that come from economies of scale. However, this can only make sense when the market for a good or a service exceeds one member state. For example, consumer preferences for new goods such as VCRs, fax machines and computers may be similar throughout the EU,[25] but there are a number of differences regarding foodstuffs and beverages, where preferences are strictly local. In those cases a potential EU standard that does not take account of these distinctions may do more harm than good. The member states of the EU are, however, obliged to notify the Commission in advance about all draft regulations and standards. If the Commission or other member states find that a new standard contains elements of NTB to trade, they may start remedial action as allowed in Articles 30 or 100 of the Treaty of Rome.

Liberalization of trade and FDI with non-EU countries potentially increases both trade with those countries and the share of foreign inputs in domestically produced 'hybrid' goods.[26] Rules of origin in general and the minimum local content requirement in particular, are used as NTBs in order to prevent goods with a high external content receiving a preferential treatment in the internal trade of the EU. However, it is increasingly difficult to determine the 'nationality' of a car. These TRIMs express the share of value added in percentages in a certain country or group of countries. Countries throughout the world are free to use rules of origin as policy measures, since the WTO does not yet regulate them. As a result, there has been a variety of practices which created difficulties for producers and traders.

A survey of TRIMs (UNCTC, 1991b) found that local content requirements are relatively more frequent than those regarding exports or employment. Although TRIMs exist in both the developed and developing countries, they are more common in the developed world.[27] TRIMs are usually concentrated in specific industries such as automotive, chemicals and computers. During an examination of 682 investment projects, the finding was that in 83 per cent of cases in which firms were required to realize TRIM objectives (local sourcing, exporting) the investors planned to do these operations anyway. Moreover the TRIMs were intruding into the mix of inputs in the production process – they were also redundant!

Rules of origin are employed in conjunction with the operation of preferential tariffs, as well as the implementation of commercial policy. Preferential rules of origin are used in a trading group to determine which goods are eligible for the agreed preferential-tariff treatment within the group. Non-preferential rules of origin take into account either the country in which the last substantial operation (the one that gave the good a new quality, that is, the one that shifted the good from one customs classification group to another) took place or the value added test or both. For assembly operations, the determination of origin is decided relative to the importance of the assembly to the whole process of production. The Kyoto Customs Convention (1973) states that unless a good is wholly produced in a country, what determines the origin of a good is the country where the 'last' substantial process took place.[28]

The EU rules of origin are based on Council Regulation 802/68 which states four criteria for determining the origin of a good. Origin is obtained in the country:

- where the last substantial operation is performed;
- that is economically justified;
- in an undertaking equipped for the purpose; and
- resulting in the manufacture of a new product or representing an important stage of manufacture.

The WTO is supposed to draft new standards for the determination of origin that would be universally applicable. Until then, the EU will continue to employ the idea of the Kyoto Convention with one important difference. The EU will determine origin of the good according to the country where the last 'economically justified' operation took place. This gives considerable scope for the arbitrary interpretation of origin rules.

Once a government spots a good that is or may be suddenly imported into its country, it often introduces an anti-dumping tariff. Foreign exporters can circumvent this barrier by locating the final, often screwdriver stage of production, in the tariff-imposing country. To counter this action, the home authorities may request that the goods produced domestically must have a certain local content in order to obtain the preferential treatment. Once the original supplier of the good meets this requirement, the local authorities may go further, as was the case with the EU control of imports of Japanese integrated circuits (microchips). Chips merely assembled in the EU would not qualify for domestic treatment. The EU rules of 1989 link the origin of microchips to the place where the diffusion process takes place. Assembly and testing follow the diffusion process and they contribute to the final value of the chip approximately as much as diffusion. There are two reasons for this decision of the Commission regarding rules of origin for integrated circuits. First, such rules require that a part of the manufacturing process takes place in the EU. That brings an inflow of foreign investment and creation of local high-quality jobs. Second, the intention is to support EU producers of microchips, as some of them perform diffusion in the EU, while assembly and testing takes place in external countries where labour costs are lower. In this case, the EU defined the origin of the good by the place where the 'most' (rather than the 'last') substantial production process takes place. Origin is determined by the R&D stage and the capital equipment that is used in the production of such goods, rather than by the place of transformation of goods. Such rules do not regard Ricoh photocopiers made, in fact assembled, in California as goods that originate in the US. Rather, the EU looks at the (Japanese) origin of essential parts such as drums, rollers, side plates and other working equipment. Once the origin of these machines is ruled to be Japanese, the EU has an arsenal of NTBs to curtail imports of these goods from the US. That has provoked tensions in trade with the US.

Yet another complication in the calculation of value added and shares of different countries in the final origin of a good derives from fluctuations in rates of exchange. What rate of exchange should be used for the calculation of value added: the one on the date of importation of inputs or the one on the date when the final good is exported into the EU? The issue arose when Switzerland exported ballpoint pens (made from American components) to France in 1983. The EU Court of Justice decided in favour of the first date.

Controversies about origin were confined for a long time to trade in goods. Nowadays, they became relevant for trade in services too. What determines the 'nationality' of traded services? Many of them are based on wide international networks. None the less, certain criteria are emerging. They include place of incorporation, location of headquarters, nationality of ownership and control, as well as the principal place of operation and intellectual input.

Rules of origin have introduced controversies, heated debates and tensions in international trade. In a highly globalized international economy where TNCs are increasingly involved in foreign production, rules of origin make less and less sense. They may bring distortions in investment decisions, reduce international trade and bring more bad than good results.

Non-tariff barriers contribute to the costs that accrue from the non-competitive segmentation of the market. They encourage import substitution and discourage rationalizing investment. The anticipated benefits that would come from the elimination of NTBs include increased competition with its effects on improved efficiency, economies of scale and the consequent reduction in unit costs of production for an enlarged market, as well as increased specialization. The outcome of this process would be an increased average living standard.

The *Extramet* anti-dumping case (C-358/89) between two French firms is very instructive. Following a complaint by Péchiney, the Commission imposed an anti-dumping duty of 22 per cent on imports of calcium metal originating in China and the Soviet Union in 1989. The importer, Extramet, claimed that the only producer (Péchiney) of calcium metal in the EU suffered self-inflicted injury by refusing to supply the good to the importer. Such anti-competitive behaviour by Péchiney was an abuse of dominant position. The difficulties of Péchiney came from poor management and high fixed costs. Although it was artificially high, the price of the only producer of the good in the EU was used as the basis for calculating the anti-dumping duty. Hence, imports from abroad seemed to be at dumping prices which provoked the introduction of the anti-dumping duty. There was, however, no suggestion that there was an association between Extramet and any of the exporters concerned. The EU Court of Justice, therefore, ruled in favour of Extramet in 1991.

A study by Emerson *et al.* (1988) illustrated the possible benefits that may accrue, under certain conditions, from the completion of the EU Programme

1992. The total EU gross domestic product in 1985 (the base year for most estimates) was ECU 3,300 billion for the 12 member states. The direct cost of frontier formalities to the private and public sector may be 1.8 per cent of the value of goods traded in the EU or around ECU 9 billion. The cost to industry of identifiable barriers, such as technical regulations, may be 2 per cent of the surveyed companies' total costs, which comes to around ECU 40 billion. Liberalization of public procurement would bring gains of ECU 20 billion, while liberalization of the supply of financial services would save a further ECU 20 billion. Gains due to economies of scale would reduce costs by between 1 and 7 per cent, yielding an aggregate cost saving of ECU 60 billion. A downward convergence of presently disparate price levels may bring gains of about ECU 40 billion under the assumption of a much more competitive and integrated EU market. The estimates offer a range of gains starting from ECU 70 billion or 2.5 per cent of the EU GNP, to ECU 190 billion or 6.5 per cent of the EU GNP. The same, one-time gains, for the 1988 GNP would give a range of ECU 175 to 255 billion. These figures are unlikely to be overestimates for they exclude important dynamic effects on economic performance, such as technological innovation and the introduction of new goods and services which is difficult to predict. There was no general opposition to the completion of the EU internal market by the end of 1992, for the opponents to the plan could not offer an alternative strategy that would make up for the losses forgone from preserving the *status quo*.[29]

3 The European Union in the world economy

The influence of the EU on the world economy is profound, as it is the principal world trade partner for both goods and services. In 1990, EU merchandise trade represented 21 per cent of world trade,[30] while the same share for the US and Japan was 17 per cent and 10 per cent respectively. The relative openness of a country to trade may be, in part, revealed by the share of trade in GDP.[31] The share of imports in the EU GDP in 1991 was 24 per cent (if internal imports are included, without it the share was 10 per cent). At the same time, the share of imports in the GDP of the US and Japan were 9 and 7 per cent, respectively. The exports side shows a similar picture. In 1991, the share of exports in the GDP of the EU was 22 per cent. In the US and Japan, the corresponding shares were 7 and 9 per cent, respectively.

The EU is also very important in world trade in services. In 1990, the share of the EU in world trade in commercial services was 27 per cent, compared to the US share of 'only' 16 per cent and Japan of 10 per cent.

The above data show that the EU is strongly linked to and interdependent with the world economy. As for the size of its GDP, it is comparable to that of the US and almost double that of Japan. As shown above, the EU has a higher degree of trade openness[32] than either of those two countries and so exerts a strong, even decisive, influence on international economic relations, in terms of both formal (trade negotiations) and actual (trade and investment flows).

Considering the geographical structure of trade in 1993, the developed market economies accounted for around 55 per cent of EU trade. That is around 7 per cent more than in 1980.

Table 7.4 External trade of the EU with major groups of foreign partners in select years

Partner	Imports Million ECU				Imports Share in total (%)				Exports Million ECU				Exports Share in total (%)			
	1980	1988	1993	1994	1980	1988	1993	1994	1980	1988	1993	1994	1980	1988	1993	1994
1 EFTA	48,079	90,653	109,606	123,722	17.0	23.4	22.6	22.9	55,261	96,434	106,344	119,419	25.5	26.5	22.0	22.2
2 OPEC	76,882	31,851	39,538	40,768	27.2	8.2	8.1	7.5	39,264	31,198	40,394	37,160	18.1	8.6	8.4	6.9
3 ASEAN	7,198	12,203	25,667	29,965	2.5	3.1	5.3	5.5	5,433	10,689	22,920	27,763	2.5	2.9	4.7	5.2
4 ACP countries	20,744	17,541	14,570	18,565	7.3	4.5	3.0	3.4	17,048	15,551	16,442	14,900	7.9	4.3	3.4	2.8
5 Other developing countries	129,233	116,617	143,244	160,691	45.7	30.1	29.5	29.7	89,296	113,634	167,764	184,401	41.2	31.2	34.8	34.2
Total extra-EU trade	282,532	387,891	485,975	540,145	100.0	100.0	100.0	100.0	216,670	363,910	482,588	538,987	100.0	100.0	100.0	100.0

Source: Eurostat (1996)

4 Imports

Energy and raw-material price hikes in the 1970s increased the share of developing countries as EU suppliers. A relative fall in the prices of primary commodities during the 1980s significantly reduced the EU imports share of the developing countries (mainly OPEC) and, at the same time, relatively increased the share of the developed market economies. Statistical data are provided in Tables 7.4 and 7.5, respectively. In 1994, the group of EFTA countries was the largest supplier of EU imports (23 per cent of the total). It was followed by the US (17 per cent of the EU total). As a supplier of the EU market, the Japanese share was 9 per cent in 1994.[33] The share of developing countries (a very heterogeneous group) followed different paths. As a group, their share fell from 46 per cent in 1980 to 30 per cent in 1994. The share of the OPEC countries fell from 27 per cent (1980) to 7 per cent in 1994. The shares of Latin America and Africa also declined in the same period, but Hong Kong, Singapore, South Korea and Taiwan almost tripled to reach over 6 per cent of EU imports in 1994. The transition economies of central and eastern Europe supplied a relatively modest share of EU imports (4 per cent), but it is slightly increasing.[34]

There was a shift in the product composition of the EU imports over time. Food, raw materials and primary products were continuously displaced by manufactured goods. Manufactured goods accounted for 54 per cent of EU imports in 1980, while in 1993, they increased to 70 per cent. The major reasons for those changes could be traced in the energy- and resource-saving technologies, changes in relative prices, the high degree of self-sufficiency in temperate-climate farm goods (mainly as a consequence of the CAP) and increases in imports from the newly industrialized Asian countries.

Table 7.5 Top 15 individual trading partners of the EU: imports in select years

Country	Million ECU (current prices)				Share in total imports (%)			
	1980	1988	1993	1994	1980	1988	1993	1994
1 United States	47,735	68,349	86,276	93,183	16.9	17.6	17.8	17.3
2 Japan	13,968	41,618	47,649	48,821	4.9	10.7	9.8	9.0
3 Switzerland	15,746	29,572	36,118	38,729	5.6	7.6	7.4	7.2
4 Sweden	11,918	21,965	23,211	27,512	4.2	5.7	4.8	5.1
5 Austria	7,136	16,881	22,290	24,645	2.5	4.4	4.6	4.6
6 China	1,974	7,005	19,538	23,012	0.7	1.8	4.0	4.3
7 Norway	8,301	12,507	17,013	19,602	2.9	3.2	3.5	3.6
8 Former Soviet Union	11,382	12,990	17,001	18,402	4.0	3.3	3.5	3.4
9 Finland	4,629	8,996	10,154	12,312	1.6	2.3	2.1	2.3
10 Brazil	4,778	9,329	8,236	10,603	1.7	2.4	1.7	2.0
11 Taiwan	2,241	8,067	10,398	10,440	0.8	2.1	2.1	1.9
12 Canada	6,393	8,415	7,886	9,188	2.3	2.2	1.6	1.7
13 S. Korea	2,079	7,240	7,735	8,688	0.7	1.9	1.6	1.6
14 Saudi Arabia	27,619	5,470	9,174	8,594	9.8	1.4	1.9	1.6
15 South Africa	6,779	12,528	8,615	6,756	2.4	3.2	1.8	1.3
Total above	172,678	270,932	331,294	360,487	61.1	69.8	68.2	66.7
Other countries	109,854	116,959	154,681	179,658	38.9	30.2	31.8	33.3
Total extra-EU imports	282,532	387,891	485,975	540,145	100.0	100.0	100.0	100.0

Source: Eurostat (1996)

5 Exports

The merchandise export side developed in a similar way to the imports side of the balance of trade (Tables 7.5 and 7.6, respectively). In 1994, EFTA was the major single destination of EU exports, 22 per cent, followed by the US at 18 per cent. Exports to Japan more than doubled between 1980 and 1994 to reach 4.9 per cent of the total, but countries such as Switzerland (8 per cent of EU exports) and Austria (6 per cent) each represented a more significant exports outlet fot the EU than Japan in 1994. Exports to developing countries fell from 41 per cent in 1980 to 34 per cent in 1994. Within the diverse group of developing countries, the relative share of EU exports between 1980 and 1994 was on decline from 18 to 7 per cent for the OPEC countries, from 8 to 3 per cent in ACP countries, but EU exports share to the newly industrialized Asian countries more than doubled to 7.6 per cent in the same period. Central and eastern European transition countries received only 8.7 per cent of EU exports in 1993.

Table 7.6 Top 15 individual trading partners of the EU: exports in select years

Country	Million ECU (current prices)				Share in total EU exports (%)			
	1980	1988	1993	1994	1980	1988	1993	1994
1 United States	27,760	71,809	84,059	95,087	12.8	19.8	17.4	17.6
2 Switzerland	22,702	35,881	38,919	42,995	10.5	9.9	8.1	8.0
3 Austria	11,389	22,514	29,431	32,139	5.3	6.2	6.1	6.0
4 Japan	4,810	17,020	22,573	26,583	2.2	4.7	4.7	4.9
5 Sweden	11,980	21,132	21,579	24,209	5.5	5.8	4.5	4.5
6 Hong Kong	2,166	6,772	11,299	13,134	1.0	1.9	2.3	2.4
7 China	1,784	5,802	11,302	12,509	0.8	1.6	2.3	2.3
8 Former Soviet Union	7,808	10,114	14,769	12,177	3.6	2.8	3.1	2.3
9 Norway	5,273	8,515	9,979	11,311	2.4	2.3	2.1	2.1
10 Poland	2,892	2,756	9,872	10,825	1.3	0.8	2.0	2.0
11 Canada	3,542	10,124	8,468	9,459	1.6	2.8	1.8	1.8
12 Turkey	1,917	5,225	11,531	8,871	0.9	1.4	2.4	1.6
13 Singapore	1,756	4,067	7,593	8,843	0.8	1.1	1.6	1.6
14 Saudi Arabia	7,833	7,572	9,453	8,749	3.6	2.1	2.0	1.6
15 Taiwan	886	4,460	7,573	8,729	0.4	1.2	1.6	1.6
Total above	114,498	233,763	298,400	325,620	52.8	64.4	61.8	60.4
Other countries	102,172	129,147	184,188	213,367	47.2	35.6	38.2	39.6
Total extra-EU imports	216,670	362,910	482,588	538,987	100.0	100.0	100.0	100.0

Source: Eurostat (1996)

The composition of EU merchandise exports remained without change over the 1980–1993 period. Manufactured goods accounted for almost 90 per cent of exports. More than 40 per cent of the entire exports was machinery and equipment goods. That was followed by chemicals and consumer goods. Unlike on the imports side (raw materials or fuel) where price developments have a relatively strong effect on trade flows,[35] prices of EU merchandise exports fluctuate relatively little.

6 Balance of trade

With rare exceptions, the trade balance of the EU with extra-EU countries was always in deficit during the past decades. It is often forgotten, however, that the mere balance of trade does not show a country's gain (or loss) from trade. What matters for the gains from trade to materialize is the *volume*, rather than the balance of trade. The larger the volume of trade, the larger the international impact on competition and allocation of resources. Bearing this in mind, the EU fares well. Its imports from third countries increased 22 times in nominal terms from ECU 24 billion in 1958 to ECU 540 billion in 1994. Exports of the EU to external countries also increased 24 times in nominal terms from ECU 22 billion in 1958 to ECU 538 billion in 1994.

7 Intra-EU trade

The most important effect on trade that results from economic integration is an *expansion in the size of the market* and an increase in the *security of access* to a group of otherwise separate national markets. The internal trade of a group of integrated countries is often taken to be one of the first indicators of the extent of their integration. The EU and NAFTA were the exceptions among the market based integration groups regarding the volume of internal trade.[36] Intra-EU trade was 60 per cent of total trade in 1992, up from 36 per cent in 1958. Apart from the ASEAN where internal trade in the same year was around 20 per cent, the share of internal trade in all other integration groups was around 10 per cent or much less.

The establishment of a full customs union in the EU in 1968 eliminated tariff and quantitative restrictions on internal trade. That was a year and a half before the target date set in the Treaty of Rome. Compared with the pre-1957 period, tariffs presented an important part of the final price of traded goods. As there were few NTBs, there was a strong and positive impact on an increase in internal trade and economies of scale. The goods that were affected most from this internal trade liberalization were passenger cars, chemicals (including pharmaceuticals), tyres, office machines and home electrical equipment. However, the expansion of internal trade in the EU as an integration-prone development needs to be clarified further. The increase in the relative share of internal trade is due partly to the enlargement of the EU and, partly, to commercial and other policies of the EU.

IV ECONOMIC RELATIONS WITH THE EFTA

1 Introduction

The (economic) relations between the EU and the EFTA could be split into four distinct periods. First, came the creation of both institutions. Second, was the shrinking of the EFTA and the first enlargement of the EU. Next, was the creation of the European Economic Area (EEA) and, fourth, is the full membership of select EFTA countries in the EU.

The origin of the relations between the EU and EFTA date from the late 1950s. A central role in those relations was played by Britain. Having seen that the

European Coal and Steel Community (ECSC) countries were determined to continue with an overall economic integration, Britain proposed in 1956 the creation of a free trade area in manufactured goods in the OEEC (a predecessor of the OECD). The ECSC countries rejected that proposal since it was one-sided. Britain would obtain free access for its manufactured goods in the market of the 'group of six', without giving reciprocal access for farm goods from the continent into its market.

As a response to the creation of the EEC, Britain gathered the 'other six' countries[37] that signed the Stockholm Convention about the creation of the European Free Trade Association (EFTA). This association was organized according to the wishes of Britain. A small secretariat (only around 70 people) was without any supranational authorities and it is the only body of the EFTA. Agriculture is excluded from the arrangement, so that its entire business refers to manufactured goods only. Apart from the elimination of tariffs on internal trade, there was almost no other intervention by the EFTA. Market forces were left to do the job of integration. There were no common policies whatsoever. Therefore, the history of the EFTA appears to be without event. The important things, i.e., market-induced specialization, happened at such a micro level as to escape the commentator's eye (Curzon Price, 1988, p. 100). However, all that does not mean that the group was not doing nicely in economic terms. Their average GDP per capita was always (significantly) higher than the same indicator in the EU.

As a purely commercial arrangement (tariff and quota-free internal trade in the manufactured goods),[38] the EFTA did not have any grand expectations regarding integration compared to the EEC. The reasons for such a situation are simple to find. The EFTA countries are in geographical terms very dispersed, they were at different levels of development and, most importantly, the EFTA countries trade very much more with the EU than with their EFTA partners. From the outset, the aim of the EFTA was *not* to create strong integration links among its members, *but* rather to find a mutually satisfactory cohabitation with the EU. In other words, the free trade area among the seven EFTA countries was only a means towards an end, rather than an end in itself (Curzon Price, 1987, p. 4). Bearing in mind that the EFTA countries intended to neutralize the impact of the creation of the EU on its trade, it appears that the EFTA succeeded in its aim.

Just one year after the establishment of the EFTA, Britain (the most important EFTA member country) submitted its application for full membership to the EU (then the EEC). The EFTA looked still born. It assumed a kind of a negative identity. Members of the EFTA started to seem from some distance as not-yet-in-the-EU.

The agreement about the entry of Britain, Denmark, Ireland and Norway into the EU (ECSC, EEC and Euratom) was signed in January 1972 after lengthy and difficult negotiations. The agreement stipulated a 5-year transition period, quotas for imports of food (butter and cheese from New Zealand) to Britain, the British contribution to the EU budget (because of the disproportionately large share of trade with the non-EU countries) and the association of the countries and territories with 'special' relations with the new members into the EU system.

Britain, Denmark and Ireland supported the Accession Agreement, but this failed to win the support of the Norwegians in a referendum. The EU acquired three new members on 1 January 1973. On the same date came into effect the Brussels' series of *bilateral* agreements of July 1972 between the EU and the rest of the EFTA countries on a free trade area for manufactured products, since Britain and Denmark left the EFTA on the day of their entry into the EU. The small EFTA countries partly stepped into the EU. It was a long-wished objective of Austria since the interpretation of Article 4 of its State Treaty at that time did not permit economic partnership with Germany. In the post-cold war era, there is now a liberal interpretation of that provision.

2 European Economic Area

One of the most striking features of economic relations between the EU and the EFTA was that it was without tensions. It is that light that one needs to view the creation of the world's largest free trade zone, the EEA, that came into being on 1 January 1994, one year behind schedule. The EEA consisted of 18 developed market economies with 372 million people. What the EEA did in practice was to extend the EU single market for manufactured goods and services to the six (Austria, Finland, Iceland, Liechtenstein, Norway and Sweden) of the seven[39] EFTA countries. The six EFTA countries adopted the EU competition rules and they were included in the EU market for public procurement.

As a group, the EFTA has been the major trading partner of the EU. Its share in EU merchandise imports was 18 per cent (ECU 11 billion) in 1970, while its share in EU exports of goods was 26 per cent (ECU 14 billion) in the same year. In 1994, the share of the EFTA countries in EU imports was 23 per cent (ECU 124 billion), while the share in EU exports was 22 per cent (ECU 119 billion). The EU has always had a trade surplus with the EFTA. Sometimes, as in the period 1986–1988, that surplus has been quite substantial. In the first half of the 1990s, the EU had a deficit in trade with the EFTA.

The EEA was originally envisaged to be a kind of waiting room which would keep the EFTA countries 'out' of the EU for (quite) some time, at least until the provisions of the Maastricht Treaty were absorbed in the EU. The EFTA countries that take part in the EEA are subject to EU laws without the political clout to influence it. Hence, five (Austria, Finland, Liechtenstein, Norway and Sweden) of the seven EFTA countries applied for full membership of the EU. Austria, Finland and Sweden approved the arrangement in national referendums and entered the EU on 1 January 1995. Norway's voters, however, just as happened in 1972, declined to join the EU. If this is the case, then what is the the longer-term value of the EEA? Would an EFTA that consists of Iceland, Liechtenstein, Norway and Switzerland (not a member of the EEA) be a viable trade organization?[40]

The EEA was inspired by the EU Programme 1992 (prompted by the White Paper or Cockfield Report of 1985) which was expected to create a genuine single market for the free movement of goods, services, capital and people. The EFTA countries were concerned about their competitive position in the post-1992 unified EU market. Their trade conditions would worsen unless an arrangement with the EU could be found. Hence, the first contacts between the EU and EFTA about a change/improvement in their economic relations date from 1989. The Agreement on the establishment of the EEA between the EU and the EFTA was signed in May 1992. One of its objectives was to contribute to the creation of conditions for the eventual reunification of all the European nations in the (distant) future.

The Agreement on the EEA is comprehensive.[41] It includes, first and foremost, four basic freedoms of movement (for goods, services, capital and people) in the 18-country area. Agriculture, fisheries and common financial policies are not covered by the Agreement.[42] Second, come horizontal policies, a catch-all title for a variety of areas such as environment, research and development, education and consumer policy. Last, are the legal and enforcement provisions. Areas that are out of the scope of the EEA Agreement are the EMS, or a monetary union, common defence and foreign policy, as well as EU moves towards political union. An interesting feature of the EEA Agreement is that, in general, it did not have a transition period. The *acquis communautaire* was applied without delay, except in a few specified cases. Let us consider the major features of the Agreement.

3 Free movement of goods

Trade between the two groups of countries was initially burdened by the existence of various tariff and NTBs (quantitative restrictions and technical standards were the most prominent). After the departure of Britain, Denmark and Ireland from the EFTA, and their entry into the EU in 1972, all EFTA countries concluded *bilateral* free trade agreements for manufactured goods with the EU. The curiosity is that the EU did not treat the EFTA countries as a unit. Hence the bilateral approach to those countries.

The 1972 Agreements eliminated most of the tariff and NTBs. The EEA Agreement introduced a new dimension into relations between the EU and the EFTA, as the EFTA was recognized by the EU for the first time as a unit. The EEA Agreement abolished all the remaining obstacles to trade in manufactured goods between the partners. The *Cassis de Dijon* principle (1979) would apply to trade in the EEA. That means that all the goods that are legally produced and traded in one of the EEA countries would be freely accepted for imports and sale in the other 17 EEA countries. The exceptions include those that are hazardous to the health and life of humans, animals, plants and environment, as well as not in the consumer interest.

Special trade provisions of the deal include the following:

- In order to ease EEA internal trade, border controls would remain for random checks, but customs formalities would be simplified.
- Rules of origin determine which goods are eligible for preferential trade treatment. They allow for the full cumulation of the EEA origin.
- There would be no discriminatory tax treatment on imported goods from EEA partners. The imposed domestic taxes on imported goods may not be higher than taxes on comparable domestic goods. This measure is supposed to remove the national protective shields and to increase efficiency.
- State aid in the EEA are proscribed. None the less, there is the possibility of allowing state aid in special cases that take into account justified economic and social motives.
- There is also a general escape clause to free trade. If vital national interests are endangered, the government of the country in danger may restrict imports. These cases are not expected to be frequent.

- State monopolies may seriously endanger competition. The EEA countries need to adjust them in such a way that they do not discriminate in either the production or distribution of goods. The Scandinavian EFTA members consider their state monopolies on liquor important for health and social reasons, so they were allowed to stay, but they may not discriminate against suppliers from other EEA countries.

The EEA was supposed to have a profound effect in the area of public contracts. The annual value of public procurement in the EEA was around ECU 600 billion. The national markets for public procurement in the EU were divided as three-quarters of the contracts were awarded to domestic suppliers. The opportunity opened up by the EEA is to increase competition in this large and lucrative market, promote efficiency, lower prices and, ultimately, benefit taxpayers. In the single EEA procurement market tenders must be advertised in the *Official Journal of the Community*. The information must be in detail and the requirements have to be founded on EU standards. Only those bidders that offer either the lowest price or the most economically advantageous terms can win the contract. Regarding enforcement of the procedure, a reviewing body is empowered to correct violations, suspend contracts and award damages.

4 Free movement of persons

Citizens of the EEA have an unrestricted freedom of movement within the area. Their residence may depend on employment in the relevant country. Retired people and students are covered by special provisions. With the exception of certain jobs in the public sector, workers and self-employed persons have the right to be employed throughout the EEA. They may not be discriminated on the basis of their nationality regarding employment, pay or other working conditions. Social security benefits obtained in any EEA country may be both accumulated and freely transferred within the group. This was a big concession that was granted by the EFTA countries. As a rule, the EFTA countries may be the receiving countries for labour that originates from the EU. The EFTA countries often have significantly higher average income than EU countries, hence they would be the preferable destinations for a labour force that is willing to migrate.

5 Free movement of services

More than a half of those employed in the developed market economies are in services. An important accomplishment of the EEA is that it grants a full freedom for the provision of services throughout the area. As such, it goes beyond the traditional free trade arrangements that usually limit themselves to a free trade in manufactured goods.

Liberalization in the supply of financial services (banking, insurance) in the EEA is supposed to increase competition and bring gains to consumers. Single licensing would ease the establishment of branches and subsidiaries in the EEA. A bank that is authorized to operate in one EEA country may establish its operation in any other EEA country without asking for a prior licence in the other EEA host country. The home country that has given the first permit is in charge of supervising the whole (EEA) operation of the financial institution.

Transport services were protected for a very long time in the EU. The EEA introduced non-discriminatory access in its transport market. To support the new freedom in the transport market, the EEA participants agreed to harmonize their technical standards (weight of vehicles, dimensions etc.). This is all expected to increase competition and benefit consumers, not only through lower prices, but also through a wider choice, higher efficiency and improved safety.

6 Free movement of capital

Linked with the freedom to supply services is a full liberalization of capital mobility in the EEA. It is meant to enhance the efficiency of industries by extending choice and lowering the cost of capital. This freedom is an important achievement of the EEA. It also aims at the elimination of exchange controls and freedom for FDI. As real estate investment has been the most restrained forms of FDI in the EFTA countries, they were given some time to fully comply with these rules. A standard escape clause about restrictions on capital movements applies in the EEA too. A country may introduce controls if the domestic capital market and/or balance of payments are in danger.

7 Other provisions

Both the EU and the EFTA countries were determined not to limit their relations in the EEA to the four freedoms of movement. They incorporated other areas of common interest into the deal. These include:

- research and development (in order to enhance competitiveness);
- small and medium-sized enterprises (extend contacts through the Business Co-operation Network);
- social policy (safety at work, improvement in working and living conditions, equal treatment of men and women);
- education (introduction of numerous student exchange programmes);
- consumer protection (product safety, door-to-door selling);
- statistics (steps towards the creation of a common system of European statistics); and
- environment (reducing pollution as it does not recognize borders).

8 Institutions

In order to ensure the smooth and efficient operation of the EEA, there was an agreement to establish the following seven institutions:

- *EEA Joint Committee* to exchange information among partners and to take decisions (it holds monthly meetings);
- *EEA Council* which is the highest political body as it is comprised of the EEA ministers and the *EU Commission*, to give political guidance to the EEA by consensus (it meets twice a year);

- *EFTA Standing Committee* which is to receive information from various expert groups to assist the EFTA countries in reaching a common position in the EEA Joint Committee;
- *EFTA Surveillance Authority* which would make sure that the EEA is properly implemented on the side of the EFTA, while the same role at the EU side would be performed by the Commission;
- *EFTA Court* which will, together with the EU Court of Justice safeguard the accurate operation of the EEA Agreement;
- as there is no transfer of sovereignty to the EEA in the form of legislative powers (the parliaments of the EFTA countries have the right to approve new legislation), the *EEA Joint Parliamentary Committee* would be an important forum for the discussion of parliamentary matters; and
- *EEA Consultative Committee* which is comprised of the members of the EU Economic and Social Committee and the EFTA Consultative Committee, it is to consider the EEA social and economic matters.

9 Conclusion

Compared with the EU the EFTA countries are small in economic terms, practise a more liberal trade policy (imports of cars, for example) and have a highly specialized economic structure.[43] None the less, the per capita income in the EFTA is higher than the average in the EU. The EFTA countries had an interest in staying out of the EU since they did not have to accept the CET of the EU which is at a higher level than their own tariffs on external trade. Participation in the EU could, potentially, bring some losses in trade with external partners to the EFTA states. This damage could be compensated for by integration and security of market access gains to the EU. In addition, the EFTA countries did not have to take part in the controversial CAP which in some cases (for example, Switzerland or Finland) offers smaller subsidies to the farm sector than is the case in the EFTA countries. The cost of staying outside the EU would include sacrificing the chance to influence the shaping of economic policies of the new generation in the EU. However, this view is based on the assumption that small countries are in reality, being asked for their opinion and, more importantly and optimistically, that that opinion is (very) respected. In any case, a relatively detailed discussion of the EU trade arrangement with the EFTA was necessary as it may present one of the possible ways in which relations between the EU and transition countries of central and eastern Europe may develop in the future, with the exception of a free movement of people.

V ECONOMIC RELATIONS WITH THE UNITED STATES

1 Introduction

As there are no preferential trade agreements between the US and the EU, America is placed at the very bottom of privileges in trade that the EU offers to its external partners. The US does not treat the EU in trade relations any differently. The framework for trade between the two partners was essentially set through the GATT/WTO. In spite of those 'low-level' concessions in trade, as a single country, the US has continuously been the major foreign supplier of the EU. In 1994, 17 per cent (ECU 93 billion) of the EU external imports came from the US. On the exports side, the US was always the country that was the major exports outlet for the EU. In 1994, 18 per cent (ECU 95 billion) of the EU exports to third countries went to the US. Almost invariably, the EU had a negative trade balance with the US. A noted exception was the period 1984–1988 when the EU had a trade surplus.

2 Problems

The one economic sector that has constantly, since the early 1960s, and that will continue to, create tensions in trade relations between the EU and the US is agriculture. The introduction of the CAP had two consequences that led to conflict in trade relations between the two partners. First, it introduced domestic subsidies in the EU that artificially increased domestic production of farm goods and, hence, reduced imports. Second, excess domestic production of farm goods created surpluses that were exported abroad with large export subsidies. The access of the US exporters of farm goods to third markets (Mediterranean countries) was/is jeopardized by EU farm policy. The entry of Greece, Spain and Portugal to the EU further reduced farm exports outlets to the US. During 1979–1980, the US provided 47 per cent of total farm imports to Portugal, the same share was 28 per cent to Spain and 13 per cent to Greece (Yannopoulos, 1988, p. 118). These strong tensions in the past, that were on the brink of becoming 'trade wars', may be defused by the implementation of the Uruguay Round deal.

Banking is another bone of contention between the two partners. A single banking licence permits a bank that is legally instituted in one EU country to operate freely in any other EU country. In order to allow foreign banks to benefit from this advantage, the EU asks for reciprocal treatment (in particular in the establishment of subsidiaries) in the country of origin of the bank in question. There are, however, certain financial activities in the US that are not granted to US banks. The US would not permit foreign (EU) banks to engage in financial operations in the US market that are not allowed to the domestic banks. One needs to distinguish between *strict* reciprocity in which all practices are the same in either country and reciprocity of *national treatment*. Under strict reciprocity, the home authorities would have to administer different regulations to each class of foreign firms determined by the origin of (the majority) of its owners. A reasonable application of this system is hardly possible (Gray and Walter, 1991, pp. 139–139). If national treatment is applied, then foreign banks are allowed to engage in the same businesses that are permitted to the local banks.

So much about the 'sins' of the EU. In its self-perception, the US still sees and portrays itself as the most open major trading nation in the world. That may not easily correspond to reality. The first and the major concern of the EU in its economic relations with the US, is *unilateralism*[44] in US external economic relations. Unilateralism has always been epitomized by the lack of confidence and discontent of the US with the GATT rules and dispute settlement procedures. The multilateral trading system may be placed in great jeopardy by the continued resort to unilateral dispute settlement because of the vicious circle of retaliation and counter-retaliation. No other important EU trading partner has similar legislation. The WTO would, however, restrain the unilateral resolution of disputes in trade and require members to align their domestic legislation with the Uruguay Round Agreement. Contrary to that, a recent Presidential Executive Order in the US has undertaken to renew the unilateral Super 301 trade legislation (European Commission, 1994, p. 7). Such measures increase uncertainty and potentially reduce economic interaction with the US and seriously question the WTO dispute settlement system.

The US intends to secure and improve access for its goods, services and investment in foreign markets through sector-specific[45] negotiations with foreign countries. Those arrangements, according to some in the US, need to cover structural barriers that are still outside the WTO scope and they ought to be supported by a credible threat of retaliation. A widely disputed 'enforcement' tool is Section 301 of the US trade law (1974) and its modification, Super 301 (1988).[46] They epitomize the thinning pledge of the US to multilateralism in international trade relations.[47] The controversy about those legal means that promoted 'aggressive unilateralism' in international trade relations has provoked a heated debate both in the US and abroad. This policy is *unilateral* because the US is allowed to define its own register of unfair trade practices employed by foreigners. This includes a number of those that are not specifically outlawed by the WTO. Hence, the US may determine on its own if a foreign partner is 'guilty of unfair trade practice' and request direct negotiation with US representatives, instead of arbitration by a multilateral organization. The policy is also *aggressive* as the US may threaten to and actually impose retaliation measures in order to carry out its objectives (Tyson, 1992, pp. 255–258).[48] The US would disregard international trade rules and act as an investigator, prosecutor, jury, judge and executioner, all at the same time. Instead of listing foreign countries and their unfair trade practices, the renewed Super 301 has a 'milder and less insulting form'. The renewed Super 301 asks the US Trade Representative to list only the practices that present barriers to trade.

The American trade policy is a model of hypocrisy. Whenever a domestic lobby is unhappy about imports of foreign (read: Japanese) goods, the US casts aside all national free trade principles and flexes its negotiating muscles in trying to control trade. America needs to be reminded that bilateral deficits primarily indicate differences in savings rates, productivity and the comparative advantages of countries. The implementation of the Uruguay Round dispute settlement mechanism would limit the use of Super 301 legislation. None the less, the 301 would remain on the shelf and within a hand's breadth of the US administration. Will it follow international and multilateral rules in trade or will it yield to the pressures of the day coming from powerful domestic lobbies and reach to the shelf for 301 in the future?

Another problem is the *extraterritorial* enforcement of US legislation (e.g., the Cuban Democracy Act, re-export control and the Marine Mammal Protection Act). Linked to unilateralism, this issue jeopardizes the sovereignty of partner countries. In addition, it may lead to tremendous legal complications. If the objective is to create a negotiated (free) multilateral trading system, then one country should not impose its standards on others, no matter how noble they are.

Next is the *national security* consideration. The US continues to restrict its trade and investment barriers by national security arguments which, in effect, aspire to introduce or prolong protectionism. In general, the argument for national security may be valid. Every country has the right to defend itself. However, what bothers the

EU is the vague and scarcely defined notion of national security. The penumbra of such an ambiguous term and a lack of transparency provide a fertile soil for the multiplication of various 'protectionist mushrooms'.[49]

Public procurement is the fourth general problem. The 'buy America' legislation and practice discriminates or even excludes foreign firms from that lucrative market at both federal and state levels. The Buy America Act of 1933 overrides US international obligations (European Commission, 1994, p. 31). Some progress was achieved when the US and the EU signed a Memorandum of Understanding in May 1993. The US has agreed to waive the application of the Buy America Act for goods, works and other services above a certain threshold at the federal level and for electrical utilities. The EU wants to reach a more comprehensive agreement in the future.

Fifth are *high tariffs* for certain imported goods. Although the implementation of the Uruguay Round Agreement would reduce the overall tariff burden for exports into the US, tariffs still remain high (up to 40 per cent) for textiles, clothing, footwear, tableware and glassware. High tariffs (25 per cent) are also applied in America on imports of two-door multi-purpose vehicles. Although the United States Court of International Trade ruled in May 1993 that these vehicles are passenger cars to which a tariff of 2.5 per cent is to be applied, the US government has appealed against that ruling.

Tax legislation may have negative effects on trade and FDI. This legislation includes reporting requirements, corporate taxes, as well as a luxury and gas guzzler tax on cars imported from the EU.

Another problem is the *multiplicity of standards*. These reduce the potential economic and technical links among partners and diminish the benefits from economies of scale in fragmented markets. The EU and the US are engaged in consultations in order to advance cooperation and reduce potential conflicts in this area.

Eighth is the issue of *intellectual property rights* that has already provoked several disputes between the two partners. The continuing discrimination against non-US products based on the Tariff Act of 1930 (Section 337), in spite of the GATT Panel ruling to the contrary, irritates the EU. There is hope that the implementation of the Uruguay Round Agreement on Trade Related Intellectual Property Rights may contribute to the resolution of some of those matters.

The *national treatment* of foreign TNCs operating in the US is not complete. These TNCs are treated differently regarding joint ventures or participation in federally funded R&D projects, as well as performance requirements. If the US Congress continues to press for conditional national treatment, that would jeopardize the flow of FDI from the EU into the US, as that location would become less attractive.

The following problem concerns the application of US *countervailing duties* and *anti-dumping measures*. According to the EU, in the application of countervailing duties the US did not follow reasonable procedures and methodology. As a result, the EU had to ask the GATT Panel about the issue. As for the anti-dumping measures, they are allowed by the WTO, but their restrictive effect on trade needs to be kept to a minimum. Regarding these two problems, the EU is most concerned about their effects on its exports of steel to the US.

In the fields of *agriculture, fisheries, services, telecommunications and broadcasting*, the Uruguay Round Agreement has brought some relief, but there are still significant obstacles to sales in the US market. That is most obvious in the areas of telecommun-ications, broadcasting and services.

Last are the direct and indirect *support measures* that the US offers to its domestic shipbuilding and aircraft industries. For example, the US applies a 50 per cent *ad valorem* tax on non-emergency repairs to domestically owned ships outside the US. In addition, the Jones Act of 1886, effectively closed the US market to imports of high-speed catamaran passenger and car ferries.

3 Conclusion

To look only at trade relations between the EU and the US may not give a full picture of economic relations between the two partners. A number of American TNCs have operated in the EU for several decades. They have concluded that the most favour-able way to take advantage of EU market opportunities is to locate, produce and market there, rather than to export. Hence, the 1992 Programme that aimed at enhancing EU competitiveness would benefit all TNCs that are operating in the region. That would, of course, harm certain exporters in the US, unless they adjust to the new situation. Finally, economic relations between the EU and the US would be shaped in the future more by the (sectoral) commercial interests of the partners, than on the political and strategic aspects of their 'special' relations.

VI TRADE RELATIONS WITH JAPAN

Just as in the case of the US, there are no pereferential trade arrangements between the EU and Japan. Regarding privileges, Japan is, together with the US, at the bottom of the league as far as concessions from the EU to third countries are concerned. In fact, Japan is often at the heart of various NTBs that the EU imposes or intends to impose.[50] Overt and covert Japanese treatment of the EU is not much different. Despite low-level preferences in trade, Japan is after the US, the most important single trading partner of the EU. In 1994, 9 per cent (ECU 49 billion) of EU imports from third countries came from Japan. Compared with 1970, when the share of Japan in the EU imports was 3 per cent (ECU 2 billion), that represents an increase of 24 times in nominal terms over the period of 24 years. On the exports side in 1994, Japan was the destination for 5 per cent (ECU 26 billion) of the EU merchandise exports. The EU has always had a negative trade balance with Japan. In 1970, that deficit was ECU 0.7 billion. It was continuously increasing to reach an annual level of ECU 22 billion in 1994 alone. The always increasing deficit has been the focus of trade disputes between the EU and Japan.

Access to goods, especially those targeted by Japanese industrial policy like cars, electronics and machine tools, has enormously benefited consumers in the EU. That has had a positive spillover effect on the acceleration of the restructuring of those industries in the EU. The problem is that in tackling the enormous trade deficit with Japan the EU often stresses protectionism, rather than the domestic industrial adjustment and increases in exports to Japan. This policy by the EU may introduce frictions in trade with the US on two fronts. First, Japan may shift more of its exports to the US and, second, the output of Japanese companies that operate in the US may be regarded by the EU as being Japanese, rather than American, in origin.

It is inevitable that sooner or later Japan is going to become a mature creditor country. That is, one that takes more earnings each year from its past foreign investment than it invests abroad. At that point, Japan would shift from being a net exporter to a net importer. Once the Japanese seek to repatriate their foreign investment income, demand for the yen would increase and make it more expensive. This, in turn, would make it easier for foreigners to sell in Japan. Such a scenario depends, however, on the savings behaviour of the Japanese and many aspects of the Japanese economic policy (Lipsey and Smith, 1986, p. 12). When this happens, protectionism may recede in the EU and America. This is all for the long term. In the meantime, the EU and the governments of its member countries are hard pressed by the short-term problems of employment and structural adjustment, as well as by elections.

It is true that Japan has to be very much more receptive to EU merchandise. Japanese business organizations and their relations with each other on the one hand, and with the Japanese government on the other, comprise the major barrier to entry into the Japanese domestic market. Overt impediments to trade may be relatively easy to identify and could be challenged by the WTO rules. There are, however, covert structural barriers in the Japanese market which fall outside WTO rules. That may be remedied by enforceable multilateral regulations on competition, restrictive business practices and policies that offer the Japanese companies a preferential advantage in the domestic market (Tyson, 1992, p. 83). However, Japan need not be the only culprit, for a trade deficit that creates frictions in trade. The importing countries, in particular the US, need to put their economies in balance and reduce domestic budget deficits which have a strong impact on the balance of trade. Even if all the Japanese barriers to trade were eliminated overnight, the budget deficits of the importing countries would remain. Japan would still have a trade surplus.[51] Exports from Japan are concentrated in several groups of goods in which Japan excels. Exports from the EU and the US are much more diversified and compete in many cases with the developing countries in the Japanese market.

Knowing that the 1992 Programme is partly aimed at them, many Japanese TNCs decided to settle in the EU in order to become local EU residents before 1993. That was most obvious in the late 1980s. They feared the possible creation of a 'Fortress Europe' that would discriminate against foreigners. These protectionist worries were not the only ones that prompted a surge of Japanese FDI in the EU. The 1992 Programme demanded it. A frontier-free EU offers possibilities for reaping the economies of scale, so there is an incentive to take advantage of that opportunity. An entry of foreign firms may prompt other domestic EU enterprises to adjust to the new situation and increase competitiveness.

VII ECONOMIC RELATIONS WITH THE TRANSITION ECONOMIES OF CENTRAL AND EASTERN EUROPE

1 Background

The relative share of the transition economies in world trade has been on the decline for quite some time. This share reached 8 per cent in 1988. The transition countries exchanged around a half or more of their trade within the CMEA before its formal demise in 1991. The economic shift towards a market based system and a decentralized decision-making process are again making the transition countries able to take advantage of being fully included in that market based international trading system. However, success in integrating the transition economies into the international trading system depends on at least two factors. The first one is the transformation of their economic system towards a market based one; the other one hinges on the openness of western markets for goods and services from transition countries.

One of the significant features of the transition process is a change in the direction of trade. After the collapse of the CMEA, transition countries redirected their trade westwards in a relatively short period of time, in particular towards the EU. Although a change in the pattern of trade took place, a portion of goods released from CMEA trade, may not easily find market outlets in the EU. Those goods may not always satisfy the quality, quantity, design and other standards that prevail in the EU. In addition, goods that may be potentially important as export items for transition countries are often regarded as 'sensitive' in the EU.

Initially, transition countries were at the very bottom of the EU pyramid of preferences. Only Romania and the former Yugoslavia benefited from the EU generalized scheme of preferences (GSP). Other transition economies were facing every trade obstacle for exports to the EU. Hence the Soviet policy of keeping friendly countries in the camp not only through political and military means, but also through economic ties was lavishly assisted by the trade policy of the EU.

In order to curtail the technological capabilities of the socialist countries, the west established the Coordinating Committee on Multilateral Export Controls (COCOM). Its objective was, during and after the cold war, to prevent the transfer of high technology to socialist countries which would enhance their fire-power.[52] As that was not necessary after the collapse of socialism, the COCOM was replaced by the Wassenaar Agreement[53] which includes Russia. The Secretariat of the new organization started work in Vienna in 1996. The purpose of the new body is to control and prevent trade in technology for atomic, chemical and bacteriological weapons, in particular, to areas of tension and countries (such as Iraq, Iran, North Korea and Libya) that may abuse them.

EU trade with the transition economies was relatively small up until the mid-1970s. After that period it increased to reach 12 per cent (ECU 55 billion) of EU imports and 12 per cent (ECU 48 billion) of EU exports in 1989 the last pre-transition year. In 1990, owing to the transition induced sharp deceleration in economic activity in the east, trade fell sharply. In that year the share of EU imports from these countries was only 6.7 per cent (ECU 31 billion), while the share of EU exports fell to 6.8 per cent (ECU 28 billion). After the initial shock, the relative share of EU imports from the transition economies recovered to reach 9 per cent (ECU 49 billion) in 1994, while the share of EU exports to these countries increased to 9 per cent (ECU 49 billion) in the same year. Among the individual transition economies, the EU had the biggest and continuous trade deficit with countries of the former Soviet Union.

2 Links

Formal links between the EU and the transition countries did not exist for a very long time. This was one of the obstacles to trade liberalization between the two economic groups. The two opposing economic blocs and systems were discriminating against each other. There was little that the east was able to offer to the west in return for MFN status in trade. That continued until the end of the cold war in 1989. The transition process introduced a significant change in those relations. From piecemeal assistance and trade concessions, certain transition countries won Association Agreements with the EU in the new situation. It all started with the EU granting the GSP, over Trade and Cooperation Agreements, to the Association Agreements. Interest in supporting the transition economies in their reform efforts was amplified by the fact that the EU has an unprecedented opportunity to reshape Europe and make it a better and safer area.[54]

It was as late as in 1989, but as early as the start of the transition process, that trade relations between the two regions started to 'normalize'. The G-7 and the EU took the first step to assist transition countries in their reform towards a market-type system, as well as to regulate relations in 1989. It was a unilateral decision to grant GSP and to curtail certain quantitative restrictions on trade with transition countries. Subsequently, most of the transition economies were removed from the list of state-trading countries.

The second step in the formalization and normalization of economic relations between the two groups was the conclusion of Trade and Cooperation Agreements with those transition countries that did not have them.[55] Albania, the Baltic states and Slovenia conducted trade with the EU on the basis of such Agreements. The trade provisions of these Agreements provide for reciprocal MFN treatment and trade concessions, they remove specified quantitative restrictions and aim at a further liberalization of mutual trade. This type of Agreement was concluded between the EU and the former USSR in 1990. After the disintegration of that country, most of the newly independent states accepted the obligations coming from that Agreement in 1992.

In order to coordinate western aid to Hungary and Poland in their transition process to a market-based economic system, political pluralism and democracy, the EU started a PHARE programme in 1989. Assistance from this programme was later extended to Albania, the Baltic states, Bulgaria, the Czech Republic, Romania, Slovakia and Slovenia. The PHARE programme aimed at an improvement in access to markets, promotion of investment, adjustment in the farm sector, food aid, environmental protection and vocational training. Its focus was the development of and support to the private sector in the transition countries.

3 Association Agreements

The latest step in the liberalization of economic relations brought Association Agreements (Europe Agreements) between the EU and select transition countries. Short of full membership, EEA and ACP deals, these Agreements[56] are supposed to be the most favourable arrangements that the EU can offer to foreign countries. These Agreements mention in the Preamble the possibility of full membership for transition countries in the EU in the (distant) future.

Different agreements offered to transition economies reflect the extent of the reform process achieved in these countries. Although the need to aid transition countries through trade concessions is recognized and some actions are taken to create free trade areas between EU and select transition countries, there are NTBs that seriously hinder exports from transition economies to the EU. This is most obvious in goods in which transition countries have a comparative advantage, such as steel, textiles, clothing, bulk chemicals and farm products.

Association agreements between the EU and Hungary, Poland and the former Czechoslovakia[57] reward these countries' transition efforts and achievements. These countries enjoyed the fastest ever climb on the EU pyramid of trade privileges. The goal of these agreements is the establishment of a free trade area in manufactured goods between the partners within a maximum period of 10 years from the entry into force of the agreements. They also provide for improved access for certain farm goods. All this is expected to reinforce the reform process in the transition countries and increase stability in relations between the partners. Although the ratification process is still incomplete, the Interim Agreements implemented trade provisions, save for sensitive goods, of the Association Agreements from March 1992. As the EU had exclusive authority for trade matters, it was able to implement this part of the association agreements. This has instantly improved the access of goods from transition economies to the EU market.

The agreements are asymmetric, as the EU removed all quotas, while the elimination of tariffs is supposed to take place over a period of up to five years. The concessions to the transition counterparts also included a slower pace of tariff elimination of up to nine years. There are provisions that refer to trade in 'sensitive' commodities. In textiles, for example, tariffs are to be eliminated within six years, while the existing quotas need to disappear in five years. At the end of the 10-year transition period there would be no special treatment for textiles in trade among these partners. The Association Agreements eliminated national quotas for trade in iron and steel. In agriculture, there are only reciprocal concessions for select goods.

Other major provisions of the Association Agreements refer to political dialogue among partners (that does not cost anything in the EU budget), as well as safeguard measures. During times of recession and when the jobs are at stake, there is an increased pressure on the authorities to introduce protectionist measures against foreign suppliers. The Agreements stipulate that if EU producers are seriously injured, or if there are dangerous developments within an EU industry that jeopardizes economic activity in the EU, then it is permissible for the EU to undertake (unspecified) safeguard measures. So, uncertainty prevails!

Rules of origin provide a potential benefit to the associated countries. It is not only goods that originate from either of the associated countries or from the EU that are entitled to preferential treatment, but the Agreements also allow for cumulation of origin among the four associated countries. Although this may sound like a concession, on the cost side of the coin, this interferes with the input mix in production. Instead of procuring inputs that may have superior features (price, quality, design), firms may be coerced by the origin rules to select inputs that qualify for preferential treatment in exports.

There are strong arguments in support of a kind of re-establishment (reintegration is not a favoured term in the east) of broken economic ties among the transition countries. The Central European Free Trade Association, the Visegrad Group,[58] was created by the Czech Republic, Hungary, Poland and Slovakia in May 1993. The following month, the three Baltic states signed a free trade agreement among themselves. Regarding concessions in trade, the EU may think about a larger-scale cumulation of origin for goods coming from transition economies in the future. A proposal of the Commission for the future does not go as far as to include the cumulation of origin of goods from all transition economies for preferential treatment. Rather, it intends to offer something less ambitious. That is, a cumulation of origin for all goods that originate from associated transition countries and the remaining EFTA countries.

Anti-dumping rules set a procedure for dealing with this problem. Imports of goods from transition economies were often sensitive to complaints that they competed on the basis of low (predatory or subsidized) prices.[59] The officials from transition countries often argue that their merchandise is not dumped on foreign markets. Lower prices for their goods indicate lower costs of production compared to the EU. None the less, anti-dumping duties may be introduced either if dumping (including unauthorized subsidies) continue, or when there is no satisfactory solution within 30 days after the matter has been referred to the Council, or in exceptional circumstances.

Most of the anti-dumping actions against transition economies deal with sensitive goods. These products (agriculture, textile, steel and bulk chemicals) are the production lines in which transition countries have relative advantage in trade. Most exports from transition economies are concentrated in those goods, although they present only a small share of EU imports and consumption. For example, even in the sensitive iron and steel trade, the EU imports from transition countries was less than 3 per cent of the apparent EU consumption (Economic Commission for Europe, 1994, p. 154). Because of such a stance on dumping in the EU, uncertainty in trade relations with the transition region continues! That is unfriendly both regarding domestic and foreign investment. Investment will not be undertaken if firms fear that their exports output will be subject to protectionist proceedings in the EU.

None the less, one should not downgrade the impact of Association Agreements on the transition countries. These Agreements introduce an element of stability into otherwise potentially volatile trade relations. An important point is that the EU accepted certain bold and liberalization-prone steps even in trade in sensitive goods. The Agreements offer some vision for economic relations in a distant future. This view is supported by a general view that concessions in trade may be the most effective way in which the west can help transition countries in their difficult, but in the longer term rewarding, transition process.

This transition process does not progress in all transition countries at the same pace. Most of the countries that emerged from the former Soviet Union are the ones that lag behind the central European transition economies. Therefore, the EU intends to conclude Partnership and Cooperation Agreements with most of the former Soviet countries. This type of accord would offer more than the usual trade and cooperation agreement, but it falls short of the benefits offered by association agreements. One bargaining problem is that Russia wants to be treated as if it were a WTO member country. The EU cannot accept this, prior to the establishment of a market economy in Russia. That is important since market rules on costs and prices on goods and services still do not follow market principles. What may emerge is a safeguard and/or an evolutionary clause that Russia may get a free trade agreement in industrial goods with the EU, if it enters into and adheres to the rules of the WTO. In the meantime, the EU has offered the countries of the Commonwealth of Independent States the TACIS (Technical Assistance for the Commonwealth of Independent States) programme which is similar to PHARE (Poland, Hungary: Assistance for Economic Researching) given to the central European transition countries.

4 Entry into the European Union

A discussion about the relations between the EU and the transition countries would be incomplete without a reference to the possible entry of these states into the EU. 'Any European state may apply to become a Member of the Union' (Article O of the Maastricht Treaty).[60] That is the only Maastricht Treaty-based (sufficient) condition for a country to be considered for full membership of the EU. In addition to that explicit (Treaty-based condition), there are several necessary and tacit, requirements for entry.

First, the applicant country must have a market economy. Second, it needs to have a stable democratic political system.[61] Third, it has to accept and implement (during the negotiated transition period) all of the prevailing EU legislation, i.e., it has to accept the *acquis communautaire*.[62] Last, the entry should not jeopardize the EU's financial resources.[63] All those necessary conditions for entry into the EU reveal that the Union has very high discretionary powers and flexibility to select the would-be members. With this in mind, even the chances of the most advanced transition countries seem bleak for quite some time in the future, *unless* and until the rules change and the economic situation in the transition countries improves. The EU has neither the intentions nor the funds to include countries that have an economic structure that would revert to agriculture or primary commodities. Such an EU attitude may be hypocritical since the west took almost half of a century to encourage those countries to join the free market and democratic world! The message is: don't hold your breath, Czechs, Hungarians, Poles Slovenes and Slovaks – and others! An optimistic scenario is that if all goes well, meaning a smooth negotiation and adjustment process, it will take the most advanced transition countries some 20 years to become full members of the EU.

The revision of the Maastricht Treaty during the IGC (1996–1997) may amend, clarify and, perhaps, ease the rules for entry. Therefore, a better window of opportunity for the central and east European transition countries may exist in the future. None the less, there are many political minefields, as the reform of the CAP, regional and social funds are politically explosive. Eastern enlargement of the EU would, in fact, be a farm enlargement, to a large extent. A powerful agricultural lobby in the EU would object to the cost of this enlargement being paid by EU farmers.

The field where a coordination and, even, unification of action between the EU and the four prospective member countries is most likely in the future is politics. It does not cost the EU money, while the four or so transition countries may feel that some progress is being made between them and the EU. None the less, the most that the east Europeans can hope for in the long term is a kind of an arrangement similar to the one that was implemented between the EU and most of the EFTA countries (European Economic Area) in 1994.

An entry, in particular, an early entry into the EU may cause a serious external shock for any transition country. Their economies are not yet fully adjusted to the market-type economic system[64] and their manufacturing and services sectors are still fragile.[65] Such an entry into the EU without a full macroeconomic stabilization and modernization of the output structure, may be disastrous for transition countries. They would not be able to withstand competition with the EU producers in most industries. (The example of the former East Germany after the reunification with the western part of the country is quite instructive.) That would shatter the chances for a further development of their young social and political democracies. Transition fatigue is obvious in all the transition countries. That is exemplified in the return of the ex-communists to office. Therefore, the entry into the EU in (a distant) future needs to be thoroughly thought over and coupled with serious preparations. The EU needs to assist transition countries in order to invest in its own peaceful and prosperous neighbourhood in the future. The question is no longer whether transition countries need to be incorporated into the EU. Rather, it is, how costly is it going to be to existing EU members, and when and how long is it going to take?

Transition economies need to 'catch up' in economic development with the EU. It is in the interest of the EU to help them achieve that. For example, if a transition country such as Poland starts at 60 per cent of the Portuguese level and if the continuous annual rate of growth of GDP in that transition country is 4 per cent, while Portugal's is 2 per cent, it would take that transition economy more than 20 years before it catches up with Portugal (CEPR, 1992, p. 65; Baldwin, 1995, pp. 477–478). One has to remember that in the first half of the 1990s only a few transition economies showed positive and relatively modest rates of growth.[66] An open market access,[67] coupled with various forms of technical and financial assistance can do a much better job than long and favourable declarations. Clearly stated demands by the EU (including a tentative timetable) on what transition economies need to do in order to join the EU would make unpopular domestic stabilization policies acceptable to the citizens in the transition region. These criteria need to be interpreted in such a way that they do not become barriers to entry.

Various agreements between EU and transition countries offer preferential treatment and introduce 'order' into their economic relations. It is a very positive step in relation to the pre-transition era, although it should not be an end in itself. Further unilateral steps need to be taken at the end of the EU if the transition process continues. However, when jobs are in question, in particular during recession and in pre-election times, short-term considerations in the EU may overshadow the longer-term gains!

5 Conclusion

A plethora of agreements that the EU has with the transition countries offers an improved access to the EU market. Those technical agreements are a paradise for lawyers and consultants. This variety of arrangements may complicate life. What may happen in the future is that the EU would like to replace the glut of agreements with a single one, at least for the distinct groups of transition countries. These economies may slowly be on the way towards the European Economic Area (the EU arrangement with some of the remaining EFTA countries). None the less, there is a lot of anxiety in relations between the EU and the transition economies as there are still risks and uncertainties in the transition region. That is why the transition economies now have partnership with the EU instead of membership.

VIII DEVELOPING COUNTRIES

1 Introduction

The EU has relatively advanced trade relations with a very heterogeneous group of developing countries. In 1970, 37 per cent (ECU 23 billion) of extra-EU merchandise imports came from the developing countries, while 31 per cent (ECU 17 billion) of extra-EU deliveries went to those countries. The EU had a trade deficit with the developing countries of ECU 6.7 billion. Trade relations gradually expanded with two sharp jumps in the EU imports during the two shocks in the 1970s and a sharp fall in trade in the mid-1980s. In 1993, 30 per cent (ECU 143 billion) of external supplies of goods came from the developing countries. On the exports side, the developing countries absorbed 35 per cent (ECU 168 billion). The EU had a surplus in trade with the developing countries of ECU 24 billion. In general, the EU consistently had a trade deficit with the developing countries, so the trade surplus in 1993 is more the exception than the rule.

The EU deals with a preferred, select group of developing countries. These are basically some of the former colonies of the EU member states. The 70 African, Caribbean and Pacific (ACP) countries contributed 8 per cent to EU merchandise imports and 7 per cent to exports of EU goods in 1970. In 1993, the same shares were 3 per cent (ECU 14 billion)[68] for the EU imports and 3 per cent (ECU 16 billion) for the EU external exports. Although the ACP countries have enjoyed the most privileged treatment in trade with the EU among all the developing countries, their relative share in trade with the EU has been declining. In 1993, the ACP countries exported to the EU as much as Norway (ECU 17 billion) did, but less than China (ECU 19 billion). Before examining the reasons for this fall, we shall look at the development of relations between the EU and the ACP countries.

2 From colonies to Yaoundé

With the exception of Luxembourg, all the founding member states of the EU have a colonial legacy. France and Belgium insisted on the inclusion of the (then) colonies in the community-to-be. The association of colonies was one of the most difficult issues during negotiations on the creation of the Community in 1955–1956. On this issue, as well as regarding most of the others, France called the tune. France did not want the CET to be applied to trade with the Francophone countries in Africa. In addition, at that time, Algeria was considered to be part of France.

France was substantially aiding its own colonies (mainly in Africa) and wanted the community-to-be, in particular Germany, to share that burden. France accepted Germany's requests for free trade (a customs union), only after Germany accepted the demands of France regarding the association of colonies and the special arrangements for agriculture. The European Development Fund (EDF) was created with an initial $581 million. All countries of the 'six' contributed to the EDF according to the allocated quota (France and Germany had a quota of 40 per cent each) to assist the development of the associated external territories.

The fourth part of the Treaty of Rome (Articles 131–136) relates to the association of the non-European countries and territories with which 'the six' had 'special relations'. The deal signed with the Associated African States[69] and Madagascar (AASM) referred to the period 1958–1963. Preferences offered by the EU to the AASM were: the gradual elimination of tariffs on imports to the EU on the basis of reciprocity, financial aid from the EU, secured access to the EU market and guaranteed prices (higher than those on the world market) for the exports of the traditional tropical products. Temperate agricultural commodities were not included in the deal as the farm policy of the EU was in the process of formation.

With decolonization, many African states became independent. New and more formal types of legal instruments were necessary to link the EU and an increasing number of 'overseas countries and territories' with which the EU countries had 'special relations'. The former colonial powers intended to retain economic (and political) influence over their ex-colonies in order to prevent Soviet intrusion into that region. They linked the newly independent states (former colonies) to the EU, not under Articles 131–136, but under Article 238 of the Treaty of Rome. After negotiations, the Agreement on trade and aid was concluded in Yaoundé, Cameroon (Yaoundé Convention) between 18 African states (south of the Sahara) and Madagascar on one side, and the EU on the other.

In Yaoundé I (1964–1969), the EU gave preferences in trade and development aid to partner developing countries. On the one hand, France and the formerly associated countries wanted to formalize the already existing preferences and, on the other hand, Germany and the Netherlands wanted to extend preferences to all developing countries in order to avoid selective discrimination among countries in the developing world. The objective of Yaoundé I was a free entry of imports of manufactured goods from the 18 countries to the EU under the principle of reciprocity and non-discrimination between the six; guaranteed prices for tropical agricultural products coupled with free access to the EU market; and, finally, an increase in aid from the EU (the EDF disposed of $730 million).

During the negotiations (1968–1969) to renew the Yaoundé Convention, the partners[70] had the same intentions as those that prevailed during the Yaoundé I period. The only important change that Yaoundé II (1969–75) introduced was an increase in the amount allocated to the EDF ($900 million) and the possibility for the developing-partner countries to obtain $100 million loans for industrialization from the European Investment Bank (EIB).

While assessing the Yaoundé Conventions one has to note the doubling of the absolute volume of trade between the partners from $933 to $1,817 million between 1958 and 1969, respectively. The relative share of the Yaoundé countries in the total EU imports, however, decreased from 5.5 per cent (1961) to 3.2 per cent (1971). At the same time EU exports to the group fell from 5.5 per cent to 3.4 per cent in the same period (Coffey, 1982, p. 15). In spite of preferences in trade to the group of developing countries, these trends show a relative increase in trade of the EU with *other* partners. In part, these changes are also due to the relative increase of prices for industrial goods and the relative fall of prices of primary commodities at the time.

3 Lomé Agreements

3.1 Introduction

The Yaoundé Conventions were directed almost exclusively to the former French colonies. After the British entry of the EU in 1973, this country wanted to include its own former colonies from Africa, Asia, the Caribbean and the Pacific, to the EU (Yaoundé) preferences. No less important was concern about the unsatisfactory trends in trade between the Yaoundé countries and the EU that was not mitigated by the two Conventions. All that turned attention to alternative ways of regulating relations between the EU and select developing countries. The attention was directed towards stabilizing developing countries' exports earnings and diversifying the economic structure (industrialization).

3.2 Provisions and impact

Forty-six African, Caribbean and Pacific (ACP) countries negotiated with the EU a new and wider agreement in relation to the preceding ones. The ACP countries exist as an organized group only in relations with the EU. Lomé, the capital of Togo, was the place where the Agreement named Lomé I was signed in 1975. Lomé I (1976–1980) has had three extensions so far: Lomé II (1980–1985), Lomé III (1985–1990) and Lomé IV (1990–2000). Later deals had several changes and amendments to the first agreement. The two most relevant features that led to the renegotiations of Lomé I were the following ones. First, most of the participating African states stagnated in their development during the Lomé I period. Second, Africa is vulnerable to economic influences over which it does not have control such as fluctuations in the price for primary commodities. The number of developing countries that have entered the chain of Lomé agreements expanded from 46 (Lomé I) to 58 (Lomé II) over 65 (Lomé III) to 70 in Lomé IV.[71]

Lomé IV deals with a number of areas from agriculture to the environment to culture. The core of the EU and ACP cooperation, however, may be found in the areas of trade, financial aid and special facilities (Stabex and Sysmin). Lomé IV was concluded for a 10-year period (1990–2000) that was split into two 5-year subperiods. It maintained the major terms of the previous Lomé deals with certain updates. One is the introduction of a human rights 'suspension clause'. If any of the essential human rights are violated in the ACP country, the EU may suspend development aid.

Almost all (99.5 per cent) goods that are exported by the ACP countries to the EU have free access (no duties or quotas) to the EU market. The EU has not asked for reciprocity from the ACP for these preferences in trade. None the less, those concessions may be misleading regarding the generosity of the EU. They refer to goods that are *currently* exported, but they do not refer to the products which might be exported after the (industrial) development of the ACP states. As for the rest of the ACP goods (0.5 per cent) they represent products that directly compete with the farm commodities covered by the CAP. A relatively generous nominal non-tariff treatment of imports from the ACP countries in the EU market, conceals the fact that almost two-thirds of the ACP exports would enter the EU tariff-free anyway. For example, 63 per cent of imports from the ACP countries would enter the EU free of tariffs through the MFN and GSP treatments in 1991 (*European Economy*, 1993a; p. 68).

The founders of the Lomé agreements thought that the preferences given by the EU to the ACP exporters would boost their shipments. Hence, that would accelerate economic growth and development in the ACP states. However, those expectations were not met at all.

Table 7.7 shows the share of ACP countries in total imports of the EU and the share of ACP countries in the EU imports from other developing countries during the period 1958–1994. In spite of relatively favourable trade treatment in the market of the EU compared with most other trading partners, the share of the ACP countries in the EU imports was, generally, on a steady decline from 10 per cent in 1958 to 3 per cent in 1994. The share of the ACP countries, as a proportion of EU imports from other developing countries, fell by two-thirds in the same period. That took place in spite of the fact that they have not been subject to full blown competition from other, in particular Asian, developing countries. That shows that other, non-preferred, developing countries were doing much better in the EU market than the select ACP group did. What the non-ACP group of developing countries did was to diversify their economic structures and widen and upgrade the composition of export goods. In addition, the increase in relative importance in the EU trade of other developing countries was due to changes in the relative price of crude oil since the early 1970s.[72]

Table 7.7 Share of ACP countries in EU imports, 1958–1993 (%)

Imports	1958	1975	1985	1990	1993	1994
1 ACP share in total external imports of the EU	10.5	7.4	7.5	4.3	3.0	3.4
2 ACP share in the EU imports from other developing countries	30.0	9.4	24.4	17.2	11.3	11.4

Source: Eurostat (1996)

The relative fall in trade between the ACP and EU hides the fact that some of the ACP countries, such as Ivory Coast or Cameroon, increased and diversified their exports to the EU during the 1980s, although their performance declined in the 1990s. The bulk of ACP exports to the EU is made up of one commodity, crude oil. Nigeria is a kind of informal leader of the ACP countries in negotiations with the EU, because of the large volume of trade with the EU (21 per cent of total ACP exports to the EU in 1993). All other ACP countries together make up the rest. It should be noted that imports of crude oil receive duty-free treatment, so that the Lomé deals do not offer any extra impetus for the ACP exports of this primary commodity.

The reason for such unfavourable developments in ACP exports to the EU include a high concentration of ACP countries in the production and exports of traditional tropical agricultural products, as well as to the weakness in the productivity and quality of the manufactured goods compared with those from Asia and Latin America. In addition, it should not be forgotten that both the EU and its member states initially promote industrialization in ACP countries, but they restrict imports of the products of these industries as soon as the ACP countries become competitive on the world market. An example of this policy was the EU warning to Mauritius to accept the 'voluntary export restraint agreement' for textiles.

What Lomé deals offered to the ACP group was, in fact, a preferential duty-free access for goods to the EU market, without formal reciprocity. The EU has the right to introduce safeguard measures in case of the need for 'external financial stability'. The EU considers the ACP countries as a single group. That is very important regarding the origin of the goods exported to the EU. The GSP offers preferences to each developing country, however, the developing countries are not taken to be a single unit. In that respect the Lomé arrangement has an advantage over the GSP.

3.3 Financial aid

The aid package that was offered to the ACP countries by the EU during the first half of the duration of the deal (1990–1995), disposed of ECU 12 billion. Allocated resources for the period 1996–2000 were ECU 14.6 billion.[73] Most of that amount (61 per cent) was reserved for the *programmable* aid. That included national and regional indicative programmes, as well as support for structural adjustment. The national indicative programmes of each ACP country refer to the development programmes and projects that are planned. Similar programmes exist at a regional level. A novel feature introduced by Lomé IV is that there is a straight reference to the environmental (drought, desertification) impact of the financed projects. Most of the rest of funds represents *non-programmable* aid that is granted to ACP states on a case-by-case basis. This includes the Stabex, the Sysmin, risk capital, emergency aid and assistance to refugees.[74] Although there was a substantial nominal increase in the available funds for the first five years of Lomé IV over Lomé III (over 40 per cent) if one considers the increase in the ACP population together with inflation, the real growth in the available resources (if there was any) was quite small.

The feature that represented an entirely new point in relations between the north and south was the system for the Stabilization of Export Earnings from Agricultural Commodities (*Stabex*).[75] It was introduced in Lomé I and upgraded in the agreements that followed. If a country exports a small number of primary commodities and if the price of these commodities fluctuate on the international market, the exporting country experiences changes in export earnings. The EU introduced the Stabex in order to stabilize earnings of the ACP countries that come from the exportation of tropical agricultural commodities. The intention of the EU was to inject into the economies of the ACP countries an amount of funds that would be received from the EU market if unexpected circumstances (a decrease in price) had not occurred. An ACP country is eligible for the stabilization of exports earnings (receipt of funds) if:

- an eligible exports commodity contributed at least 5 per cent to the total exports earnings of all goods to all destinations (in the case of least developed, landlocked and island ACP countries, the corresponding threshold is 1 per cent); and
- if the exports earnings were decreased by 4.5 per cent of the reference level[76] (for the least developed countries the threshold is 1 per cent).

A transfer from the Stabex is meant to stabilize exports earnings, but the destabilizing element is a long lag between the fall in exports earnings and the actual transfer, as well as a shortage of Stabex funds.

Stabex disposed of ECU 1.5 billion during 1990–1995.[77] The number of tropical agricultural commodities that are covered by Stabex was extended from 29 (Lomé I), to 44 (Lomé II), Lomé III covered 48, while Lomé IV covers 49 basic agricultural and fishing products that ACP countries export to the EU.[78] The list includes almost all ACP agricultural export commodities, so one cannot expect a large expansion of it in the future. The bulk of all transfers (over a half) went on the support of only a few commodities such as oils and fats (groundnuts and related products such as groundnut oil) and tropical beverages (coffee and cocoa). Such a high concentration of the disbursements of funds, however, was not the idea of the founders of the Stabex. The funds received from the Stabex may be spent either in the sector that recorded the loss of exports earnings or in other (farm) sectors for the purposes of diversification. The recipient ACP country is obliged to send a report to the EU Commission on the use of the transferred funds within a year. Failing that, the Council of Ministers may suspend the application of decisions on subsequent transfers until the ACP state has provided the required information.

The Compensatory Financing Facility introduced by the IMF in 1963 was to finance the fall in the developing countries' exports earnings from primary products. The fall in exports earnings eligible for financing has to be the consequence of circumstances beyond the control of the developing countries. That might look, at first sight, similar to the Stabex scheme. However, there are crucial differences between the two systems. The IMF gives support in dealing with the balance-of-payments problems in general. The IMF takes into account the general situation of the balance of payments of the country. Stabex, on the contrary, considers only the specific commodity fall in exports earnings. The amount of funds that can be received from the IMF is limited by the country's quota, while transfers from Stabex are limited by the funds that are allocated to it by the EU.

3.4 Has the Lomé Convention benefited the ACP countries?

If the ACP countries have been continuously marginalized with regard to EU trade relations over the past several decades, the question is, were the Lomé arrangements of any advantage to the beneficiary countries? Although there is no counter-factual world that would disclose what would have happened without the Lomé deals, terms of trade would have been much worse for the ACP countries without the Lomé regime. The Lomé deals could have supported trade and development of the ACP countries only if these countries had a sufficient manufacturing capacity to take advantage of the offered opportunities. Failure to process primary goods and add value is the chief cause of the relative decline of the ACP countries in imports to the EU (Cosgrove, 1994).

Concluding the discussion on EU relations with the ACP countries, one must concede one crucial fact. The Lomé and other preferrential deals were not offered to the ACP countries either because of economic efficiency or because of altruism. Rather, the deals were offered to the ACP countries, even at a certain cost to the EU, because the beneficiary countries were 'natural' targets for the intrusion of communist interest at the time. The Lomé scheme was a product of the cold war.[79] After the disappearance of the Soviet empire and the cold war, has the reason for Lomé vanished too (Curzon Price, 1994, pp. 4–5)? Apparently, it has, as there is no clear evidence that the beneficiary countries really gained from the various concessions. The older and more complex the system becomes, the more administrative resources it absorbs. Many working hours were lost by firms, by customs, by forgers of origin certificates, by checkers of forgeries, etc. If those countries had been offered MFN treatment, the new system would have been more efficient from the resource-allocation point of view, as well as cheaper to run (Curzon Price, 1996, pp. 73–74).

The ACP countries no longer feature high on the EU priority list. Economic adjustment (reallocation of resources) relies principally on domestic resources and capabilities. A degree of support from international organizations including the EU, may be the best answer to the enormous economic and social problems in the ACP countries. Putting aside the Lomé preferences that produce, after all, only a marginal effect on the beneficiaries, the ACP, as well as other developing countries, may wish to place more emphasis on the WTO and multilateralism in the future, as there is an obvious risk of 'donor fatigue'.

4 Trade in bananas

The international market for bananas is of great importance for the developing countries that export them. World imports of bananas were worth $5.0 billion in 1993. Compared with other imported foodstuffs in the same year, that was below the trade in coffee ($7.4 billion), but more than imports of either oranges and related fruits ($3.2 billion) or cocoa beans ($2.1 billion)(FAO, 1994). As an agricultural product, banana cultivation is generally confined to the tropical developing countries. They are mainly in Latin America, the Caribbean, Africa and certain Asian countries such as the Philippines. Major banana consumers are the industrialized countries in the temperate zone. Bananas are also produced in the EU in Crete, as well as in overseas departments such as the Canary Islands, Guadeloupe, Madeira and Martinique. As EU domestic production does not satisfy internal demand either by quality or quantity, bananas are imported from abroad (this represents two-fifths of world imports).

Prior to 1993, Belgium, Denmark, Ireland, Luxembourg and the Netherlands were importing bananas predominantly from Latin America. The only border measure was the 20 per cent *ad valorem* tariff. Germany has always had a tariff-free quota for imports of bananas from all sources. Britain, France, Greece, Italy and Portugal limited imports of bananas by licences and other quantitative restrictions. Spain had a closed domestic market for banana imports.

The objective of the 1992 Single Market Programme was to increase competition, widen choice and reduce prices for goods and services in the EU market. This means that all overseas goods that enter the EU need to circulate freely in the internal market. The final outcome of the Programme is expected to be an increase in welfare. The rules of the Programme needed to be applied also to the EU-internal market for bananas. That meant that the previous national import systems had to be abandoned in favour of a common one. Regulation 404/93 introduced a common market organization for bananas in July 1993.

The new banana-imports regime of the EU that entered into force in 1993 had two basic purposes: the creation of a single internal market for bananas and securing the access to the EU market for bananas from the ACP countries. The EU domestically produced bananas (Crete, Canary Islands and overseas departments) have a general annual quota of 854,000 tonnes. Each producing region has a specific quota derived from the quantities produced in the best year prior to 1991. The basic features of the new import system include the following provisions:

- A general annual tariff-free quota for the *traditional* imports from the ACP countries is 857,700 tonnes. That is around 15 per cent more than the situation prior to 1993.
- Imports from ACP countries over and above the traditional level is called the *non-traditional* imports. It faces a specific tariff of ECU 100 per ton.
- Imports from all other countries, mainly from Latin America (the 'dollar area bananas') has an annual EU quota of 2.1 million tonnes (following the entry of Austria, Finland and Sweden, the quota was increased to 2.5 million tonnes).[80] This quota was roughly equal to EU imports of bananas prior to 1993. These imports face a specific tariff of ECU 100 per tonne.
- Any annual EU imports over and above the 2.5 million tonnes quota faces a duty of ECU 850 per ton (for ACP countries, it is ECU 750 per ton).

Detailed specifications on conditions of trade in general, such as quantity, quality, preferences, charges, penalties, etc. reduce uncertainty. However, such managed trade removes one problem (uncertainty), but introduces another one (too much certainty or rigidity). It distorts market signals and (mis) leads entrepreneurs down blind alleys (Curzon Price, 1994, p. 3).

The Commission issues import licences for bananas according to previous levels of imports. Although they are issued free of charge, there is a secondary market for those licences among traders that experience an excess or drop in demand. The Framework Agreement (1994) allows the four exporting countries to employ export licences. Hence, in order to export to the EU, traders must obtain both export and import licences! EU importers must import at least 30 per cent of bananas from ACP countries.

The new EU system for the importation of bananas introduced equity regarding the treatment of the domestic consumers, although at potentially higher prices, at least in Germany. As for the producers of bananas, the system is inefficient. The EU import quotas favour preferential suppliers (ACP) over the domestic consumers (Read, 1994, p. 232). The efficient and highly competitive 'dollar area' producers of bananas, both regarding price and quality, may be handicapped by the new EU system. Some production of bananas may be diverted from the 'dollar area' into the ACP countries, not on the grounds of efficiency, but on the grounds of the discriminatory administrative preferences of the EU. At the same time, the favoured ACP countries may have certain medium- and long-term costs as their inefficient production structure is being supported. This may postpone structural adjustment of their economies for the future, when the cost of such reallocation of resources may be much higher. In any case, the EU system for the imports of bananas will be subject to alterations in the future. Domestic consumers *may* be reluctant to pay more and get lower-quality bananas from the inefficient (marginal) sources than would be the case if they were able to acquire bananas from the 'dollar area' suppliers. In their fight against the 'special relations' of the domestic administration with the preferred countries, the domestic consumers *may* get support from the giant TNCs such as Castle & Cooke, Del Monte and United Brands and the government of their parent country (US) that have strong interests in the 'dollar area' countries. The EU banana-trade regime has already instigated a complaint to the WTO which may easily last several years.

The new (complicated) banana regime cost the EU consumers an estimated $2.3 billion a year. However, currently only $0.3 billion reaches the target developing countries, the rest 'disappears' in the distribution process (Borrell, 1994, p. 24). One may interpret the cost of the policy as a readiness by EU consumers to give aid to ACP producers. If that is so, a better policy for both the EU and ACP producers would be for the EU to accept a free trade in bananas and give a half of the cost of the policy to ACP countries in outright grants!

5 Generalized System of Preferences

Just like the Lomé Conventions, the GSP was a product of the 'cold war'. Negotiations about the GSP took place under the auspices of the UNCTAD during 1964–1971. The GSP were supposed to offer two solutions. First, the domestic market of many developing countries is too small for the internationally competitive operation of a number of manufacturing industries. The GSP had to stimulate exports from the developing to the developed countries and increase the flow of funds to the developing partners through trade (indirectly), rather than aid and loans (directly). Second, the intention was to counterbalance the preferential trade agreements between the EU and the select group of the developing countries (Yaoundé group).

The scheme is *generalized* because it is granted to the developing countries by most industrialized ones, and because it includes all industrial (manufactured and semi-manufactured) goods as well as specific processed agricultural commodities. It is *preferential* because the exported goods from the developing countries enjoy an advantage over similar exports from the industrialized countries. Commodities that have undergone only limited processing (inputs) are charged lower duties than finished goods. The more sophisticated the commodity, the higher the effective tariff protection. The developing countries consider that such a tariff structure in the advanced countries makes industrialization and exporting from developing countries difficult. The developing countries always asked for a preferential tariff (and non-tariff) treatment for their industrial products and components in exports to the advanced countries. What the GSP offered to the developing world is a tariff-free treatment (up to a certain quota) of manufactured exports. At the same time, the developed countries charge customs duties on identical imports from other developed countries. The GSP offers preferences to the developing countries that are equal to the difference between the preferential (lower) GSP tariff and the 'standard' tariffs charged on imports of the same manufactured commodities from the developed countries. A continuous reduction in tariffs under the auspices of the GATT/WTO that are charged under the MFN clause, lead to the devaluation of preferences in trade that the GSP offers to the developing countries.

One of the basic rules of the WTO is that the participating countries must, in general, extend to each other the most favourable terms negotiated with any other single partner (MFN clause). The only exception is when the preferential terms are the result of an agreement to form a free trade area or a customs union (Article XXIV). The reasons for the exception of the GSP from the WTO rules was a recognized need to increase the exports earnings of developing countries and to support their industrialization and modernization.

The EU introduced GSP in 1971, Japan followed suit during the same year, while the US did the same in 1976. In general, most of the OECD countries grant GSP preferences. The beneficiary countries were, until relatively recently, all of the developing countries. Unfortunately, the GSP is not a single consistent generalized system offered by donor countries. Rather, it is a myriad of individual schemes offered by each developed country. The GSP is not a contractual agreement such as Lomé deals. It is a preference that is granted unilaterally. It can also be modified in the same, unilateral, way. All developing countries ought to receive, in principle, preferences in trade from the developed countries without reciprocity.

The application of GSP has many restrictions. The GSP does not generally apply to trade in farm, textile and leather goods. The US and Japan have excluded textile products from their GSP, while the EU has included these goods into its own GSP, but only to those developing countries that accept the 'voluntary export restraint agreement'. The duration of the EU GSP was 10 years. However, this period was insufficient for most of the developing countries to industrialize and develop. Therefore, the duration of GSP was extended.

Every year the EU reviews its GSP and determines the import quota for each commodity covered by the scheme. Once the quota is used in full, the EU applies a tariff on further imports. The level of the quota is determined by the 'sensitivity' of the good. The producer's lobby in the EU is able to move some 'non-sensitive' and 'semi-sensitive' commodities into the group of 'sensitive' commodities and decrease the GSP quota accordingly.

The EU has two priorities regarding GSP for the period 1995–2005. First, as a tool of development, the GSP needs to be directed towards the neediest, i.e. poorest countries. This means that the EU will implement 'graduation', a programme of transfer of preferential margins from relatively advanced to poorer developing countries. This is to avoid the problem of a high concentration of beneficiary exporting countries supplying a large share of the total GSP exports. Over half the benefits of the GSP in 1983 accrued only to four relatively advanced beneficiary countries: Hong Kong, South Korea, Taiwan and Brazil (Karsenty and Laird, 1986, p. 10).[81] The purpose of graduation is to enlarge export opportunities for the least-developed countries.[82] In addition, another objective was to dilute a high concentration of GSP benefits on a few relatively advanced developing countries. As such, the graduation programme is not trade oriented, but development oriented. Second, as an instrument of economic development, the GSP needs to take into consideration broader objectives, such as social and environmental concerns. None the less, the new 10-year scheme would not introduce extra benefits to the developing countries over and above the ones reached in the Uruguay Round combined with the existing GSP.

A country that wants to receive the GSP treatment from the EU has to submit a certificate of origin showing that the whole or a substantial part of the value was added (production and/or transformation) in the exporting country. The EU grants a cumulative origin principle to the ACP countries, as well as to some of the integration schemes of the developing countries (ASEAN and the Andean Pact). The majority of the developing countries did not get any benefit from the GSP since they did not have the commodities (industrial base) to help them take advantage of the GSP.

A serious problem with the GSP is its complexity. It is sometimes so complicated that the system itself can represent an NTB. During business negotiations, neither exporters from the developing countries, nor the EU importers know if the GSP will be implemented. This is because data about tariff-free quotas may not be readily available, which introduces an element of instability.

Overall, the developing countries have had, at best, only modest trade (and development) gains from the GSP. Tariffs by the EU and other GSP sponsors are at relatively low level. Hence, the margins of preference and a limited commodity coverage of the GSP do indeed offer relatively small advantages in trade to the developing countries. An estimate for 1983 concluded that imports by the GSP donor countries from the beneficiary developing countries were only 2 per cent higher than they would have been otherwise (Karsenty and Laird, 1986, p. 9). If such a situation does not change, the developed countries may soon face a choice between an increase in the importation of goods from the developing countries or an inflow of immigrants from the same source.

Although the second EU GSP scheme expired at the end of 1990, its application was extended until the end of 1994 because of the pending outcome of the Uruguay Round negotiations. A new EU GSP scheme for manufactured goods was put in place in 1995 for a period of four years. The new scheme has four features:

- The quotas on GSP imports from the previous system were completely replaced by tariff modulation. Duties on imports of very sensitive products (textiles and clothing) would be reduced by 15 per cent, the reduction for sensitive products is 30 per cent, while for non-sensitive ones it is 65 per cent.
- The EU will apply the policy of graduation. GSP would be reoriented towards low- and medium-income countries which so far have had little benefit from the system.
- An additional margin of preference would be granted to countries that comply with certain labour (freedom of association, minimum-age employment, collective baragaining) and environment standards (forest management).
- GSP may be withdrawn if there is a violation of human rights in the beneficiary country.

The immediate benefit of the new GSP system is that it is much simpler to operate than previous ones, and it abolished disruptive quotas.

6 Economic relations with other developing countries

EU contractual relations with the *Mediterranean* countries are much less comprehensive than those with the ACP group. The Mediterranean countries are together with the transition countries of central and eastern Europe, the EU's closest neighbours. In 1994, the EU traded with the Mediterranean countries around three times more than with the ACP group. One of the major stumbling blocks in trade relations was the fact that the Mediterranean countries produce similar agricultural commodities (wine, olive oil, citrus fruits, vegetables) to the ones produced in southern Europe, in particular Greece, Italy, southern France, Spain and Portugal, as well as textiles.

In the late 1960s the EU concluded trade agreements with Greece, Turkey,[83] Israel, Tunisia, Algeria and Morocco, but it was only in 1973 that the EU introduced its Global Strategy towards the Mediterranean countries. The reasons for this late start were, on the one hand, France's insistence on relations with the select group of the developing countries (ACP) and, on the other hand, Dutch and German objections to such selectivity. As for Italy, there was a problem that agricultural production would be jeopardized by a more liberal treatment of imports from the south Mediterranean countries.

Bearing in mind its special historic, economic, political and strategic interest in the Mediterranean region, the EU delivered its 'Global Strategy'. The main features of this policy were proposals to create a free trade area in industrial goods between the EU and each country in the Mediterranean region, industrial cooperation, technical and financial aid, as well as concessions in farm imports to the EU that do not interfere (much) with the CAP. The most striking feature was that the EU wanted free trade in industrial goods, while on the other hand, did not either allow for a free movement of labour or permit free trade in agricultural goods in which the Mediterranean countries have comparative advantages.

Countries included in the 'Global Strategy' were the Maghreb countries (Morocco, Algeria and Tunisia), Mashreq countries (Egypt, Jordan, Lebanon and Syria), Israel, Libya, Turkey, Cyprus, Malta and the former Yugoslavia. Greece, Spain and Portugal were included in this strategy before their entry to the EU in 1981 (Greece) and 1986 (Spain and Portugal).[84] What these countries were offered by the EU was duty-free access for their manufactured goods, various concessions in imports of agricultural commodities, EU grants, and loans from the EIB.

So far the EU has concluded two generations of agreements with the Mediterranean countries. They range from non-preferential treatment, over cooperation to association. The main features of these deals are EU concessions in trade. The EU and Cyprus concluded negotiations in 1987 about the creation of a customs union. This was the first such agreement between the EU and an outside country. In 1995, the EU concluded association agreements with Israel, Morocco and Tunisia. Similar agreements are in preparation for a few other countries. There was a grand conference in the same year in Barcelona between the Mediterranean and EU countries (27 in total) that was supposed to strengthen peace and prosperity of the region, as well as bring free trade across the Mediterranean by 2010. In addition, the EU offered an aid package of ECU 4.7 billion and loans from the EIB. However, the basic objective of such moves by the EU were two. First, to create the economic and social conditions that prevent emigration from south Mediterranean countries into the EU and, second, a fear of Islamic fundamentalism. Time will tell if this move by the EU has been too little, too late!

The EU is very dependent on the imports of Middle Eastern oil. The vulnerability of the EU in this regard was obvious during the Yom Kippur war of 1973. The EU wants to secure oil supplies through the Euro–Arab dialogue. This dialogue has a very strong political element, derived from the Arab states. If Arab countries unite in their relations with the EU, they will be able to win important concessions from the EU in the short run. However, due to deep-rooted divisions and hostilities among the Arab countries about the general issue of who is going to lead the Arab world, this outcome is a very long way from reality. Apart from Morocco and Tunisia, most other Arab countries' major export item is oil, which enters the EU duty free.

Until British entry of the EU (1973) the Commonwealth countries enjoyed tariff preferences on the British market. After British entry, the EU concluded cooperation agreements with *Bangladesh, India, Nepal, Sri Lanka and Pakistan*. The agreements provide for reductions in tariffs, consultation and an exchange of information. These countries in the Indian sub-continent were excluded from the Lomé deals, not because they were more developed relative to other ACP countries, but because they were comparatively large countries with a sufficient manufacturing capacity to present a competitive threat to the EU manufacturers. The EU signed a similar agreement with the Association of South East Asian Nations (ASEAN)[85] in 1980 which was aimed at the promotion of trade, technical cooperation and a stimulation of investment in the ASEAN region. *China* is also a beneficiary of an agreement from this family. EU agreements with countries in *Latin America* are recent in origin. The EU intends to penetrate the huge markets of the countries in the 'Green Continent'. In doing that, the EU needs to keep in mind the strategic interests of the US in the region. Beneficiaries of agreements with the EU are the Andean Pact,[86] MERCOSUR[87] countries, Mexico and a number of Central American countries. The deals often offer 'special' treatment for exports of sugar, jute and cocoa products from countries such as Bangladesh, India and Sri Lanka.

7 Conclusion

EU trade policy towards developing countries has two basic elements: concessions and aid. The EU depends on imports of raw materials, so it needs secure supplies and good export outlets for its manufactured goods. Hence the need for the development of cooperation with developing countries. None the less, trade has lost a lot of relevance for EU relations with the ACP countries.

The development cooperation policy of the EU was very selective regarding preferences in trade and aid. This policy was Afrocentric (especially Sub-Saharan Africa). Out of all developing countries, the Lomé deals included (only) a half of them. None the less, many of the ACP countries are among the poorest countries in the world and they got certain preferences in trade and aid. Because of the proximity of the transition economies of central and eastern Europe, the EU is shifting its trade and aid focus eastwards. There is a kind of donor fatigue with the countries of the south as decades of preferences in trade and around ECU 30 billion of aid to the ACP region produced little positive result. In fact, the lone-wolf development policies by the 'Asian tigers'[88] proved to be much more productive than the policies of 'pampering' through preferences in trade and aid. Therefore, one should not be surprised to find out that many developing countries would be advised to help themselves in future as there will be little direct aid available.

The EU policy towards the select 70 ACP developing countries is embodied in the chain of Lomé agreements. However, the developing countries which remained out of the Lomé preferences did better in trade and exports to the EU than the 70 ACP countries. The EU continues to import raw materials from ACP countries, while ACP countries import industrial commodities from the EU. Lomé has not changed these trends. This may have led some observers to look at the Lomé conventions as a failure. However, this conclusion may not be fully substantiated as certain ACP countries expanded the range of goods in exports. Although relations under the Lomé deals were deemed to be the ones of equality and interdependence, they turned to be a system of unilateral preferences and aid to the ACP countries from the EU.

France has succeeded in keeping out of Lomé deals with Asian countries that were former British colonies. What the EU can offer to the developing countries which are not included in the Lomé deals are the GSP and cooperation agreements. The EU has concluded various trade agreements with the Mediterranean countries, with countries of the Indian sub-continent, ASEAN and in Latin America. The 70 ACP countries and France would like to see the Lomé agreements as a permanent means of EU–ACP cooperation. The ACP group would like to get larger funds from the EU and its member countries. At the same time, the ACP countries would not like an expansion in the Lomé membership since this would mean a loss of their position in the EU market.

The EU helps the development of industrial activity in the developing countries, but as soon as exports from these countries become competitive, the EU imposes imports restrictions (the best example was the Multifibre Agreement). Probably the most suitable way of helping developing countries would be to grant certain preferences in trade for a limited period of time. That could be coupled with a particular, conditional aid package in order to develop the enterpreneurship in the developing countries.

The Lomé agreements were as much praised as criticized. They were condemned because they cover only half of the developing countries and because they do not solve the problem of trade in textiles and temperate agricultural commodities. Stabex is, without any doubt, the most important innovation in the economic relations between the north and south. None the less, its coverage of export commodities is limited and its budget often short of funds.

The post-1992 EU may have little direct effect on the developing countries. If the result of the Programme is an acceleration of economic growth in the EU, that may have a potential spillover effect on an increase in imports to the EU from the developing countries. In fact, this has taken place regarding imports from certain Asian developing countries. The biggest impact of the 1992 Programme on the developing countries may not necessarily be traced in trade, although the developing countries may be adversely affected in the short run by the new EU standards (environment, for example) that could be met only at relatively high costs. The greatest effect may be found in investment diversion. No matter how small those flows were/are to the developing countries, they *may* be diverted both to the EU because of the growth effects, and to the transition countries of central and eastern Europe because of the new type of EU trade arrangements with this region. FDI may be diverted from the developing countries, but will not necessarily be. The determinants for the location of FDI to the developing countries and the EU are quite different. While FDI in the developing countries is resource-oriented, foreign investors look in the EU for a wide and rich market, skilled human resources, sophisticated technology and last, but not least, rationalization of their transborder business operations.

Apart from some agricultural commodities, the EU is more or less an open market for the commodity exports from the developing countries. The paradox is that the most successful exporters have been the developing countries that suffered the highest EU exports restrictions![89] This suggests that the EU border protection was a relatively small barrier to the developing countries' exports. Bigger obstacles were unfavourable domestic conditions and policies in the developing countries such as distorted exchange rates, inadequate incentives and poor infrastructure (Pohl and Sorsa, 1994, p. 150).

IX CONCLUSION

The external trade policy of the EU is founded on liberal principles. So much for trade philosophy. In practice, the EU has taken important liberalizing steps, even in sensitive areas. However, the problem is that these bold steps have been confined only to select countries. The EU has considerable discretionary power to differentiate (even discriminate) among its trade partners by offering or not offering different types of trade and other agreements. Although member countries of the EU are members of the WTO that stands for multilateralism, the EU 'rewards' its foreign friends by special bilateral trade agreements.

Internal protectionist lobbies in the EU are quite strong. Farmers are the most obvious example. They are followed by both manufacturers, whose output, and trade unions, whose jobs, are 'jeopardized' by a surge of foreign imports (steel, for example). Their influence is strong during recessions. There are constant opportunities to employ 'temporary' safeguard measures as allowed by both the Treaty of Rome (Article 109i) and Article XIX of the GATT. This introduces uncertainty in trade relations.

The Agreements that the EU offers to its external partners have several common features, but only two are most striking. First, as a rule, deals basically refer to liberal, even free trade regimes for manufactured goods. Agricultural goods are generally excuded from coverage, although there may be select (reciprocal) concessions. Second, if partners are on a lower level of economic development than the EU countries (developing countries or transition countries, but not the EFTA), the EU offers asymmetric deals. That means the EU gives bigger concessions (including aid and technical assistance) and/or implements them at a faster pace than their counterpart. As for direct aid, it may be expected to shrink in the future because of budgetary restrictions in the donor countries. This should not be a cause for much concern (one may even be indifferent to such a change) as there is little, if any, evidence of the impact of aid on economic growth and efficiency. Of course, a certain level of aid will always be necessary, but only for a small group of the poorest and neediest countries. However, the EU started introducing clauses about human rights in its trade deals with external countries. If they are violated, the EU reserves the right to suspend its concessions.

The EU offered the most favourable economic treatment to those EFTA countries that take part in the EEA. On the pyramid of economic privileges (Figure 7.4), the EEA partners are followed by the ACP countries (Lomé Agreement). Below are

Figure 7.4 Pyramid of trade privileges (hierarchy of trade regimes)

those countries with Association Agreements (six transition economies and several Mediterranean countries). They are succeeded by countries with Trade and Cooperation Agreements. Further down are countries that are privileged with the GSP and, then, the countries that are offered MFN status.

The EU took bold steps to open up its market in many sensitive goods in trade with certain transition countries. As in trade with the EFTA, the EU is entitled to introduce protective measures in certain cases. That introduces uncertainty in trade relations with all trading partners. None the less, access to the EU market from the EFTA and transition countries is better than what was in place before the new set of rules were introduced. The new arrangements increased legal order into their relations.[90]

Most of the recent international conflicts in commerce among the major trading partners (EU, US, Japan and the newly industrialized countries) can be found in trade in specific goods. They deal with industrial policy and free competition (standards, subsidies, dumping, origin, market access, public procurement), intellectual property rights and TRIMs. Translated into plain English, these conflicts mainly arise with high-technology goods. It is hard to imagine that the major world trading partners are interested in coordination (not to mention harmonization) of their domestic competition, industrial, R&D and technology policies in the near future. These goods and many fast-growing and lucrative services linked to them (telecommunications or data processing, for example) encompass an ever growing share in international trade and provide super-normal profits (rents) to those that are ahead of other competitors. Being ahead of the others gives a chance to set standards that may prevail for a long time in the future. As the manufacturing of those goods and production of services is based on market imperfections (economies of scale, sunk costs, R&D), frictions in trade in these goods may not be excluded in the future, unless there is the reliable and effective conflict resolution mechanism that the new WTO is supposed to provide.[91]

NOTES

1 All statistical data were taken from Eurostat sources, unless stated otherwise.
2 Common instruments of EU commercial policy include the common external tariff, quantitative restrictions, customs valuation regulation, rules of origin, anti-dumping and countervailing policy, common trade arrangements with external countries and measures to counter the violation of intellectual property rights.
3 The removal of internal border controls achieved by the 1992 Programme made Article 115 ineffective. In any case, the authorization of actions (most of them referred to trade in textiles) based on this Article were in a steady decline during the 1980s. From over 300 authorizations in 1980, they had more than halved by the end of the decade.
4 One of the crucial French demands during the negotiations that led to the signature of the Treaty of Rome was an association of its overseas territories. France was a big colonial power at that time and wanted its colonies, predominantly in Africa, to get preferential status in the EU. At the same time, Germany and Italy wanted to secure their traditional suppliers for bananas and coffee. So, a liberalization of trade within the EU coexisted with 'special' trade relations with select external countries.
5 This section gives no more than a brief outline of the theory of customs unions. For a broader treatment of the issue, an interested reader is advised to consult Jovanović (1992 and 1997a) and Robson (1987).
6 This is a part of the reason why highly protected countries, such as those in eastern Europe before the transition period had, in general, a poor export performance in western markets.
7 The seven rounds of tariff negotiations under the auspices of the GATT were: the Geneva (1947), Annecy (1949) and Torquay (1950–1951) Rounds, the Dillon Round (1959–1962), the Kennedy Round (1963–1967), the Tokyo Round (1973–1979) and the Uruguay Round (1986–1994).
8 A TRIM is a new name for the 'old' performance requirements.
9 These grey-area measures insulate users from exchange rate fluctuations. Hence, market signals get distorted.
10 The developed market economies granted the developing countries an exception from reciprocity. Although this might have been a concession given to the developing world, in some cases, indeed, this 'concession' excluded the developing countries from negotiations about certain trade issues. As these countries graduate in their development process, as the newly industrialized Asian countries have done, there is an understandable demand that there needs to be an exchange of concessions between these countries and the developed market economies. This has, in fact, taken place, during the Uruguay Round.
11 The Cairns Group includes most of the countries that are significant exporters of agricultural products.
12 Exceptions to immediate tariffication are granted to Japan and South Korea in their imports of rice. These countries are supposed to double their imports of rice in six years and apply tariff rates of zero to 25 per cent.
13 The formal name of the MFA is the Arrangement Regarding International Trade in Textiles. This derogation from GATT rules started as a short-term trade measure with restraints on trade in cotton textiles in 1961, but it was subsequently broadened to include

wool and man-made fibres, hence the name MFA. There were around 30 countries involved in these *bilateral* deals. They all ended in 1994. Since then, WTO rules apply.

14 The EU should be concerned about the huge imports of textiles from China. It was never covered by the MFA and China is not (yet) a member country of the WTO.

15 Past experience shows that GATT-sanctioned retaliations were the exception, rather than the rule.

16 Countervailing duties are the trade devices of strong partners (anti-dumping duties are too, but to a lesser extent). Tariffs and quotas are available to all countries. Opponents of the use of countervailing duties in the US have urged Canadian firms to start countervailing cases against the US, in order to show that the Americans also subsidize. Canadian enterprises responded that if they do that, the Americans will find some other way to retaliate against them (Lipsey, 1991, p. 100).

17 Exceptions are primary goods.

18 Non-tariff barriers have continuously irritated international trade relations. The most striking manifestation of international concern about the reduction of NTBs can be found in the extended scope of the Uruguay Round of tariff negotiations beyond the 'traditional' GATT agenda. On the regional scale the EU White Paper (1985) and the subsequent Single European Act (1987) intended to complete the internal EU market and create an economic area without frontiers. For the residents of the EU of course. This ambitious programme intended to eliminate or reduce substantially NTBs that hinder the free creation and operation of economic activities in the EU.

19 For example, in the field of financial services, the US is excused from the application of the MFN clause.

20 The introduction of a new good does not depend only on fixed costs and expected benefits, but also on substitution and complementarity with those goods that already exist on the market.

21 See Chapter 5 on competition policy.

22 A supplementary tax 'replaced' the Poitiers customs clearance procedure in January 1983.

23 It was the US demand to exclude agriculture from the Agreement that created the GATT. Later on, that act caused a backlash against the US in trade with the EU and Japan. We shall return to this issue in the discussion about trade relations between the EU and the US.

24 Between 1989 and 1991, the annual imports of Japanese cars into Italy more than doubled from 10,000 to 22,000 (*The Financial Times*, 5 August 1991).

25 Around a third of manufactured goods that are traded in the EU are covered by harmonized standards. The rest is covered by national ones.

26 An example are cars produced by Nissan in Britain. France limited imports of Japanese cars to 3 per cent of the domestic market and claimed that the Nissan Bluebird cars produced in Britain were Japanese in origin. There was an earlier informal guideline for the local content of the Japanese cars produced in the EU. Those cars would have preferential (domestic) treatment in the EU market if the local EU content was at least 60 per cent. To get this national treatment, France asked for an increase to 80 per cent of the EU origin in 1988. In order to qualify for national treatment in the EU, the cars produced (assembled) need to have an 80 per cent local (EU) content.

27 For example, national governments in the EU can make cash grants in the priority industries of up to 60 per cent of the cost of investment. In the US, more than 24 states offer and compete with substantial grants (and grant equivalents) in order to attract the location of world-scale manufacturing projects. These grants are increasing. Michigan offered state and local incentives worth $120 million ($14,000 per job) to attract Mazda in 1984; Indiana offered $110 million ($51,000 per job) to Subaru-Isuzu in 1986; Kentoucky offered $325 million ($108,000 per job) to Toyota in 1989 (UNCTC, 1991b, pp. 73–74).

28 Packaging and dilution with water do not alter the essential features of a good, so they are not taken as important elements that change the origin of goods.

29 The analysis of Emerson was based, in part, on shaky assumptions. There are those that disagree with Emerson's conclusions because of their *underestimation* of the effects of the 1992 Programme. Baldwin (1989) thought that the one-time gains would be translated into

a substantial 'medium-term growth bonus'. Others disputed Emerson's conclusions because they thought that the expected results were *overestimates* by a factor of two or three (Peck, 1989, p. 289).

30 This share excluded the intra-EU trade. If trade among EU member countries is included, then EU share in world trade would increase to 39 per cent.

31 This needs to be qualified as large countries may be, but not necessarily are, diversified in production, hence they have a relatively smaller 'natural' propensity to trade relative to small (specialized) countries.

32 The openness of an economy can be measured by the ratio of trade (exports, imports or both) to GDP. Openness depends on a number of factors that include economic policy, size of the economy, diversification of the economy, level of economic development, proximity of trading partners, climate, tastes and historical ties.

33 After a sharp increase in the share of EU imports from 5 per cent in 1980 to 11 per cent in 1988, the imports share of Japan has been declining.

34 Just as a matter of comparison, the share of Switzerland in the total EU external imports was over 7 per cent in 1992.

35 As prices of basic raw materials including oil are usually denominated in dollars, fluctuations in the rate of exchange for the dollar adds an extra element to the actual change in price for these goods.

36 The share of internal trade in the NAFTA was 45 per cent in 1993. In the non-market based integration group such as the former CMEA, internal trade was large, but declining from 62 per cent in 1960, down to 59 per cent in 1970, over 54 per cent in 1985 to 38 per cent in 1990.

37 Apart from Britain there were Denmark and Norway, as well as the neutral countries: Austria, Sweden and Switzerland. Portugal joined the group a little later and took part in the establishment of the organization. Iceland joined in 1970. Finland became an associated member in 1961, while it entered the group in 1986 as a full member.

38 The EFTA refers only to manufactured goods. Agricultural goods are left out of the agreement. That was not very popular in those countries with a relatively developed agricultural and fisheries sector, such as Denmark, Norway and Portugal.

39 Switzerland does not take part in the EEA. The major reason is that Switzerland feared a large inflow of foreign labour. Liechtenstein entered the EEA in 1995, but had to renegotiate its customs union with Switzerland, as the EU was afraid that Swiss goods would enter the EEA through Liechtenstein without restrictions.

40 It is not likely that an EFTA consisting of only three countries that are far away from each other would be a viable commercial organization. None the less, a successful economic adjustment of the transition economies may prepare these countries for the EFTA membership, as a waiting room for full entry to the EU in the distant future. However, to enter the EFTA, the eligible transition economies need to submit their application, and the EFTA needs to take into account the views of the EU in its decision-making.

41 The 129 Articles-long Agreement has around 1,000 pages, supplemented by over 1,400 EU laws (on 12,000 pages). That is *acquis communautaire* in practice. As a matter of comparison, the original Treaty of Rome that created the EEC in 1958 with all its Annexes and Protocols has a little less than 250 pages.

42 Although farm goods are the chief exception to the free movements of goods agreement in the EEA, they are not fully excluded. Both the EU and the EFTA are committed to liberalizing trade in farm goods in the spirit of WTO arrangements.

43 The 1992 Programme that is supposed to increase the specialization of EU producers would bring little, if any, gains to EFTA countries as they are already highly specialized.

44 Political considerations for the introduction of protection in the US are presented in Finger *et al.* (1982).

45 Contrary to such selective reciprocity that inspires the creation of regional trading blocs, the WTO stands for a broad-based exchange of concessions in international trade relations.

46 Super 301 was designed to provide a quick response retaliation and to send strong signals to foreign partners. That was a reaction to the long and costly delays common in the application of Section 301.

47 Another anti-multilateral signal that the US is sending is a resort to regionalism in trade relations.

48 In general, most of the recent frictions in international trade come from conflicts in trade in specific goods, rather than from the conduct of global policies that distort trade. In that light, the polemic about the 301 legislation raised three basic issues: has the US the right (legal/moral) to circumvent the WTO rules and to prosecute, judge and retaliate unilaterally? What would be the consequences if other countries follow a similar unilateral path? Do small trading partners have any chance to refuse to negotiate in such circumstances?

49 There may be a controversy regarding protectionism in the US. Supporters of the issue may argue: how protectionist is a country that had an average monthly trade deficit of $11.3 billion in the period 1990–1993?

50 Although NTBs are common in trade in industrial goods between the EU and the US on the one hand, and Japan, on the other, the NTBs are *not* as common in trans-Atlantic trade relations.

51 On a purely commercial level, foreign firms have shown a lack of sales efforts in Japan. Compared with the number of Japanese sales offices abroad, foreign firms have only an eighth of that number, while regarding staff, foreigners have only one-twentieth of the people stationed in Japan compared with Japanese stationed overseas (El-Agraa, 1988, pp. 84–85).

52 The goods whose trade was followed by the COCOM were divided in three lists: nuclear related exports, conventional weaponry and dual use (civil or military) goods and technologies.

53 Wassenaar is a suburb of The Hague.

54 As a reminder, the share of transition countries in imports of the EU in 1993 was 8 per cent (roughly the share of Switzerland alone). On the exports side, the fraction of transition economies was 8.7 per cent, which was roughly the same as the share of Switzerland (8 per cent) and similar to that of Austria (6 per cent) alone.

55 Trade and Cooperation Agreements entered into force for Hungary in 1988, Poland 1989, former Czechoslovakia 1990, while for Bulgaria and Romania it was in 1991.

56 Europe Agreements were signed with Hungary, Poland and the former Czechoslovakia in 1991. The interim agreements entered into force in 1992. Bulgaria and Romania concluded Association Agreements in 1994, while the Baltic states did the same in 1995 and Slovenia in 1996.

57 After the dissolution of Czechoslovakia in 1993, the two successor states renegotiated their original Agreement with the EU.

58 The major problems of the Visegrad Group include the following two. First, this integration arrangement means different things to different countries. The Czechs see it as a purely free trade area-to-be by the year 2000. Others would like it to be a bit more than that. Second, internal trade is relatively small. More than half of the total trade of member countries is with the EU.

59 In many instances, these goods do not compete on non-price grounds, such as quality or design.

60 Article 237 of the Treaty of Rome regulates the same issue in an identical way.

61 This means a multi-party parliament, rule of law and respect of human and minority rights. This also includes good neighbourly relations and no territorial disputes. Regarding the last request, not a single transition country passes this test. None of the EU countries fare well here. Just think of Northern Ireland.

62 This includes around 11,000 laws and regulations of the EU.

63 If there are no changes in EU policies and if the four Visegrad countries enter the EU, various estimates state that annual transfers from the EU to the four countries combined will be between ECU 20 and 30 billion. (A short survey of select studies is given by Baldwin, 1995, p. 477.)

64 With the possible exception of the Czech Republic and Slovakia, not a single transition country had a well developed market system even before they became centrally planned economies.

65 The EU may even think about excluding agriculture from the possible entry talks with the transition economies, although that is the sector where these countries may have comparative advantages. Alternatively, if the farm sector is included in negotiations, it may receive a longer transition period, just as was the case with the deals with Spain and Portugal.

66 Davenport (1995, p. 20) reported the results of several studies that attempt to estimate the necessary annual investment requirement of the central European countries in order to double GDP per capita over 10 years. Various estimates are between US$ 103 and 344 billion! One wonders where that money would come from.

67 Groups of manufactured goods that the EU protects most from imports from transition countries include: iron and steel, non-ferrous metals, glassware, footware, clothing, rubber and chemicals.

68 Nigeria alone exported to the EU goods (mainly oil) worth ECU 3 billion in 1993.

69 These were the African states south of the Sahara.

70 Mauritius joined the original AASM group of 18 countries in 1972.

71 Following the admission of Eritrea to the ACP group, its membership comprises 70 countries.

72 A sharp criticism of the ACP group came from the Secretary-General of the ACP group, Edwin Carrington, who said: 'We of the ACP have talked a lot, philosophised a lot, we have studied a lot, we have met a lot. We have not done much else (*The Courier*, March–April 1990, pp. 18–19)'.

73 Lomé I disposed of ECU 3.4 billion, Lomé II had ECU 5.7 billion, while Lomé III offered ACP countries ECU 8.5 billion.

74 Apart from aid through the EU, member states have their own bilateral aid programmes. In some instances, such as in France, one of the determining factors for the allocation of aid is which language is spoken in the beneficiary country.

75 A similar system, called Sysmin, exists for mining products. It was introduced by Lomé II.

76 The reference level is calculated on the basis of average exports earnings during the period of six preceding years less the two years with highest and lowest figures.

77 The Stabex disbursed during Lomé I ECU 382 million, ECU 557 million during Lomé II and ECU 925 million during Lomé III.

78 Important commodities for the Lomé countries that are not included in the Stabex list are sugar, tobacco, citrus fruit and beef.

79 The US has always publicly argued in favour of a free multilateral trading system. The Lomé and similar deals were running against such an ideal. The US was, however, silent about them because of strategic considerations. None the less, in spite of a strong cold war influenced preference in trade towards select developing countries, France (and Belgium) would argue in favour of retaining certain trade preferences for their former colonies.

80 As a result of the Second Banana Panel in the GATT (1994), the Framework Agreement between the EU and four exporting countries (Colombia, Costa Rica, Nicaragua and Venezuela), these four exporting countries were allocated half of the 2.5 million tonnes quota.

81 The key products that benefited from the GSP treatment were those based on labour, rather than capital related technologies. The major ones were perambulators, toys, sporting goods, footwear and telecommunications apparatus.

82 For example, South Korea 'graduated' in the EU GSP plan. Hong Kong, South Korea, Singapore and Taiwan 'graduated' in the US GSP scheme

83 Upgrading trade arrangements with Turkey in the second half of the 1990s to a customs union may benefit more exporters from the EU than from Turkey! Most trade barriers against Turkish goods by the EU were eliminated many years ago.

84 One should note that Jordan and Portugal were included in this strategy, although these countries do not border the Mediterranean Sea.

85 Brunei, Indonesia, Malaysia, the Philippines, Singapore, Thailand and Viet Nam.

86 Bolivia, Colombia, Ecuador, Peru and Venezuela.

87 Argentina, Brazil, Paraguay and Uruguay.

88 Other examples include Japan, China and Switzerland.

89 Look at Table 7.3 and find China, Taiwan, Brazil and South Korea. The comparison, however, may not be fully justified as some of the four countries are very large ones. So too are India, Pakistan and Nigeria!

90 International trade liberalization in the post-1960s period, as well as extension of the GATT into new areas such as services could have been slower in absence of the 'challenge' posed by the evolution of the EU (Blackhurst and Henderson, 1993, p. 412). A similar conclusion is reached by Krugman (1995, p. 181). None the less, there are certain reasons to suppose that the impact of the EU on the multilateral trading system has not been entirely benign (Winters, 1994, p. 602).

91 An analysis of trade conflicts in high-technology industries is provided by Tyson (1992).

8

REGIONAL POLICY

I INTRODUCTION

The prevailing attitude towards regional policy was one of non-intervention until the economic crisis of the 1930s. As the allocation of resources is perfect in a situation of free trade,[1] intervention in the form of regional policy is not necessary. Such a 'classic' premise has not, however, passed the test of time. The reasons for the alteration of the classic idea included not only transport costs, but also other market imperfections such as economies of scale or externalities. In those circumstances, an industrial policy is generally directed towards an increase in national or regional production potential and capabilities through a (supposedly) efficient allocation of resources from the national standpoint.[2] The objective of a regional policy is, however, to influence the distribution of the created wealth and to contribute to the easing and eventual solution of the 'regional problem'. In spite of intervention in regional affairs, there has appeared a recent move towards abandoning or, at least, easing and changing intervention in regional matters.

There is still controversy regarding the question of what constitutes the 'regional problem'. If taken together, there are several elements that may provide an insight into this issue. First, there is the situation when different regions grow at uneven rates for a long period of time, so the policy action endeavours to reduce that problem. Second, intervention may also aim at an equalization of consumption or GDP per capita among different regions. Third, the government may be interested in a relatively equal access of the population throughout the country/union to an adequate level of public goods and services. Another concern of the public authorities may be to include a spatially stable distribution of economic activities and population in order to avoid negative externalities.

Governments intervene in regional matters at least because of the following three reasons:

- *equity* (this social motive is based on public pressure on the government to try to achieve a 'proper' balance and an 'orderly' distribution of national wealth among different regions);
- *efficiency* (the desire to employ, sustain and increase national economic potential and capabilities); and
- *strategic behaviour* (public authorities want to control the comparative advantages of the country).

287

Intervention in the form of a regional policy is not a simple task as there are constant changes in technology, competition and demography.

This chapter is structured as follows. Section II spells out basic theoretical ideas regarding regional policy in particular in an integrated area. That is followed by a consideration of objectives and instruments of a regional policy in section III. Various aspects of regional policy in the EU are the subject matter of section IV. The conclusion is that the EU has to pay attention to regional matters, in particular, because of the fact that in an EMU balance-of-payments disequilibria are replaced by regional disparities.

II THEORY

The neo-classical or convergence school of thought argues that the 'regional problem' is not a problem at all. A free movement of goods, services and factors would, under certain assumptions, equalize factor earnings and living standards in all regions. In spite of this, even the *laissez-faire* governments may be seriously tempted to intervene in the economy as the adjustment process may work so slowly that it may not be politically acceptable. Another school has emphasized growing disparities, rather than equalization among regions. Imperfect markets with economies of scale, constrained mobility of factors or externalities may increase the attractiveness of already advanced areas and widen regional gaps, rather than reduce them.

Determinants of industrial location include consideration about: access to raw materials, energy and labour; access to markets; competition; government (dis)incentives; and the cost of transport. Advances in transport and communication technologies have made transport costs rarely the most important determinant for the location of business. While considering feasible spots, a firm may prefer a least-cost location and ignore the demand side of the function. In the reverse case, a firm may emphasize demand and neglect everything else. In practice, a firm considers both of these issues simultaneously.

The urbanization of society is one of the important features of the modern world. One of the reasons for this development is a declining share of labour relative to capital in agriculture. Another incentive for urbanization comes from the fact that many manufacturing and service operations depend on access to public services, in particular, in countries that are known for intervention. That is why lobbyists cluster in cities such as Brussels. Footloose industries are less reliant on natural inputs. In some cases they may place more emphasis on proximity to final markets, which further contributes to the urbanization trend.

Industrial development was shaped in the past by a host of economic and historic factors. Many of them were quite accidental.[3] Historically, attractive locations for setting up business were at a crossroads or at the mouth of a river. During colonial times, the ruling powers obtained natural resources from their provinces. In many cases they prevented the development of manufacturing in colonies as they wanted to secure these outer markets for the exports of the domestic manufactured goods. The local competition was eliminated. If some development of manufacturing activities took place it was usually in port cities, and was limited to primary processing.

Once a business activity begins to grow in an area, and if the system is flexible, then it attracts other enterprises to the region. The location of a firm was influenced in the past both by the endowment of immobile local resources and by the flow of mobile factors. A modern firm is highly mobile in its search for profitable opportunities, not only within its region or country, but also internationally. For a footloose firm, the advantages of one location in relation to others are much more human oriented than subject to resource endowments. Up until the 1960s it seemed to be more efficient to move people to jobs by migration. The footloose element of many modern industries supports production in relatively small and flexible units. Hence, there is an arbitrary and uncertain component in the location of firms for these industries. Locations that are close to consumers save in the transport costs of final output, while other locations may save in the cost of production. In some cases, costs of inputs, economies of scale and forwarding outlays may favour peripheral locations, while in others a preference may be for the ones that are close to consumers.

As products mature, the production cycle can make some previously unattractive locations for business interesting for consideration. Innovation is the process by which inventions are put into commercial use, while technology transfer is the process by which new products are transformed into 'old' goods elsewhere. An increasing number of new goods in the north usually creates demand all around the world. Hence, the relative price of northern goods rise in relation to the prices of southern commodities. It is profitable to invest in the north, so capital moves there from the south. Similarly, technology transfer shifts at least a part of demand towards goods produced in the south. This catch-up by the south, makes a certain amount of capital move there, so the relative income of southern workers increases. This process may 'hurt' the technical leader. Therefore, northern countries have an interest in continuously innovating, not just to grow, but in order to maintain their real incomes (Krugman, 1990a).[4]

There is, however, a drive that may help out the lagging regions in an integrated area. Suppose that the initial elimination of barriers to the movement of goods, services and factors in a common market spurs an inflow of factors to already industrialized areas where they benefit from economies of scale and externalities. If all the barriers to internal trade and factor movements are eliminated or become insignificant, firms may benefit from economies of scale and externalities in other (less advanced or peripheral) regions where the variable costs of production are potentially lower than in the centre of the manufacturing or service activity (Krugman and Venables, 1990, p. 74). In this case, the less developed region or a country that takes part in a common market is likely to gain on two counts. First, its industries get firms that benefit from economies of scale and, second, their former industrial structure that was typified by a lack of open competition is altered. Therefore in theory, economic integration may, but not necessarily will, bring greater benefits to the regions/countries that lag in their development behind the centre of economic activity. However, if production linkages (forward and backward) are strong and internal to an industry such as in chemicals or financial services, and imperfect competition prevails, then economic integration will trigger agglomeration tendencies. If those linkages are not limited to a relatively narrow industry group, but are strong *across* industries and sectors, then integration will produce agglomeration tendencies in select spots. If labour is not mobile, the whole process will tend to open up new, and widen existing, regional wage differentials

(Venables, 1995). Although this may produce de-industrialization tendencies in the peripheral regions, this does not mean that integration is not desirable. Education and regional policies increased the attractiveness of Spain as a location for various manufacturing industries. That was discovered not only by external, but also by EU investors.[5]

Others, however, argue that the outcome may be reversed from the one just described, and that an active regional policy is necessary, especially in an EMU. An outflow of migrants would discourage an entry of new businesses into the region which would further weaken the economic position of the area in question. None the less, such a vicious circle has not materialized in the EU. What seems likely to be the case in the EU is that the regional disparities slowly narrowed until the early 1970s; this was followed by a decade-long period of widening of regional gaps; and after this the regional gap among the member countries more or less stabilized.[6]

The national rate of growth of capital stock (without FDI and foreign loans) depends on home savings and investment. Suppose now that one region/country initially accumulates more capital than the other. In the following period both regions grow, but the one with more capital grows faster than the one with less. As manufacturing capital grows, the relative prices of manufacturing goods fall. After a certain period of time, there is a point where the lagging region's industry cannot compete internationally and it begins to shrink. Once this process starts, the new theory of trade and strategic industrial policy suggests, there is no check. Economies of scale may drive prices down in the capital-abundant region and the lagging region's manufacturing industry disappears. In this model, relatively small beginnings can have large and irreversible final consequences for the manufacturing structure of a country, its competitiveness and trade (Krugman, 1990a, pp. 99–100). A lesson for the EU is that the 1992 Programme provided certain opportunities for a concentration of firms in select hot spots,[7] as well as for the rationalization of business operations. In the US, for example, there is a high concentration of the aircraft industry around Seattle, electronics in Silicon Valley, and cars around Detroit. However, once the concentration of business becomes too high, there are negative externalities such as pollution, congestion and an increase in the price of land. This may have an impact on the spread and decentralization of businesses and their shift to other regions as firms may wish to leave the 'threatened' regions.

There are many causes of regional disequilibria. These include market rigidities such as a relatively low mobility of factors; geographical determinants; differences in the availability of resources; the education of management and training of labour; regional economic structure (in some regions declining industries, in others growing ones); institutional factors such as the centralization of public institutions (Paris is an obvious example); and national wage setting in spite of differences in productivity (Vanhove and Klaassen, 1987, pp. 2–7). Regional disparities appear in numerous forms. They include not only differences in income levels per capita, rates of growth or rates of unemployment, economies of scale, externalities, output and consumption structures, productivity, but also age structure, population density and the pattern of migration.

Regional policy is basically aimed at influencing economic adjustment in the four (theoretical) types of regions.

- Regions with a relatively high share of agriculture in production and employment. These are usually underdeveloped rural areas with relatively low levels of income, high levels of unemployment and a poorly developed infrastructure.
- This policy tries to have an adjustment impact in regions whose former prosperity was founded on industries now in decline, such as coal, steel, shipbuilding or textiles. These are the regions that failed to keep pace with changes in technology and were unable to withstand external competition (in some instances because of excessive protection). In the event of recession, labour in these regions is the first to be made redundant.
- Regions with a high concentration of manufacturing have congestion and pollution problems. Of course, in these areas benefits exist from the joint use of goods and services that are available. Regional policy may, however, try to reduce the existing congestion and pollution and/or prevent their further increase.
- Regional policy helps the solution of adjustment problems in frontier regions which are far from the strongest areas (poles of growth) of a country's or union's economic activity.

The above discussion has shown that there is a great deal of uncertainty regarding the impact of international economic integration on regional matters. One thing, however, needs to be mentioned here. Having a 'peripheral' location is not an irreversible economic fact. Its impact can be mitigated and, even reversed, as has been successfully shown by countries such as Australia or Japan. What matters most for economic competitiveness is the efficient development and employment of the most precious economic factor: human capital!

Jobs can be located in the regions where there are people with suitable qualifications, training and experience. Therefore, regions with unskilled labour cannot be expected to attract a significant proportion of industries that use modern technologies that employ trained labour and educated management. The location of business near large and/or growing markets saves in transport costs. If returns to scale were constant, as the neo-classical theory assumed, this could have equalizing tendencies for factor-owners' rewards in different regions. With economies of scale, these tendencies may increase, rather than decrease, regional disequilibria.

Convergence in the level of development among different regions is not a self-operating process. It works easier during an economic recovery, than during recessions. Lagging regions/countries usually have a higher proportion of both 'sensitive industries' and public enterprises than the prosperous ones. Therefore, they may be hit harder by a recession and budgetary restrictions than other regions.

Around the 1960s the regional problem was usually tackled with supply-side subsidies for the provision of infrastructure and reallocation of various (public) manufacturing and service industries. Foreign competition, in particular from the newly industrialized countries, placed in jeopardy a number of industries that failed to adjust. As there had been little success with earlier efforts to solve the regional problem,[8] coupled with austerity programmes in public finances, there was a major change in regional policies during the 1980s. Outright subsidies were reduced or slashed and the policy was supplemented by a system that is supposed to make the lagging regions more self-reliant and that supports indigenous development. This included the development of human resources, attraction of private investors (in particular foreign ones) and provision of technical services.

Recent research introduces a great deal of apprehension regarding the introduction of a regional policy. The long-term rate of regional convergence is quite comparable across countries, in spite of highly different efforts to promote regional equality (Barro and Sala-i-Martin, 1991; Sala-i-Martin, 1994).

III OBJECTIVES AND INSTRUMENTS

A region may be more easily discerned than defined. The definition of a region depends on the problem which one encounters. A region is both a geographical phenomenon with its distinctions from others; it also has political, governmental and administrative features; and it is an ethnic and social concept with its human and cultural characteristics. A region is also an economic concept with its endowment factors, their combinations and mobility. Therefore, a region can be defined in theory as a geographic area that consists of adjoining particles with similar unit incomes and more interdependence of incomes than between regions (Bird, 1972, p. 272). A region of a country or an economic union may be thought of as an open economy.

Regional policy is intervention by the state in order to influence the 'orderly' distribution of economic activity and to reduce social and economic differences among regions. It was usually a reactive (*ex post*) policy which primarily tried to reduce the existing regional disparities, rather than a policy that primarily prevented the creation of new regional disequilibria.

Trade liberalization and/or economic integration can provoke economic adjustment (reallocation of resources). Enhanced competition may force certain regions to embark upon a painful, but potentially rewarding, transfer of resources from unprofitable into profitable economic activities. These regions often blame integration or trade liberalization for adjustment 'pains'. However, such an objection may not always be justified. The most basic reason for the painful adjustment process is due to prior protectionism. The policy of long and excessive sheltering of the domestic economy reduces the pace of the reaction of local enterprises to international structural pressures and, hence, increases the cost of adjustment in the future. The adjustment costs may certainly be there, but the benefits *may* more than compensate for the effort!

Relatively low wages may attract investment into the region; however, there may, at the same time, be certain agglomeration and concentration tendencies in other regions. If there is a nationwide setting of wages, that may act as a structural barrier working against the lagging regions. As there is no flexibility in the level of wages among various regions in spite of differences in productivity, the less developed areas do not have the capacity to respond to this situation. One may not know in advance where the balance will tilt. Certain developed regions may become more developed, while some less developed regions/countries may become poorer (if nothing is done to alleviate the situation), but certain less developed regions may join the group of advanced ones.

The objectives of a regional policy are various, but their common denominator is that they aim at the utilization of a region's unemployed or underemployed resources and potential, the attraction of missing factors, and increases in output and incomes.

In a congested or polluted area, this policy restricts the expansion of firms and stimulates exit from the region. In the developing countries, the primary concern is economic development. This is most often coupled with regional imbalances, but their solution is not as high on the agenda as increases in economic potential. In areas of economic integration, the problem of regional (in)equalities is of great concern. Countries are reluctant to lag in their development behind their partners for a long time. This is of great concern in monetary unions (the goal of the EU) where there are no balance-of-payments disequilibria, but rather regional disparities.[9] Depressed regions/countries can no longer resort to devaluation as there is a single currency, while advanced regions/countries may not always be willing to finance regional disequilibria without proof that there is structural adjustment taking place in the regions assisted.

The first justification for a regional policy (intervention that aimed at assisting the process of economic adjustment), as contrasted with free market adjustment, can be found in the structural deficiencies of regions. These include: market rigidities, conditions of access to the market and the structure of output. When there exist such imperfections, a free market system is 'unable' to achieve satisfactory equilibrium from the social standpoint in the short and medium term, so there may be a need for intervention in order to increase output.

Regional imports consists of goods and services. In France, for example, most of the country's regions purchase financial, insurance, legal and other services from Paris. All this may not be quantified with ease. A reduction in a region's exports, for instance, may be obvious from the outset. Regional solutions to these disequilibria are inhibited by rules of competition and by the existence of a single currency. Hence, the second 'justification' for regional intervention in an economic union.

The third reason for intervention may be found in the employment of factors. The neo-classical theory of international trade usually assumes a free and full international mobility of factors which ensures full employment. However, even Adam Smith noted that a man is the most difficult commodity to transport. During recession, the employment situation is difficult everywhere, therefore the potential advantages of some regions that are abundant in labour are removed. Reduced mobility of labour prevents the equalization of discrepancies in economic unions. Hence, growth in one region may create conditions for even higher growth in the same region and increase inequalities among regions (the polarization effect). This may, however, act as a 'locomotive' for development in other regions as there may be increased markets there for food, economies of scale and innovation (the spread effect). In order to accept the argument that there are benefits from the spread effect, one must assume that there is a complementarity between the regions in question.

In the situation which is closer to reality and which includes economies of scale, large sunk costs, externalities and other market failures, adjustment does not happen according to such a relatively smooth neo-classical expectation. The regional absorption capacity of new technologies requires continuous learning, adaptation, development of human capital and established industrial culture. Therefore, the introduction of new technologies may be quite risky. That is why certain technologies diffuse quite slowly among regions. The reallocation of resources induced by the spread effect works at a (much) slower pace than may be politically acceptable, hence the need for intervention.

The fourth rationale could be found in the 'need' for compensation. Two opposing forces brought by economic integration affect regional development. The first one, specialization, leads to a convergence in regional incomes. Backward regions tend to specialize in labour intensive production according to their comparative advantage. This can have as a consequence a faster increase in wages in those regions than in the rich ones. The second force includes economies of scale and externalities. It can lead to a divergence in regional incomes. As integration extends the size of the market, firms take advantage of economies of scale and externalities. The EU 1992 Programme gave certain incentives for the concentration of businesses. This may benefit some regions more than the others; in fact, there is a possibility that certain (small and backward) regions may actually be hurt by integration if there are no instruments for compensation. Hence, another justification for a regional policy.

Subsidies may be one of the tools of a regional policy. However, a distribution of subsidies is always subject to political pressures. The final disbursement of subsidies often reflects more the balance of political powers than the comparative (dis)advantage of a region. At the end of the process, regional policies executed in such a way may do more harm than good, or at best, they may have a dubious effect. None the less, public policies in the backward regions, such as support for education, infrastructure, select public goods and help for the creation of small and medium-sized businesses in the form of loan guarantees for starting up have the potential for making a positive contribution to regional development.

The fifth reason for intervention may be found in the improved allocation of resources. Free markets usually direct capital towards already developed regions in the short and medium term. Private investors tend to increase the speed of the safe return of the funds they invested and to save as much as possible on investment in infrastructure. It may be understandable why they direct their funds towards the already advanced regions. These tendencies of agglomeration (adjointing locations of linked productions), where the developed tend to be more developed while the underdeveloped remain at best where they are, have significant private benefits on the one hand, as well as social costs and benefits on the other. A society may reap the benefits of large-scale efficient production. However, if private entrepreneurs are not impeded in their decision-making by a government policy, the location of their business may introduce significant social costs, such as pollution, congestion and traffic jams in some regions, and unemployment and increased social assistance in others.

The sixth reason for intervention may be found in the improvement in stabilization (macroeconomic) policy. Regional differences in rates of unemployment may reduce the possibilities for the control of inflation and the manipulation of stabilization policy. The reduction of inflation in some regions may increase unemployment in others. This may not always be the desired outcome. Diversified regions with a variety of employment opportunities would be able to adjust in a less painful way than specialized regions with the entrenched market rigidities.

The seventh justification for having a regional policy is that it may reduce public expenditure in the assisted region in the long run. Public support to firms to locate in certain regions may propel economic activity in these regions. Unemployment may drop, so welfare payments may be reduced and tax receipts may be increased and spent on something else in the long term. In addition, 'employment' in public services used to provide a shelter to the unemployed. Such artificial employment may be reduced or even eliminated once the private sector (with superior wages) starts thriving in the assisted region.

The eighth rationale points out that regional policy is targeted at regions with some disadvantage (underdevelopment, unemployment, obsolete output structure or pollution). The benefits of a regional policy are not confined only to the assisted area. Part of the benefit is enjoyed by other regions through externalities. The advantaged area of a regional policy is larger than the assisted area itself. That is why the Germans or the Swedes have some interest in helping out the Irish or Portuguese. Integration may be enhanced, unwanted migration of labour may be prevented, factors may be employed in a more effective way and there may be important non-economic gains.

Finally, apart from the above arguments for regional policy that mostly deal with 'economic' efficiency, there are political grounds which are at least as important as the economic ones. Solidarity, tolerance and the perception of a common future are the core of any social community. A mitigation of economic disparities among the constituent regions may be the necessary reason for the unity of a state or an economic union. That is relevant as the costs and benefits of international economic integration tend to be unequally spread among the participating countries in a situation of market imperfections. Arguments for equality demand the solution and/or mitigation of intolerable or growing differences in the distribution of wealth among the population which lives in different regions. The national political system does not always take fully into account the needs of backward regions. For example, the national system of setting wages may on the one hand significantly reduce wage-cost advantages for many regions, while, on the other hand, welfare expenditure can contribute to a greater regional equilibrium. Complete equalization in the standards of living in different regions is neither possible nor desirable because it may relax incentives for change and improvement. What is needed in regional matters is a continuous adjustment of regional development within commonly agreed guidelines, as well as protection of the standard of living which is accepted as desirable by the group.

Regional intervention may be quite costly. In addition, there may be in-efficient replication of certain efforts at various levels of government. Therefore, one may use the subsidiarity argument in favour of an EU regional policy. The EU is best placed to coordinate various regional actions, improve their efficiency, and to collect and transfer resources from prosperous to backward regions in the EU.

The goals of regional policy, such as balanced growth, equal shares in the social and cultural progress of the society, solidarity, regional distinctiveness and stability, are vague and may not be accurately measured. Specific objectives such as job creation, reduction in unemployment, housing and development of infrastructure introduce fewer problems in quantification. In the implementation of a regional policy care has to be given in the selection of policy tools to ensure that the policy does not evolve into protection of the existing economic structure, as that prevents structural adjust-ment and the efficient division of labour.

Instruments of regional policy are often directed towards entrepreneurs and factor owners. They can be employed either directly (support of existing or shifting towards new business activities) or indirectly (improvement in infrastructure). Their joint effects may increase employment, investment and output in the assisted regions, at least in the short term.

The dilemma of the state may be to stimulate regional development through private investment, on the one hand, and/or to invest directly in production and infrastructure for which there is no interest in the private sector. The available policy tools include those that provide incentives and disincentives to firms to move into or out of specific regions. Major instruments include: regional allocation of capital, investment, infrastructure, output, social security and wage subsidies; vocational training; public procurement and provisions of goods, services and infrastructure; reductions in interest rates; tax concessions; decentralization of government offices, education and health services; reductions in energy and public transportation costs; free locations; licences for the location of business; and trade protection.

If offered, cash grants may be preferred regional policy instruments to reduced tax liabilities. Grants apply directly to all firms, while reduced tax liabilities help only those that are profitable. Trade restrictions are not the wisest instruments of regional policy. The costs fall on the whole economic union, while they bring benefits to one or only a few regions.

Disincentives for regional expansion in congested areas are a relatively novel feature. In Britain, for example, they appeared in the form of Industrial Development Certificates that could be obtained prior to expansion or location in non-assisted regions. However, after the second oil shock, as unemployment increased, these certificates were abandoned as an instrument of regional policy. In France, for instance, there were certain constraints on the expansion of manufacturing and service industries in the Paris region. They included a special tax on office floor construction and authorizations for large-scale investments.

The policy of moving workers to jobs views the regional problem exclusively as one of unemployment. It ignores the fact that other problems in a region may be worsened further by this 'forced' mobility of labour. The productive part of the population moves out of the region while the consuming part remains in it. The local tax base may not be able to provide funds in order to cover the costs of local health care, schools and other social services. The overall situation may be worsened by the multiplier effect. In the advanced regions that receive the migrants, there may also be created new disequilibria. The new population increases congestion and rents for certain types of housing which may diminish the quality of life there.

Unemployment rates can be one of the most telling indicators of regional variation. If labour mobility is relatively low, then the movement of jobs to workers may reduce regional disparities in unemployment. Against this action is the fact that it may increase costs as alternative locations may not be optimal for the efficient conduct of business. However, as more industries become footloose, these costs to firms may diminish. Improvements in infrastructure, including training of labour and education of management, together with the spread of timely information, can help the location of footloose industries which are at the beginning of their product cycle in the assisted regions.

IV EUROPEAN UNION

1 Introduction

International economic integration may, in certain cases, aggravate the situation of already backward and peripheral regions in comparison with previous circumstances. This is recognized in part by the existence of national regional policies. None the less, having a peripheral location does not mean that a country is destined to have a poor economic performance. The accumulation and efficient employment of human (and physical) capital is the most important factor for a nation's economic performance. Although countries such as New Zealand, Australia, even Japan or South Korea have relatively unfavourable geographical locations regarding major transport routes, the irreversibility of their 'peripheral' position has been mitigated and more than compensated for by the accumulation and efficient employment of national human and physical capital. The location of Spain at the fringe of the EU was alleviated by an expansion of infrastructure and further development of human and physical capital. There is an expectation that Greece and Portugal, as well as the prospective new-comers from the transition region, will do the same in the future.

An economic union's regional policy can be justified at least on the grounds of harmonization of national regional policies and (re)distribution of wealth within the group (subsidiarity principle). Policy coordination at the central level is defended on the grounds that it prevents clashes of different national regional policies with common objectives. The policy needs to ensure, at the very least, that existing regional problems are not made worse by economic integration, otherwise the less developed regions/countries would have no incentives to participate in the project.

2 Legal base

Alongside national regional policies the EU has its own role in the fight against regional disparities. The Treaty of Rome did not explicitly request the introduction of a common regional policy. That was the consequence of the prevailing confidence in the free market solutions to regional problems at the time of its drafting. The Preamble of the Treaty says that the member countries intend to ensure harmonious development by narrowing the differences between regions and promoting the development of the least favoured areas. This was also confirmed in Article 2. Article 39 seeks special treatment for different agricultural regions; Article 49 requests balanced employment in order to avoid threats to standards of living in the various regions; Article 75 notes that the policy in the area of transport should not have negative effects in certain areas; Article 92 permits state aid to regions with low standards of living; while Article 198e empowers the European Investment Bank (EIB) to provide guarantees and loans for projects in the less developed regions. The initial expectation was that a removal of barriers to trade and factor movements would be sufficient in order to avoid regional problems. An active regional policy and free trade could not be easily reconciled. As time passed and the EU enlarged, regional problems became more acute and brought changes during the 1970s that were epitomized in the creation of a special European Regional Development Fund (ERDF) in 1975.

The Single European Act introduced Article 7c that recognized the need that the Commission may propose appropriate and temporary arrangements to help the efforts of countries which are at a lower level of development, during the period of the establishment of the internal market. As for the economic and social cohesion of the EU, Article 130a asks for the promotion of the harmonious development of the EU including 'reducing disparities between the various regions'. Article 130b demands the coordination of economic policies among the member states and authorizes the EU to support the achievement of these objectives through the Structural Funds (Guidance Section of the EAGGF, ERDF and ESF).

The Maastricht Treaty also recognized the need for intervention in regional matters. Article 130d created a Cohesion Fund for financial contributions to the projects in the poorer member countries. The fund was endowed with ECU 15 billion for the period 1993–1999.[10]

3 Evolution

The evolution of the regional policy of the EU can be divided into three broad phases. Regional issues did not feature high on the agenda among the original six member countries of the EU. At that time, only Italy was concerned about the regional problem because of the southern part of the country. That is why there was hardly any regional policy in the EU until 1973. Following the entry of Britain, Denmark and Ireland in the same year, the situation changed in the enlarged EU. The second phase in the development of regional policy began after the first enlargement of the EU. Britain was particularly interested in having regional issues included in the EU. Hence were created the first tools for the implementing the policy, in the form of the ERDF. The entry of Greece and later Spain and Portugal in 1986, amplified the desire and the need for an EU regional policy. This policy mainly benefits the EU-rim countries (Britain, Greece, Ireland, Italy, Portugal and Spain), just as the CAP favours the 'northern' countries.[11] The third phase started with the reform of policy and the ERDF in 1988. The idea of an EMU gave a fresh impetus for further development of regional policy.

Following the first enlargement of the EU, the new regional conditions of the EU were officially analysed for the first time in the *Report on the Regional Problems of the Enlarged Community* (the Thomson Report) of 1973. The Report identified two types of regions in the EU that have problems. First, there are the farming regions that are located in the periphery of the EU. The Italian Mezzogiorno or Ireland fit into this group. In both regions there is a relatively high long-term structural unemployment and dependence on farming. Second, the problem regions are also the ones that have a high proportion of regional output and employment in the declining industries. These problem regions have a slow rate of shifting resources out of those industries and a relatively high level of long-term structural unemployment. Certain regions in Britain fit into this group. A renegotiation of the British entry and the concerns of Italy and Ireland led to the creation of the ERDF in 1975 under Article 235 of the Treaty of Rome. However, the ERDF will provide resources for regional development that are only *additional* to the sources that are available for regional development from the national funds.

4 Regional discrepancies

Difference in economic development among regions exist in every country, but at the EU level they seem much larger. Less-developed regions in one country may have distinctive characteristics from less-developed regions in others, including large variations in income. In addition, congestion in southern Italy is greater than that in south-west France. Table 8.1 presents GDP per capita in the EU countries at market prices during the period 1990–1994 ordered according to the relative level in 1994. The comparison of the relative difference in GDP per capita among regions and countries at current exchange rates may well overestimate the real difference between advanced and backward regions or countries. The difference between Luxembourg as the richest country according to this measure and Portugal as the least developed was 3.8 : 1 in 1994.

Table 8.1 GDP per capita in ECUs, 1990–1994

Country	1990	1991	1992	1993	1994
Luxembourg	21,770	23,100	24,860	26,860	28,520
Denmark	19,970	20,310	21,080	22,160	23,660
Germany	18,690	17,400	18,890	20,100	21,150
Austria	16,140	17,100	18,190	19,450	20,670
France	16,690	17,140	17,950	18,630	19,460
Belgium	15,200	15,970	17,000	17,850	18,870
Sweden	21,130	22,460	22,080	18,130	18,850
Netherlands	14,940	15,570	16,300	17,270	18,070
Finland	21,290	19,570	16,290	14,160	16,230
United Kingdom	13,450	14,240	14,000	13,930	14,780
Italy	14,950	16,130	16,284	14,490	14,750
Ireland	10,070	10,410	11,110	11,330	12,440
Spain	9,950	10,950	11,390	10,430	10,380
Greece	6,340	6,880	7,160	7,410	7,630
Portugal	5,350	6,350	7,450	7,324	7,430
EU (15)	14,890	15,400	15,970	15,940	16,650
US	17,430	18,280	18,150	20,970	21,720
Japan	18,690	21,860	22,680	28,720	30,950

Source: EUROSTAT (1996)

A useful device for overcoming part of the problem associated with the inter-country comparison of GDP at market prices can be found in the current purchasing-power standard (PPS). This statistical indicator is based on the relative prices of a basket of representative and comparable goods. The PPS represents more adequately the real level of local purchasing power and it often gives a significantly different result from the ones given in current ECUs, in particular when there are serious changes in the rates of exchange. As the PPS is not affected (in the short term) by fluctuations in the exchange market, it is more appropriate to use this indicator for countries such as Greece, Italy, Portugal and Spain, than the current ECU values. Significant differences between data given in current ECUs and the ones in the PPS are assigned to the differences in price levels in the member countries of the EU. If the price levels in an individual member country are higher than the EU average, then the GDP

Table 8.2 GDP per capita, purchasing power standard in ECUs, 1990–1994

Country	1990	1991	1992	1993	1994
Luxembourg	21,620	23,250	24,580	25,420	26,140
Denmark	15,300	16,480	16,650	17,740	18,810
Belgium	15,190	16,210	17,300	17,950	18,540
Austria	16,650	17,380	17,100	17,720	18,480
France	16,200	17,270	17,710	17,420	18,120
Germany	17,050	16,070	17,080	17,150	17,890
Netherlands	14,820	15,510	16,060	16,310	16,900
Italy	14,900	15,920	16,470	16,120	16,770
United Kingdom	14,610	14,790	15,500	15,800	16,660
Sweden	17,010	16,880	15,700	15,590	16,140
Finland	16,200	15,540	13,760	14,400	15,210
Ireland	10,400	11,290	12,250	12,830	13,970
Spain	10,940	11,990	12,160	12,330	12,790
Portugal	8,680	9,710	10,410	10,940	11,220
Greece	8,430	9,040	9,610	10,000	10,160
EU (15)	14,730	15,220	15,760	15,840	16,520
US	20,550	21,180	22,440	22,750	23,890
Japan	16,270	17,760	18,720	18,900	19,278

Source: EUROSTAT (1996)

per capita is higher in current ECUs than according to the PPS. The reverse is true for countries that have a GDP per capita in current ECUs below the EU average. In those countries, the PPS gives a higher value than the GDP in current prices.[12]

Table 8.2 provides data on the differences in GDP per capita in the EU at purchasing power standard during the period 1990–1994. This kind of presentation changes, to an extent, the picture of the relative wealth of countries in comparison with Table 8.1. The difference in average real income according to this indicator was between the richest Luxembourg and the poorest Greece (2.6 : 1 in 1994). These contrasts are also an indication of differences in the level of economic development, while disparities in unemployment rates may be one of the indications of a relatively poor capacity to adjust to various economic shocks. It also has consequences for the regional problem as local output is below its potential.

The two tables reveal an interesting feature. That is, the relative decline of Britain, the world economic leader in the nineteenth century. While according to the GDP per capita in current prices Italy closely approached Britain during the period of observation, according to the purchasing power standard, Italy was on a higher level of development than Britain throughout the 1990s. If one adds the impact of global warming, Britain would soon join the 'olive-oil zone' of the EU that is bothered with regional problems.[13]

Data for 1992 in the PPS[14] reveal that the most developed regions of the EU, the ones with per capita GDP of 150 per cent or more of the EU average (100), were Hamburg (196 per cent), Darmstadt (174 per cent), Brussels (174 per cent), Paris (169 per cent), Vienna (166 per cent), Oberbayern (157 per cent), Luxembourg (156 per cent) and Bremen (155 per cent). On the other hand, the most backward regions were the ones that had GDP per capita 50 per cent or less than the EU average (100). They were the five new German *Länder* (38–44 per cent, each); Greek regions of Voreio Aigaio (45 per cent) and Iperios (47 per cent); French overseas departments of Guadeloupe (37 per cent) and Réunion (45 per cent); and Portuguese regions of Alentejo (41 per cent), the Azores (41 per cent), Madeira (44 per cent) and Centro (48 per cent). There are regional differences within countries too.[15] These discrepancies may be capable of dividing the EU. The objective of the EU is to mitigate the existing and prevent the creation of the new regional imbalances.

In spite of the relative backwardness measured by the differences in GDP per capita relative to the average in the EU, the most thriving parts of the EU can be found in sizeable parts of both Spain and Portugal.

5 Action

Local regional policies that are carried out by member states and their regional authorities, on the one hand, can have an advantage over EU regional policy because the local authorities may be better informed about local needs and problems. On the other hand, the EU is better placed to coordinate regional, as well as other national policies. In addition, the EU may contribute its own resources, introduce common priorities and standards, and also take into account regional interests when it reaches certain policy decisions. The EU has to make sure through the employment of the rules of competition that the member governments do not distort competition by a 'subsidy war'. Normally, the EU puts a ceiling on the permitted subsidy per establishment and/or a job created in various regions.

The ERDF was established in 1975. Its expenditure was allocated to the member states in fixed quotas. These national quotas were set according to the following four criteria:

- the national average GDP per capita had to be below the EU average;
- the assisted region had to have an above-average dependence on farming or a declining industry;
- there had to be structural unemployment in and/or emigration from the region;
- EU policies such as free trade had a detrimental impact on the region.

In simple terms, the governments of the member states had to submit regional projects to the EU to meet the allocated financial quota and to commit certain funds themselves to these projects, and the EU funds were obtained. The EU did not have any on the selection process. It was simply reacting to national initiatives. There was also a minuscule non-quota part of the ERDF which absorbed only 5 per cent of the resources. The EU was able to use these funds freely. Such a situation was criticised and the ERDF was reformed in 1985.

The reformed ERDF divided its funds among the EU member states by indicative ranges instead of fixed quotas as was the earlier case. Those indicative ranges only guarantee that the government would receive the minimum range over the period of three years if it submitted a sufficient number of quality projects. The projects submitted would be evaluated according to criteria that are consistent with the EU priorities and objectives. The intention of the EU is to receive a greater number of applications in order to increase competition among various proposals. The ERDF support may be up to 55 per cent of the public expenditure on regional projects, it is allowed to co-finance programmes and it may prop up the development of the indigenous potential in regions. The ERDF also attempts to mobilize local resources because it is increasingly difficult to attract private investment from wealthy to poor regions. Additional attention is devoted to coordinating both member countries' regional policies and the EU policies that have an impact on regions (CAP, trade, environment, for example).

A further modification of EU regional policy came after putting into effect the Single European Act (1987) and the entry of Spain and Portugal that intensified the regional problem. The Act introduced a new Title into the Treaty of Rome on Economic and Social Cohesion. Article 130a requests the promotion of harmonious development in the EU and 'reducing disparities between the level of development of the various regions'. Article 130b asks for a coordination of economic policies among the member countries and authorizes the EU to support those actions and objectives set out in Article 130b through Structural Funds. Apart from these grant-awarding funds, the EU has loan-awarding institutions (EIB and ECSC) that are also involved in regional projects.

Special regional problems emerged in the EU in 1986 after the entry of Spain and Portugal. Therefore, during the preparations for the enlargement, the EU introduced the Integrated Mediterranean Programme in 1985. The goal of this coordinated Programme was to help the Mediterranean regions of the EU (Greece and southern regions of Italy and France with a combined population of around 50 million) to adjust to competition from the two new member countries. The Programme disposed of ECU 4.1 billion in grants and ECU 2.5 billion in loans over a period of seven years. It integrated all available sources of finance on the levels of the EU, national, regional and local authorities. In addition, it coordinated other policies of the EU. The Programme was not aimed only at the adjustment of agricultural production (olive oil, wine, fruit, vegetables), but also at the adjustment of existing and the creation of new SMEs. Alternative employment for jobs lost in agriculture was to be found in services (tourism) and SMEs. Apart from the border regions of Finland, the entry of three developed countries (Austria, Finland and Sweden) in 1995 has not introduced new regional distortions in the EU.

The adjustment of the regional policy and the ERDF that took place in 1988 had one basic objective. It was to improve the coordination of various structural funds in order to support the 1992 Programme. The 1988 reform introduced the following six basic *principles*:

- member countries are to submit plans according to priority objectives;
- there needs to be a partnership between the administration on the local, regional and national level;
- the EU measures play only an additional role;
- there needs to be compatibility with other EU policies such as competition and environment;
- different EU policies need to be coordinated; and
- resources need to be concentrated on the least-developed regions.

At the same time, five priority *objectives* of the regional policy included:

- promotion of the development of the backward regions (objective 1);

- economic adjustment and conversion of the production structure in the regions that were affected by a large-scale industrial decline (objective 2);
- fight against structural unemployment (objective 3);
- promotion of the employment of the young (objective 4); and
- structural adjustment in agriculture, in particular in the regions that are affected by the reform of the CAP and fisheries (objective 5a); and promotion of development in rural areas (objective 5b).

Another decision in the reform package was to more than double the resources of Structural Funds from ECU 6.3 billion in 1987 to ECU 14.1 billion in 1993.[16] None the less, those funds had to be only an additional regional expenditure to the one undertaken by national governments. The objective was to make the structural policy a policy tool with a real impact, to move from *ad hoc* project to multiannual programme financing, to increase the predictability of the policy (as the funds were planned for a period of five years) and increased partnership with the authorities that are involved in the regional policy at all levels of government. In practice, all these tasks turned out to be quite bureaucratic; the methodology for the designation of regions that had to receive assistance permitted a high degree of political influence, so the coverage of the assisted areas was wider than was originally planned and support was less concentrated (Bachtler and Mitchie, 1993, pp. 722–723).

The provisions that regulate the operation of the Structural Funds were revised in 1993. The main thrust of the 1988 reform was, none the less, preserved. Alterations included only a simplification of the decision-making procedure and its greater transparency; the planning period over which the Structural Funds operate was extended to six years (1993–1999); the resources for the period 1994–1999 would total ECU 144.5 billion; and there was an inclusion of a few new regions that are eligible for the assistance.

As always when there is a disbursement of funds, the Commission has to be careful. It has to find a balance between its intention to have effective policies that do not introduce distortions that may be damaging for the EU in the long term, on the one hand, and subsidy-seeking regions and firms on the other. To be eligible for EU assistance, the disadvantaged region has to have per capita GDP of 75 per cent or less of the EU average. In reality, the application of this official ceiling was quite 'flexible' as aid was given also to the regions that had average income of 80 per cent of the EU average.

The regional policy of the EU is just a supranational addition to, instead of being a partial replacement of various national regional policies. Its first shortcoming is that the ERDF is modest in relation to regional needs. It should not be forgotten, however, that the regional policy of the EU is a relatively novel facet. It is improving through time. The share of Structural Funds was almost a third of the entire expenditure from the EU Budget in 1994. The effort to reduce disparities between rich and poor countries in the EU is great in circumstances of relatively slow growth and cuts in expenditure. Another brake in the development of the regional policy are the national governments as they prevent, in some cases, greater involvement of the EU in their own regional affairs. A greater degree of coordination of national economic policies may avoid squandering scarce EU funds. Through various kinds of EU expenditure (for example, farm outlays) the poor in relatively wealthy EU countries (such as Germany and France) are subsidising rich landowners in relatively poor countries like Portugal. Thus, coordination of national and EU policies is necessary.

There could appear a tendency of redirection of structural spending from rural to urban areas. Regional problems are starting to concentrate in the urban areas of the backward regions. The beneficiaries of economic integration in the EU are urban areas in the central regions. This process created disadvantages also in the urban areas, but in the *other* regions of the EU. That is because the EU is a heavily urbanized group of countries.

The impact of the 1992 Programme on regional disequilibria in the EU is ambiguous. There is an identification problem. First and foremost, one needs to answer difficult questions: what are the short- and long-term effects of the 1992 Programme on the regions and, then, what is the impact of the changes on the regional disequilibria that would have happened on their own? If the longer-term effects of Programme 1992 include liberalization of EU trade, then output may continue to be concentrated in the already advanced regions in order to benefit from positive externalities (this implies a fall in output and wages in the less advanced regions). However, internal trade liberalization may reallocate some of the EU production activities towards the periphery in order to take advantage of lower wages and other production costs there. As the outcome is uncertain in a situation with market imperfections, the effects of Programme 1992 on the regions will be debated for quite some time in the future.

Traditional forms of the national regional policy started to decline from the early 1990s in most of the member countries of the EU. Denmark, for example, abolished all regional development grants and loans in 1991. The Dutch have restricted their regional assistance to a relatively small part of the country in the north. Owing to budgetary constraints, France had to scale down its regional aid. Germany has severely curtailed regional policy in the western part of the country, while placing priorities in the new eastern *Länder*. Even the less developed countries such as Greece and Ireland had to be careful with their regional expenditure because of the restrictions that originate in recession. The new spirit of national regional policies in the EU countries includes (Bachtler and Michie, 1993, p. 721–722):

- reduction of the importance of regional policy in the northern countries;
- transfer of responsibilities to regional and local levels;
- automatic aid is replaced by discretionary assistance; and
- increased involvement of the Commission in regional matters, in particular, through the rules on competition.

Contemporary regional policy also includes the local development of producer services. That is the feature that started to be slowly incorporated in this policy only in the latter half of the 1980s. None the less, the creation of jobs in new manufacturing businesses, their extension in existing ones or the relocation of businesses still account for the major part of regional intervention. The Commission may authorize investment aid of up to 75 per cent net-grant equivalent in the least-developed regions. The same limit is 30 per cent in other areas where aid is allowed. The upper limit for aid in the least-favoured areas is intended to increase the competitiveness of these regions in attracting private investment. In practice, the country that has such regions within its confines may face severe budgetary problems and lack the necessary funds to finance projects in those areas. Hence, the impact of this concession is significantly eroded. In any case, a relatively high proportion of the allowed aid of up to 75 per cent may seriously question the share of the commercial risk that is borne by the private firm (Yuill *et al.*, 1994, p. 100).

As time passes, one may observe the expanding sway of the Commission in EU regional matters. It is mainly exercised through the rules on competition.[17] National governments also conduct regional policies; however, they are increasingly becoming selective and make sure that the policy provides value for money. In addition, outright general assistance to the regions is being replaced by transparent grants for capital investment.[18]

There is concern among member countries that the Commission relies heavily on quantitative indicators in the designation of areas for assistance and that it does not take into consideration to a sufficient degree the specific circumstances of each area. For example, unemployment data in rural areas may hide the 'real' regional problem as there may be strong emigration tendencies from those areas. Unemployment rates that are below the national average do not reflect a buoyant local economy, but rather a lack of local job opportunities. The quantitative approach by the Commission may be justified on the grounds that it must be impartial. The Commission can be questioned in its work by the European Parliament or by the Court of Justice so it must have certain justification for its action. Although the quantitative criteria play an important role in the first phase of the consideration of the problem by the Commission, the second phase of analysis provides for a greater flexibility and consideration of other, more qualitative elements (Yuill *et al.*, 1994, pp. 98–100).

6 Mezzogiorno

Forty years of regional policies in Italy have failed to deliver any sizeable and continual catching-up by the Mezzogiorno[19] with the rest of the Italian economy. One of the policy tools that were used to support industrialization in the region were legal provisions that requested public corporations to direct the majority of their investments towards the south. These firms were regarded in the receiving area more as providers of jobs (hence, as supporters of the local demand) than as contributors to the growth of the national economy. As such, a relatively low efficiency of investment in the Mezzogiorno does come as no surprise at all. Because of those 'results' there was growing pressure for a reconsideration of public policy towards the south, as well as an open opposition to this policy from northern regions of the country (Padania).

During the first half of the 1950s GDP per capita in the south of Italy was around 55 per cent of the north and centre of the country. The same ratio was 57 per cent in the second half of the 1980s. In spite of this, the Mezzogiorno cannot be described as a 'poor' region, in particular, in terms of its consumption. The artificially high levels of consumption are supported by large transfers of resources from outside the region. Therefore, the Mezzogiorno may be described as a structurally dependent economy (*European Economy*, 1993a, p. 21–22).

Development of infrastructure should not be undertaken without close coordination with other policy measures. For example, poor transport links may 'protect' local industries in the backward regions as was the case in southern Italy. Once the

Autostrada del Sole was built, that led to a chain of bankruptcies in the local food, textiles and clothing businesses.

The regional problem of the Mezzogiorno cannot necessarily be solved by dealing with the lack of funds or improving the infrastructure, but, rather, by considering the non-material sphere. One of the major obstacles may be found in the absence of an 'entrepreneurial culture'. In addition, a survey of TNCs that already operate in or consider investment in the Mezzogiorno revealed that the main disincentives to foreign investors in the region include the existence of criminal organizations and political factors. A lack of infrastructure featured highly only for those TNCs that had not yet established their branches in the region. Factors that contributed to the attractiveness of the Mezzogiorno included the availability of relatively low-cost labour (both quantity and quality), the availability of land, as well as various public incentives to set up business operations there.[20]

Dissatisfaction with previous regional policies conducted since the 1950s, pressure from the northern regions and the involvement of the Commission in regional and competition affairs, contributed to the introduction of Law 488 in December 1992. This Law effectively abolished special intervention (*intervento straordinario*) for the Mezzogiorno and extended the coverage of the policy (grant-based support) also to the centre-north of Italy. This means that regional policy in Italy is no longer tantamount to the policy directed to the southern part of the country. The abolition of the special treatment for the Mezzogiorno may be taken to be as one of the most significant developments in regional policies during the past four decades.

V CONCLUSION

If a country or an economic union has differences in the levels of development and/or living standards among the constituent regions that do not have at least a tendency towards equalization, then such a country/economic union may not be considered to have a well integrated economy. Therefore, all countries and economic unions have a certain commitment to reduce regional disequilibria for various economic and, more importantly, non-economic reasons. The aims of EU regional policy are to reduce existing and prevent new regional disparities. If a regional policy is to be effective, then the authorities at all levels of the government have to coordinate their activities in order to influence decisions about the allocation of resources. In spite of these coercive powers, regional policies of countries have had relatively limited achievements. It should come as no surprise that the achievements of the EU regional policy which often relies more on persuasion and on certain funds than on coercion, is scanty indeed.

Regional policy has been based on a number of compromises, hence the purity of principles suffered. Past attempts to shape regional policy relied mainly on the alleviation of transport and communication costs through the expansion of infrastructure, as well as the mitigation of agglomeration disequilibria. More recently, attention has shifted towards a greater self-reliance of the regions that are lagging in development, as well as the enhancement of the competitiveness of enterprises in those regions.

Demand, technology and supplies of factors often change. Regions that fail to adjust continuously to the new challenges remain depressed. One of the broad objectives of regional policy is to help redistribute economic activity among different regions. Its impact may not be measured easily, as it is no a simple task to construct a counterfactual world that would specify what would have happened without this policy. The difference between the actual and the counterfactual situation may be attributed to regional policy.

Raw materials are traded without major restrictions, while manufacturing industry and services are protected. On these grounds, the resource exporting regions (countries) may be supporters of free trade in a country or an economic union, because they would be able to obtain manufactured goods at more favourable terms of trade.

The question, however, arises as to whether regional policy increases or decreases market imperfections. In the second-best world, all answers are possible, but not always desirable. If the costs of such policy are less than the benefits which it brings, then the policy is justified. The rationale for a regional policy, which basically redistributes income (equity), must be found in solidarity among regions that constitute countries and/or the EU, as well as the fact that the benefit area is larger than the assisted region.

There are at least three major arguments in favour of EU regional policy. First, in absence of policy instruments such as tariffs, NTBs, devaluation or rate of interest, regions that are not able to adjust as fast as the rest of the EU face increases in unemployment and decreases in living standards. In this situation, there is some justification for the demand for short-term fiscal transfers at the EU level to ease the adjustment process. The possibility of such transfers in unforeseen cases ought to be permanent in an EMU. Otherwise, when in need, the regions that are in trouble may not be sure that other partner countries would provide resources on a case-by-case basis. EMU may not be able to operate efficiently without an effective regional policy. Structural Funds are expected to involve around 35 per cent of the EU budget in 1999. Second, coordination of national regional policies at the EU level (subsidiarity) can avoid self-defeating divergent regional programmes that were taken in isolation. Third, footloose industries, economies of scale and externalities do not guarantee that integration would bring an equitable dispersion of economic activities. Some guidance for economic adjustment and allocation of resources in the form of regional policy may be necessary. Expanding Structural Funds are employed in the EU in order to preserve unity with diversity in the group.

It is hard to locate the point where regional competition distorts competition beyond the interest of the EU. Hence uncertainty over regional policy will continue in the future. There are many arbitrary elements in the policy, as well as special cases. The regional policy of the EU has revealed its limitations. It is still an unconsolidated policy with deficient policy instruments. If this is so in the case of integrating the 15 current member countries that are on the road to establishing an EMU, the situation will be worse if certain central European transition countries join the EU in the future. A solution to the regional development problem, as well as to achieving a certain balance among various regions is an urgent, difficult, but highly rewarding challenge for the EU in particular in the light of moves towards an EMU. Instability in regional policy at national and EU level seems likely to continue. It is plausible that a trend towards decentralization in the creation and execution of regional policy will continue in the future. There is, however, a risk in the expansion of regional incentives that may compete with each other. In contrast to decentralization in national regional policy, EU regional policy has continued to widen its coverage and scope.

NOTES

1 The tacit assumption has always been that there are no transport costs.
2 A strategic industrial (and trade) policy is based on a number of assumptions that include non-retaliation by foreign partners and (perfect) information and forecasts.
3 Remind yourself with the examples of Boeing, the film industry in California and Nestlé (Chapter 6 on industrial policy, note 14, p. 212).
4 See the section on innovation in Chapter 5 on competition policy.
5 See Chapter 9 on capital mobility.
6 The economic history of integrated states such as the US points to the fact that integration is associated with regional convergence which predominates over economic divergence in the long run. This process is rather slow, around 2 per cent a year, but it is sustained over a long period of time (Barro and Sala-i-Martin, 1991, p. 154).
7 See the discussion of mergers an acquisitions in Chapter 5 on competition policy.
8 This should not be taken to suggest that regional policy is ineffective in general terms. Given the means and the structure of the problem in the case of the EU, however, the policy has not yielded significant positive results.
9 See Chapter 2 on monetary policy.
10 The funds would be spent according to the following ranges: Spain (52–58 per cent), Greece and Portugal (16–20 per cent each) and Ireland (7–10 per cent).
11 Federal countries such as the US, Canada, Australia or Switzerland have different regional policies from that in the EU.
12 The difference between the GDP per capita and according to the PPS is particularly striking in the case of the memorandum country of Japan.
13 Britain changed its regional policy during 1980. The most important features of this alteration included the following three elements. First, the regional disequilibria started to be seen as a problem of a *region*, rather than a *national* issue. Therefore it needed to be resolved by indigenous development, rather than by a transfer of resources and business activity from elsewhere. Second, direct subsidies for employment were replaced by a system of regional aid programmes based on employment creation through improved competitiveness. Third, the policy became increasingly reliant on employment cost-effectiveness (Wren, 1990, p. 62).
14 Eurostat (1995), 'Statistics in focus: regions', No. 1.
15 In Finland, for instance, the southern regions of Åland and Uusimaa (including Helsinki) are the most prosperous. GDP per capita there is 120 per cent of the EU average (100). The rest of the country has an income 90 per cent of the EU average.
16 The European Coal and Steel Community has established its own influence in the regions that are involved in coal, iron and steel industries. Loans were given for the retraining and redeployment of workers, as well as for modernization of the industry. The European Investment Bank has been giving loans for such projects in the less developed regions of the EU.
17 See Chapter 5 on competition policy.
18 Regional support started to include producer services and incentives for the introduction of innovations such as licences or patents.
19 Mezzogiorno is the area south of Lazio.
20 *Business Europe*, 31 May 1991, p. 3.

9

CAPITAL MOBILITY

I INTRODUCTION

The purpose of this chapter is to shed light on longer-term capital mobility and foreign direct investment (FDI) in the EU.[1] In principle, FDI requires freedom of establishment and, if possible, the national treatment in foreign markets. It is a distinct type of international capital flow as it has a strong risk-taking and, most often, industry-specific dimension. In addition, it is coupled with a transfer of technological know-how, as well as management and marketing skills.

Capital moves among countries in the form of portfolio and direct investment. Portfolio investment is most often just a short-term movement of claims which is speculative in nature. The main objectives include an increase in the value of assets and relative safety. This type of capital mobility may be induced by differences in rates of interest. The recipient country may not use these funds for investment in fixed assets which may be repaid in the long run, so these movements of capital may be seen by the recipient country as hot, unstable and 'bad'. Volatility of portfolio investment complicates their analysis. The large number of portfolio investments, made in many cases by brokers, obscures who is doing what and why.

Foreign direct investment permits the investor to acquire a lasting, partial or full, control over the investment project. The investor does not only employ own funds, but also knowledge and management. These investments are long-term in nature. They may increase the productive capacity of the economy, so they are often lured by host countries as something which is becoming, cold and 'good'. FDI may not be found in perfectly competitive markets, hence market imperfections may explain them. They include expected profits, market presence (particularly where markets grow rapidly), avoidance of tariff and NTBs, integration of operations in different locations, economies of scale, externalities and differences in taxation. FDI is a better way to obtain foreign capital than loans. Funds are often invested in longer-term projects and managed by experts. The project debt is serviced only to the extent that profit is made, which is not the feature of foreign loans.

Foreign direct investment is often the result of decisions by transnational corporations (TNCs). Therefore, FDI may be a relatively good proxy for the investment activities of TNCs (keeping in mind that TNCs may control operations abroad by simply giving licences).

There are three main types of TNC activities. They involve investments that are: import substituting, resource based and rationalized (Dunning, 1988, p. 54). *Import substituting* investments seeks new markets, but they replace trade. They are influenced by the relative size and growth of the foreign market in which the investment is made, the relative costs of supplying that market through imports or local production, as well as the relative advantage of engaging in direct local production or licensing.

Resource based investment is motivated by the availability and cost of both natural resources and labour in the target location. As the products of such investments are often exported abroad, the economic climate in foreign markets, transport costs and barriers to trade influence the attractiveness of such investment to TNCs.

Rationalized investments are seeking efficiency. They are, just like resource based investments, complementary to trade. Their attractiveness is found in cost considerations. They are influenced by the ease with which intermediate or final products (linked to economies of scale and specialization) can be traded on international markets. The case in question is the US loss of competitiveness as a site for the labour intensive production and where the domestic enterprises from this part of manufacturing locate abroad.

On the one hand, there is the search by efficiency-seeking enterprises, particularly some TNCs, for seamless and wide international markets regarding trade and investment. *Globalization* of economic activity is making national frontiers less divisive than a few decades ago. Such world-wide economic integration and integrated international production of goods and services whereby competitors are in each others' back yard are made possible by the expansion of information and telecommunication technologies.[2] That process is sometimes inverted, on the other hand, by the spread of *regionalism* (in the developing world) pushed by relatively inefficient firms and many governments that are driven by short-term election interests, even though the conditions for a relatively successful integration process such as at in western Europe, may be largely absent. Regional integration (a second-best solution) may resolve conflicts through positive cooperation but, if pushed to the limit, it may undermine multilateral (first-best) trade and investment systems and fragment the world economy into conflicting regional blocs. Regionalism and globalization/multilateralism do not necessarily need to conflict. If the regional blocs adopt fairly liberal external trade and investment policies, and if they cooperate, the general outcome may be overall welfare-enhancement.[3]

The structure of this chapter is as follows. Section II considers the impact of intervention on the attraction of FDI. Section III sheds light on the impact of integration on the operation of TNCs and *vice versa*. Legal grounds for FDI in and out of the EU and the evolution of those flows are contained in section IV. The conclusion suggests that regarding FDI, there were mainly agglomeration tendencies in the EU.

II INTERVENTION[4]

If market imperfections permit rents (above average profits), then the governments of the integrated countries may wish to intervene. A larger market of an integrated area may be more able to absorb the cost of intervention owing to the spread of such costs than could be the case with individual countries acting alone. For instance, a simplified (prisoners' dilemma) example is presented in Table 9.1. Suppose that there are just two firms capable of producing aircraft:[5] British Aerospace in Britain and Aérospatiale in France. Assume also that due to sunk costs, R&D and economies of scale, only one firm can produce aircraft efficiently (profitwise) within the EU and that public authorities prefer to purchase domestically made goods. The numbers in Table 9.1, then show the profit of the two firms. If there is no intervention by the government, the firm that moves first captures the market and makes a profit. If both produce: both lose; if neither produce: there is neither gain nor loss. The example is important since if only one country has the ability to produce aircraft, the government of the other may then try to persuade a foreign TNC to settle within its borders, thus putting the potential competitor from the partner country out of business. That is a strong case for joint treatment of TNCs by the integration groups.

Table 9.1 Profit in the aircraft industry, without intervention

France \ Britain	Production	No production
Production	−3; −3	10; 0
No production	0; 10	0; 0

Now suppose that there is no domestic producer of aircraft in Britain and that the domestic government[6] decides that it may be sensible to have aircraft production located at home and to move first to strategically and irreversibly pre-empt any other player.[7] Reasons may include employment, export and prestige, but also, and more importantly, various externalities, including obtaining the leading edge in one of the high-technology industries and national pride. The government decides to invite Boeing to come to Britain. As bait, it offers various subsidies and protection to capture the aircraft market in the integration arrangement with France.[8] The major reason for the subsidy is not simply to increase export sales, but rather to improve terms of trade and secure rents for the home firm, a cluster of related domestic enterprises and, finally, for the country itself. Of course, such a policy may have a considerable balance-of-payments effect in the medium and long term. Hence, the structure of markets and operations of TNCs are significant. Engineering comparative advantages of countries and firms are becoming more important in modern footloose industries and are eroding, to an extent, inherited comparative advantages.[9] Basically, this is how the new trade theory explains the success of Japan.[10]

What is important here is that the neo-classical model deals with the given and perfect resources and capabilities, while the new theory studies market imperfections and government intervention in a dynamic set-up that suppresses market constraints and pushes economic frontiers outwards. It considers economies of scale, externalities, differentiated products, changing technology and FDI. These are all features of the modern manufacturing. The new theory questions the proposition that free markets may successfully take advantage of potential benefits in the new situation. Such an approach is different from the neo-classical one where TNCs were, by definition, excluded from consideration. The assumption in free markets is that there is no ground for transborder business activities since the allocation of resources is perfect (first-best solution). The new theory explains that countries can trade not only when their resource endowments and production capabilities are *different*, as in the neo-classical situation, but also when their resource endowment and production capabilities are *identical*. The case in question is intra-industry trade (i.e., intra-EU trade in cars).

One thing, however, ought to be clear from the outset. The new theory does not replace the neo-classical one. What it does, is to consider market imperfections that can be mitigated by intervention which may introduce an adjustment instrument into an already highly imperfect situation.

Table 9.2 discloses profits of the two producers when the government of Britain subsidizes its (foreign owned/controlled) firm with monetary units that equal 5. If the firm in Britain decides to produce, it will always have the advantage over its potential French rival.

Table 9.2 Profit in the aircraft industry, with intervention

France \ Britain	Production	No production
Production	−3; 2	10; 0
No production	0; 15	0; 0

When market imperfections exist, the government of Britain can influence allocation of resources and specialization. None the less, to make correct choices in the selection of national champions, the government ought to be competent and possess correct information, otherwise there may be costly commercial failures, such as the French–British Concorde project or computers in France. Many governments in east Asia successfully intervened in the economy. But governments in many east-European and developing countries were intervening much more, yet in many cases these countries did not have economic success comparable to east Asia. In any case, intervention is eased when the number of potentially competing firms is small and production output is standardized.

In any case, governments need to keep in mind that general favours (subsidies) that are handed out to the domestic firms may trickle out to foreign beneficiaries, located within the confines of the jurisdiction of the government that offers subsidies. A better policy may be to subsidize the development and upgrading of the domestic human capital as footloose capital is increasingly being attracted, among other factors, by the local availability of skilled, highly trained and experienced labour and management.

In the advanced countries such as the US, more than 24 states offered and competed with substantial grants (and grant-equivalents) in order to attract the location of world-scale manufacturing projects. These grants are increasing. Michigan offered state and local incentives worth $120 million ($14,000 per job) to attract Mazda in 1984; Indiana offered $110 million ($51,000 per job) to Subaru-Isuzu in 1986; Kentucky offered $325 million ($108,000 per job) to Toyota in 1989 (UNCTC, 1991a, pp. 73–74); Alabama gave $252 million ($168,000 per job) to Mercedes-Benz in 1993; while North Carolina handed out $130 million ($108,000 per job) to BMW. In spite of strict rules of competition, countries in the EU are sometimes allowed to hand out 'incentives' to TNCs to settle within their confines. Britain gave $89 million ($29,675 per job) to Samsung in 1994, while France granted $111 million ($56,923 per job) to Mercedes-Benz and Swatch in 1995 (UNCTAD, 1995, p. 18). These kind of subsidies are well beyond the financial capabilities of developing countries.

This simple model of strategic investment, industrial and trade policy is based on the expectation that the subsidized home production of a tradeable good or service shifts monopoly profits (rents) to the home country and to the firms owned/controlled by it. Those profits ought to be over and above the cost of the subsidy. If those domestic firms are affiliates of foreign TNCs, then the effect on the home country's welfare may be uncertain. No matter the circumstances, the expectation that profit shifting may enhance the home country's welfare holds *only* when foreign countries do not retaliate against domestic subsidies. A cycle of retaliation and counter-retaliation would make everyone worse off. In addition, when there is a liberal treatment of FDI, bilateral trade deficits may point to misleading signals. For example, if Japan (or any other country) invests in China in order to take advantage of cheap labour and export output to the US, bilateral deficit in trade between the US and Japan may shrink, but the same deficit may increase trade between the US and China.

III TRANSNATIONAL CORPORATIONS AND INTERNATIONAL ECONOMIC INTEGRATION

Many business activities entail high costs, uncertainties and face rapid changes in technology and demand, so the operation of such activities in relatively small markets may not be commercially viable from the efficiency point of view. As worldwide free trade may not be achieved in the short or medium term (if ever), as the first-best neo-classical solution suggests, international economic integration may be an attractive second-best policy option. Such integration, although to an extent an inward-looking strategy, widens/pools the markets of the participating countries. Larger and growing markets provide greater confidence than relatively smaller ones to both domestic and foreign investors.

Domestic markets in most of the countries are so small that even a high protection of growth-propelling manufacturing industries and services aimed at supplying the local market may not be viable from the point of efficient employment of resources. By supplying a larger market provided by the integration arrangement, participating countries may increase production, capacity utilization, employment and investment; reduce vulnerability to external shocks; capture economies of scale; improve bargaining positions in international markets; and increase average standards of living. Those results are viewed in comparison to the situation in which all countries act alone under heavy domestic protection.

Production and distribution of goods and services in an integrated area does not take place exclusively by domestic firms, but also by TNCs and their affiliates. This point adds to the theoretical analysis an extra element that brings it closer to the real world, but it also introduces certain analytical drawbacks to the pure and simple theoretical models. In an early work, Mundell (1957) argued that within the HOS theoretical model, trade in goods and trade in factors may substitute each other. Markusen (1983) has shown that the flow of factors (operations of TNCs) are complementary to international trade, rather than substitutes, and that the proposition by Mundell may be only a special case. In any case, FDI is due to market imperfections, since in the free-trade case the allocation of resources is perfect and there are no grounds for FDI whatsoever. None the less, TNCs provide for powerful enterprise-created links that may integrate national economies.

There are at least five basic theories that explain why firms engage in transborder business activities and become TNCs.[11] First, the motivation to control foreign firms may not come from the need to employ assets in a prudent way in foreign markets, but rather to remove competition from other enterprises. Such a *market-power* approach by TNCs was advocated by Hymer (1976). The problem with such an argument is that most of the TNCs (measured by their number) are small and medium-sized. There were around 40,000 parent firms with over 250,000 foreign affiliates in 1995 (UNCTAD, 1995a). That shows that to become a TNC, a firm need not be a monopolist or an oligopolist at home and try to exercise that power abroad. If there is strong competition in the market for differentiated goods and services and an easy substitution is possible (perfumes, soaps, watches, clothing, vehicles, passenger air transport, to mention just a few examples), then the market-power argument for the transnationalization of business is weakened.

Second, while the market-power model excludes potential rivals from competition, the *internalization* theory holds that an arm's-length relation among individual firms is in some cases less efficient (e.g., trade in technology) than an intra-firm cooperative association. Profits may be maximized by means of an efficient and friendly intra-firm trade in intermediaries that eliminates sometimes excessive transaction costs (middlemen, exchange-rate risk, infringement of intellectual property rights, bargaining costs) when the business is conducted through the market. In these circumstances a hierarchical organization (an enterprise) may better reward parties in the longer term, as well as curb bargaining and incentives to cheat, than markets and external contractors. While Hymer conceives TNCs as vehicles for reaping monopoly profits and for the internalization of pecuniary externalities, the internalization model looks at TNCs as a mode of business organization that reduces transaction costs and internalizes non-pecuniary externalities. This model of FDI may be convincing in come cases, but it may not explain the structure and location of all FDI flows, since in addition to the internalization possibilities there ought to be ownership-specific and locational advantages for FDI.

Third, the *eclectic paradigm* (Dunning, 1988, pp. 42–45) explains the transborder business activities of TNCs (production of goods and services) as a mix of three factors. First, in order to produce abroad and be successful, a TNC must have or control income-generating ownership-specific and mobile advantages (such as superior technology, brand name, access to wide markets, etc.) compared with the local firms (including other TNCs) in the potential host country. Second, there must be opportunities for the internalization of ownership-specific advantages. It should be in the interest of the enterprise to transfer those advantages abroad within its own organization, rather than sell the right to use those advantages to other firms located in the country of the intended production. Third, locational (non-mobile) advantages refer to the gains of comparative or location-specific advantages of the target country. They refer both to the spatial distribution of resources and to those created by the government.[12] If a firm possesses/controls ownership-specific advantages, then it may use licensing to penetrate foreign markets. In the case of both ownership-specific and internalization advantages, such an enterprise may use exports as a means of entering foreign markets. It is only where an enterprise is able to take *simultaneous* advantage of ownership, internalization and locational advantages, that it will employ FDI as a means of operating in foreign markets.

Fourth, the *product-cycle* model reasons that mature (and, perhaps, environmentally unsound) lines of production of goods (there is no explicit reference to services) are being passed on to the developing countries. That is why transnationalization of business takes place. Such an argument cannot pass the test of recent developments. There is a heavy concentration of FDI in developed countries and the majority of developing countries are relatively neglected in FDI flows. In addition, countries start investing abroad at a much earlier stage of their development than before. The newly industrialized countries and many other developing countries are investing abroad. In many cases those investments are in the developed world. That may be prompted by the desire to be present in the developed countries' markets (closer to the customers), near the source of the major technological developments, as well as the strength of a host country's domestic currency.

Fifth, the *competitive international industry* model for the transnationalization of business refers to oligopolistic competition within the same industry and reactions to business moves by the rivals. SMEs may, in their business actions, act independently. Large firms care for the actions of their rivals, i.e., they act strategically (pay attention to the likely reaction of their competitors to their own actions). What Exxon does in Europe, Shell will (try to) do in the US. Competition is not 'cutthroat', but rather 'stable' among several oligopolies.

One of the main drives of transnationalization of business is a search for wider and/or growing markets. It assumes that property rights are secured in the host country. That is why nearly 80 per cent of all FDI stock is within the developed economies. Developing countries and those in transition regions face, therefore, very tough competition in attracting TNCs. Integration extends markets for the participating countries and it may be expected *ex ante* that some TNCs may favour integration among countries.

Integrated countries may obtain benefits from TNC activity. Those gains, specific to the operation of TNCs within the area, include not only tangible resources (transfer of capital on more favourable terms than could be obtained on capital markets, tax receipts, economies of scale, sourcing of inputs from local suppliers and employment) that it provides at lower cost than through the market, but also various intangible assets such as new technologies in production and management that make existing resources more productive, positive externalities in production through linkages, international marketing networks that can overcome barriers for exports into foreign markets, new ideas, clustering of related firms, training of labour and competition. The pecuniary element of those spillovers is quite difficult to measure and could easily escape the attention of a non-economist. Monopolization, restrictive business practices, increased sourcing from the parent country with a negative impact on the balance of trade, transfer pricing, transfer of profits abroad[13] and polarization may be found on the other side of the benefits coin. All of them affect the allocation of resources that does not always have a favourable impact either on the integrated country or on the whole group.

Foreign ownership and control of domestic output facilities is often seen by the man in the street as a cost (if it is a cost at all) to the domestic economy that is brought by TNCs. A more convincing argument against the operation of TNCs is that they behave in the market in an anti-competitive way through various business practices such as predatory pricing, monopolization or transfer pricing.

One of the host country's arguments against the TNCs is their internal (transfer) pricing system.[14] TNCs internalize intermediate product and service[15] markets. Prices in trade among different sister enterprises are arrived at by non-market means.[16] For example, if technology transfer is measured by international payments of royalties and fees, then around 80 per cent of payments are undertaken on an intra-firm basis (UNCTAD, 1994, pp. xxi–xxii). By doing so, TNCs may shift profits out of countries with relatively high taxes to those with lowest corporate taxes (tax avoidance)[17] or they may oust competition by cross-subsidizing product lines. In order to shift profits, vertical TNCs may overprice imports of inputs and underprice exports. This pricing system may distort flows of trade. One way to control the operation of the TNCs in the host country may be to request that the internal pricing system between the parent and subsidiary should be as if they were two separate companies. The enforcement and control of this request may be seriously endangered if there are no substitutes for these internally traded goods. Another solution may be to harmonize fiscal systems in countries where TNCs operate. None the less, a note of caution needs to be added. Transfer pricing is perhaps used much more than TNCs are willing to admit, but much less than is supposed by the outsiders (Plasschaert, 1994, p. 13).

Internalization of intermediate goods or services markets within TNCs is not always done with the primary goal of avoiding taxes on corporate profits. If a TNC wants to maintain high quality in the supply of its goods and services, then local or out-of-the-firm suppliers may not necessarily be able to meet the high standards requested by the TNC. Hence, the reason for keeping production (and pricing) internal to the TNC. None the less, fiddling with transfer pricing is more widespread in the developing countries than in the developed world. The balance-of-payments position often forces developing countries to control flows of foreign exchange. Strict controls may induce TNCs to manipulate with transfer pricing in order to protect and/or increase profits. The developing countries are not well equipped to first detect and, second, control manipulations with internal prices of TNCs.

A potential case against TNCs is that they rely heavily on the R&D of their parent companies and/or head offices that may charge this in a way which may not be controlled by the host country. This can make both subsidiaries and host countries too dependent on foreign R&D and technology. Is this really the case? Some empirical research has shown that subsidiaries had more R&D in Canada than other domestic Canadian firms (Rugman, 1985, p. 486). European elevator companies keep their R&D for elevators for tall buildings in the US because this country has many tall buildings. While there is historical evidence that the major part of R&D used to take place in the headquarters of TNCs, this is no longer the case on a large scale. In many instances foreign subsidiaries developed technologies that benefited the parent firm. For example, IBM's (US) breakthroughs in superconductor technology took place in Switzerland; Hoffmann-La Roche (Switzerland) developed important new pharmaceuticals in New Jersey (US); Toshiba made advances in audio technology in their British labs; and Matsushita has R&D facilities for air-conditioners in Malaysia. Affiliates of foreign TNCs in the US look a lot like the domestic firms. There are no signs of headquarters effects (Graham and Krugman, 1991, pp. 72–74; 117).[18]

A small country often does not have the available resources for basic research in relation to a big one. By imports of technology a small country may have access to the results of a much larger volume of R&D wherever carried out. It can be both complementary and supplementary to R&D already undertaken in the domestic economy. Relying on the domestic operation of foreign-owned TNCs is a wiser choice for a risk-avert country than being dependent on foreign supplies of the same good that is produced elsewhere.

There is, however, a tendency to decentralize R&D within TNCs. One reason is the reduction in costs of research, while the other is the exploitation of host countries' incentives to R&D (subsidies, tax breaks, secure contracts). The basic research may remain in the headquarters while subsidiaries apply development according to the local demand. It is often forgotten that many firms that create knowledge are not always either TNCs or big. The only condition for their creation is that they operate in a competitive environment which is often lacking in small countries.

It is, however, a goal of countries to set (realistic) objectives in relation to integration: to see how TNCs fit into the picture; to structure their entry, operation and exit; as well as to negotiate deals. In addition, if the integrated countries master the production of goods and services to such an extent that it increases their international competitiveness, these firms within the area may go abroad and themselves become TNCs. They may improve the employment of home resources and enter new markets beyond the confines of the market of the integrated area.

Suppose that a TNC as a monopolist exports a good to a group of integrated countries protected by a common binding quota. If, in addition, that TNC decides to locate within the integrated area, it may choose to produce there any quantity of the good it wishes. In such a case, the integration scheme (as a whole, but not necessarily every part of it) may gain significantly since there is an additional employment of domestic factors, while domestic consumers also gain since the price of the good falls. In another example, when there are local firms competing with a TNC in the home market, the location of the TNC within the integrated area may benefit both consumers (price falls) and resource utilization since home firms ought to improve competitiveness if they want to remain in business. If such a process works well, then one may not justify restrictions to the operation of foreign TNCs in an integrated area (be it in the developed or developing world).

An arrangement that integrates countries may improve the terms of trade of the group with the rest of the world. If the price of a good or service that is imported to the group falls after integration, then such an arrangement increases the rents of the scheme to the detriment of the ones previously made by foreign firms. Suppose that country A and country B integrate. If a TNC outside the integration scheme that produces good X is located in country B prior to integration and continues to operate there after the integration arrangement is formed, then the price of good X may fall due to the possible competition in the integrated market or increased efficiency that comes from economies of scale. If country A starts importing good X from country

B, then there are benefits additional to trade creation for country A. The rents of the TNC dwindle, while the surplus of country A's consumers rises. That consequence of integration, from the standpoint of country A, is called the *foreign profit diversion effect*. When there is another TNC producing good Y in country A that starts to be exported to the partner country B after integration, then, from the point of country A, there is an opposite effect named *foreign profit creation effect* (Tironi, 1982, pp. 155–156).

The foreign profit creation/diversion effects are of vital importance to schemes whose economic structures are dominated or influenced by TNCs. That may be the case in the countries that are involved in the globalization of international business, as well as in many developing countries. If countries such as that integrate, then TNCs are mostly interested in favourable foreign profit-creation effects. Suppose that there are two countries that contemplate integration and that each has in its market a different TNC that manufactures the same undifferentiated good. If the leverage of the two TNCs on decision making is significant in the two countries, then the TNCs may collude and undermine integration efforts.

Governments usually respect the opinions of the business community, in particular, if that business has a noticeable impact on the welfare of the country. Hence, in some cases, TNCs may even play one government against another and continue with inefficient (from a resource allocation point of view), but profitable, production for them.[19] That is one of the reasons why the arrangements that integrate developing countries may include provisions that refer to TNCs. None the less, the policy stance of an integrated area towards TNCs depends on the basic objectives of the group. If the basic objective of the group is an increase in *employment*, then ownership of the firms does not matter at all. FDI is, after all, an investment. If the goal of the group is to *shift rents* towards integrated countries, then it does matter who is the owner of the manufacturing and service facilities.[20]

International economic integration brings expanded markets, as well as new business opportunities and concerns. Hence, TNCs may enter such an expanding area, under certain conditions, and increase FDI by the creation of 'tariff factories'.[21] In addition to such an *investment creation effect*, new prospects for improved business without tariffs and quotas on trade within the region may prompt local firms to rearrange production facilities within the group. That may produce the *investment diversion effect*, that is, increased FDI in certain countries of the group and diminished FDI in others.

If the integrated market of (developing) countries is still small enough for the establishment of the cluster of related suppliers, then major gainers may be TNCs that assemble goods and/or perform only limited (usually final) manufacturing operations. Such a tendency may be enhanced when the integrated countries have relaxed rules of origin for goods that qualify for liberal treatment in the internal trade. Although the internal trade of the group increases, so does the extra-group import content of the traded goods. Broad regional deepening of production linkages does not take place. Estimates of the potential increase in trade ought to refer to the dual pattern of trade (imports of components from abroad and exports of finalized goods within the group) and discount the gross increase in the internal trade of the region. Instead of the expected relative reduction in the dependency on external markets, integration on such terms may have a completely opposite effect.

Governments of potential host countries may compete with each other with subsidies offered to TNCs in order to elicit their location. In such a game, TNCs may benefit since their bargaining power is enhanced. One outcome may be that TNCs locate in each country, supply the local protected market, engage in parallel production on a scale that is sub-optimal from a resource allocation point of view, while these countries lose interest in the integration process. Such a game requires a common competition policy, joint industrialization programme and treatment of TNCs in a group of (developing) countries, otherwise the linkages with the suppliers from the local economy and integration partner country may be, indeed, superficial. Integration may lead to a structure of production that is dominated by firms alien to the integrated group. A potentially positive absorption and spread of changes in the market (created by the involvement of TNCs) by local enterprises does not take place.

Transnational corporations have an interest in promoting integration among developing countries that have small markets, but only under the condition that these firms were not involved in the countries concerned prior to integration. In medium and large developing countries, the position of TNCs may be quite different, since TNCs do not seek integration among countries of such size. In fact, they may be a major obstacle to the forceful integration of developing countries. The primary concern of TNCs may not be efficiency in production, but rather the likely reactions of other TNCs, as well as an intention to avoid conflicts (UNCTAD, 1983, p. 12).

Transnational corporations treat their business in different countries as a single market operation. Therefore, their financial service is always centralized as it may best meet the needs of the firm as a whole.[22] It represents the backbone of overall efficiency. This is most pronounced in the case where ownership-specific advantages of a TNC generate high returns. Other operations such as employment, wage and labour relations are always decentralized within TNCs. Labour markets are local and often highly regulated, so decentralization of these issues is the optimal policy for the TNCs. Multi-plant coordination of business is one of the greatest advantages of TNCs. For example, Nike (an American 'producer' of sports goods) keeps its R&D in Oregon, but subcontracts the actual manufacturing of those goods in some 40 locations, principally in Asia. If wages increase in one country, Nike moves production into another.

It is argued that TNCs invest most often in the fast-growing manufacturing industries such as electronics and pharmaceutical industries. These industries fall into foreign hands. Foreigners may thus harm the host country by interfering with sovereignty. An example is when the US introduced a ban on the export of technology for the gas pipeline from the former Soviet Union to western Europe in the early 1980s. Many subsidiaries of the American firms in western Europe were adversely affected by this decision. It is much harder for a host country to hit the parent country of a TNC through a subsidiary.

Contemporary technologies complicate the assessment of the employment impact of FDI. Modern technologies substitute capital for labour. A 'greenfield' entry on a new site adds to employment in the host country if it does not put domestic competitors out of business. A takeover of an existing firm does not necessarily increase employment and it may reduce it if this firm rationalizes its existing activity (Buckley and Artisien, 1987, p. 212). A subsidiary may start as a unit for marketing the final good. If it develops further, it may become a product specialist which may increase employment (direct and indirect) of certain types of labour.

Transnational corporations may introduce technologies which use relatively more resources in short supply (capital) and relatively fewer of the factor which is abundant (labour) in the host country. TNCs may offer relatively higher wages to qualified domestic labour in order to attract it. This labour may flow from the host country's firms into TNCs. However, this may be due, in part, to the fact that home firms do not value properly a resource that is in short supply. Vacancies in domestic firms may be filled by less well trained labour which may have an adverse effect on the growth of production in the host country. Although technologies used by TNCs in the host countries may not be the most up-to-date, they may be better than those currently in use in developing countries.

Takeovers are most attractive to those enterprises which have wide international marketing networks. They are appealing to the businesses that are interested in penetrating the widest possible market. This is actually enhanced if the acquiring (or merged) enterprise is not linked to any industrial grouping which helps to avoid conflicting interests. That is why the Anglo-Saxon TNCs dominate cross-border mergers and acquisitions in Europe.

IV EUROPEAN UNION

1 Legal base

The provisions of Article 52 of the Treaty of Rome give unrestricted right to the residents of any member state to establish their business anywhere in the EU. Other stipulations, such as Article 67, commit the member countries to abolish all restrictions on the movement of capital which belongs to the residents of the EU. Article 68 requires that national rules governing the capital and money markets must be implemented in a non-discriminatory manner. According to Article 71, any new restrictions should be avoided. A safeguard clause is contained in Article 73. If movements of capital lead to disturbances in the capital market in any member country the Commission shall authorize that state to take protective measures. Articles 67–73 were operational till the end of 1993. As of 1 January 1994 they were replaced by new provisions (Articles 73a–73g) from the Maastricht Treaty. Article 73b prohibited all restrictions on the movement of capital both within the EU and between the member states and third countries. While 'endeavouring to achieve the objective of free movement of capital between Member States and third countries to the greatest extent possible...the Council may...adopt measures on the movement of capital to or from third countries involving direct investment'. Qualified majority is necessary for these 'measures'. If, however, these measures involve a step back in the EU law concerning the liberalization of the movement of capital from or to third countries, this Article requires unanimity in the Council. A safeguard clause is contained in Article 73f. If movements of capital to or from third countries cause or threaten to cause serious difficulties in the operation of economic and monetary union, the Council may apply protective measures against third countries for a period not exceeding six months. Monetary and payment sanctions against third countries are covered by Articles 73g and 228a, respectively. Article 92 prevents the member states from outbidding each other with subsidies. Furthermore, Article 109*i* allows a member country to take the necessary protective measures in the event of a sudden crisis in the balance-of-payments. The scope of the measures may only be that it needs to be strictly necessary to remedy these sudden difficulties. None the less, the Council has the authority to amend, suspend or abolish such national protective measures.

Coupled with the provisions on monetary union, free capital mobility established by the EU means that the national monetary independence of the member countries was lost to a considerable degree. For example, if all things are equal, an increase in a member country's interest rate relative to those in the outside world, meant to cool the economy and curb inflation, would, in fact, expand the domestic quantity of money. Many TNCs would invest funds in that country in order to profit from higher rates of interest. In a reverse case, when a country lowers its rates of interest with the intention of stimulating economic activity with cheap loans, that would, in fact, contract the available funds, as TNCs would move financial resources to countries with higher rates of interest (Panić, 1991, p. 212).

2 Issues

The establishment of the EU, as mark 1 in the integration process, and its relative dynamism provoked an expansion of TNCs from the US, which invested in this region during the 1960s and 1970s. The implementation of the 1992 Programme, as mark 2 in the integration process, and the completion of the internal market was likely to increase investment by the Japanese TNCs in the EU. However, the actual involvement also depended, in part, on the evolution of the tariffs and NTBs in the EU.

While mark 1 in the integration process eliminated (among other things) tariffs on internal trade, the objective of mark 2 was an elimination of NTBs on internal trade. That was supposed to increase the efficiency of production (rationalized investments), reduce transaction costs, increase competition and demand, and also harmonize standards. That required certain adjustments of internal production in the EU. The rationale for the existence of 'tariff factories' was removed. Therefore, investment in production that avoided internal EU barriers was significantly reduced or eliminated altogether. In any case, mark 2 was expected to increase the operation, cooperative agreements, strategic alliances and investment of TNCs that originate from the EU. An additional effect would be investment creation. In the longer term, they would look like those in America that take full advantage of economies of scale.

There was an initial fear by foreign TNCs that the EU may create 'Fortress Europe' and protect its home market with the 1992 Programme. Some of them rushed to establish themselves in the EU before this potential 'discrimination' took place. Target enterprises in the EU were thus overvalued to the extent that other locations, most notably in the US, became more attractive. In spite of that, the EU continued to be an interesting location for FDI, so foreign TNCs also sought to enter into strategic alliances with the EU firms.

Horizontally integrated TNCs such as 3M responded to integration in the EU by specialization of production in their plants. 'Post it' notes are made in its British plant, while scotch tape is produced in its German unit. Previously, 3M produced a wide range of goods in each country in order to predominantly serve the local market. Vertically integrated TNCs such as Ford responded to the new opportunities by vertical specialization. Differentials and gear boxes are produced in France, while engines are made in Spain. In addition, there emerged a special kind of relation among the competing firms. A removal of NTBs on internal trade and liberalization of public procurement 'forced' inter-firm specialization in similar goods. For example, ICI (Britain) specialized in marine, decorative and industrial paints, while BASF (Germany) did the same in automobile paints (Dunning, 1994a, pp. 296–297).

3 Evolution

Unlike the Exxon-Florio amendment (1988) in the US that gave the President the right to block mergers, acquisitions or takeover of domestic firms by foreign TNCs when such action is supposed to jeopardize national security, the EU does not have a common policy regarding FDI. Only Article 52 of the Treaty of Rome gives the right of establishment to businesses throughout the EU for the nationals of any member state. Japan is also without many formal barriers to inward FDI. None the less, the real obstacles to FDI in Japan are not found in the legal sphere. They exist in the cost 'doing business in Japan', such as close and strong informal links among businesses, tight labour markets, language barriers and difficulties in obtaining the necessary data.

The impact of the creation of the EU on the attraction of FDI from the US was at the centre of early studies of the relation between integration (or, as it was then called, 'tariff discrimination' introduced by the EU and EFTA) and FDI. The expectation was that the allocation of FDI would be influenced by integration. In particular that the establishment of the EU would lure TNCs to locate in this region. Scaperlanda (1967, p. 26) found, in the examination of the American FDI trend in Europe between 1951 and 1964, that the formation of the EU has not attracted a large share of the American FDI. Since 1958, the value of FDI from the US in the EU was $3.5 billion, while in non-EU Europe, it was $4.0 billion. Factors such as familiarity with the country in which the investment is to be located, differences in the application of technology and the financial liquidity to fund foreign investment, outweighed the influence of the creation of the EU on the pattern of FDI. In addition the American TNCs were more interested in the French market than the one of the EU(6).

Instead of calculating the trend in FDI for the whole period 1951–1964, merging both 'before' and 'after' the EU effects (as did Scaperlanda) and masking investment shifts, rather than revealing them, Wallis (1968) broke the period of analysis into two sub-periods. The share of American FDI in the EU moved along a continuous and increasing path in the period 1951–1964 with a kink in 1958. Before 1958, the EU share increased by 0.73 per cent a year, while after 1958, the average annual increase was 2.70 per cent.

D'Arge (1969, 1971a, 1971b) tried to determine the impact of European integration on American FDI in the EU and EFTA. The effect of the formation of a trading bloc on FDI may be along the following three lines:

- it may be a one-time (intercept) shift in trend,
- a gradual increase in trend (slope shift), or
- a combination of the other two.

The data showed that in the case of the EFTA, there was a positive intercept shift (a one-time effect), while in the period following the creation of the EU, there was a combination of shifts in both slope and intercept. Scaperlanda and Reiling (1971) suggested that European integration has not crucially influenced and changed American FDI flows in this region. This was based on a similarity of trends in FDI between the EU and EFTA after 1959, although there was a presumption that the EU would have a greater effect than EFTA. None the less, one thing has to be kept in mind here. At that time, Britain was the country that received the largest share of American FDI. It was also a member of EFTA (not the EU). Therefore, the early studies of the impact of integration on FDI do not show a clear picture regarding the relation between the two variables. A clarification of the situation, however, came latter on. Evidence was found that in the case of American FDI in the EU, size and growth of market played an important role (Goldberg, 1972, p. 692; Scaperlanda and Balough, 1983, p. 389).

Econometric modelling of FDI is a formidable task. The results of various models depend much on the assumptions, so that the conclusions may be only tentative. Nevertheless, there is general support for the hypothesis that tariff discrimination or integration influence FDI. But this cannot be translated into a statement that an x per cent change in tariffs will induce a y per cent change in FDI. Therefore, strong policy recommendations on the basis of such models are reckless (Lunn, 1980, p. 99).

Recent studies report that the net effect of international economic integration has been to increase both internal EU and non-EU investment in the Union. The elimination of import duties on internal EU trade encouraged non-EU investors to locate in the Union (Dunning and Robson, 1987, p. 113). An elimination of NTBs (1992 Programme) prompted both EU and non-EU TNCs to invest in the Union.[23]

The 1992 Programme prompted TNCs to rationalize their operations in the EU. The absence of any reference to TNCs from the official reports generated by the Single European Act such as Emerson *et al.* (1988) and the Cecchini Report (1988) comes as a surprising omission. The assumption in those reports seems to be that international specialization and trade is carried out by firms whose operational facilities are confined to a single country. Growth and predominance of TNCs in most areas of economic activity make this kind of analysis inappropriate (Panić, 1991, 204).

Britain has always been a relatively attractive location for TNCs although its economic performance relative to other major countries has mostly been poor. What was the reason for that interest? Regional incentives were no more generous than in the rest of the EU.[24] The English language was often mentioned as one of the reasons for that interest, although large TNCs were always able to afford to transcend the language barrier. Location in Britain was supposed to serve as a springboard to the rest of the EU, but so could be locations in other member countries. Where Britain, however, scores high, is that it has a labour force that is relatively low paid (compared to other major countries in the EU), it has a good industrial infrastructure, and social and political stability.

The Japanese TNCs were quite inclined to invest in Britain. However, they preferred to build new factories in rural areas, rather than take over the existing plants. They also preferred takeovers to joint ventures. The advantages of the 'greenfield' entry was that previous managerial habits and labour relations were not inherited (Sharp and Shepherd, 1987, p. 60). In fact, where the Japanese TNCs had a clear comparative advantage they preferred greenfield starts, while where their comparative advantage was weaker, they were involved in alliances and joint ventures.

4 Flow of foreign direct investment[25]

Table 9.3 summarizes intra-EU(12) FDI flows during the period 1984–1993. Panel A presents annual outflows of FDI in the individual member countries, while panel B gives data on the FDI that were received by other EU-partner countries. The first striking feature of Table 9.3 is the discrepancy between the data in the two panels. In 1992, the difference between the total outflows in panel A and inflows in panel B was over ECU 15 billion. That was a half of the recorded inflow in panel B!

There are many causes of this asymmetry. These range from different definitions of FDI to the variety of collection systems and methods. The major cause of this

Table 9.3 Geographical breakdown of intra-EU(12) flows of FDI, 1984–1993 (ECUs millions)

	1984	1985	1986	1987	1988	1989	1990	1991	1992	1993
					A Outflows					
Belgium/										
Luxembourg	−1,063	−499	−957	−1,179	−3,806	−5,363	−7,996	−4,390	−7,174	−5,642
Denmark	−8	6	−72	177	−136	−499	−155	−252	−590	−103
Germany	−632	−617	−589	−438	−1,372	−4,907	−7,576	−7,433	−7,665	−3,957
Greece	−15	−114	−136	−102	−86	−242	−229	−330	−381	−300
Spain	−573	−597	−1,170	−1,523	−1,892	−3,397	−4,880	−5,338	−5,035	−3,775
France	−1,215	−1,236	−1,434	−1,346	−4,426	−3,949	−4,262	−3,597	−6,753	−3,782
Ireland	−141	−279	−61	−160	−300	−1,087	−2,233	−4,105	−1,789	−1,804
Italy	−970	−488	−1,105	−769	−1,276	−2,341	−2,196	−1,740	−3,103	−2,276
Netherlands	2,803	−698	−2,799	−1,291	−3,789	−4,555	−5,102	−2,588	−8,532	−5,958
Portugal	−82	−186	−114	−190	−314	−734	−888	−974	−1,192	−503
United										
Kingdom	−1,886	−1,629	−2,847	−5,243	−2,595	−7,703	−10,054	−7,426	−3,753	−6,257
Intra-EUR12	−278	133	−36	−252	−228	−958	572	697	−14	7
not allocated										
EUR12	−4,059	−6,204	−11,319	−12,316	−20,219	−35,736	−44,998	−37,477	−45,981	−34,350
					B Inflows					
Belgium/										
Luxembourg	878	368	379	1,460	2,163	1,970	2,481	3,958	4,984	3,323
Denmark	110	105	186	177	290	542	438	949	671	129
Germany	657	1,234	2,033	1,534	2,119	4,771	8,089	8,681	7,303	8,949
Greece	9	6	2	1	4	−2	14	−4	10	3
Spain	16	32	67	167	235	604	551	469	287	362
France	713	627	933	3,211	5,031	9,232	8,479	7,143	7,293	3,401
Ireland	26	37	55	65	258	448	548	561	345	353
Italy	491	218	583	661	1,162	924	1,687	1,501	3,266	1,988
Netherlands	318	539	2,784	1,453	6,757	5,518	7,083	6,141	2,955	2,018
Portugal	5	14	2	4	26	41	63	227	368	222
United	1,108	2,425	2,503	3,421	6,151	8,522	3,953	2,791	3,266	6,583
Kingdom										
Intra-EUR12										
not allocated	36	88	52	217	217	664	207	−87	18	7
EUR12	4,366	5,694	9,579	12,371	24,414	33,234	33,592	32,332	30,765	27,338

Source: European Union Direct Investment 1984–93, Luxembourg: Eurostat, 1995

disequilibria is thought to be the inclusion or exclusion of reinvested profits in FDI statistics. Only Britain, France, Germany, Italy, the Netherlands and Portugal produce statistics on reinvested earnings. Another source of this asymmetry is the recording of short-term loans. Certain countries may register some of them as FDI, while others do not. Yet another source of variance includes borrowing on the local market. These investments do not appear in balance-of-payments data, while if the country uses company surveys for the collection of data on FDI, these loans may be recorded there. Other causes of difference include factors such as exchange rates, date of recording and accounting for authorized and actual investment. Therefore, the EUROSTAT suggests the use of average FDI data for analysis and practical purposes. These data are given in Table 9.4.

The preferred locations for internal-EU(12) FDI were, according to Table 9.4, Germany, France, Britain, Benelux[26] and Spain (Panel B).[27] Apart from Spain, those countries were at the same time the major internal investors in the EU. Annual internal FDI flows in the EU were at relatively low levels in the mid-1980s. Those flows, however, quadrupled from ECU 10.4 billion in 1986 to ECU 39.3 billion in 1990. Since then, annual flows had ups and downs, but the important observation is

Table 9.4 Average intra-EU(12) flows of FDI, 1984–1993 (ECUs millions)

	1984	1985	1986	1987	1988	1989	1990	1991	1992	1993
A Outflows										
Belgium/ Luxembourg	−635	−299	−691	−1,655	−1,754	−3,322	−3,077	−4,220	−6,607	−2,698
Denmark	−122	−164	−257	−278	−362	−1,081	−649	−886	−845	15
Germany	−1,168	−1,318	−2,587	−1,610	−2,762	−5,811	−9,577	−10,018	−8,243	−8,869
Greece	−9	−6	−2	−1	−5	1	−16	5	−10	−3
Spain	NA	NA	−118	−270	−355	−759	−1,023	−1,116	−259	−836
France	−827	−593	−1,368	−3,639	−5,945	−9,718	−11,409	−7,963	−9,458	−4,575
Ireland	−25	−37	−55	−65	−255	−408	−548	−561	−345	−353
Italy	−642	−761	−1,144	−998	−1,709	−1,528	−3,250	−1,317	−3,022	−3,316
Netherlands	−1,262	−955	−2,483	−1,998	−3,797	−5,410	−6,459	−6,386	−4,545	−4,118
Portugal	−3	−8	2	8	−46	−48	−83	−275	−415	−151
United Kingdom	554	−1,701	−1,723	−1,730	−5,221	−6,071	−3,100	−2,211	−4,616	−5,935
EUR12	−4,213	−5,949	−10,449	−12,344	−22,317	−34,485	−39,295	−34,904	−38,373	−30,844
B Inflows										
Belgium/ Luxembourg	749	655	743	1,265	3,417	5,006	6,454	5,068	7,094	5,749
Denmark	−8	−7	35	−127	70	422	269	398	582	308
Germany	694	580	926	250	1,317	3,952	4,235	4,566	4,386	2,181
Greece	15	111	136	102	86	248	229	294	381	300
Spain	NA	NA	1,741	1,976	2,844	4,239	6,062	5,736	4,660	4,028
France	1,316	1,245	1,431	1,654	4,348	5,262	4,009	4,133	7,387	5,652
Ireland	141	280	62	160	301	1,069	2,233	4,105	1,789	1,804
Italy	867	935	769	1,310	2,020	2,015	2,085	1,230	2,262	2,266
Netherlands	−1,098	520	1,881	1,315	3,151	3,817	4,542	2,015	5,512	4,977
Portugal	99	202	150	230	424	895	1,135	1,192	1,154	758
United Kingdom	559	609	2,560	4,085	4,228	7,081	8,327	6,517	3,159	2,825
EUR12	4,213	5,949	10,449	12,344	22,317	34,485	39,295	34,904	38,373	30,844

Source: European Union Direct Investment 1984–93, Luxembourg: Eurostat, 1995

that they have always been (well) above ECU 30 billion. For the 'core' countries of the EU the acceleration in the FDI trend (1986–1990) coincided with the implementation of the 1992 Programme. Firms wanted to consolidate their competitive position prior to full implementation of the Programme. Internal flows of FDI in the EU, therefore, point to agglomeration tendencies.

Before mark 2 in the integration process, the endogenous EU firms had, in general, primarily a national orientation, while foreign-owned TNCs (mainly American) had a pan-European business perspective. The removal of NTBs that came with the 1992 Programme aimed at addressing this disequilibria in the European-business operation. It had an obvious and positive impact on internal FDI flows from 1989. The EU internal FDI flows became more important than outflows from the EU to third countries. Another interesting observation is that the southern countries such as Greece and Portugal were largely left out of the EU-internal flows of FDI.

EU member countries were investing not only within the group, but also outside it. At the same time, the EU was an attractive location for foreign investors too. Data on extra-EU(12) FDI flows are given in Table 9.5. Apart from 1990 and 1992, the EU was a net exporter of FDI. None the less, foreign investors have increased their interest in the EU. That was due to the 1992 Programme. However, Thomsen and Nicolaides (1991, p. 103) argued that the 1992 Programme had not influenced the *quantity* of FDI in that period in the EU, but rather its *timing*.

If Table 9.5 is compared with Table 9.4, intra-EU FDI flows became more important for the EU than external ones from 1989. From that year EU investors started to invest more within the EU than outside it. Before that, economic integra-

Table 9.5 Extra-EU(12) flows of FDI, 1984–1993 (ECUs millions)

	1984	1985	1986	1987	1988	1989	1990	1991	1992	1993
					A Outflows					
United States	−11,537	−10,061	−17,772	−23,885	−22,120	−24,053	−7,155	−9,232	−6,523	−10,167
Japan	−294	−34	−104	12	−247	−682	−911	−341	−432	1,168
EFTA	−952	−722	163	−1,789	−2,593	−1,992	−3,226	−2,471	−2,729	−4,028
OPEC	153	−104	−565	−56	−343	−1,801	74	−1,502	−550	−1,060
ACP	−19	−120	−66	−155	−269	−322	−211	−650	−743	191
EX-COMECON	−1	−6	−12	−9	−74	−113	−244	−1,304	NA	NA
Extra-EUR12	−17,407	−15,105	−21,932	−30,670	−31,680	−33,282	−20,527	−26,732	−17,764	−21,854
					B Inflows from					
United States	2,951	1,788	2,660	2,337	2,551	9,846	9,178	5,411	11,619	9,044
Japan	390	719	465	1,572	2,584	4,354	5,406	1,682	1,816	1,662
EFTA	1,663	1,838	3,258	3,833	8,509	8,351	11,284	6,883	4,036	3,634
OPEC	149	421	−543	−119	912	110	306	453	664	440
ACP	155	61	40	104	15	52	−14	164	171	150
EX-COMECON	75	18	15	16	18	83	274	201	NA	NA
Extra-EUR12	6,152	5,711	7,119	12,991	18,141	27,943	32,753	20,933	22,551	21,029

Source: European Union Direct Investment 1984–93, Luxembourg: Eurostat, 1995

tion was only one factor that influenced FDI flows from the EU countries within and out of the EU. Other factors, such as exchange rates, especially of the US dollar, might have played a more prominent role. While the liberalization of internal EU trade had a strong impact on trade integration, FDI flows point out that until 1989 integration was stronger on the global plane than on the regional one.

The US and EFTA countries have always been both the major targets for FDI from the EU and, at the same time, the major sources of FDI coming into the EU. The US share of total foreign FDI in the EU was 33 per cent during the period 1984–1993. The EFTA countries' fraction was 31 per cent and the one of Japan was 11 per cent during the same period.[28] Total services received 63 per cent of all FDI inflows (the largest part went to finance and banking), while the EU manufacturing sector was the target for 31 per cent of the flows during 1984–1993 period.

The US was the preferred location for outward FDI from the EU. This country received 58 per cent of all EU outgoing FDI flows during the period 1984–1993. The share of the EFTA was 8 per cent, while that of Japan was 1 per cent in the same period. An interesting feature is the fact that EU investors withdrew ECU 1.2 billion from Japan in 1993. Outgoing FDI from the EU were distributed 'more equally' among the economic sectors in the target countries, as both services and manufacturing got 40 per cent of FDI, respectively. Such large global inter-penetration of FDI reduces the chances that regional arrangements may turn into closed blocs. A 'hostage population' of TNCs may reduce the fear of retaliatory measures. Extensive FDI links between the US and the EU assisted in the relaxation of potential conflict between the two partners regarding market access. The same is not yet true with Japan. There is hope that Japan will mature as a foreign investor in the future and that potential conflicts with that country will be defused. A drive towards a reciprocal treatment of FDI with Japan (or any other country) may not be highly productive. It is generally accepted that TNCs bring benefits that more than compensate for the possible costs. The EU is, after all, the major source of FDI so the demand for a reciprocal treatment may be counter-productive. The principle of reciprocity in FDI often means the aligning of regulations upwards (reciprocal treatment in trade is often different, as it levels down trade provisions).

Major EU investors in the non-EU countries were Britain, Germany, France and the Netherlands during the period 1984–1993 (Table 9.6). Those were, at the same time, the major destination countries for the extra-EU FDI. In addition to those countries, external investors were also interested in the Benelux countries and Spain. The experience of Spain is valuable for other EU-rim countries. The country improved its infrastructure, it has an unimpeded access to the EU market and has a relatively abundant qualified and cheap (according to the EU standards) labour force. As such, it provided an attractive springboard for those external TNCs interested in operating on a pan-EU market. A pronounced interest in Spain by external investors points to a relative spread of external FDI in the EU.

The EU countries started slowly to invest in the transition countries of central and eastern Europe. This is the only region in the world where international business has not yet expanded on a large scale. Therefore, some TNCs may wish to locate part of their activities in that region instead of certain other areas of the EU. Southern member countries of the EU may feel neglected because of outgoing FDI into the transition region, no matter how small these flows are. Such fears are, however,

Table 9.6 Contribution of EU(12) member countries to external FDI flows, 1984–1993 (ECUs millions)

	1984	1985	1986	1987	1988	1989	1990	1991	1992	1993
					A Outflows from					
Belgium/ Luxembourg	60	52	−605	−545	−1,839	−1,145	−1,175	−370	−511	−1,469
Denmark	−222	−147	−390	−219	−297	−397	−415	−835	−710	−1,234
Germany	−2,978	−4,020	−5,364	−5,266	−5,961	−4,515	−5,369	−4,884	−5,157	−4,440
Greece	−48	−190	−63	−9	−8	1	−3	2	−20	−4
Spain	NA	NA	−241	−227	−552	−415	−733	−1,116	−731	−796
France	−1,747	−2,379	−3,531	−3,483	−3,958	−6,205	−6,864	−7,801	−2,898	−4,644
Ireland	−100	−108	−40	−86	−598	−835	−22	−997	−524	32
Italy	−1,512	−598	−865	−495	−1,144	242	−1,031	−4,362	−1,597	−1,530
Netherlands	−1,011	−2,373	−1,029	−3,607	−2,612	−5,182	−4,497	−3,179	−4,645	−3,155
Portugal	−11	−17	−5	−6	−2	−15	−26	−60	−67	−3
United Kingdom	−9,627	−5,105	−9,799	−16,728	−14,710	−14,819	−392	−3,130	−903	−4,609
EUR12	−17,407	−15,105	−21,932	−30,670	−31,680	−33,282	−20,527	−26,732	−17,764	−21,854
					B Inflows to					
Belgium/ Luxembourg	64	507	151	693	1,282	1,868	1,355	1,774	1,727	3,343
Denmark	32	159	156	151	422	640	567	637	210	911
Germany	115	295	246	215	−383	1,670	2,187	440	735	1,410
Greece	−27	134	207	87	63	90	79	75	76	60
Spain	NA	NA	1,076	1,338	1,799	2,127	2,956	2,139	2,081	1,846
France	1,387	1,677	1,386	2,056	1,813	2,100	3,365	4,287	4,287	2,929
Ireland	−30	330	1	327	174	399	964	1,353	77	1,291
Italy	927	30	−456	1,745	3,063	291	3,020	1,288	1,022	1,410
Netherlands	139	507	938	664	947	2,704	3,013	2,807	2,762	809
Portugal	135	122	47	97	211	365	586	520	370	284
United Kingdom	1,996	623	3,366	5,619	8,748	15,690	14,661	5,612	9,204	7,260
EUR12	6,152	5,711	7,119	12,991	18,141	27,943	32,753	20,933	22,551	21,090

Source: European Union Direct Investment 1984–93, Luxembourg: Eurostat, 1995

exaggerated. The southern part of the EU should not worry, at least not in the medium term. Most transition countries still have such distortions that it will take them a long time to restructure. The alleged general 'exodus' of FDI and EU jobs is not well founded, although some EU industries may have certain adjustment pressures. If relatively low wages are a decisive factor for FDI in transition countries, the EU would have already been flooded with cheap goods from those countries. Factors other than wages influence the competitiveness of firms. These include productivity and capital stock. Therefore, southern EU member countries are still ahead of most of the transition countries in these matters. In addition, the Mediterranean region of the EU still has other advantages over the transition countries. Southern EU countries have direct access to the growing single EU market with more than 370 million consumers whose wealth is growing. They also have hard currencies, liberal treatment of TNCs and unrestricted capital mobility. Those are features that most transition countries still lack.

Another advantage of the EU Mediterranean region can be found in economies of scale. This part of the EU is characterized by a lot of SMEs. Those firms have a chance to grow efficiently in the single market of the EU and benefit from economies of scale. Large European firms have already enjoyed considerable advantage from economies of scale. Hence, SMEs, and countries in which they prevail, have long-term potential for greater gains from the 1992 Programme.

The newly industrialized countries may also wish to invest in the EU in order to be present in a growing and affluent market, as well as to have access to new technology. As for the TNCs from transition countries located in the EU, they can be expected to be active in trade-supporting services. Apart from that, most of these TNCs are not expected to have either technological or managerial or financial capacity to enter the EU on a large scale in any other way in the near future.

V CONCLUSION

A popular perception, based on shoddy economics, is that the export of goods is beneficial for the country and, therefore, needs to be supported, while the import of (certain) goods is perceived to be dangerous as it may jeopardize the national output and employment potential.[29] FDI is, however, treated in a different way. Outflows are deterred as there is a fear that exporting capital means exporting exports, causing an outflow of jobs, while inflows are to be welcomed! Capital mobility has its costs and benefits. If they are desirable, they should be stimulated, otherwise they should be taxed and/or controlled. Simultaneous inflows and outflows of FDI in integrated countries is possible and quite likely. This was confirmed in 1989 when intra-EU flows of FDI became more important than EU investment in third countries. FDI inflow may, however, be significant even without formal integration. Just look at the trans-Atlantic FDI flows. TNCs primarily follow the opportunities for making profits in large and growing markets in the long term. Therefore, economic integration is *a*, rather than *the* cause of FDI.

The loss of the international competitive position of the EU in relation to the US, Japan and the newly industrialized countries (in several lines of production) in the 1970s and 1980s, has increased both interest in and the need for the strengthening of the competitiveness of TNCs that come from the EU. These TNCs are the key actors for the improvement of the international competitiveness of the EU. Ambitious public research programmes in the EU, whose funds well exceed similar ones in the US and Japan, can help the EU first to catch up and later to improve its position *vis-à-vis* its major international competitors.

American FDI in the EU were market seeking in the 1950s and 1960s. The same was the case with Japanese FDI in the 1970s and 1980s. As the EU consumers were not able to purchase what they wanted because of NTBs, Japanese TNCs invested in the EU in order to satisfy existing and growing local demand. TNCs from both source countries have always been looking at the EU market as a single unit. Their advantages over the local EU enterprises included in certain cases not only a superior capability to innovate products and technologies, manage multi-plant production and supply, but also a willingness, experience and ability to serve consumers from close proximity, rather than through exports, that was often favourite method of operation of many national firms in the EU. There is, however, at least one difference between the Japanese and American FDI in the EU. A half of Japanese FDI was concentrated in banking and insurance in the early 1990s. At the same time, more than a half of the American FDI was in the manufacturing industry. Therefore, the

Japanese FDI has relatively little impact, at present, on the EU manufacturing industry, while the same is not true for the American TNCs (Buigues and Jacquemin, 1992, p. 22). Such focus of the Japanese investors may come as a surprise as this country has advantages in electronics and vehicles. A concentration of Japanese FDI in financial services (rely on human, rather than physical capital) both in the EU and the US is, however, a partial reflection of Japanese balance-of-payments surpluses and appreciation of the yen.[30]

In order to avoid a weakening of the competitive position of EU firms in global markets, the EU may follow two courses, although there may be a strong appeal to employ a mix of the two. First, the EU may increase protection of domestic firms against foreign TNCs through measures such as rules of origin, local content requirements and other TRIMs. Second, the EU may open its domestic market and welcome foreign, in particular, Japanese TNCs to settle their operations in the EU. As widely argued, EU firms in a sizeable part of its manufacturing industry are less efficient than their counterparts in the US and Japan. Suppose that the EU adopts a liberal economic policy. If EU firms adjust and withstand competition from foreign TNCs, they may in relative terms gain more from market liberalization than their foreign competitors.

The incomplete internal market in the EU was the major cause of a sub-optimal production structure in the region. All economic agents, including TNCs, behave as welfare maximizing units in the long term, subject to given conditions. These private agents should not be criticized for their actions, which may not conform with public objectives. The completion of the internal market in the EU, which included a removal of NTBs, assisted in the rationalization of production and enhanced location-specific advantages of the EU. This would continue to increase both the size and growth of the EU market, which may, in turn, further increase investment expenditure in the region.

As one of the major players in the international capital mobility scene, the EU would like to see multilateral rules for FDI. Those rules would include the right of foreigners to invest and operate competitively in all sectors of the economy; only few exceptions from the general rule should be allowed; there should be no discrimination of foreign investors based on their origin; a 'standstill' commitment would prevent the introduction of new restrictions; and there should be a 'roll-back' principle to gradually eliminate national (or group) measures that run counter to the liberalization of FDI rules.

NOTES

1 Any firm that owns or controls assets in more than one country may be called a transnational corporation. It is a wider concept than FDI since it includes non-equity business participation in another country. As for the amount of FDI, the total world outward stock (the production potential) was an estimated $2.6 trillion in 1995, while the worldwide outflows of FDI in 1995 reached $230 billion. The distribution of the stock of FDI is asymmetrical. Around three-quarters of FDI stock is located in developed countries, while two-thirds of FDI stock in the developing countries is concentrated in ten countries (UNCTAD, 1995a). The sectoral distribution of FDI reveals that the industries that are absorbing the largest slices of FDI are those dominated by high technology and highly qualified personnel. The reasons for such a distribution may be found in the excessive transaction costs of arm's-length contacts through the market, thus internalization of those links within a firm seems to be a more effective business choice.

2 Trade is relatively more concentrated within regions than FDI. This suggests that trade plays a more prominent role in intra-regional integration arrangements, while FDI has a greater influence on global integration (UNCTAD, 1993, p. 7).

3 The pace of international trade liberalization since the 1960s as well as the extension of the GATT into new areas, such as services and agriculture, might have been much slower in the absence of the challenge posed by progress of EU integration. The debate should not be between regionalism and multilateralism, but rather between liberalism and interventionism (Blackhurst and Henderson, 1993, p. 412).

4 See the chapters on industrial policy (6) and competition (5).

5 Other examples of goods with similar and significant economies of scale and sunk costs to which the same example applies include submarines, spaceships, telecommunication equipment, satellites, radars, missiles, precision instruments, earth-moving equipment, high-speed trains, large boilers, turbines and very fast computers.

6 The role of government as an organizing force in a market economy is increasingly being re-examined. Although there is a desire to reduce it intervention, the fact is that those countries in which the government has exerted a strong and positive influence have had the most impressive economic performances over the past two decades (Dunning, 1994a, p. 1).

7 According to an influential view, no matter what a government does in order to influence competitiveness and increase exports in the short run, would cause an adjustment of the exchange rate and factor prices in the long run (Johnson and Krauss, 1973, p. 240). The new theory disputed such an approach and argued that in the presence of increasing returns to scale, externalities and the economies of learning, the policy of the government does matter. Such a policy may introduce, if handled properly, irreversible advantages for the country in question.

8 In order to intervene/subsidize in an intelligent way, the government needs a lot of information which is quite costly to obtain. This includes not only information about technology and demand, but also the reactions of other governments and TNCs. If successful, strategic policy is a magnificent one. In practice, a subsidy in one country may provoke retaliation in another in the form of a subsidy or a countervailing duty. The retaliation and counter-retaliation chain makes everyone worse off. Integration may offer certain advantages to developing countries in a situation like that. It may inspire these countries to negotiate the distribution of strategic industries within the area or attract TNCs in order to maximize positive externalities and reduce unnecessary subsidies. The basic argument for intervention may be that without intervention in an area and owing to imperfections, there may be *under-investment* in a strategic industry. If, however, intervention is inept, *over-investment* may be the consequence.

9 For example, trade within the EU is to a large extent of an intra-industry character. It is much more driven by economies of scale, than by the 'classic' comparative advantages of these countries.

10 If pushed to the limit, a national reaction to a monopoly in a foreign country is the creation of a national monopoly. That is fighting fire with fire (Curzon Price, 1993, p. 394)!

11 Dunning (1993) and Pitelis and Sugden (1991) provide a survey of the opinions on the nature of a TNC.

12 For example, governments may change over time the availability, quality and cost of the domestic factors. The disposable tools for this policy include the training of labour and the education of management, R&D, science, transport and communication infrastructure, and tax policies.

13 The transfer of profits out of the country takes place when TNCs do not find the country in question a promising location for the reinvestment of earnings. Such a transfer may send a warning signal to the government that something is wrong in the economy and that something needs to be done about it.

14 Intra-company pricing refers to transactions among related units of the same firm. Not every manipulation of transfer prices increases the overall profits of the entire company, as these extra revenues stem from sales to outside customers (Plasschaert, 1994, p.1).

15 Trade in services is expanding. Monitoring internal prices for services is a much more complex task than inspecting the same prices for goods by the employment of free market criteria.

16 Firms are reluctant to comment and release data on their internal prices. Hence, this is very much a grey area for research.

17 Tax avoidance is a means that does not break any laws, as this practice may be possible according to positive regulations. Tax evasion is different, as it violates laws. In practice, the difference between the two practices is often ambiguous.

18 TNCs that come from the US and operate in the EU reported annual R&D of almost $2,500 per employee in 1989. In contrast, Euroaffiliates of the Japanese TNCs reported R&D per employee of around $725 in the same year (Gittelman et al., 1992, p. 18). The reasons for such behaviour by Japanese TNCs include a relatively strong headquarters effect as the Japanese FDI in Europe is a relatively novel feature compared with FDI from the US that has been present in the region on a larger scale since the 1950s. In addition, Japanese TNCs may be more involved in the EU in relatively mature manufacturing industries and services where R&D expenditure is not as high as in other activities.

19 In a situation where TNCs do not dominate in the economy of a country or an integrated group of countries, then, of course, their impact may be marginal. The situation, however, in virtually all present-day regional groupings of developing countries is that TNCs play a dominant role (Robson, 1987, p. 209).

20 An educated management and trained labour force (domestic human capital) is what matters for the country, rather than ownership of the business (Reich, 1990). Tyson (1991) disagreed with such a view and argued that ownership still mattered. This position, however, opposes the traditional US stance that favours free trade and the flow of capital.

21 The creation of tariff factories within an integrated area is a strategy that TNCs pursue not in order to take advantage of their efficiency or to employ a foreign resource (resource efficiency), but rather to benefit from (or avoid) the shield provided by the common external tariff and NTBs. That may be one of the reasons why Japanese TNCs were eager to establish their presence in the EU, prior to the full implementation of the 1992 Programme, and become EU residents in order to avoid the fear coming from the possible creation of 'Fortress Europe'.

22 For example, Pirelli (Italy) coordinates and guarantees its global financial duties from a Swiss affiliate which is in charge of finance for the whole corporation. The US affiliate of Siemens (Germany) transmitted daily financial data to headquarters that is in charge of global financial management (UNCTAD, 1993, p. 124).

23 The diversity of views expressed in the debate on the effect of European integration on FDI were surveyed by Yannopoulos (1990).

24 Government incentives influenced TNCs such as Ford to make new investments in the north-west of the country and Wales. Honda, Nissan and Toyota benefited from public grants as they settled in regions with unemployment problems. However, these allowances were equally available in Britain to other firms from the EU or third countries, whether they were from car production or other industries.

25 All data in this section are based on EUROSTAT (1995), *European Union Direct Investment 1984–93*, Luxembourg: Eurostat.

26 One has to be careful when interpreting the data for countries such as Luxembourg (or Switzerland). These countries often act only as intermediary locations for the inflow and outflow of funds.

27 There was an increased flow of FDI in EU-rim countries in 1991.

28 More than a half of all Japanese FDI is located in the US.

29 Through trade a country obtains useful things from abroad. Therefore imports are a gain, rather than a cost. To pay for imports, the country has to send its useful goods and services abroad. In these terms exports are a cost, rather than a gain!

30 A distinct feature of Japanese FDI in manufacturing is that Japanese TNCs tend to invest in countries that have a certain advantage in the target manufacturing industry. For instance, Japanese FDI in machinery and precision instruments went to Germany, FDI in the production of cars went to Britain, while FDI in glass, stone and clay products went to Belgium (Yamawaki, 1991, p. 232).

10

LABOUR MOBILITY

I INTRODUCTION

Mobility of labour or labour responsiveness to demand has been a significant facet of economic life for a long period of time. Labour has not only moved among regions, but also among economic sectors. In the late 1950s, agriculture employed around 20 per cent of the labour force in most industrialized economies. In the 1990s, agriculture employs less than 5 per cent of the labour force in these countries.

The theoretical assumption that labour has a greater degree of mobility within a country than among countries may not always be substantiated. Inter-country mobility of labour between Ireland and other developed English speaking countries was, perhaps, much greater than internal Irish labour mobility. None the less, labour mobility should not always be taken in its 'technical' meaning of pure movements of persons from place A to place B. One has to bear in mind that these are the people that move with their skills, knowledge, experiences and organizational competence.

Outside of common markets, international labour migration is characterized by a legal asymmetry. The Universal Declaration of Human Rights (1948), Article 13, denies the right to the country of origin to close its borders to *bona fide* emigrants. This country may not control the emigration flows according to its interest. The country of destination, however, has an undisputed right to restrict the entry of immigrants, although this is not explicitly mentioned in the Declaration. In these circumstances migration flows are determined by demand. So, the will to move is a necessary condition for labour migration, but it is not a sufficient one.

This chapter is structured as follows. Sections II and III consider the costs and benefits of labour migration for countries of origin and countries of destination, respectively. Section IV deals with labour mobility in the EU. The conclusion is that labour migration will be relatively high on the agenda over the coming decades because of unfavourable demographic trends in the EU and various push factors in the neighbouring regions.

II COUNTRY OF ORIGIN

If political instability and economic problems (push determinants) overcome the propensity to stay in the homeland (pull factors), then there are several reasons for international migration of labour. The most significant ones include the possibility of finding a job which may be able to provide improved living standards, as well as better conditions for specialization and promotion. In these complex conditions migrants act as utility maximizing units, subject to push and pull forces.

The migration of labour has its obstacles. They may be found both in receiving and in countries of origin. Socio-psychological obstacles to migration may include different languages, recognition of qualifications, climate, religion, customs, diet and clothing. Such barriers to migration were high in the nineteenth century for intra-European mobility of labour. That was one of the reasons why Europe was a source of significant emigration. In addition, socio-psychological obstacles may be one of the reasons why Japan has almost closed borders for legal immigration. Economic obstructions include the lack of information about job openings, conditions of work, social security, legal systems, systems of dismissal (last in, first out) and the loss of seniority. During recession and unemployment periods there may be nationalistic, racial and religious clashes between the local population and immigrants. Trade unions may lobby against immigration, as well as to drive immigrants away.

Countries of origin experience significant losses of manpower. Migrants are usually younger men who want to take the risk of moving. These regions may have the tendency of becoming feminine and senilized. Potential producers leave while consumers remain behind. The countries of origin lose a part of their national wealth which was invested in raising and educating their population. If the migrants are experienced and educated, then their positions may often be filled by less sophisticated staff. The result is lower productivity and lower national wealth.

The brain-drain argument is not convincing in all cases. Many of those who migrate cannot always find adequate jobs in their home countries. The physician who leaves Burkina Faso is one example. This country needs more medical services. A Mozambican astro-physicist is quite another. That country has few labs, telescopes and large computers, so it cannot utilize the qualifications of the expert. It makes sense for this skilled person to go abroad and possibly send some money to his country of origin. However, if computer programmers emigrate from Mozambique, there is no point in this country importing computers, and without the advent of new technology it will remain backward indefinitely! If the migrants return after a (long) period abroad, some of them may be old and/or ill, so they become consumers. This all may reduce the local tax base and increase the cost of social services to the remaining population.

Apart from these costs, countries of origin may obtain certain short-term gains from emigration. The movement of labour reduces the pressure caused by unemployment, and reduces the payment of unemployment benefits (if they exist). Possible remittances of hard currency may reduce the balance-of-payments pressure, and if migrants return they may bring back hard currency savings and new skills which may help them to obtain or create better jobs. This may help the development efforts of the country.

If some countries do not have exportable goods they have to export labour services (if other countries want to accept that) in order to pay for imports. However, there is an asymmetry in the perception of labour mobility. When the rich north wants to send workers abroad, then that counts as trade in services. When the poor south wants to do the same, it is regarded as immigration!

The volume of possible remittances depends on the number of migrants, the length of their stay and incentives. The shorter the stay of migrants abroad, the higher the probability that they will transfer or bring all their savings to their home countries. During short stays abroad, they intend to earn and save as much as possible. If they stay abroad for a longer period of time, then they may wish to enjoy a higher standard of living than during relatively short stays. They reduce the volume of funds which are potentially remitted to their countries of origin. If the country of origin offers incentives for the transfer of these movies in the way of attractive rates of interest, rate of exchange, allowances for imports and investment, and if there is overall stability, then there is a greater probability that such funds will be attracted.

III COUNTRY OF DESTINATION

The supply of local labour and the level of economic activity determine the demand for foreign labour in the country of destination. A country may permit an inflow of foreign labour, but this country must bear in mind that those are the people who come with all their virtues and vices. Foreign workers may face open and hidden clashes with the local population. The host country population may dislike foreigners because they take jobs from the domestic population,[1] they bring their customs, increase congestion, depress wages and because they send their savings abroad, to mention just a few reasons. In certain cases, such as the migration of retired persons from Scandinavia to Spain or from Canada to Florida, this should not be regarded as migration in response to wage differentials. These migrants do not work, they just spend and enjoy their life savings, creating a permanent demand for certain services and jobs for the locals.[2]

The country of destination has obvious benefits from immigration. The migrants are a very mobile segment of the labour force. Once they enter a country, they are not linked to any particular place. Mobility of the local labour in the EU is quite low.[3] This is often due to a number of factors: reluctance to leave relatives and friends; spouses who have jobs they do not want to give up; children who go to schools to which they are attached; and homes which are still under mortgage.

The mobility of migrant labour within the country of destination has an impact on the national equalization of wages. Every subsequent wave of immigration depresses the wages offered to earlier immigrants. Foreign labour that is legally employed need not necessarily be cheaper than local workers as there is legislation requiring the payment of fair wages to all. However, foreign labour is more easily controlled by management. Local labour may not have language barriers to moving within the home country.

In general, the country of destination may acquire labour which is cheaper and whose training has not been paid for by the domestic taxpayers. Migrants increase the demand for housing, goods, pay taxes (which may exceed what they receive in transfer payments and public services) and take jobs that are unattractive to the domestic labour at the rates offered. These are posts in the open air, in mines, foundries, construction, garbage collection, cleaning, hotels, restaurants and other monotonous jobs. The posts which are most threatened by migrants are the ones that are usually modestly paid. Migrants compete for these vacancies with the local youth and women who may have reduced opportunities for work. While offering lower wages for those jobs, the countries of destination may partially reduce the price of inputs (labour) and partially increase competitiveness, at least in the short run.

Migrant workers may not know the language of the host country, so these people may not be able to take part in the social life. The only place where they can demonstrate themselves as creative beings may be in production. These workers may sometimes work at a faster and better pace than the domestic ones. This may provoke clashes with the local workers as new production norms may be increased. Migrants may leave after a while, while the locals may be tied by these norms for a long time. Employers sometimes prefer to conclude direct agreements with migrant workers than to employ domestic labour. It is not only that the migrant workers are working for lower wages than the domestic labour in the absence of legal protection, but also that foreigners may be dismissed with less consequences for the employer. Alternatively, foreign workers' permits may not be renewed.

IV EUROPEAN UNION

It needs to be stated from the outset that the EU has no common policy regarding labour migration. Article 48 of the Treaty of Rome provides for the freedom of movement of workers within the EU. It also abolishes any discrimination among workers that are citizens of the member states.[4] In addition, Article 8a provides the citizens of the EU with an unrestricted right to move and reside within the territory of the EU. As for visas for non-EU nationals, Article 100c, authorizes the Council to take decisions on that issue.

Following the Second World War, migrations of people in Europe had four distinct phases. First came the period from 1945 to the early 1960s. People moved because of the adjustment to circumstances after the end of the war, as well as to the process of decolonization. For example, 12 million Germans were forced to leave central and eastern Europe. Most of them settled in Germany. Colonial powers such as Britain, Belgium, France and the Netherlands were affected by return migration from European colonies and the inflow of workers from former overseas territories. There were over a million French residents of Algeria that resettled in France during and after the Algerian war of independence. The second phase of the movement of people had an overlap with the preceding one. It lasted from 1955 to 1973. Labour shortages in certain countries created opportunities for migrant workers. Labour from Italy, Spain, Portugal, Greece, Turkey, former Yugoslavia, Morocco and Tunisia was migrating northwards, mainly to Germany and France. Around 5 million people moved northwards during this period. Then came the third period of restrained migration from 1973 to 1988. Following the first oil-price shock and the connected economic crises and social tensions, the recruitment of foreign labour was abruptly stopped. The policies that were encouraging return migration were not working. The foreign population in the EU was, however, increasing as family members were joining workers that were already in the EU. In addition, these residents had higher birth rates than the local population. The fourth phase started in 1988. It was linked with the dissolution of socialism, economic transition and ethnic wars. Hundreds of thousands of refugees and asylum seekers, as well as economic immigrants, moved to EU countries. Germany alone received 1.5 million new immigrants in 1992 (Zimmermann, 1995, pp. 46–47).

Conventional wisdom states that an abolition of barriers to international migration of labour will bring an increase in labour flows in relation to the previous situation.

This hypothesis can be tested in the case of the EU. The total number of intra-EU migrants of the original six member countries was around half a million prior to 1960 which increased to a little over 800,000 in 1968. This volume of migrant workers remained almost constant until the early 1980s, and since then it decreased to 650,000 migrants. All other intra-EU migrations were national (from southern to northern Italy or from western regions of France into Paris), rather than inter-state. The inevitable conclusion is that the creation of the EU has not significantly changed intra-EU labour migrations. While intra-EU trade has increased, intra-EU migrations have decreased. Trade and migration of labour were substitutes (Straubhaar, 1988).

The explanation for greater migrations of labour from non-EU countries than within the EU can be found, in part, in the differences in production functions and barriers to trade among countries. The more similar the structure and the level of development between countries and the lower the barriers to trade, the greater will be the substitution effect between trade and labour migration. This also explains the migration of labour from Italy just after the creation of the EU, as well as the subsequent reduction in this flow.

The decline in intra-EU labour mobility during the 1980s can also be explained by the significant improvements in the state of local economies. Labour migration from Italy has slowed down since 1967. The same has happened in Greece since the early 1970s. Similar tendencies can be observed with Spain and Portugal since the mid-1980s. In addition, traditional countries of emigration, such as Italy or Greece, themselves became targets for significant legal and illegal immigration. North Africans and Albanians were entering Italy in a clandestine way, while Greece was a destination for similar migration by the Albanians. A certain number of Bulgarians, Serbs, Poles and Russians entered Greece legally, but stayed there after their permits expired.[5]

An interesting feature is Italy's transition over the past three decades from a net exporter to a net importer of non-European, mainly Mediterranean, illegal labour. Illegal immigrants work in, and contribute to, a growth in the informal economy. Costs of labour are both lower and more flexible in the black economy. This encourages firms to shift resources from the legal economy to the informal one. However, the technology available is less efficient in the underground economy. Hence, such immigration makes possible a transfer of capital (and labour) towards the informal economy. This may be favourable for firms that avoid tax obligations, but it is damaging for the economy as a whole (Dell'Aringa and Neri, 1989, p. 134).

There is a special type of international mobility of labour which is often overlooked. Many TNCs mandate that their employees circulate and spend time in various affiliates in order to keep the corporation internationally and personally integrated. The staff often move at regular intervals. Although this is recorded in statistics as international mobility of labour, it occurs within the same firm.

Exact data on the flow of migrants are deficient. Therefore, Table 10.1 simply presents estimates of stock data of the population and migrants in the EU in 1993.[6] There were more than 5 million EU migrants and over 11 million non-EU immigrants in the EU in 1993. This volume of immigrants may prompt some to look at immigrants as the sixteenth nation of the EU. The migration of labour can be a significant feature even if countries are not formally integrated. More than two-

Table 10.1 Population and immigrants in the EU in 1993 (thousands)

Country	Total residents	Nationals	Total migrants	Migrants from EU	Migrants from non-EU
Austria	7,796	7,278	518	79	439
Belgium	10,068	9,159	909	542	367
Denmark	5,181	5,001	180	41	139
France	56,652	53,055	3,597	1,322	2,275
Finland	5,055	5,009	46	12	34
Germany	80,975	74,479	6,496	1,719	4,777
Greece	10,350	10,150	200	64	136
Ireland	3,563	3,473	90	—	—
Italy	56,960	56,037	923	160	763
Luxembourg	395	—	—	—	—
Netherlands	15,239	14,482	757	189	568
Portugal	9,865	9,743	122	33	89
Spain	39,048	38,655	393	181	212
Sweden	8,692	8,193	499	187	312
United Kingdom	57,222	55,202	2,020	770	1,250
EU	368,978	350,187	16,874	5,268	11,345

Source: Eurostat (1995)

thirds of migrants (a wider notion than migrant workers) in the EU up to the mid-1970s came from the non-member, mostly Mediterranean, countries. Despite all the enlargements of the EU, in 1993 more than two-thirds of all migrants in the EU still come from the non-member countries.[7] Apart from the non-EU migrants who have legal working permits, there are probably an estimated 10 per cent extra illegal immigrants.

The government is a significant employer in all EU countries. Therefore, many jobs may be closed to foreigners even if they are citizens of EU partner countries. This potential obstacle to employment has been removed by the EU Court of Justice ruling that only those positions which are linked with national security may be reserved for domestic labour. It would be absurd to argue that a person loses skills, experience and knowledge after crossing a border. In order to facilitate labour mobility, in particular of highly educated labour, the EU sets qualitative (content of training) and quantitative (years of study, number of course hours) criteria which diplomas must meet in order to be awarded and mutually recognized.

Recessions now rarely affect only one country. During the times of economic slow-downs the unemployed EU labour stayed in its country of origin. This was because the chance of finding employment abroad was smaller than at home. If there were some gaps between supply and demand in the labour market, labour migration from third countries closed them, rather than the internal EU flows. Reduced EU-internal labour migration was due to a trend which was levelling income and productivity rates among the original six member countries, as well as the growth in the other EU countries which created domestic demand for labour. Hence, the expectation that the creation of a common market would significantly increase long-term intra-group migrations of labour was refuted in the case of the EU.

The free movement of people is one of the cornerstones of the single market in the EU. It is also one of the visible symbols for people in the street that European integration works. Therefore, most of the EU countries signed an accord on the free circulation of people in a small Luxembourg village of Schengen in 1985 (the deal was revised in 1990). The core of the Schengen Agreement was to shift passport controls from internal frontiers to external EU borders, to set uniform visa policy, to increase cooperation among the national authorities that deal with the issues, as well as to coordinate asylum policies.[8] Once in, all the people may move freely in the Schengen countries. However, the non-EU nationals may work only in the country that gave them the visa.

After many delays the Agreement was put into effect in seven EU countries[9] in March 1995. The introduction of the deal, in practice, was coupled with many delays (for example, by the creation of the Schengen Information System, a common database for wanted people and stolen goods). Once put into effect, it faced certain difficulties. Confronted with a wave of Islamic terrorist attacks, France effectively pulled out of the main commitment of the deal in June 1995. The country introduced land-border controls because of the fear of terrorism.[10] This was also why Britain stayed out of the arrangement. No matter how genuine these fears of terrorism, drug smuggling and illegal immigration are, the truth is that, as a rule, terrorists and drug smugglers with their cargoes are not caught on borders, but rather inside the country after tip-offs to the authorities. Another setback to the spirit of Schengen came when Spain threatened to suspend the key provisions of the Agreement after a Belgian court failed to authorize the deportation of two suspected Basque terrorists to Spain in 1996. Perhaps the largest proportion of illegal immigrants enter EU countries legally with short-term visas. Once those visas expire, they go 'underground'. Other EU and non-EU countries (Iceland and Norway) are considering entering the Schengen Agreement. However, confidence in the Agreement has been seriously undermined.

V CONCLUSION

Major labour movements took place from the Mediterranean countries into the EU during the 1960s and early 1970s. The exception was Italy which has been in the EU since its establishment. Internal labour mobility in the EU has not played a significant role in European integration, in spite of relatively significant differences in average wages (and productivity) among countries. However, a new type of human mobility has emerged in the EU. It pertains to students and research staff supported by the EU.

The first generation of migrants is now ageing. The migration issue is no longer one of labour movements, but rather of integrating these people into the host countries. Almost half of the migrant population was born in the host countries. This generation is confronted with different cultures, and they are often in search of their identity. Their future depends on training and legal security regarding residence and employment rights in the receiving country. Certain EU countries, such as Britain, France, Ireland and Italy allow dual citizenship. Others, such as Germany or Denmark, request that people relinquish their former citizenship to become German or Danish. If a Turk gives up his citizenship, he or she has to forgo rural property rights in Turkey. This is one of the reasons why Turks in Germany give careful consideration to becoming German.

An efficient EU immigration policy needs to be regulated by economic instruments. That may be based in the future on two possible pillars (Straubhaar and Zimmermann, 1993, p. 233):

- The labour market needs to determine the volume of worker migration. There should be no legal restrictions for economically motivated migration. As soon as the migrant has a job, he or she should be allowed to enter the EU country. If the person is out of a job for a specified period (such as 6 or 12 months), the local authority, may withdraw the residence permit to that person. Migrants may be offered the opportunity to purchase citizenship and pay for that over a fixed period of time.
- The authorities need to set quotas for non-economically motivated (mass) migration such as refugees and asylum seekers.

The stagnating level of population in the EU, combined with prosperous economic conditions in comparison with the adjoining regions, create strong economic incentives for migration into the EU. Uncertainties regarding the transition process in central and eastern Europe create additional incentives for labour mobility towards the EU. The same holds for certain south Mediterranean countries where Islamic fundamentalism is connected with instability.[11] These are important reasons for keeping migration relatively high on the policy agenda in the coming two decades. In addition, the EU will have to compete for mobile professionals from the outside world.

NOTES

1 In a static world, free immigration of labour lowers (or prevents the increase of) the real wages of certain wage-earners in the receiving country.

2 There is a fine difference between immigration and an immigrant policy. The former refers to the admission of foreigners into the receiving country. An immigrant policy deals with the treatment of residing foreigners. Neither of the two policies is well grasped in EU countries.

3 It is estimated that labour is almost three times more mobile among the federal states of the US if compared with labour mobility within individual EU states. There are relatively good reasons for the American geographical rootlessness. The US is a very homogenized country indeed. If you push it to the limit, no matter where you go there, the supply of goods and services is almost identical. Most of the American cities, towns and villages look similar. That may be one of the most important reasons why the majority of Americans move so easily and so often.

4 The rights of non-EU migrant workers depend on the bilateral agreement between their country of origin and the country of destination.

5 Unrestricted immigration in current conditions is out of the question. A highly restrictive immigration policy would provide incentives for illegal immigration. One of the consequences of illegal immigration is insecurity and the exploitation of the migrants, hence it has to be discouraged.

6 Migrants include migrant workers and members of their families that reside with them in the country of destination.

7 The difference from the data presented in Table 10.1 and the ones by Straubhaar (1988) come from the likely underestimation of the stock of migrants by Straubhaar, who relied only on the working permits issued by the country of destination.

8 The Dublin Convention (1990) of the 12 member countries provided for a joint procedure for asylum seekers. The Convention has reconfirmed the Schengen Agreement on this issue.

9 Benelux, France, Germany, Portugal and Spain. Greece and Italy signed the Schengen Agreement but they have not yet implemented it.

10 The French were refusing to implement the agreement on the grounds that terrorists might escape the vigilance of some of their co-signatories. In truth, France's hostility predates its recent experience of terrorism and owes more to the right-wing National Front's criticism of Schengen.

11 Important questions remain. Is the size of the Mediterranean sea sufficient to protect Europe from these troubles? Should the EU do more to prevent an uncontrolled mass immigration from the region? Does that include investment in the democratic institutions in these countries and investment in production in order to keep people employed there? Does it include more concessions in trade to these countries? Would that jeopardize the EU textile industry which relies in part on the labour imported from the south Mediterranean countries?

11

SOCIAL POLICY

I INTRODUCTION

The objective of social policy in a country is to ensure, at least, a socially acceptable minimum standard of living for all its population. Hence, social policy goes beyond employment related issues. It touches people not only when they are at work, but also when they are outside of it or without it. Social policy deals with problems which include wages, unemployment insurance, the welfare system, pensions, health, education, as well as the professional and geographical mobility of labour. The short-run redistributive (security) goal of this policy does not necessarily clash with economic adjustment. In the long run these two objectives supplement each other. There will be no security without adjustment and no adjustment without a certain security in the long run. Social policy should not prevent the economic system from adjusting. On the contrary: it ought to stimulate shifts from low productivity economic structures to those that demand a qualified and highly productive labour and management.

The foundations of a social policy may be traced to the nineteenth century when the social security system was introduced. Between the wars, there was increased concern that economic and social risks should be shared by the whole society. After the Second World War and up to the 1970s a sustained and relatively high rate of economic growth, as well as favourable demographic structure made possible a big increase in social policy expenditure in most developed countries. This has not involved great political costs because the governments' budgets were able to sustain such outlays without too much trouble. Since the recession of the early 1970s, it became obvious that social expenditure was growing so dear that it posed a threat to the adjustment of the entire economic system. This situation demanded reform. Social policy has been transformed from a safety net designed to ease economic adjustment to a concept whose role is to provide citizens with something approaching property rights or entitlements to the status quo (Courchene, 1987, pp. 8–9). There are attempts to change the welfare state (high degree of income protection and social insurance) into a competition state. However, once the social system is there, it is very hard to reform it downwards. When France tried to do that at the end of 1995, the result was the worst wave of strikes since 1968! In a situation of continuous budgetary deficits, this system can no longer be afforded. Otherwise, it will remain fixed at the present situation and economic adjustment will be unable to take place. The social cost of preserving everybody's entitlement without any conditions would be endless.

This chapter is structured as follows. Section II outlines the general possibilities for the reform of social policy. Section III is devoted to the social policy of the EU. Specific consideration is given to the legal base for the policy, its evolution and the European Social Charter. The conclusion is that the EU has very limited powers in the social sphere and that there is a certain confusion about its role in this policy in the future.

II A NEW BUDGETARY SUSTAINABLE SOCIAL POLICY

Public authorities, no matter whether regional, national or at the level of the EU, often become a resort for the rescue of the unsuccessful. As soon as a firm, industry, region or a social group perceives or encounters a difficulty, instead of adjusting they ask first for government intervention. This pressure can be quite strong. However, the budgetary situation drives all public authorities to think more about how to reform social policy and its expenditure than about whether to reform this policy or not.

A society should create the conditions for the attainment of a minimum standard of living of the entire population, including the guarantee of a minimum income, but to such an extent that it does not downgrade the values and incentives to work, move and acquire new knowledge, nor to such an extent that it impedes economic adjustment and growth. Expenditure should be coupled with the social ability to pay and should not overtax the most enterprising and propelling agents that push the economic and social life of the society ahead. Social policy should be coordinated with other economic policies in order to increase its effectiveness. There are no disputes about these issues, whatsoever, but difficulties arise about how to achieve these goals in an 'equitable' way.

For instance, overviews of the British welfare system stressed that it should be changed because it was incomprehensible, uncoordinated, unnecessarily expensive to administer, a chief cause of unemployment, discriminatory, arbitrary, unfair, deteriorating instead of improving, that it penalized marriage and subsidized family breakup, and also de-stabilized and divided society (Courchene, 1987, p. xv). At least some of these aspects of social policy are, unfortunately, not restricted only to the British social system.

The system of unemployment insurance is one of the first on the agenda for the reform. This system often downgrades the value of work in some societies. Short-term employment and reliance on longer unemployment insurance eligibility periods is a tolerable way of life for some segments of the population. If wages are relatively low for some workers, while unemployment benefits are close to their wages, then a proportion of this group of wage-earners may shift to the welfare-recipient segment of the population. Incentives to work, move, retrain and education may be weakened or eliminated. Unemployment benefits were created to cushion against short-term difficulties when labour was passing between jobs. Hence, they are not a suitable means for the correction of structural or long-term unemployment. A reform should introduce a link between the duration and level of unemployment benefits for relatively younger and middle-age groups of unemployed to their vocational retraining and length of previous work, as well as introduce incentives for reallocation.

Human capital (employment) management has to ensure that there is a balance of employment over an economic cycle, that the age, sex and qualification distribution of the employed is adequate, and that there is a passing on of knowledge and experience among employees. Part-time and fixed-term contracts, as well as the hiring of outside specialized firms may be useful and flexible methods of achieving a balance of manpower and meeting the needs of all firms, in particular SMEs.

Structural unemployment, in particular among the young and women, is an indicator of poor vocational training. In addition, this unemployment should not be considered in the traditional way, i.e. labour is either in or out of full-time work. There is potentially substantial scope for part-time employment, for example, students or young mothers who are happy to work a couple of hours a day as they are not in the position to accept different types of contracts. The creation of such jobs need to be encouraged. They introduce flexibility both on the supply and demand side of the market and they need not (although they may) evolve into permanent posts. Supporting legal and fiscal instruments can be important incentives along these lines.

Structural unemployment results from a failure of firms (and government policies) to adapt to changing circumstances. Firms or entire industries produce goods that are not in demand, operate with excessive production costs or cannot withstand competition from abroad. Another, cyclical type of unemployment, comes from a lack of demand. Economic activity fluctuates, consumers may feel insecure at certain times, they save more and spend less, hence there is a lack of the demand that has a cyclical impact on employment. The stated objective of the EU is to make its industries more competitive and to ease the problem of structural unemployment, as well as to assist in the geographical and professional mobility of labour.[1]

Education is another major field for reform. This is important because human knowledge services become increasingly relevant in economic life. Knowledge is the cornerstone of modern manufacturing and services industries. Hence, education should be coordinated with the needs of firms. Employers increasingly demand highly trained labour and educated management. Experience suggests that the nineteenth-century approach by the Luddites to an introduction of new technology and its modern version of opposing a shift to new technologies is mistaken. The countries that were most successful in creating new jobs, such as the US and Japan, were also the ones that made the fastest adjustment and shift towards a knowledge-based, high-technology economy. None the less, compared to those two countries, social solidarity in the form of maintaining income of certain social groups is higher in the EU. However, everything has its price. There are new moves away from social assistance to the disadvantaged towards the creation of jobs, as social-expenditure schemes depend on productive jobs. The EU was involved for a long time in the neutralizing management of unemployment instead of being involved in the creation of new jobs.

The higher education of students is expensive and is becoming increasingly so. On the one hand, top experts may be attracted to private industry, so universities should keep their offers to the brightest teachers and students relatively high. On the other hand, to maintain up-to-date libraries, computers and their software, labs, equipment and various consumables become increasingly expensive. During periods of budgetary cuts which hit hard universities and their research institutes, these schools may not always rely only on public funds and random donations. The only way to solve this financial problem on a more permanent basis may be to increase tuition fees. Everyone who wants post-secondary education should have free access to make an attempt at this in the first year. Those that want and are eligible to go further, may face higher tuition fees. It may be appropriate that students bear a larger share of their education costs. Students are, of course, one of the most needy groups of the population. They should be assisted by a well endowed public system of loans at favourable conditions.

Health care is a social sub-system which will be most difficult to reform. Every society pays a great deal of attention to the health system. It has immense social value. Free access to a minimum of health care personifies one of the most fundamental values of equality in modern societies. On these grounds, the expenditure for health care, in particular, in ageing societies (a pan-European feature), may not be easily reduced. The only window for reform may be found in the partial charging of medical care by those in relatively high-income groups.

III EUROPEAN UNION

1 Legal base

The Treaty of Rome does not exclude social issues, but they are not mentioned often in the text. A relatively small space is devoted to social policy in the Treaty of Rome, reflecting the belief that the impact of social policy on the operation of the EU was not of primary importance. The EU acquired wider powers in the area of social policy with the Single European Act and the Maastricht Treaty which amended the original Treaty of Rome. The Preamble of the updated Treaty of Rome refers to continuous increase in the standard of living as the basic goal of the EU. Article 2 states the objectives of the EU that include a high level of employment and social protection, as well as raising the standard of living and quality of life. Articles 48 to 51 introduce a free movement of labour among the EU countries and also guarantee eligibility for and aggregation of social-insurance benefits. As for education, Article 41 suggests a coordination of efforts in the sphere of vocational training, while Article 57 seeks the mutual recognition of diplomas and other certificates of formal education.

The Commission has to use high standards while regulating health, safety, environmental and consumer protection (Article 100a). Articles 117 and 118 introduce cooperation among member countries regarding standards of living, vocational training, employment, social security and protection of health in the workplace. Improvements in the working environment (health and safety of workers) and the harmonization of conditions are covered by Article 118a. Article 118b gives the authority to the Commission to 'endeavour to develop the dialogue between management and labour at European level'. Article 119 introduces the principle of equal pay for equal work between men and women. Articles 3 and 123 created the European Social Fund with the objective of improving employment opportunities, raising the standard of living and increasing both the geographical and the occupational mobility of workers. General education and vocational training are covered by Articles 126 and 127, respectively. The member states are in charge of the organization of general education and curricula, while the EU is responsible for the promotion of cooperation among member states, developing the European dimension in education with an emphasis on languages, encouraging mobility of students and teachers, and promoting youth exchanges. Article 130*a* sees economic and social cohesion as both a prerequisite and an instrument of harmonious development. Article 130*b* asks both the governments of the member countries to conduct and coordinate economic policies in such a way as to attain the objectives set out in Article 130*a* and the EU to support those objectives through its Structural Funds.

2 Evolution

One of the first legal documents which the EU delivered in 1958 was the social insurance system for migrant workers who are citizens of EU member countries. The basic principles are that these workers have the same social insurance rights as workers from the host country, that social insurance contributions may be freely transferred among EU countries and that social insurance contributions will be taken in their aggregate amount.

The objective of the European Social Fund (ESF) established in 1961, as the main instrument of the EU social policy, is to improve employment opportunities, to contribute to raising the standard of living and to increasing the mobility of labour both between occupations and between regions. The extremely high priority given to the easing of unemployment is because this problem has been the most important social issue in the EU since the mid-1970s. The fight against unemployment was later reinforced by the other two Structural Funds. The results of most forecasts point to the fact that unemployment would remain a problem in the EU for quite some years to come.

Social policy, however, usually covers a much wider group of issues than those awarded to the ESF. Apart from the involvement in unemployment and education/training issues that are partly covered by the ESF, a 'standard' national social policy intervenes in a much larger number of issues which include health and welfare. At the beginning of its operation, the ESF was merely reimbursing half of the costs of vocational training and relocation of workers in the member countries. However, two problems were obvious. Interventions were retroactive and they were concentrated in the country that had the greatest expenditure is these fields (Germany).

The ESF was reformed in 1971 when it was allowed to intervene in the field of vocational training with an emphasis on the young, under 25 years of age, and to intervene in regions with ailing industries and structural unemployment. After the reform around 90 per cent of expenditure went on the occupational mobility of workers, while the remainder was spent on geographic mobility. The subsequent reform of the ESF in 1984 reserved 75 per cent of its resources for the training and employment of the young under 25 years of age. The most disadvantaged regions were guaranteed 45 per cent all of appropriations. The ESF covers up to half of the eligible costs, but never more than the total public expenditure of the country concerned. In support of adults, the fund gives priority to women, to the long-term unemployed, the handicapped and migrants from within the EU. The ESF has had a minor, but growing, role in ameliorating the EU's unemployment problem. A popular argument is that the ESF has never had enough funds to satisfy all the demands which exist in the region. This is not, in fact, the case. Although the ESF has a serious task to perform, part of its problem is the way it operates. Funds totalling ECU 47 billion are available for the period 1993–1999. The allocation is decided before the actual social programmes. Therefore, a large amount of funds, ECU 1.6 billion (28 per cent of the annual allocation in 1994) have remained unspent![2]

There were around 19 million people unemployed in the EU (11 per cent of the workforce) in 1996. Half of them are long-term unemployed. The young, under the age of 25, are hit hard since 20 per cent of this group are without a job. In addition, a high concentration of unemployed is in the group of unskilled workers. The countries that have the highest rates of unemployment (Spain, Ireland) are not the ones with the oldest and most mature manufacturing sectors. Unemployment is a major problem in countries with a relatively large and low-production farming sector.

Social security benefits may have a significant impact on the level of wages. If employers are required to pay relatively high social security contributions, then they can lower wages and vice versa. Different levels of expenditure on social security contributions among countries may have an influence on competition among countries in the short run. When unemployment is relatively high and long-term, various tax revenues are affected in a negative way, demand for social expenditure increases, and budget deficits are harder to cut. In addition, taxes and social security contributions on labour in the EU countries (30 to 50 per cent of labour costs) are higher than in the US or Japan. National labour markets are over-regulated in Europe. That is one of the reasons why significantly fewer new jobs are created in the EU than in the US, where the regulation of the labour market is easier. None the less, regulation is primarily at the *national*, rather than at the EU level, hence the EU need not necessarily be blamed for the failure of efforts to ease the unemployment problem.

The European system for exchanging job information (Sedoc) was set up in order to increase mobility of labour among member countries. Many employers, however, did not list their vacancies with Sedoc and other labour exchanges since they consider such applicants as having poor work histories.

A pessimistic or, as some may call it, a realistic, expectation is that there are perhaps around 10 million unemployed young Europeans in the 1990s. They are at the bottom of the EU pool of labour and due to their poor training they will remain unemployable! This problem may be somehow easy to overlook while they are still young. But, once they create their own families, they will constitute distinct underclass. That is why the ESF has been concentrating more on the problem of youth unemployment since 1984 than on anything else. Incentives to vocational training, geographical mobility and flexible employment laws may represent a long-term solution to this problem. None the less, the employment policy ultimately remains the responsibility of member states. A coordination of national policies in this field started in the form of exchanges of information, experience and resolutions.

The EU has not done much about education in the past. There was an EU programme in 1976 which intended to promote cooperation in higher education in the region, to standardize teaching courses, to increase the access to education throughout the EU and to improve and widen the teaching of languages that are spoken in the member countries. The EU required member states to offer classes for the children of migrant workers in order to give them the opportunity to receive some education in the culture and in the language of their country of origin. Since the

1980s the EU education and youth-exchange programmes have been expanding and they have included:

- PETRA: vocational training for young people and their teachers;
- FORCE: improvements in the quality of training;
- COMETT: cooperation between universities and industry;
- ERASMUS: mobility of university students and teachers, as well as joint courses;
- YOUTH FOR EUROPE: exchanges of 15- to 25-year olds;
- LINGUA: language training;
- TEMPUS: cooperation with central and eastern European universities;
- SOCRATES: exchange of students and pupils.

In many cases linked with the social issues (and, hence, social philosophy), the EU was long on statements, but short on action as economic constraints were not taken into consideration. The Social Action Programme of 1974, for example, called for a full and better employment, improvement in living and working conditions, as well as the participation of workers and employers in the EU decision-making process through the Standing Committee on Employment. Due to economic crisis and introverted economic strategies, the Programme did not have any notable achievements.

3 The European Social Charter

The European Social Charter (1989) was controversial from the outset. It outlined basic rights of EU workers and was adopted as a political declaration by all EU member states with the exception of Britain. The Charter provides for 12 basic rights:

1 The right to work in the EU country of one's choice.
2 The right to a fair wage.
3 The right to improved living and working conditions.
4 The right to social protection under prevailing national systems.
5 The right to freedom of association and collective bargaining.
6 The right to vocational training.
7 The right of men and women to equal treatment.
8 The right of workers to information, consultation and participation.
9 The right to health protection and safety at work.
10 The protection of children and adolescents.
11 The guarantee of minimum living standards for the elderly.
12 Improved social and professional integration for the disabled.

The objective of the Charter is to lay down political foundations for a minimum common legislation in the area of labour affairs. Although without a legal force, the Charter presents a political obligation. Most of the Charter's provisions are not disputable at all. Controversies arise regarding 'fair wages' that may be interpreted as an intention to introduce an EU-wide minimum wage; and the regulation of working hours, holidays and workers' participation which all may jeopardize the flexibility so essential in labour markets.

Britain was not in favour of the Charter, because of a fear that the Commission would use it as a foundation for various proposals and for legislation in the social sphere. As such, it may impose uniformity in labour legislation on countries that have different traditions and economic structures (labour regulation in smelting may need a different model from tourism). Freedom of contract and flexibility in the labour market, important components of competitiveness, would be restrained. For example, Britain thinks that is would be better that employers and employees negotiate the length of the working week, than to have uniform EU-wide rules.

The Commission of the EU proposes binding regulation on health and safety at work. The reason is that there are tens of thousands of workers that are killed or injured at the workplace each year. Although the objective of the EU is to support the creation of jobs, that need not be achieved at the cost of reduction in health and safety. These are areas without disputes among the member countries. Problems, however, arise with part-time employment. The Commission intends to propose that part-time employees receive the same benefits as full-time workers. Britain is the strongest opponent of such a policy, since excessive regulation may discourage the creation of part-time jobs.[3]

Many workers prefer longer night shifts over a shorter period of time than shorter shifts over a longer period of time. If working time is regulated, then workers would lose the freedom to negotiate their working time. The need for choice and flexibility in the labour market beneficial both to employees and to employers is something that the Commission often forgets. Uniform laws that do not provide for flexibility may press hard SMEs that not only need flexibility, but are also the major employers of labour. Moreover, SMEs also employ the most disadvantaged groups of workers such as the young and women.[4] In addition, there is an increasing demand by enterprises for temporary workers hired from specialized firms, rather than taking on permanent staff.

EMU would bring the elimination of separate national currencies. Without them, countries have a limited arsenal of means to adjust to sizeable economic disparities. Countries may introduce flexible wages, give incentives to mass migration and/or employ transfer payments. A recent example of Germany, however, has shown that wages were inflexible, mass migration was hardly tolerable, while transfer payments were damaging. Instead of creating conditions for a greater flexibility in the labour market, the EU is bracing itself with the Social Charter!

Firms with a longer-term perspective may perceive the prospect of paying firing costs ('golden handshakes', retirement pensions etc.) as a 'tax' on hiring – a drain on profits, causing a disincentive to take on new labour in the future. The Social Charter may add to unemployment and usher protectionism in two ways. First, regulation has its costs in the reduction of flexibility in the labour market and the decline in competitiveness compared with countries that have a lighter regulatory burden and can make their businesses adapt, change and grow. Second, if EU regulation is adjusted upwards to the standards that prevail in the northern countries, then southern EU countries would need transfer of funds to make up for the loss of growth. The EU commitment to free trade would be placed in jeopardy (Curzon Price, 1991, pp. 130–131).

If the social dimension of the harmonization of labour laws includes an upward adjustment, then this would increase the costs of production in those countries with a relatively lax legislation (south), economic growth would suffer and there would be a demand for protection. Conversely, if member countries are left alone to set their labour laws, harmonization through competition may produce a downward adjustment. Over-regulation of the labour market (north) would be eased, costs of production would fall, competitiveness would be enhanced and there would be positive impact on growth. It is only in this way that high wages can be sustained in the longer term with a reasonable degree of openness of the economy.

The 1994 Directive requested that firms with more than 1,000 employees should set up consultative works councils if at least 150 of employees work in two or more EU countries. The Directive affects around 1,200 EU enterprises. Its objective is to improve the right of workers to be kept informed and consulted. Participation of workers in the affairs of their firms, even though it only takes the form of consultation and exchange of information, may well increase the cohesion and moral and improve productivity. Certain affected enterprises such as Canon or Panasonic assert that the councils fit neatly into their (Japanese) standards of collective responsibility. Volkswagen has a positive experience with works councils as a means for spreading information. Although Britain opted out of the Social Charter, United Biscuits, a British firm, set up its own works council.

In spite of those developments firms worry about two issues related to works councils. First come costs. The meeting of the councils have to take place once a year. However, if mergers, acquisitions and relocations that affect employees take place, then there would need to be additional meetings. The costs to enterprises of running works councils would soar. Second are relations between works councils and trade unions. There is a fear that works councils would lead to EU-wide collective bargaining. The current degree of integration in the EU does not yet permit efficient wage bargaining on this level. Centralized wage bargaining by the EU is, however, unlikely. It is doubtful that national trade unions would relinquish their local bargaining rights to a higher tier. In the future, it is likely that both the unions and employers would like to keep the extent of works councils quite limited. However, the greatest peril that the works councils pose is that they may curb the development of more flexible ways of maintaining the flow of information between management and employees.

Besides the Directive on works councils, more legislation is in the pipeline. It includes granting the same benefits regarding pay, holidays and other rights to part-timers as are given to the full-time staff. Such strengthening of employees' rights represents a potential threat during times of relatively high unemployment and job insecurity. This may hit SMEs enterprises hardest (those up to 250 employees), as they may refrain from taking on staff. There were around 17 million SMEs in 1995, employing 70 per cent of the EU labour force.

IV CONCLUSION

The demand for social expenditure is almost insatiable. The expenditure for these services may be increased during periods of prosperity, at lowest political cost, as was the case in the 1960s. During economic slow-downs and budgetary deficits, the social services which have mushroomed have to be reformed. Unemployment insurance is more of an income-support instrument than oriented towards labour adjustment. This should be changed in favour of mobility of labour, in particular, that of younger people, both among occupations and regions. Sometimes it is better to give a pension to 60-year-old workers than to provide dole money to teenagers and tweenagers.

Coverage of the EU social policy is limited. Intervention has been much less of a well organized policy and much more a mix of various social issues that the member states were willing to transfer to the EU. The 'loose' character of social policy comes from the legal provisions that are, in certain cases, aspirational rather than operational. Its major concern was in the past and will remain at least until the end of the decade, the alleviation of the unemployment problem. But one needs to remember that (un)employment policies and major instruments to deal with the problem are still in the hands of *national* governments. Other aspects of the policy include geographical and professional mobility of labour, safety at work and educational exchanges.

The effects of social policy may not be measured directly. Indirectly, social policy has its impact on the length of life expectancy, reduction of illiteracy, increase in training and the safety of workers. All this increases the production potential of a country. Average life expectancy of the EU population is increasing. For men at birth it was 63.9 years in 1950, while in 1991 it increased to 72.8 years. Women live longer. Their average life expectancy at birth was 68.3 years in 1950, and 79.4 in 1991. Therefore, national social protection systems will have to be adjusted over the coming two decades because of the ageing population in the EU and the consequent increase in the demand for social care. Due to demographical changes the EU labour fource will shrink after 2010. Part of the solution to the problem may be found in selective imigration policy, in particular, from transition countries.

Calls for a radical change in the EU social policy have gone. The real danger stems from the fact that without the reform of social policy, member countries and the EU may encounter problems in the present and future with methods which were designed in and for past times. The best way to solve unemployment problems is for member states and the EU to work together towards the achievement of the common goal: greater flexibility in the labour market. The problem is that the participating countries may not wish to abandon their own rights in this policy and transfer them to the union level. Politicians in a number of EU countries often support in private the British stance on social (and other) issues. Freedom in their public statements is limited because of political (coalition) commitments, hence Britain presents a convenient scapegoat.

If the labour-related laws are going to be set and harmonized on the EU level, while wages and social security contributions are left to member states, then that may create some perplexing problems. Moreover, when disputes arise, the EU Court of Justice will have to rule on these messy issues! The Medium-term Social Action Programme (1995) reflected the fact that there was absolutely no consensus among industry, unions or member states about the requirements of the EU social policy. Confusion in the area of the EU social policy will continue!

NOTES

1 See the chapters on industrial policy (6) and labour mobility (10).
2 Only publicly authorized agencies (training agencies, trade unions etc.) may apply for allocations from the ESF. As they play the role of both fox and hound at the same time, that creates the temptation for fraud. For example, 36 Portuguese trade union officials were charged in 1995 with setting up a fake training company in order to get subsidies. The funds received went into paying the bills of the trade union. There are no penalties for countries that spend funds on ineligible projects (*The Economist*, 27 January 1996, p. 30).

3 Certain low-paid jobs in services, such as packing assistants in supermarkets, janitors or car washers, have all but disappeared in the EU, but not in the US. If European employers are required to provide such a fluctuating labour force with excessive benefits, they would prefer to relinquish these services.

4 A certain margin of preference to women applicants for jobs has been an unwritten practice in many of the EU countries. This was especially true in the northern part of the EU in spite of a 1976 Directive requiring equal treatment of both sexes. The European Court of Justice ruled (1995) that jobs quotas were not allowed. The case in question (landscape gardening) arose when the German state of Bremen gave jobs to women ahead of equally qualified men.

12

ENVIRONMENT POLICY

I INTRODUCTION

A clean and healthy environment has been taken by many to be a ubiquitous good for a long time. The ecological system was assumed to balance itself in a more or less satisfactory way, hence there was no need for public intervention in those matters. That is the reason why public concern about the environment was mainly limited to declarations.[1] Such an attitude has, however, changed over time. The formal corner-stone in the evolution of global concern about the environment was the UN Conference on Human Environment that took place in Stockholm in 1972. The Conference reached an agreement on the universal responsibilities regarding the global environment and produced a large set of recommendations that would guide policies all around the world in this field. Relatively recent environmental disasters such as Seveso (Italy, 1976), Bhopal (India, 1984) and Chernobyl (Ukraine, 1986) have increased global awareness about the impact and damage that can be inflicted on the environment and the natural balance.

This chapter is structured as follows. Section II considers select theoretical issues that are linked with environmental policy. Section III presents foundations, principles and new initiatives in the environmental policy of the EU, as well as the impact of agriculture on the environment. The conclusion is that the environmental policy of the EU is still unconsolidated, but there are opportunities for it to develop in the future.

II ISSUES

Public intervention in the field of environment and the control of pollution is limited by at least two obstacles. The first barrier to an effective public intervention rests on the imperfect information that is available to the government. For example, the administration needs data on the possible negative effects of a chemical. This information is often obtained from the affected chemical company. That firm has an incentive to provide incomplete, misleading or even false data to the government in order to influence the outcome of the policy in its own favour. The work of the government is made even more difficult as scientists often disagree on the acceptable or environmentally safe level of emission of pollutants, i.e., up to what level of pollution the environment may be expected to cope with on its own, and the point beyond which harm may start. Therefore, it is often hard for the government

353

to set those standards. Imperfect information leads us to the second obstacle to an effective public intervention in the area of environment. As information is often deficient, public decision-makers have a wide margin for discretion. Therefore, the bureaucrats are subject to lobbying. Such influence is strong from the organized and potentially affected (chemical or power-generating) industries which may often distort government decisions and laws in their favour. The voice of the (unorganized) consumers and general public has been quite low for a long time. An entry of the 'greens' into political life, the inclusion of environmental issues in the programmes of established political parties, and organizations such as Greenpeace are all slowly changing the balance of power between the business community and the general public.[2]

The accepted basis for environmental policies in the OECD countries is the polluter-pays principle from 1972. The Earth Summit in Rio de Janeiro (1992) reaffirmed this principle, but added that states have common, although differentiated obligations. Although the polluter-pays principle may seem just on the surface, its universal application may encounter problems. If producers are in the position to pass on the costs linked to environment management expenditure to their consumers, the users of goods or services are the ones that pay for those costs. While the developed countries may have the capacity, means and will to apply the principle in practice, problems arise on the side of the developing countries as they are price-takers for their goods on the international market. In many cases they may not be able to pass on those costs to their consumers and finance the necessary compliance with international standards and demands. Hence the need for a global action (and funds) regarding environmental issues. Examples of such global action include the Montreal Protocol on Substances that Deplete the Ozone Layer (1987); the Basel Convention on the Control of Transboundary Movements of Hazardous Wastes and Their Disposal (1989); and the Convention on International Trade in Endangered Species of Wild Fauna and Flora (1973).

Pollution is not only a regional, but also a trans-frontier, trans-regional, and global phenomenon. For example, the quality of the Dutch drinking water taken from the Rhine depends on substances that entered the river in the upstream countries. Similarly, there is a partial link between vehicle exhaust gases in Britain and damage that acid rain does to the Black Forest region in Germany.

High environment-related standards may bring a potential danger of 'eco-protectionism' as a new type of NTB in international trade. Countries or their groups with relatively strict domestic environmental standards prevent or make difficult imports of affected goods produced in countries where these standards are low. There are, however, a number of valid reasons for a variation in standards among countries. They include not only differences in climate, but also level of development and population density. Countries with relatively lax environmental standards such as Malaysia, the Philippines, South Korea or Thailand have not received foreign investment in polluting industries, although one could expect that it may become the case (Charnovitz, 1995, p. 19).

It is sometimes alleged that compliance with environmentally sound standards may increase costs of production and, hence, jeopardize the international competitiveness of goods. Various purification gadgets and changes in technology to make the production process cleaner cost money. However, do they put a country's competitiveness in peril? A World Bank study of the impact of the environment-related expenditure on competitiveness of countries that have relatively high expenditure on those projects brought interesting results. For example, it was found that Germany, a country with strict environmental standards and relatively high national expenditure on these matters, maintained international competitiveness in environmentally sensitive goods in the 1970s and 1980s, in spite of increases in environmental expenditure. In addition, the study found little systematic relationship between higher environmental standards and competitiveness in environmentally sensitive goods. In general, developed countries have maintained their comparative advantage in these goods (Sorsa, 1994).

International trade agreements that link countries have, for a long time, avoided environmental issues. For instance, Article 27 of the EFTA convention has as its objective an expansion of trade in fish, but without any reference to conservation. Similarly, for years the GATT promoted trade in tropical goods, but without due respect for the environment. Following the Rio Declaration (1992), future arrangements will take ecological issues into consideration. None the less, there is an unresolved issue on the global scale. It concerns the settlement of disputes. Trade arrangements deal with the settlement of commercial disputes, while environmental issues have been left aside.

III EUROPEAN UNION

1 Foundation

The Treaty of Rome does not lay grounds for a common EU policy on the environment. That reflects the prevailing neglect of the environmental matters at the time of its drafting. The general authority for *any* policy is, however, given in the catch-all Article 235. None the less, EU action has been evolving. A few months after the Stockholm Conference, the EU Summit in Paris (1972) provided the groundwork for an EU environmental policy. The polluter-pays principle was adopted and 5-year environment programmes were launched. These programmes were initially attempts to harmonize national legislation on the environment in order to prevent distortions in competition, but later on, the programmes became more ambitious. Since that time, the EU has adopted over 200 legally binding documents in the field of environment.

Together with the signing of the Treaty of Rome (1957) that set the foundations of the EU, another Treaty was also signed. This is the Treaty that established the European Atomic Energy Community (Euratom). The potential benefits, as well as perils of atomic energy were recognized, hence at that time the six countries wanted to put a legal control over ownership, trade, research and employment of nuclear power. The potential negative impact of this source of energy on the environment was recognized by the Treaty. Article 2 requests the establishment of 'uniform safety standards to protect the health of workers and of the general public'. In addition, Article 30 requests the introduction of basic health and safety standards linked with atomic energy.

The Single European Act (1986), Articles 130r–t, introduced a Title on the environment into the Treaty of Rome. Those articles were reaffirmed and some of them revised in the Maastricht Treaty (1991). The objectives of EU environmental policy include preserving, protecting and improving the quality of the environment; protection of human health; prudent exploitation of natural resources; and promotion of international measures that deal with global environmental problems. Although the polluter-pays principle is still applied, there is provision for EU assistance if the costs of the agreed EU action fall disproportionately on the authorities of one or more member states. Common measures in the field of environment may not, however, prevent member states maintaining or introducing more stringent national protective measures.

2 Principles

The EU environmental policy rests on four principles:

- *Prevention*: The EU intends to prevent all environmental damage through preventive action. All planning and decision-making processes that affect the environment such as motorways or power plants have to take into account the impact on the natural habitat in order to avoid the need for any corrective action in the future.
- *Rectification*: Pollution has to be tackled at its source and as promptly as possible. In cases where it cannot be entirely eradicated, it needs to be kept at the lowest possible level.
- *Polluter pays*: Prevention, cleaning and compensation for pollution should be borne, in principle, by those that cause it. The rationale for this principle is to provide a stimulus not to pollute at all or, if necessary, to do that with as 'clean' technologies as possible and in the least harmful way. There is, none the less, a possibility of EU assistance if common measures to protect the environment impose unequal costs on certain countries, for example in the south of the EU where the previous rules were lax.
- *Inclusion*: Environmental aspects have to be considered whenever the EU decides about all other common policies.

Although the principles are there, their application and new eco-legislation should avoid segmenting the EU market. None the less, if the application of the spirit of the *Cassis de Dijon* case cannot be applied in the EU in environmental issues for reasons that include differences in climate or national (im)possibilities of absorbing costs, then EU eco-legislation needs to be coupled with funds and loans to those (southern) countries that are forced to implement such laws.

3 Common Agricultural Policy and the environment[3]

The Common Agricultural Policy (CAP) has been one of the longest and most profound common policies of the EU. In essence, it guaranteed both high prices for select farm products and also purchases at these prices. The production and, especially, the overproduction of farm goods may have an adverse effect on the salinization and erosion of soil. An excessive usage of fertilizers, pesticides, herbicides, phosphorus, minerals, nitrogen and fossil fuels pollute ground, water[4] and food with chemicals. That also reduces the number of species of plants and animals in their natural habitat. If, however, the implementation of environmental laws increases the cost of production and decreases output, the producers may (but not necessarily will) weaken their competitive position. An additional environment-unfriendly aspect of the CAP was that crops that were traditionally rotating, such as pulses, oats and fodder, are disregarded by the CAP. The price policy has created a virtual monoculture that has upset the long established farm balance. In addition, milk and other animal-based goods extend the creation of animal manure which is a rich source of nitrogen.

Everyone that drove around England noticed the impact of the CAP on the environment and the traditional landscape. The sight of sheep and cattle in fields and meadows disappeared. That was a direct consequence of the increasing intensification of livestock husbandry and a shift of land into cereal production. The bright yellow colour of the ripening crop is, however, distinctive and alien to the traditional English landscape. In addition, the CAP price policy gave incentives to farmers to increase output and change the countryside. They drained ponds and uprooted hedgerows and footpaths to provide land to plough (Atkin, 1993, pp. 128–130).

The intention of the MacSharry Reform (1992) was to reduce farm output in the EU. If this takes place, there would be a positive externality on the environment in the region as it is expected that there would be a drop in the use of pollutants. That would be felt mostly in the northern regions of the EU as the (large) farmers there employ chemically-based methods of production to a larger extent than farmers elsewhere in the EU. However, a fall in the EU output, may increase the price of certain farm goods on the international market. As a consequence, there may be an expansion of agricultural output in the Cairns group of countries and the US. Hence, the demand for polluting chemicals in these countries may increase. While there may be some improvement in the environment of the EU, there may be a degradation of the quality of the environment elsewhere in the world.

If there are cases in which farm production does not respond to incentives or when the damage to the environment is extreme, then regulatory measures may be an efficient policy instrument. Changes that are being considered by the EU in this respect include certification and registration of chemicals used in agriculture, restrictions of the chemical content in foodstuffs, as well as the dissemination of information and knowledge to traders and users of farm chemicals about their impact on the environment, food and health.

All those problems were considered, and part of the MacSharry Reform brought the Agri-environmental Programme. It recognized both the role that farmers play in the protection of rural areas and the need to compensate for that role. This Programme envisioned premiums for the employment of non-polluting methods of production (organic farming), conversion of farmland into parks, development of leisure activities, protection of the scenery, conservation of bio-diversity and training in the protection of environment. All these activities, together with tourism, will create alternative local jobs that will compensate, at least in part, for the loss of jobs in direct farming. Member states draft their zonal programmes and then, submit them to the EU for approval. As these programmes are a relatively new feature, there is not enough evidence for their evaluation. None the less, agri-tourism is growing. For instance, Parco dell'Orecchiella in Tuscany is becoming a popular destination for visitors. That gives additional business and employment to the region.

4 New policy initiatives

As transport, agriculture, tourism and manufacturing have consequences on the environment, a successful environmental policy should be developed and implemented by everyone and not simply by the ministry of the environment. Sustainable development has to meet the needs of the present generation without compromising the ability of future generations to meet their own needs. Therefore, while it is true that the EU started with a series of Action Programmes on the Environment in 1973, these remained more haphazard statements of intent which had little serious impact on the substantive activities of the EU. A striking example of this lack of consideration for environmental consequences is the 1992 Programme. The implementation of the internal market went ahead without attention to its impact on the environment until 1989. In that year an EU task force studied the environmental impact of the 1992 Programme which supplemented the Cecchini Report. The latter concluded that an increase in output would have a negative impact on the environment because expansion in the production of waste and pollution would result from increased road haulage. Hence, the optimistic results of the Cecchini's Report had to be adjusted, i.e. reduced by the size of the damage done to the environment.

A shortage of raw materials and a lack of landfields resulted in the creation of policies for waste management and recycling. The EU Directive on packaging and package waste (1994) was an attempt to harmonize national packaging laws;[5] in addition it set recycling targets. At least half of paper, board, glass and metal packages have to be recovered (taken back from consumers) and 25–45 per cent recycled by the year 2001. The Fifth Environmental Action Programme selected around 200 chemicals that are going to be examined for environmental soundness. It is reckoned that some 50 chemicals will be subject to risk-reduction programmes prior to the year 2000. There is also a strategy to reduce the consumption of energy in cars and households, as well as to switch to non-fossil fuels in order to reduce the emission of CO_2. Following the Montreal Protocol and the London and Copenhagen amendments, there is a commitment to reduce gradually and eliminate completely consumption and production of all ozone depleting substances. Technical standards, taxation, green point and other eco-labelling instruments are additional instruments of environmental policy.

In a consideration of a case regarding the Danish law on the packaging of drinks (the provision was that drinks should be marketed in returnable bottles), the EU Court of Justice ruled in 1988 that the protection of the environment took priority over the rules of free trade. This may be an important precedent for similar cases in the future (Weale and Williams, 1993). The EU has an eco-audit Directive (1993) that encourages industrial firms to introduce voluntarily eco-audit schemes. The objectives of these schemes are to determine how well the management and equipment is performing; verification of compliance with local, regional, state and EU environmental provisions; and minimization of risks of pollution. In addition, the Commission entered into voluntary environmental agreements with industry on several occasions. One agreement covered the labelling of cleaning products, while several others dealt with the reduction in the use of chlorofluorocarbons (CFCs) in different industries. However, the European Parliament is sceptical about the effectiveness of voluntary agreements as a means to achieve policy objectives.

Management of forests is an important part of environmental policy. It should be ensured that timber originates from sustainably managed forests. The idea about the afforestation of farmland in the EU as a part of the reform package came from the Mansholt's Plan (1968). The MacSharry Reform simply reinvigorated it. As afforestation deals with the medium and long term, its scope and effect cannot be evaluated at present. If, for example, the policy uses premiums for the alteration of landscape with fast-growing poplars, then there may appear a surplus production of soft wood which would jeopardize the position of traditional and non-subsidized growers. The local programmes need to emphasize indigenous types of forests that will increase the consumption of nitrates already in the soil, prevent erosion of land, create jobs in the timber industry, reduce surpluses of farm goods, and beautify the local landscape – all at the same time. Special subsidies to chestnut and oak planting need to be high on the agenda for consideration. Although the overall benefits of such schemes are self-evident, doubtful financial pledges introduce a degree of uncertainty into their future. Unfortunately, short-sighted decision-makers fail to see that the programmes such as these will have to be undertaken in the future, but their cost will then be higher than it is at present.

IV CONCLUSION

Public concern and action over environmental issues has increased since the 1970s. It is not only limited to the local concerns such as the revitalization of a lake or the preservation of an endangered species of birds, but it also includes global issues such as the depletion of the ozone layer.

Market forces do not take into account environmental issues that are often linked with longer-term considerations. Environmental externalities, however, do become recognized, so the previous 'benign neglect' policy is evolving into an active approach. Intervention in environmental affairs may be costly in the short term, but the overall pecuniary and other longer-term non-financial gains more than compensate for that shortfall. There may also be short-term direct gains from environmental programmes. Examples include benefits from savings in the consumption of energy.

Strong industrial lobbies and general reductions in public expenditure create a certain anxiety over the future extent of environmental policies. For example, the noble goals of the EU Agri-environmental Programme may be slowed down by the lack of resources. None the less, increased public awareness, pressure and research, as well as the involvement of the producers of the environmentally related goods may provide compelling forces for the expansion of environmental policies.

Although there were certain important steps in the creation of the environmental policy in the EU, this policy is still rather vague. That does, however, not come as a surprise. A policy on the environment is one of the youngest EU ideas. Once it is there, it will have the tendency to grow, just as other EU policies did. So far, the policy has been long on declaration and short on action, in particular regarding the CAP. Insecure funds to support the policy reflect both general restraints on public expenditure and a concentration of public authorities on more immediate short-term issues. None the less, the demand for leisure is increasing. People are able, ready and willing to pay for a nice walk in the picturesque countryside. Care for the environment also creates jobs. Coupled with the increasing general consciousness about the conservation of a clean, healthy and sustaining environment, this policy will be high on the EU agenda in the future.

NOTES

1 This neglect does not mean that environmental problems were neither existing, nor obvious. Everyone in Europe was aware of the problems for the elderly and sick created by London smog in the past.
2 The expansion of activities regarding environmental issues provided an incentive to the development of those industries that manufacture environment-related goods. One firm's expensive obligation is another's chance for profit. The major buyers of these products are municipalities, power and water-producing companies, mining and manufacturing firms.
3 See Chapter 4 on the CAP.
4 Water drained from surface soil brings phosphates into rivers. This stimulates the expansion of algae that consume oxygen in water. This may kill aquatic life, including fish. Such pollution has been observed in many rivers in north-western Europe and in Lombardy.
5 For example, Belgium applied a packaging tax, Denmark had a deposit-refund scheme, while Germany used a labelling system.

13

TRANSPORT POLICY

I INTRODUCTION

The size of the market determines, in static terms, the opportunities for the division of labour and specialization. Market size is, on the other hand, limited by natural and human imposed barriers to trade. The impact of natural obstacles to trade such as distance or geography could be moderated by the construction of new roads, railways, bridges, tunnels and ports. In addition, a fall in costs of transport per unit of transported good (or per passenger) reduces barriers that may exist between two or more places. International economic integration is able to mitigate or even eliminate the impact of artificial barriers to trade such as tariffs, quotas, taxes and NTBs. Developed and relatively cheap transport and communication links among states are necessary conditions for successful economic integration.

There was little intervention in trade during the nineteenth century. None the less, markets among many countries remained detached because of relatively high costs of transport and a lack of full and timely information about opportunities for trade. Since then, heavy public investment in infrastructure has shortened the distance between various markets.

Classic models of international economic integration have excluded the space dimension from considerations (alternatively, when transport costs were included, they were assumed to be equal to zero). Although increasing productivity reduces cost per unit of transported goods, this was not entirely legitimate. Transportation distances vary because of new markets; and speed (and price) of delivery depends on the method of transport. In addition, the transport industry is a significant contributor to the GDP and employment. In a standard case, transport costs have the same effect on the final price of goods and trade as tariffs. When the cost of transport is reduced (as with the reduction in tariffs), new trade among states may be created.

Transport services have at least four characteristics. First, there is public intervention regarding rates, investment in infrastructure, taxes, subsidies and conditions for operations (safety, dimensions of vehicles, pollution and the like).[1] It is most pronounced in railways, the mode of transport that is almost entirely monopolized.[2] Second, transport services are significant employers of labour and consumers of capital goods and energy. Third, the demand for transport services depends on the level of economic activity and income. The supply of these services is, however, inelastic in the short term. Fourth, transport services play a crucial role in the successful operation and competitiveness of an economy.

361

Consideration in this section concentrater on road transport[3] where the EU has made the most determined efforts to secure the adoption of common policies. Air and maritime transport have a strong international (rather than regional) character and national regulation. For a long time they have escaped EU scrutiny. The section is structured as follows. After the legal base for the common transport policy in the EU, there is a consideration of its modest evolution. The EU has ambitious plans to be involved in various aspects of the transport policy, that are slowly evolving. The stumbling blocks in the future will be the lack of huge funds necessary for the financing of trans-European networks.

II EUROPEAN UNION

1 Legal base

Apart from trade and agriculture, transport was the only major industry to which the Treaty of Rome devoted a special Title. The inclusion of transport policy in the Treaty of Rome was the request of the Dutch who have a special interest in this economic activity. Articles 3 and 74, respectively, state that the creation of a common transport policy is one of the objectives of the EU. Apart from this general request, there are no other instructions about the nature of a common transport policy. However, the Council of Ministers is charged by Article 75 to lay down common rules for the policy. For internal EU transport, Article 79 outlaws any discrimination regarding rates or conditions for carriage of the same goods over the same transport links on the grounds of destination or origin of goods. The question of aids is regulated by Articles 77 and 80, respectively. Basically, unless authorized by the Commission, state aids are forbidden. Articles 129*b* to 129*d* refer to trans-European networks. The EU is empowered to contribute to the establishment and development of trans-European networks in transport, telecommunications and energy infrastructures. The objectives include a promotion of interconnection and interoperability of national networks, standardization and cooperation with third countries on projects of mutual interest. In addition, Article 130*r* obliges the EU to conduct environment friendly policies.

2 Evolution

Transportation is one of the most important economic activities in the EU. It contributes around 7 per cent to the GDP of the EU. In addition, this service industry employs directly around 7 million people in the EU of 15 countries. Its impact on the economy of the EU is amplified by the fact that almost 3 million people work in the production of transport related equipment. As such, suppliers of transport services were able to establish contacts with and influence on the policy-makers.

Transport is an evolving and growing industry. This is not only the consequence of changes in technology (fuel-saving and environment friendly engines, or very fast trains), but also because of the changing structure of manufacturing. New production methods reduce stocks, become flexible and depend on varied and rapid delivery services. Shipment sizes are being reduced, but deliveries became more frequent. Storage is being passed on from firms' warehouses to supply trucks. Firms increasingly prefer to locate away from congested urban areas, to run multi-site business operations, so they depend on a reliable transport system for inputs and the delivery of goods to major markets. Increased professional mobility and a rise in personal income, coupled with increased holiday time, has also boosted demand for travel.

The Schaus Memorandum (1961)[4] was the first attempt to introduce a common transport policy in the EU. The Memorandum suggested an elimination of impediments to the creation of a common market in transport services; the national markets for transport services ought to be open; and that there should be attempts to create conditions for free competition in the provision of transport services. At the time when transport markets were highly regulated, Schaus' ideas were highly controversial and were 'set aside'. Another attempt by the Commission to advance its transport policy was in 1973. The central element was the call to establish a system that would improve transport infrastructure, promote social progress, increase safety and reduce costs. The Council, again, made no formal response to the proposal. The Commission continued with its efforts to create a common transport policy and came up with a new set of proposals in 1983. In essence, the new proposals provided principles for a comprehensive internal market in transport activity. In spite of a few attempts by the Commission to initiate the creation of a common transport policy, this policy failed to appear in the EU even 15 years after the end of the transition period in 1968. Transport policy still remained under the control of national governments.

Developments in the policy of transport were prevented by different perceptions about how policy in this area needs to be structured. Certain countries such as France and Germany saw transport as an industry that has to contribute to wider social and regional policy objectives. Britain, on the other hand, regarded transport as an industry that is no different from others and that should be treated accordingly. The consequence was that an EU policy has never been established.

The lack of progress regarding the creation of the common policy in transport was such that the European Parliament (supported by the Commission) took the EU Council of Ministers to the Court of Justice in 1983. The charge was that the Council failed to act on the basis of Article 75. The ruling of the Court (1985), confirming the charge by the Parliament, was a landmark in the development of the EU transport policy. The Council was obliged to take the necessary measures in order to go ahead with the creation of an obligatory, but still missing, common policy. Consequently, direct measures towards the creation of a common transport policy (such as an elimination of segmented national markets, phased removal of licences and the granting of cabotage[5] rights) and indirect ones (a removal of checks on internal frontiers)[6] were included in the 1992 Programme.

3 Future

Following the landmark ruling of the Court (1985) and the 1992 Programme, the Commission tried to set out a global approach to the development of a common transport policy. Its Communication, *The Future Development of the Common Transport Policy* (Commission of the European Communities, 1992), spells out policy action for the future. There are seven major objectives:

- *Proper operation of the internal market.* This includes removing restrictions on cabotage for the EU-residing operators.
- *Intermodal competition and complementarity.* The thrust of this objective is that users have to pay the full cost of the transport service. It may be quite difficult to implement: for example, in urban public transport or railway lines that are servicing small, backward and distant rural areas. The provision of such services have always been subsidized within the functions of social, regional and cohesion policies.
- *Development of trans-European networks.* This is a medium- and long-term objective. The networks are supposed to become the 'arteries through which the economic lifeblood' of the EU flows. They should become major routes along which people, goods and services flow. As such, they will further economic integration, ease communication, shrink distances and bring peripheral regions into easier and cheaper contact with central areas. In order to operate those networks in an efficient way, the provision of these services need to be liberalized, they must be technically compatible and any possible bottlenecks have to be eliminated. Most of the projects, however, require massive investment. This is a major obstacle to their realization. The expectation that the private sector is going to be the major investor may not be fulfilled. The very long-term nature of the projects, their sky-high costs, as well as bad experience of private-sector financing of infrastructural projects such as the Channel Tunnel may act as important obstacles for the involvement of the private sector in these projects.
- *Protection and conservation of the environment.* Transport is responsible for around 25 per cent of the total EU emission of CO_2, one of the greenhouse gases that contributes to global warming. The EU set an interim target for the stabilization of CO_2 emission by the year 2000 at 1990 levels, and a reduction in years beyond. This would require an increase in the efficiency of fuel consumption (Commission of the European Communities, 1992, p. 61).
- *Safety.* Each year accidents cause around 50,000 deaths and more than 1.5 million injuries on the roads of the EU[7] (Commission of the European Communities, 1992, p. 65). The direct annual costs of these accidents is around ECU 15 billion. This annual amount needs to be increased by an additional ECU 30 billion in lost output. Safety improvements are a legitimate area for EU concern. There was a chain of directives regarding the harmonization of standards for brakes, lighting, windshields, sound levels, dimensions and weights of commercial vehicles and the like. The EU intends to promote better training of drivers, to increase the awareness of dangers of driving while intoxicated or tired, and to encourage 'calm driving'. Technical measures to reduce the high toll in human and economic terms, include improvements in the safety of vehicles and roads.
- *Social issues.* The EU intends to further the implementation of the Social Charter in the area of transport. In addition, there must be an obligatory period of rest for drivers (for example, by the introduction of the tachograph as 'the spy in the cab'), a regulation of working time and other conditions, as well as training.
- *External relations.* The intention of the EU is to cooperate first and foremost with Switzerland on transport issues. Because of the lack of a land frontier with Greece, certain Balkan nations will also be included in the list of those countries which will participate in a common transport policy.

As already noted, the provision of transport services throughout the EU has been highly regulated and restricted. This resulted in a very inefficient system and losses when trucks had long return journeys without any cargo. There were, however, bilateral licences and quotas for the provision of transport services that were negotiated among member countries each year. In order to tackle the problem, certain EU permits were introduced. Although they presented a positive step forward in the market for transport services in the EU, they had a limited effect as their number was relatively small compared with the demand. A secondary (black) market for licences evolved. The 1992 Programme introduced a substantial change. The Council decided in 1988 that as of 1993 any operator holding a national licence could carry on with operations in the EU with the exclusion of cabotage. In addition, it was decided that road haulage operators will be able to provide cabotage throughout the EU from 1998.[8]

Air transport has traditionally been highly regulated and dominated by a flagship carrier. Hence, the actual performance of national carriers had little impact on their competitiveness. Demands for reductions in public expenditure in the 1990s contributed to privatization trends in the air transport industry. Britain and the Netherlands followed more liberal policies in this industry than other EU countries. National governments started permitting foreign airlines to purchase stakes in national air carriers. There is a possibility that smaller carriers (from southern EU countries) are going to be absorbed by larger EU carriers.

III CONCLUSION

If compared with the trade policy of the EU or the CAP, a common transport policy does not exist, but it is slowly evolving. Its delayed, but undisputed development started in 1985 following the ruling of the Court of Justice against the Council of Ministers. One has to note here that the EU has always been involved in the financing of transport infrastructure in one way or another. None the less, this has been more on an *ad hoc* project-by-project basis than as a part of a coherent common transport policy. The role of the EU in financing transport infrastructure will be reinforced in the future by the setting up of trans-European networks.

Another turning point in the creation of a (common) transport policy came with the 1992 Programme. Policy emphasis moved away from the elimination of NTBs towards the broader objective of the smooth operation of a transport system within the single market. The result is a more open market, free of bureaucracy, which is helping firms to increase their efficiency and competitiveness. The medium-term objective of the EU is to integrate national transport networks into a coherent European transport system, to remove bottlenecks and to forge previously missing links. It may be expected that the Commission will propose and carry out a more active policy in the area of transport (if national governments permit) on the grounds of subsidiarity, cohesion, regional development, safety, protection of the environment and social issues.

NOTES

1 Public authorities often use subsidies and discriminatory rates for the transport of goods and passengers to and from select regions with disadvantages, as an aid to the development of and employment in those areas.

2 A loss-making and highly subsidized train transport system was revived following the opening up of high-speed TGV train service between Paris and Lyon in 1981. Since then, this development has boosted similar train services on the major railway routes in the EU.

3 Around 70 per cent of all merchandise transport in the EU is by road; railways carry around 19 per cent; while the share of inland waterways is around 9 per cent.

4 Commission of the European Economic Community, 1961.

5 Granting cabotage right to foreigners occurs when country A allows operators from country B to provide internal transport services in country A. It represents a profound move towards the full freedom to provide transport services.

6 A Single Administrative Document, introduced in 1988, replaced up to 70 different forms that were previously necessary for lorries crossing internal frontiers in the EU. The Document is also valid for EFTA countries.

7 Almost 2 million people have been killed and almost 50 million people injured in traffic accidents in the EU since its creation!

8 Cabotage would also be allowed for air transport from 1998.

14

CONCLUSION

The objective of this book was to look into the origin, evolution, operation and prospects for economic integration in the EU. The evolution of the EU can fit into five broad periods. First was creation and growth (1957–1968); in the second came consolidation and enlargement (1969–1973); third was the period of Eurosclerosis (1974–1984); then arrived the great leap forward, the so-called Euroactivism (1985–1992); once this ended, the latest period has now become a venture into the unknown (1993–). It is worthwhile noticing that IGC have marked some of these periods as milestones. IGCs provide rare opportunities to redesign the EU and are therefore particularly important.

The first conference (the term IGC is of relatively recent origin) based on the Schuman/Monnet Plan, started in 1950, culminating with the signing of the Treaty of Paris that created the ECSC; the second one began in 1955 in Messina and ended up with the Treaty of Rome; the third one was initiated in 1970 in order to revise Article 203 of the Treaty of Rome on the financing of the budget; the fourth one was launched in 1985 and led to the Single European Act; the fifth and the sixth IGCs started simultaneously in 1990. One dealt with the extension of the Single European Market to the EMU, while the other focused on political union. They both produced the Maastricht Treaty. The seventh IGC started in Turin in March 1996. Its goal is to prepare the EU for the coming decades and to make it more manageable once it increases the number of member countries. This IGC, which may last until the end of 1997, is a planned step because the Maastricht Treaty was only an intermediate stage on the long road to deeper integration. It may slow down the grand plans presented in the Maastricht Treaty regarding EMU, but the EU may come out better organized. In fact, reorganization of the structure may absorb most of the work of the IGC.

'Euroactivism' is over and the EU is passing through a period of crisis. On the political front, it has been unable to solve the neighbouring Yugoslav black hole, which showed just how minor a role the EU plays in resolving serious international crises (although other countries and organizations did not fare much better). In the economic field, it does not seem capable of creating new jobs and reducing unemployment. As for the EMU as structured in the Maastricht Treaty, its implementation will not take place in the near future.

In addition, coverage of many EU policies such as those ones in social, regional, taxation, environment or transport areas is still limited. These policies have been based on a number of compromises, which have affected the purity of their principles. Intervention has been much less of a well-organized policy and much more a mix of various issues that the member states were willing to transfer to the EU. The 'loose' character of these policies also comes from the legal provisions that are in certain cases aspirational, rather than operational.

Regarding trade and global competition issues, the EU has suffered a relative loss of competitiveness in comparison with the US in computers and aerospace industries; Japan in cars and consumer electronics; and developing countries in textiles and apparel, as well as a potential loss in a number of other industries which provided the impetus for the 1992 Programme. Businesses reacted to the single market programme by consolidations through mergers and acquisitions, as well as joint ventures. Programme 1992 enhanced the dynamic process of competition by easing market segmentation and, somewhat paradoxically, increasing concentration in business. This concentration permitted economies of scale and an increase in technical efficiency in production. In addition, it enhanced R&D through a joint sharing of high costs. As widely argued, EU firms in a sizeable part of its manufacturing industry are less efficient than their counterparts in the US and Japan. If the EU does adopt a liberal economic (including trade) policy, if EU firms adjust and withstand competition from foreign TNCs, they may in relative terms gain more from market liberalization than their foreign competitors.

An increase in internal EU competition that came through the elimination of internal NTBs provided opportunities for the EU to benefit from the so far unexploited economies of scale that would reduce, over time, costs of production and increase global competitiveness, not only in manufacturing, but also in services. This would all provide an additional longer-term bonus to investment and growth of the EU economy. Hence, not only innovating firms and those that use state-of-the-art technologies, but consumers, too, are able to benefit from the challenges provided by increased competition. The dynamic segment of labour may gain from the integration process as trade and competition would not determine *if* there are jobs, but rather *which* jobs are available.

As far as unification of the market is concerned, there is a burning question: is the EU aiming at an almost totally homogenized market, with similar tastes and lifestyles, such as the US exhibits? Apart from several exceptional spots, no matter where one moves in the US, one may see almost everywhere the same types of towns and villages, and virtually the same general type of life or diet. That may be the reason why the Americans move so easily within their own country. This form of integration is not necessary or even possible in Europe. It is hardly conceivable in Europe to have almost identical flavours of pasta or steak (*bistecca Fiorentina*) both in Tuscany and Lapland, as is the case with McDonald's hamburgers in Chicago and San Diego.[1] There need to be various measures to preserve unity with diversity in the EU as long as people want that and are able and ready to pay for it. How far we can go with integration is up to the people to decide in ballot boxes.

It must not be forgotten, though, that European integration contributed to international trade liberalization in the post-1960s period. In addition, the extension of the GATT into the new areas such as services could have been slower in the absence of the 'challenge' posed by the evolution of the EU. None the less, there are certain reasons to suppose that the impact of the EU on the multilateral trading system has not been entirely benign (for example, in agriculture).

The lifecycle of goods is shortening and the situation in the market changes rapidly. Innovation, technology and the skills of the labour force are key factors in competitiveness. Therefore, there should be more emphasis on education as the most valuable asset that a country or region can have, that is, human capital, to solve problems and shape comparative advantage for and in the future. The EU has to do much more in the area of increasing human skills, experiences and organizational competences than has been the case so far.

A topic that will be high on the EU agenda is eastern enlargement. Interest in the support of the transition economies in their reform efforts is emphasized by the fact that the EU has an unprecedented opportunity to reshape Europe and make it a better and safer area. The EU should not fear opening-up to the east because of the impact on jobs. The effects would be felt not in quantity, but rather in the quality of jobs. A revision of the Maastricht Treaty during the IGC may change and ease the rules for the entry of select transition countries. None the less, there are many political minefields such as reform of the CAP, regional and social funds. Eastern enlargement of the EU would be, in fact, a kind of farm enlargement, to a considerable extent. A powerful agricultural lobby in the EU would resist that cost of enlargement being paid by EU farmers.

As a matter of fact, limits to further integration in the EU can be found essentially in national politics. EU member states are among the oldest in the world, they have differences not only in social, legal and tax structures, but also in history and climate. None the less, the connecting tissues among those countries are economic and political interests. These *national* political obstacles are supplemented by *nationally* regulated and rigid labour markets and high taxes. Hence, certain barriers to integration are more within the member states, than at the EU level! The problem is that the participating countries may not wish to abandon their own rights in economic policies and transfer them to the Union level.

Policy-makers tend to forget that in economic integration sovereignty is most often pooled, rather than given up. For instance, politicians in a number of EU countries often support in private the dissenting British stance on various issues in the EU. Freedom in their public statements is often limited because of constraints such as political (coalition) commitments or because of the 'smallness' of their country: Britain represents, therefore, a convenient scapegoat for caution (read: slowness) in economic integration. Economic integration is a highly charged political process which requires caution, gradualism and, more than anything else, the political will which economic theory may not predict.

The general conclusion is that there is considerable room for improvement in economic integration in the EU, as well as for the reform of policies such as the CAP. If certain grand approaches to integration such as EMU as based on the Maastricht Treaty (and on criteria which are not known in the theory of international monetary integration) fail,[2] then that does not mean that the idea of European integration is doomed. On the contrary. There are many other possible scenarios for it, including monetary integration. Perhaps, a less ambitious plan for monetary integration, set for a longer period of time than the one established by the Maastricht Treaty may produce a better and more stable EU in the future, and also preserve unity with diversity in the region, which is the only guarantee of success.

Those (few) who decided to specialize in European integration during the late 1970s and first half of the 1980s (including the present author) were asking themselves at that time of Eurosclerosis if their choice of subject was correct. Those who embark upon studying European integration now can at least be sure that their efforts will not be vain.

NOTES

1 Italians *scusate* for the inappropriate comparison of your cuisine with American hamburgers – the intention here was simply to make a point!
2 There have been many failures in the reform of the CAP, one of the key EU policies, and European integration has survived.

BIBLIOGRAPHY

Adams, G. (1983). 'Criteria for US industrial policy strategies', in *Industrial Policies for Growth and Competitiveness* (eds G. Adams and L. Klein). Lexington: Lexington Books, pp. 393–418.

Adams, G. and A. Bolino (1983). 'Meaning of industrial policy', in *Industrial Policies for Growth and Competitiveness* (eds G. Adams and L. Klein). Lexington: Lexington Books, pp. 13–20.

Adams, G. and L. Klein (1983). 'Economic evolution of industrial policies for growth and competitiveness: overview', in *Industrial Policies for Growth and Competitiveness* (eds G. Adams and L. Klein). Lexington: Lexington Books, pp. 3–11.

Armington, P. (1969). 'A theory of demand for products distinguished by place of production', *International Monetary Fund Staff Papers*, pp. 159–178.

Armstrong, H. (1985). 'The reform of European Community regional policy', *Journal of Common Market Studies*, pp. 319–343.

Atkin, M. (1993). *Snouts in the Trough*. Cambridge: Woodhead.

Audretsch, D. (1989). *The Market and the State*. New York: New York University Press.

——(1993). 'Industrial policy and international competitiveness', in *Industrial Policy in the European Community* (ed. P. Nicolaides). Dordrecht: Martinus Nijhoff, pp. 67–105.

Bachtler, J. and R. Michie (1993). 'The restructuring of regional policy in the European Community', *Regional Studies*, pp. 719–725.

——(1995). 'A new era in EU regional policy evaluation? The apprisal of the structural funds', *Regional Studies*, pp. 745–751.

Badaracco, J. and D. Yoffie (1983). '"Industrial policy": it can't happen here', *Harvard Business Review*, (November–December), pp. 97–105.

Balassa, B. and L. Bauwens (1988). 'The determinants of intra-European trade in manufactured goods', *European Economic Review*, pp. 1421–1437.

Baldwin, R. (1989). 'The Growth effects of 1992', *Economic Policy*, pp. 248–270.

——(1995). 'The eastern enlargement of the European Union', *European Economic Review*, pp. 474–481.

Barro, R. and X. Sala-i-Martin (1991). 'Convergence across states and regions', *Brookings Papers on Economic Activity*, pp. 107–182.

Bayliss, B. (1985). 'Competition and industrial policies', in *The Economics of the European Community* (ed. A. El-Agraa). Oxford: Philip Allan, pp. 209–227.

Bayliss, B. and A. El-Agraa (1990). 'Competition and industrial policies with emphasis on competition policy', in *Economies of the European Community* (ed. A. El-Agraa). New York: St Martin's Press, pp. 137–155.

Bean, C. (1992). 'Economic and monetary union in Europe', *Journal of Economic Perspectives*, pp. 31–52.

Bellamy, C. and G. Child (1987). *Common Market Law of Competition*. London: Sweet & Maxwell.

Bhagwati, J. (1989). 'United States trade policy at the crossroads', *World Economy*, pp. 439–480.

Bianchi, P. (1995). 'Small and medium-sized enterprises in the European perspective', *International Journal of Technology Management* (Special Publication), pp. 119–130.

Bird, R. (1972). 'The need for regional policy in a common market', in *International Economic Integration* (ed. P. Robson), Harmondsworth: Penguin, pp. 257–277.

Blackhurst, R. and D. Henderson (1993). 'Regional integration agreements, world integration and the GATT', in *Regional Integration and the Global Trading System* (eds K. Anderson and R. Blackhurst). New York: Harvester Wheatsheaf, pp. 408–435.

Blais, A. (1986). 'Industrial policy in advanced capitalist democracies', in *Industrial Policy* (ed. A. Blais). Toronto: University of Toronto Press, pp. 1–53.

Boner, R. and R. Krueger (1991). *The Basics of Antitrust Policy.* Washington: The World Bank.

Borrell, B. (1994). 'EU bananarama III', World Bank Policy Research Working Paper 1386.

Brander, J. (1987). 'Shaping comparative advantage: trade policy, industrial policy and economic performance', in *Shaping Comparative Advantage* (eds R. Lipsey and W. Dobson). Toronto: C.D. Howe Institute, pp. 1–55.

Brander, J. and B. Spencer (1985). 'Export subsidies and international market share rivalry', *Journal of International Economics*, pp. 83–100.

Buckley, P. and P. Artisien (1987). 'Policy issues of intra-EC direct investment', *Journal of Common Market Studies*, pp. 207–230.

Buigues, P. and A. Jacquemin (1992). 'Foreign direct investment and exports in the Common Market', paper presented at the Japanese Direct Investment in a Unifying Europe, conference held in INSEAD, Fontainebleau, 26–27 June 1992, mimeo.

—— (1994). 'Foreign direct investment and exports to the European Community', in *Does Ownership Matter* (eds M. Mason and D. Eucarnation). Oxford: Clarendon Press, pp. 163–197.

Buigues, P. and A. Sapir (1993). 'Market services and European integration: issues and challenges', *European Economy Social Europe*, No. 3, pp. ix–xx.

Campagni, R., P. Cheshire, J. de Gandemar, P. Hall, L. Rodwin and F. Suickars (1991). 'Europe's regional-urban features: conclusions, inferences and surmises', in *Industrial Change and Regional Economic Transformation* (eds L. Rodwin and H. Sazanami). London: Harper-Collins, pp. 301–315.

Canzoneri, M. and C. Rogers (1990). 'Is the European Community an optimal currency area? Optimal taxation versus the cost of multiple currencies', *American Economic Review*, pp. 419–433.

Carlén, B. (1994). 'Road transport', *EFTA Occasional Paper No. 49*, pp. 81–111.

Carliner, G. (1988). 'Industrial policies for emerging industries', in Strategic *Trade Policy and the New International Economics* (ed. P. Krugman). Cambridge: MIT Press, pp. 147–168.

Cecchini, P. (1988). *The European Challenge 1992 – The Benefits of a Single Market.* Aldershot: Wildwood House.

CEPR (1992). *Is Bigger Better? The Economics of EC Enlargement.* London: CEPR.

Chang, H. (1994). *The Political Economy of Industrial Policy.* London: Macmillan.

Charnovitz, S. (1995). 'Regional trade agreements and the environment', *Environment*, pp. 16–20 and 40–45.

Chaudhry, P., P. Dacin and P. Peter (1994). 'The pharmaceutical industry and European Community integration', *European Management Journal*, pp. 442–453.

Cnossen, S. (1986). 'Tax harmonization in the European Community', *Bulletin for International Fiscal Documentation*, pp. 545–563.

—— (1990). 'The case for tax diversity in the European Community', *European Economic Review*, pp. 471–479.

—— (1995). 'Reforming and coordinating company taxes in the European Union', paper presented at the conference Changing Role of the Public Sector: Transition in the 1990, Lisbon, 21–24 August 1995.

Cobham, D. (1989). 'Strategies for monetary integration revisited', *Journal of Common Market Studies*, pp. 203–218.

Coffey, P. (1982). *The Common Market and Its International Economic Policies.* Amsterdam: Europa Institute.

Commission of the European Communities (1992). *The Future Development of the Common Transport Policy*. Brussels: European Union.

Commission of the European Economic Community (1961). *Memorandum on the General Lines of the Common Transport Policy* (Schaus Memorandum). Brussels: European Economic Community.

Cooper, C. and B. Massel (1965). 'A new look at customs union theory', *Economic Journal*, pp. 742–747.

Corden, W. (1972). *Monetary Integration*. Princeton: Essays in International Finance, Princeton University.

Cosgrove, C. (1994). 'Has the Lomé Convention failed ACP trade?', *Journal of International Affairs*, pp. 223–249.

Courchene, T. (1987). *Social Policy in the 1990s, Agenda for Reform*. Toronto: C.D. Howe Institute.

Currie, D. (1992). 'European monetary union: institutional structure and economic performance', *Economic Journal*, pp. 248–264.

Curwen, P. (1995). 'The economics of social responsibility in the European Union', in *The Economics of the New Europe* (ed. N. Healey). London: Routledge, pp. 188–205.

Curzon Price, V. (1981). *Industrial Policies in the European Community*. London: Macmillan.

——(1987). *Free Trade Areas? the European Experience*. Toronto: C.D. Howe Institute.

——(1988). 'The European Free Trade Association', in *International Economic Integration* (ed. A. El-Agraa). London: Macmillan, pp. 96–127.

——(1990). 'Competition and industrial policies with emphasis on industrial policy', in *Economics of the European Community* (ed. A. El-Agraa). New York: St Martin's Press, pp. 156–186.

——(1991). 'The threat of "Fortress Europe" from the development of social and industrial policies at European level', *Aussenwirtschaft*, pp. 119–138.

——(1993). 'EEC's strategic trade-cum-industrial policy: a public choice analysis', in *National Constitutions and International Economic Law* (eds M. Hilf and E. Petersmann). Deventer: Kluwer, pp. 391–405.

——(1994). 'The role of regional trade and investment agreements', paper presented at the conference 'Policies dealing with the EU–LDC relations in view of the transition in central and eastern European countries', The Netherlands Economic Institute, Rotterdam, 16–17 May 1994.

——(1996). 'The role of regional trade and investment agreements', in *Transition in Central and Eastern Europe* (eds A. Kuyvenhoven *et al.*). Dordrecht: Kluwer, pp. 69–88.

d'Arge, R. (1969). 'Note on customs unions and direct foreign investment', *Economic Journal*, pp. 324–333.

——(1971a). 'Customs Unions and Direct Foreign Investment', *Economic Journal*, pp. 352–355.

——(1971b). 'A Reply', *Economic Journal*, pp. 357–359.

Davenport, M. (1995). 'Fostering integration of countries in transition in central and Eastern Europe in the world economy and the implications for the developing countries', Geneva: UNCTAD / ITD 7, 31 October 1995.

Defraigne, P. (1984). 'Towards concerted industrial policies in the European Community', in *European Industry: Public Policy and Corporate Strategy* (ed. A. Jacquemin). Oxford: Clarendon Press, pp. 368–377.

de Ghellinck, E. (1988). 'European industrial policy against the background of the Single European Act', in *Main Economic Policy Areas of the EEC – towards 1992* (ed. P. Coffey). Dordrecht: Kluwer, pp. 133–156.

de Grauwe, P. (1975). 'Conditions for monetary integration – a geometric interpretation', *Weltwirtschaftliches Archiv*, pp. 634–646.

——(1991). 'The 1992 European integration program and regional development policies', in *Trade Theory and Economic Reform: North, South and East* (eds J. de Melo and A. Sapir). Cambridge, MA: Basil Blackwell, pp. 142–153.

——(1994a). *The Economics of Monetary Integration*. Oxford: Oxford University Press.

——(1994b). 'Towards EMU without the EMS', *Economic Policy*, pp. 149–185.

—— (1995). 'The Economics of convergence towards monetary union in Europe', Discussion Paper No. 1213, CEPR, London.

de la Fuente, A. and X. Vives (1995). 'Regional policy and Spain', *Economic Policy*, April, pp. 13–51.

Dell'Aringa, C. and F. Neri (1989). 'Illegal immigrants and the informal economy in Italy', in *European Factor Mobility* (eds I. Gordon and A. Thirlwall). New York: St Martin's Press, pp. 133–147.

Delors, J. (1989). *Report on Economic and Monetary Union in the European Community.* Brussels: European Community.

Dertouzos, M., R. Lester and R. Solow (1990). *Made in America.* New York: Harper Perennial.

Donges, J. (1980). 'Industrial policies in West Germany's not so market-oriented economy', *The World Economy*, pp. 185–204.

Dosi, G. (1988). 'Sources, procedures and microeconomic effects of innovation', *Journal of Economic Literature*, pp. 1120–1171.

Dosi, G., K. Pavitt and L. Soete (1990). *The Economics of Technical Change and International Trade.* New York: Harvester Wheatsheaf.

Dowd, K. and D. Greenaway (1993a). 'Currency competition, network externalities and switching costs: towards an alternative view of optimum currency areas', *Economic Journal*, pp. 1180–1189.

—— (1993b). 'A single currency for Europe?', *Greek Economic Review*, pp. 227–244.

Drabek, Z. and D. Greenaway (1984). 'Economic integration and intra-industry trade: the EEC and CMEA compared', *Kyklos*, pp. 444–469.

Dunning, J. (1988). *Explaining International Production.* London: Unwin Hyman.

—— (ed.) (1993). *The Theory of Transnational Corporations (The United Nations Library on Transnational Corporations).* London: Routledge.

—— (1994a). 'Globalization: the challenge for national economic regimes', *Discussion Paper* No. 186, Department of Economics, University of Reading.

—— (1994b). 'MNE activity: comparing the NAFTA and the European Community', in *Multinationals in North America* (ed. L. Eden). Calgary: University of Calgary Press, pp. 277–308.

Dunning, J. and P. Robson (1987). 'Multinational Corporate Integration and Regional Economic Integration', *Journal of Common Market Studies*, pp. 103–124.

Economic Commission for Europe (1994). *Economic Survey of Europe in 1993–1994.* New York: United Nations.

EFTA, (1993). *Pattern of Production and Trade in the New Europe.* Geneva: EFTA.

Eichengreen, B. (1993). 'European monetary unification', *Journal of Economic Literature*, pp. 1321–1357.

El-Agraa, A.M. (ed.) (1985). *The Economics of the European Community.* Oxford: Philip Allan.

—— (1988). *Japan's Trade Frictions.* London: Macmillan.

—— (ed.) (1990). *The Economics of the European Community.* New York: St Martin's Press.

—— (ed.) (1994). *The Economics of the European Community.* New York: Harvester Wheatsheaf.

Emerson, M., M. Auejan, M. Catinat, P. Goybet and A. Jacquemin (1988). 'The economics of 1992', *European Economy*, March.

European Commission (1994). *1994 Report on US Barriers to Trade and Investment.* Brussels: European Union.

European Communities (1973). *Report on the Regional Problems of the Enlarged Community.* Brussels: European Community.

—— (1985). *Completing the Internal Market (White Paper).* Luxembourg: European Community.

—— (1991). *XXth Report on Competition Policy.* Brussels: European Community.

—— (1993). *The Community Budget: The Facts in Figures.* Brussels: European Community.

European Economy (1989). *International Trade of the European Community.* No. 39.

—— (1990a). *One Market? One Money.* No. 44.

—— (1990b). *Social Europe*. Special Edition.

—— (1991). *The Economies of EMU*. Special edition No. 1.

—— (1993a). *The European Community as a World Trade Partner*. No. 52.

—— (1993b). *The Economic and Financial Situation in Italy*, No. 1.

—— (1994a). *Competition and Integration; Community Merger Control Policy*. No. 57.

—— (1994b). *EC Agricultural Policy for the 21st Century*, No. 4.

FAO (1994). *FAO Yearbook: Trade 1992*. Rome: FAO.

Faulhaber, G. and G. Tamburini (1991). *European Economic Integration*. Boston: Kluwer.

Finger, M., K. Hall and D. Nelson (1982). 'The political economy of administered protection', *American Economic Review*, pp. 452–466.

Fleming, M. (1971). 'On exchange rate unification', *Economic Journal*, pp. 467–486.

Folkerts-Landau, D. and D. Mathieson (1989). *The European Monetary System in the Context of the Integration of European Financial Markets*. Washington: IMF.

Fraisse, R., B. Cazes, F. Descoyette and J. Levet (1993). 'France: shaping factors', in *The European Challenges Post-1992* (eds A. Jacquemin and D. Wright). Aldershot: Edward Elgar, pp. 203–233.

Freeman, C. (1994). 'The economics of technical change', *Cambridge Journal of Economics*, pp. 463–514.

Frohberg, K. (1994). 'Assessment of the effects of a reform of the common agricultural policy on labour income and outflow', *European Economy*, No. 5, pp. 179–206.

Geroski, P. (1987). 'Brander's "Shaping comparative advantage": some comments', in *Shaping Comparative Advantage* (eds R. Lipsey and W. Dobson). Toronto: C.D. Howe Institute, pp. 57–64.

—— (1988). 'Competition and innovation', in Commission of the European Communities, *Studies on the Economics of Integration*. Brussels: European Community, pp. 339–388.

—— (1989). 'European industrial policy and industrial policy in Europe', *Oxford Review of Economic Policy*, pp. 20–36.

Geroski, P. and A. Jacquemin (1985). 'Industrial change, barriers to mobility, and European industrial policy', *Economic Policy*, pp. 170–218.

Gittelman, M., E. Graham and H. Fukukawa (1992). 'Affiliates of Japanese firms in the European Community: performance and structure', paper presented at the Japanese Direct Investment in a Unifying Europe, conference held in INSEAD, Fontainebleau, 26–27 June 1992, mimeo.

Goldberg, M. (1972). 'The determinants of U.S. direct investment in the E.E.C.: a comment', *American Economic Review*, pp. 692–699.

Graham, E. and P. Krugman (1991). *Foreign Direct Investment in the United States*. Washington: Institute for International Economics.

Gray, P. and I. Walter (1991). 'The integration of the EC market for financial services and the US banking and insurance industries', in *Europe and America, 1992* (ed. G. Yannopoulos). Manchester: Manchester University Press, pp. 128–149.

Greenaway, D. and C. Milner (1987). 'Intra-industry trade: current perspectives and unresolved issues', *Weltwirschaftliches Archiv*, pp. 39–57.

Grilli, E. (1993). *The European Community and the Developing Countries*. Cambridge: Cambridge University Press.

Gros, D. (1989). 'Paradigms for the Monetary Union of Europe', *Journal of Common Market Studies*, pp. 219–230.

Grossman, H., G. Koopmann and A. Michaelowa (1994). 'The new World Trade Organization: pacemaker for world trade', *Intereconomics*, (May–June), pp. 107–115.

Grubel, H. (1967). *International Monetary System*. Harmondsworth: Penguin Books.

—— (1970). 'The theory of optimum currency areas', *Canadian Journal of Economics*, pp. 318–324.

Hagedoorn, J. and J. Schakenraad (1993). 'A comparison of private and subsidized R&D partnerships in the European information technology industry', *Journal of Common Market Studies*, pp. 373–390.

Hague, D. (1960). 'Report on the proceedings: summary record of the debate', in *Economic Consequences of the Size of Nations* (ed. E. Robinson). London: Macmillan, pp. 333–438.

Hamilton, B. and J. Whalley (1986). 'Border tax adjustment and US trade', *Journal of International Economics*, pp. 377–383.

Harris, R. (1985). *Trade, Industrial Policy and International Competition*. Toronto: University of Toronto Press.

Hartmann, M. (1994). 'The effects of EC environmental policies on agricultural trade and economic welfare', in *Agricultural Trade and Economic Integration in Europe and North America* (eds M. Hartmann, P. Schmitz and H. von Witzke). Kiel: Vauk, pp. 150–170.

Hay, D. (1993). 'The assessment: competition policy', *Oxford Review of Economic Policy*, pp. 1–26.

Hayek, F. (1978). *New Studies in Philosophy, Politics, Economics and the History of Ideas*. London: Routledge & Kegan Paul.

Hewitt, A. (1984). 'The Lomé Conventions: entering a second decade', *Journal of Common Market Studies*, pp. 95–115.

Hill, T. (1977). 'On goods and services', *Review of Income and Wealth*, pp. 315–338.

Hindley, B. (1991). 'Creating an integrated market for financial services', in *European Economic Integration* (eds G. Faulhaber and G. Tamburini). Boston: Kluwer, pp. 263–288.

Hymer, S. (1976). *The International Operations of National Firms: A Study of Direct Foreign Investment*. Boston: MIT Press.

Jacquemin, A. (1984). European Industry: *Public Policy and Corporate Strategy*. Oxford: Clarendon Press.

——(1990a). 'Mergers and European policy', in *Merger and Competition Policy in the European Community* (ed. P. Admiraal). Oxford: Basil Blackwell, pp. 1–38.

——(1990b). 'Horizontal concentration and European merger policy', *European Economic Review*, pp. 539–550.

——(1991). 'Collusive behaviour, R&D and European competition policy', in *European Economic Integration* (eds G. Faulhaber and G. Tamburini). Boston: Kluwer, pp. 201–235.

Jacquemin, A. and J. Marchipont (1992). 'De nouveaux enjeux pour la politique industrielle de la Communauté', *Revue d'économie politique*, pp. 69–97.

Jacquemin, A., and A. Sapir (1991). 'The internal and external opening-up of the Single Community Market: efficiency gains, adjustment costs and new Community instruments', *International Spectator*, pp. 29–48.

Jacquemin, A. and D. Wright (1993). 'Corporate strategies and European challenges post-1992', *Journal of Common Market Studies*, pp. 525–537.

Jansen, M. (1975). *History of European Integration 1945–75*. Amsterdam: Europa Institute.

Johnson, C. (1984). 'The idea of industrial policy', in *The Industrial Policy Debate* (ed. C. Johnson). San Francisco: Institute for Contemporary Studies.

Johnson, H. and M. Krauss (1973). 'Border taxes, border tax adjustment, comparative advantage and the balance of payments', in *Economics of Integration* (ed. M. Krauss). London: George Allen and Unwin, pp. 239–253.

Jovanović, M. (1992). *International Economic Integration*. London: Routledge.

——(1995). 'Economic integration among developing countries and foreign direct investment', *Economia Internazionale*, pp. 209–244.

——(ed.) (1997a). *International Economic Integration: Critical Perspectives on the World Economy – Theory and Measurement* (Volume I). London: Routledge.

——(1997b). *International Economic Integration: Critical Perspectives on the World Economy – Monetary, Fiscal and Factor Mobility Issues* (Volume II). London: Routledge.

——(1997c). *International Economic Integration: Critical Perspectives on the World Economy – General Issues* (Volume III). London: Routledge.

——(1997d). *International Economic Integration: Critical Perspectives on the World Economy – Integration Schemes*(Volume IV). London: Routledge.

Karsenty, G. and S. Laird (1986). 'The generalized system of preferences: a quantitative assessment of the direct trade effects and of policy options'. UNCTAD Discussion Paper 18. Geneva: UNCTAD.

Kay, J. (1990). 'Tax policy: a survey', *Economic Journal*, pp. 18–75.

Kemp, M. and H. Wan (1976). 'An elementary proposal concerning the formation of customs unions', *Journal of International Economics*, pp. 95–97.

Kenen, P. (1969). 'Theory of optimum currency areas: an eclectic view', in *Monetary Problems of the International Economy* (eds R. Mundell and A. Swoboda). Chicago: Chicago University Press, pp. 41–60.

——(1995). 'Capital controls, the EMS and EMU', *Economic Journal*, pp. 181–192.

Keynes, J. (1923). *A Tract on Monetary Reform*. London: Royal Economic Society.

Komiya, R. (1988). 'Introduction', in *Industrial Policy of Japan* (eds R. Komiya, M. Okuno, K. Suzumura). Tokyo: Academic Press, pp. 1–22.

Krugman, P. (1990a). *Rethinking International Trade*. Cambridge: The MIT Press.

——(1990b). 'Protectionism: try it, you'll like it', *International Economy* (June–July), pp. 35–39.

——(1993). 'The current case for industrial policy', in *Protectionism and World Welfare* (ed. D. Salvatore). Cambridge: Cambridge University Press, pp. 160–179.

——(1995). 'The move toward free trade zones', in *International Economics and International Economic Policy: A Reader* (ed. P. King). New York: McGraw-Hill, pp. 163–182.

Krugman, P. and A. Venables (1990). 'Integration and the competitiveness of peripheral industry', in *Unity with Diversity in the European Economy: the Community's Southern Frontier* (eds C. Bliss and J. Braga de Macedo). Cambridge: Cambridge University Press, pp. 56–75.

Lall, S. (1994). 'The east Asian miracle: does the bell toll for industrial strategy?', *World Development*, pp. 645–654.

Lancaster, K. (1980). 'Intra-industry trade under perfect monopolistic competition', *Journal of International Economics*, pp. 151–175.

Leamer, E. (1984). *Sources of International Comparative Advantage*. Cambridge: The MIT Press.

Levin, R., A. Klevorick, R. Nelson and S. Winter (1987). 'Appropriating the returns from industrial research and development', *Brookings Papers on Economic Activity*, pp. 783–820.

Linder, S. (1961). *An Essay on Trade and Transformation*. Uppsala: Almquist & Wiksells.

Lipsey, R. (1957). 'The theory of customs unions: trade diversion and welfare', *Economica*, pp. 40–46.

——(1960). 'The theory of customs unions: a general survey', *Economic Journal*, pp.496–513.

——(1987a). 'Models matter when discussing competitiveness: a technical note', in *Shaping Comparative Advantage* (eds R. Lipsey and W. Dobson). Toronto: C.D. Howe Institute, pp. 155–166.

——(1987b). 'Report on the workshop', in *Shaping Comparative Advantage* (eds R.G. Lipsey and W. Dobson). Toronto: C.D. Howe Institute, pp. 109–153.

——(1991). 'The case for trilateralism', in *Continental Accord: North American Economic Integration* (ed. S. Globerman). Vancouver: The Fraser Institute, pp. 89–123.

——(1992). 'Global change and economic policy', in *The Culture and the Power of Knowledge* (eds N. Stehr and R. Ericson). New York: De Gruyter, pp. 279–299.

——(1993a). 'Globalisation, technological change and economic growth', Annual Sir Charles Carter Lecture, mimeo.

——(1993b). 'The changing technoeconomic paradigm and some implications for economic policy', Canadian Institute for Advanced Research, Vancouver, mimeo.

——(1993c). 'Canadian trade policy in relation to regional free trade agreements: CAFTA, NAFTA and WHFTA', Canadian Institute for Advanced Research, Vancouver, mimeo.

——(1994). 'Markets, technological change and economic growth', Canadian Institute for Advanced Research, Vancouver, mimeo.

Lipsey, R. and K. Lancaster (1956–7). 'The general theory of the second best', *Review of Economic Studies*, pp. 11–32.

Lipsey, R. and M. Smith (1986). *Taking the Initiative: Canada's Trade Options in a Turbulent World*. Toronto: C.D. Howe Institute.

Lipsey, R. and M. Smith (1987). *Global Imbalances and US Policy Responses*. Toronto: C.D. Howe Institute.

Lunn, J. (1980). 'Determinants of US Direct investment in the EEC', *European Economic Review*, pp. 93–101.

——(1983). 'Determinants of US Direct investment in the EEC', *European Economic Review*, pp. 391–393.

MacDougall, G. (1977). *Report of the Study Group on the Role of Public Finance in European Integration*. Brussels: European Community.

McFetridge, D. (1985). 'The economics of industrial policy', in *Canadian Industrial Policy in Action* (ed. D. McFetridge). Toronto: University of Toronto Press, pp. 1–49.

Machlup, F. (1979). *A History of Thought on Economic Integration*. London: Macmillan.

McKinnon, R. (1963). 'Optimum currency area', *American Economic Review*, pp. 717–725.

——(1994). 'A common monetary standard or a common currency for Europe? The fiscal constraints', *Rivista di Politica Economica*, pp. 59–79.

Markusen, J., (1983). 'Factor movements and commodity trade as complements', *Journal of International Economics*, pp. 342–356.

Mason, M. (1994). 'Elements of consensus: Europe's response to the Japanese automotive challenge', *Journal of Common Market Studies*, pp. 433–453.

Meade, J. (1973). 'The balance of payments problems of a European free-trade area', in *The Economics of Integration* (ed. M. Krauss). London: George Allen and Unwin, pp. 155–176.

Molle, W. (1990). 'Regional policy', in *Main Economic Policy Areas of the EEC – Toward 1992* (ed. P. Coffey). Dordrecht: Kluwer, pp. 63–99.

Morita, A. (1992). 'Partnering for competitiveness: the role of Japanese business', *Harvard Business Review* (May–June), pp. 76–83.

Mundell, R., (1957). 'International trade and factor mobility', *American Economic Review*, pp. 321–335.

——(1961). 'A theory of optimum currency areas', *American Economic Review*, pp. 321–325.

——(1994). 'European monetary union and the international monetary system', *Rivista di Politica Economica*, pp. 83–128.

Nevin, E. (1985). 'Regional policy', in *The Economics of the European Community* (ed. A. El-Agraa). Oxford: Philip Allan, pp. 338–361.

Nicolaides, P. (ed.) (1993). *Industrial Policy in the European Community*. Dordrecht: Martinus Nijhoff.

Nicolaides, P. (1994). 'Why multilateral rules on competition are needed', *Intereconomics*, pp. 222–218.

Nicolaides, P. and A. van der Klugt (eds) (1994). *The Competition Policy of the European Community*. Maastricht: EIPA.

Noël, E. (1993). *Working Together – The Institutions of The European Community*. Luxembourg: European Communities.

OECD (1995). *Agricultural Policies, Markets and Trade in OECD Countries*. Paris: OECD.

Panić, M. (1988). *National Management of the International Economv*. London: Macmillan.

——(1991). 'The import of multinationals on national economic policies', in *Multinationals and Europe 1992* (eds B. Bürgenmeier and J. Mucchelli). London: Routledge, pp. 204–222.

Peck, M. (1989). 'Industrial organization and the gains from Europe 1992', *Brookings Papers on Economic Activity*, pp. 277–299.

Pelkmans, J. and P. Robson. (1987). 'The aspirations of the White Paper', *Journal of Common Market Studies*, pp. 181–192.

Petith, H. (1976). 'Agriculture, manufacturing and terms of trade effect of European integration', *Recherches Économiques de Louvain*, pp. 119–133.

Pinder, J. (1982). 'Causes and kinds of industrial policy', in *National Industrial Strategies and the World Economy* (ed. J. Pinder). London: Croom Helm, pp. 41–52.

Pinder, J., T. Hosomi and W. Diebold (1979). *Industrial Policy and International Economy*. New York: The Trilateral Commission.

Pitelis, C. and R. Sugden, eds (1991). *The Nature of the Transnational Firm*. London: Routledge.

Plasschaert, S. (1994). 'Introduction: transfer pricing and taxation', in *Transnational Corporations: Transfer Pricing and Taxation* (ed. S. Plasschaert). London: Routledge, pp. 1–21.

Pohl, G. and P. Sorsa (1994). 'Is European integration bad news for developing countries?', *World Bank Research Observer*, pp. 147–155.

378

Prais, S. (1981). *Productivity and Industrial Structure.* Cambridge: Cambridge University Press.

Pratten, C. (1971). *Economies of Scale and Manufacturing Industry.* Cambridge: Cambridge University Press.

—— (1988). 'A survey of the economies of scale', in *Studies on the Economics of Integration, Research on the Costs of Non-Europe,* vol. 2, Brussels: European Communities, pp. 11–165.

Prest, A. (1983). 'Fiscal policy', in *Main Economic Policy Areas of the EEC* (ed. P. Coffey), The Hague: Martinus Nijhoff, pp. 58–90.

Read, R. (1994). 'The EC internal banana market: the issues and the dilemmas', *The World Economy,* pp. 219–235.

Reich, R. (1982). 'Why the U.S. needs an industrial policy', *Harvard Business Review,* (January–February), pp. 74–81.

—— (1990). 'Who is us?', *Harvard Business Review,* (January–February), pp. 53–64.

Robson, P. (1983). *Integration, Development and Equity.* London: George Allen and Unwin.

—— (1987). *The Economics of International Integration.* London: George Allen and Unwin.

Romer, P. (1994). 'New goods, old theory and the welfare costs of trade restrictions', *Journal of Development Economics,* pp. 5–38.

Rosenberg, N., R. Landau and D. Mowery (eds) (1992). *Technology and the Wealth of Nations.* Stanford: Stanford University Press.

Rosenblatt, J., T. Mayer, K. Bartholdy, D. Demekas, S. Gupta and L. Lipschitz (1988). *The Common Agricultural Policy of the European Community.* Washington: IMF, Occasional Paper 62.

Ruding Committee (1992). *Conclusions and Recommendations of the Committee of Independent Experts on Company Taxation.* Luxembourg: European Communities.

Rugman, A. (1985). 'The Behaviour of US Subsidiaries in Canada: Implications for Trade and investment', in *Canada/United States Trade and Investments Issues* (eds D. Fretz, R. Stern and J. Whalley). Toronto: Ontario Economic Council, pp. 460–473.

Sala-i-Martin, X. (1994). 'Regional cohesion: evidence and theories of regional growth and convergence', CEPR Discussion Paper, No. 1075.

Salvatore, D. (1994). 'European monetary problems and the international monetary system', *Rivista di Politica Economica,* pp. 129–147.

Sapir, A. (1992). 'Regional integration in Europe', *Economic Journal,* pp. 1491–1506.

—— (1993). 'Structural dimension', *European Economy Social Europe,* No. 3, pp. 23–39.

Sapir, A., P. Buigues and A. Jacquemin (1993). 'European competition policy in manufacturing and services: a two speed approach?', *Oxford Review of Economic Policy,* pp. 113–132.

Sarris, A. (1994). 'Consequences of the proposed common agricultural policy reform for the southern part of the European Community', *European Economy,* No. 5, pp. 113–132.

Scaperlanda, A. (1967). 'The EEC and US Foreign investment: Some Empirical Evidence', *Economic Journal,* pp. 22–26.

Scaperlanda, A. and R. Balough (1983). 'Determinants of US Direct investment in Europe', *European Economic Journal,* pp. 381–390.

Scaperlanda, A. and E. Reiling (1971). 'A Comment on a Note on Customs Unions and Direct Foreign investment', *Economic Journal,* pp. 355–357.

Schmalensee, R. (1988). 'Industrial economics: an overview', *Economic Journal,* pp. 634–681.

Sengenberger, W., G. Loveman and M. Piore (eds) (1990). *The Re-emergence of Small Enterprises: Industrial Restructuring in Industrialised Countries.* Geneva: ILO.

Sharp, M. and K. Pavitt (1993). 'Technology policy in the 1990s: old trends and new realities', *Journal of Common Market Studies,* pp. 129–151.

Sharp, M. and G. Shepherd (1987). *Managing Change in British Industry.* Geneva: ILO.

Sidjanski, D. (1992). *L'Avenir Fédéraliste de L'Europe.* Paris: Presses Universitaires de France.

Siebert, H. (1991). 'Environmental policy and European Integration', in *Environmental Scarcity: The International Dimension* (ed. H. Siebert). Tübingen: J.C.B. Mohr, pp. 57–70.

Sinn, H. (1990). 'Tax harmonization and tax competition in Europe', *European Economic Review,* pp. 489–504.

Sleuwaegen, L. (1987) 'Multinationals, the European Community and Belgium', *Journal of Common Market Studies,* pp. 255–272.

Sorsa, P. (1994). 'Competitiveness and environmental standards', World Bank Policy Research Working Paper 1249.

Straubhaar, T. (1988). 'International labour migration within a common market: some aspects of EC experience', *Journal of Common Market Studies*, pp. 45–62.

Straubhaar, T. and K. Zimmermann (1993). 'Towards a European migration policy', *Population Research and Policy Review*, pp. 225–241.

Swinbank, A. (1993). 'CAP reform, 1992', *Journal of Common Market Studies*, pp. 359–372.

Tavlas, G. (1993a). 'The theory of optimum currency areas revisited', *Finance and Development*, June, pp. 32–35.

——(1993b). 'The "new" theory of optimum currency areas', *The World Economy*, pp. 663–685.

Thomsen, S. and P. Nicolaides (1991). *The Evolution of Japanese Direct Investment in Europe*. New York: Harvester Wheatsheaf.

Thygesen, N. (1987). 'Is the EEC an optimal currency area?', in *The ECU Market* (eds R. Levics and A. Sommariva). Toronto: D.C. Heath, Lexington Books, pp. 163–189.

——(1993). 'Towards monetary union in Europe-reforms of the EMS in the perspective of monetary union', *Journal of Common Market Stuidies*, pp. 447–472.

Tironi, E. (1982). 'Customs union theory in the presence of foreign firms', *Oxford Economic Papers*, pp. 150–171.

Trebilcock, M. (1986). *The Political Economy of Economic Adjustment*. Toronto: University of Toronto Press.

Tyson, L. (1987). 'Comments on Brander's "Shaping Comparative Advantage": creating advantage, an industrial policy perspective', in *Shaping Comparative Advantage* (eds R. Lipsey and W. Dobson). Toronto: C.D. Howe Institute, pp. 65–82.

——(1991). 'They are not us. Why American ownership still matters', *The American Prospect*, (Winter), pp. 37–49.

——(1992). *Who Is Bashing Whom? Trade Conflict in High-technology Industries*. Washington: Institute for International Economics.

Tyson, L. and J. Zysman (1987a). 'American industry in international competition', in *American Industry in International Competition* (eds J. Zysman and L. Tyson). Ithaca: Cornell University Press, pp. 15–59.

——(1987b). 'Conclusion: what to do now?', in *American Industry in International Competition* (eds J. Zysman and L. Tyson). Ithaca: Cornell University Press, pp. 442–447.

UNCTAD (1983). *The Role of Transnational Enterprises in Latin American Economic Integration Efforts: Who Integrates with Whom, How and for Whose Benefit?*. New York: United Nations.

——(1993). *World Investment Report: Transnational Corporations and Integrated International Production*. New York: United Nations.

——(1994). *World Investment Report: Transnational Corporations, Employment and the Workforce*. New York: United Nations.

——(1995a). 'Incentives and foreign direct investment', TD/B/ITNC/Misc.1, 6 April 1995.

——(1995b). *World Investment Report*. New York: United Nations.

UNCTC (1990). *Regional Economic Integration and Transnational Corporations in the 1990s: Europe 1992, North America and Developing Countries*. New York: United Nations.

——(1991a). *World Investment Report: The Triad in Foreign Direct Investment*. New York: United Nations.

——(1991b). *The Impact of Trade-related Investment Measures*. New York: United Nations.

——(1991c). *Government Policies and Foreign Direct Investment*. New York: United Nations.

van der Voude, M., C. Jones and X. Lewiss (1994). *E.C. Competition Law Handbook*. London: Sweet & Maxwell.

Vanhove, N. and L. Klaassen (1987). *Regional Policy: A European Approach*. Aldershot: Avebury.

Varian, H. (1984). *Microeconomic Analysis*. New York: Norton.

Vaubel, R. (1990). 'Currency competition and European monetary integration', *Economic Journal*, pp. 936–946.

Venables, A. (1995). 'Economic integration and the location of firms', *American Economic Review* (Papers and Proceedings), pp. 296–300.

Viner, J. (1950). *The Customs Union Issue*. London: Stevens and Sons.

von Cramon-Taubadel, S. and H. Thiele (1994). 'EU agriculture: reduced protection from exchange rate instability', *Intereconomics*, 6 (November–December), pp. 263–268.

Waer, P. (1994). 'European Community rules of origin', in *Rules of Origin in International Trade* (eds E. Vermulst, P. Waer and J. Bourgeois). Ann Arbor: University of Michigan Press, pp. 85–194.

Wallis, K. (1968). 'The EEC and United States Foreign Investment: Some Empirical Evidence Re-examined', *Economic Journal*, pp. 717–719.

Weale, A. and A. Williams (1993). 'Between economy and ecology?. The Single Market and the integration of environmental policy', in *A Green Dimension for the European Community: Political Issues and Processes* (ed. D. Judge). London: Frank Cass, pp. 45–64.

Werner, P. (1970). *Report to the Council and the Commission on the Realization by Stages of Economic and Monetary Union in the Community*. Luxembourg: European Community.

Whalley, J. (1987). 'Brander's "Shaping comparative advantage": remarks', in *Shaping Comparative Advantage* (eds R. Lipsey and W. Dobson). Toronto: C.D. Howe Institute, pp. 83–89.

Winters, A. (1994). 'The EC and protection: the political economy', *European Economic Review*, pp. 596–603.

World Bank (1993). *The East Asian Miracle*. New York: Oxford University Press.

Wren, C. (1990). 'Regional policy in the 1980s', *National Westminster Bank Quarterly Review*, pp. 52–64.

Yamawaki, H. (1991). 'Discussion', in *European Integration: Trade and Industry* (eds A. Winters and A. Venables). Cambridge: Cambridge University Press, pp. 231–233.

Yannopoulos, G. (1988). *Customs Unions and Trade Conflicts*. London: Routledge.

——(1990) 'Foreign direct investment and European integration: the evidence from the formative years of the European Community', *Journal of Common Market Studies*, pp. 236–259.

——(ed). (1991). *Europe and America, 1992*. Manchester: Manchester University Press.

Yuill, D., K. Allen, J. Bachtler, K. Clement and F. Wishdale (1994). *European Regional Incentives, 1994–95*. London: Bowker.

Zimmermann, K. (1994). 'European migration: push and pull', *Proceedings of the World Bank Annual Conference on Development Economics 1994*, pp. 313–342.

——(1995). 'Tackling the European migration problem', *Economic Perspectives*, pp. 45–62.

Zysman, J. (1983). *Governments, Markets and Growth*. Ithaca: Cornell University Press.

INDEX